SPECTRUM ANALYSIS

IN ITS APPLICATION TO

TERRESTRIAL SUBSTANCES,

AND

THE PHYSICAL CONSTITUTION OF THE HEAVENLY BODIES.

FAMILIARLY EXPLAINED BY

DR. H. SCHELLEN,

DIRECTOR DER REALSCHULE I. O. COLOGNE, RITTER DES ROTHEN ALDERODENS IV. KL.,
ASSOCIATE OF SEVERAL LEARNED SOCIETIES.

TRANSLATED FROM THE SECOND ENLARGED AND REVISED GERMAN EDITION BY

JANE AND CAROLINE LASSELL.

EDITED, WITH NOTES, BY

WILLIAM HUGGINS, LL.D., D.C.L., F.R.S.

WITH NUMEROUS WOODCUTS, COLORED PLATES, AND PORTRAITS; ALSO ÅNGSTRÖM'S AND KIRCHHOFF'S MAPS.

NEW YORK:
D. APPLETON AND COMPANY,
549 & 551 BROADWAY.
1872.

EDITOR'S PREFACE.

THE daughters of my friend, Mr. Lassell, F. R. S., President R. A. S., having asked me to edit their translation of this work, I consented the more readily to accede to their wish because Dr. Schellen's book appeared to me valuable as a popular account of a new branch of scientific investigation.

I have to remind the readers of the book that I am not responsible for the views of the author, nor for the relative importance which he has given to the work of different investigators in the same field of research. I have added some notes, which are distinguished from those of the author by being enclosed within brackets. The absence of an editorial note is not, however, to be understood in every case as giving my sanction to the statements of the text. This remark applies in particular to the section on the "Influence of Temperature and Density on the Spectra of Gases," in which are several statements which appear to need confirmation. Since this part of the translation passed through my hands, Ångström has published a note* in which he shows that Wüllner is mistaken in the different spectra which he describes as belonging to hydrogen and to oxygen.

* *Comptes Rendus*, August, 1871, and *Phil. Mag.*, November, 1871.

I regret that the author has reversed the practice of the principal spectroscopic observers, and placed the red end of the spectrum opposite the reader's left hand, and not, as in the maps of Kirchhoff, Ångström, and others, on the right-hand side of the page.

In so new a science there must be necessarily many points not finally settled, but this circumstance does not detract from the great merit of the book as a popular treatise on Spectrum Analysis.

WILLIAM HUGGINS.

UPPER TULSE HILL, *December*, 1871.

TRANSLATOR'S PREFACE.

THE original of the following work was introduced to our notice by Mr. Huggins, to whom we had appealed for information as to the best elementary book on the Spectroscope; and, while engaged in its perusal, the interest we felt in the subject suggested the idea of undertaking the translation of the work. Just as we had completed our labors, the second German edition made its appearance, and this necessitated so entire a revision of the whole work as to occasion considerable delay.

In order to render the work as complete as possible, we have, at the suggestion of the editor, given in an Appendix Mr. Stoney's important paper "On the Cause of the Interrupted Spectra of Gases," and Prof. Young's valuable catalogue of the lines observed in the spectrum of the chromosphere. We have besides inserted in the body of the work an account of the total eclipse of 1870, a copy of Ångström's maps of the solar spectrum, a view of the corona from a photograph by Mr. Brothers, and a representation of some of the solar prominences from a drawing by Prof. Respighi.

We are glad to have the opportunity of expressing our thanks to Messrs. Hanhart for the care they have taken in the reproduction of the several lithographic plates, especially for the admirable way in which they have represented Ångström's maps; also to Mr. Pearson, for the careful manner in which he has conducted the engraving on wood of Kirchhoff's maps, so as to represent them in several tints, a task in which he has been materially assisted by the great accuracy of the printers, Messrs. Watson & Hazell.

JANE AND CAROLINE LASSELL.

Ray Lodge, Maidenhead, *December*, 1871.

PREFACE TO THE SECOND EDITION.

THE present work is founded upon a series of lectures delivered by the author during the winter of 1869, before the "Vereine für wissenschaftliche Vorlesungen," in this city. Its object is, on the one hand, to give a clear and familiar representation of the nature and phenomena of Spectrum Analysis, enabling an educated person not previously familiar with physical science to become acquainted with the newest and most brilliant discovery of this century; and, on the other hand, to show the important position which Spectrum Analysis has acquired in the pursuit of Physics, Chemistry, Technology, Physiology, and Astronomy, as well as its adaptability to almost every kind of scientific investigation.

The general reader will be introduced by this book into a new realm of science, the dominion of which has extended in a few years over all terrestrial substances, and even beyond them to the most distant parts of the universe. He will learn to decipher the new language of *Light*, which, by unequivocal signs, yields him information not only concerning the nature of terrestrial substances, but also of the physical constitution of the heavenly bodies. The professor of science will find in these pages many details for the arrangement of apparatus by which to exhibit the various spectra and their characteristic phenomena to a large audience, and present to them a view of those splendid discoveries, the direct sight of which can only be enjoyed by the few who possess an instrument for the purpose.

To facilitate the due appreciation of the results which have been obtained by the application of Spectrum Analysis to the heavenly bodies, the author has given with each class of objects a summary of the information hitherto furnished by the telescope, and has sought to give a glance in passing at the progressive development and partial transformation of the heavenly bodies.

The great interest that has everywhere been excited by the first edition of this work has made a second edition necessary within the period of a year. The author has given his attention to the careful revision of each section, which he has in many cases enlarged and enriched by the discoveries made by Spectrum Analysis generally, but more especially in its application to the observation of the sun. Great prominence has been given to the detailed explanation of the various methods employed in the practical working of the spectroscope.

In conclusion, the author acknowledges with grateful thanks the valuable assistance rendered him by various scientific men who have kindly communicated to him the results of their labors, among whom he would especially mention Messrs. Huggins, Secchi, Lockyer, Zöllner, Janssen, Morton, and Young. His thanks are also due to the publisher, who has watched over with so much care and interest the typographical department, as well as the execution of the numerous and elaborate illustrations.

THE AUTHOR.

COLOGNE.

CONTENTS.

PART I.

ON THE ARTIFICIAL SOURCES OF HIGH DEGREES OF HEAT AND LIGHT.

PAGE

1. Introduction . . . 3
2. The luminous power of flame . . . 6
3. The Bunsen burner . . . 10
4. The magnesium light . . . 13
5. The oxhydrogen flame . . . 16
6. Drummond's lime-light . . . 19
7. The electric spark . . . 20
8. The induction coil . . . 23
9. Luminosity of gases: Geissler's tubes . . . 24
10. The voltaic arc: the electric light . . . 27
11. The electric lamp . . . 31

PART II.

SPECTRUM ANALYSIS IN ITS APPLICATION TO TERRESTRIAL SUBSTANCES.

12. Light . . . 39
13. Analogy between light and sound . . . 40
14. Analogy between musical sounds and colors . . . 45
15. Refraction of light . . . 47
16. Refraction of monochromatic light by a prism . . . 53
17. Refraction of the different colors by a prism . . . 57
18. The solar spectrum . . . 60
19. The spectra of the lime-light and the electric light . . . 64
20. Recombination of the colors of the spectrum . . . 69
21. Influence of the width of slit on the purity of the spectrum . . . 70
22. The continuous spectra of solid and liquid bodies . . . 71
23. The spectra of vapors and gases . . . 72

PAGE

24. Spectrum apparatus 78
25. Mode of measuring the distances between the lines of the spectrum. 85
26. The compound spectroscope 89
27. Browning's automatic spectroscope 93
28. Prism of comparison, or reflecting prism 96
29. Designation of the lines of the spectrum 101
30. Various methods for exhibiting the spectra of terrestrial substances 103
31. Influence of temperature and density on the spectra of gases . 114
32. Influence of the temperature of gases on the width of the lines of the spectrum 121
33. Influence of temperature on the delicacy of spectrum reactions . 122
34. The colors of natural objects 125
35. Absorption of light by solid bodies 128
36. Absorption of light by liquids 129
37. The Sorby-Browning microspectroscope 133
38. Absorption of light by gases 140
39. Relation between the emission and absorption of light . . . 142
40. Reversal of the spectra of gases 144

PART III.

SPECTRUM ANALYSIS IN ITS APPLICATION TO THE HEAVENLY BODIES.

41. The solar spectrum and the Fraunhofer lines 159
42. Kirchhoff's scale of the solar spectrum 164
43. Ångström's normal solar spectrum 165
44. Coincidence of the dark Fraunhofer lines with the bright spectrum lines of terrestrial elements—Kirchhoff's maps 168
45. Kirchhoff's theory of the physical constitution of the sun . . 173
46. The atmospheric lines in the solar spectrum as observed by Brewster and Gladstone 176
47. The telluric lines in the solar spectrum and the spectrum of aqueous vapor, as observed by Janssen 179
48. The solar spots; the faculæ and their spectra 184
49. Total solar eclipses 206
50. Photographic pictures of total solar eclipses 209
51. The total solar eclipse of August 18, 1868 215
52. The total solar eclipse of August 7, 1869 232
53. The prominences and their spectra 242
54. The corona and its spectrum 251
[The total solar eclipse of 1870] 254

PAGE

55. THE TELESPECTROSCOPE, AND METHOD OF OBSERVING THE SPECTRA OF THE PROMINENCES IN SUNSHINE 262
56. THE CHROMOSPHERE AND ITS SPECTRUM 272
57. MODES OF OBSERVING THE PROMINENCES IN SUNSHINE—FORM OF THE PROMINENCES 288
58. MEASUREMENT OF THE DIRECTION AND SPEED OF THE GAS-STREAMS IN THE SUN 307
59. SPECTRUM ANALYSIS OF THE HEAVENLY BODIES—STELLAR SPECTROSCOPES . 317
60. SPECTRA OF THE MOON AND PLANETS 333
61. SPECTRA OE THE FIXED STARS 337
62. SECCHI'S TYPES OF THE FIXED STARS 342
63. COLOR OF THE STARS—DOUBLE STARS AND THEIR SPECTRA 350
64. VARIABLE STARS 353
65. NEW OR TEMPORARY STARS 357
66. INFLUENCE OF THE PROPER MOTION OF THE STARS IN SPACE UPON THEIR SPECTRA 362
67. SPECTRA OF NEBULÆ AND CLUSTERS 367
68. COMETS AND THEIR SPECTRA 386
69. FALLING STARS, METEOR-SHOWERS, BALLS OF FIRE AND THEIR SPECTRA . 403
70. SPECTRUM OF LIGHTNING 421
71. SPECTRUM OF THE AURORA BOREALIS 423

APPENDIX A 429
"On the Cause of the Interrupted Spectra of Gases," by G. Johnstone Stoney, M. A., F. R. S.

APPENDIX B 435*
"Preliminary Catalogue of the Bright Lines in the Spectrum of the Chromosphere." By C. A. Young, Ph. D., Professor of Astronomy in Dartmouth College.

LIST OF WORKS ON SPECTRUM ANALYSIS 440

ILLUSTRATIONS.

FIG.		PAGE
1.	Combustion of a Steel Watch-spring in Oxygen	7
2.	Bunsen's Gas-burner	11
3.	Bunsen's Heat-Lamp with Blow-pipe	12
4.	Grant and Solomon's Magnesium-Lamp.	14
5.	Prof. Morton's Magnesium-Lamp	15
6.	Gas-bag for Oxygen or Hydrogen	17
7.	Oxyhydrogen Blow-pipe. (Drummond's Lime-light)	18
8.	The Electric Spark	21
9.	The Electric Spark intensified by a Condenser	22
10.	Electric Egg	24
11.	Geissler's Tube	25
12.	Plücker's Tube	25
13.	Bunsen's Battery	26
14.	The Electric Light	28
15.	Projection of the Voltaic Arc	29
16.	The Carbon-points of the Electric Light. (Highly magnified)	30
17.	Foucault's Electric Lamp	32
18.	The Siren	42
19.	Savart's Toothed Wheel	44
20.	Refraction	49
21.	Path of the Rays through a Medium with Parallel Sides	50
22.	Refraction through Glass of Parallel Surfaces	51
23.	Refraction exhibited on a Screen	52
24.	Projection of the Slit, and Displacement of the Rays by Refraction	53
25.	The Prism	54
26.	Prism mounted on Stand	54
27.	Path of Ray of Light through a Prism	55
28.	Refraction of a Ray of Light by a Prism	56
29.	Viewing Objects through a Prism	57
30.	Divergence of the different colored Rays in passing through a Prism	58
31.	Prism of Bisulphide of Carbon	61
32.	Exhibition of the Solar Spectrum	61
33.	Indivisibility of the Pure Colors of the Spectrum	63
34.	Projection of the Spectrum of the Lime-light	65
35.	Browning's Electric Lamp	68

FIG.		PAGE
36.	Action of the Double Prism	68
37.	Recombination of the Colors of the Spectrum	69
38.	Influence of the Width of Slit on the Purity of the Spectrum	70
39.	Volatilization of Metals in the Electric Light	73
40.	Ruhmkorff's Electric Lamp	75
41.	The Simple Spectroscope	79
42.	Indivisibility of the Pure Colors of the Spectrum	79
43.	Neutralization of Refraction and Dispersion	80
44.	Amici's Direct-vision System of Prisms	81
45.	Herschel's Direct-vision Prism	82
46.	Herschel-Browning's System of Prisms	83
47.	Janssen-Hofmann's Direct-vision Spectroscope	84
48.	Janssen's Direct-vision System of Prisms	84
49.	Browning's Miniature Spectroscope	85
50.	Graduated Scale in Spectroscope	86
51.	Micrometer for measuring the Distances between the Lines	87
52.	Compound Spectroscope	90
53.	Kirchhoff's Spectroscope, by Steinheil	91
54.	Large Spectroscope of the Kew Observatory	92
55.	Path of a Ray through Nine Prisms	93
56.	Browning's Automatic Spectroscope	95
	[Automatic Spectroscope used by Huggins]	97
57.	The Prism of Comparison, or Reflecting Prism	99
58.	The Prism of Comparison	99
59.	The Double Spectrum	100
60.	Hofmann's Prism of Comparison	101
61.	Table of Spectra according to Kirchhoff and Bunsen	102
62.	Mitscherlich's Spectrum Wick	106
63.	Mitscherlich's Apparatus for Permanent Spectra	107
64.	Morton's Apparatus for Monochromatic Light	108
65.	Intensifying the Electric Discharge by a Leyden Jar	109
66.	Browning's Intensifying Apparatus	110
67.	The Becquerel-Ruhmkorff Apparatus	112
68.	Stand for Plücker's Tubes	113
69.	Spectra of the Various Orders	117
70.	Glass Vessel for Absorbent Liquids	130
71.	Spectra of Absorbent Substances	131
72.	Observations of Absorption	132
73.	The Sorby-Browning Microspectroscope	133
74.	Section of the Microspectroscope	134
75.	Adjustments for the Slit in the Microspectroscope	135
76.	Micrometer for measuring the Absorption Lines	137
77.	Scale for the Microspectroscope	138
78.	Absorption Bands of Human Blood	139
79.	Glass Globe for Absorbent Vapors	141
80.	Reversal of the Sodium Line (seen with the Spectroscope)	145
81.	Reversal of the Sodium Line (projected on a Screen)	148
82.	Volatilization of Sodium in the Electric Light	149
83.	Bunsen's Apparatus for the Absorption of the Light of Sodium	151

FIG. PAGE
84. Absorption of the Sodium-Flame 152
85. Fraunhofer's Solar Spectrum 160
86. Solar Spectrum with Prisms of Flint Glass, Crown Glass, and Water . 162
87. The Solar Spectrum with Kirchhoff's Scale 164
88. Ångström's Normal Solar Spectrum. (Portion with the Line-F) . . 167
89. Coincidence of the Fraunhofer D-lines with the Lines of Sodium . 170
90. Coincidence of the Fraunhofer Lines with the Lines of Iron and Calcium . 171
91. Coincidence of the Spectrum of Iron with sixty-five of the Fraunhofer Lines, 172
92. The Brewster-Gladstone Solar Spectrum, with the Atmospheric Lines . 177
93. Janssen's Spectrum of the Sun on the Meridian and at the Horizon. (Telluric Lines) 181
94. Spectrum of Sirius on the Meridian and at the Horizon. Spectrum of the Sun on the Meridian and at the Horizon 182
95. The Telluric Lines in the Solar Spectrum after Ångström . . . 183
96. Solar Spot seen through a large Telescope by Secchi at Rome, April 3, 1858 185
97. Granules and Pores of the Sun's Surface, after Huggins . . . 186
98. Solar Spot, after Nasmyth, with three Bridges of Light . . . 187
99. Solar Spots, after Capocci; Furrows in the Penumbra . . . 187
100. Faculæ in the Neighborhood of a Spot, after Chacornac . . 188
101. Group of Solar Spots observed and drawn by Nasmyth, June 5, 1864 . 190
102. The Great Solar Spot of 1865. (From 7th to 16th October) . . 191
103. Solar Spot of July 30, 1869 192
104. Solar Spot of July 31, 1869 193
105. Spiral Solar Spot observed by Secchi 195
106. Changes in the Appearance of a Spot caused by the Rotation of the Sun 197
107. The D-lines in the Spectrum of a Solar Spot 198
108. Spectrum of the Solar Spot of 11–13th April, 1869, observed by Secchi, 201
109. Total Solar Eclipse of August 7, 1869 208
110. Browning's Photographic Telescope 210
111. Path of the Rays through the Telescope 211
112. Eye-piece Tube of the Photographic Telescope 212
113. Slide of the Photographic Telescope 213
114. Total Solar Eclipse of July 18, 1860. (Photographed by De la Rue) . 214
115. Zone of the Total Eclipse of August 18, 1868, from Aden to Torres Straits . 216
116. Total Solar Eclipse of August 18, 1868. (Observed at Aden.) (Picture 1) 220
117. Total Solar Eclipse of August 18, 1868. (Aden.) (Picture 2) . . 221
118. Total Solar Eclipse of August 18, 1868. (Aden.) (Picture 3) . 222
119. Union of the Prominences in one Drawing 223
120. Tennant's Photographic Pictures collected into one Drawing. (Guntoor, August 18, 1868) 224
121. Total Solar Eclipse of August 18, 1868, at Mantawaloc-Kekee . . 226
122. Solar Eclipse of August 18, 1868, observed from the Steamer Rangoon . 228
123. Solar Eclipse of August 18, 1868, observed at Wha-Tonne by Stéphan, 229
124. Solar Eclipse of August 18, 1868, observed at Mantawaloc-Kekee . . 230
125. Union of the Prominences in one Drawing—(Total Eclipse of August 7, 1869) 236
126. Photographic Picture of the Corona, August 7, 1869 . . . 238
127. The Corona of the Eclipse of August 7, 1869, at Des Moines . . 239
128. Gould's Drawing of the Corona of August 7, 1869—(4h. 58m.) . . 240
129. Gould's Drawing of the Corona of August 7, 1869—(5h. 0m.) . . 241

FIG.		PAGE
130.	Various Spectra of the Prominences	243
131.	Young's Telespectroscope	247
132.	Spectrum of the Prominences	248
133.	Young's Observation of the Prominence-Spectrum	248
134.	Sketch of a Prominence by means of its Spectrum Lines	264
135.	Lockyer's Telespectroscope	266
136.	Lockyer's Telespectroscope constructed by Browning	267
137.	Method of observing the Prominences	268
138.	Merz's Simple and Compound Spectroscope	270
139.	The Spectrum of the Sun's Disk (below) and that of the Chromosphere (above) near the C-line	273
140.	The Spectrum of the Sun's Disk and that of the Chromosphere near the D-line	274
141.	The Spectrum of the Sun's Disk and that of the Chromosphere near the F-line	274
142.	Covering of the dark C-line with H α	278
143.	Partial Covering of the dark F-line with H β	279
144.	Changes in the Line H β after Lockyer	280
145.	Changes in the Line H β after Young	281
146.	Reversal of the C- and F-lines	282
147.	Young's Observation of the Reversal of the D-lines	283
148.	Huggins's First Observation of a Prominence in Full Sunshine	293
149.	Solar Prominences observed by Zöllner	295
150.	Lockyer's Observation of Various Prominences	298
151.	Young's Observation of Various Prominences	300
152.	Young's Observation of a Chain of Prominences	301
153.	Solar Storm observed by Lockyer March 14, 1869. (Picture 1)	301
154.	Solar Storm observed by Lockyer March 14, 1869. (Picture 2)	302
155.	Changes in the Form of a Prominence	303
156.	Respighi's Observations of the Prominences round the entire Limb of the Sun	305
157.	Direction and Speed of the Gas-streams in the Sun	310
158.	Displacement of the F-line; Velocity of the Gas-streams in the Sun	311
159.	Movement of a Gas-vortex in the Sun	314
160.	Unequal Displacement of the Greenish-blue Hydrogen Line (H β)	315
161.	Merz's Object-glass Spectroscope	319
162.	Merz's Object-glass Spectroscope. (Mounting of the Prism)	320
163.	Merz's Object-glass Prism	321
164.	Huggins's Stellar Spectroscope. (Perspective View)	322
165.	Huggins's Stellar Spectroscope. (Horizontal Section)	323
	[Grubb's Automatic Spectroscopes]	323
166.	Huggins's Stellar Spectroscope. (Partial Vertical Section)	324
167.	Secchi's Stellar Spectroscope	326
168.	Secchi's Large Telespectroscope	328
169.	Huggins's Large Telespectroscope	329
170.	Merz's Simple and Compound Spectroscope	330
171.	Merz's Simple Spectroscope	331
172.	Browning's Miniature Spectroscope	331
173.	Browning's Hand-Spectroscope	332

FIG.		PAGE
174.	Spectrum of Uranus	335
	[Spectrum of Uranus, after Huggins]	336
175.	Spectrum of Aldebaran (α Tauri) and that of Betelgeux (α Orionis) compared with the Solar Spectrum and Spectra of Terrestrial Elements	340
176.	Secchi's Types of the Fixed Stars	344
177.	Spectrum of Sirius	345
	[Spectrum of a Red Star, after Huggins]	349
178.	Spectrum of the Star A of α Herculis	353
179.	Spectra of the Component Stars of the Double Star β Cygni	354
180.	Variability of a Star according to Zöllner	355
181.	Spectrum of the Temporary Star T Coronæ Borealis. (May 15, 1866)	360
182.	Displacement of the F-line in the Spectrum of Sirius	364
183.	The Great Nebula in Orion	368
184.	Central and most brilliant Portion of the Great Nebula in the Sword-handle of Orion, as observed by Sir John Herschel in his 20-foot Reflector at Feldhausen, Cape of Good Hope (1834–1837)	369
185.	The Large Magellanic Cloud	370
186.	Nebula of the Form of a Sickle (H. 3239)	371
187.	Spiral Nebula (H. 1173)	372
188.	Spiral Nebula in Canes Venatici (H. 1622)	372
189.	Transition from the Spiral to the Annular Form	373
190.	Annular Nebula in Lyra	373
191.	Nebula with several Rings (H. 854)	374
192.	Elliptical Annular Nebula (H. 1909)	375
193.	Elongated Nebula (H. 2621)	375
194.	Double Nebula (H. 3501)	376
195.	Annular Nebula with Centre (H. 2552)	376
196.	Planetary Nebula with two Stars (H. 838)	377
197.	Planetary Annular Nebula with two Stars (H. 464)	377
198.	Planetary Nebula (H. 2241)	377
199.	Planetary Nebula (H. 2098)	378
200.	Stellar Nebula (H. 450)	378
201.	Spectrum of Nebula (H. 4374)	378
202.	Spectrum of Nebula compared with the Sun and some Terrestrial Elements	379
203.	Planetary Annular Nebula in Aquarius, with Spectrum	383
204.	Stellar Nebula (H. 450)	384
205.	Spiral Nebula (H. 4964), with Spectrum	384
206.	Annular Nebula in Lyra, with Spectrum	385
207.	Donati's Comet on July 2, 1858	388
208.	The July Comet on July 3, 1861	388
209.	Donati's Comet on October 5, 1858	389
210.	The July Comet on July 2, 1861	390
211.	Position of the Tail of a Comet as regards the Sun	390
212.	Orbit of Donati's Comet	391
213.	The July Comet on June 30 and July 1, 1861	392
214.	Spectrum of Tempel's Comet (1866)	395
215.	Spectra of Brorsen's and Winnecke's Comets compared with the Spectra of the Sun, of Carbon, and of the Nebulæ	396
216.	Winnecke's Comet (II., 1868)	398

FIG.		PAGE
217.	Huggins's Apparatus for observing the Spectra of Hydrocarbons	400
218.	Balls of Fire seen through the Telescope	408
219.	Orbit of the Meteor-Shower of the 10th of August	410
220.	Orbit of the November Meteor-Shower	412
221.	Orbits of the August and November Meteor-Showers. (Orbits of Comets III., 1862, and I., 1866)	416
222.	Browning's Meteor Spectroscope	418
223.	Spectrum of the Aurora Borealis, after Zöllner	427

LIST OF PLATES.

		To face PAGE
I.	TABLE OF SPECTRA	FRONTISPIECE.
II., III.	KIRCHHOFF'S MAPS OF THE SOLAR SPECTRUM	165
IV., V., VI.	ÅNGSTRÖM'S MAPS OF THE SOLAR SPECTRUM	168
VII.	TOTAL SOLAR ECLIPSE (INDIA)	225
VIII.	TOTAL SOLAR ECLIPSE (NORTH AMERICA)	235
IX.	SOLAR SPECTRUM AND SPECTRUM OF THE PROMINENCES DURING A TOTAL ECLIPSE	251
X.	CORONA PHOTOGRAPHED AT SYRACUSE BY MR. BROTHERS	259
XI.	SOLAR PROMINENCES OBSERVED BY ZÖLLNER	303
XII.	SOLAR PROMINENCES OBSERVED BY YOUNG	303
XIII.	SOLAR PROMINENCES OBSERVED BY RESPIGHI	306

LIST OF PORTRAITS.

	PAGE
ROBERT WILHELM BUNSEN	103
DR. JOSEPH VON FRAUNHOFER	159
GUSTAV ROBERT KIRCHHOFF	164
WILLIAM HUGGINS	337
P. ANGELO SECCHI	342

PART FIRST.

ON THE ARTIFICIAL SOURCES OF HIGH DEGREES OF HEAT AND LIGHT.

ON THE ARTIFICIAL SOURCES OF HIGH DEGREES OF HEAT AND LIGHT.

1. Introduction.

THE total eclipse of the sun in India of the 18th of August, 1868, was an event which, it will be remembered, excited extreme interest in the scientific world, and led to a large expenditure of money and labor in order that a new method of investigation — Spectrum Analysis — might be applied to those mysterious phenomena invariably present at a total solar eclipse, the nature and character of which the unassisted powers of the telescope had proved themselves inadequate to reveal. The brilliant results obtained at this eclipse were fully confirmed by the more recent observations made in North America during the total eclipse of the 7th of August, 1869, and the records of those eclipses laid before the various scientific societies clearly assert the triumph of spectrum analysis. On this account the new method of investigation has excited great interest in all cultivated circles, and therefore a familiar and comprehensive exposition of the details of spectrum analysis, in which is shown the great value of this method of research in every department of physical science, seems not uncalled for.

By *spectrum* is not understood in physics a spectre or ghostly apparition, as the verbal interpretation of the word might well lead one to suppose, but that beautiful image, brilliant with all the colors of the rainbow, which is obtained when the light of the sun, or any other brilliant object, is allowed to pass through a triangular piece of glass—a prism.

The unassisted eye can perceive no difference in the light

from the heavenly bodies and that from various artificial sources, beyond a variation in color and brilliancy; but it is quite otherwise when the light is viewed through a prism. There are then formed very beautiful colored images or spectra, the constitution and appearance of which depend upon the nature of the substance emitting the light. The different appearances presented by these colored images are so entirely characteristic, that to every substance, when luminous in a gaseous form, there corresponds a peculiar spectrum which belongs only to that particular substance.

It follows, therefore, that when the spectra of different substances have been determined once for all, by previous researches, and have been recorded in maps or impressed upon the memory, it is easy in any future investigation to recognize at once, from the form of the spectrum which a body of unknown constitution presents, the individual substances of which it is composed.

This statement presents in general terms the nature of spectrum analysis. It analyzes bodies into their constituent parts, not as the chemist, with alembics and retorts, with reagents and precipitates, but by means of the spectra which these substances give when in a state of intense luminosity.

Spectrum analysis in no way supplants the methods of chemical analysis hitherto in use; for its function is neither to decompose nor to combine bodies, but rather to reconnoitre an unknown territory, and to stand sentinel, and signalize to the physicist, the chemist, and the astronomer, the presence of any substance brought beneath its scrutiny.

With what acuteness, with what delicacy does spectrum analysis accomplish this task! When the balance, the microscope, and every other means of research at the command of the physicist and the chemist utterly fail, one look in the spectroscope is sufficient in most cases to reveal the presence of a substance. If a pound of common salt be divided into 500,000 equal parts, the weight of one of these portions is called a milligramme. The chemist is able, by the use of the most delicate scales and the application of special skill, to determine the weight of such a particle; but, in doing so, he comes close upon the limits of his power of detecting by chemical means the presence of sodium, the chief element in common salt. But if that small milligramme be subdivided into three million parts, we arrive at so minute a particle that all power of discerning it fails, and yet even this excessively small quantity is sufficient to be recognized with certainty in a spectroscope. We have but to strike together the pages of an old dusty book in order to perceive immediately, in a spectroscope placed at some distance, the flash of a line of yellow light which we shall presently learn is an unfailing sign of the presence of sodium.

It was to be expected that so sensitive a means of investigation, from which no known substance can escape, would very soon lead to the tracking out and discovery of new elements which, till then, had remained unknown, either because they are scattered very sparingly in nature, or stand out with so little that is characteristic, from some other substances, that the imperfect chemical methods hitherto in use have not been able to distinguish them.

This expectation was brilliantly realized even by the first steps taken in this direction. The two Heidelberg professors, Bunsen and Kirchhoff, to whom we are indebted for the discovery of spectrum analysis and its application to practical science, very soon discovered, with their new instrument, two new metals, Cæsium and Rubidium, to which two others, Thallium and Indium, have been since added.

But all the brilliant and astounding results which spectrum analysis has furnished in the provinces of physics and chemistry have been far surpassed by its performances in that of astronomy. Newton's law of gravitation has given us the means of calculating the courses of the heavenly bodies, of projecting the orbits of the earth, the planets and comets, and of predicting their relative positions in these orbits, together with the accompanying phenomena of the ebb and flow of the tides, and the eclipses and occultations of the heavenly bodies. But this same gravitation chains man to the earth and forbids him to leave it. It is, therefore, only on the wings of light that news reaches him of the existence of those numberless worlds by which he is surrounded. The light alone, which proceeds from these stars, is the winged messenger which can bring him information of their being and nature; spectrum analysis has made this light into a ladder on which the human mind can rise billions and billions of miles, far into immeasurable space, in order to investigate the chemical constitution of the stars, and study their physical conditions.

Until within a few years, the telescope was the only means by which these investigations could be carried on, and the intelligence derived from this source concerning the stars and nebulæ was very scant, being confined to but partial information of their outward form, size, and color.

Since the year 1859, spectrum analysis has entered the service of astronomy, and its performances for the short space of eleven years are, in the most widely-differing ways, perfectly astounding.

It is possible by means of a prism to decompose into its component parts the light of the sun, the planets, the fixed stars, comets and nebulæ, and thus obtain their spectra in the same way as that of earthly luminous substances. By a careful comparison of the spectra of the stars with the well-known spectra of terrestrial substances, it can be determined, from their complete agreement or disagreement, with a certainty almost amounting to mathematical precision, whether these substances do or do not exist in those remote heavenly bodies.

The foregoing statements present in general terms the essence and scope of spectrum analysis. Its starting-point is the spectrum of each individual substance, and in order to obtain this it is requisite that the substance should not only be luminous, but should emit a *sufficient quantity* of light. Dark bodies are not available for spectrum analysis; if they are to be submitted to its scrutiny, they must first be brought into a state of vivid luminosity.

To avoid later interruptions and repetitions, it will be desirable, before entering upon the subject of spectrum analysis, to review with brevity the means afforded by chemistry and physics for rendering luminous all substances gaseous and non-gaseous, and even the least fusible metals.

2. The Luminous Power of Flame.

The immediate cause of the luminosity of flame has not yet been fully ascertained, notwithstanding the many investigations that have been made with this object. If a glass receiver (Fig. 1) be filled with oxygen, and a lighted piece of phosphorus be plunged into it from above, the phosphorus will burn with great energy and give out a dazzling light. In the same manner most metals previously raised to a glowing heat, as, for instance, a steel watch-spring, will burn in pure oxygen, with the development of an intense light.

FIG. 1.

Combustion of a Steel Watch-spring in Oxygen.

If, on the contrary, a stream of gas issuing from a reservoir of hydrogen be ignited in free air, it will burn with a scarcely perceptible flame. The flame produced by oil, petroleum, and coal-gas is very brilliant, while that from spirits of wine is faint.

What occasions this difference?

The chemical process of the combustion of phosphorus and of hydrogen is the same, namely, the combination of these substances with oxygen; the amount of heat evolved is also not very dissimilar; the difference, therefore, appears to lie only in the nature of the products of combustion. In the case of phosphorus this product appears as a solid body, in the form of a dense white cloud (phosphoric acid); in the case of hydrogen gas, the product of combustion is invisible, because it is water in a gaseous form—that is to say, steam.

This remark applies, with few exceptions, to all combustion which takes place at very high temperatures. A flame which contains neither *solid* matter as a product of combustion, nor yet a *foreign solid* body in a state of incandescence, is, as a rule, but little luminous, even when the temperature of combustion is very high; therefore, at a similarly high temperature, glowing solid or liquid bodies emit far more light than gaseous substances do; the fewer solid particles there are in a flame the less brilliant will be its light. The scarcely perceptible flame of burning hydrogen gas will immediately become luminous if any solid body be heated in it to incandescence.

If a spiral platinum wire be held in the flame it shines brightly; the glowing wire is clearly seen, and conveys the impression that the light is not due to the hydrogen flame, but to the glowing white-hot metal. The heat generated by the chemical combination of the hydrogen gas with the oxygen of the air renders the platinum incandescent, and it is the glowing platinum wire, not the flame, which emits the intense light.

If a grain of common salt be dropped into the dull flame, it flashes up brightly with a yellow light. The salt is dispersed into a million of the smallest particles, all of which glowing in the flame can no longer singly be distinguished: they thus give the appearance to the hydrogen flame as if it shone of itself.*

For the illustration of this point it is unnecessary to make any artificial experiments, since the flame of common gas, which, owing to its great brilliancy, is universally employed for domestic and other uses, is well suited to the purpose. Coal-gas is a chemical compound of hydrogen gas and carbon, though it is often contaminated to a more than necessary extent with other substances.

Carbon, after oxygen certainly the most precious of all substances, alike valuable in its crystal form of diamond as in its dirty black form of coal, is not distinguishable in common gas, for through its combination with hydrogen it has lost its brilliant sparkle as well as its black color, and it then appears as a transparent gas, not indeed as an independent body, but in the most intimate chemical combination with hydrogen, as carburetted-hydrogen gas.

If this gas be ignited as it streams out of an ordinary burner, in contact with the atmospheric air, the greater part of its oxygen is taken up by the hydrogen in the gas, and a considerable quantity of carbon, for which there is not sufficient oxygen pres-

* [This experiment is more satisfactorily made by the introduction into the flame of a finely-divided solid which is not decomposed, as is the case with salt. Some of the light when salt is employed is due to the luminous vapor of sodium.]

ent, is thrown down. Combustion takes place almost entirely near the edge of the flame, where it is in contact with the oxygen of the air; in the middle, the gas is merely decomposed by the heat of the combustion, and in this heat the very finely-separated particles of carbon which have been precipitated are in a state of brilliant incandescence. It is to these glowing particles that the gas-flame owes its illuminating power. In order to see them, it is only necessary to hold a cold substance, such as a china saucer, in the brilliant part of the flame; the disengaged carbon covers the saucer in the form of the finest soot.

The same thing occurs in the burning of tallow, stearine, oil, or petroleum; in the lighting of candles or lamps the combustible substance is first decomposed, and then, by the heat of combustion, combinations of carburetted hydrogen arise in the form of gas. When the oxygen is insufficient, only a small portion of carbon is immediately burnt, and that at the edge of the flame, where a great development of heat takes place; here the product of combustion is a gas (carbonic acid), and therefore the edge of the flame gives but little light; in the inner part, however, where there is a want of oxygen, the solid particles of carbon attain a white heat, and only as they escape out of the flame burn by the high temperature of the edge. It is, therefore, the incandescent solid particles of carbon that give to the flame its illuminating power.

Easy, therefore, as it is to give brilliancy to a non-luminous flame, it is no less easy to deprive a brilliant gas-flame of its luminosity; all that is required is to mix such a quantity of oxygen or atmospheric air with the gas before it is burnt, that the oxygen penetrates into the inner part of the flame, and burns all the carbon present in the gas. When this happens, the flame instantly ceases to be luminous, and is found nearly under the same conditions as the flame of pure hydrogen gas. With a sufficient quantity of oxygen the combustion of the hydrogen, as well as of the carbon, goes on with unusual rapidity in all parts of the flame at once; the natural consequence of this is that, on account of the incomparably greater development of heat, the non-luminous gas-flame is much hotter than the luminous one; it is now a heat-flame, and a source of heat instead of light.

In opposition to these facts, there are others which prove that the presence of solid particles in a flame is by no means necessary in order to give it luminosity. Frankland has shown that, when hydrogen is burnt in oxygen under a pressure gradually increasing up to twenty atmospheres, the feeble luminosity of the flame becomes gradually argumented, until, at a pressure of ten atmospheres, it is bright enough to allow of a newspaper being read at the distance of two feet from the flame. A similar increase of brilliancy is observed in the combustion of carbonic-oxide gas in oxygen under pressure; and, under similar conditions, bisulphide of carbon burns in oxygen, or in nitric-oxide gas, with an intense light, though no solid particles are present in the flame. Frankland maintains, therefore, that the luminosity of a coal-gas flame is not due to the presence of solid particles of incandescent carbon, and that the soot deposited on a porcelain saucer from a gas-flame is not solid carbon, but a conglomerate of the densest light-giving hydrocarbons. He has proved that the very clear flame of coal-gas is perfectly transparent, from the fact that he sent the intense electric light through such a flame on to a screen, without the least trace being perceived of any solid incandescent particles of carbon.

While Frankland considers the luminosity of the flame to depend mainly on the *density* of the burning gas, St.-Claire Deville ascribes it chiefly to the *temperature* of the combustion which is dependent upon the density of the gas.

Whatever may be the cause of luminosity in an incandescent body, this fact is certain, that incandescent, solid, and liquid bodies possess a much geater brilliancy, and emit a much more intense light, than gases do when rendered luminous under ordinary pressure; and that the luminous power of gases increases in proportion to the pressure to which they are subjected, by which their density is increased, and they approach more nearly the condition of fluids.

3. The Bunsen Burner.

The correctness of the foregoing statements may be easily shown by a lamp of Bunsen's construction (Fig. 2), which is absolutely required in all researches with spectrum analysis. This burner causes a rapid combustion of the particles of carbon in coal-gas, and so generates a high degree of heat, and this is accomplished by allowing the gas which enters the lower part of the lamp to mix plentifully with atmospheric air before passing up the tube to feed the burner. For this purpose, the lower chamber S is perforated, so that the outer air enters freely while the gas is burning. The gas takes up here a sufficient quantity of air, and then rises with it to the top of the tube *a a*.

FIG. 2.

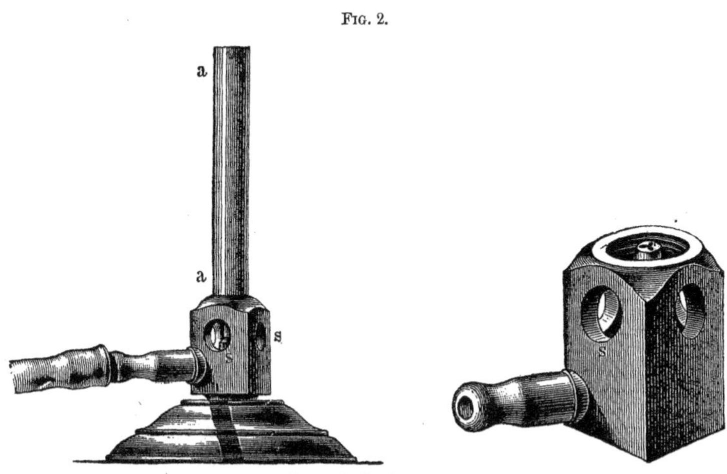

Bunsen's Gas-burner.

The flame gives no light, but its heat is very considerable; if the supply of outer air be intercepted by closing with the fingers the openings to the mixing-chamber S, the flame immediately becomes luminous, and throws down particles of carbon in abundance, which was not the case before, as no soot whatever is deposited on a china saucer by the non-luminous heat-flame.

If the burner be contrived, as is very desirable when working with the spectroscope, so that the entrance of air to the gas can be shut off at will, either entirely or partially—which is easily effected by turning round a perforated ring—then the same burner serves to give alternately a luminous or a heat flame. When the ring cuts off the supply of air to the gas by closing the openings to the mixing-chamber, the flame shines brightly, like any ordinary gas-flame; when, on the contrary, the ring is turned to allow the air to pass into the mixing-chamber, the luminosity ceases, and the flame becomes a heat-flame.

The heat of this flame is so intense that it is capable of converting many substances, which it may be desirable to examine by spectrum analysis, into a gaseous condition, causing them to emit sufficient light to yield a clearly perceptible spectrum. But a far greater heat may be attained if the atmospheric air, instead of being left to mix itself with the gas, be forced in by means of a powerful blow-pipe. A contrivance of this kind is seen in the gas blow-pipe (Fig. 3); the gas from the pipe G enters a wide

Fig. 3.

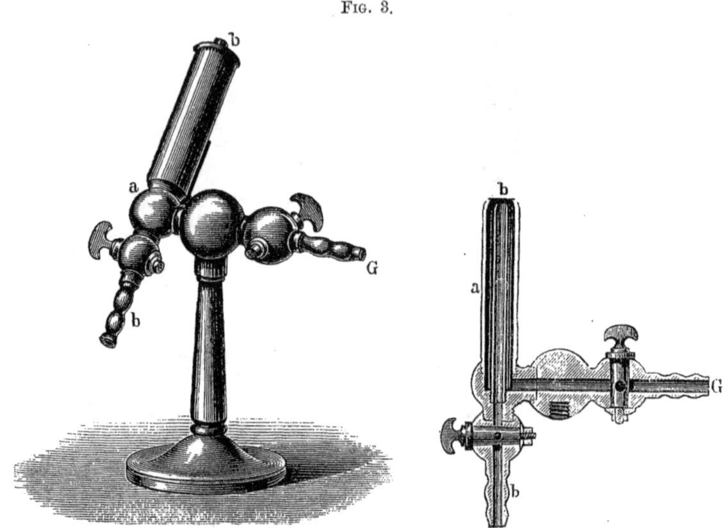

Bunsen's Gas Blow-pipe.

tube *a*, which is closed at the lower end by a stopcock, and is made to turn on a pivot round the stand; the gas passes through, and escapes at the farther end. In the middle of this tube *a* runs a second narrower tube *b b*, through which the atmospheric air is forced into the stream of gas by means of a bellows and an elastic tube. The gas-flame receives so much oxygen in this way, not only round the edge, but also in the centre, that an enormous quantity of heat is generated by the complete combustion of the hydrogen and carbon. Over the escape-end, a tube slides up and down, and partly by this means, and partly by the cocks, the degree of heat in the flame can be regulated at will. The greater the quantity of gas which can be burnt in a given space, and the greater the energy and the rapidity of the combustion, the greater also will be the amount of heat evolved. For this reason, in the great laboratories, the atmospheric air is forced by a special air-pump into a strong iron receiver of the capacity of several quarts, where it is subjected to a pressure of one and a half or two atmospheres. If this compressed air be allowed to escape along with a copious stream of gas from a common tube, in the same manner as we have just described, the flame becomes one of such intense heat, owing to the rapid and complete combustion of so large a quantity of carburetted hydrogen, that it has power to melt in a few minutes considerable quantities of the least fusible metals, as, for example, a couple of pounds of platinum.*

4. The Magnesium-Light.

There are some substances, such as potassium, sodium, etc., which have so great an affinity for oxygen that they wrest it even out of its most intimate combinations in order to form with it a new substance—a process accompanied by a development of both light and heat. Among these substances, magnesium is especially distinguished for the extraordinary amount of heat and light which it thus produces. This metal is white like silver, and of remarkable metallic brilliancy; it is very light, but somewhat heavier than water, so that it will not float upon its surface. When heated in the air up to a certain temperature, it ignites, and burns, at the expense of the atmospheric oxygen, with a white and dazzling light on which, when near, the eye cannot bear to look.

Magnesium burns with great rapidity, and the solid product of combustion—solid incandescent magnesia—emits a very intense light; it partly rises in the air in the form of white smoke, and partly falls as white powder to the ground. Though the luminous power of the sun be 524 times greater than that of the magnesium-light, the activity of its chemical rays is only about five times as great. This light is therefore peculiarly adapted for the photographic representation of objects which are badly lighted, of works of art in dark palaces and churches, of underground buildings, and of small landscape pictures, such as representations of moonlight, etc. It is well known that the Roman catacombs, and the dark tomb-chambers in the interior

* [For the melting of platinum, air and hydrogen or oxygen and coal-gas should be used.]

of the pyramids, have afforded fine photographic pictures by the aid of the magnesium-light.

Unfortunately, the price of this costly metal is still high, and stands now at 20*s*. per ounce.* It may be assumed that the ordinary magnesium wire burns about one grain and a half in a minute, in value about a half-penny, and evolves a light which in intensity is equal to seventy-four stearine-candles, of which five go to the pound. From these experimental data it may easily be calculated that the *unit of light* in the combustion of magnesium does not cost much more than its equivalent in stearine-candles.

For the magnesium-light to be of practical use, the combus-

Fig. 4.

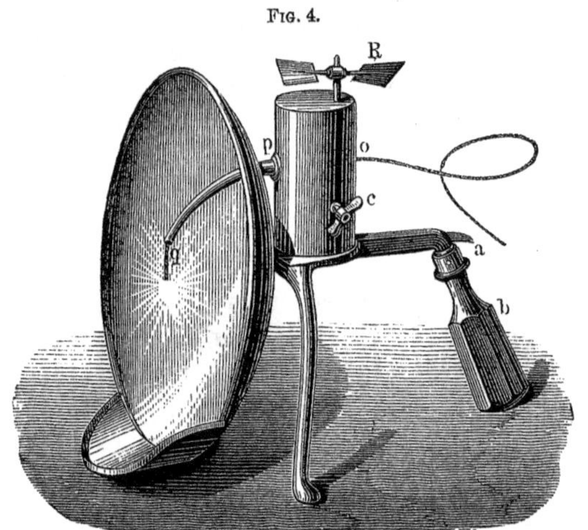

Grant and Solomon's Magnesium-Lamp.

tion must be under control, and the light so arranged that its concentrated rays can be thrown in any direction. The lamp constructed by Grant and Solomon accomplishes this object with tolerable success. It consists (Fig. 4) of a clock-movement enclosed in a case, which, when wound up by the key *c*, and set in motion, turns two small cylinders, placed one over the other. The magnesium wire enters the case from a coil at *o*, where it passes between the cylinders, and is pushed forward at a uniform speed through the small brass tube *p q*. The orifice *q* of this

* [The price in Hopkin and Williams's (5 New Cavendish Street, W.) catalogue is 12*s*. per ounce for magnesium in powder for burning.]

tube is in the focus of a silvered concave mirror, so that, when the wire *q* is ignited, all its light is thrown forward; by means of the handle *b* the lamp can be turned in any direction.

The adjustable fan R serves to accelerate or retard the speed of the clock; the works are set in motion by pressing down the button *a*, and stopped by pressing the button in the contrary direction.

In order to carry away rapidly the magnesia formed by the burning magnesium, an artificial draught is arranged, which, as the front of the lamp is enclosed by a glass door, escapes into a chimney above, through the space between it and the reflector, while the outer atmospheric air is allowed a free entrance by an opening beneath. The magnesium-vapor rises up the chimney, and thus the reflecting mirror, and the room in which the combustion takes place, escape contamination from the fumes. Another excellent lamp of this kind, contrived by Prof. Morton, of Philadelphia, is represented in Fig. 5. The clock-work is

FIG. 5.

Prof. Morton's Magnesium-Lamp.

placed at the lower part of the case at the back, above which stand two reels of magnesium wire. In the front part of the case are fixed the two cylinders through which, by means of clock-work, the bands of magnesium are pushed beneath the chimney toward the opening in front, where they are ignited. The atmospheric air is allowed a free entrance to the place of combustion, both in front and at the sides, so that a powerful draught is created, by which the fumes of magnesia are carried up the chimney.* In the lower part of the chimney, below the light, work eccentric cutters, by which the ashes formed by the combustion are removed from time to time. Above the chimney is placed a bent tin tube of from three to six feet in height, over which is fastened a bag of gauze or muslin, which, without presenting any perceptible hinderance to the current of air, prevents the magnesia-dust from escaping. By this contrivance the light is preserved from the prejudicial influence of the vapors; it exceeds in brilliancy that of the lamp described above, and burns with steadiness and regularity.

We have dwelt the longer on this light, since magnesium plays so important a part in spectrum analysis; but the heat which its combustion generates cannot be used for volatilizing other substances and rendering them luminous, as its brilliancy is so great as to completely overpower their light. Under these circumstances we must seek for a flame which, with the least possible luminosity, shall yet evolve sufficient heat to fuse most metals; such a flame chemistry furnishes us in the oxyhydrogen blow-pipe.

5. The Oxyhydrogen Flame.

In the Bunsen burner the combustion of coal-gas ensues slowly and incompletely: slowly, because the hydrogen in combination with carbon is supplied only in small quantities; incompletely, because the gases are not mixed in due proportions, and the nitrogen of the air presents a hinderance. If, on the contrary, pure hydrogen gas be previously mixed with as much pure oxygen as will insure its complete combustion (two volumes of hydrogen with one of oxygen), oxyhydrogen gas is obtained, which when ignited explodes with a fearful noise, and

* [When the light of burning magnesium is observed spectroscopicelly, in additon to a brilliant continuous spectrum, the bright lines of the vapor of magnesium are seen, and also other lines which Huggins found in the light of magnesia heated in the oxyhydrogen flame, and which appear to belong to volatilized magnesia. The light of magnesium burning in air seems to have a threefold source, luminous vapor of magnesium, luminous vapor of magnesia, but chiefly incandescent solid magnesia from the combination of the metal with the oxygen of the air.]

occasions sometimes the destruction of the strongest vessels. The heat evolved by this combustion is the greatest which can at present be produced by *chemical* means, and it is sufficient to accomplish the fusion of substances which have borne unchanged the action of the hottest furnaces.

To make use of the intense heat of this flame without encountering the danger of an explosion, the gases must not be mixed before ignition, nor allowed to flow out of the same common reservoir, as in that case the flame would spread into the interior, and cause the ignition of the whole quantity. It is necessary so to arrange the apparatus that the gases shall reach the emission-tube from separate vessels, and be allowed to mix only immediately before escaping from the burner.

The simplest arrangement of this kind is similar to that of the gas blow-pipe in Fig. 3, but with this difference, that the section of the two tubes should bear more nearly the relation of two to one. The gases are stored in two separate gas-bags * (Fig. 6),

Fig. 6.

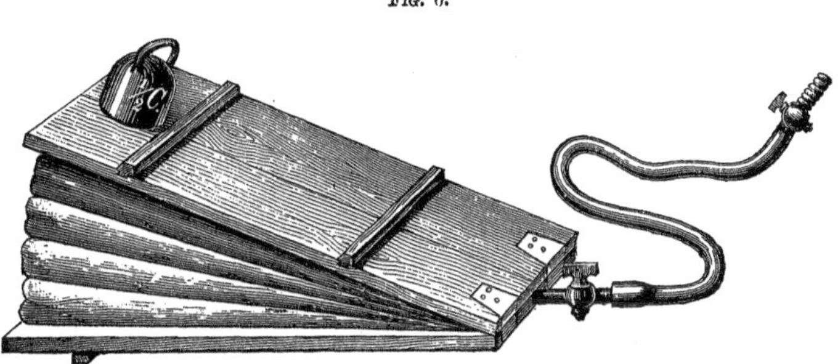

Gas-bag for Oxygen or Hydrogen.

whence they reach the lamp by means of pressure. The outer wide tube of the lamp must be placed in connection with the hydrogen reservoir, and the inner narrow one with that containing oxygen ; both the tubes should be fitted with a fine brass-wire netting, to prevent the flame retreating into the inside, or

* [More convenient than the bags, in which the gases can be kept with safety but a very short time, are the wrought-iron vessels which may be purchased of Mr. Ladd, Beak Street, London, filled with the gases condensed to about twenty atmospheres. These iron bottles contain sufficient gas to maintain an ordinary oxyhydrogen light for from six to eight hours. They can be refilled with condensed gas at a small expense.]

the gas extending from one tube to the other, from any cause, such as the diminution of pressure in the reservoirs.

A very convenient arrangement for such an oxyhydrogen lamp, or blow-pipe, is made by fixing on to a stand the burner C (Fig. 7), with its two tubes S and W conveying oxygen and hydrogen, the upper part of the tube C being inclined sideways, and so connected with its lower portion that it can be turned in any direction. If a carrier be connected to the piece E, which may be made to approach the burner, and furnished at the end with a contrivance for holding things, such as a socket, pincers, a small plate, etc.; and further, if a screw with rackwork be so applied that the whole upper part E may be moved up and

Fig. 7.

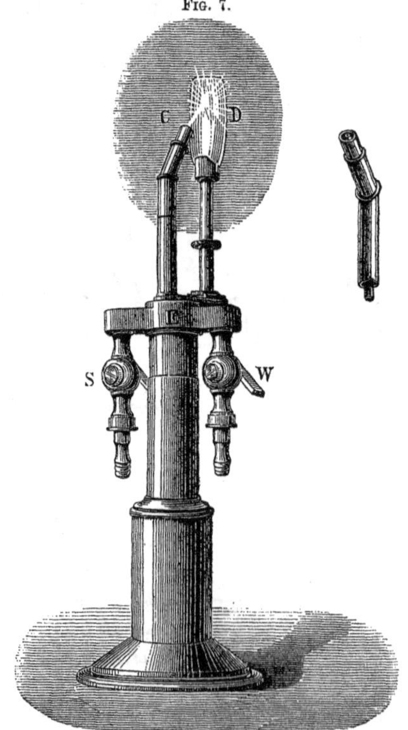

Oxyhydrogen Blow-pipe.—(Drummond's Lime-light.)

down—we obtain an apparatus which can be used for heat as well as light, and which, on account of its being so easily manipulated, may be employed for many practical purposes.

To produce the oxyhydrogen flame, it is necessary to open first the cock W, and allow the hydrogen to flow out for a few seconds before igniting it, that it may expel the atmospheric air remaining in the elastic tube; the hydrogen burns, under the pressure of the weight lying upon the bag of gas (100 lb.), in a long, faintly-luminous flame. The oxygen-cock S may now be carefully opened—the entrance of the oxygen into the hydrogen flame being generally announced by a very faint explosion—and on gradually fully opening the tap the flame becomes shorter and more pointed, until its luminosity almost entirely ceases; if the excess of hydrogen gas be now shut off by turning the cock W, there will be immediately formed the small, pointed, non-luminous flame of the oxyhydrogen blow-pipe.

It would carry us too far from our present purpose were we to describe the range of wonderful experiments in combustion which are made with the oxyhydrogen blow-pipe in the lecture-rooms of chemists; two of these will suffice to show the powerful heat produced by this flame:

If a thick wire of platinum, a metal very difficult to fuse, be held in the flame, it melts immediately like wax. If a bundle of steel wires be placed in the flame, the iron sputters about in a thousand brilliant sparks like a shower of fire, and great molten drops of the glowing metal fall to the ground from time to time, and run about in all directions.

6. Drummond's Lime-light.

In order to make the oxyhydrogen flame a source of intense light, a cylinder, D (Fig. 7), of well-burnt lime is placed upon the socket of the lamp, and the flame directed against its upper part; it begins at once to glow, and throws out a dazzling light.

The oxyhydrogen light, or Drummond's lime-light as it is sometimes called, after its discoverer, attains a still higher intensity, if a piece of magnesium or zirconia be substituted for the cylinder of lime—an arrangement that has often been adopted in the public illuminations in Paris. While the lime cylinder slowly consumes in the oxyhydrogen lamp, so that fresh surfaces must be constantly presented to the flame, the piece of zirconia does not waste, and remains unchanged, in spite of the most intense incandescence.*

* [Huggins found, in the spectrum of the light from lime placed in the oxyhydro-

As the heat as well as the light of the oxyhydrogen flame depends upon the quantity of the burning gases, it is difficult to estimate the temperature with accuracy. In a lamp in which the diameter of the outer tube (hydrogen) is four-tenths of an inch, and that of the inner one (oxygen) one-fifth of an inch, the strength of the light is at least equal to that of 180 stearine-candles; the temperature at which platinum melts is about 1,470° C. (2,678° Fahr.); but the heat of this flame under ordinary pressure is estimated by Bunsen to be 2,800° C. (5,070° Fahr.).* As the oxyhydrogen light and the magnesium light are employed in a variety of ways—not only in public illuminations, but also in theatrical displays, in the exhibition of dissolving views, and in the gas-microscope—so the non-luminous flame renders important service to spectrum analysis on account of its extraordinary heat, in which many substances may be rendered luminous in a state of vapor.

The facility with which oxygen gas can now be produced in large quantities, and the possibility of employing ordinary coal-gas in place of pure hydrogen gas, combine to render the oxyhydrogen flame a cheap mode of developing an extraordinary degree of heat and light, easy and safe to manage, and sufficient in most cases to exhibit, even to a large audience, the physical principles of spectrum analysis, and its various methods of application.†

7. The Electric Spark.

To attain, however, the greatest amount of heat and light

gen flame, bright lines similar to those which are seen when chloride of calcium is heated in the flame of the Bunsen burner, and which belong probably to volatilized lime, and not to the vapor of calcium. These lines show that a portion of the lime is volatilized by the heat. No lines were seen in the spectrum when zirconia was employed; this earth, therefore, appears to be fixed at the temperature of the oxyhydrogen flame.]

* [Pouillet gives 3,082° F. as the melting-point of platinum. By calculations founded upon the amount of heat ascertained by Andrews and others to be emitted during the combustion of a given weight of hydrogen, and the experiments of Regnault upon the specific heat of oxygen, hydrogen, and steam, it has been shown by Bunsen that the temperature of the oxyhydrogen flame cannot exceed 14,580° F., but the actual flame-temperature, as shown by the experiments of Deville and Bunsen, is probably from 4,500° F. to 6,000° F.]

† [The oxyhydrogen lamp is sufficient for the exhibition on a screen of the colored photographs of the drawings of spectra, but, when it is desired to exhibit the spectra of metals, the electric lamp should be employed.]

which can at present be produced, we must leave the province of chemistry, with its processes of combustion, and turn to that of electricity, where we are encountered by a host of phenomena, accompanied by an intense degree of light and heat.

When the electric spark flashes from the thunder-cloud to the earth, it illuminates the country around with a blinding light; it ignites and melts on its way the least fusible materials; in lightning we have the greatest heat and the most intense light which the powers of our earth are able in general to produce. But we can make no use of this electric discharge; we are scarcely even able to escape its destructive influence, and to prescribe to the lightning its appointed path from the cloud to the earth. We must, therefore, under such circumstances, confine ourselves to the electric discharge as produced by artificial means.

Besides the well-known machines which excite electricity through the friction of a glass disk, there has been added of late a contrivance called an induction machine, which yields a rich supply of electric force, and gives a spark of intense brilliancy. In all electrical motors arranged for exhibiting light, sparks are formed between two metallic poles or pieces of wire (Fig. 8),

Fig. 8.

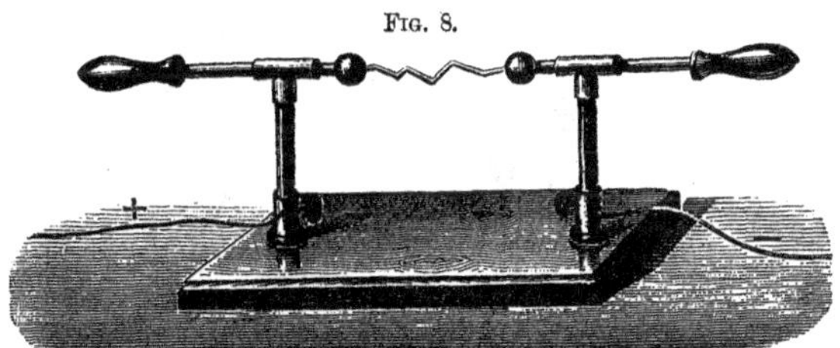

The Electric Spark.

which are placed in contact with those parts of the machine which collect the positive and negative electricity. By the mutual attraction of the two electricities, and the struggle for union, there ensues a tension of electricity at the end of the metal poles when they are separated from each other; if this be so strong that the obstacle presented by the stratum of air between the metallic conductors is overcome by it, then the electricities are instantly united, and the union takes place in that form of light and heat which is called the *electric spark*.

The amount of heat thus generated depends upon the degree

of tension and the quantities of electricity by the union of which it is produced; but, in most cases, it is so great that small particles of the metal poles are volatilized and become luminous. The glowing metallic vapor affects the color of the spark, which therefore appears with various kinds of light, according to the nature of the conductors. These phenomena afford us, in aid of our researches with spectrum analysis, a very simple method of volatilizing and raising to a high degree of luminosity most of the

Fig. 9.

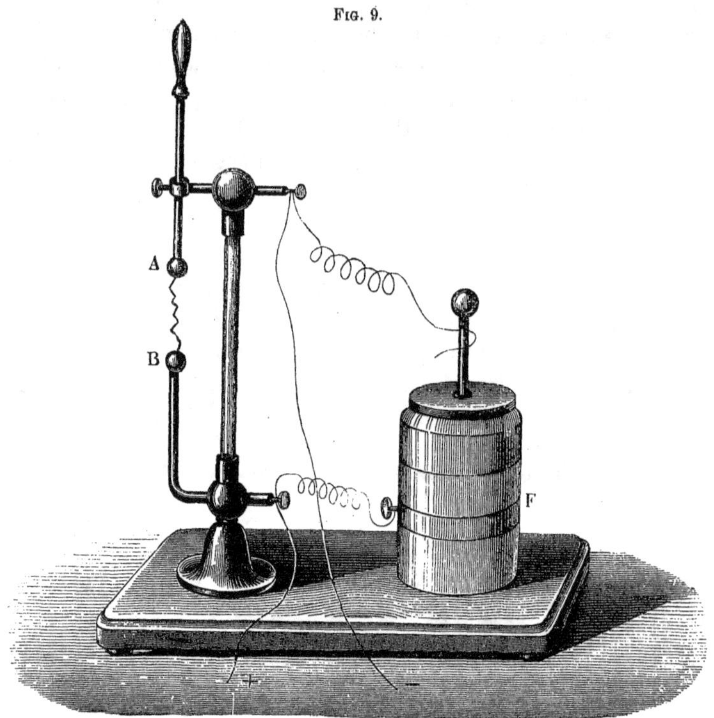

The Electric Spark intensified by a Condenser.

metals and other substances which are conductors of electricity. To obtain the same result with liquids, it is only necessary, as will hereafter be more fully described, to place one of the metal poles in the liquid to be examined, and to bring the other sufficiently near the surface for the spark to pass from it to the liquid. By the heat of the spark a small portion of the liquid is volatilized and made luminous.

If the spark supplied by these machines be insufficient, and a higher degree of heat be desired, an intensifying apparatus, such as a Leyden jar, F, or a condenser, must be placed between the two metal conductors A, B (Fig. 9); the spark passes between A and B only when the condenser has become charged, and the heat evolved is in proportion to the amount of electricity collected in the condenser.

Gases can also be made luminous by the electric spark, if enclosed in glass tubes and the spark sent through them. The discharge then takes a different color, according to the nature of the gas: in hydrogen gas it appears a purple-red; in chlorine, green; in nitrogen, violet; in oxygen, white; but this method is not advisable in general, because the heat of the spark is insufficient at the ordinary pressure to render a large quantity of gas luminous; it will presently be seen how this object may be attained by rarefying the gas.

8. The Induction Coil.

Among the most powerful motors of electricity is that apparatus which, by means of a comparatively weak electric current acting on every part of a thin wire many thousand feet in length, and completely insulated, produces electric sparks of such length and tension that they may bear comparison even with lightning. The small instruments of this kind, which are frequently employed in medical practice, are known by the name of Induction Coils. Those of larger size are called, after their inventor, Ruhmkorff's Induction Coils, and are now so constructed that with moderate dimensions they give sparks from twelve to sixteen inches in length.

If a long strip of gummed paper be strewed with copper filings, and brought, when dry, in connection with the poles of the induction coil, the current runs over the whole path of the filings, and passes from one particle to another with such rapidity as to give to the chain of successive sparks the appearance of one long stream of lightning. In this way sparks can be formed of from twelve to sixteen feet in length, which by their form, brilliancy, and loud report, bear the closest resemblance to lightning.

For most purposes of spectrum analysis, an induction coil of moderate strength is sufficient; the poles are constructed of platinum, because this metal is able to withstand the heat of the sparks which, when the instrument is in operation, pass between them with a loud, crackling noise, and follow each other in such quick succession that they appear as one continuous stream of light of intense brilliancy. As the induction coil, when once set to work, is self-acting, it is much more suited to the requirements of spectrum analysis than those machines which supply electricity only so long as their glass disks are in revolution.

9. Luminosity of Gases—Geissler's Tubes.

Experience has long shown that gases in a rarefied condition are good conductors of electricity, while they are without exception bad conductors when in a state of greater density. At the time when Bunsen and Kirchhoff first introduced spectrum analysis into science, it was known that in an egg-shaped glass vessel (Fig. 10) in which the air had been rarefied by an ordinary air-pump to a pressure of from $\frac{1}{12}$ to $\frac{1}{5}$ of an inch of mercury, the electric current would pass with the greatest readiness, in the form of a luminous arch, between the metal knobs enclosed in the air-tight vessel, even when the knobs were eight or ten inches apart—an envelope of blue light surrounding the ball by which the negative current entered, and a brush of reddish light being emitted from the positive ball.

Fig. 10.

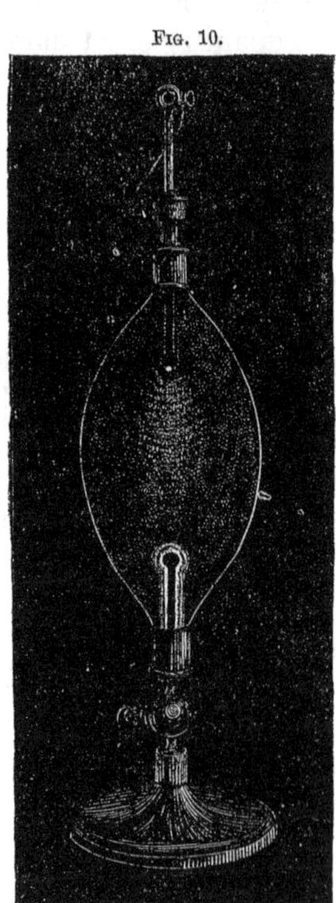

Electric Egg.

If small quantities of the vapors of certain substances, such as alcohol, phosphorus, or turpentine, be introduced into the glass vessel before rarefying the air, the spray of light will not merely be colored according to the nature of these vapors, but there will be also a series of dark stripes breaking crossways through the light, which, therefore, as it disperses from the metal knobs, will no longer be continuous, but be interrupted by dark strata.

The study of these phenomena has been simplified and considerably extended since Dr. Geissler, of Bonn, by a new method of rarefying air, succeeded in producing a vacuum in glass tubes, in which the gases to be investigated could be enclosed in a state of extreme attenuation, and which, by means of two platinum wires soldered at the end of the tubes, could be brought into connection with the poles of an induction coil.

These phenomena vary exceedingly, according to the form and composition of the glass of which each portion of the tube is composed, but especially according to the nature of the gas enclosed, and its degree of tenuity. Fig. 11 shows a compound Geissler's tube of this kind; when in contact with the poles of the induction coil, and the gas rendered luminous by the passage of the electric current, those portions of the tube which are filled with rarefied atmospheric air, or nitrogen, emit a beautiful red light; carbonic acid and carburetted hydrogens give green and white tints; in a dark room these tubes present a splendid spectacle by the alternate strata of dark and brilliant parts, the purity of the colors, and the variety of forms into which the glass has been manufactured.

Fig. 12.

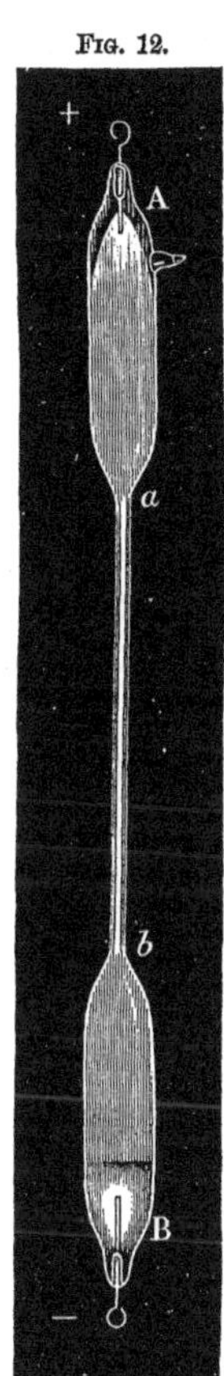

Plücker's Tube.

Fig. 11.

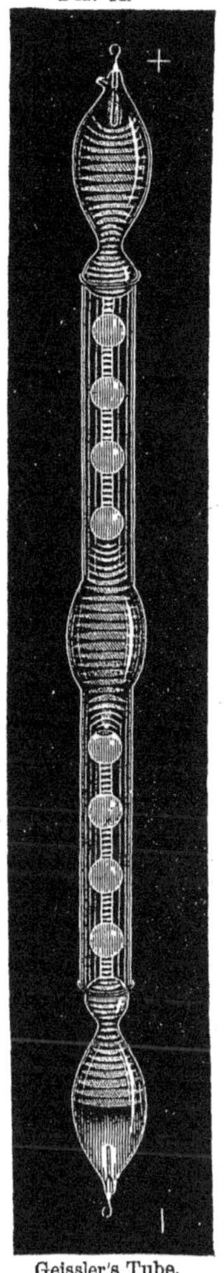

Geissler's Tube.

Geissler's tubes furnish a very convenient means for rendering any gas luminous; but the intensity of the light emitted by the gases when enclosed in these tubes is for the most part too small for the purposes of spectrum analysis, for the spectrum of such a tube can be examined only when every other light is withdrawn. Prof. Plücker, of Bonn, who, among the various scientific men distinguished for their labors in the development of spectrum analysis, holds a foremost place, and whose researches on the spectra of gases are of the highest value, concentrated this faint light by causing the electricity to pass through rarefied gas confined in a very small space, and this he successfully accomplished by substituting very narrow capillary tubes for the wider ones previously used.

Let us examine a series of Plücker's tubes as prepared for the purposes of spectrum analysis. The first of these is almost reduced to a vacuum—at least the small amount of gas in it does not produce a greater pressure than $\frac{1}{250}$ of an inch of mercury: the second tube (Fig. 12), where the central portion *a b* is capillary, encloses extremely rarefied hydrogen gas, the third nitrogen, the others oxygen, chlorine, carbonic acid, and minute traces of the vapors of iodine, sulphur, quicksilver, selenium, etc. If these tubes be brought singly into connection with an induction coil, in order

Fig. 13.

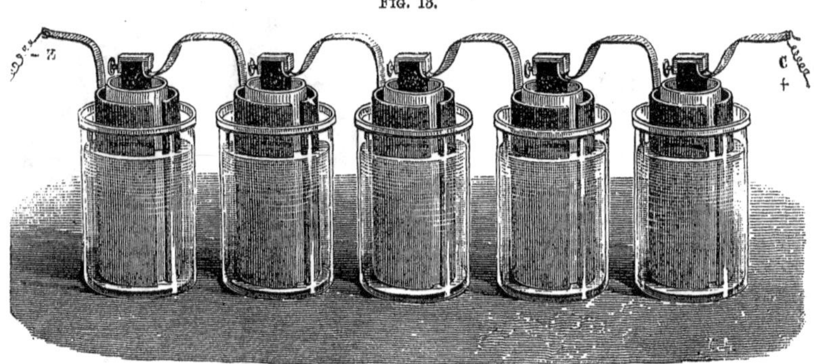

Bunsen's Battery.

that the current may pass between the platinum wires A and B, and render the gas enclosed luminous, the first tube shows no appearance of light, although the wires are barely separated $\frac{1}{25}$ of an inch, and the spark could be discharged in air at the distance of two or three inches. It therefore follows that the electric current requires a material conductor for its transmission from one wire to the other, and that it cannot pass where there is no trace of either gas or vapor—that is to say, *in vacuo.* In the other tubes, however, the light passes through the narrow portion *a b* with considerable intensity, and is visible at some distance as a sharply-defined line, bearing a very decided color peculiar to the luminous gas. These tubes, therefore, supply a means of rendering gases and vapors luminous; they emit under the influence of the electric current a brilliant line of light which is well adapted for observations of the spectrum of the enclosed gas.*

10. The Voltaic Arc—The Electric Light.

It will be well now to turn our attention for a short time to that source of electricity which is able to evolve the highest degree of heat with the most intense light—namely, the voltaic arc, or the electric light. When the poles, C, Z, of a powerful voltaic battery, such as a Bunsen battery, of fifty or sixty elements (Fig. 13), are connected by means of two metal wires with two pieces of carbon, *a*, *b* (Fig. 14), and these brought into contact, the electricity generated by the battery is discharged between them through the carbon, which is nearly as good a conductor as the metal. If these pieces of carbon be pointed at the ends, an extraordinarily intense light is emitted on the passage of the current at the points of contact, and they may be separated one or two tenths of an inch without interrupting the discharge.

If the copper wires K, Z, from the poles of the battery, be connected with the metal rods A, B, in which the carbon-points *a*, *b* are fixed, the electric current cannot break through the stratum of air between these points so long as they are not in contact, though this would easily be effected were the electricity of high tension from an electrical machine or an induction coil. If the upper metal rod A, which carries the negative carbon, be brought down so as to bring the two points in contact, there starts out at the same instant a bright point of light, which, in proportion as the poles are separated one-tenth of an inch or more, increases in extent and power, filling a large space with its brilliancy: the light is suddenly extinguished if the carbon-points are still farther separated. If, by pushing down the movable rod A, the points are again brought into contact—reproducing the light—then separated a little, and the machine left to itself, it

* [For simply viewing the spectra of the gases in these tubes, a spectroscope may be dispensed with. It is only necessary to view the brilliant line of light through a prism held before the eye.]

Fig. 14.

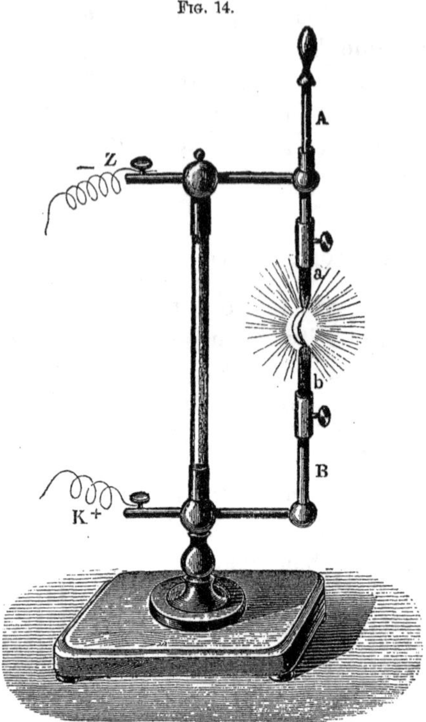

The Electric Light.

will be seen after a while, by the use of a dark glass, that the distance between the points increases, and that their form is constantly changing; after a short time the light goes out of itself, because the distance between the points has become so great that the electric current can no longer overcome the resistance of the intervening stratum of air.

It is not prudent to expose the eye to a near inspection of this dazzling light, and dark glasses prevent the delicate changes which are taking place from being observed with sufficient distinctness; it is therefore advisable, after the example of Le Roux, to throw upon a white screen an enlarged image of the glowing carbons by means of a magnifying-glass, when the appearance of the incandescent carbons and the intervening arc of flame may be observed from a distance without injury to the eyes.

For this purpose the room must be darkened, and a somewhat different arrangement employed for holding the carbon-points in the lamp A (Fig. 15.)* This apparatus is provided,

FIG. 15.

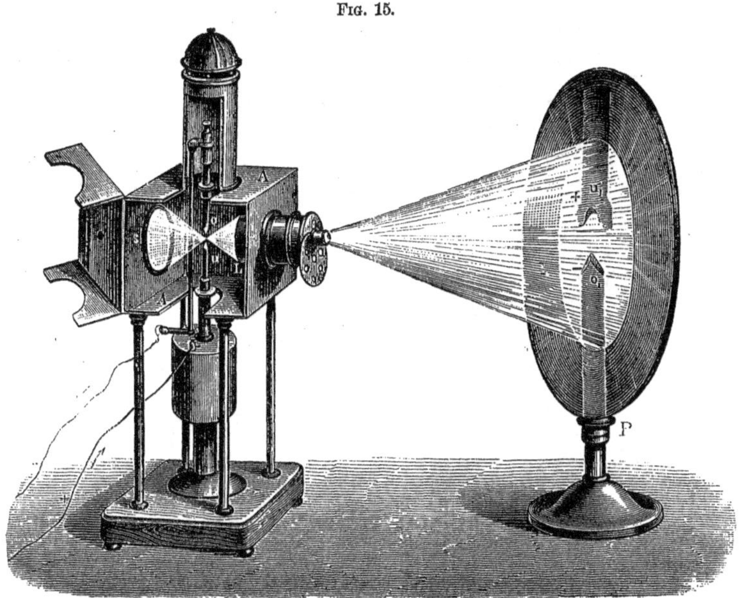

Projection of the Voltaic Arc.

like a magic lantern, with a lens, L, of suitable focal distance, placed in front, and a concave reflecting mirror, S, behind; a diaphragm with different-sized holes is placed before the lens, in which an opening of medium size (about one-eighth of an inch) is selected, the electric current allowed to enter, and the lens pushed backward and forward until the magnified image of the carbon-points is quite distinct on the white paper screen P, placed about thirteen feet from the lamp. With this image (Fig. 16), in which the carbon-points are magnified one hundred times, and made to appear the length of six feet, the slight changes going on in them can be easily observed. It will be noticed at the first glance that the intense light is emitted by the incandescent carbon, and that the arc of flame flickering between the

* In the drawing, this is made to appear open at the side, to show the arrangement of the carbon-points *o u*, the lens *L*, and the reflector *S*. In reality, the lamp is shut close up after receiving the carbon-holder.

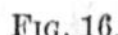

Fig. 16.

The Carbon-points of the Electric Light.—(Highly magnified.)

points—called the *voltaic arc*—is comparatively little luminous. It will be remarked also that one of the carbon-points begins to increase at the expense of the other; that which first loses its point and wastes the fastest is always the one which is in connection with the positive pole (the carbon-pole) of the battery. Very intensely bright particles pass from time to time from the positive to the negative carbon; little globules are to be seen running about on the surface of the carbon—globules of melted silica, a substance always to be found even in the purest carbon;

these are the enemies of the electric light, for they give by their motion a certain irregularity to the arc of flame, and, as they are much less brilliant than the carbon, they considerably abate the intensity of the light. Should these globules, by their restless movements, reach the hottest part of the points where the strongest light is emitted, their rapid motion is made known by a hissing noise, but unfortunately also by a sudden diminution of the light.

When the carbon-points have become so separated that the voltaic current has difficulty in passing, by means of the incandescent particles, through the air from one pole to the other, the strength of the current suddenly diminishes, and in like proportion the light begins to wane. This is at last extinguished, because the electric current can no longer build itself a bridge out of the glowing particles, on account of the distance, of perhaps half an inch, by which the points are then separated.

It is evident from what has been stated that the electric light is certainly very intense, but also very uncertain, and that a special contrivance is required to make the electric arc a source of continuous and steady light. In order to adapt it to optical purposes—such as projecting an image on a screen to be seen by a number of spectators in the same way as sunlight or Drummond's lime-light is employed—a further contrivance must be added, to insure the fixed position of the light by keeping the carbon-points not only at the same distance from each other, but also in the same position relatively to the lenses forming the image, notwithstanding the continual consumption of the carbon.

11. The Electric Lamp.

The ingenuity of scientific and practical men has succeeded in overcoming most of these difficulties, by the construction of various kinds of apparatus by which the point of light between the carbons may be kept steadily in the same place for hours together, provided the carbon employed be quite pure, and the strength of the battery tolerably uniform. But all these lamps, among which those of Foucault and Serrin hold the first place, are extremely complicated, and require constant watching while in use, on account of the extreme difficulty in procuring carbon of the requisite purity and hardness.

The electric lamp constructed by Duboscq, of Paris, on Foucault's plan (Fig. 17), is a masterpiece of mechanism, and is in every way suitable for the combustion of metals and the exhibition of spectra. Without entering into all its mechanical details,

Fig. 17.

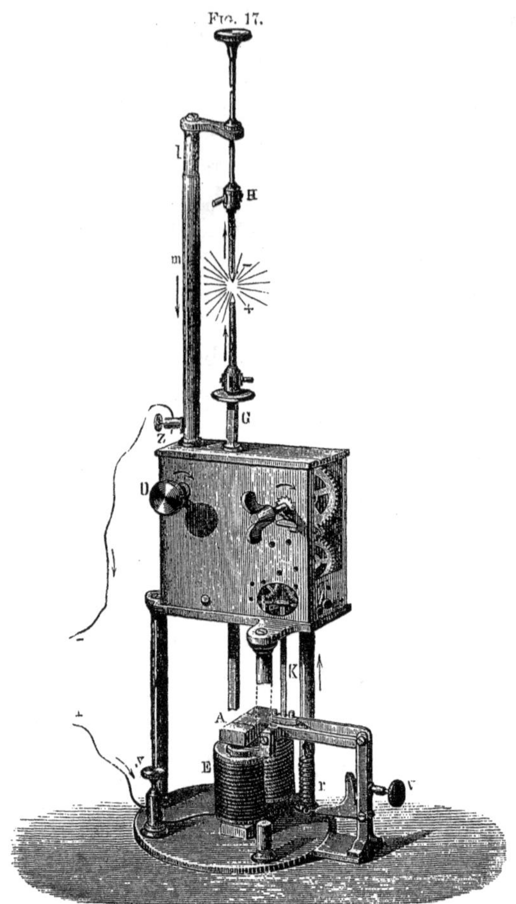

Foucault's Electric Lamp.

it is sufficient here to remark that the works are regulated by the magnetic power of the voltaic current in such a way that, in proportion as the carbon-points are separated by the waste of combustion, the carriers G and H are again made to approach.

The wires from the battery are connected with the lamp by

the binding screws *y*, *z*, and so arranged that the current must pass through the coil of the electro-magnet E, to reach the carbon-holders G, H. It is easy by means of the screw V so to regulate the armature, A, of the electro-magnet with its spring *r*, that it shall remain drawn down when the carbon-points are at the proper distance, about one-tenth of an inch: by the drawing down of the armature, the rod K lays hold of a portion of the wheel-work, and holds it still. When, in consequence of the combustion of the carbon, the distance between the points increases, the strength of the voltaic current diminishes, and the magnet E, becoming weaker in the same proportion, lets loose the armature, A, before the points have become so far separated as to break the current. The rod K by this movement is pushed aside, and sets the clock-work free, which, beginning to act, pushes the two racks G and *l* (which latter is movable up and down the tube *m*), carrying the holders, G and H, at a different rate of motion in opposite directions, so that the rod G, connected with the positive pole, is moved nearly twice as fast upward as the rod *l* is sent downward. The carbon-points have scarcely again approached, when the voltaic current and the power of the electro-magnet are raised to their original strength, the armature is attracted, and the clock-work stopped. By this mechanism the carbon-points can never be so far separated as to cause the extinction of the light, for the holders are moved at a rate proportional to that at which the waste of carbon takes place—the lower positive carbon being consumed twice as quickly as the upper negative one—and therefore the light is not only made continuous by this mechanism, but is kept immovably at one and the same place. By means of the screw D, the racks G and *l* can be moved independently of the clock, and by a third screw, to be found on the opposite side of the instrument, the upper rack, *l*, can be also moved by itself. In this way the experimenter has the power, before applying the electric current to the lamp, to place the arc of light in that position in the apparatus which the lens may require. The second function of the clock is to separate, without the interference of the experimenter, the carbon-points, which must be brought into close contact in order that the voltaic arc may be formed between them, and the carbon attain its highest incandescence. The separation is accomplished by the racks G and *l*, which before moved forward, being made to go backward by means of two connected cog-wheels, which can work them in either direction, a contrivance which helps to make the electric lamp one of the most complicated but at the same time one of the most ingenious and complete instruments employed in the illustration of physical science.*

The intensity of the heat and light from the voltaic arc depends upon certain circumstances, but principally upon the amount of electricity generated, and therefore on the number and nature of the elements employed, and on the purity of the carbon-points. With a medium-sized battery, consisting of 50 or 60 of Bunsen's or Grove's elements, the light varies from that of 400 to 1,000 stearine-candles, according to the purity of the carbon-points, and their distance from one another. Fizeau and Foucault have compared the chemical power of the electric light with that of the sun, by means of iodized silver plates, and found that the electric light from a Bunsen battery of 46 elements could be expressed by the number 235, supposing sunlight at noon on an August day to be represented by 1,000.

The light from a Bunsen battery of 100 elements produces much discomfort to the eyes; according to Despretz, a single glance, even with the naked eye, is sufficient, when 600 elements are employed, to occasion considerable injury to the eye, and a long-continued headache. Even when only 60 elements are used, it is desirable to avoid looking directly at the naked light, and to protect the eyes with deep-blue spectacles during the experiments.

We are now in possession of all the sources of light and heat requisite for a complete exhibition of the laws and phenomena which relate to the spectrum analysis of terrestrial substances and the heavenly bodies. We shall employ in our illustrations, according to the nature of the subject, sometimes the Bunsen burner, sometimes the oxyhydrogen or the Drummond light, sometimes the induction coil and Geissler's and Plücker's tubes, and also frequently the electric light. The phenomena of spectrum analysis can be easily shown with simple means to a small circle of spectators, where every one can approach the apparatus

* [Mr. Ladd constructs a form of electric lamp specially adapted for the exhibition of spectra. The lantern is provided with two movable openings, by one of which the image of the voltaic arc may be projected on the screen, and by the other the spectrum of the light sent through one or more prisms may be thrown on the same screen.]

and the experimenter's table ; but their exhibition before a large audience, numbering many hundred persons, requires extraordinary means of demonstration, and the use of the strongest light and the most powerful heat that can be produced by artificial means.

PART SECOND.

SPECTRUM ANALYSIS IN ITS APPLICATION TO TERRESTRIAL SUBSTANCES.

SPECTRUM ANALYSIS IN ITS APPLICATION TO TERRESTRIAL SUBSTANCES.

12. Light.

ALTHOUGH the theory of light is now so completely understood that we are able to explain the most complicated optical phenomena, yet an elementary reply to the question, What is the nature of light? still presents some difficulty. We perceive the operation of this power of Nature in all directions and in the most manifold ways; the sun, as it stands in full splendor in the heavens, pours forth but a single tone of color over the earth, and yet the individual objects in the landscape appear in the most varied and glorious tints. What, then, are these colors? How are they developed out of the white light which the sun and other luminous bodies emit?

We need not seek to avoid answering this question if we can succeed in giving a clear insight into the phenomena of spectrum analysis; for we have already intimated that the world of color is the peculiar province of this new method of investigation.

The approaches to science are frequently obstructed by strange propositions, discouraging and apparently contradictory, which seem, to the uninitiated, like those ghosts that haunted the way by which Dante and his heavenly guide descended to the realms of the departed; with a little courage, however, we may easily traverse this dreaded path, seize hold of the harmless apparitions, and make friends first with one and then with another as we approach them.

We will therefore boldly grasp the proposed inquiry: if the answer to it cannot be exhaustive, it will at least contain material enough to incite to further reflection, and perhaps also afford the necessary basis for a more easy comprehension of the elaborate theories which are enunciated in physical treatises.

According to the theory generally received at present, the whole universe is an immeasurable sea of highly-attenuated matter, imperceptible to the senses, in which the heavenly bodies move with scarcely any impediment. This fluid, which is called *ether*, fills the whole of space—fills the intervals between the heavenly bodies, as well as the pores * or interstices between the atoms of a substance. The smallest particles of this subtle matter are in constant vibratory motion; when this motion is communicated to the retina of the eye, it produces, if the impression upon the nerves be sufficiently strong, a sensation which we call *light.*

Every substance, therefore, which sets the ether in powerful vibration is luminous; strong vibrations are perceived as intense light, and weak vibrations as faint light, but both of them proceed from the luminous object at the extraordinary speed of 186,000 miles in a second, and they necessarily diminish in strength in proportion as they spread themselves over a greater space.

Light is not therefore a separate substance, but only the vibration of a substance, which, according to its various forms of motion, generates light, heat, or electricity.

13. Analogy between Light and Sound.

This representation of the nature of light ceases to be surprising when we come to compare the vibrations of ether with those of atmospheric air, and draw a parallel between light and sound—between the eye and the ear.

A string set in vibration causes a compression and rarefaction of the surrounding air; in front of it the air is pushed together and condensed; behind it the vacuum it creates is filled up by the surrounding air, which thus becomes rarefied for the moment.

* The hypothesis, that atmospheric air in a condition of extreme attenuation is to be placed in the room of ether, is yet too vague and too little supported by optical phenomena to be here entertained.

This periodic movement of the air is transmitted to our ears at the rate of about 1,100 feet in a second; it strikes against the tympanum, and occasions, by its further impulse on the auditory nerves and brain, the sensation we call *sound*. Air in motion, by its influence on the organs of hearing, is the cause of sound; ether in motion, by its influence on the organs of sight, is the cause of light. Without air, or some other medium whereby the vibration of bodies can be propagated to our ears, no sound is possible. As a sonorous body throws off no actual substance of sound, but only occasions a vibration of the air, so a luminous body sends out no substance of light, but only gives an impulse to the ether, and sets it in vibration.

A musical sound, in contradistinction to mere noise, is produced only when the impulses of the air reach the ear at regular intervals; if the intervals between the impulses are not sufficiently regular, the ear is only conscious of a hissing, a rushing, or a humming noise; a musical sound requires perfect regularity in the succession of impulses.

The pitch of a musical note depends on the number of impulses in a given time—as, for instance, in a second; the greater the number of vibrations in a second, the higher will be the note produced. When the single impulses are fewer than 16 or more than 40,000 in a second, the ear is no longer sensible of a musical sound: in the first case it either perceives only an undefined deep hum, or else it distinguishes the individual strokes upon the tympanum and becomes sensible of them as distinct blows; in the latter case there is an impression of a sharp but equally indefinite shrill or hissing noise. The limits of susceptibility of the ear for musical sounds lie between 16 and 40,000 impulses per second. The number of vibrations in a second given by a normal tuning-fork was determined in the year 1859 to be 435 in a temperature of 15° C. (59° F.)*

The truth of the foregoing statements may be easily proved in the following manner: A disk of zinc, A, Fig. 18, is fastened to an axis which can be set in rapid rotation by means of a cord working over a large wheel. The disk is perforated with eight

* [The number of vibrations of a C tuning-fork is 512. The deepest tone of orchestral instruments is the E of the double bass with $41\frac{1}{4}$ vibrations. Some organs go as low as C′ with 33 vibrations, and some pianos may reach A with $27\frac{1}{2}$ vibrations. In height the piano-forte reaches to a^{iv} with 3.520. The highest note of orchestra is probably d^{v} of the piccolo-flute with 4.752 vibrations.]

series of holes placed along eight concentric circles, of which only four are given in the drawing: the holes are of the same size in each circle, and at equal distances from each other, so that their number increases in each ring from the centre to the edge.

Fig. 18.

The Siren.

When the disk, by means of the large wheel, is set in uniform motion at the rate of one revolution in a second, and one circle of the holes is blown upon with considerable force through a glass or metal tube, B, a note is heard: by blowing upon the next series higher, the note is of a higher pitch; a lower set of holes gives, on the contrary, a deeper note; so that, if all the rings were blown upon in succession from the lowest upward, the distinct notes of the complete octave would be heard.

This apparatus has received the name of the Siren; her "notes are not indeed ensnaring, nor does she threaten philosophers with the dangers of the Homeric heroes by the seductive charm of her voice;" on the contrary, she sings nothing but truth, if only a willing ear be lent to her song.

What is it that here produces the sound? The mere revolution of the disk makes no noise; the motion of the air by the blowing through the tube first elicits the notes. When by the rotation of the disk the current of air strikes against an opening, it presses through it, pushing the air before it and condensing it; this impulse reaches the ear at once, and strikes upon the tympanum: the current of air immediately afterward comes against the solid part between the holes, by which it is interrupted. If the circle blown upon contain twenty-four openings, the ear would receive twenty-four impulses at every revolution of the disk; and if the disk made twenty revolutions in a second, the ear would receive $20 \times 24 = 480$ impulses in the same interval. The outside circle has twice as many openings as the innermost one; it therefore furnishes with the same speed of rotation $20 \times 48 = 960$ impulses in a second.

The ear cannot distinguish the individual impulses when they exceed sixteen in a second; the impressions they then produce become blended together, the one following the other so instantly that the sensation in the ear is that of one continuous impulse or sound.

The *pitch* of a note is thus seen to depend entirely upon the number of successive impulses following each other at the same uniform rate, its *strength* upon the force of the impulse. With a stronger blast, the pitch of the note remains unchanged, but the tone becomes more piercing, while, if a ring containing a greater number of holes be blown upon, the pitch rises till in the last circle, with double the number of openings, the octave of the same note is heard that was given by the innermost circle.

It is true that the cause of sound is not the same in all musical instruments; sometimes it is the vibration of strings, or elastic prongs, sometimes stretched membranes, or, again, columns of air confined in tubes which create at regular periods a condensation and rarefaction of the air; but in every case a note can only be produced by similar impulses recurring at regular intervals, conveyed by the air to the organs of hearing.

Savart exhibited the cause of sound in another way which is not less instructive than the one just described. Instead of the perforated disk, he made use of a wheel provided with 600 teeth, which could be set in very rapid rotation in the same manner as the disk, and, as the wheel revolved, the teeth were allowed to press against the edge of a card. To make this experiment it is only necessary to substitute a toothed wheel for the perforated disk, as shown in the apparatus in Fig. 19, and while the wheel is in rapid revolution to hold a thin card or a piece of pasteboard against its toothed edge. The card is bent a little by each tooth as it goes by, and springs back to its first position as soon as it is released by the passing of the tooth: the motion of the card is communicated to the surrounding air, and reaches the ear in consequence of the regular revolution of the wheel, in the form of waves of air, or of condensations and rarefactions of the air following each other at regular intervals.

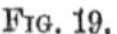
Fig. 19.

Savart's Toothed Wheel.

When the wheel is turned slowly, there is heard only a succession of taps, or isolated impulses of the card, distinctly separable one from another, which do not as yet unite to form a musical sound. In proportion, however, as the rapidity of the rotation is increased, the number of impulses increases also, and they unite in the ear to produce musical notes rising continually in pitch. A small recording apparatus fixed to the axle of the toothed wheel gives the number of revolutions in a second; if this number be multiplied by 600, the number of teeth on the wheel, the result gives the number of condensations of air striking the ear in a second. It is easy by this means to determine the number of vibrations the ear receives in a second from a note of any given pitch, and thus to verify the results obtained by the perforated disk.

It will now be easier to understand the motion of ether, and its mode of operation on the organs of sight. Ether as well as air can be set in regular vibrations, and even in such a manner that the phases of condensation and rarefaction are repeated at regular periods of time. The difference between the vibrations of the air and the ether is occasioned by the remarkable delicacy and elasticity of the latter, which not only permits a greater rapidity in the propagation of motion than is possible with the coarse and heavy particles of air, but also allows the number of vibrations per second to be immensely greater, so that their number has to be reckoned by billions.

14. Analogy between Musical Sounds and Colors.

Colors are to the eye what musical tones are to the ear. A certain number of ether-impulses in a second against the retina of the eye are necessary to produce the sensation of light: if the number of these waves pass above or below a certain limit, the eye is no longer sensible of them as *light*.

The first sensation of these vibrations on the part of the eye commences at about 450 billion impulses in a second, and the eye ceases to perceive them when they have reached double this number, or about 800 billion: in the first case the impression produced is that of dark red, in the latter of deep violet.

The greater the number of vibrations in any given time, the more rapidly must the single impulses succeed each other; it may be concluded, therefore, that the different colors are only produced by the different degrees of rapidity with which the ether-vibrations recur, just as the various notes in music depend upon the rapidity of the succession of vibrations of air. The vibrations which recur most slowly—amounting, however, to at least 450 billion in a second—give the sensation of red; those recurring more rapidly produce that of yellow; and, if the rapidity with which the impulses succeed each other continue to increase, the sensation becomes in succession green, blue, and violet, with which last color the human eye becomes insensible to the ether-motion, which, however, is still very far from having attained its limit of rapidity.

The gradation of the colors from red through yellow, green, and blue, to violet, is to the eye what the gamut is to the ear; and it is therefore not without reason that we speak of the tone and harmony of color. To the physicist the words color and tone are only different modes of expression for similar and closely-allied phenomena; they express the perception of regular movements recurring in equal periods of time—in ether producing colors, in air musical sounds; in the former instance by means of the organs of sight, in the latter by the organs of hearing—movements of extreme rapidity in ether, of more moderate speed in air.

But it will be asked, What becomes of those vibrations which are above and below the limits of the eye's sensibility to light and color? Do they wander about purposeless and unnoticed? By no means: forces are proved to exist in the rays of the sun, and other intensely luminous bodies, which cannot be perceived by the eye. Those slower vibrations which, though they are reckoned by billions in a second, do not yet amount to 450 billion, are made apparent to us in the sensation of heat, which is also the result of oscillatory movement—radiant heat being, like light, propagated without the aid of foreign bodies. Those vibrations, on the other hand, which have a velocity greater than that by which deep violet is produced—at which color the eye's susceptibility to light ceases—reveal themselves by their powerful chemical action; they succeed each other too rapidly for the visual nerves to be any longer conscious of the impulses, but they have the power of working chemical changes, and the decomposition of various substances can be undoubtedly traced to the agency of these invisible rays. An English physicist has succeeded in moderating the excessive velocity of these vibrations by means of certain substances, and in this way has brought some of the invisible chemical rays within reach of the eye's susceptibility.*

* [Fluorescent substances possess this property. The peculiar blue light diffused from a perfectly colorless solution of sulphate of quinine was observed by Sir John Herschel, and the colored light diffused from various vegetable solutions and essential oils was subsequently examined by Sir David Brewster. To Prof. Stokes, however, is due the true explanation of these phenomena; he showed that the blue light of the solution of quinine consists of vibrations brought within the limits of the power of the eye which were originally too rapid to be visible. If a fresh infusion of the bark of the horse-chestnut be placed beyond the limits of the visible spectrum of sun-

Dove describes, in his own ingenious manner, the course of the vibrations as they produce successively sound, heat, and light, as follows:

"In the middle of a large darkened room let us suppose a rod, set in vibration and connected with a contrivance for continually augmenting the speed of its vibrations. I enter the room at the moment when the rod is vibrating four times in a second. Neither eye nor ear tells me of the presence of the rod, only the hand, which feels the strokes when brought within their reach. The vibrations become more rapid, till, when they reach the number of thirty-two in a second,* a deep hum strikes my ear. The tone rises continually in pitch, and passes through all the intervening grades up to the highest, the shrillest note; then all sinks again into the former grave-like silence. While full of astonishment at what I have heard, I feel suddenly (by the increased velocity of the vibrating rod) an agreeable warmth as from a fire diffusing itself from the spot whence the sound had proceeded. Still all is dark. The vibrations increase in rapidity, and a faint-red light begins to glimmer; it gradually brightens till the rod assumes a vivid-red glow, then it turns to yellow, and changes through the whole range of colors up to violet, when all again is swallowed up in night. Thus Nature speaks to the different senses in succession; at first a gentle word audible only in immediate proximity, then a louder call from an ever-increasing distance, till finally her voice is borne on the wings of light from regions of immeasurable space."

15. Refraction of Light.

Light does not, like sound, require a ponderable material for its propagation; it comes to us from the remotest regions of space, and it penetrates the vacuum we may create in our laboratories with the greatest ease. But, when light passes through a stratum of air, through water or glass, a portion of the ether-motion appears to be destroyed—*absorbed*, and this absorption is so much the greater, the farther the distance the light has to

light admitted through a slit into a dark room, it becomes beautifully luminous, in consequence of the power which it possesses to lower the invisible ultra-violet vibrations into light which can affect the eye.]

* That is to say, the tympanum is pressed in sixteen times, and sixteen times withdrawn; therefore, sixteen blows are received upon the ear.

travel through these bodies. Thus objects are seen with perfect distinctness through a thin sheet of glass, while through a thick piece they are less clearly visible, and are sometimes almost obliterated.

So long as light passes through a completely homogeneous medium possessing the same density throughout, it is transmitted in a straight line; but it is quite otherwise when it passes from one medium to another of different constitution. When, for example, a ray of light coming through the air strikes upon the surface of water, or upon a sheet of glass, and afterward passes through these denser substances, it deviates from its straight course the moment it touches the new medium, excepting only when it falls perpendicularly to the surface separating the two media.

This deviation of the ray of light from its straight course is called *refraction:* it occurs in all cases where light passes obliquely from one medium to another of different density or constitution. If a straight stick be held half in air and half in water, the portion that is in the water does not seem to be the straight continuation of the upper part; the rod appears as if it were bent at the surface of the water.

The laws of refraction can be deduced with strict consistency and with mathematical precision from the theory of light which has been already enunciated; for our purpose, however, it will suffice to consider in detail only the most important of them. If, for example, the ray R I, Fig. 20, pass from the air into water at I, it will pursue its path through the water, not in continuation of the straight line R I, therefore not in the direction of I R', but in that of I S, which is nearer than I R' to the perpendicular I Q erected on the surface of the water at the point I. The refracted ray I S remains in the same plane R I Q formed by the incident ray R I with the perpendicular I Q, and in this plane the angle R I Q formed by the ray R I with the perpendicular Q P in the rarer medium (air) is, with very few exceptions, greater than the angle S I P formed by the ray I S with the perpendicular Q P in the denser medium (water, glass, etc.). On passing from a rarer into a denser medium the ray is usually bent *toward* the perpendicular in the denser medium; and, conversely, on passing out again from the denser into the rarer medium, it is bent *from* the perpendicular.

The relative proportions of the two angles R I Q and S I P may be ascertained by describing a circle with any radius from the point I, and letting fall the perpendiculars T U and S P from the points of intersection T and S upon the line Q P. These

FIG. 20.

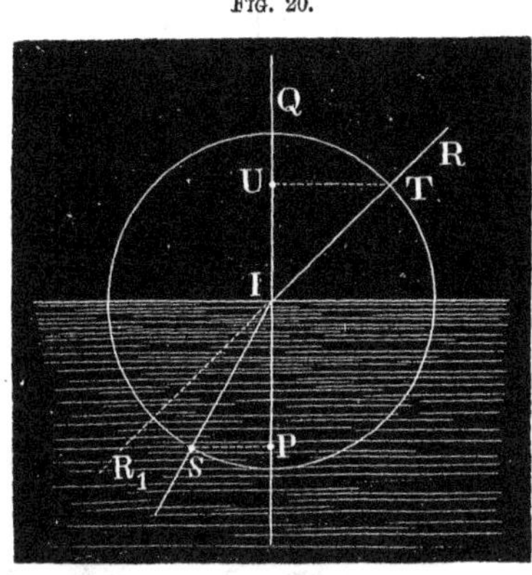

Refraction.

perpendiculars are called the *sines* of the angle which they enclose; thus, T U is the sine of the angle of incidence T I U, and S P is the sine of the angle of refraction S I P, and the sines are subject to the following universal law of refraction: *For the same two media the proportion of the sines of the angles of incidence and refraction is a constant quantity, whatever the angle of incidence.*

This proportion (T U : S P) is, for example, for air and water as 4 to 3, whence it follows that at whatever angle the ray R I in the air may strike the surface of the water, the refracted ray I S will be so deflected that T U shall be to S P in the proportion of 4 to 3. This invariable ratio between the sines is called the *index of refraction* of the media. The index of refraction for air and water is therefore expressed by 4 : 3, or more accurately by 1.34; for air and glass by 3 : 2, or 1.53. As the index of refraction varies according to the nature of the medium, it will necessarily have a very unequal value for different kinds of glass; it is, for example, for air and crown glass 1.534, while for air and dense flint glass it is 1.645; the refracting power, therefore, of flint glass is much greater than that of crown glass under similar conditions.

If a ray of light, as S I in Fig. 21, be transmitted from the air through a medium, M M, with parallel sides—for example, through a plate of glass—then a simple construction deduced from the preceding law will show that the incident ray S I will be diverted at I toward the perpendicular I N, in the direction I R; but that, on its emergence from the glass at R, it will again deviate to an *equal* amount from the perpendicular R N[1], so that, in whatever direction the incident ray S I may fall, the emergent ray R F always remains parallel to it. A spectator at F, on the opposite side of the glass plate M M, would receive the incident ray S I in the direction R F, and would see the luminous point S, whence the ray S I emanated, in the direction R S[1], so that this point would appear in a different place, S[1], to that which it really occupies.

Fig. 21.

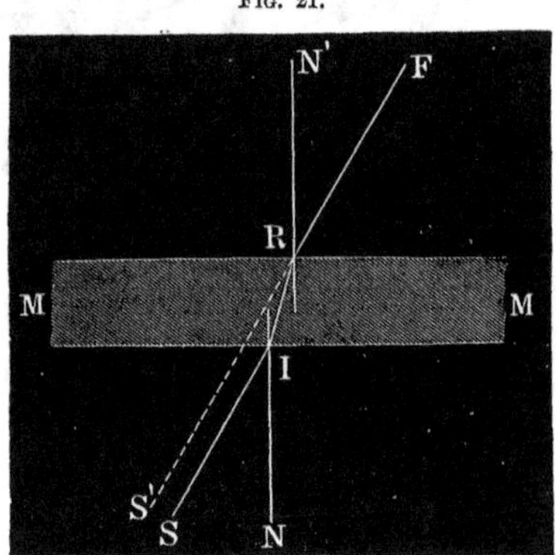

Path of the Rays through a Medium with Parallel Sides.

By the same principle can the daily phenomenon be explained that in looking through a window, though the rays pass from the air through the glass before reaching the eye, the outside objects do not appear either distorted or broken, as is the case with the stick held in water. Refraction does, in fact, occur in all those places where the line of sight is not perpendicular to the pane of glass. The objects are, notwithstanding, free from distortion, because the incident and emergent rays are parallel, though they do not form continuous straight lines; consequently, as the displacement of the rays is everywhere the same, the objects appear through the window in the same relative positions as when viewed without the interposition of the glass. It may be easily proved that the images of all objects seen through a window-pane are really displaced, and appear in a different position from the one they actually occupy, by comparing one part of them seen through air alone with another part seen through glass. As this displacement is but small through thin glass, it will be well, in making the experiment, to choose a piece of thick glass, and always to look at the objects obliquely. If a piece of thick glass, Fig. 22, be laid on any drawing so as only to cover one half, in order that one part may be seen through air and another through glass, the displacement of the portion under the glass will be seen clearly when the drawing is looked at obliquely.

FIG. 22.

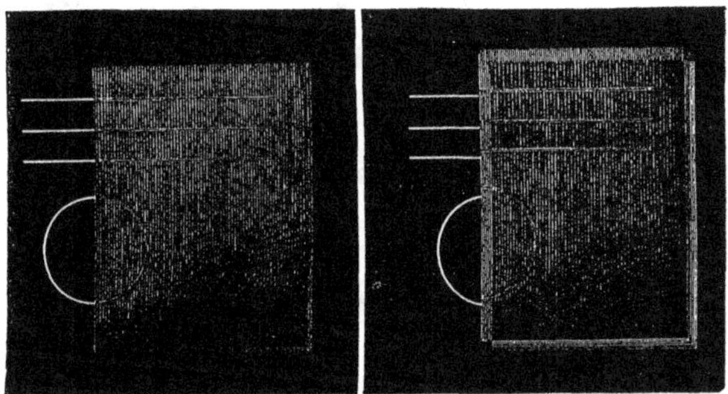

Refraction through Glass of Parallel Surfaces.

The refraction of light may be demonstrated to a large audience in the following manner, by the use of the oxyhydrogen light (Part I., p. 19): The oxyhydrogen lamp is placed in the same lantern which was used for the representation of the electric light (Part I., Fig. 15). The rays emitted by the incandescent lime, K, are rendered parallel by the lens L (Fig. 23) in the inside of the lantern, and in this form they pass through the ring R, across which is fixed a brass arrow. By means of another lens, L_1, placed at the same height as the arrow, but at some distance from it, an enlarged inverted image, P P, of the arrow is obtained upon the screen, and the image may be made perfectly distinct by adjusting the lens.

A rectangular parallelopiped bar of glass, *a a*, is then held against the arrow, so that the parallel rays of light passing through the ring are perpendicular to the sides of the glass.

FIG. 23.

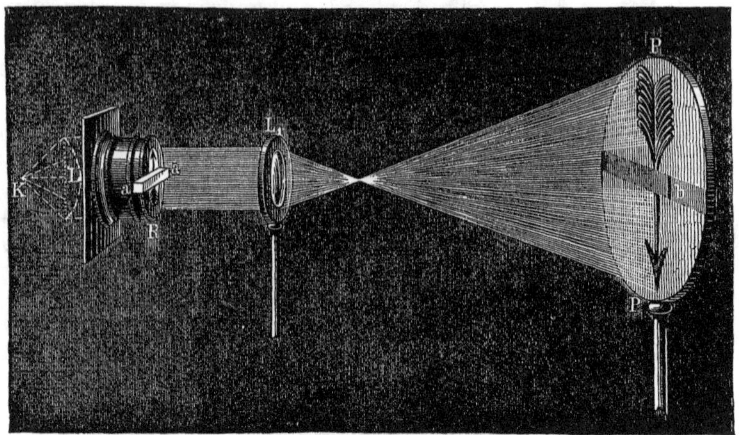

Refraction exhibited on a Screen.

No change is perceived in the image of the arrow itself; only the part where the glass bar depicts itself is somewhat less illuminated than the rest of the screen, which is caused by the absorption of a portion of the light in passing through the thick glass. It may be concluded, therefore, that those rays of light which pass through the glass, perpendicularly to its sides, have not been diverted from their straight course.

If, however, the glass bar be held obliquely against the arrow, the rays of light proceed no longer in a straight course between it and the lens L_1, but are turned on one side, as may be seen in the corresponding piece of the image of the arrow *b*, which appears displaced sideways from the shaft.

The same phenomenon is seen, if, instead of an opaque arrow, a disk, in which there is a narrow vertical slit, be inserted in front of the lantern. A B in Fig. 24 represents the enlarged image of the slit upon the screen, a bright sharp line. If the glass bar *g* be held flat against the disk, so that the rays of light passing through the slit are perpendicular to the surfaces of the glass, there appears only a slight dimness in the corresponding spot C of the image, in consequence of the partial absorption of the light by the glass. If, however, the glass be inclined against the slit, the corresponding portion of the image is displaced to the right or left, according to the inclination of the glass bar, and the image of the slit appears broken. If the experiment were repeated with a cube of glass twice the thickness in place of the half-inch glass bar, the absorption and displacement of the light would be much more strikingly exhibited.

FIG. 24.

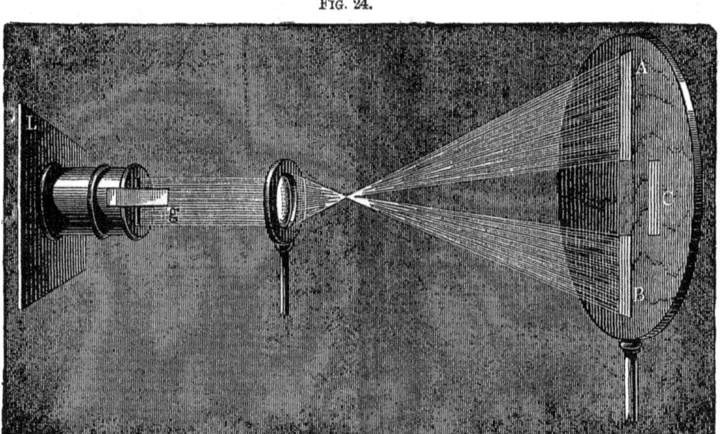

Projection of the Slit, and Displacement of the Rays by Refraction.

16. REFRACTION OF MONOCHROMATIC LIGHT BY A PRISM.

Let us now consider what occurs when with two media of unequal density, such as air and glass, the outside surfaces of one of them, instead of being parallel, form an angle with each other, as, for instance, in a three-sided glass prism, Fig. 25. For the convenient handling of such a prism, so that it may be turned about without the glass surfaces being touched, it is usually mounted on a brass stand, as shown in Fig. 26, when the edges where the surfaces unite can be placed at will in a horizontal or vertical direction.

In order to follow the path of a ray of light through a prism, let A B C, Fig. 27, represent the section of a prism standing on its base, and let the ray D *e* fall in the plane of the section upon the surface A B. The ray on entering the glass is bent toward the perpendicular *f e* in the direction *e h*. After passing through the prism in a straight course, it is again bent at *h* on emerging into the air, and is permanently deflected from the perpendicular *g h* in the direction *h* E. The ray D *e* therefore takes the direction D *e h* E when a prism is interposed in its path, while, were the prism removed, it would pursue its original course along the straight line D D_1.

FIG. 25.

The Prism.

It will thus be seen that the incident ray D *e* is deflected by the prism neither in a straight line nor in a parallel direction: theory and experience have both established that *in every case* the

FIG. 26.

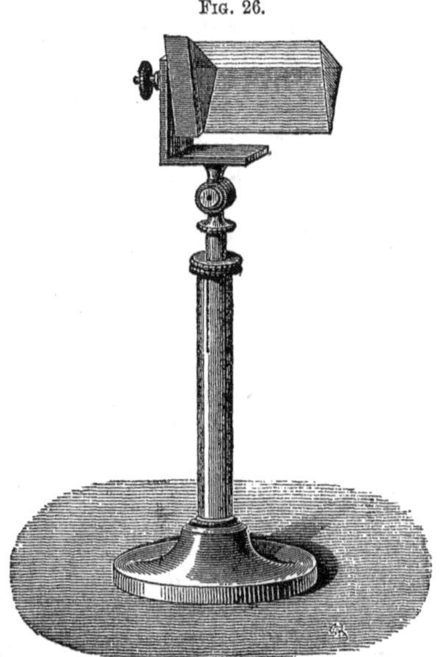

Prism mounted on Stand.

incident ray is diverted from its original straight course in such a manner that the emergent ray is bent toward that surface of the prism (the base) through which it does not pass. The edge A opposite the base C B is called the *refracting edge;* the solid angle B A C formed at that point, the *refracting angle;* and the angle formed by the emergent ray (*h* E) with the course D D_1 of the incident ray is called the *angle of deviation*, or *angle of refraction.*

Fig. 28 will illustrate this more clearly: the incident ray S I passes through the prism after its first refraction at I in the direction I E; it becomes refracted a second time as it emerges at E, and then proceeds in the direction E R. In all the three figures the dotted lines I N and E N[1] are drawn perpendicular to the surfaces of the glass; the ray is deflected in the denser medium of the glass toward this perpendicular, while it is bent away from it in the rarer medium of air, so that the angle it makes with the perpendicular is always greater in the air than in the glass. In the second figure the incident ray S I passes unrefracted through the prism in the direction I E, because S I is perpendicular to the surface of the prism. In the third figure the incident ray S I and the emergent ray E R form the same angle with the surfaces of the prism, in which position there occurs the smallest divergence of the emergent ray E R from the direction of the incident ray I S, and this is therefore called the position of *Minimum of deviation.*

Fig. 27.

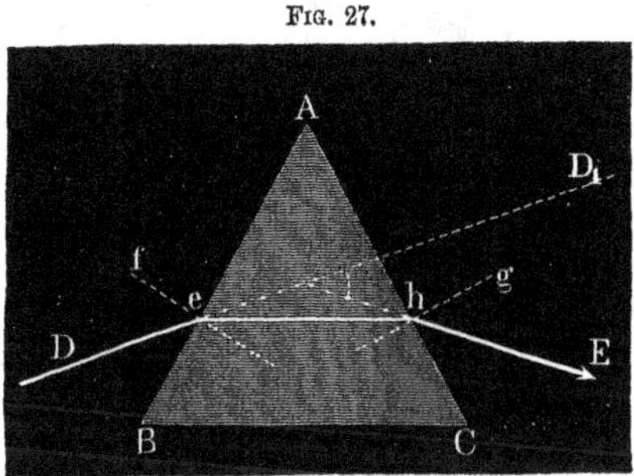

Path of a Ray of Light through a Prism.

A luminous point is seen, as is well known, in the direction in which the rays proceeding from it reach the eye. If, therefore, the rays from a candle (Fig. 29) are made to pass through a prism before reaching the eye, and the prism so placed that the

FIG. 28.

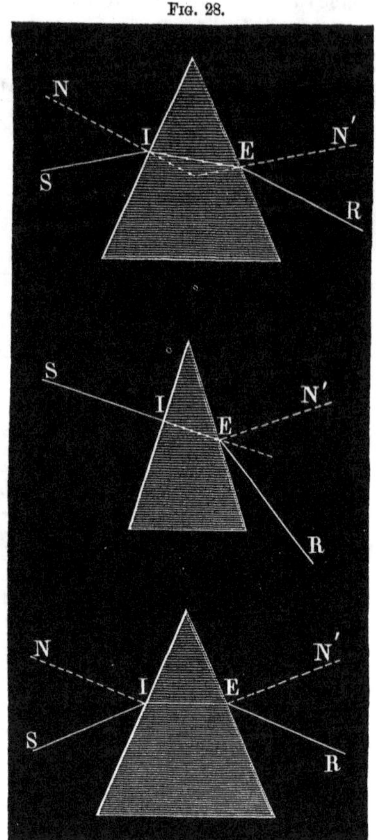

Refraction of a Ray of Light by a Prism.

rays are bent down toward the base, the eye sees the flame in the direction of the emergent rays—that is, in a higher position than it really occupies. If, on the contrary, the prism be turned round so that the base is uppermost, the rays of light will be bent upward, and the eye on receiving them will see the flame in a lower position.

Fig. 29.

Viewing Objects through a Prism.

17. Refraction of the Different Colors by a Prism.

We have hitherto paid no attention to the nature of a ray of light, and have therefore only made acquaintance with those phenomena of refraction which are common to rays of every description. Let us now consider the behavior of the different colored rays in their passage through a prism.

For this purpose let a diaphragm in which is a circular hole of about one-eighth of an inch in diameter be placed immediately in front of the lantern A, Fig. 30, and the aperture covered with a thin piece of glass *m*, colored red with oxide of copper. By interposing the lens L, a small, red circle A_1, the image of the aperture A, will be seen immediately opposite on the screen S S. If the glass prism *n p o* be inserted in the path of the ray between

L and A_1, in the place indicated in the figure, the red circle on the screen will move from A_1 to R. The light from A which fell upon the prism in the direction A B is thus considerably

Fig. 30.

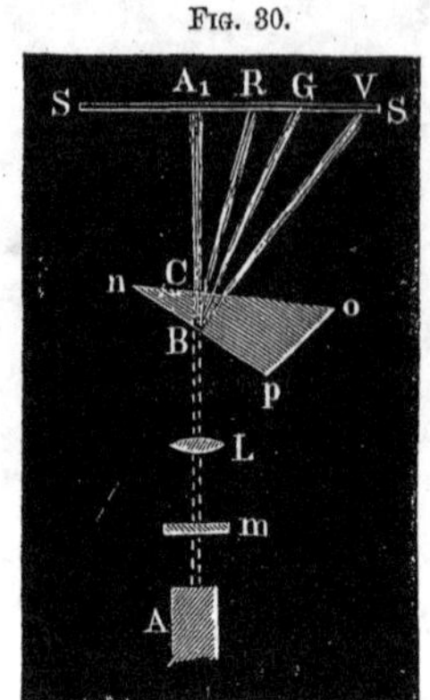

Divergence of the different colored Rays in passing through a Prism.

diverted from its straight course A A_1, so that the emergent ray C R has moved farther away from the edge *n*, where the two refracting glass surfaces unite, and has approached the opposite surface *p o*, the base of the prism.

If green light be examined by the interposition of a green glass, the ray emerging near C no longer falls upon the screen at R, but at the point G, which lies still nearer the base of the prism *p o*, from which it may be concluded that green light diverges more than red does from the original direction. If, finally, a violet glass be placed before the aperture, the violet ray is yet more refracted by its passage through the prism than the green was, for it strikes the screen at V. This experiment may be repeated with orange, yellow, blue, and other colored glass; and it will be found that the place of the image on the screen changes with every color, that the red light is the least, and the violet the most refracted, and that the refrangibility of the different colors continues to increase from red through orange, yellow, green, and blue, to violet.

We are now able to tell beforehand what will happen if a ray of light composed of several colors be allowed to pass through a prism. The individual colors will be separated by the first refraction on entering the prism, and they will be much more widely dispersed as they leave it; the incident ray will be decomposed into as many colors as it consists of, and each color will follow its own particular path from the first entrance of the light into the prism. All the colored rays can be distinguished one from another upon the screen, as they group themselves according to the order already given.

These simple experiments show that rays of light of different colors possess different degrees of refrangibility; red light is not so much diverted from its straight course by refraction as violet is: the former, therefore, is less refrangible than the latter. This different behavior of red and violet light is, as is clearly shown by the undulatory theory, a necessary consequence of the unequal rapidity of the ether-vibrations, which we have already recognized as the cause of the different colors. In red light the number of vibrations striking the eye in a second is about 450 billion, in violet 800 billion; as deep and shrill musical sounds are propagated in the same medium with the same rapidity, so the different colors travel with the same velocity. If the latter be taken at 42,000 German geographical miles, or 316,365,000,000 millimetres in a second, the length of each wave—that is to say, the distance between two succeeding condensations of ether—of red light will be 0.000703 of a millimetre, and of violet light 0.000395 of a millimetre.* If, therefore, different colored rays pass from one medium to another—as, for instance, from air to glass—the rays of shortest wave-length, namely, the violet, are more easily influenced by the increased resistance which the glass offers to the passage of the light, and are consequently more refracted than those of greater wave-length, namely, the blue, the green, the yellow, and the red rays.

* [Prof. Tyndall, in his "Notes on Light," gives the following numbers:

"The length of a wave of mean red light is about 1-39000th of an inch; that of a wave of mean violet light is about 1-57500th of an inch. The velocity of light being taken at 192,000 milos in a second, if we multiply this number by 39,000 we obtain the number of waves of red light in 192,000 miles; the product is 474,439,600,000,000. All these waves enter the eye in a second. In the same interval 699,000,000,000,000 waves of violet light enter the eye."

It must be remembered that the new determination of the value of the solar parallax by the observations of Mars, which agrees closely with the results of a rediression of the observations of the transit of Venus by Mr. Stone and Prof. Newcomb requires that the usually received velocity of light should be reduced by about one twenty-seventh part, and may be taken at 185,000 miles per second. This velocity agrees nearly with the result obtained by Foucault from direct experiment.]

As each color has a length of wave peculiar to itself, so also has it a particular degree of refrangibility; and therefore a beam of light which is composed of several colored rays must be decomposed by refraction into its individual colors, since each single ray is deflected or refracted in a different degree. The mingled rays of light travelling along one common road, which appeared to the eye before refraction as a light of one color, are separated by its agency according to their several degrees of refrangibility, and afterward proceeding in distinct paths they are distinguished by the eye as separate colors.

When a monochromatic ray — red, for instance — passes through a prism, the amount of its dispersion does not depend merely on the rapidity of the ether-vibrations, or length of wave, but is also considerably influenced by the nature of the substance of which the prism is composed, and the angle formed by the two surfaces through which the light passes. There is, under similar circumstances, a greater amount of refraction in a prism of bisulphide of carbon than in one of glass, and the refractive power varies, as we have seen, with the kind of glass of which the prism is formed. For the purposes of spectrum analysis, prisms of dense flint glass with an angle of from 45° to 60° are generally employed; but, if the highly-refractive properties of the substance, bisulphide of carbon, be required, it will be necessary to make use of a hollow prism (Fig. 31), formed of plane pieces of plate glass cemented together, in which the liquid may be held.

The question now presents itself as to how colorless, that is to say white light, is affected by its passage through a prism. It is well known that the light coming to us from the sun at noon in a clear sky is called pure white light. This light, however, is not always at our disposal, least of all in a public lecture-room; we will, therefore, before entering upon any experiments with artificial light, briefly review the results obtained by the prismatic analysis of the light of the sun.

18. The Solar Spectrum.

If a ray of sunshine be allowed to pass through a small round hole in the window-shutter of a darkened room, as is shown in Fig. 32, there will appear a round white spot of light, exactly in the direction of the ray, upon a screen placed opposite the opening, as will be seen indicated by the dotted lines in the figure.

FIG. 31.

Prism of Bisulphide of Carbon.

A very different appearance will be presented if the ray of light be made to fall upon a prism. The ray is at once deflected from

FIG. 32.

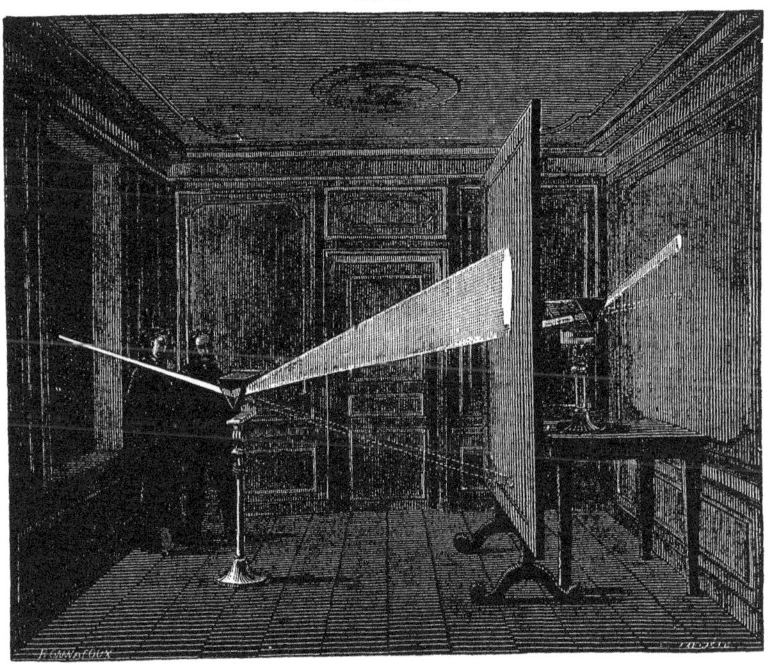

Exhibition of the Solar Spectrum.

its straight course upward, that is to say, toward the base of the prism, and away from the sharp edge of the refracting surfaces, which, as represented in the drawing, are turned downward: on its emergence from the prism it no longer remains one single ray, as it entered the window-shutter, but is separated into very many single-colored rays, which, as they continue to diverge, form upon the screen an elongated band of brilliant colors, instead of the former round white image of the sun. In this brilliant band the individual colors blend gradually one into the other, beginning at that end lying nearest the direction of the incident ray (the lowest end in the figure), with the least refrangible color, a dark and very beautiful red; this passes imperceptibly into orange, and orange again into bright yellow; a pure green succeeds, which is shaded off into a brilliant blue, and this gives place to a rich deep indigo; a delicate purple leads finally to a soft violet, by which the range of the visible rays is terminated. A faint picture of this magnificent solar image is given in No. 1 of the Frontispiece; this is called the *Spectrum.** In the above-mentioned colors of the solar spectrum the eye discerns numberless gradations, which pass imperceptibly from one to another; and since language does not suffice to give separate names to each of these, we must content ourselves with designating only the seven principal groups, which are known as the colors of the spectrum.

This experiment furnishes conclusive evidence that white light is not simple and indivisible, but composed of innumerable colored rays, each of which possesses its own peculiar degree of refrangibility, and therefore, on refraction, pursues a separate path. The prism analyzes white light; the result is the separation of all the colored rays of which it is composed, and the consequent formation of the colored image called the *Spectrum.*

The decomposition of sunlight by refraction is shown in various phenomena known to the ancients as well as ourselves, though they were not able, as we are, to trace them back to their true cause. The rainbow, with its pure but delicate colors, the sparkle of the cut jewel in its brilliant flashes, the play of color emitted by cut glass, and the prismatic facets of crystal lustres as the sun shines upon them, the glow of the clouds and high moun-

* Of the dark lines represented in this plate we shall not have occasion to speak till we reach Part III.

tain-peaks in the various-colored light of the rising and setting sun—all these effects are occasioned by the decomposition of white light by its refraction on passing through glass in a prismatic form, through drops of liquid, or through vapor.

The colors of the solar spectrum possess a purity and brilliancy to be met with nowhere else; they are all perfectly indivisible, and cannot be further decomposed, as may be easily proved on attempting to analyze a colored ray by means of a second prism. If a small round hole be made in the screen in any portion of the image of the spectrum, the extreme red, for instance (Fig. 28), a red ray passes through it, and appears upon the opposite wall as a round spot of red light, precisely in the same direction as the red rays left the prism on the other side of the screen. If a second prism be interposed in the path of the ray that has passed through the screen, the ray will suffer a second refraction, and the image be thrown upon another place (higher up in the figure) on the wall; this new image, however, is simply red, like the incident ray, and by a careful adjustment of the prism shows no elongation, but appears perfectly round. Fig. 33 shows this phenomenon with the central color of the spectrum. The ray falling on the prism *s* is decomposed into a colored spectrum at A B, and a small pencil of these colored rays will not be further decomposed by the second prism *p*, but only diverted. The same thing occurs with all the colors of the spectrum without a single exception, which proves that the colors separated by the prism are not capable of further decomposition, and are therefore indivisible and homogeneous.

The decomposition of white light into its colored rays is called *dispersion;* the dispersion of light is therefore to be clear-

FIG. 33.

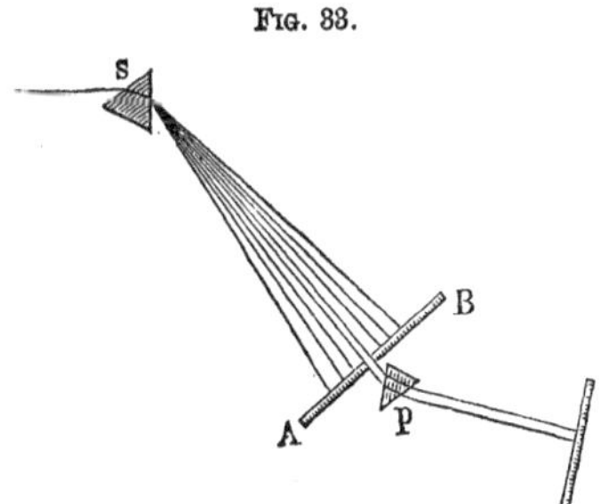

Indivisibility of the Pure Colors of the Spectrum.

ly distinguished from *refraction*. The latter, as we have seen, varies in amount with every kind of color; it is greatest in the violet, and smallest in the red rays. The amount of dispersion, to which we shall again refer in a closer analysis of the solar light, is determined by the *length* of the spectrum, or, in other words, the distance between the extreme red and violet rays. As the nature of the reflective substance of a prism—for example, the kind of glass of which it is made—and its refracting angle each exert an influence upon the amount of refraction, in a similar manner do the same conditions also affect the amount of dispersion, or the length of the spectrum; it may, however, be remarked here that refraction and dispersion are not increased or diminished in equal proportions.

The different colors are not present in the solar spectrum in the same proportions, and consequently they assume very unequal lengths in the spectrum. If the whole length of the solar spectrum be divided into 100 equal parts, the proportions of the colors will be as follows: red 12, orange 7, yellow 13, green 17, blue 17, indigo 11, and violet 23.

The unequal brilliancy of the different colors of the spectrum is apparent even to a superficial observer, and Fraunhofer found by careful measurements that, if the greatest intensity of light which lies between yellow and green were expressed by 1,000, the light of orange would amount to 640, the middle red to 94, the outer red to only 32, the green to 480, blue to 170, between blue and violet to 31, and violet only to 6.

19. The Spectra of the Lime-light and the Electric Light.

In the absence of sunlight, Drummond's lime-light (Part I., p.19) may be analyzed by a prism in the following manner: Let the lantern L (Fig. 34), which has been already described, be placed on a table T T, 5 feet long and 16 inches wide, turning on a pedestal F, and the lime-light lamp introduced, in front of which is inserted a diaphragm *d*, provided with a contrivance for allowing the light to pass out of the lantern through a narrow slit. Opposite the lantern, at a distance of 12 or 15 feet, place two paper screens S S_1, 8 feet square, inclined to each other at a wide angle; let the lime-cylinders then be raised to incandescence by means of the the oxyhydrogen gas, the room be

Fig. 34.

Projection of the Spectrum of the Lime-Light.

completely darkened, and the table T T so turned that the tube *d* of the lantern be perpendicular to one of the screens (S). Then let a double convex lens *l*, of 4 inches diameter, and about 12 inches focus, be placed between the slit *d* and the screen S, at a distance of about 12 inches from the slit, so as to throw the rays issuing from the slit upon the screen S in the form of a sharp and magnified image, d^1, of the slit *d*. Close behind this lens *l*, a flint-glass prism P of 60°, 2½ inches high and 2 inches broad, must be placed in the direct path of the rays,* when there will instantly appear on the second screen S_1 a magnificent spectrum, about 3 feet long and 16 inches wide, exhibiting the whole range of colors as shown in No. 1, Frontispiece. Owing to the distance of the screen, the spectrum is displaced very considerably from the spot d^1, where the rays fell when unbroken by the prism; the red lies nearest to that straight line, the violet is the farthest removed from it; the former is therefore the least refracted, and the latter the most so. The individual colors succeed each other without the slighest interruption; their limits are not sharply defined, they rather blend gradually one into the other, and thus form an unbroken, or *continuous* spectrum.

As the lantern L may obstruct the view of the screen S_1 to some of the spectators, the top of the table T T can be turned upon its pedestal F, so as to throw the spectrum upon the screen S. Instead of turning the table, the colored rays as they leave the prism *p* might be received upon a flat mirror, and thrown by reflection on to the second screen; but the spectrum would lose in intensity by this reflection, inasmuch as a reflected image is always fainter than the object. The table might even be turned farther round still, and the prism be directed toward the spectators, when the rays could be thrown by means of the mirror to any part of the room.

In order to obtain a pure spectrum, the width of the slit must not exceed one-sixteenth of an inch; were it widened, the spectrum would greatly increase in splendor and brilliancy, but it would be perceived on a careful examination that the colors in the middle were neither so pure nor so clearly separated one from another as before, and that in the centre the light had become almost white.

* This position of the prism is the most advantageous, because the loss of light is least; the spectrum would be nearly as good if the prism were moved 11 or 12 inches from the lens.

Instead of the spectrum being received upon the side of the paper screen fronting the audience, and reflected thence so as to be visible to the spectators, a *transparent* screen may be advantageously used, behind which is placed the lamp. By this means the screen is visible without interruption from the lantern or experimenter, and every arrangement much simplified. A very suitable material for such a screen is thin tracing-paper, which may be had about two yards wide of any length, or fine white muslin sewn together in breadths, and made transparent by damping before each experiment. By fastening the screen to a roller, it may be easily moved out of the way when the attention of the audience is to be directed to the lantern or prism.

The spectrum of the electric light may be thrown upon the screen in the same manner as that described for Drummond's lime-light. The electric lamp, as described before (Part I., p. 32), is substituted for the oxyhydrogen-gas lamp in the lantern,* Fig. 35; and the two adjustable carbon-points connected by copper wires with an electric battery of 50 Bunsen's or Grove's large elements. As soon as the current passes through the carbon-poles, the electric arc is formed, and the white light pouring through the slit produces, by means of the lens *l* (Fig. 34), a well-defined image of the slit upon the screen. If the flint-glass prism *p* be again placed in the path of the rays behind the lens, the wonderfully beautiful spectrum of the electric light appears thrown sideways on the screen, in place of the white image of the slit. By slightly increasing the width of the slit, the spectrum gains considerably in brilliancy, and the colors are so clear and brilliant that the spectrum would still be bright, were the light spread over a surface even two or three times as large. It will be desirable to enter somewhat further into this experiment, because practically it is often necessary to produce a great dispersion of light, and thus obtain a very extended spectrum, in order that its various details may be examined with sufficient minuteness.

For this purpose the flint-glass prism is replaced by one of bisulphide of carbon (Fig. 35), which produces a spectrum of the same breadth but of almost double the length of the former one.

* The electric lamp and lantern represented in the drawing is constructed by Browning especially for this purpose, and is much simpler and cheaper than that by Duboscq.

Fig. 35.

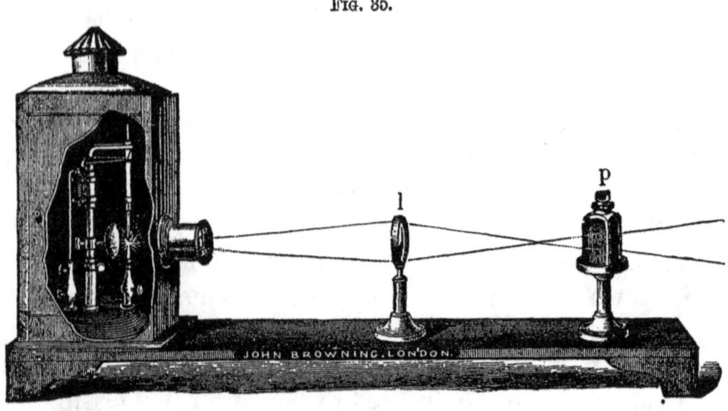

Browning's Electric Lamp.

Immediately in front of this prism p (Fig. 36) is placed the prism of flint glass p_1, so arranged as to throw the rays upon the second prism p in a manner similar to that in which it had itself received the light from the lens (the prisms forming an angle of about 100°

Fig. 36.

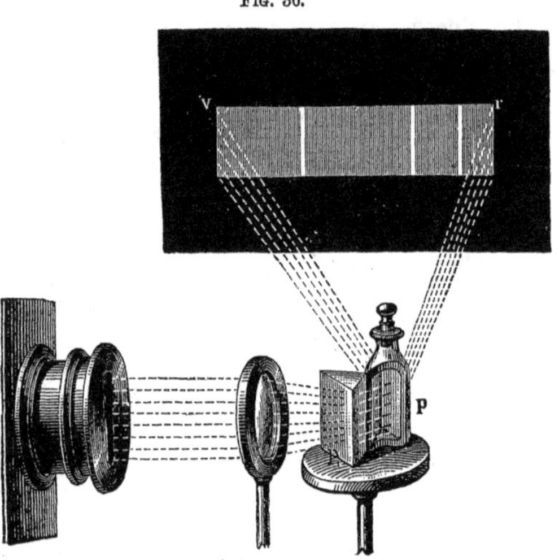

Action of the Double Prism.

with each other); in this way the spectrum is extended to the length of about eight feet, and diverted more than 90° to one side: the colors, however, though still very visible, and easily distinguishable one from another, have yet lost much of their original brilliancy. A combination of two prisms of bisulphide of carbon would extend the spectrum still farther, but the brightness would be diminished in the same proportion.

In many scientific investigations, not merely two, but sometimes four and even as many as eight prisms, with angles varying from 45° to 60°, are employed, according to the strength of the light.

20. Recombination of the Colors of the Spectrum.

If white light be actually composed of the colors contained in the spectrum, then the recombination of the same colors must reproduce white light. The simplest method of collecting several rays of light into one point is by a convex lens or a burning-glass. If the sun's rays fall perpendicularly on such a glass, the refraction they suffer in their passage through it causes them to converge to one point—the focus. To accomplish by this means the recombination of the colored rays of the spectrum of the electric light, a cylindrical lens must be interposed between the

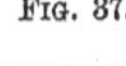

Fig. 37.

Recombination of the Colors of the Spectrum.

prism and the screen on which the spectrum of the small line of light issuing from the slit is extended to a length of some six feet: this lens is a convex lens of peculiar form, which possesses the property of recombining in a point all the rays issuing from each point of the line of light passing through the slit after dispersion by the prism, and therefore of representing the whole of the rays of that short line of light again as a small line. When, therefore, this lens (Fig. 37) is placed at a proper distance behind the prism, the colors of the spectrum disappear from the screen, and are replaced by a short line of light, some few inches in breadth, white in the middle and slightly colored at the edges. As this color indicates that the large screen is not in the focus of the lens, a smaller one is placed nearer to it, upon which the image appears as a purely white, very narrow line of light, in which all the colored rays issuing from the prism have been recombined, and the white light reproduced out of which they originated.

21. Influence of the Width of Slit on the Purity of the Spectrum.

The spectrum of white light is the richer and purer in color the narrower the slit is made: the truth of this statement will be easily proved by the following considerations. The ray of white-light $a\ a_1$ (Fig. 38), falling on the prism P from the ex-

Fig. 38.

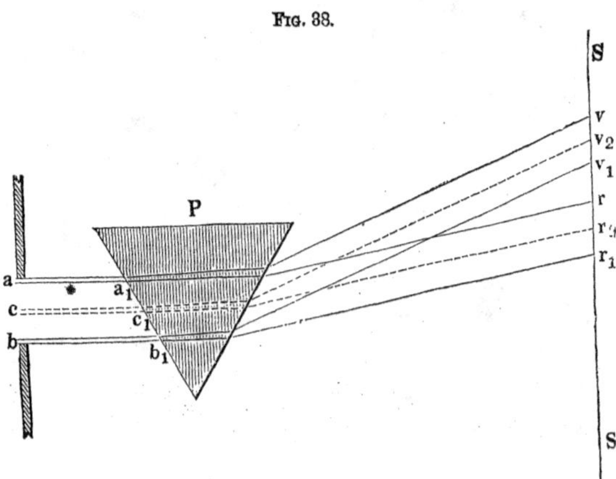

Influence of the Width of Slit on the Purity of the Spectrum.

treme end a of the slit $a\ b$, produces a complete spectrum $r\ v$, which contains between r and v, or red and violet, all the colors of the spectrum. In the same manner the ray $b\ b_1$, proceeding from the other end of the slit b, exhibits also a complete spectrum, r_1 v_1, with all its colors. Between these two ends a and b are many other points, emitting light, which increase in number according to the width of the slit; out of these let us select for consideration the point c_1, the ray from which, c c_1, forms another spectrum, r_2 v_2, between the two outer spectra, r v and r_1 v_1 which it is evident falls partly over the two other spectra between the two points r_2 v_2. While in the portions v v_2, r_2 r_1, there are parts of the pure spectra formed by the rays a a_1 and b b_1, there are to be found in the portions v_2 r_2 of the compound spectra v r_1 the superposed colors due to the whole slit, and their colors being no longer separately distinguishable, produce on the eye the impression of a confusion of tints. The spectrum of white light, therefore, emitted through a wide slit is only pure or of one color at the extreme ends, in the red and in the violet rays; in the middle a mingled light prevails, composed of all possible groups of rays, and which, therefore, might be decomposed afresh into its constituent parts by a second prism.

On this account it is important to pay the greatest attention to the width of the slit in all practical applications of spectrum analysis: as a rule, it should never be wider than the intensity of the light to be examined absolutely requires. The contrivances for the regulation of the width of slit are mostly very simple; the purity of the spectrum, however, is not merely affected by the width of the slit, but also by the smoothness of its edges, since a few particles of dust even on the edges of the slit are sufficient to produce a number of dark streaks along the whole length of the spectrum, which greatly impede observation.

22. The Continuous Spectra of Solid and Liquid Bodies.

When the carbon-points used for the production of the electric light are carefully prepared, and completely free from all extraneous substances, the light is purely white, being emitted exclusively by solid particles of carbon in a state of incandescence. The spectrum of this light is, therefore, continuous like that of incandescent lime; it is unbroken by gaps in the colors, or by sudden transitions from one color to another, and is uninterrupted by either dark or bright bands.

All other incandescent bodies, whether solid or liquid, give a similar spectrum, the colors being distributed in the order represented in the Frontispiece, No. 1. If, instead of the lime-light, the magnesium-light (§ 4), the light of an incandescent platinum wire, or the flame of coal-gas in which light is produced by incandescent particles of carbon, be analyzed by the prism, continuous spectra are always obtained, but with this difference, that the various groups of color are not always distributed in exactly the same proportion in each individual spectrum; and therefore, according to the kind of light employed, sometimes red, sometimes yellow, and sometimes violet predominates. Only in very rare instances do incandescent solid substances emit with any preëminent strength an isolated set of colored rays, as is the case with the very rare substance, Erbia. It may therefore be considered that, as a rule, where there is a *continuous spectrum without gaps, and containing every shade of color, the light is derived from an incandescent solid or liquid body.*

23. The Spectra Vapors and Gases.

Very different spectra are obtained when the source of light is not an incandescent *solid* or *liquid* body, but a *vapor* or a *gas* in a glowing state. Instead of a continuous succession of colors, the spectrum then exhibits a series of distinct bright-colored bands, separated one from another by dark spaces.

As gases and vapors in a luminous state emit much less light than do solid bodies, the exhibition of their spectra on a screen before a large audience is restricted to those substances which give by their volatilization in the oxyhydrogen flame, or electric lamp, a luminous vapor of sufficient brilliancy to form a spectrum clearly visible at some distance, notwithstanding the distance of the screen from the slit, and the loss of light by its passage through the lens and the thick prism. For this purpose, the vapors of copper, zinc, brass, silver, cadmium. sodium, thallium, etc., are particularly suited.

Although the oxyhydrogen flame is adapted for these experiments, inasmuch as it emits scarcely any light, yet the electric lamp is much more suited to the purpose, because it generates a far greater degree of heat, therefore volatilizes more rapidly the above-named substances, and brings them to a higher state of luminosity. In order to exhibit these spectra, the apparatus described in § 19, and drawn in Fig. 35, is employed; the lower carbon-pole of the lamp is replaced by a half-inch cylinder, *u*, Fig. 39, of pure carbon, the upper end of which is slightly hollowed, and it is fixed precisely in the focus of the lantern-lens. In the hollowed end of the carbon is laid a piece of zinc the size of a pea, and the upper pole, *o*, is brought down until it comes in contact with it, when the electric current instantly passes through the carbon, and the intense heat produced quickly volatilizes the zinc. If the upper carbon-pole *o* be now withdrawn to form an arc of flame, and it be raised somewhat higher than was the case during the former experiment, so that the carbon may glow less, and the light be almost exclusively that of the luminous zinc-vapor, there will be seen on the screen, not the

FIG. 39.

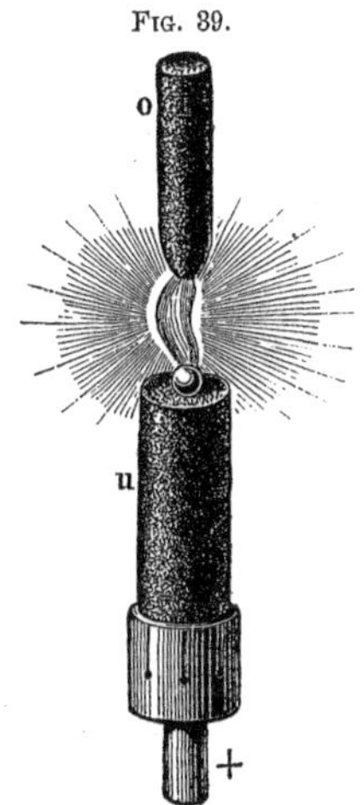

Volatilization of Metals in the Electric Light.

spectrum of incandescent zinc, but that of the vapor of zinc which constitutes the arc of light seen between the carbon-poles. It will be at once perceived that this spectrum differs essentially from the continuous spectrum already described; it consists, in fact, of only one red band and three very beautiful bright-blue bands. The faintly-colored band, which forms as it were a background to these bright stripes, is due to the glowing carbon, some of the white light of which reaches the screen; on opening the lantern, the zinc-vapor is seen rising in the form of a blue cloud.

The carbon which has become contaminated by the zinc may be replaced by a fresh cylinder, in the cavity of which is laid a piece of copper, and the electric current again allowed to pass: a spectrum of quite another kind appears on the screen, consisting of three bright bands which were not present in the zinc spectrum, while the red and blue stripes which characterized the latter have disappeared.

Instead of the carbon-cylinders, thick rods or wires of zinc, copper, etc., may be employed: the spectra are then more decided and brilliant, but are very evanescent, lasting only for a moment, because the metals burn away the instant there is contact, and the electric current is then interrupted.

The inquiry now suggests itself whether the ether-waves which produce the colors in the spectra of zinc and copper would suffer any reciprocal interference were the same experiment to be made with brass, a substance composed of zinc and copper; or whether each material in this alloy would emit independently its own peculiar colors, so that the spectrum of the compound substance would consist of the superposed spectra of the component metals? In order to obtain an answer to this question, it is only necessary to lay a piece of brass in the cavity of a fresh cylinder of carbon, and apply the electric current. A magnificent spectrum meets the eye, in which can be recognized at once not only the red line and three bright-blue bands of the zinc, but also the three green bands of the copper. The rays from the volatilized constituents of an alloy do not therefore interfere with each other; each vapor, even when in combination with other vapors, emits its own system of colored rays, which in passing through a prism separate from one another in consequence of their unequal refrangibility, and appear as a system of disunited columnar bands, forming an interrupted or discontinuous spectrum.

To avoid the tedious and troublesome operation of changing the lower carbon-cylinder, Ruhmkorff, of Paris, has fitted to the lamp the contrivance shown in Fig. 40, which will be easily understood by comparing it with Duboscq's regulator (Fig. 17). The clock-work is dispensed with, as, during the few moments necessary for the volatilization of a small piece of metal, the arc of light between the upper carbon *o* and the lower carbon *u* is very slightly removed from the focal point of the lens, and by turning the screw *a*, the whole of the upper portion of the lamp may be raised and lowered at will, and the arc of light thus kept continuously in the focus of the lantern lens. Six carbon-cylinders, instead of one only as in Fig. 39, are here employed, arranged in a circle upon a small plate, which by means of the carrier G is made to revolve, so that, by simply turning the plate round, any one of them may be brought exactly under the carbon-cylinder *o*. This cylinder can be raised or lowered by means of

Fig. 40.

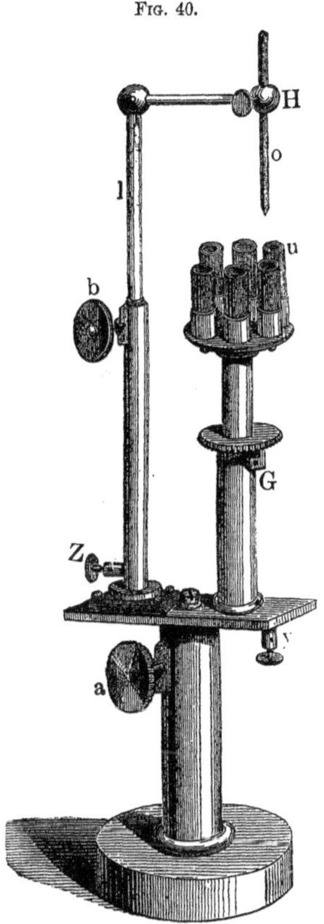

Ruhmkorff's Electric Lamp.

the screw *b*, so that if before the experiment six different metals be placed upon the carbon-cylinders, by merely turning the plate, and if necessary by turning the screws *a* and *b*, each metal may be volatilized in the arc of flame, and the spectrum of its glowing vapor obtained.

The characteristic feature of spectra obtained from luminous vapors or gases is the want of continuity in the succession of the colors. Such a spectrum is composed of distinct colored bands, irregularly arranged, with dark spaces between them, and is therefore called a *discontinuous spectrum*, a *spectrum of bright lines*, or a *gas-spectrum*.

The spectra of the vapors of sodium, lithium, cæsium, and rubidium are represented in Nos. 2, 3, 4, and 5 of the Frontispiece, while those of oxygen, hydrogen, and nitrogen gas are shown in Nos. 6, 7, and 8. They exhibit at a glance the great difference which exists between the continous spectrum (No. 1) of incandescent solid and liquid bodies and the discontinuous spectra of gases. The vapor of sodium (No. 2) under ordinary circumstances, and when not exposed to an extremely high temperature, gives a spectrum consisting only of one bright orange line, which, however, will be seen to be double by the use of sufficient dispersive power. The spectrum of luminous lithium-vapor (No. 3) consists only of two colored lines or bands, one a brilliant red and the other a faint-yellow line. Much more complete is the spectrum of cæsium; at a sufficiently high temperature the luminous vapor exhibits from ten to thirteen clearly distinguishable lines, three of which are visible even at a low temperature. Of these three lines two are blue and one yellow; the remaining yellow and green lines do not appear as individual bands until the temperature is sufficiently high to cause the glowing vapor to emit light of the requisite intensity, as before this heat is attained they run one into the other so as to give a faint show of color in the manner of a continuous spectrum.

It is desirable to supplement the observations previously made with the spectrum of brass by the two following experiments: Let a grain of sodium be laid upon the lower cylinder, and the electric current allowed to pass through it to the upper carbon-pole. The sodium is quickly volatilized in the arc of flame, and the spectrum already described (Frontispiece, No. 2) appears on the screen, a single stripe of bright yellow. Let the current now be interrupted, and two fresh carbon-cylinders introduced, on the lowest of which is laid a grain of common salt, and the current reëstablished. Common salt is a compound of chlorine and sodium, and it might be expected from the experiment with brass, the spectrum of which was made up of the combined spectra of its two components, zinc and copper, that the spectrum of salt would similarly consist of the spectrum of chlorine gas and that of the vapor of sodium: this, however, is evidently not the case, for only the same yellow bands appear which were given by the metallic sodium, occupying precisely their former position on the screen; while of chlorine, which when isolated gives a very characteristic spectrum, there is nothing whatever to be seen.

The same thing occurs with other metals that combine with chlorine, as may be seen if a mixture of the chlorides of lithium, barium, magnesium, and thallium, be placed on the upper surface of a somewhat wider cylinder of carbon. As the current passes from pole to pole, these substances are volatilized in the arc of flame, and on contracting the slit a little a number of closely-arranged colored bands are seen, some of which—as, for instance, the red of the lithium and the bright green of the thallium—stand out with especial distinctness. If a second prism (Fig. 32) be interposed, so as to lengthen the spectrum to about six feet, the individual stripes appear less bright, but more sharply divided one from another; by widening the slit, the stripes increase a little in brilliancy. Those who are familiar with the simple spectra of lithium, barium, magnesium, and thallium, will not find it difficult to recognize each separate substance in the compound spectrum produced by the mixture of these substances; here again, however, the spectrum of chlorine is not present, at least it is not visible.

If the various compounds of such metals as sodium, calcium, etc.—for example, chloride of calcium, iodide of calcium, nitrate of lime, etc.—be in the same way subjected to spectrum analysis, the spectrum of the metal is alone obtained, and never that of the other constituents; the spectra of the vapors of metals assert themselves with such marked prominence that the spectrum of any non-metallic substance with which they are in combination either does not appear at all, or else is so overpowered by the clear and brilliant lines of the spectrum of the metal as not to be perceived.*

* See Appendix A, "On the Cause of Interrupted Spectra of Gases," by G. Johnstone Stoney, M. A., F. R. S.

24. Spectrum Apparatus.

The thought is perhaps rising in the minds of many who have accompanied us thus far, that the production of the spectrum of a substance for the purposes of analytical examination is encumbered with great difficulties and many troublesome details, involving too much labor to be available for the use of the chemist and the physicist. This is, however, not the case ; if in our mode of illustration a powerful galvanic battery and the electric lamp with its revolving table and large screen have been employed, it has been only to show how, by the extraordinary heat and light of the voltaic arc, the simple phenomena on which spectrum analysis is based can be made visible to many hundred spectators at once in a large lecture-room. When, however, the light from the heated vapors need not be greater than is required for a single observer, the whole electric apparatus may be dispensed with, and the simple Bunsen burner (Fig. 2) substituted ; indeed, in many cases, a powerful spirit-flame is sufficient to exhibit the gas-spectrum of a substance. The slit and the prism may then be reduced to small dimensions ; in place of the large screen of paper that reflected the light, the small sensitive screen of nerves—the retina of the human eye—becomes the surface on which the spectrum is received ; and the whole cumbrous contrivance occupying so much space is replaced by a small spectrum apparatus as trustworthy as it is easy to manipulate.

Every spectrum apparatus or spectroscope, exclusive of the source of light, is composed of an adjustable slit, a contrivance (collimating lens) for rendering the rays parallel that have passed through the slit, and a prism. In order that the instrument may be used at any hour of the day, all light except that under examination must be excluded from the prism, and therefore the slit, lenses, and prism, are enclosed in a tube, or, if the prism be too large, the latter is fitted with a separate cover. Further, as the spectrum on emerging from the prism is but little longer than the width of the slit, and only becomes of some length as the distance from the prism increases, a magnifying-glass is introduced, in order that the eye, though at but a small distance from the prism, may see the spectrum of a sufficiently large size, and the spectrum therefore is not observed with the naked eye, but through the medium of a telescope of moderate power.*

It has been already mentioned that the colored rays composing the spectrum form an angle with the incident rays as they

FIG. 41

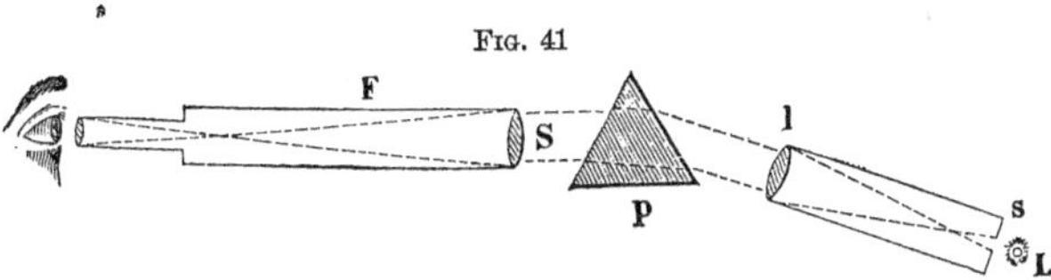

The Simple Spectroscope.

enter the prism. It is therefore necessary, in observing the spectrum, that the tube of the telescope directed to the outer surface of the prism should be placed in a different direction to the tube carrying the slit and the lens. A spectroscope arranged in this way is shown in Fig. 41. The light emitted from L, after passing through the slit *s* and the collimating lens *l*, reaches the prism *p* in parallel rays; it is there diverted as well as decomposed, whereby the spectrum S is seen through the telescope F in a direction very different from that of the tube *s l*. This arrangement has the inconvenience that in conducting a research with spectrum analysis the eye cannot be directed straight at the light, and therefore the spectrum can only be found after some search for it by moving the instrument backward and forward.

FIG. 42.

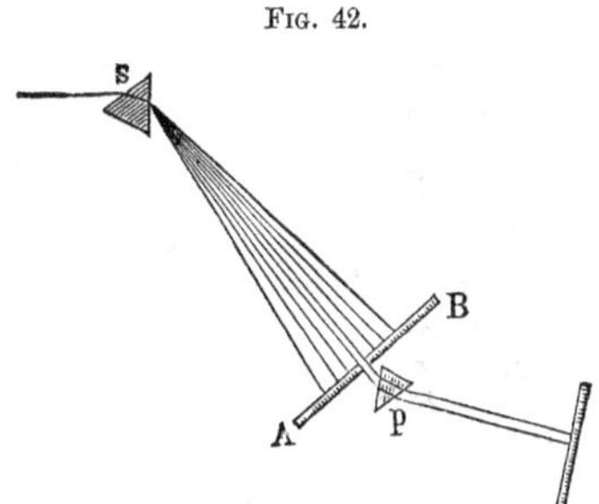

Indivisibility of the Pure Colors of the Spectrum.

* [The telescope is necessary not only for magnifying the spectrum, but also for enabling the eye to receive the whole of the light passing from the collimating lens through the prisms. Without a telescope the eye receives so much only of the beam of parallel rays as is contained in the area of the pupil of the eye.]

A spectroscope would therefore be obviously more convenient if the slit, lens, prism, and telescope, were all in a straight line, so that it would only be necessary, in observing with it, to direct the instrument like a telescope to the light to be examined, in order to observe the spectrum.

On reconsidering the action of a prism *s*, Fig. 42, it will be easy to understand that the various colored rays receive a different amount of deviation according to the position of the prism as regards the incident ray; it can be readily shown by calculation that of all the emergent rays that one suffers the least deviation which, as in E R, Fig. 28, makes the same angle with the prism as the incident ray S I makes with the surface upon which it falls. When a prism is so placed that the colored ray in the spectrum suffering least deviation is the one which possesses the mean wave-length—about 0.000549 of a millimetre (*vide* p. 59)—which is situated between the yellow and the green, the prism is then said to be in the position of *minimum deviation;* strictly speaking, however, the prism has a special position of minimum deviation for each colored ray. The angle formed by this central emergent ray with the incident ray is the measure of the refractive or *deviating* power of the prism, while the length of the spectrum is the measure of its *decomposing* or *dispersive* power.

Fig. 43.

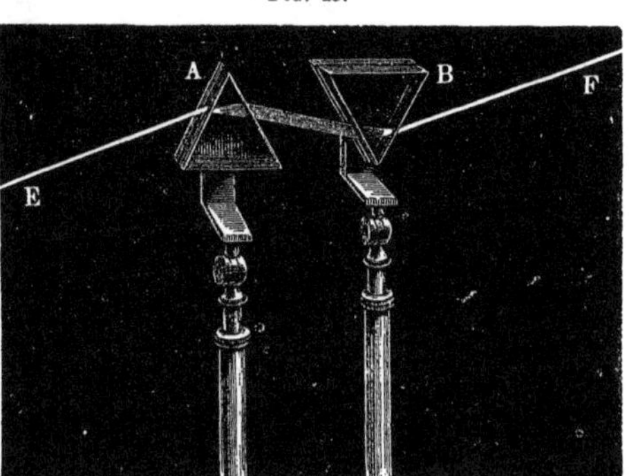

Neutralization of Refraction and Dispersion.

If two prisms, A and B (Fig. 43), of similar composition and equal refracting angle, be placed in reversed positions, the incident ray E, of white light, will be refracted by the first prism A, and decomposed into its colored rays; the second prism B, however, which refracts in an opposite direction, destroys the first divergence, and reunites the incident colored rays into a single emergent ray F. If the ray F be received upon a screen, there will appear a white image, tinged at the upper edge with red, and at the lower with violet light, because at the extreme edges of the image the colors are not superposed. In this case the second prism B has neutralized both the refraction and the dispersion of the first prism, and the action of this system of prisms is very nearly the same as that of a thick piece of glass with parallel sides.

Now, if the dispersive power of a prism varied in the same

Fig. 44.

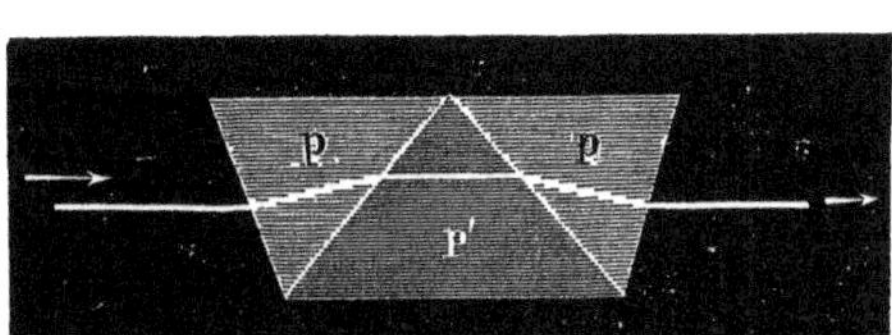

Amici's Direct-vision System of Prisms.

proportion as its power of refraction, then, whatever the kind of glass employed for the prisms placed as in Fig. 43, and whatever might be their refracting angles, when they were so placed as to neutralize refraction, their power of dispersion or capability of forming a spectrum would be likewise destroyed. In other words, the formation of a spectrum would always be connected with the deviation of light from its straight course, and it would not be possible by means of a system of prisms to receive the spectrum of a luminous object—for example, a flame or a star—when viewed in a straight line.

In reality, however, this is not the case. The dispersive power of various kinds of prisms is not in equal proportion to the refractive power; a flint-glass prism, for instance, gives with an equal amount of refraction of the central rays a spectrum of much greater length than can be obtained from one of crown glass. It is therefore possible so to combine and place in reversed positions, as in Fig. 43, two prisms of different refracting angles, one of flint, and the other of crown glass, that the refraction of the incident rays shall be entirely counteracted, while the greater dispersive power of the flint glass shall only be partially destroyed by the crown glass, and consequently a spectrum formed by the remaining rays. If a bright object be looked at through such a system of prisms, in a rectilinear direction, its spectrum will be seen in the line of sight; the colors will, of course, not be so widely dispersed as would be the case were the object looked at in an oblique direction through the flint-glass prism alone.

Compound prisms of this kind, or more especially systems of prisms which show a spectrum when held in a straight line between the source of light and the observer's eye, are called *direct-vision* prisms.

Such an arrangement of the spectroscope was approximately accomplished by Amici, in 1860, by a judicious combination of two crown-glass prisms, with a third prism of flint glass of 90° interposed. By this construction the rays of mean refrangibility suffer no divergence, so that a luminous object may be viewed in a rectilinear direction, and a spectrum be obtained, since the dispersion produced by the flint-glass prism in one direction is greater than that produced by the two crown-glass prisms in the opposite direction.

Fig. 45 exhibits another form of direct-vision prism, contrived by Prof. A. Herschel for the observation of meteors. The ray of light E undergoes two total reflections from the inner surfaces of the prism before it emerges from it in the

Fig. 45.

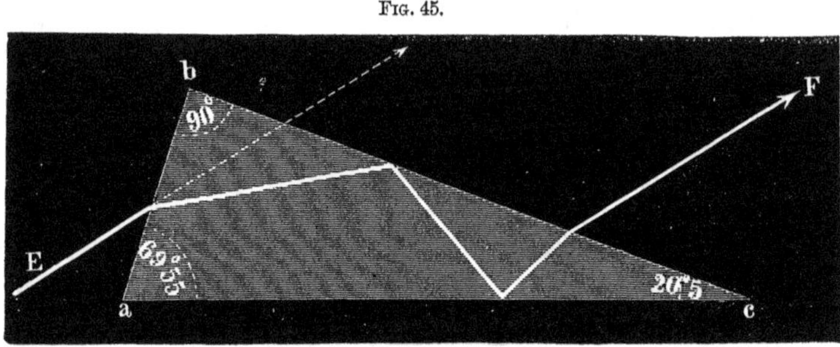

Herschel's Direct-vision Prism.

form of the spectrum F, in a direction parallel to E. The construction, however, of such a prism is surrounded with difficulties, since the action of each surface is required in the course of the rays, and it is exceeding difficult to attain sufficient accuracy in the angles *a* and *c*.

Browning, the optician, has overcome these difficulties by combining two such prisms. In the Herschel-Browning system of prisms (Fig. 46), the ray F, which emerges from the first prism A in a direction parallel to the incident ray E, is brought back again by the second prism B to the direction of the incident ray, so that the central emergent colored rays G form an exact prolongation of the incident ray E.

Janssen, of Paris, adopting Amici's construction, has produced, with the help of the excellent optician Hofmann, a direct-vision spectroscope, which, from the facility with which it can be used, its moderate price, and the great purity and length of the

FIG. 46.

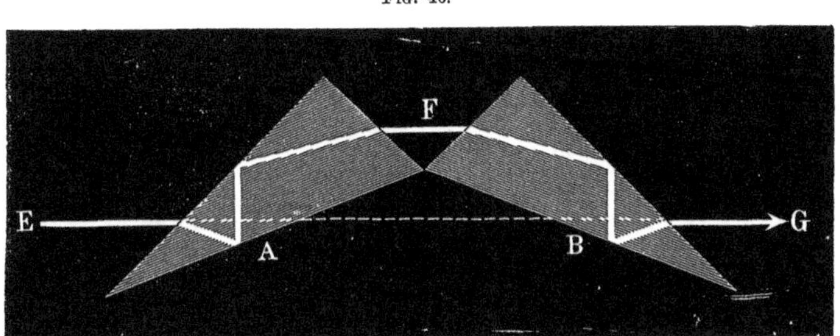

Herschel-Browning's System of Prisms.

spectrum it produces, has become an instrument indispensable to the chemist, the physicist, and the astronomer.

Janssen's direct-vision spectroscope, Fig. 47, has the appearance of an ordinary telescope, and can either be held in the hand while in use, or placed, when steadiness is required, upon a small revolving stand. The several parts are sketched in the drawing above the instrument, in the same positions that they occupy within the tube. In front, at the end which is directed toward the source of light, is the slit S, formed of two steel edges,* which can be easily widened or contracted by means of the screw V and an opposing spring. At L the collimating lens *l* is inserted, by which the rays diverging from the slit S are rendered parallel, and thrown upon the five prisms *p*. Of these, which are drawn in detail in Fig. 48, the first, third, and fifth, are of crown glass, while the second and fourth are of flint glass, and they form

* [Mr. Rutherfurd employs the unalterable substance obsidian for the edges of the slit.]

7

so perfect a system from the accurate adjustment of the angles of the prisms, that the emergent central colored rays F have pre-

FIG. 47.

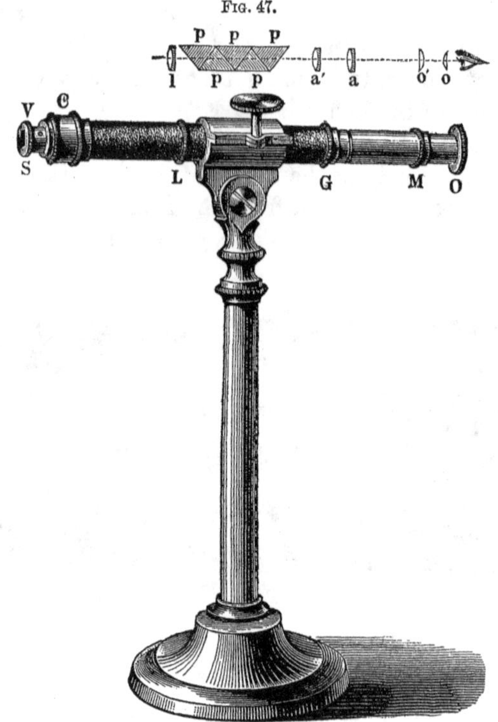

Janssen-Hofmann's Direct-vision Spectroscope.

cisely the same direction as the incident rays E, and therefore pass in a straight line through the tube L G M O, in which the compound prisms occupy the space between L and G. The lenses *a′* and *a* behind G form the object-glass; *o′* and *o* in the small

FIG. 48.

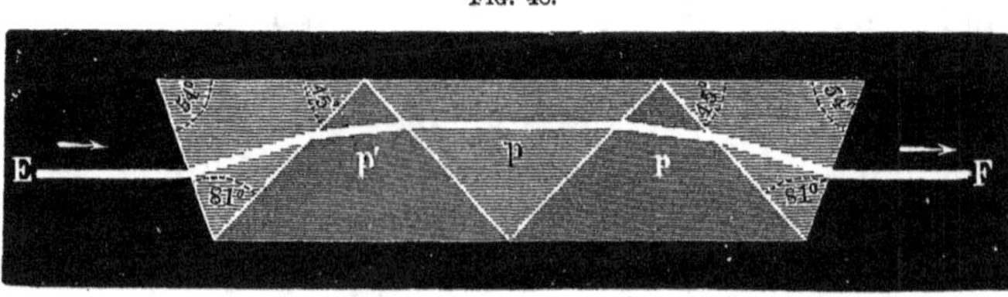

Janssen's Direct-vision System of Prisms.

sliding-tube O, the eye-piece of the telescope through which the spectrum is observed.

Browning has manufactured another direct-vision spectroscope, with seven prisms, which commends itself by the excellence of its performance, the facility of its use, the smallness of its di-

FIG. 49.

Browning's Miniature Spectroscope.

mensions, the purity of color, and its low price. A sketch of it is shown in Fig. 49; the slit is simply regulated by turning round a ring at the end of the tube, and the spectrum is observed direct without a telescope. The length of this admirable little instrument is only about 3½ inches, and is, therefore, very deservedly called the miniature or pocket spectroscope.

25. MODE OF MEASURING THE DISTANCES BETWEEN THE LINES OF THE SPECTRUM.

We have already seen that the spectra of luminous vapors consist of one or more colored bands, and that it is not difficult from the distribution of these lines in the spectrum to recognize the substance by which such a spectrum is produced. Experience teaches that the single lines forming the spectrum of any given substance never fall in the same places as those of another substance, the spectrum of which may be shown at the same time; but, owing to the immense number of these lines (in iron, for example, according to Ångström and Thalén from 460 to 500), they approach each other so closely, especially when the spectrum is not much spread out, that it is necessary to have a contrivance in a spectrum apparatus for determining the relative places of the single lines, and for measuring with precision the amount of separation one from the other.

The number and relative position of these lines is, indeed, always the same in a given apparatus for any one substance as long as the temperature remains the same, however variously the substance may be combined with other bodies; but, by the use of prisms of greater dispersive power, or of a larger number of prisms, or by increasing the refracting angle of the prisms or the size of the telescope, these positions are altered, so that the *actual* amount of separation between any two lines in the spectrum of any substance varies according to the arrangement of the spectrum apparatus. This alteration extends even to the *relative* distances of the various lines in one and the same spectrum; when the whole spectrum of a substance is by any means extended two or three times its original length, the single lines do not all separate one from the other in the same proportion. On this account

Fig. 50.

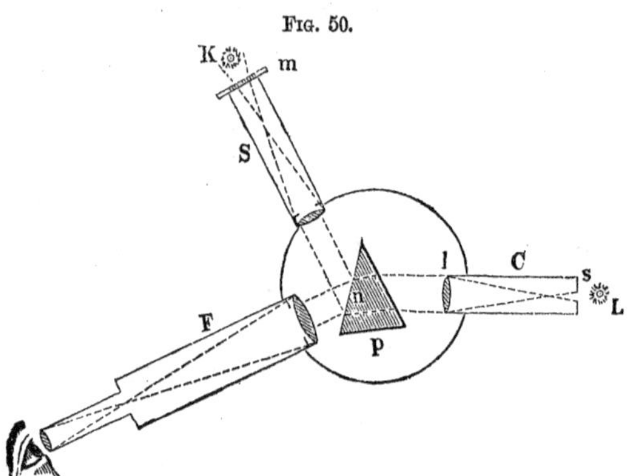

Graduated Scale in Spectroscope.

the same substance does not yield, in different spectroscopes, spectra identical throughout; the estimation of this difference is therefore one out of many reasons why it is requisite to have some means of measuring the distance of the individual lines one from the other, and of determining their relative positions.

The simplest and most usual arrangement of this kind is illustrated in Fig. 50. C is again, as in Fig. 41, the tube enclosing the slit *s*, and the collimating lens *l*; *p* is the prism, and F the telescope. To this is added a third tube S, which is with the others fastened to a stand, and lies with them on a horizontal plane. At the extreme end of this tube is fixed a reduced millimetre scale *m*, photographed on glass of about one-fifteenth the original dimensions, which is provided, according to the size of the apparatus, with a larger or smaller number of fine divisions. The tube S is inclined in such a manner toward the surface of the prism *n*, on which the telescope is directed, that its axis and that of the telescope form the same angle with the surface of the prism; consequently the scale *m* is, in obedience to the laws of light, reflected by the outer polished surface of the prism in the direction of the axis of the telescope, and its magnified image is seen in the telescope F at the same time as the spectrum to be observed. The scale *m* is bordered on both sides with tinfoil, and illuminated from without by a candle, K, or a small gas-flame, so that its image is seen with complete distinctness the whole length of the spectrum; and, as its black divisions are parallel to the colored bands, the amount of separation between any two of these bands may easily be read off in parts of the graduated scale.

In the direct-vision spectroscope, Fig. 47, a small glass scale placed in the eye-piece of the telescope is seen projected upon the spectrum, and by means of this scale the position of the lines of the spectrum may be measured.

A contrivance preferable to any fixed scale is that by which a well-defined mark of some kind—as, for instance, a fine wire or cross-wires, or two points facing each other, or a line of light, etc.—is made to move along the spectrum in the inside of the tube, and the amount of motion accurately measured externally by means of a micrometrical arrangement. This micrometer consists, principally, of a sliding-plate *a*, Fig. 51, provided with a slit or fine metal wire, an underplate, *b b*, on which the first plate

FIG. 51.

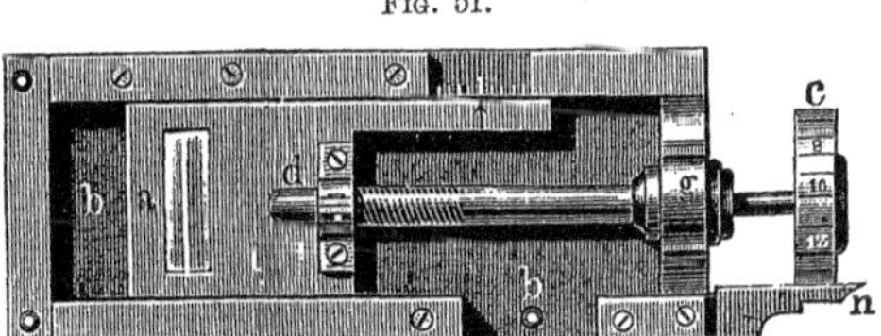

Micrometer for measuring the Distances between the Lines.

travels, and an exceedingly fine screw *d*, the head *c* of which is engraved after the manner of a divided circle. This screw, which is held firmly at *g*, works into the screw-plate *d* attached to the slide *a*, in which the mark is fixed, which it moves to the right or left upon the lower plate. In order to measure accurately the amount of motion, the value of a screw-thread must be ascertained, and the screw-head *c* be so divided as to mark off parts of an entire revolution. If, for instance, one revolution of the screw is half a millimetre in value, and the circumference of the screw-head *c* be divided into fifty equal parts, the displacement of the mark by a complete revolution of the screw amounts to half a millimetre, consequently a displacement amounting to one division of the screw-head is equivalent to only $\frac{1}{50}$ of a half-millimetre, or to $\frac{1}{100}$ of a millimetre. The screw-head *c* works close to the sharp edge *n*, by which parts of a revolution can be read off, while the number of complete revolutions are registered by means of the indicator on the slide *a* being brought over the divisions marked on the underplate *b b*. The micrometer is so connected with the eye-piece of the telescope in the spectrum-apparatus that the slide *a*, with its indicator, is in the inside of the tube, while the screw-head *c* and the divisions numbering the complete revolutions are visible on the outside. The micrometer-mark is seen projected upon the spectrum in the field of the telescope, and may be brought over any part of it by turning the screw. In this way, it is possible, by moving the indicator from one line of the spectrum to another, to determine accurately the distance between any two lines by the divisions marked on the screw-head.

Another mode of determining the relative positions of the lines of a spectrum consists of a telescope provided with cross-wires, or a line of light which can be moved on an axis from one line to another, and the angle measured which is described by this motion. In this case the distance between the lines is denoted by the angle; it will be seen at once that for any given instrument it is easy to calculate the real distance between the lines from the angles measured.*

* [Two new forms of spectroscopes, in which the positions of the lines can be rapidly registered, were constructed for observations of the solar eclipse of December, 1870.

Prof. Winlock contrived a form of instrument in which the positions of the observing telescope, when directed to different parts of the spectrum, are recorded by marks upon a plate of silvered copper.

Mr. Huggins communicated to the Royal Society the following description of the instrument taken by him to Oran:

"The short duration of the totality of the solar eclipse of December last led me to seek some method by which the positions of lines observed in the spectrum of the

26. The Compound Spectroscope.

The reader is now in a position to understand the use of the various parts of a complete spectrum-apparatus, Fig. 52, espe-

corona might be instantly registered without removing the eye from the instrument, so as to avoid the loss of time and fatigue to the eye of reading a micrometer-head, or the distraction of the attention and other inconveniences of an illuminated scale.

"After consultation with the optician Mr. Grubb, it seemed that this object could be satisfactorily accomplished by fixing in the eye-piece of the spectroscope a pointer which could be moved along the spectrum by a quick-motion screw, together with some arrangement by which the position of this pointer, when brought into coincidence with a line, could be instantly registered.

"I was furnished by Mr. Grubb with an instrument fulfilling these conditions, and also with a similar instrument with some modifications by Mr. Ladd, in time for the observation of the eclipse.

"Unfortunately, at my station at Oran, heavy clouds at the time of totality prevented the use of these instruments on the corona; but they were found so convenient for the rapid registration of spectra, that it appears probable that similar instruments might be of service for other spectrum observations.

"In these instruments the small telescope of the spectroscope is fixed, and at its focus is a pointer which can be brought rapidly upon any part of the spectrum by a screw-head outside the telescope. The spectrum and pointer are viewed by a positive eye-piece which slides in front of the telescope, so that the part of the spectrum under observation can always be brought to the middle of the field of view. The arm carrying the pointer is connected by a lever with a second arm, to the end of which are attached two needles, so that these move over about two inches when the pointer is made to traverse the spectrum from the red to the violet. Under the extremity of the arm fitted with the needles is a frame containing a card, firmly held in it by two pins which pierce the card. This frame containing the card can be moved forward so as to bring in succession five different portions of the card under the points of the needles; on each of these portions of the card a spectrum can be registered.

"The mode of using the instrument is obvious. By means of the screw-head at the side of the telescope, the pointer can be brought into coincidence with a line; a finger of the other hand is then pressed upon one of the needles at the end of the arm which traverses the card, and the position of the line is instantly recorded by a minute prick on the card. A bright line is distinguished from a dark line by pressing the finger on both needles, by which a second prick is made immediately below the other. In all cases the position of the line is registered by the same needle, the second needle being used to denote that the line recorded is a bright one.

"It was found that from ten to twelve Fraunhofer lines could be registered in about twelve seconds, and that, when the same lines were recorded five times in succession on the same card, no sensible difference of position could be detected between the pricks registering the same line in the several spectra.

"It is obvious that, by registering the spectra of different substances on the card, a ready method is obtained of comparing the relative position of the lines of their spectra.

"Each spectroscope was furnished with a compound prism made by Mr. Grubb, which gave a dispersion equal to about two prisms of dense glass, with a refracting angle of 60°."]

cially the three tubes directed to the prism at different angles, as in that constructed by Kirchhoff and Bunsen. The eye of the observer is placed in the axis of the telescope directed to that surface of the prism from which the light emerges in the form of the spectrum; the opposite surface of the prism receives through the slit and collimating lens the light emitted from the object to

Fig. 52.

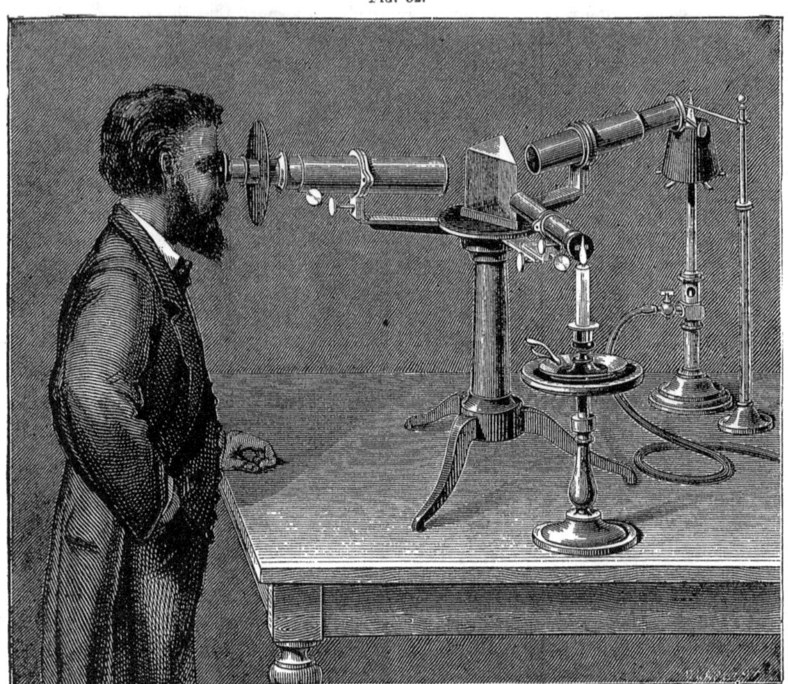

The Compound Spectroscope.

be examined; at the side of the observer is the tube carrying the illuminated scale, or the micrometer-screw, so that the mark coinciding with any division of the scale may be placed on any line of the spectrum.*

In most spectrum investigations the dispersion obtained by a flint-glass prism of 45° or 60° is sufficient to show the chief characteristics of the spectrum; should this not be the case, however,

* The description of the microspectroscope, telespectroscope, and meteor-spectroscope, will be given farther on

the dispersion must be increased by the use of several prisms, a method already explained in reference to Fig. 36.

Kirchhoff employed in his investigations on the solar spectrum an excellent apparatus constructed by Steinheil, of Munich, in which, instead of only one prism of flint glass, four such prisms were employed, and a telescope possessing a magnifying power of 40°. Each of the four prisms (Fig. 53), three of which had a

Fig. 53.

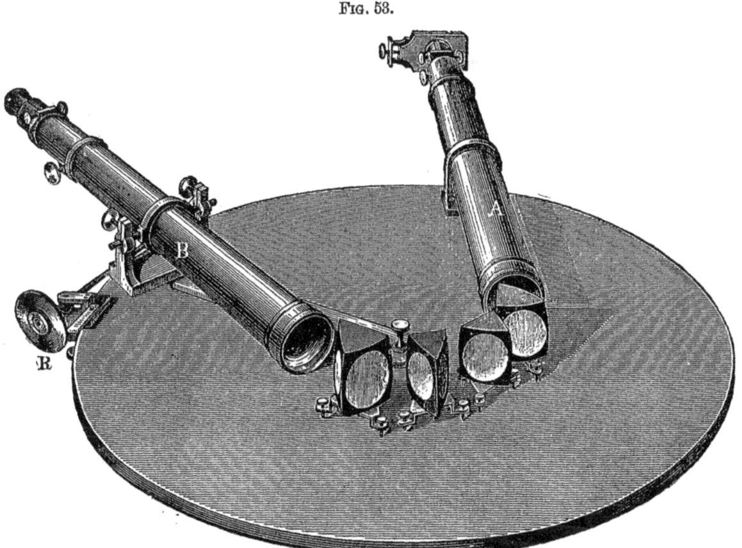

Kirchhoff's Spectroscope by Steinheil.

refracting angle of 45°, and the fourth of 60°, was cemented on to a small brass tripod, and could thus be easily placed in the right position on a horizontal iron table. The tube A carried at the end, directed toward the sun, the slit, and the prism for comparison, which will be described hereafter (Fig. 57); the telescope B, which received the widely-diverging rays of the solar spectrum from the last prism, could be moved by means of a micrometer-screw R, on a divided circle, so as to determine the distance between any of the dark lines in angular measure.

This amount of elongation of the spectrum has been, however, surpassed: Thalén employed six flint-glass prisms, each having an angle of 60°; Gassiot went as far as eight, Merz even

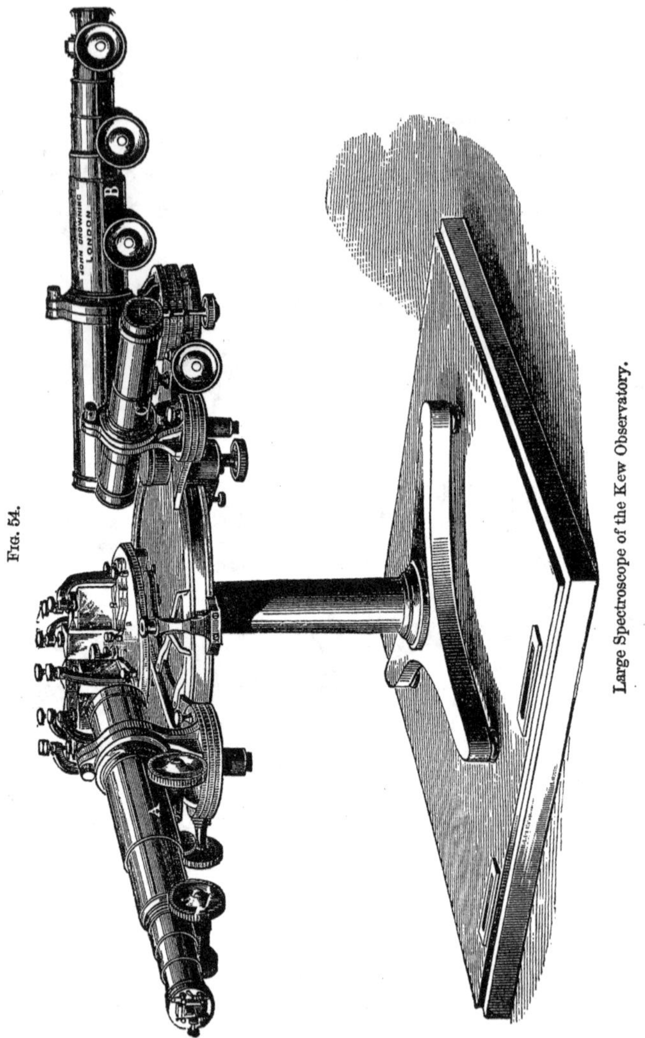

Fig. 54.

Large Spectroscope of the Kew Observatory.

to eleven prisms of glass, while Cooke made use of as many as nine prisms of bisulphide of carbon. Fig. 54 shows one of the largest spectroscopes yet made, constructed by Browning, and used by Gassiot at the Kew Observatory for the investigation and delineation of the solar spectrum. The tube A carries the collimating lens, the slit, and the prism for comparison; the nine prisms rest, as in Kirchhoff's instrument, on small plates provided with levelling screws upon an iron table; B is a telescope of high magnifying power; C, a tube fitted with a scale (compare Fig. 50). The slender ray of light entering the first prism from the slit and collimator-tube A passes through the range of nine prisms as shown in Fig. 55, and finally emerges from the last prism and enters the telescope B in the form of a widely-dispersed ray or an elongated spectrum. The power of a spectrum-apparatus, however, does not depend alone upon the *number* of the prisms, but also quite as much upon the dispersive power of each prism. In the workshops of the celebrated optician Merz, of Munich, prisms have been manufactured lately of the densest lead glass, having a specific gravity of 4.75; one of these prisms with a refracting angle of 60° is quite as efficient as the four prisms together employed in Kirchhoff's instrument, Fig. 53.*

FIG. 55.

Path of the Ray through the Nine Prisms.

27. BROWNING'S AUTOMATIC SPECTROSCOPE.

Spectroscopes consisting of several prisms are usually adjusted by finding the minimum of deviation for the *brightest* rays—those, for instance, situated between the yellow and the green—

* [Very dense glass has the disadvantage of not being colorless. In lead glass the absorption of light due to this cause is almost wholly confined to the part of the spectrum more refrangible than F.]

for each prism which is then permanently secured to its supporting plate. There are, however, two objections to this arrangement. In the first place, only those rays for which the prisms are specially adjusted are seen under the most favorable circumstances, because they only pass through each prism in a line parallel to the base. In the second place, since the last prism is immovable, while the telescope travels in an arc from one end of the spectrum to the other, the object-glass of the telescope receives the full light only when it is directed to the central part of the spectrum; and, on the contrary, only a part of the light falls on the object-glass when the telescope is directed to one end of the spectrum, either the red or the violet.

Now, it is easy to see that in observing the ends of the spectrum it is most important that the object-glass should receive the whole of the light, since it is just these terminal colors that have least brilliancy. This can only be accomplished by the prisms being made adjustable for the minimum of deviation for those rays which are under examination.

Bunsen and Kirchhoff, therefore, in their investigations of the solar spectrum, attached the prisms of their compound spectroscope (Fig. 53) to the ground-plate by means of movable supports, and altered the position of the prisms for every color of the spectrum; it is needless to remark that such an arrangement involved much trouble and inconvenience.

This inconvenience is removed in Browning's automatic spectroscope, by so connecting the prisms with each other and the telescope, that, on placing the instrument on any particular color, the prisms, without any interference from the observer, will be simultaneously and automatically adjusted for the minimum of deviation for that color.

Fig. 56 shows the arrangement of the various parts of the automatic spectroscope. Of the prisms, numbered from 1 to 6, the first only is fastened to the ground-plate P P, the others are connected to each other by hinges at the corners of the triangular metal holders forming the base. A metal rod *a*, provided with a slit, is attached to the middle of this base, by means of which each prism can move round a central pin common to the whole set. The prisms are arranged in a circle round this pin, which again is fastened to a swallow-tailed movable bar, *s s*, about two inches in length, situated under the plate P P. If, therefore, the central pin be moved, the whole system of prisms moves with it, and the amount of motion communicated to each prism varies in proportion to its distance from the first prism,

Fig. 56.

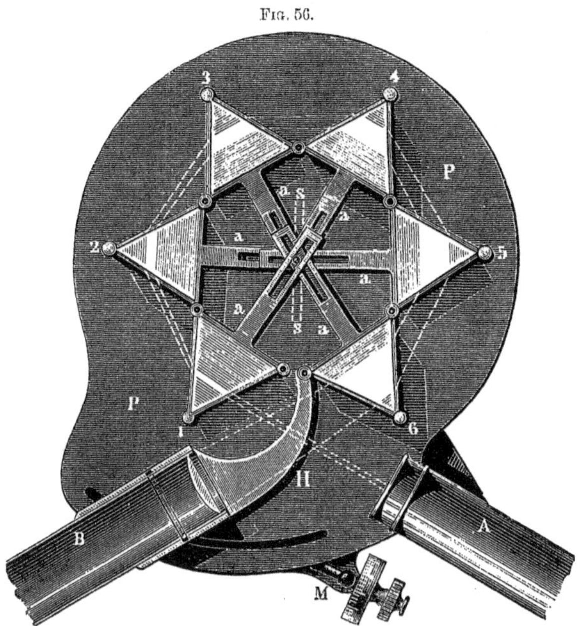

Browning's Automatic Spectroscope.

which is stationary; if, for instance, prism 2 moves 1°, the third prism is moved 2°, the fourth 3°, the fifth 4°, and the sixth 5°. The tube of the telescope B is fastened to a lever H, which is connected by a hinge with the last prism, No. 6. At the other end of this lever, or on the carrier of the telescope B, works the micrometer-screw M, by turning which the tube B can be directed upon any part of the spectrum issuing from prism 6. This lever is so adjusted that, to whatever angle the telescope is turned, the amount of movement for the last prism shall be twice as great. The rays emerging from the middle of this last prism fall perpendicularly upon the centre of the object-glass of the telescope; the rays issuing from the collimator A, and falling upon the first stationary prism 1, pass through the individual prisms in a line parallel to their base, and arrive finally on their emergence from the last prism, 6, in the direction of the optical axis of the telescope, whether it be directed upon the central or the terminal colors of the spectrum; the object-glass is consequently always filled with light. As the tube B is turned toward any color of the spectrum, the lever H sets at the same time all the prisms in motion, in such a manner that each adjusts itself to the minimum angle of deviation.

The automatic spectroscope shows a great advance in the construction of compound spectroscopes, and has already been acknowledged as such by all authorities on this subject.*

28. Prism of Comparison, or Reflecting Prism.

By means of a careful examination of the spectrum-lines of all known substances in which attention has not only been given to

* [Automatic spectroscopes, possessing these advantages in a greater or less degree, had been constructed previously by Littrow, Rutherfurd, Prof. Young, and Mr. Lockyer. An independent method adopted by Grubb is thus described by him:

"The spectroscope as exhibited is in an unfinished state, having been sent to Mr. Huggins for arranging some small matters of convenience, such as the dividing of Sector, Reading microscope, etc.

"It consists of a combination of four compound prisms and two semi-compound prisms, all made use of twice, the total power of the instrument therefore being equal to ten compound prisms, each having a dispersion of about 9°, that is, a total dispersion of about 90°, probably the largest ever obtained. The observing and collimating telescopes are respectively 6 and 4½ inches focus, and 1 inch aperture, the section of pencil actually in use being 1 inch by : 0.6 inch. This is perfectly constant from end to end of the spectrum, as the prisms are automatically worked.

"The prisms are 2¼ inches high, being just twice the height required for the section of the pencil: the lower half being made use of for the first course of rays, the upper for the backward course.

"Referring to the diagrams (the same letters of reference apply to both), the dotted lines represent those levers, etc., which are situated in a different plane, being at the back of the spectroscope. The right-angled prism of reflection (0) is applied only on the upper half of the first semi-compound prism (1), so that it does not interfere with the first course of the rays, which utilize only the lower half of the prisms.

"The parallel rays from the collimator enter the lower half of the first semi-compound prism without refraction, this prism (1), therefore, is stationary. They then pass through four entire compound prisms, 2, 3, 4, 5, and one semi-compound, 6, from which by two internal total reflections in the prism of reflection, 7, they are passed to the upper half of the prisms, by which they return through the four entire compounds and two semi-compounds, and are finally received, emerging from the first fixed semi-prism, by the right-angled prism of total reflection 0, and so passed to the observing-telescope, which is placed at right angles to the collimator merely as a matter of preference. Any other position can be utilized if desired.

"The prisms and automatic arrangement are contained in an air-tight box, and the brightness of the lines, but also to the exact measurement of their relative distances, accurate drawings have been made of the spectra of various substances, some of which are given in the Frontispiece and in the table, Fig. 61. If these tables be pro-

both observing and collimating telescopes are stationary, considerable advantages in such a powerful spectroscope, and allowing of great compactness..

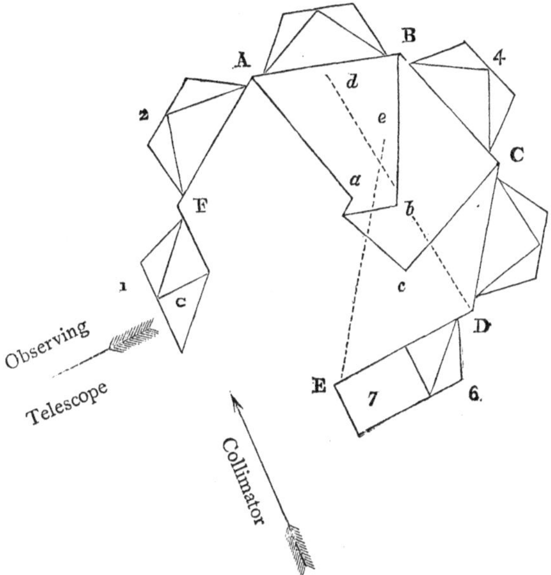

"The several parts of the spectrum required to be examined are brought into the field by acting on the sector, which carries the automatic arrangement, each line being exactly in minimum deviation when brought to the centre of the field.

"The sector reading by a vernier to 10 seconds of arc divides the spectrum into about 20,000 parts.

"The mechanical arrangement of the automatic movement is that which we made a model of during Mr. Huggins's visit here last spring, and decided upon as giving the most constant and reliable results.

"The motion is given to the chain of prisms entirely by a system of levers which will be easily understood from the diagrams.

"The first three movable joints of chain A B C are connected by levers to the studs, *a*, *b*, *c*, fixed in a circular disk, which is rotated through 60° by the toothed sector and pinion. The pins being fixed at their proper radii, draw the several prism tables through the required angle, the levers forming tangents in their mean position. The last two joints D and E were found geometrically to describe most accurately arcs of circles; they have therefore been attached to levers working on fixed centres at back of spectroscope, shown in the drawing by dotted lines.

"The whole system of the automatic movement is composed of hardened steel vided with a millimetre scale, by which the distance between any two lines can be determined, they form a valuable standard of comparison in doubtful cases when examining the spectrum of an unknown substance. But, in an ordinary spectroscope, no great dependence can be placed on the measures made with the photographic scale, for the breadth of the lines depends upon the width of the slit, and this may vary with each observer; the measurement, too, and subsequent comparison of a spectrum with the spectra represented in the tables, requires too much time, besides being laborious and uncertain, while in many cases the spectrum to be examined is very evanescent, or perhaps appears under circumstances that make comparison with the tables either impracticable or quite untrustworthy in its results.

In all such cases, it is well to employ a contrivance of Kirchhoff's, by which only one half of the slit is employed for the spectrum to be examined, and the other half made use of for receiving a second spectrum from the incandescent vapor of a well-

pivots, working in hardened steel bearings, a system which can obviously be made to work with the greatest accuracy and constancy.

"The delicate steel parts of slit have been electro-gilt, to preserve them from oxidation. The jaws (of gold plate) are drawn asunder by a double wedge, acted upon by a screw, so as to preserve the axis of collimation. They are pulled together by a

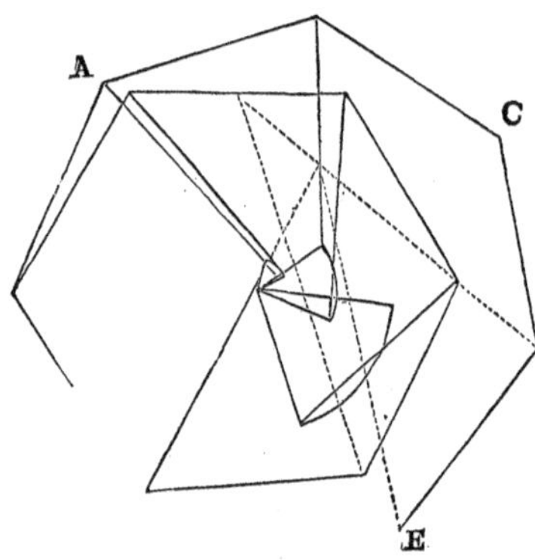

spring at the back. The micrometer-head of screw is divided into forty parts, each division being equivalent to $\frac{1}{40000}$ of an inch of opening.

"The slots in the table of the spectroscope have nothing whatever to do with the guiding of the chain of prisms. They are merely to allow of the junction of the two systems of levers working in different planes."—*Monthly Notices of Royal Astronomical Society*, vol. xxxi., p. 36.]

known substance, which can then be compared directly with that under examination. For this purpose the upper half of the slit remains free, and can, as shown in Fig. 57, be made wider or narrower at will by means of the micrometer-screw. In front

FIG. 57.

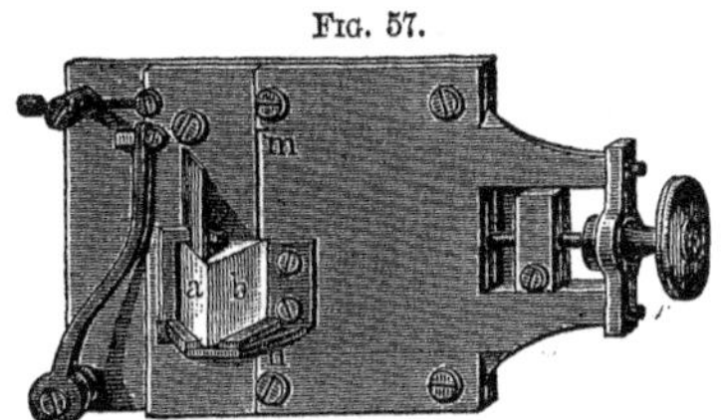

The Prism of Comparison, or Reflecting Prism.

of the lower half is placed a small equilateral glass prism, *a b*, which is movable, and which cuts off from this portion of the slit all the rays of light falling directly in front of it.

A reference to Fig. 58, which gives a horizontal section of the vertical slit and prism of comparison, will easily explain its action. F is the source of light whence the rays pass straight through the upper half of the slit above the surface of the small prism, and form a spectrum according to the usual action of an inverting telescope, in the lower half of the field of view. At one side, on a level with the prism, is placed the flame L, either a Bunsen burner or a spirit-lamp in which the substance is volatilized, the spectrum of which is needed for comparison with that formed by the light F. The rays from L falling at right angles on the surface *d f*, will be totally reflected as by a mirror from the prism-surface *d c* at the point *r*, and will emerge from the prism in the direction *r s*, pass at *s* through the lower half of the

FIG. 58.

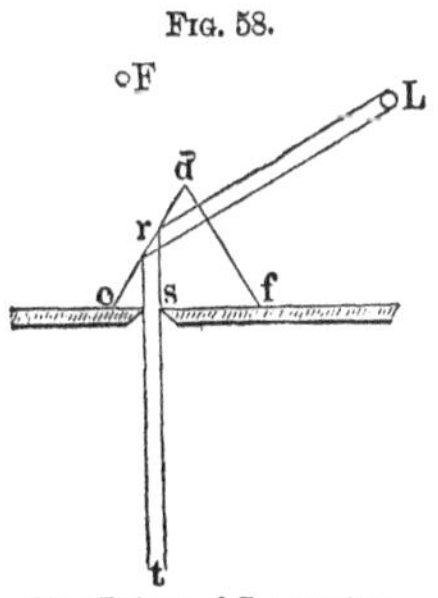

The Prism of Comparison.

slit, and fall in the direction *s t* on the lower half of the principal prism in the inside of the tube, in the same manner as the rays from F fell on the upper half.* In this way the spectra *o* and *u* of the two flames F and L are seen in juxtaposition in the same field of view as shown in Fig. 59, where for greater clearness it is represented as it would appear if both images were thrown upon a screen. In reality, as the spectra *o* and *u* are seen through a telescope direct without a screen, their positions are reversed, so that the spectrum *o* from the upper half of the slit is seen below, and the spectrum *u* from the lower half is seen above. If the same substance be volatilized in the two flames F and L, the

Fig. 59.

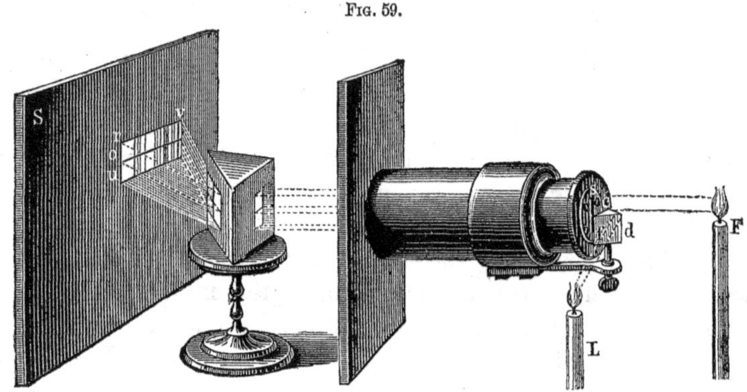

The Double Spectrum.

corresponding lines of one spectrum will fall in exact prolongation of those of the other, because two pencils of rays of the same constitution will produce precisely similar spectra with the same width of slit, the same prism, and the same position of the telescope.

If, therefore, the presence of a certain substance be suspected in one of the flames—for example, in F—and from its spectrum, received through the upper half of the slit, there remains some doubt as to its nature, a small quantity of the supposed substance is volatilized in the second flame L, and a comparison made between the juxtaposed spectra. If there be a complete coincidence

* [The light passing through each half of the slit is not restricted to the corresponding part of the prism, but, since it consists of diverging rays, spreads itself over the collimating lens and then passes through the prism as a beam of parallel rays of the same diameter as the lens.]

between the lines of the upper and lower spectra, they both belong to one and the same substance; while, in the case of want of coincidence, the body to be tested does not contain the same substance as that with which it is compared. From the extreme sensitiveness of the eye to the exact coincidence of two lines in two spectra produced under similar circumstances and observed at the same time, this mode of comparison forms one of the most important methods of spectrum analysis.

FIG. 60.

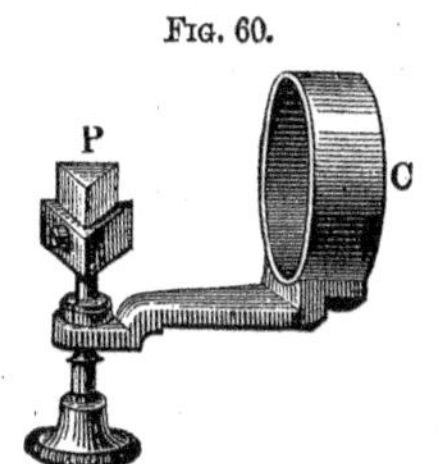

Hofmann's Prism of Comparison.

Fig. 60 shows how the small prism of comparison P can be easily applied to a direct-vision spectroscope (Fig. 47) by means of the sliding-ring C. It will be understood that, instead of the second flame, the electric spark or one of Geissler's tubes filled with a known gas may be employed; the importance of this method, when applied to the spectrum investigations of the sun, the fixed stars, nebulæ, and comets, can only be fully entered into when this part of the subject comes under discussion.

For the ready comparison of various spectra, it is convenient to have always at hand the means of producing the spectra of known elements. For this purpose small wax or tallow candles are prepared, the wick of which is impregnated with the various metallic compounds of chlorine, and they are employed as a secondary source of light in the manner above described.

29. DESIGNATION OF THE LINES OF THE SPECTRUM.

Not only the number of the spectrum-lines of a substance, but also the degree of their intensity, is deserving of careful attention. As the brilliancy of the lines increases with the temperature, so, as a rule, it is those lines which are particularly prominent at a high degree of heat that are the first to appear at

Fig. 61.

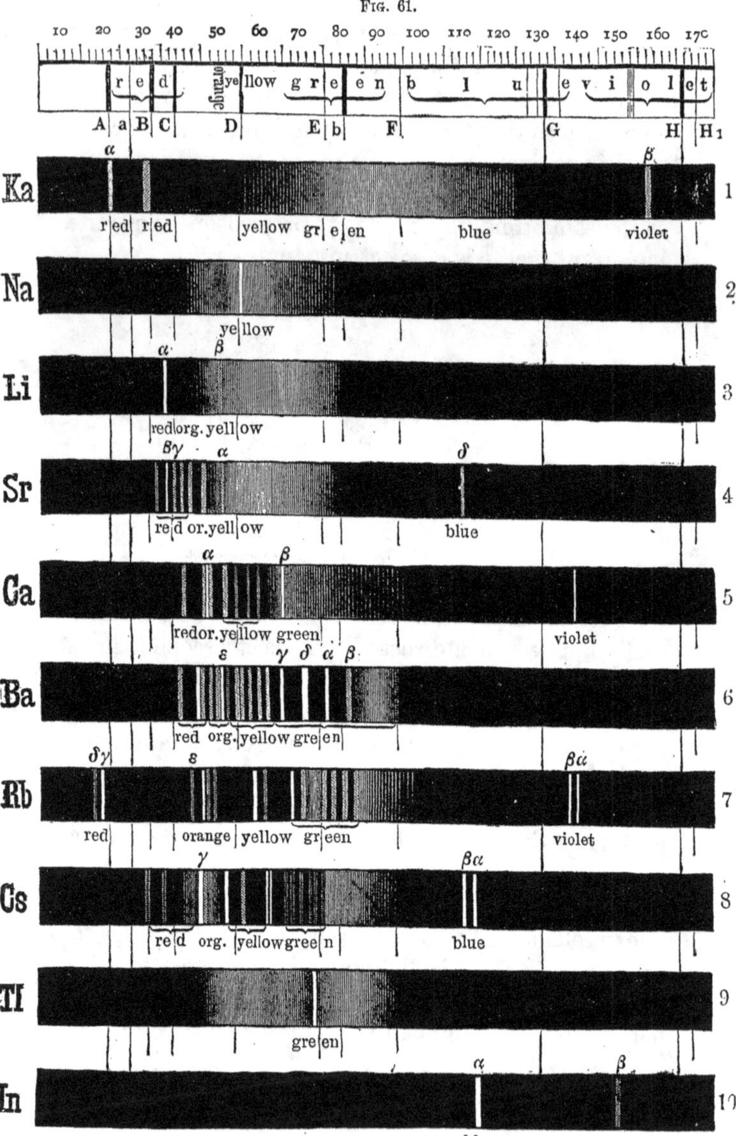

Table of Spectra according to Kirchhoff and Bunsen.

a low temperature. These prominent lines, therefore, are the most suited for the recognition of a substance, and on this ground are called the *characteristic* lines. Such lines, according to their

Robert Wilhelm Bunsen.

degree of brightness, are designated in each substance by the letters of the Greek alphabet, α, β, γ, δ, etc., being affixed to the chemical sign denoting the substance. The spectrum of potassium (Fig. 61, No. 1) has two characteristic lines, one red and one violet; the former, as the most intense, is therefore designated Ka, α, the latter by Ka, β. The brilliant red line of lithium (Fig. 61, No. 3, Frontispiece No. 3) is called Li, α, the fainter orange line Li, β; the characteristic lines of the spectrum of barium (No. 6) are in the green; those of cæsium (No. 8, Frontispiece No. 4) Cs, α, and Cs, β, are blue; those of rubidium (No. 7, Frontispiece No. 5) Rb, α, Rb, β, violet, and Rb, γ, Rb, δ, dark red; the most intense line of hydrogen gas (Frontispiece No. 7) is red, and is designated by H α, the greenish-blue line nearly equal to it in brightness by H β, and the much fainter violet line by H γ, etc.

The table in Fig. 61 exhibits the spectra observed by Kirchhoff and Bunsen as follows: 1, Potassium; 2, Sodium; 3, Lithium; 4, Strontium; 5, Calcium; 6, Barium; 7, Rubidium; 8, Cæsium; 9, Thallium; 10, Indium, collated for easy comparison, with a statement of the color of the individual lines, and a scale for determining their relative distances. The colors marked above No. 1 represent the solar spectrum, in which the black lines designated A, B, up to H, will be hereafter explained.

30. Various Methods for exhibiting the Spectra of Terrestrial Substances.

The spectra of incandescent *solid* and *liquid* bodies are *continuous*, and resemble each other so closely, that only in a very few instances can they be distinguished; spectra of this kind are, therefore, not suitable for the recognition of a substance, though they authorize the conclusion, as a rule, that the substance is either in a solid or liquid state. Only the discontinuous spectra, consisting of colored lines which are obtained from a gas or vapor, are sufficiently characteristic to enable the observer to pronounce with certainty, by the number, position, and relative brightness of these lines, the chemical constitution of the vapors by which the light has been emitted. It follows from this circumstance that spectrum analysis deals preëminently with the investigation of gas-spectra, and that, for the examination of a substance which does not exist in Nature in the form of gas or vapor, the first step must be to place it in this condition.

Use of the Bunsen Burner.

The temperature at which substances are volatilized varies greatly; while the heat of an ordinary spirit-lamp is sufficient for many, such as potassium and sodium, for others, especially the heavy metals and their compounds, the great heat of the electric spark is requisite. In many cases, however, the temperature of the non-luminous flame of the Bunsen burner is sufficient to volatilize the substances intended for examination, and to cause them to emit a light sufficiently intense to give a brilliant spectrum.

A Bunsen burner, as shown in Fig. 2, is therefore one of the necessary requisites for spectrum investigation. In using the lamp, the air is first shut off below, and a pure, continuous spectrum of the luminous flame obtained by an accurate adjustment of the telescope and a careful setting of the slit. To prevent flickering, the lower part of the flame is surrounded, as shown in Fig. 52, by a hollow cone of sheet-iron; by the introduction of atmospheric air the flame is then rendered non-luminous, and only the upper very hot point of the flame made use of, into which the substances to be tested are brought from the side by means of a thin wire of platinum, a metal on which this temperature has no influence. When the spectrum appears, the focus of the telescope must be adjusted immediately, and the slit narrowed sufficiently to insure the bright-colored lines being sharply defined. In the Bunsen burner, spectra can only be obtained from the metals potassium, sodium, lithium, strontium, calcium, barium, cæsium, rubidium, copper, manganese, thallium, and indium, and from these most readily when they are in combination with chlorine, in which state they are most easily volatilized.*

* [In the case of some only of these metals can the spectrum of the metal itself be obtained by heating their chlorides in the flame of the Bunsen burner.

Some time ago Roscoe and Clifton investigated the different spectra presented by calcium, strontium, and barium, and they "suggest that, at the low temperature of the Bunsen flame or a weak spark, the spectrum observed is produced by some compound, probably the oxide of the difficultly-reducible metal; whereas at the enormously high temperature of the intense electric spark these compounds are split up, and thus the

The method of introducing the substances to be examined into the flame by means of a platinum wire has this drawback, that the spectrum is visible only for a very short time, and in

true spectrum of the metal is obtained. In none of the spectra of the more reducible alkaline metals (potassium, sodium, lithium) can any deviation or disappearance of maxima of light be noticed on change of temperature." In a recent paper "On the Spectra of Erbia and some other Earths," Huggins, after describing the bright lines seen in the spectra of some earths when incandescent in the oxyhydrogen flame, remarks:

"The question presents itself as to the nature of the vapor to which the bright lines are due in the case of the earths, lime, magnesia, strontia, and baryta. Is it the oxide volatilized? or is it the vapor of the metal reduced by the heat in the presence of the hydrogen of the flame? The experiments show that the luminous vapor is the same as that produced by the exposure of the chlorides of the metals to the heat of the Bunsen gas-flame. The character common to these spectra of bands of some width, in most cases gradually shading off at the sides, is different from that which distinguishes the spectra of these metals when used as electrodes in the metallic state.*

"As the experiments recorded in this paper show that the same spectra are produced by the exposure of the oxides to the oxyhydrogen flame, Roscoe and Clifton's suggestion that these spectra are due to the volatilization of the compound of the metal with oxygen is doubtless correct.

"The similar character of the spectrum of bright lines seen when erbia is rendered incandescent would seem to suggest whether this earth may not be volatile in a small degree, as is the case with lime, magnesia, and some other earths. The peculiarity, however, of the bright lines of erbia, observed by Bahr and Bunsen, that they could not be seen in the flame beyond the limits of the solid erbia, deserves attention. My own experiments to detect the lines in the Bunsen gas-flame, even when a very thin wire was used, so as to allow the erbia to attain nearly the heat of the flame, were unsuccessful. The bright line in the green appears, indeed, to rise to a very small extent beyond the continuous spectrum, but I was unable to assure myself whether this appearance might not be an effect of irradiation.

"It is perhaps worthy of remark that the chlorides of sodium, potassium, lithium, cæsium, and rubidium, give spectra of defined lines which are not altered in character by the introduction of a Leyden jar, and which, in the case of sodium, potassium, and lithium, we know to resemble the spectra obtained when electrodes of the metals are used. Now, all these metals belong to the monad group; it appeared, therefore, interesting to observe the behavior of the other metal belonging to this group.

"Chloride of silver when introduced into the Bunsen flame gave no lines. The chloride was then mixed with alumina, which had been found to give a continuous spectrum only, and exposed to the oxyhydrogen flame, but no lines were visible. When, however, the moistened chloride was placed on cotton and subjected to the induction spark without a jar, the true metallic spectrum was seen, as when silver electrodes are used.

"The behavior of silver, therefore, is similar to that of the other metals of the monad group. Now, the difference in basic relations which is known to exist between

* "For the spectra of metallic strontium, barium, and calcium, see Phil. Trans., 1864 p. 148, and Plates I. and II. Both forms of the spectra of these substances are represented by Thalén in his Spektralanalys.' "

many cases the bright lines flash out only to vanish again immediately. In order to observe the spectrum for a longer time, it is necessary, therefore, to be constantly introducing new material into the flame—a tedious and troublesome process.

To overcome this difficulty and obtain a permanent spectrum, Mitscherlich has devised the following expedient: A solution of the substance to be examined is introduced into a small glass vessel *a* (Fig. 62), closed at the top and bent round at the lower end, which terminates in a narrow tube *b*. In this opening is placed a bundle of very fine platinum wire *c*, tightly held together by a wire of platinum, and secured into the tube by the bent position of the wires. By capillary attraction, the liquid is continually drawn through the opening by the platinum wick to the place of volatilization. A series of such tubes may be ranged round the circumference of a revolving table *d* (Fig. 63),

Fig. 62.

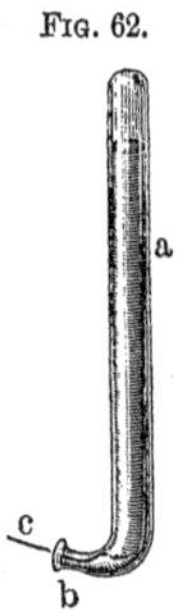

Mitscherlich's Spectrum Wick.

so that the platinum wick of any one of them can be brought at will into the flame of the Bunsen burner *h*, placed near the edge of the table. An addition of acetate of ammonia to the solution assists the capillary action of the platinum wick, which, when rightly placed in the flame, allows of the spectrum being continuously observed for nearly two hours.

the oxides of the monatomic and polyatomic metals would be in accordance with the distinction which the spectroscope shows to exist in the behavior of their chlorides; the chlorides of the polyatomic metals would be more likely to split up in the presence of water into oxides and hydrochloric acid.

"In the case of some of the oxides and chlorides, one or more of the lines appeared to agree with corresponding lines in the metallic spectra; it may be, therefore, that under some circumstances, as in the case of magnesium burning in air, the metallic vapor and the volatilized oxide may be simultaneously present."]

Not less complete, and more generally applicable, is the following contrivance by Morton, of Philadelphia, which, intended principally for the production of *monochromatic* (homogeneous) light on a large scale, is also employed in spectrum researches for bringing a continuous supply of greater quantities of the substances to be examined into the Bunsen flame. The apparatus consists of four or five ordinary non-luminous Bunsen lamps A B (Fig. 64), fixed into one common-gas tube D, and enclosed below, where the supply of air is received, by a covering of tin C D. At one side of this case is a wide opening C, through which the point F of a disperser E supplies a stream of vapor by the heat of a spirit-lamp, or else a stream of air is driven through the tube F, by means of bellows or an India-rubber ball, in the manner of an ordinary spray apparatus. Close under the orifice of the pointed tube F is a glass tube which reaches down into a glass vessel containing a solution of the substance to be exam-

FIG. 63.

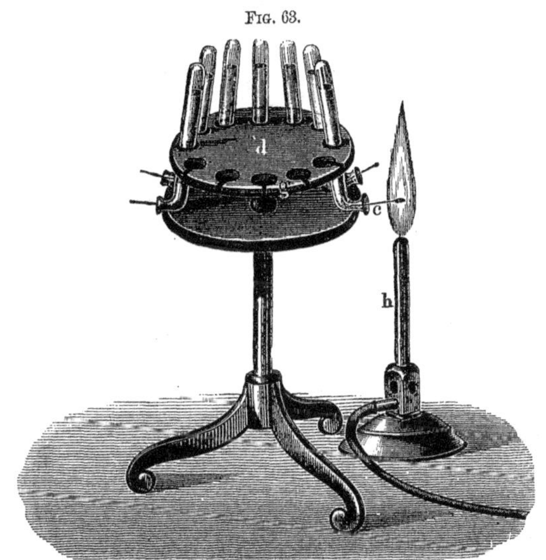

Mitscherlich's Apparatus for Permanent Spectra.

ined. The stream of air or vapor forces some of the liquid in the vessel G up the vertical glass tube, and disperses it; the fine particles, mixed with a sufficient quantity of atmospheric air, are driven forcibly through the orifice C into the tin case, where they are mingled with the coal-gas and are volatilized at the mouth of the burners. By this method, Morton has produced monochromatic light of various kinds on a large scale, especially the yellow light of sodium, by the use of a solution of common salt, which, with a suitable disposition of sixty such sets of burners, he employed for the production of magic effects on the stage.

Application of the Induction Coil.

When the heat of the Bunsen burner is not sufficient to volatilize the substance to be investigated, recourse must be had to those sources of still greater heat that have been already described

Fig. 64.

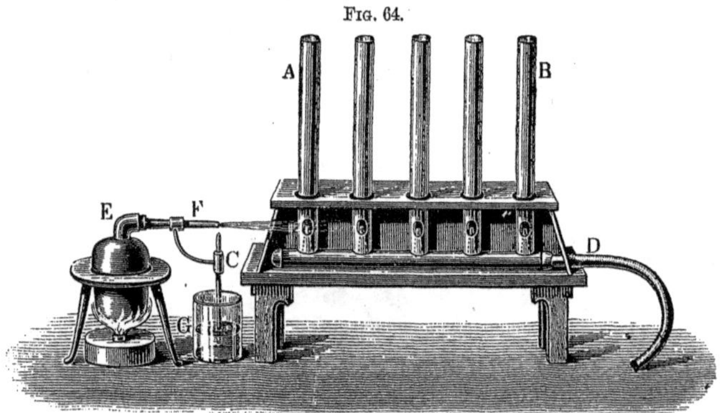

Morton's Apparatus for Monochromatic Light.

(oxyhydrogen flame, p. 16, the voltaic arc, p. 27, the induction coil, p. 23), among which the induction coil deserves the preference on account of its greater facility of management. The apparatus is employed in the usual manner by moistening the ends of the platinum wires, between which the spark passes, with the substance to be investigated, and examining the spectrum of the spark, or, when this heat is insufficient, by intensifying the spark through the interposition of a special condensing apparatus (p. 23).

In general, however, the effect of this method is to produce two different spectra, which are superposed, one of the gas in which the spark passes, and the other of the metal forming the poles. If electrodes of different metals be employed, and the spark be allowed to pass always through the same gas, the spectrum of the luminous gas appears as if it were a background upon which the more intense spectra of the metals are well relieved.

The way in which a Leyden jar is interposed for intensifying the spark is easily understood by reference to Fig. 65. M is the end of the induction coil, which, to insure a discharge of some intensity, is supplied with electricity from a powerful Bunsen battery of from six to eight elements (Fig. 13). The extremities of the coil are fastened into the insulated binding screws 1 and 2. From the first (1) of these pass two wires, one (4) to the binding-screw *d*, and the other to the knob K, in connection with the inner coating of the intensifying jar R; from the second (2) also pass two wires, one to the binding-screw *a*, and the other (3) to O, where it is connected by means of the copper disk T with

FIG. 65.

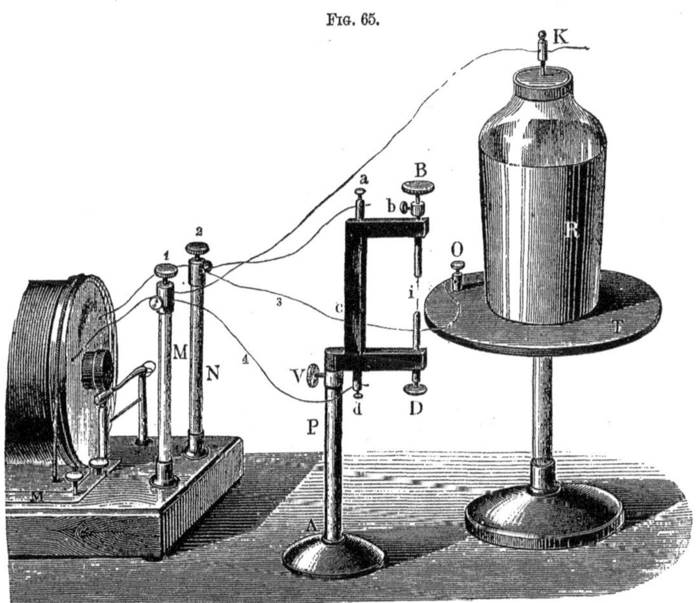

Intensifying the Electric Discharge by a Leyden Jar.

the outer coating of R. B and D are wire holders for the reception of the metals, the spectra of which are to be examined, or for the insertion when necessary of platinum wires, the ends of which may be smeared with the substances to be investigated. The upper metallic arm *a b* B is insulated from the lower arm *d*

D by the intervening piece of ebonite, so that the equalization of the opposite electricities accumulated in 1 and 2 can take place only through the wires B and D at *i*, and the spark can only pass when the quantity of electricity accumulated in the jar R is of such an intensity as to enable the discharge to break through the stratum of air between the wires B and D. Sparks produced in this way are shorter than those not intensified, but far more powerful; they are very bright, and of so intense a heat that all metals may be raised to incandescence in them and volatilized; the spectra thus obtained are unfortunately not steadily visible, for, owing to the discontinuous action of the machine, they flash out momentarily with every fresh spark, and by their inconstant light interrupt investigation.*

Browning has much improved and simplified this method of introducing a Leyden jar into the current of an induction coil by

FIG. 66.

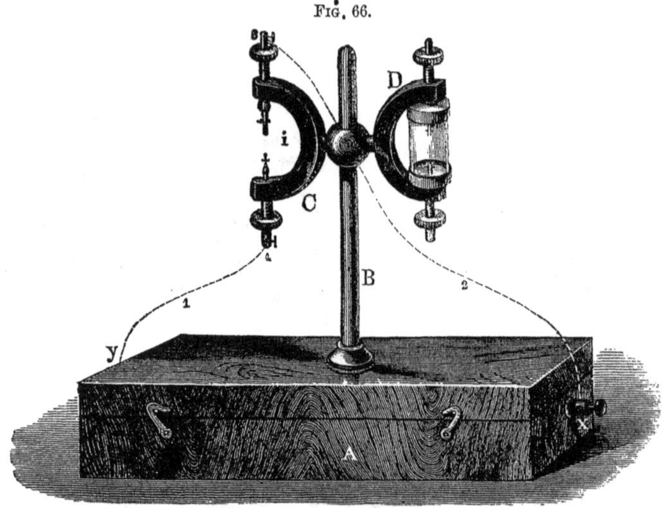

Browning's Intensifying Apparatus.

substituting plates of ebonite for the glass jar. When these are coated on both sides with tin-foil, they act like a Leyden jar. Browning places from four to six of such plates in layers entirely insulated one from another, enclosed in a case A, seen in Fig. 66.

* [The difficulty is easily removed by such an arrangement of the power of the coil relatively to the size of the jars, that the discharges succeed each other with a rapidity sufficient to produce a persistent impression on the eye.]

By a simple mechanical contrivance inside the box, one or more of these intensifying plates can be used as required. The brass rod B, with the two ebonite holders C, D for wire or glass, is screwed on to the lid of the case, and is placed within the box when the condenser is not in requisition. The substances to be investigated, or the metal wires, are inserted between the platinum forceps 3 and 4, from the binding-screws of which the conducting wires 1 2 lead to the poles *x y* of the ebonite plates projecting from the box. The whole apparatus is by means of the same binding-screws placed in connection with the wires (1, 2, Fig. 65) of the induction machine. The ebonite holder D is fitted for the reception of glass tubes or other vessels provided with conducting wires—the details of which will be given hereafter—and by the help of a spring, of Geissler's tubes, so that the spectrum of the substances they contain, whether in a liquid or gaseous condition, may be brought under examination.

The first successful contrivance for the examination of the spectra of liquids, and of substances in a state of solution, is due to Séguin, of Grenoble, whose plan has been greatly extended and very variously applied by Becquerel. The contrivance, as arranged by Ruhmkorff and Browning, for convenient use, consists of several glass vessels, b, b_1, b_2 (Fig. 67), five or six inches in height, and rather more than an inch in width, inserted in the small table A B; these vessels are fused at one end, while at the other they are closed by corks. A platinum wire fused into the lower end of the vessels, and projecting into the inside, places the liquids they contain in connection with the *negative* pole of the induction coil, while a second platinum wire, fused into the narrow glass tubes a, a_1, a_2, passes through the corks from above, and, projecting one-twentieth of an inch from the small tubes, remains some tenth of an inch distant from the surface of the liquids. By connecting the binding-screws 1 2 on one side with the inductor, and on the other side, as shown in the figure, with the platinum wire b of the first vessel, and a_2 of the last vessel, and by placing the other wires in connection, a with b_1, a_1 with b_2, etc., the electric current may be made to pass through all the liquids, and by the passage of the spark between the upper platinum wires a, a_1, a_2, and the liquids, the substances in solution may be volatilized in the heat, and their various spectra obtained at the same time.

When the action of the induction coil is so regulated that the interruption of the current and consequent passage of the spark takes place in rapid succession, the spectrum remains almost perfectly free from disturbance, and the apparatus works for hours

Fig. 67.

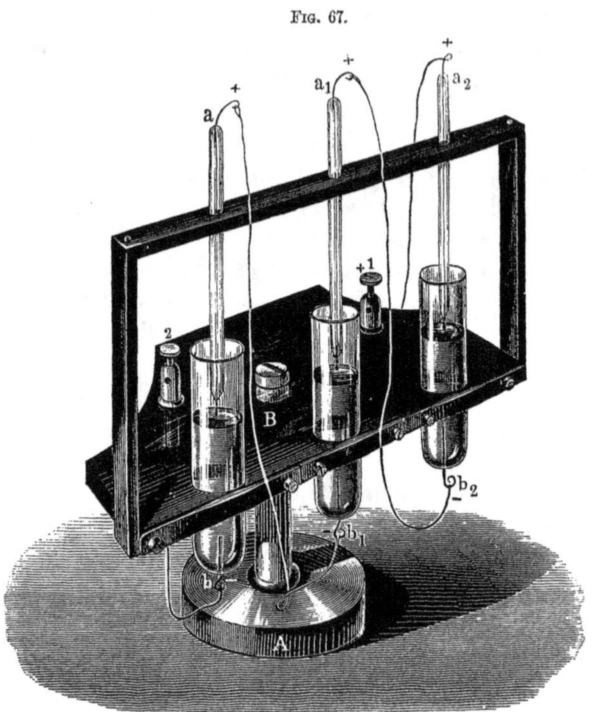

The Becquerel-Ruhmkorff Apparatus.

together like an intense heat-lamp constantly fed with the substances to be investigated. As, however, by the rapid succession of sparks the liquids in the smaller glass tubes often become considerably heated, wider tubes should be employed when the apparatus is to be used for many consecutive hours.

For these experiments, solutions of the various metallic compounds of chlorine in pure water are the most suitable; when in a concentrated form they produce spectra of great intensity, but weak solutions will give spectra that are easily to be recognized. The spark is colored more or less intensely, according to the nature of the metal held in solution. The following metals give great brilliancy to it: chloride of sodium (yellow); chloride of strontium (red; chloride of calcium (orange); chloride of magnesium (green); chloride of copper (greenish-blue); chloride of zinc (blue); but various other compounds of barium, potassium, antimony, manganese, silver, uranium, iron, etc., give also very remarkable colorings, and corresponding characteristic spectra. It is one advantage of this method of investigation, that the spark from platinum wires produces no direct spectrum of platinum, inasmuch as the heat is not sufficiently great to volatilize this metal completely.

For the investigation of the spectra of gases, either Plücker's tubes (Fig. 12) may be employed, for which, besides the glass tubes provided with platinum or aluminium wires, a special quicksilver air-pump is requisite; or Angström s plan may be adopted, in which the electric discharge from a Leyden jar or induction

Fig. 68.

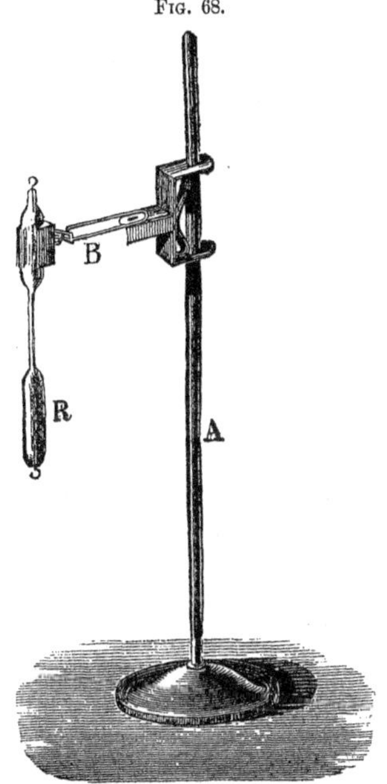

Stand for Plücker's Tubes.

machine is allowed to pass between two points of one and the same metal enclosed in glass tubes, which are filled with the gases to be examined. In the first case, the tube R, filled with highly-rarefied gas, is placed within the spring clamp B, lined with cork, and movable upon the stand A (Fig. 68), which at the same time revolves upon its horizontal axis, and therefore serves to place the tubes vertically or horizontally, as may be required; when the electric discharge passes through the tube, the enclosed gas becomes luminous, and shines in the narrow part of the tube with an intense light; it is only necessary then to bring the slit of the spectroscope as near as possible to the tube in a position parallel to its length, to recognize at once a distinct spectrum of the gas. In the other plan, where the spark passes between two points of metal in the gas to be investigated, the gas or metal spectrum is more or less brilliant according to the distance of the points one from the other; the spectrum of the gas should therefore be observed in the middle between the metal points, where it is most distinctly marked and most easily distinguished from the discontinuous spectrum of the metal.*

31. Influence of Temperature and Density on the Spectra of Gases.

Bunsen and Kirchhoff have proved that the degree of heat of the flame in which a substance is volatilized and made luminous has no influence on the position of the colored lines of the spectrum, but that it affects considerably their number and brightness. As the brightness increases with the temperature of the flame, it often happens that bright lines will appear in the spectrum of the same substance at a high degree of heat which were scarcely to be seen, or indeed were invisible, at a lower temperature. The spectrum of thallium, a metal recently discovered by spectrum analysis, consists of a single bright-green line when volatilized in a Bunsen burner; but, if the electric spark be allowed to pass between two thallium wires, many other lines

* [A convenient method of observing the spectra of gases at the atmospheric pressure is to cause the induction spark to pass between wires sealed in a glass tube which is drawn into an open capillary point at one end, and at the other is connected with the vessel in which the gas is slowly produced. The glass tube should be cut away in front of the wires, the edges ground flat, and a small plate of glass held air-tight over the opening by elastic bands, an arrangement which permits of any deposit on the inside of the tube being easily removed. By this method fresh portions of gas are constantly exposed to the spark, which is of importance when some compound gases are under examination, and some sources of impurity, which are possible when the gas is collected, are avoided.]

become visible at the far higher temperature of the spark, among them a set of violet-colored bands at some distance from the bright-green line. Lithium in a moderate temperature gives only the one magnificent red line already alluded to; at a higher temperature a faint-orange line makes its appearance, and at the extreme heat of the voltaic arc Tyndall was the first to notice, during a lecture at the Royal Institution, the further addition of a bright-blue band. The principal red line (Ka) of potassium can be made to appear and disappear according as the temperature is increased or diminished. By the use of an ordinary Bunsen burner producing a moderately high temperature, this line is always apparent in the spectrum of potassium; but if the temperature be raised by the use of bellows it immediately disappears.* If a few grains of common salt be dropped into the flame of a Bunsen burner, there is emitted an intense light of one color, producing a spectrum of one single yellow line. If the temperature of the flame be raised by a further supply of oxygen, the brilliancy of this line is immediately augmented, and the number of colored lines so much increased as to approach somewhat to a continuous spectrum.† If Debrai's heating apparatus be made use of, and the sodium-vapor raised to the temperature of 2500° C. (4532° Fahr.), the bright lines become so

* [The red line is present with the intense heat of the induction spark, and is double. In addition, Huggins observed about sixteen lines, which are marked in his maps, when the induction spark was taken between electrodes of metallic potassium. When metallic lithium was employed, only one line of moderate intensity was seen in addition to the three strong lines which distinguish this substance.]

† [In 1863 Huggins observed that when an induction spark is passed between electrodes of sodium, in addition to the well-known double line, three other pairs of lines and a nebulous band make their appearance in the spectrum. The two more prominent of these are not far from air-lines, and with an instrument of insufficient dispersive power might easily be confounded with them. He showed that these lines really belong to sodium, and not to accidental impurities.

There is also at least one bright line between the well-known lines coincident with D. He describes his comparison of this spectrum of sodium with the solar spectrum thus:

"So numerous are the fine lines of the solar spectrum, and so difficult is it to be certain of absolute coincidence, that I hesitate to say more than that the pair of lines 818 and 821 (of the scale of the maps in Phil. Trans., 1864) appeared to agree in position with Kirchhoff's lines 864.1 and 867.1; and of the pair 1169 and 1174, one appears to coincide with a line sharply seen in the solar spectrum, but not marked in Kirchhoff's map, which would be about 1150.2 of his scale, and the other with Kirchhoff's line 1154.2. The other pair and the nebulous band are too faint to admit of satisfactory comparison with solar lines."]

9

numerous that the different colors run one into the other, and produce a continuous spectrum. The former yellow sodium flame has become white, and contains rays of every degree of refrangibility.

Plücker and Hittorf obtained similar results in their researches on the spectra of luminous gases and vapors, whereby they proved the existence of two different spectra (of the first and the second order) in hydrogen, nitrogen, oxygen, phosphorus, sulphur, selenium, etc. The spectrum of the first order is a continuous one, with shaded bands; that of the second order consists of narrow bright lines on a dark background: the former appears with an electric discharge of moderate tension, while the latter belongs to a high temperature, such as can be produced in Geissler's tubes by the electric spark at a high tension.

Still, however, in some cases where the same kind of electric discharge is employed, different spectra are obtained according to the degree of density given to the gas enclosed in the tubes. Wüllner has followed out these investigations with hydrogen, oxygen, and nitrogen, and obtained, according to their degree of density, from two to four spectra for each of these gases.

The following remarkable phenomena are exhibited by hydrogen with the use of one of Ruhmkorff's large induction machines, set in action by a battery of six of Grove's elements, and with the occasional introduction of a Leyden jar (Fig. 65): When the pressure to which the gas is subjected is much less than one-twentieth of an inch of mercury, the spectrum is discontinuous, consisting of six groups of extremely bright lines in the green. When the density of the gas increases, there appears *temporarily*, by the use of a simple induction current not too strong, a *spectrum of bands*, I. order (Fig. 69, No. 1), which, however, on the pressure of the gas amounting to one-twentieth of an inch, soon changes into the *spectrum of lines* designated by Plücker as II. order (Fig. 69, No. 2), and consisting of the three lines H α (vivid red), H β (bright green-blue), and H γ (blue-violet, and fainter than the others). (Compare Frontispiece No. 7.)* When the pressure on the gas exceeds that of one-tenth of an inch, a bright light appears in the red, and in two places in the green, and with an increase of pressure the spectrum assumes more and

* A fourth line, H δ (violet), was discovered by Ångström in this spectrum, which corresponds with the dark line in the solar spectrum marked *h*.

more the character of a spectrum of bands (I. order) extending from orange to blue, but still crossed by a series of bright lines between H α and H β. Up to a pressure of eight inches this spectrum retains its full brilliancy, but, as the pressure increases to sixteen inches, it gradually loses in intensity, without its gen-

FIG. 69.

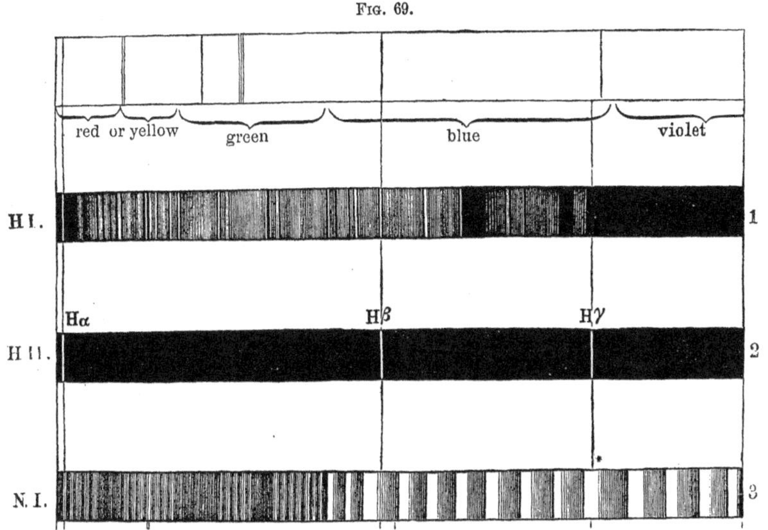

Spectra of the Various Orders.

eral character being essentially altered, excepting that the individual lines, as was observed by Plücker, begin to widen.

If the pressure be still further increased, the spectrum becomes brighter again, the yellow and the orange gradually reappear, the line H α remains still very bright, but is somewhat indistinct at the edges. From this line, however, a completely continuous spectrum without bands extends from the orange to the violet, and is brightest where the line H β was situated. With a further increase of density the brightness of the spectrum is throughout much increased; under a pressure of twenty-nine inches, there is still a faint maximum of light perceptible at the spot H α, which, at a pressure of thirty-nine inches, almost ceases to be visible.

The spectrum is then completely continuous between H α *and* H β, like that of an incandescent solid body, only the brightness is somewhat differently distributed. The temperature of the tube is now raised so high by the heat of the gas that the sodium line appears as a bright-orange line, which is occasioned by the vapor of sodium given out by the glass. With a pressure of forty-eight inches, the whole of the continuous spectrum is really dazzling; and, even under a pressure of fifty-two inches, the electric discharge from the jar may still be passed through the tube, though it now takes place only by flashes.

The changes, therefore, through which the spectrum of hydrogen gas successively passes when the density of the gas is gradually increased from the minimum up to the maximum pressure at which the induction current ceases to pass, are as follows: 1. The spectrum of six lines in the green; 2. The temporary spectrum of bands (I. order); 3. The spectrum of three lines (II. order); 4. The more permanent and complete spectrum of bands (I. order); 5. The pure *continuous* spectrum.

That the shaded spectrum of bands (Fig. 69, No. 1) differs essentially from the unshaded continuous spectrum, is shown by Wüllner's observations with the Leyden jar. When the condenser was introduced the shaded spectrum was not visible, but, by an increase of pressure, the spectrum of the three lines, H α, H β, H γ, passed at once by a widening of the lines into the unshaded continuous spectrum; it is therefore incorrect to describe, as is often done, a spectrum of bands as a continuous spectrum of I. order, and also to speak of two distinct continuous spectra.

Oxygen exhibits nearly the same phenomena. Under slight pressure there first appears a spectrum of bands; as the pressure increases, this spectrum gives place to what Plücker has designated a spectrum of lines, which loses in brilliancy as the density of the gas increases, till, at a pressure of eight inches, it is scarcely visible. The brightness then augments, and at the same time there appears as a background an unshaded, pure continuous spectrum, which becomes so brilliant in the red and yellow as to incorporate with itself the lines of the other spectrum, which are no longer distinguished by their greater brightness.

In nitrogen, the change from the spectrum of bands (I. order) to the pure continuous spectrum is very distinctly marked, since at a certain density of the gas the spectrum of bands I. order (Fig. 69, No. 3) disappears, and is replaced by the spectrum of lines II. order upon a dark background; it is not till afterward that the background becomes quite continuous and luminous.

If it be conclusively established by these investigations of Wüllner that the various spectra of a gas are dependent upon its density, and that the continuous spectrum is formed at the greatest density and with the strongest induction current that can be made to pass, yet the answer to the question as to the dependence of these spectra upon the temperature of the gas is still left to conjecture, since the connection between the kind of electric current and the temperature of the spark or of the glowing gas has not yet been ascertained. Every thing, however, seems to point to the conclusion that the spectrum of bands (I. order) is characteristic of the lowest temperature—a conclusion which seems to be borne out first of all by the early observation of Plücker and Hittorf, who always obtained a spectrum of bands with a simple induction current, but a spectrum of lines when a condenser was introduced; and, secondly, by the observations made by Wüllner on a great variety of gases. The spectrum of lines (II. order) is the result of a higher degree of heat, the continuous spectrum that of the highest temperature. The spectrum of six lines occurs at the minimum pressure, under a similar condition of the electric discharge (by flashes or impulses) that took place with the maximum pressure; the temperature of the gas producing this spectrum is therefore in all cases higher than that by which a spectrum of bands is produced.

In conformity with this view, that the continuous spectrum appears only with the highest temperatures, such as are requisite to render luminous gas of great density, is the fact discovered by Frankland, that, as the yellow sodium-flame becomes white when burning in a stream of oxygen, and then emits rays of every refrangibility, so also does the flame of hydrogen, usually so little luminous, become a white luminous flame in compressed oxygen gas by an *increase* of temperature, when it emits a continuous spectrum.

The doubt still left by these investigations, as to whether the difference in the spectra of hydrogen is to be ascribed mainly to the influence of pressure, or to the temperature conditional on that pressure, must first be settled before it can be determined from the appearance of one or other spectrum what the amount of pressure is to which the gas is subjected, and this is rendered the more necessary by the investigations lately undertaken by Secchi concerning the various spectra of hydrogen, nitrogen, bromium, and chlorine.

Secchi sent the electric spark from an ordinary friction machine, through a tube filled with rarefied nitrogen, the tube being so constructed as to consist of three lengths of tubes of various calibres, the first portion a capillary tube, the second part one-eighth of an inch in diameter, and the third about three-tenths of an inch. When the conductor was placed in connection with one of the platinum wires from the tube, while the other wire communicated with the friction-cushion, there was seen in the capillary tube only the spectrum of I. order, consisting of narrow connected stripes or bands, giving the appearance of grooves (Fig. 69, No. 3). When, on the contrary, one of the platinum wires was connected with a metal knob, and a spark allowed to pass, while the other wire conducted to the earth, the spectrum changed according to the length of the spark. When the spark reached the length of three-quarters of an inch, the capillary tube shone with a green light, and gave a spectrum of lines, or that of II. order, while the wider portions of the tube gave a spectrum of bands of I. order. With a sufficient length of spark, therefore, three varieties of spectra may be seen at the same time; in the narrowest part of the tube the spectrum of II. order with bright lines appears, and in the two wider parts of the tube are to be seen spectra of bands or stripes. One of these latter spectra is that described by Plücker as consisting of fine groove-like bands, and the other is composed of wider bands, which are so spread out that three of them are equal to eight of the former. The same phenomena occur if instead of an electrical machine a powerful induction coil be used, and a condenser introduced into the current.

Similar results were obtained from bromine, chlorine, and hydrogen, which prove *that, in different sections of the same tube filled with gas of the same density, spectra of the various orders may be obtained at the same time.*

Now, the influence of the diameter of the tube upon the temperature of the enclosed gas is the same, no doubt, as that which occurs in the metal wires, in which it has been established that the heat increases in an inverse ratio to the square of the diameter. It therefore follows that the temperature of the gas is greatest in the capillary part of the tube, and that *under an equal press-*

ure of the gas the spectrum of bands (I. order) corresponds to a lower temperature than the spectrum of lines (II. order).

The temperatures at which these spectra of the various orders are produced are not the same for all gases. In a tube containing both nitrogen and aqueous vapor, the *lines* of hydrogen (spectrum II. order) made their appearance at the same time as the spectrum of bands I. order of nitrogen, whence it follows that the lines of hydrogen are visible in a temperature in which the lines of nitrogen do not appear.

32. Influence of the Temperature of Gases on the Width of the Lines of the Spectrum.

The width of the lines of the spectrum depends in general upon the width of the slit of the spectroscope; by widening the slit these lines also widen, without their brilliancy being affected. This width, as a rule, is not less than that of the slit, but lines wider than the slit are often observed. An exception to this rule is found in some lines in the spectra of gases when they have been produced at different temperatures. The spectrum of hydrogen occupies so important a place in the investigations of the physical constitution of the sun and other heavenly bodies, that it will be desirable here to mention the facts which relate to the widening and contracting of the three characteristic lines.

Plücker and Hittorf were the first to observe that in a narrow tube filled with hydrogen the three characteristic lines H α, H β, H γ (Frontispiece No. 7), appeared at a certain degree of rarefaction. By raising the temperature of the tube by the introduction of a Leyden jar, or other means of intensifying the electric discharge, an increase of the width of the line H γ, toward both ends of the spectrum, is first apparent, then a widening of the line H β, while H α remains almost unchanged till H γ has passed into an undefined, broad violet band, and H β has, with diminished intensity, become extended in both directions. With a pressure $2\frac{1}{3}$ inches, the spectrum of lines has already passed into a continuous spectrum; and under a pressure of $14\frac{1}{4}$ inches the intensity of the spectrum has so much increased that the red line H α, now widened into a band, is scarcely distinguishable from the rest of the spectrum.

When the gas is highly rarefied, the line H α is the first to disappear, while H β is still distinctly visible.

These observations upon pressure have been confirmed by Wüllner as follows: under a pressure of $\frac{9}{10}$ of an inch the spectrum of hydrogen consists of the three lines; with a pressure of $1\frac{7}{10}$ inch, the line H γ is considerably increased in width, H β less so, while H α remains unchanged. When the pressure is increased to 18 inches, the lines H γ and H β have so far expanded that continuous bands of color appear in their places, and H α is visible only as a wide, diffused line, until at the great pressure of 22 inches the spectrum is perfectly continuous, and H α is no longer to be recognized as a line, but is changed into a broad red space.

It was found by Secchi by employing tubes of varying calibre (§ 31) that, with a diminution of the tension and temperature of the electric spark, the width of the hydrogen lines decreased, till with the same width of slit they disappeared, or else became very fine and scarcely to be seen, in the parts of the tubes of greatest diameter, while they continued visible in the capillary portions. It therefore follows that with the same pressure on the gas a diminution of temperature is accompanied by a narrowing of the hydrogen lines, and it seems that *with a given density there is a limit of temperature at which the three bright lines of this gas disappear.* Were it possible to estimate this temperature, the amount of pressure to which the gas was subjected could be inferred. This question is involved in considerable difficulty, but is at the same time of such great importance in the investigations of the solar atmosphere that it will no doubt soon engage the attention of those physicists who have the requisite apparatus at their command.

33. Influence of Temperature on the Delicacy of Spectrum Reactions.

Bunsen and Kirchhoff discovered, in their first labors on this subject, that the spectra of alkalies and alkaline earths increased in intensity as the temperature to which they were subjected increased, but it remained uncertain whether the increased brightness resulted merely from the increased volatilization of these metals or from the consequent increased delicacy of the spectrum reactions.

Cappel has therefore lately renewed these investigations; solutions of the metallic salts were volatilized between the poles of a small induction machine giving a spark $\frac{5}{8}$ of an inch long, and by the use of Mitscherlich's glass tubes, provided with platinum wicks (Fig. 62), the spectrum made permanent for some time. A series of solutions, each half the strength of the preceding one, were prepared from a number of metallic chlorides; the spectrum of the metal which was in connection with the positive pole was continuously observed, while increasingly concentrated solutions were brought in succession into the electric current till the lines of the substance, the position of which had previously been accurately determined for that particular spectroscope, were clearly visible.

The result of these observations is given in the following table.

The second column contains the minima of metallic substance needed to produce the principal characteristic line, therefore the most sensitive line of the metal. It shows that by the use of this minimum of metallic substance the spectrum consists of only one single line, with the exception of copper, the spectrum of which, even with the smallest perceptible mixture, is composed of three lines. The third column is compiled from earlier observations, so modified that the weight of the mixtures has reference to the amount of metal contained in the compounds.

From this table it appears that, with the exception of the alkalies, the susceptibility of the spectrum reactions in the metals, inclusive of lithium, is from 40 to 3,000 times greater in the heat of the electric spark than in the temperature of the non-luminous gas-flame. Many new lines make their appearance in the spectrum of the induction spark which are not visible at a lower temperature.*

As a practical result of these investigations by Cappel, it seems to be established that the spectrum analysis of alkalies is best conducted by the temperature of the oxyhydrogen flame, and that of other metals by the electric spark. It seems probable that by the use of still higher tension, such as may be obtained by the introduction of condensers (Fig. 65), the sensibility of the spectrum reactions in a great number of metals may, in consequence of the higher temperature, be raised above the foregoing limits.

* [See note, p. 104.]

No.	Name of the Metal investigated.	Susceptibility in Milligrammes.	
		By the use of the Induction Spark.	By the use of the Bunsen Burner.
1	Cæsium	$\frac{1}{4,000}$	$\frac{1}{25,000}$
2	Rubidium	$\frac{1}{1,000}$	$\frac{1}{7,000}$
3	Potassium	$\frac{1}{400}$	$\frac{1}{3,000}$
4	Sodium	..	$\frac{1}{14,000,000}$
5	Lithium	$\frac{1}{40,000,000}$	$\frac{1}{600,000}$
6	Barium	$\frac{1}{900,000}$	$\frac{1}{2,000}$
7	Strontium	$\frac{1}{100,000,000}$	$\frac{1}{30,000}$
8	Calcium	$\frac{1}{10,000,000}$	$\frac{1}{50,000}$
9	Magnesium	$\frac{1}{500,000}$	..
10	Chromium	$\frac{1}{4,000,000}$	..
11	Manganese	$\frac{1}{200,000}$	$\frac{1}{83}$
12	Zinc	$\frac{1}{600,000}$	..
13	Indium	$\frac{1}{90,000}$	$\frac{1}{2,000}$
14	Cobalt	$\frac{1}{15,000}$	..
15	Nickel	$\frac{1}{600}$	..
16	Iron	$\frac{1}{26,000}$	..
17	Thallium	$\frac{1}{80,000,000}$	$\frac{1}{50,000}$
18	Cadmium	$\frac{1}{18,000}$	..
19	Lead	$\frac{1}{20,000}$	..
20	Bismuth	$\frac{1}{70,000}$	..
21	Copper	$\frac{1}{20,000}$	$\frac{1}{285}$
22	Silver	$\frac{1}{12,000}$	..
23	Mercury	$\frac{1}{10,000}$	..
24	Gold	$\frac{1}{4,000}$	..
25	Tin	$\frac{1}{17,000}$	..

The importance of the choice of a suitable temperature in investigations with spectrum analysis is shown by the behavior of strontium. If, for example, $\frac{1}{100}$ of a milligramme of this metal be taken, a quantity that can be detected by the ordinary mode of analysis, $\frac{1}{300}$ part of this small quantity will be shown by its spectrum analysis in the Bunsen burner; but if the electric spark be employed, $\frac{1}{5000}$ part of this last small particle may be distinguished with the greatest certainty. Cappel, therefore, rightly maintains that in searching for new metals the employment of high temperatures is very important, and that the use of very powerful induction machines, with the addition of condensers, would very probably lead to the discovery of new elements.

34. The Colors of Natural Objects.

Besides the colors of the spectrum, which are the simple elements composing white light, there is another class of colors apparent in every substance, which are therefore known as the colors of natural objects. When we see that a picture is formed by covering the canvas with various pigments, and that leaves and flowers are bright with the most beautiful tints, while white cloth becomes red, green, or blue, according to the color of the liquid into which it is dipped, we are easily led to believe that every substance carries in itself its own color, which is peculiar to it alone, and is inherent in the substance. At most, we might admit that light was requisite to render the color visible.

And yet this is not so. Were colors really something inherent in the object, every colored substance would manifestly appear always of the same color by whatever light it was illuminated. But this, as every one knows, is not the case. The beautiful violet dress which in daylight appears of the purest color seems dull and gloomy by gas-light; materials which in daylight are a bright blue are tinged with green in candle or lamp light. And what if a landscape or a colored object be viewed through a tinted glass? All colors then seem changed, without the objects in themselves being altered; if the color of the glass be intense, the various colors of the objects immediately disappear, and every thing seems shaded in the color of the glass. The same thing happens if some common salt be rubbed into the wick of a spirit-lamp, and surrounding objects viewed by the yellow light of such a flame;

the colors disappear, or lose much of their brilliancy, and every thing seems either in mere light and shade, or else of a dull gray.

These facts clearly prove that colors are not inherent in objects, that they have no independent existence, but that they are called forth by some extraneous cause.

On the other hand, these considerations show that there must be something in the objects themselves to help in the formation of color; for they in no way assume the color of the light illuminating them, but appear, as a rule, of quite a different hue.

The *natural* color of an object is that in which it appears when illuminated by the pure white light of the sun, or by daylight; it is called red or blue when it so appears by daylight. Now, if an object be illuminated by white light, and yet appear of another color, the cause of the change must be looked for in the influence which the surface of the body exercises on the ether-waves constituting white light. The effects of this influence are very different according to the nature of the coloring matter with which the object is provided; but they may mostly be reduced to one of two cases: either that a portion of the ether-motion is entirely stopped, or so considerably diminished in its passage over the ponderable atoms of the substance, as that heat instead of light is evolved; or else that the ether-waves are irregularly reflected from the surface of the object, as sometimes occurs with the waves of sound. In the first case the rays of light are said to be *absorbed;* in the latter, *scattered.*

When the surface of a body has the property of absorbing all the colors of the solar spectrum with the exception of one—red, for example—that body appears red to us by daylight because this color alone is reflected to the eye. When, on the contrary, it has the power of absorbing some of the rays—the red and orange, for instance—and of reflecting the others, namely, the yellow, green, and blue, the color of the object will then be that produced by the mixture of the unabsorbed—the reflected—colors. Now, as white light contains the whole range of colors visible in the spectrum, it can easily be understood why so many different-colored objects should be seen in nature with such an infinite variety of tints.*

* [A certain proportion of the light falling upon colored bodies is usually sent back unchanged by superficial reflection, without undergoing the elective absorption to which the color of the substance is due.]

When all the colors of white light are reflected from an object in the same proportions as they occur in the solar spectrum, the object appears white by daylight, and brilliant in proportion to the *quantity* of light it reflects. In proportion, however, as it reflects *fewer* rays of all kinds, the white loses in intensity; the object appears first gray, then dark, and at last black, when all the rays falling upon it are absorbed and none reflected.

Those objects are therefore black the surfaces of which are so constituted as to absorb all the colored rays of white light; those are white which reflect all the rays which fall upon the surface; and those are colored which reflect some of the rays and absorb others.

A white object may therefore appear of all colors: if red light falls upon it, it reflects it to the eye, and appears red; in blue light it appears blue; in green light, green, etc.; whereas a black object always appears black, whatever may be the color of the light by which it is illuminated.

We may here further remark that a colored substance assumes a different tint when illuminated by colored light, and then appears of another than its natural, that is to say, daylight color. Vermilion, for example, when placed in red light, becomes of a more fiery red; in orange or yellow light, it appears orange or yellow, but deeper in tone; green rays impart to it something of their own tint, but, as the red substance can reflect only a few of the green rays, it appears pale and dull by their light; it seems still duller and darker in blue light, and with indigo and violet it is almost black.

These phenomena are explained by the supposition that the surfaces of colored bodies possess the property of reflecting the rays of one particular color in far greater proportion than those of the other colors; they do not therefore appear black when illuminated by a light differing from their own natural color. Take, for example, a piece of paper half of which is colored a deep blue and half red: the colored rays other than the blue and red are not all absorbed: it is true that the blue piece reflects the blue rays preëminently and in greatest number, as the red part does the red rays, but the red has also the capability of reflecting other rays to a small amount. If the pure yellow light of a spirit-flame impregnated with salt be allowed to fall on the paper in a completely dark room, the paper must appear black if the coloring matter reflect only the red and blue rays, because the yellow rays of the burning sodium will be absorbed, and no other light falls upon the paper: but this is not the case. The paper only appears black on the blue part; the red half is still visibly colored, though of a decidedly yellow shade. We therefore conclude that the blue of the paper does not reflect the yellow rays, but that the red has that power in a small degree. Almost all colored objects act like the red paper; they reflect preëminently one particular color, namely, that one of which they appear by daylight; but they are able also to reflect in small quantities all other or at least some other colors, and so they vary in tint according to the kind of light in which they are seen.

The colors of objects are very rarely pure and simple like those of the spectrum; most of them are composed of several colors, and can be decomposed into their original elements by a prism. As without prismatic decomposition we are unable merely from the color of an object to say positively which colors are absorbed and which reflected, so it is equally impossible for us to decide from the color of a flame what the composition of its light may be without investigation. The light of the sun, the lime-light, the magnesium-light, the light of coal-gas, petroleum, and oil, all appear to us more or less white, and yet the spectra of the various lights differ considerably. It is true they all contain the whole range of the colors of the spectrum, from red to violet; but each color is present in very different proportions. The light from gas, oil, and candles, has less blue than that of the sun and the lime-light, and very much less violet. A blue material will therefore reflect less blue by lamp, gas, or candle light, than by daylight; the color will not only be flat and dull, but will have a touch of green in it on account of the preponderance of yellow light. Blue and violet especially receive a green tinge by candle-light, in which these colors appear much duller than in daylight; and indeed sometimes, according to the nature of the coloring matter employed, this tint is so decided that in artificial light many kinds of green cannot be distinguished from blue.

35. Absorption of Light by Solid Bodies.

By the term *absorption* we have already designated that action by which light, in its passage through certain media, or by its reflection from the surfaces of bodies, is weakened, partially retained, or entirely stopped. We found that those substances called black absorbed rays of every color and reflected no light from their surfaces, and that most substances absorbed with great avidity rays of certain colors, while they were insensitive to others. The cause of this absorption is probably due to the vibrations of the ether being communicated to the ponderable molecular particles of the substance.

Similar phenomena are noticed when light is transmitted through colored glass. When all the objects in a landscape appear red through a red glass, it is because the glass allows only the red rays to pass through, and absorbs every other colored ray: such a glass is transparent only to red light, and is opaque to every other color. But it is rarely the case that colored glass is transparent for one color only; most kinds of glass absorb rays of certain colors, and allow the others to pass through in very different proportions. The naked eye is unable to decide which of the colored rays are transmitted through a colored glass; this can only be accurately determined by analyzing the transmitted light by a spectroscope or simple prism.

If we examine by a spectroscope the transmitted light of the colored glass that we before made use of (§ 17) for obtaining red, green, and blue light, it will at once be seen that the ruby-red glass transmits some orange and even some yellow rays, as well as the red, but that it entirely absorbs the green, blue, and violet rays; the cobalt-blue glass transmits some violet and green rays, besides the blue, but absorbs all the red rays. If both glasses be laid one over the other, and a gas-flame looked at through them, it seems as if scarcely a single ray was transmitted; the red glass absorbing the green, blue, and violet rays, and the blue glass absorbing the red rays, there pass through only traces of such light as has not been entirely absorbed, and this causes the gas-flame to appear of a dull yellow. A combination of several glasses, or indeed any single glass which absorbs all the colored rays composing white light, is opaque, that is to say, black; glass of perfect transparency, absorbing absolutely none of the transmitted light, does not exist.

36. Absorption of Light by Liquids.

The absorptive power of colored liquids is in general much more decided and marked than that of colored glass. No coloring matter has yet been found which will absorb or transmit only one kind of colored rays; the colors of liquids, therefore, as seen by white light, are mixed colors, and their absorption varies exceedingly, according to the refrangibility of the light which falls upon them, and the degree of concentration possessed by the solution. Sorby, Haerlin, Hoppe, and Valentin, besides Gladstone and Huggins, have delineated a great number of well-known coloring matters and other liquids, in the course of their investigations, and have ascertained to what extent their various degrees of concentration affect the individual parts of the continuous spectrum.

If these absorption phenomena are to be exhibited before a large audience by the use of the electric or Drummond's light, it is desirable to take those colored liquids which show their absorption in a very characteristic manner, as, for instance, a solution in ether of chlorophyll—the green-coloring matter of leaves—a solution in water of the coloring matter of human blood, or a thin layer of potassium permanganate solution.

Fig. 70.

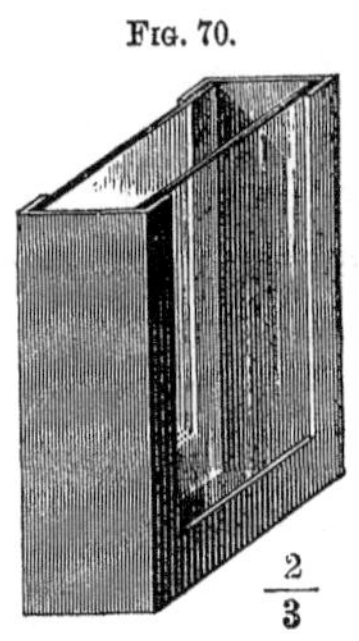

Glass Vessel for Absorbent Liquids.

If a continuous spectrum of white light about six feet long be projected in the usual way, and a glass vessel (Fig. 70) composed of flat plates containing the chlorophyll solution introduced into the path of the rays, the spectrum on the screen will be seen immediately to change. Dark bands (Fig. 71, No. 2; Frontispiece No. 10) appear in the red, as well as in the yellow, green, and violet portions, and the blue shades give place to a faint-red hue; the green chlorophyll solution does not therefore absorb the whole of the red and yellow rays, but only those which possess a peculiar refrangibility or wave-length; it exerts the same influence on most of the blue and violet rays, while it transmits unchanged all the other colors of white light.

FIG. 71.

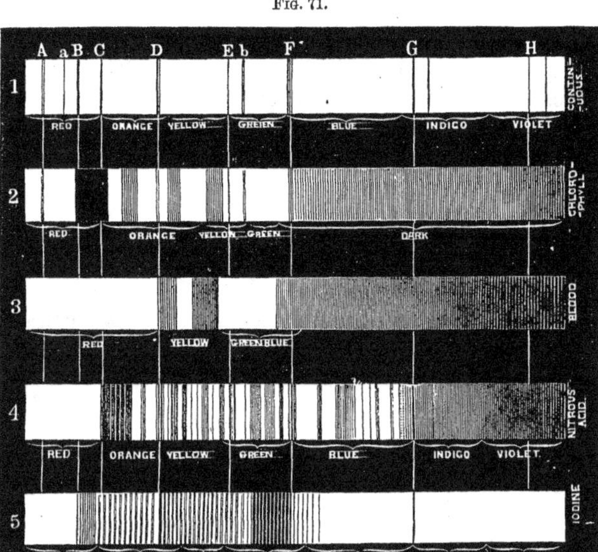

Spectra of Absorbent Substances.

If a greatly-diluted solution of fresh arterial blood be substituted for the leaf-green, the red in the spectrum will be intensified, while the blue and the violet will be nearly extinguished. Fig. 71, No. 3, shows in the yellow and commencement of the green two dark-blood bands, with a faint-green stripe interposed.

These phenomena appear in a much more striking manner if they are observed through a spectroscope instead of being projected on a screen; the colored liquid is then placed immediately in front of the slit, and the spectra viewed directly by the eye. It is needful for this purpose to have small glass troughs with parallel sides, similar to the one drawn in Fig. 70, but Stokes recommends carefully-selected test-glasses,* any of which may be

* Browning manufactures such glass tubes and vessels of every required size and shape, especially in the form of a wedge, so as to test easily the same liquid at different successive thicknesses. He also furnishes, enclosed in glass tubes, a whole series of liquids, the absorptive power of which is either remarkably great or else manifested in a peculiar way.

filled with the requisite liquid, and placed, as shown in Fig. 72, close in front of the slit by means of a supporting ring fastened to the end of the spectroscope. If the instrument with the slit not too contracted be directed toward a luminous cloud, or when this is not available toward a bright light placed immediately in front, there will appear a brilliant spectrum crossed by dark bands produced by the absorption of the liquid.

In many cases small changes produced in these coloring matters by dilution, by chemical action, or by the increase or diminution of the thickness of the stratum of liquid, are accompanied by changes in the absorption bands, so that a conclusion may be formed from the position, width, and intensity of these dark bands as to the nature of the coloring matter and the circumstances by which it has suffered alteration. The two dark-blood bands are seen in the yellow-green of a spectrum formed by either daylight or lamp-light from water infused with but a trace of blood, and which exhibits to the naked eye scarcely a perceptible tinge of yellow. On this account spectrum analysis has been called into the service of physiology and pathology, and is fitted to render valuable aid in medico-legal investigations, since it is not improbable that the spectroscope, when in connection with the microscope, will be able to detect the presence of blood or poison in many cases where the microscope alone can furnish no results, or only those of an untrustworthy character.

Fig. 72.

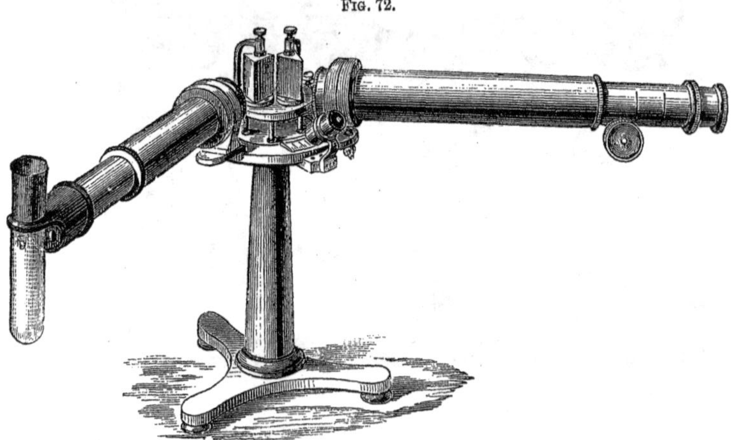

Observations of Absorption.

37. THE SORBY-BROWNING MICROSPECTROSCOPE.

The object of this instrument is to facilitate the accurate observation of the absorptive phenomena of the smallest solid and liquid bodies, such as are prepared for microscopic examination —a corpuscule of blood, for instance.* Sorby, with the assistance of Browning, has so arranged the spectroscopic part of the instrument that it can be applied to any microscope by fixing it in the place of the ordinary eye-piece so that the spectroscopic investigation of an object can be pursued without any change in the manner of using the instrument. In a complete instrument a contrivance is attached to the side by means of which the substances to be investigated may be compared with the spectra of

FIG. 73.

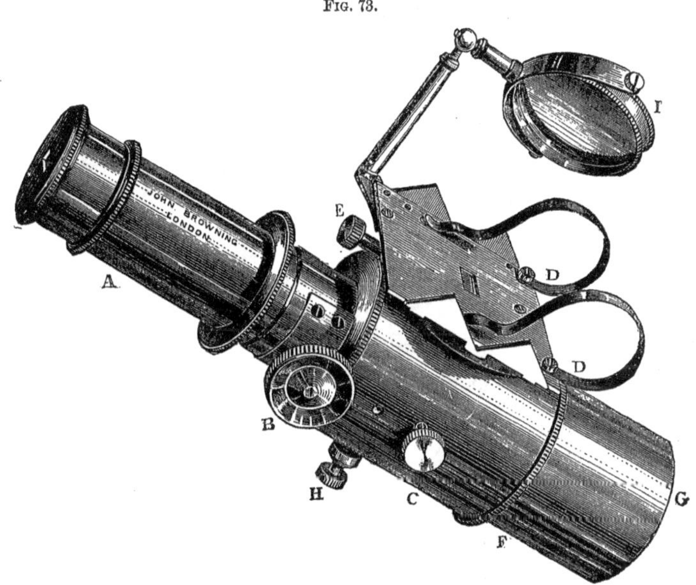

The Sorby-Browning Microspectroscope.

* [In his earlier researches with the microscope, Sorby illuminated the object to be examined by placing it in a spectrum formed on the stage of the instrument by a prism and lens placed beneath. Huggins first pointed out the method of observing the spectra of the light from microscopic objects by means of a slit and a prism placed *above* the object-glass of the microscope. (*See* "On the Prismatic Examination of Microscopic Objects," Trans. Microscopical Society, May 10, 1865.) It is on this principle that the very convenient instrument described in the text is based.]

known substances: this apparatus consists of a small stage, a prism for comparison (§ 38), and a movable scale for measuring accurately the places of the absorption bands.

Fig. 73 shows a perspective view of the whole instrument, as fitted to slide into the upper tube of the microscope in place of the eye-piece; Fig. 74 gives a section showing the internal construction; and Fig. 75 gives a section through the plane of the two screws C and H, exhibiting the slit with its contrivances for adjustment and the prism for comparison.

The tube A encloses a second tube carrying a direct-vision system of five prisms *c*, and an achromatic lens *l* (Fig. 74); by means of a milled head B, with screw-motion, this inner tube can be moved up and down, so that the slit situated in the plane of the screws C and H may be in the focus of the lens *l*; consequently the rays from the slit, after passing through the lens, fall parallel on to the prisms.

Fig. 74.

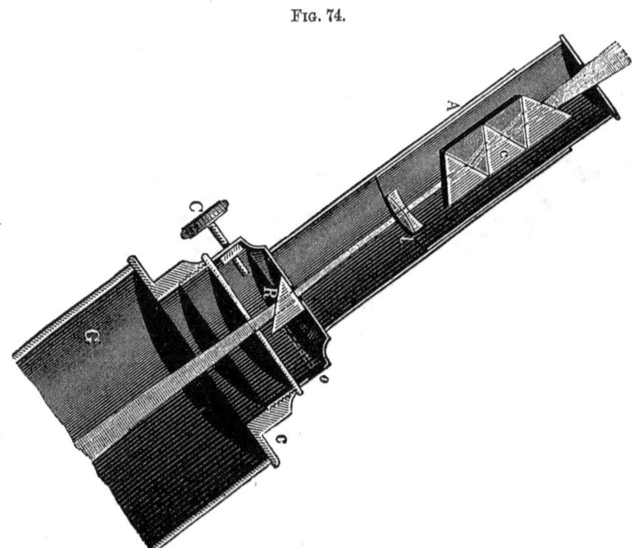

Section of the Microspectroscope.

D D is the stage on which the objects for comparison—liquids between plates of glass or in small tubes—are secured within notched edges, by means of metal springs, which hold the small glasses in such a position that the light falling on them from the side, after its passage through the liquid, reaches a square opening in the middle of the stage, whence, as Fig. 74 shows, it passes through a side opening *o* into the inside of the principal tube, and falls upon the reflecting prism R, which acts as a prism for comparison. When the apparatus for comparison is not required, the square opening in the stage D D is closed by a sliding plate by means of the screw E, so that the side-light may be shut out of the instrument.

Fig. 75 gives a section through the plane of the slit between the screws C and H. The piece *n* is fixed, while *m* is movable, by means of the screw H and an opposing steel spring, which

FIG. 75.

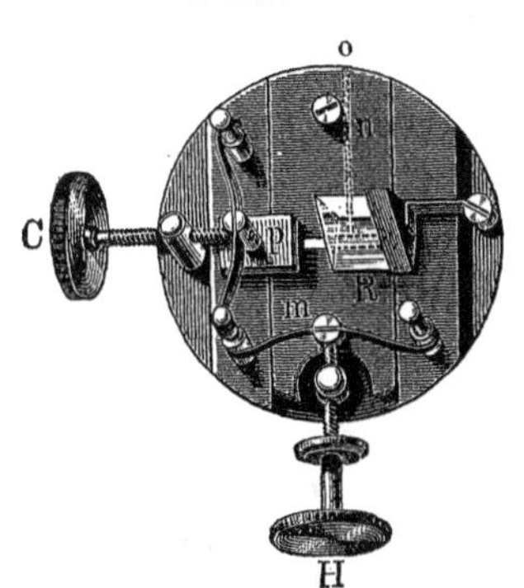

Adjustments for the Slit in the Microspectroscope.

serves to widen or narrow the slit. Close over the slit is a covering plate *p*, which is moved backward and forward by the screw C and a spring acting against it, thus enabling the slit to be lengthened or shortened. The reflecting prism R covers a part of the slit; if this slit be open, and the light from the object for comparison fall from the side at *o* upon the prism R, it will be reflected back, and be thrown upon the system of prisms *c*, together with the light coming through the open part of the slit from below (Fig. 74). In this way two spectra are received in juxtaposition, one produced by the light passing through the tube G, the other by the light which has been transmitted through the known liquid upon the stage D D.

In order to use the microspectroscope, the tube A, with the prisms, must be removed, and the tube G inserted into the eye-piece tube, so that the slit at the eye-end shall be parallel to the inner slit.* The object-glass required is then screwed into the lower part of the microscope, the object the spectrum of which is to be investigated laid upon the stage, and illuminated according as it is transparent or opaque with a mirror from below, or by means of an achromatic condenser from above, and the focus adjusted in the same manner as for an ordinary microscopic investigation, so that the enlarged image may be distinctly seen. For this purpose it is requisite that the slit, by means of the screw H, should be opened wide. The tube A, with the compound prism, is then replaced, its position regulated with regard to the slit by the screw B, and the width of the slit adjusted until a well-defined spectrum is obtained. As each portion of the spectrum possesses a refrangibility peculiar to itself, the prisms must, for the delicate absorption lines, be specially adjusted for each dark line. It need scarcely be remarked that in these investigations the lowest possible powers are employed.

When the substance to be investigated is to be compared with the spectrum of a known substance, the stage D D is employed in the manner described. If it be used in daylight, the tube of the microscope must be directed to a bright part of the sky (Fig. 73); for a better illumination of the liquids on the stage D D, especially by lamp-light, the mirror I is employed, and is so supported as to allow of its being placed in any position with respect to the opening in the stage.

For the accurate determination of the position of the absorption lines, the upper cover of the tube A is removed and replaced by another, which, as represented in Fig. 76, is provided with a lateral tube *a a*. In this tube the lens *e* can be adjusted by means of the screw *b*, while in front is a contrivance by which an opaque glass plate *d*, on which a fine transparent line or cross has been photographed, may be moved backward and forward by the micrometer-screw M (compare Fig. 51), and the amount of motion measured. In front of the opening of the tube *a a* is placed a movable mirror S, which reflects the light it receives, whether daylight or lamp-light, on to the glass plate *d*. By turning the micrometer-screw M, the light transmitted through the glass plate is thrown into the tube A A, in the form of a

* [Mr. Browning now makes the instrument with a circular aperture instead of a slit, so that the eye-cap may be placed in any position.]

bright line, and the lens *e* adjusted to such a position as to direct the image of this line upon the upper surface of the range of prisms *c*, presenting an angle of 45°, whence it is reflected in the direction of the principal tube, and reaches the eye at the same time as the spectrum. A bright line or cross is thus seen upon the spectrum, and it is not only easy, by turning the micrometer-screw M, to place the bright line precisely upon any absorption line, but also to measure accurately the relative distances between any dark lines in the spectrum by means of the divisions of the micrometer.

Fig. 76.

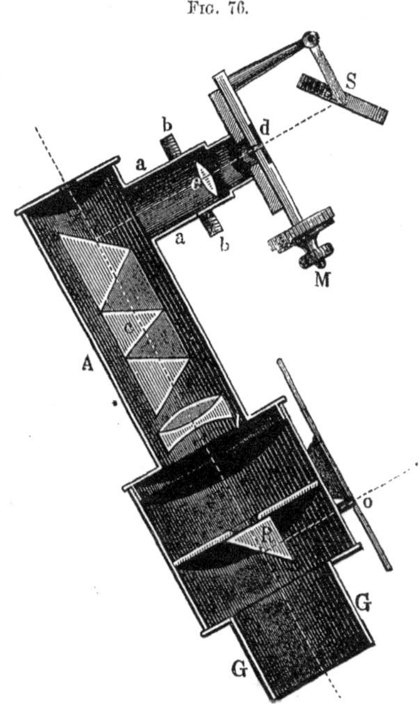

Micrometer for measuring the Absorption Lines.

In order, however, that the results given by various instruments may be compared, these divisions must not be arbitrary.

It has already been mentioned (p. 62), and will be more fully entered into in Part III., that the solar spectrum, and consequently the spectrum of daylight, is not continuous, but is everywhere crossed by numerous dark lines of varying intensity. These dark lines always occupy the same place in the scale of color in the spectrum, that is to say, each line is produced by the absorption of one and the same color, or by light of the same refrangibility, whatever may be the composition or angle of the prism. It is most advantageous to select the darkest lines in the solar spectrum to form a scale for dividing the screw-head M of the microspectroscope.

For this purpose Browning divides the screw-head M into a hundred equal parts, and determines the divisions of the scale for every instrument by a previous trial in which bright daylight is admitted from below through the slit and the tube G (Fig. 73), and these divisions are successively marked off by the indicator on the screw-head whenever the bright line of light (Fig. 76) is coincident with the individual dark lines of the solar spectrum. The dark lines are then drawn in accordance with these numbers upon a spectrum about five inches long, which is divided into an arbitrary number of equal divisions, as represented in the upper half of Fig. 77. By means of such a spectrum, the position of the absorption bands of any liquid may be determined

Fig. 77.

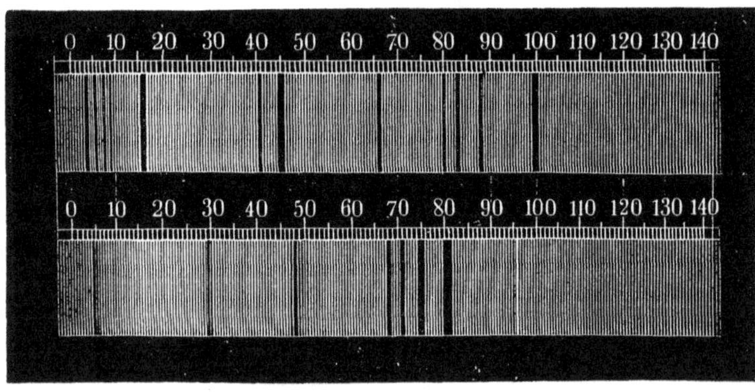

Scale for the Microspectroscope.

without difficulty, care only being taken that artificial light be employed for the formation of the spectrum, since daylight always produces the dark lines of the solar spectrum, and these might easily be confused with the absorption lines. In fact, it is only necessary, when dark bands are observed in the spectrum of a substance, to bring the line of light in the micrometer upon the spectrum (Fig. 76), and place it by means of the screw M in coincidence with the absorption lines to be measured, and then read off the number upon the divided screw-head. The numbers read off for the various lines need only be compared with the divisions of the scale of the normal spectrum, in order to determine at once the position of these lines in the spectrum for all similar investigations. Should a more complete representation of the absorption spectrum be required, it is only necessary, as shown in the lower half of Fig. 77, to draw the lines according to the numbers read off on the micrometer screw-head upon a spectrum furnished with the scale of the normal spectrum. The bright line seen at the number 96 in this lower spectrum ought to indicate that an absorption line was seen at this spot in the instrument. If, instead of the line of light a bright cross be used, the point formed by the intersection of the lines is placed in the middle of the absorption line, or, if it be a band, upon each edge in succession.

Fig. 78.

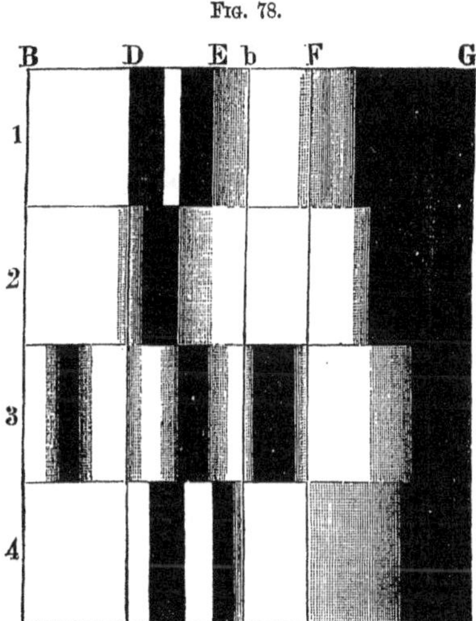

Absorption Bands of Human Blood.

Those who wish to enter more minutely into investigations of this kind will do well to begin with various solutions of blood, with madder, aniline red, fresh solution of permanganate of potash, or with other similar substances of highly absorptive power.

In Fig. 78 are shown the absorption bands of human blood

as given by Stokes; it will be seen how greatly they vary in the same substance according as it is subjected to changes or mixed with other bodies. All four spectra are the absorption spectra of human blood: No. 1 is that of fresh scarlet blood; No. 2, that of deoxidized blood (cruorine). By the action of an acid on blood the cruorine is converted into hæmatin, which gives a spectrum showing an entirely different set of bands; and hæmatin can again be oxidized and reduced, until it exhibits the dark bands shown in Nos. 3 and 4.

While Hoppe-Seyler and Valentin are already actively engaged with the absorption spectra of those substances which play an important part in physiology and pathology, Sorby has devoted himself to the investigation of articles of commerce such as dyes and wine—to ascertain its age, as well as to detect the adulteration in food, such as beer and wine, mustard, cheese, butter, etc. Spectrum analysis has thus opened a wide field of investigation to the physiologist, the physician, the botanist, the zoologist, the chemist, and the technologist, and the labors undertaken in these various departments of science have already yielded valuable results.

38. Absorption of Light by Gases.

While colorless gases only weaken the intensity of the light they transmit, and exert no selective absorptive power upon any particular rays; and while, on the contrary, colored solid and liquid bodies wholly absorb certain rays, and entirely transmit others, thus producing wide absorption bands that extend sometimes over whole groups of colors in the continuous spectrum, colored gases, differing from both, exhibit only narrow dark bands, which, like black lines, traverse not unfrequently every color in the continuous spectrum.

For the exhibition of these absorption phenomena a glass globe (Fig. 79) is employed, smoothly polished inside, and capable of being closed at both ends by pieces of plate glass. The vapors for examination are introduced into the globe by a side opening; but, if it be desirable that they should be formed during the investigation, the substances needed for their development can be placed in the vessel by removing the cover, and vaporized by a careful application of heat. The globe must be placed immediately before the prism, or close in front of the slit of the spectroscope, and in such a position in the path of the rays that they may pass through the inside of the sphere perpendicularly to the glass plates covering it.

Fig. 79.

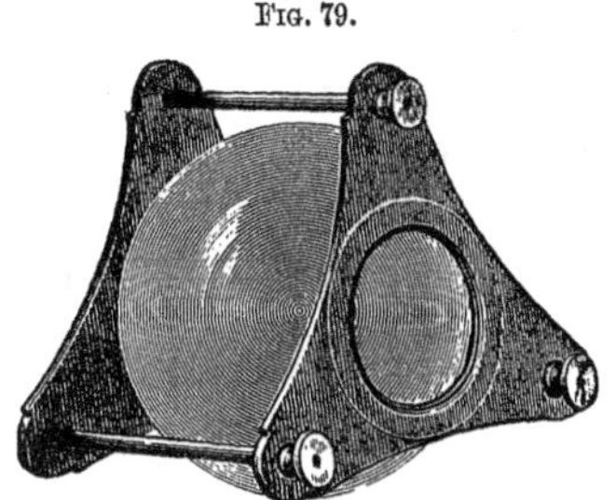

Glass Globe for Absorbent Vapors.

To exhibit the absorptive properties of nitrous-acid gas on a large scale, the electric lamp or Drummond's light must be employed, and the continuous spectrum of white light thrown upon the screen in the manner described in § 19, Fig. 34. If the globe filled with the red vapor of nitrous acid * be placed in front of the prism in the position already described, the spectrum will appear crossed by a row of dark bands, the violet end having entirely disappeared. By increasing the heat of the vapor these bands gradually become stronger, while new dark bands successively appear, until at last, when the temperature has reached a certain limit, all the colored portions of the spectrum are absorbed, and not a ray of the electric light is able any longer to penetrate the vapor. Brewster carried the process so far by a constant increase of temperature as to render the gas entirely opaque even to the power of the sun's rays. The absorption spectrum of this gas is shown in Fig. 71, No. 4 (Frontispiece No. 9).

If some pieces of iodine be placed in the globe and heated, a violet vapor is produced, through which the electric light may be made to pass. The phenomena which are then seen differ greatly from those before exhibited; by slightly widening the slit, a large piece of the spectrum, from the beginning of the yel-

* The vapor is obtained in the simplest and most convenient manner by heating nitrate of lead, a process which may take place either in a separate vessel or with care in the glass globe itself.

low to the blue, appears to be cut out, and, if the slit be contracted to obtain a purer spectrum, this broad dark belt resolves itself into numerous fine dark lines, which are seen to cross the whole of the spectrum from red to the beginning of blue. If the absorption spectrum of the vapor of iodine be examined in a test-tube glass by means of a spectroscope, the whole of the orange and yellow will be seen crossed by a great number of fine black lines, which become so numerous in the green that they can scarcely be separated one from the other, and appear to form a shaded band (Fig. 71, No. 5). With instruments of high magnifying power these dark bands are resolved into very fine lines, increasing in number and intensity toward the middle and darkest portions of the bands.

Other colored gases yield similar absorption spectra, particularly the vapors of bromine, hydrochloric acid, perchloride of manganese; also, according to Morren, of chlorine, etc., while, on the contrary, there are other vapors, such as those of sulphur and selenium, which, although colored, do not occasion any absorption bands in the spectrum.

Aqueous vapor also exercises an absorptive action upon light, and its absorption lines are very noticeable in the spectrum of the sun, and that of diffused daylight. On account of the connection of these lines with the spectrum of the heavenly bodies, the consideration of the details of their appearance must be left till we come to the discussion of the solar spectrum in Part III.

39. Relation between the Emission and the Absorption of Light

When it is remembered that solid bodies in a state of incandescence *emit* a much greater body of light than gases emit in a similar condition, and that they are able to *absorb* a much greater quantity of the light falling on them—in certain circumstances even the whole of it—through the transfer of the ether-vibrations to their ponderable atoms; when, further, it is remembered that just those substances that *give out heat* with the greatest facility, and in the fullest quantity, are also the most capable of *receiving heat* from without or *absorbing* it, the thought is suggested that there must be an intimate connection, a certain reciprocity between the power of a body to emit light (emission) and to absorb it (absorption). That the temperature of the substance has an influence on this relation between its emissive and absorptive powers is proved by the phenomena of the gas-spectra of the first, second, and third order (§ 31), as well as by the variety of absorption spectra exhibited at different temperatures by the same substance. A century ago the eminent mathematician and physicist Euler, in his "Theoria lucis et caloris," enunciated the principle that every substance absorbs light of such a wave-length as coincides with the vibrations of its smallest particles. Foucault mentioned in his work on the spectrum of the electric light, published in 1849, that owing to the impurity of the carbon-points the intense yellow sodium line appeared, and was changed into a black line when sunlight was transmitted through the electric arc. Ångström gave expression as early as the year 1853 to the general law that a gas when luminous *emits rays of light of the same refrangibility as those which it has power to absorb*, or, in other words. that *the rays which a substance absorbs are precisely those which it emits when made self-luminous.**

But all these facts remained isolated, and there was yet wanting the comprehensive grasp of a general physical law under

* [In a report to the British Association for the Advancement of Science in 1861, Prof. Balfour Stewart wrote: "In connection with this subject it may not be out of place to introduce the following extract of a letter from Prof. W. Thomson, to Prof. Kirchhoff, dated 1860. Prof. Thomson thus writes: 'Prof. Stokes mentioned to me at Cambridge some time ago, probably about ten years, that Prof. Miller had made an experiment testing to a very high degree of accuracy the agreement of the double dark line D of the solar spectrum with the double bright line constituting the spectrum of the spirit-lamp burning with salt. I remarked that there must be some physical connection between two agencies presenting so marked a characteristic in common. He assented, and said he believed a mechanical explanation of the cause was to be had on some such principles as the following: Vapor of sodium must possess, by its molecular structure, a tendency to vibrate in the periods corresponding to the degrees of refrangibility of the double line D. Hence the presence of sodium in a source of light must tend to originate light of that quality. On the other hand, vapor of sodium in an atmosphere round a source must have a great tendency to retain on itself, i. e., to absorb and to have its temperature raised by light from the source of the precise quality in question. In the atmosphere around the sun, therefore, there must be present vapor of sodium, which, according to mechanical explanation thus suggested, being particularly opaque for light of that quality, prevents such of it as is emitted from the sun from penetrating to any considerable distance through the surrounding atmosphere. The test of this theory must be had in ascertaining whether or not vapor of sodium has the special absorbing power anticipated.'" In the same connection must also be considered the experiments on the properties of radiant light communicated in 1860 by Prof. Balfour Stewart to the Royal Society.]

which the individual phenomena could be arranged. It was reserved to Kirchhoff to discover this law, and to establish triumphantly its truth, not only by mathematical proof, but also in many striking instances by experiment.

In the year 1860, he published his memoir on the relation between the emissive and absorptive powers of bodies for heat as well as for light, in which occurs the celebrated sentence: "*The relation between the power of emission and the power of absorption of one and the same class of rays is the same for all bodies at the same temperature,*" which will ever be distinguished as announcing one of the most important laws of Nature, and which, on account of its extensive influence and universal application, will render immortal the name of its illustrious discoverer.

40. Reversal of the Spectra of Gases.

From Kirchhoff's law it follows as a necessary consequence that gases and vapors in transmitting light absorb or impair precisely those rays (colors) which they themselves emit when rendered luminous, while they remain perfectly transparent to all other colored rays. Luminous sodium-vapor, for example, gives under ordinary circumstances a spectrum of one bright-yellow double line; it emits therefore this yellow light only. If the white light of the sun, the electric arc, or the oxyhydrogen-lamp be allowed to pass through the vapor of sodium, the vapor will abstract or extinguish from the white light just those yellow rays which it emitted when in a luminous state. While the greater part of these yellow rays are absorbed by the sodium-vapor, all the other rays—the red, orange, green, blue, and violet—pass through unimpaired.

The mode in which Kirchhoff conducted his experiments, which admit of certain and easy repetition by means of a direct-vision spectroscope, is shown in Fig. 80, where the apparatus is arranged in the same way as for the exhibition of the absorption spectra. L is an oil-lamp, the white light from which is decomposed into a continuous spectrum of every shade of color by the prism of the spectroscope S (p. 84). After the eye-piece of the telescope and the slit have been so adjusted as to exhibit a distinct spectrum, there is placed close in front of the slit *s* a glass-tube N, from which the oxygen of the air has been expelled by the introduction of hydrogen gas, and in which are laid some pieces of metallic sodium. The glass tube is heated by means of the spirit-lamp or gas-flame G, and part of the sodium is converted into vapor; a dark line soon makes its appearance in the bright

Fig. 80.

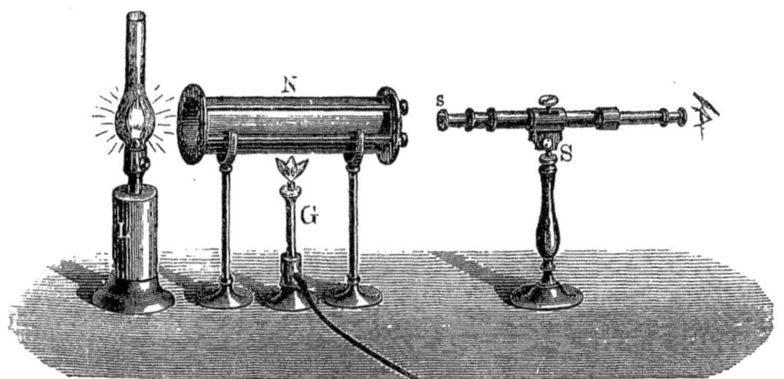

Reversal of the Sodium Line (seen with the Spectroscope.)

yellow of the continuous spectrum of the oil-lamp precisely in the place where the sodium-vapor when rendered luminous by heat shows its yellow line. For proof of this it is only necessary to replace the sodium-tube N by a spirit-flame in the wick of which some common salt (chloride of sodium) has been rubbed, and to screen the light of the lamp: the luminous sodium-vapor produces the yellow line precisely in the same place in which the yellow light was before absorbed from the continuous spectrum and the dark line formed.

The optician Ladd furnishes strong glass tubes half an inch in width, closed at both ends, and filled with hydrogen gas and a small quantity of sodium. On being slowly and gradually heated, the sodium becomes vaporized. If such a tube be held vertically close in front of the slit *s*, and the white light of a lamp, or what is preferable the light from incandescent lime, be allowed to pass through the tube containing sodium-vapor before entering the slit *s*, a dark line is visible precisely in the place of the bright sodium line. By the use of a spectroscope of strong dispersive power the bright sodium line does not appear as a single but as a double line: accordingly, in such an instrument the dark absorption line of sodium-vapor appears double, and both these dark lines occur precisely in the place where the two bright sodium lines are found when the light from sodium alone falls into the spectroscope.

In the same way, by employing the vapors of lithium, potassium, strontium, and barium, Kirchhoff and Bunsen extinguished from a continuous spectrum precisely the same bright colors which these vapors emit when luminous. Luminous lithium-vapor (Frontispiece No. 3) gives a spectrum of one intense red line and a fainter orange one; lithium-vapor absorbs also just those same colors from white light sent through it. If Kirchhoff's experiment be repeated with lithium in the same manner (Fig. 80) as already described with sodium, two unequally dark lines will appear in the continuous spectrum of the lamp-light precisely in the same places where the luminous lithium-vapor showed the two bright lines.

The important result of these investigations is therefore that the characteristic *bright* lines of sodium, lithium, etc., are changed into *dark* lines when the intense white light of incandescent solid or liquid bodies passes through the vapor of these metals. The spectrum of luminous sodium-vapor is a bright *yellow* (double) line, the rest of the field in the spectroscope remaining dark; the spectrum of an incandescent solid or liquid body, after it has passed through sodium-vapor at a lower temperature than itself, occupies, on the contrary, the whole field with its brilliant colors excepting only that one place in which the *dark* sodium line is found. As therefore the bright lines of gas-spectra are converted in these experiments into dark lines, while the dark parts of the spectrum are changed into brilliant colors by the continuous spectrum of the white light, the entire gas-spectrum seems to be reversed in respect of its illumination: for this reason the phenomenon has been called, after Kirchhoff, "*the reversal of the spectrum.*"

It has been fully proved by Kirchhoff that the difference between the temperature of the incandescent solid or liquid body giving the continuous spectrum, and that of the absorptive vapor through which its white light passes, exercises a great influence upon the reversal of the spectrum, and that the whole phenomenon rests upon the relation existing between the emissive and absorptive powers of the vapor, which relation is determined by the difference of temperature. The reversal experiments, therefore, succeed only when there is a great difference of temperature between the incandescent solid body and the absorptive vapor, and they will succeed all the more certainly the higher the temperature is of the incandescent body, and the lower that of the reversing vapor. The light of the sun, the electric arc, Drummond's lime-light, or a glowing platinum wire, may be employed in place of the lamp (L, Fig. 80). If, instead of the glass tube filled with hydrogen and sodium, etc., free sodium-vapor be employed, such as can be obtained by heating metallic sodium in a flame, this flame must not be of a high temperature. The temperature of the Bunsen burner, or even of a spirit-lamp, is too great as opposed to the heat of the oxyhydrogen lime-light; for this purpose the moderately hot flame produced by spirits of wine, diluted with as much water as it will bear, is sufficient, when with the addition of a little common salt, the sodium line in a good spectroscope, with a suitable opening of the slit, will appear black upon the colored ground of the continuous spectrum of the lime-light. If the white light of the electric arc, with its far greater heat, be used to form the continuous spectrum, the reversal of the sodium and lithium lines may be produced by volatilizing these metals in the flame of the Bunsen burner.

For the exhibition of the reversal of the sodium line on a screen, the glass tube above mentioned containing hydrogen gas and sodium is not well suited, as the sodium-vapor is not dense enough, and soon stains the sides of the glass; but, if the electric arc be used for the white light, the sodium-vapor may be produced by means of a gas-flame.

For this purpose the carbon-points should be previously moistened with a weak solution of salt, and allowed to dry again. If a continuous spectrum some three feet long be formed by the electric lamp and prism in the usual way, the bright sodium line is seen passing through the yellow, the position of which may be noted by making a mark *m* at the side. The small amount of sodium adhering to the carbon-points soon evaporates in the heat of the electric light, and the yellow line is extinguished. The gas-burner G (Fig. 81) is now placed before the slit of the electric lamp E, so that the rays of the incandescent carbon issuing from it must pass through the flame G. Before adding the sodium to this gas-flame, a perforated screen S of pasteboard is placed in front of the lens L, in order that the large screen on which the spectrum is formed shall be protected from the intense yellow light of the burning sodium: none of these preparations exert the slightest influence upon the continuous spectrum $r\ v\ v_1 r_1$ on the screen. A piece of sodium the size of a pea is placed in a platinum spoon *l*, and brought into the gas-flame; the sodium

FIG. 81.

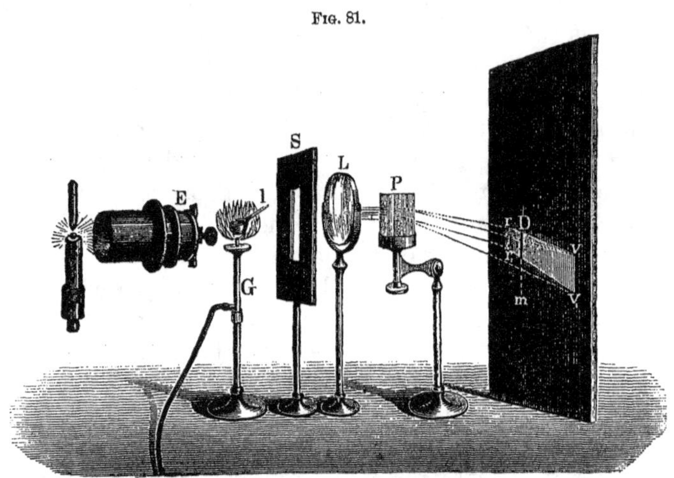

Reversal of the Sodium Line.—(Projected on a Screen.)

ignites, and forms a dense cloud of vapor through which the rays of the electric light must pass. On the screen is seen a stripe D of intense blackness, precisely in the place marked *m* where the bright sodium line before appeared; the sodium-vapor has, partially at least, absorbed or extinguished from the white light of the incandescent carbon the yellow light of the same degree of refrangibility as the sodium-vapor emitted. If the sodium be withdrawn from the gas-flame, the black line immediately disappears from the screen; if it be reintroduced, the black line again appears precisely in the same place. The sodium-vapor therefore absorbs the same light, that is to say the same colored rays, which it emits in a luminous state.

The instructive experiment of the reversal of the sodium line may be made in another way, which is not less fitted than the preceding one to give a clear illustration of certain phenomena of the solar spectrum. For this purpose the lower pole of the electric lamp is replaced by a cylinder of carbon half an inch thick, the upper surface of which, slightly hollowed out (Fig. 82), contains a piece of sodium the size of a pea. The Bunsen burner G, and the pasteboard screen S, are removed, while the lens L, the prism P, and the large screen, remain undisturbed. To prevent the intense incandescence of the carbon, and the consequent appearance of the white electric light, the two poles are separated after the first contact somewhat wider than is usual (rather more than $\frac{2}{10}$ of an inch): only a faint continuous spectrum is formed, and the lamp emits only the intensely yellow light of the burning sodium. As soon as the electric current passes, the sodium begins to glow strongly, and a single band of

FIG. 82.

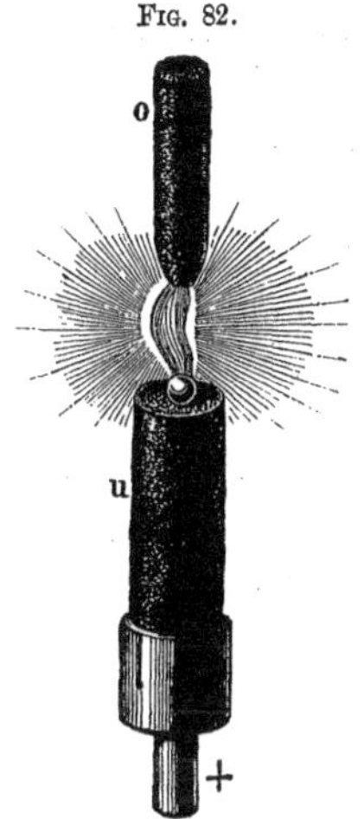

Volatilization of Sodium in the Electric Light.

brilliant yellow about two inches wide is seen upon the screen, which is the spectrum of the luminous sodium-vapor. But in a few seconds a sharply-defined deep-black line about an inch wide appears in the middle of this yellow band, while the remaining portion of the color fades away. The bright-yellow sodium line has become changed into a dark line, which continues as long as the combustion of the sodium lasts.

In this case the reversal is easily explained in the following manner: The sodium becomes first intensely heated, and its vapor emits its yellow light; immediately afterward a great portion of the sodium is converted into *vapor* by the great heat of the electric arc, and *envelops the small luminous portion about the sodium in a dense cloud of non-luminous sodium-vapor.* The yellow light of the small luminous portion of the sodium-vapor must pass through this large cloud of sodium-vapor of a lower temperature, and is absorbed by it before reaching the slit of the lamp. We may repeat the conclusive inference: *The vapor of sodium absorbs precisely the same light that luminous sodium-vapor emits.*

Without employing either the electric or Drummond's light, this phenomenon may be exhibited by the following simple but ingenious contrivance of Bunsen's: It consists (Fig. 83) of two bottles, A, B, containing zinc and common salt, and both nearly filled with a very diluted solution of hydrochloric acid. Each bottle is closed with an India-rubber stopper pierced with two holes, one of which in each stopper serves for a gas-burner of different construction.

In one hole of the lamp A is a bent glass tube *b* for the introduction of coal-gas from a common-gas pipe; in the other opening is the tube *c*, which is narrowed at the top, serving for the escape of the gas. The other lamp B is fitted up in the same manner as A, with the exception that the escape-tube *c′* is bent and terminates in a much smaller opening.

Over each of these glass tubes *c* and *c′* is a burner constructed of tin-plate, which can be moved up and down. The burner *d* of the lamp A is cylindrical below, and spreads out above in the shape of a fan, so as to form a narrow and somewhat arched slit of about an inch in length. The burner *e* of the lamp B is cylindrical throughout, and is covered with a conical-shaped chimney *h*, which slides up and down the tube *e*. As the top of the chimney has an opening only an inch in diameter, which can be still further diminished by the addition of another cover with a yet smaller aperture, the gas when ignited forms a conical-shaped pointed flame *d*, which can be reduced by means of the stopcock of the gas-tube to about an inch in length. The flame *g* of the lamp A, on the contrary, is very large and broad, owing to the size of the emission-tube *c*, and the compression of the wide burner *d f*, and presents a luminous surface of some extent.

The bottles are used for the purpose of mixing a little common salt (chloride of sodium) with the hydrogen gas formed by the action of the diluted hydrochloric acid on the zinc. The hydrogen gas as it rises mixes with the coal-gas, and carries the chloride of sodium into both flames, producing in this way the brilliant-yellow light of sodium-vapor.

Fig. 83.

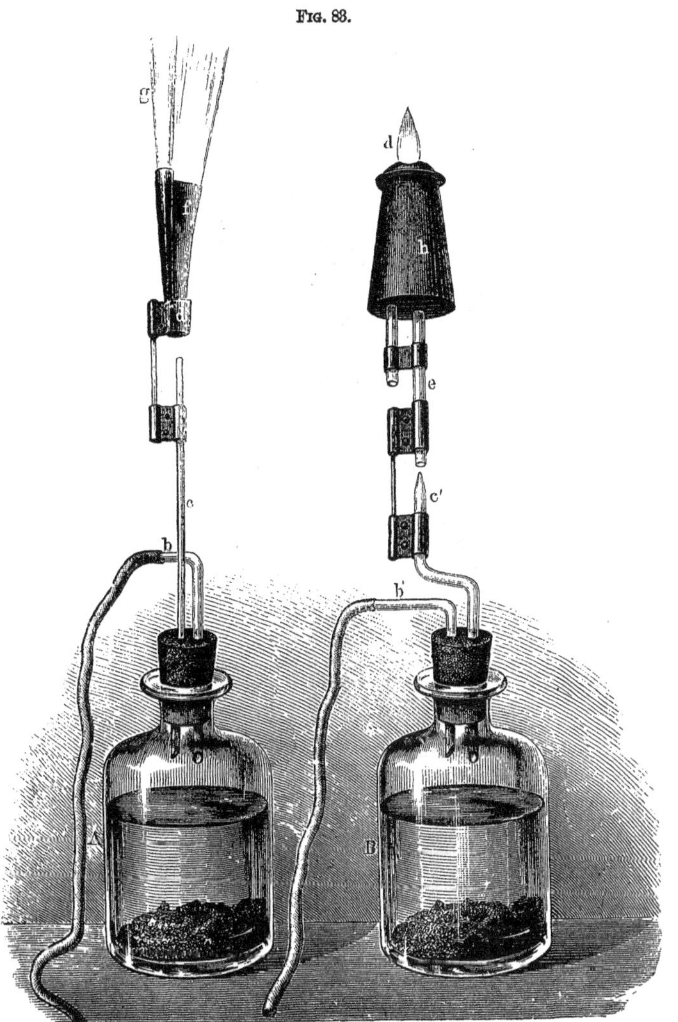

Bunsen's Apparatus for the Absorption of the Light of Sodium.

Both lamps are placed very near to each other, so near indeed that, as shown in Fig. 84, the flame *g* of the lamp A serves as a background to the lamp B. In this position the small flame *d*, notwithstanding the brilliant light of the flame *g* immediately behind it, appears quite dark and smoky, indeed almost black, when all conditions are favorable—the burner and chimney rightly placed, and the supply of gas suitably adjusted. The heat-flame *g* emits with intense brightness the light of sodium; the small sodium-flame *d* in front of it absorbs these rays as they pass through it; and, as it is much less luminous than the flame *g*, it appears dark by contrast with the bright background.

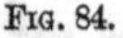
FIG. 84.

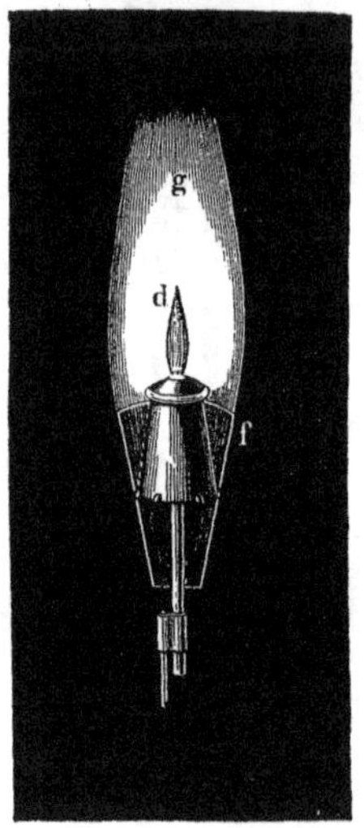

Absorption of the Sodium-Flame.

Desaga, of Heidelberg, the constructor of this apparatus, has lately much simplified it by uniting the two burners, and fixing the common supply-tube by means of a single stopper on to a larger bottle.

The experiment of reversal may be easily shown by the use of a spectroscope in the following manner: The instrument is so directed on to a spirit-lamp that when a grain of salt is dropped into the flame a well-defined spectrum consisting of the well-known yellow sodium line is formed. The flame is then brought close in front of the slit, and a piece of newly-cut metallic sodium, the size of a pea, is placed over the flame in a wire netting. The flame cannot pass the wire, yet the sodium begins at once to burn, and the brilliant-yellow sodium line is seen in the spectroscope: very soon, however, a black line appears in the same place very sharply defined against the bright background. Here also the brilliant luminous vapor of the burning sodium is enveloped in a dense cloud of feebly luminous sodium-vapor which completely absorbs the greater part of the yellow sodium-light.

We can now readily predict what appearance will be presented in the spectroscope if the light of an incandescent solid or liquid body, before entering the slit of the instrument, pass through a less highly heated atmosphere of any kind of vapor, such as that of sodium, lithium, iron, etc. The incandescent body would have produced a continuous spectrum if its light had sustained no change on the way; but in the vaporous atmosphere through which its rays must pass, each vapor absorbs just those rays which it would have emitted if luminous, thereby extinguishing these particular colors, and substituting for them dark bands in those places of the continuous spectrum where it would have produced bright lines. The spectroscope shows, therefore, a continuous spectrum extending through the whole range of colors from red to violet, but intersected by dark lines; the sodium line, the two lithium lines, the numerous iron lines, etc., appear on the colored ground of the continuous spectrum as so many *dark* lines.

Spectra of this kind are evidently *absorption spectra;* they are also called *reversed* or *compound spectra.* If a *complete coincidence* can be established in such a spectrum by means of either a prism of comparison (§ 28), or a scale (§ 25), between the characteristic *bright* lines of the gas-spectrum of a certain substance with the same number of *dark* lines, the conclusion may be admitted that, in the absorptive atmosphere which has produced the dark lines, the same substance is contained in a condition of vapor. The wide influence which this result of Kirchhoff's discovery has on the investigation of the physical constitution of the heavenly bodies, is shown by the consideration that, as the various substances of this earth can be recognized by their simple gas-spectra, so the reversed gas-spectra afford the key to the recognition of the matter of which the heavenly bodies are composed; and, indeed, so important is the part which they play in the analysis of the stellar world, that we may well be excused if we linger a while longer on this subject.

The question will occur to every one on reflection—why, if the weak sodium-flame absorb the yellow rays from the intense white light that passes through it, do not the yellow rays of the flame itself again replace the yellow sodium line? A somewhat closer investigation of all the influences at work will not only give materials for fully answering this inquiry, but afford the means also of clearly explaining the cause and true nature of the dark lines.

Let I designate the intensity of the *white* light of the incandescent solid or liquid body, taking the electric light as an example, i that of the absorptive flame, which, for the sake of simplicity, we will suppose to be a sodium-flame, and $\frac{I}{n}$ the proportion between the absorptive and the emissive powers of this flame—that is to say, $\frac{I}{n}$ is lost by absorption from the total intensity. If then the white light I pass through the sodium-flame, and suffer a loss in intensity by absorption of $\frac{I}{n}$, there will be in the place of the spectrum where the sodium line appears, which we will call D, an amount of light equal to $I - \frac{I}{n} + i$. The amount of absorption $\frac{I}{n}$ diminishes the intensity of the spectrum at the spot D, but the intensity of the sodium-flame will to a greater or less degree supply the deficiency. If the amount of the absorption were precisely equal to the intensity i, the intensity of the spectrum at the spot D would be just as great as that of the neighboring parts, and there would therefore be no interruption of the spectrum; there would neither be a dark line nor a bright line visible. If the intensity i of the sodium-flame be greater than the absorption $\frac{I}{n}$, the brightness of the spot D in the spectrum would be greater than on either side of it, and there would appear at this place a bright-yellow sodium line, although the white light had passed through the absorptive flame; the reverse will be the case if the intensity i of this flame be less than the whole absorption; the brightness of the spectrum at the spot D will then be less than that of the surrounding parts. In the last case, however, this want of light will appear as a shadow by contrast with the brightness of the neighboring places, and the usual bright-yellow sodium line will seem to be a dark line.

It will be seen further, from this investigation, that in the places where the dark absorption lines appear there is by no means a total absence of light; therefore these lines should not be described as quite black; but, in contrast with the surrounding brilliancy produced by the full undiminished light of the incandescent solid or liquid body, these lines *appear* quite black even when their brightness exceeds that of the absorbing vapor.

The whole action of the *reversal* of a bright spectrum line into a dark one rests on the proportion between the absorptive power and the compensating emissive power in the absorbing vapor: the greater the absorptive power, and the less the emissive power, further, the greater the light of the incandescent body, so much the darker will the reversed lines appear to be.

The following table will serve to elucidate the foregoing remarks, by giving four examples for the sodium line:

No.	The Intensity of the White Light is called	The Intensity of the Sodium-Flame is	The Absorptive Power of the Sodium-Vapor is	The Intensity of the Spectrum before	in	behind the Sodium Line is then	The Sodium Line appears therefore
1	2	1	$\frac{1}{4}$	2	$3 - \frac{2}{4} = 2\frac{1}{2}$	2	bright.
2	10	1	$\frac{1}{4}$	20	$11 - \frac{10}{4} = 8\frac{1}{2}$	10	dark.
3	100	1	$\frac{1}{2}$	100	$101 - \frac{100}{2} = 51$	100	darker.
4	100	1	$\frac{3}{4}$	100	$101 - \frac{300}{4} = 26$	100	very dark.

In the first case, the place D is $\frac{1}{2}$ brighter than the surrounding parts of the spectrum, therefore it appears as a *bright* sodium line. In No. 2, the brightness of the place D is only equal to $8\frac{1}{2}$, while that of either side is 10; it is therefore not so bright at D as at the side of D, and in consequence D appears dark against the surrounding parts of the spectrum. In No. 3, the contrast is still greater between the light at D 51 and that at the side 100. Finally, in No. 4, where the absorptive power of the flame is assumed to be $\frac{3}{4}$, the contrast between the strength of light, 100 and 26, is so great that the line seems almost black. The intensity with which the yellow line of sodium and the red line of lithium appear when these substances are heated in a Bunsen burner, warrants the conclusion that these metals would also absorb with great power rays of the same refrangibility, and therefore the assumed absorptive power $\frac{3}{4}$, given in the last example, is considerably below the truth.

PART THIRD.

SPECTRUM ANALYSIS IN ITS APPLICATION TO THE HEAVENLY BODIES.

Dr. Joseph von Fraunhofer.

Page 159.

SPECTRUM ANALYSIS IN ITS APPLICATION TO THE HEAVENLY BODIES.

41. The Solar Spectrum and the Fraunhofer Lines.

THE most brilliant example of a reversed spectrum—that is to say, a continuous spectrum crossed by dark absorption lines—is afforded by the sun. If an ordinary spectroscope, armed with a telescope of low power, be directed to a bright sky with a rather wide opening of the slit, a magnificent continuous spectrum will be seen, exhibiting the most beautiful and brilliant colors without either bright or dark lines. But, if the slit be narrowed so as to obtain the purest possible spectrum (§ 21), and the focus of the telescope be very accurately adjusted, the spectrum, now much fainter, will be seen to be crossed by a number of dark lines and cloudy bands. If, by the use of several prisms (§ 19), the spectrum be lengthened, and a higher magnifying power employed, these thick lines and bands will become resolved into separate fine lines and groups of lines, which are so sharply defined and so characteristically grouped, that by the help of a scale they are easily impressed upon the memory and distinguished one from another.

As early as 1802 these dark lines in the solar spectrum had been observed and described by Wollaston; later, in 1814, they were more carefully examined and mapped by Fraunhofer, of Munich; and, later still, by Becquerel, Zantedeschi, Matthiessen, Brewster, Gladstone, and others; but their origin and nature remained a mystery, notwithstanding the acutest reasoning and most painstaking researches of many able physicists, until Kirchhoff made his splendid discovery in 1859.

Fig. 85.

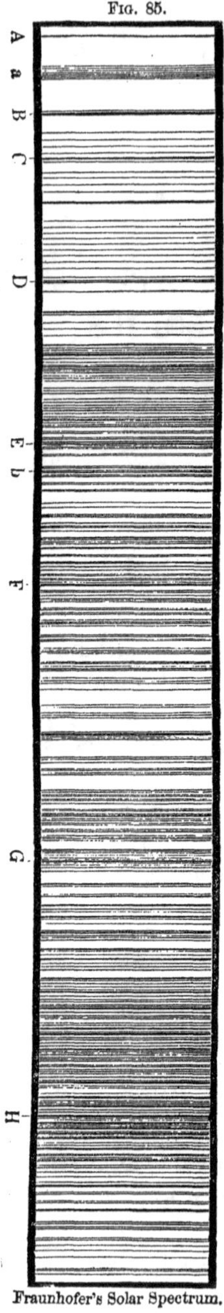

Fraunhofer's Solar Spectrum.

Fraunhofer was able to distinguish with certainty about 600 lines; he found also that with the same prism and telescope they always kept the same relative order and position, and were therefore peculiarly adapted to serve as marks for denoting the place of any single set of colored rays, and for determining the refrangibility of any particular color.

To facilitate reference to any of the innumerable colors of the solar spectrum (Frontispiece No. 11), Fraunhofer, whose drawing is accurately represented in Fig. 85, selected, out of the great number he observed, *eight* characteristic lines situated in the most important places of the spectrum, which he designated by the letters A, B, C, D, E, F, G, H; of these lines A and B lie in the red, C in the red near the orange, D in the orange, forming a double line with a high power, E in the yellow, F on the borders of the green and blue, G in the dark blue or indigo, and H in the violet. Besides these lines, there is a noticeable group *a* of fine lines between A and B, and also a group *b*, consisting of three fine lines, between E and F. It was remarked even by Fraunhofer that the position of the two dark lines in the solar spectrum, designated by him D, were coincident with the two bright lines shown by the light of a lamp, now known as the double sodium line. These dark lines of the solar spectrum have been called, after their discoverer, the Fraunhofer lines.

After Fraunhofer, Zantedeschi, Professor of Physics in the University of Padua, devoted himself to the investigation of the dark lines in the solar spectrum, upon which work he had already entered in the year 1846. He deviated from Fraunhofer's method of observation by introducing the prism between two condensing lenses; the slit was placed in the focus of one lens, while the other served to project the spectrum on to a screen. By this means he constructed an apparatus which in all essential points differed little from the spectroscope now in use.* The important sphere destined to prismatic analysis did not escape the penetration of this physicist, since in his work "Ricerche fisico-chimiche-fisiologiche sulla luce," † he thus expresses himself in speaking of the significance of the spectrum:

"The solar spectrum is the most perfect photoscope that in the present state of science can be imagined. Light itself exhibits, and registers with wonderful minuteness, the changes occurring in the constitution of a luminous body, or in the medium through which the light passes. I therefore recommend to the scientific investigator a *camera-obscura* specially adapted to these photoscopic observations. I am convinced that such investigations will prove of the highest value, not only in the study of light, but also in the departments of meteorology and astronomy. Light, which in these days is commissioned to be the painter of Nature, may also become its own delineator, since it is ever disclosing new wonders out of the mystery of its being, and revealing those constant changes which are taking place, not only in our planetary system, but throughout the whole universe."

By a careful investigation of the spectra formed by prisms of different substances, it is found that the same colors do not occupy the same proportionate space in each spectrum; with a prism of flint glass, for instance, there is proportionately less red and more blue and violet than with a prism of crown glass. The greater the difference between the refractive powers of a substance for the red and the violet rays, the greater will be the distance over which the colors are spread—in other words, the greater will be the *dispersive power*. The *length* of the spectrum

* [The ingenious use of a collimating lens, with the slit placed in its focus, by which a spectroscope is made so much more manageable, and without which arrangement many of the recent applications of this instrument would have been scarcely possible, seems to have been independently adopted by several observers about the same time. Prof. Swan made use of this arrangement in experiments on the ordinary refraction of Iceland spar in 1847; and the distinguished optician, Mr. Simms, constructed a collimator, in place of a distant slit, at the suggestion of the present Astronomer Royal, in 1848.]

† Venezia, 1846. Typ. G. Antonelli.

depends essentially upon this dispersion, and it is therefore not a matter of indifference whether a prism of flint glass, of crown glass, of water, or of bisulphide of carbon, be employed for producing the solar spectrum.

Fig. 86 exhibits clearly the various dispersive powers of the different substances, flint glass, crown glass, and water. The spectrum obtained by a flint-glass prism is about twice the length of that given by a similar sized crown-glass prism, and nearly three times the length of that from a hollow glass prism of the same form filled with water. The spectrum produced by a prism of bisulphide of carbon is very much longer than that given by a flint-glass prism, and this even is surpassed by one obtained from oil of cassia.

As the length of the spectrum is increased, the separation between the Fraunhofer lines increases also, but by no means in equal proportions. If, for example, the spectrum of the flint-glass prism were exactly twice the length of that of the crown-glass prism, the distance between any two dark lines, F and B

Fig. 86.

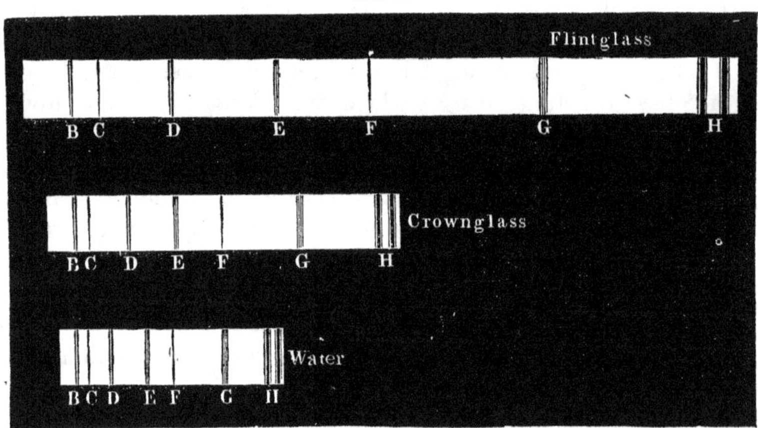

Solar Spectrum with Prisms of Flint Glass, Crown Glass, and Water.

for instance, will not be exactly twice as great in the one spectrum as in the other. In the water-spectrum F B = F H, the crown-glass spectrum is longer, but the various divisions formed by the Fraunhofer lines have not increased in equal proportions. In the water-spectrum F B = F H, while in the crown-glass spectrum F B is somewhat smaller than F H; by this latter prism, therefore, the blue and violet end is rather farther extended in comparison with the red and yellow end than by the water-prism.

This difference is still more obvious in comparing the two spectra of the water and the flint-glass prisms with an equal deviation of the light corresponding to the line B; the difference in the proportion of F B to F H is smaller in the flint-glass spectrum than in the water-spectrum, and this difference is more apparent than in the crown-glass spectrum.

It would therefore be an error to take for granted, as some have done, that the distances between individual dark lines in the spectrum change in the same proportion as the entire length of the spectrum; even if the dispersive power of any substance be known for the outside rays, or for the lines B and H, the amount of separation between the intervening lines of the spectrum cannot be deduced from this; the relative position of these lines must be specially ascertained for each refracting substance. An accurate knowledge of the peculiar conditions of the spectrum apparatus employed must therefore be acquired by every observer before he can venture to direct attention to the results of the observations made with it; he must become familiar with the precise places of all the chief lines and groups of lines seen in the solar spectrum, so that in the examination of any particular line, whether in the spectrum of a terrestrial substance or of a heavenly body, he may know at once, at least approximately, to which of the Fraunhofer lines it lies nearest.

The instrument used by Kirchhoff in his investigations on the solar spectrum is represented in Fig. 53, in connection with which it was stated that the amount of dispersion, or the length of the spectrum, increases with the number of prisms employed. By the use of such a powerful instrument a number of dark lines that appear to be single in smaller spectroscopes become resolved into several individual lines; the D-line even with a moderate power is separated into two fine lines, and shows besides a cloudy band of still further resolvability.

It is self-evident that with a great dispersion of the light, by which the spectrum is greatly lengthened, the intensity of each group of colors will be considerably diminished. By the use of a sufficient number of prisms the brilliant solar spectrum may be reduced almost to invisibility, and an excellent means is herewith provided, as will be seen later on, for reducing the excessive brilliancy of the solar light to the requisite amount when observing phenomena on the sun's limb.

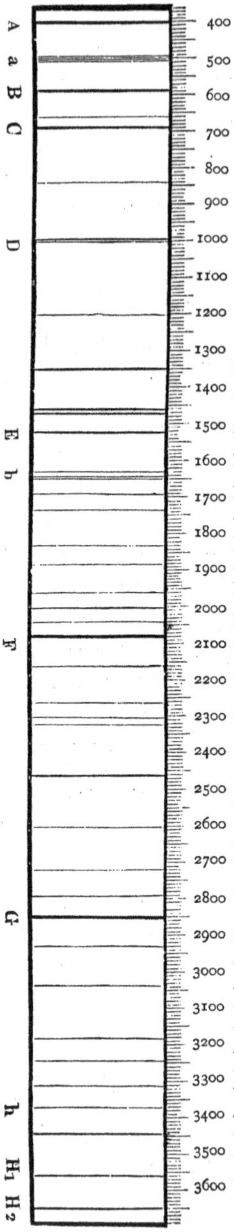

Fig. 87.—The Solar Spectrum with Kirchhoff's Scale.

42. Kirchhoff's Scale of the Solar Spectrum.

To facilitate the observation and recognition of the numerous dark lines in the solar spectrum, and to determine accurately their position and relative distances one from another, the mapping of all the visible lines must be made according to a given scale, or else in accordance with a certain scale adopted once for all, and this scale taken as a basis for measuring or estimating the place of any particular line. Kirchhoff, with an expenditure of time and trouble truly admirable, was the first to undertake these measures for certain portions of the spectrum. The instrument which he employed, consisting of four prisms, has been already shown in Fig. 53; from this drawing it will be seen that he made use of a divided circle, fixed to the head of the micrometer-screw R, by which the cross-wires of the telescope B could be brought to coincide with each of the dark lines of the spectrum. The eye-piece was so placed that the threads of the cross-wires formed angles of 45° with the dark lines; the point of intersection of the wires was, by means of the micrometer-screw R, placed in succession over every one of these lines, and the division on the screw-head (Fig. 51) read off; an estimation of the degree of intensity and breadth of the lines was recorded at the same time.

GUSTAV ROBERT KIRCHHOFF.

Page 164.

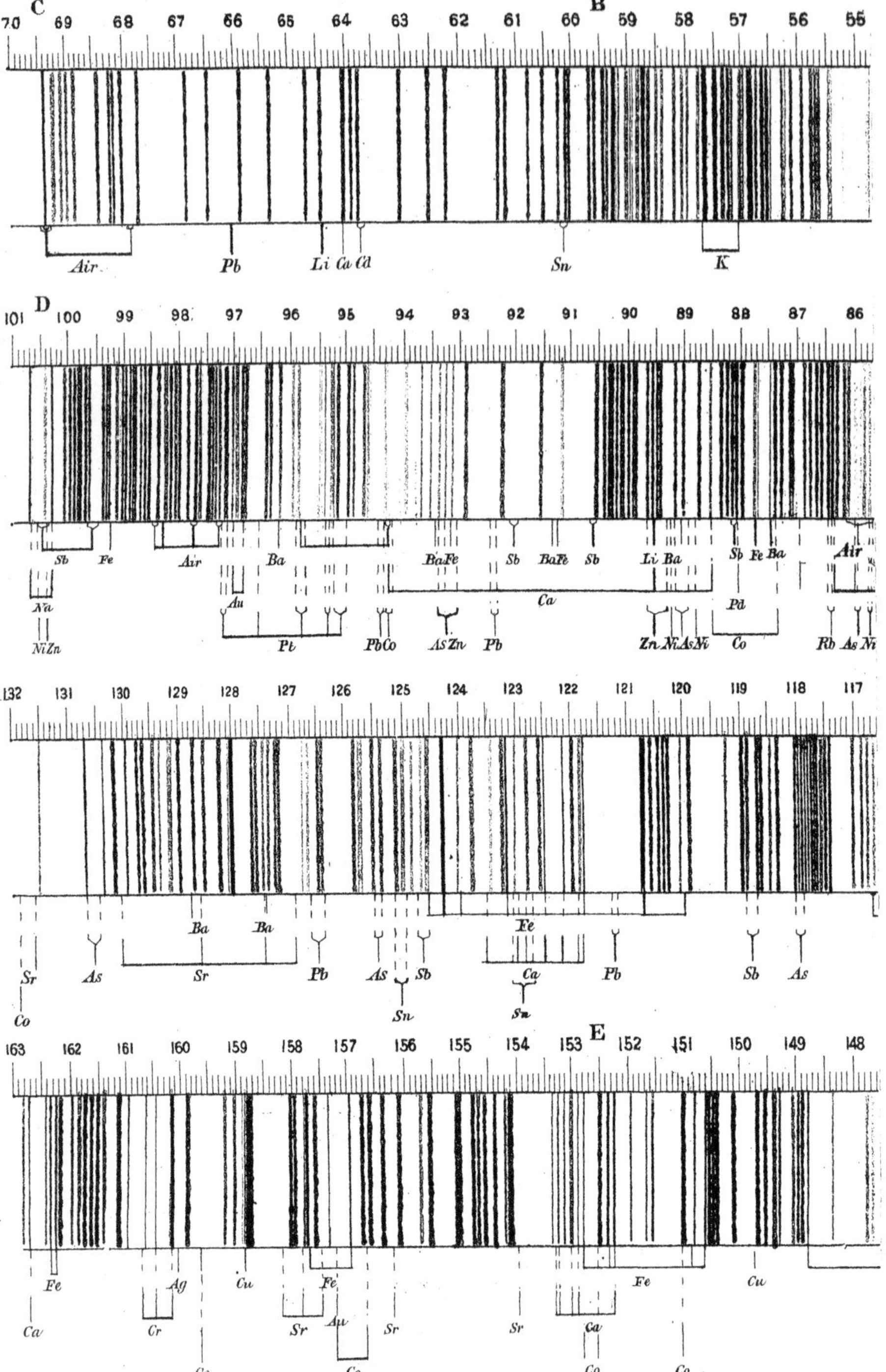

C
B
70 69 68 67 66 65 64 63 62 61 60 59 58 57 56 55
Air
Pb
Li Ca Cd
Sn
K
D
101 100 99 98 97 96 95 94 93 92 91 90 89 88 87 86
Sb Fe Air Ba BaFe Sb BaFe Sb Li Ba Sb Fe Ba Air
Na Au Ca Pd
NiZn Pt PbCo AsZn Pb ZnNiAsNi Co Rb As Ni
132 131 130 129 128 127 126 125 124 123 122 121 120 119 118 117
Ba Ba Fe
Sr As Sr Pb As Sb Ca Pb Sb As
Co Sn Sn
E
163 162 161 160 159 158 157 156 155 154 153 152 151 150 149 148
Fe Ag Cu Fe Fe Cu
Ca Cr Sr Au Sr Sr Ca
Co Co Co Co

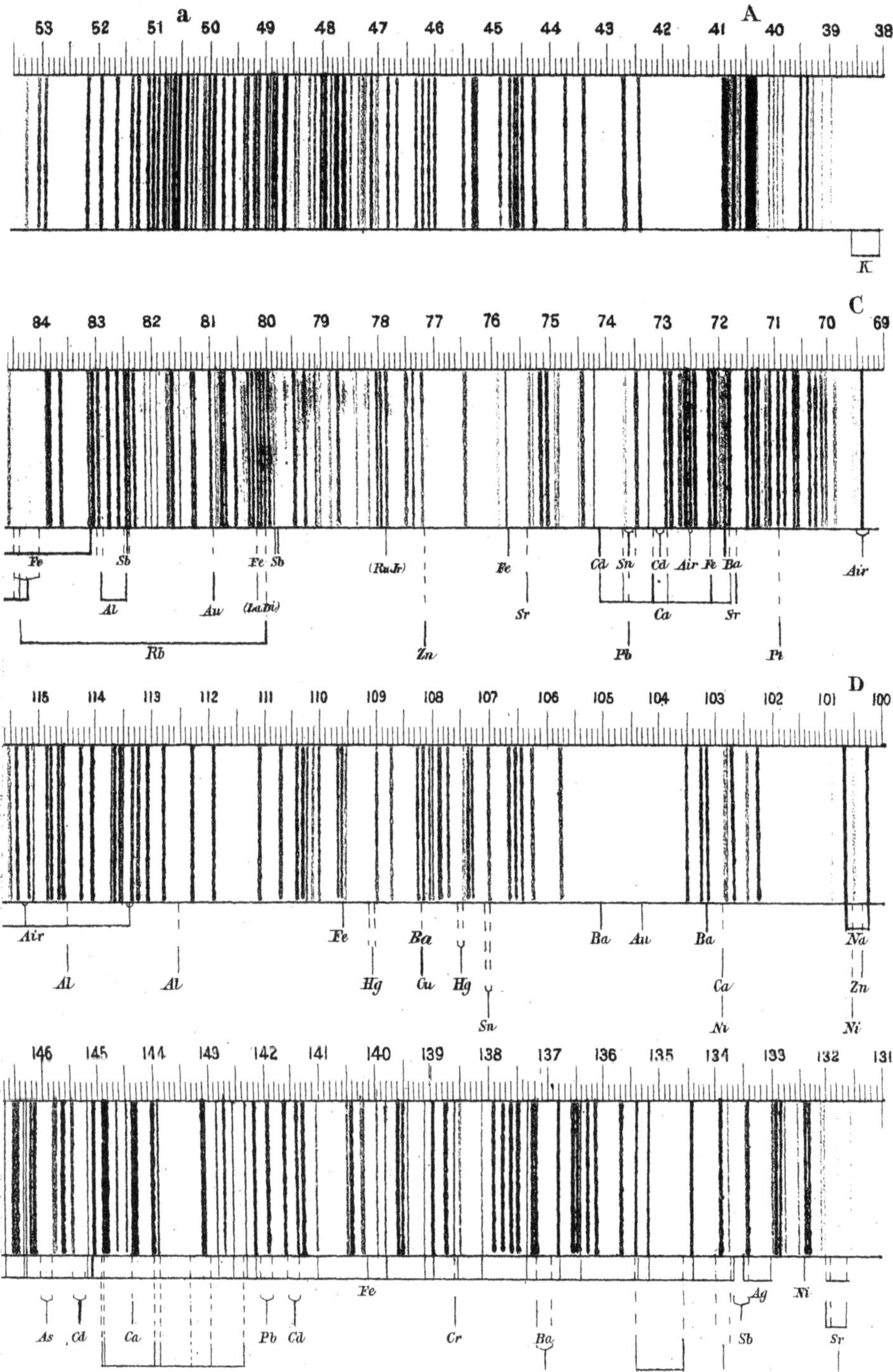

a
A
53 52 51 50 49 48 47 46 45 44 43 42 41 40 39 38
K
C
84 83 82 81 80 79 78 77 76 75 74 73 72 71 70 69
Fe Sb Fe Sb (Ru Jr) Fe Cd Sn Cd Air Fe Ba Air
Al Au (La Di) Sr Ca Sr
Rb Zn Pb Pt
D
115 114 113 112 111 110 109 108 107 106 105 104 103 102 101 100
Air Fe Ba Ba Au Ba Na
Al Al Hg Cu Hg Ca Zn
Sn Ni Ni
146 145 144 143 142 141 140 139 138 137 136 135 134 133 132 131
Fe Ag Ni
As Cd Ca Pb Cd Cr Ba Sb Sr
Co Hg Co Hg Co

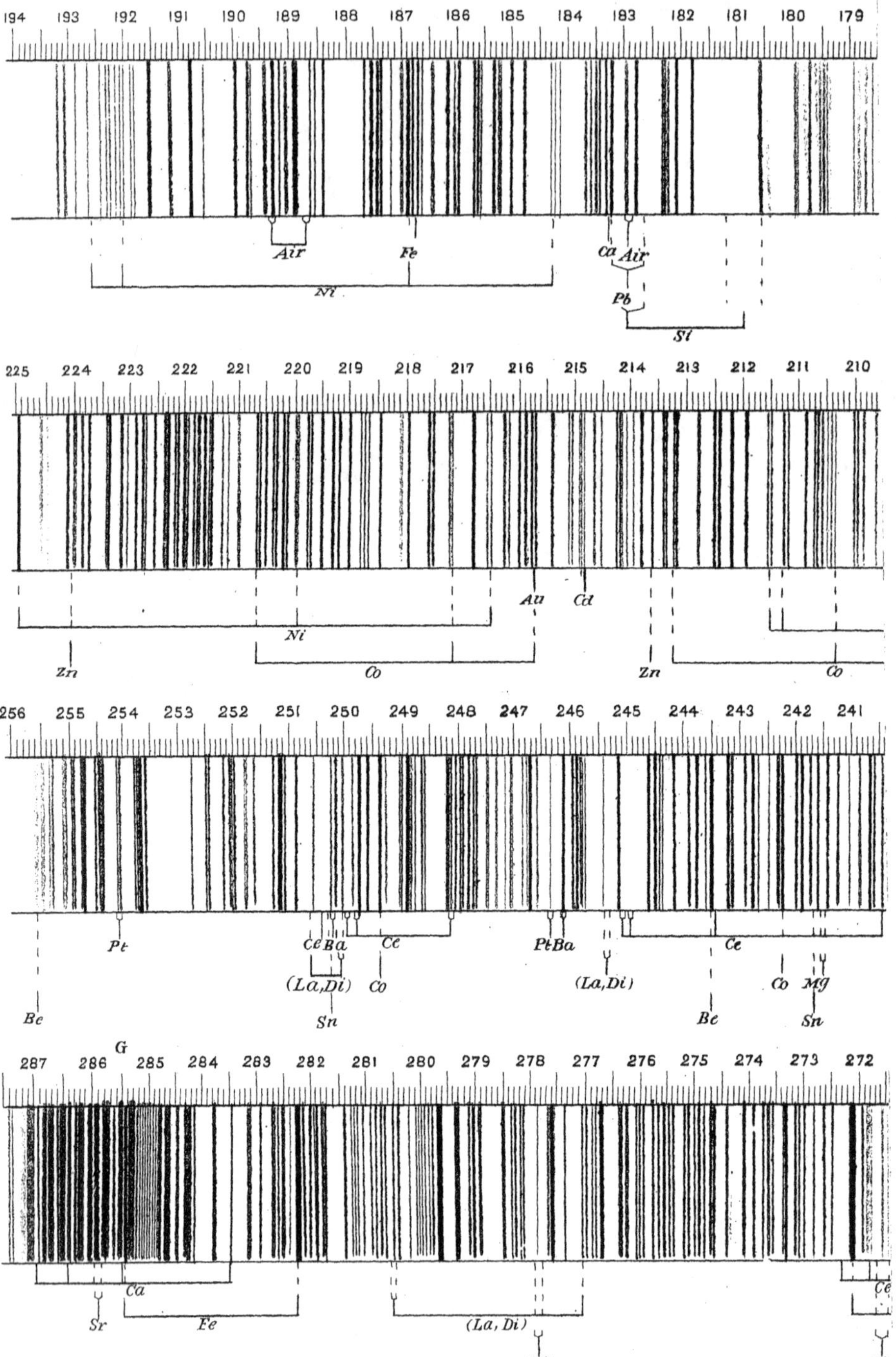
194 193 192 191 190 189 188 187 186 185 184 183 182 181 180 179
Air
Fe
Ni
Ca Air
Pb
Si
225 224 223 222 221 220 219 218 217 216 215 214 213 212 211 210
Au
Cd
Ni
Zn
Co
Zn
Co
256 255 254 253 252 251 250 249 248 247 246 245 244 243 242 241
Pt
Ce Ba
Ce
Pt Ba
Ce
(La, Di)
Co
(La, Di)
Co
Mg
Be
Sn
Be
Sn
G
287 286 285 284 283 282 281 280 279 278 277 276 275 274 273 272
Ca
Ce
Sr
Fe
(La, Di)
Hg
Pb

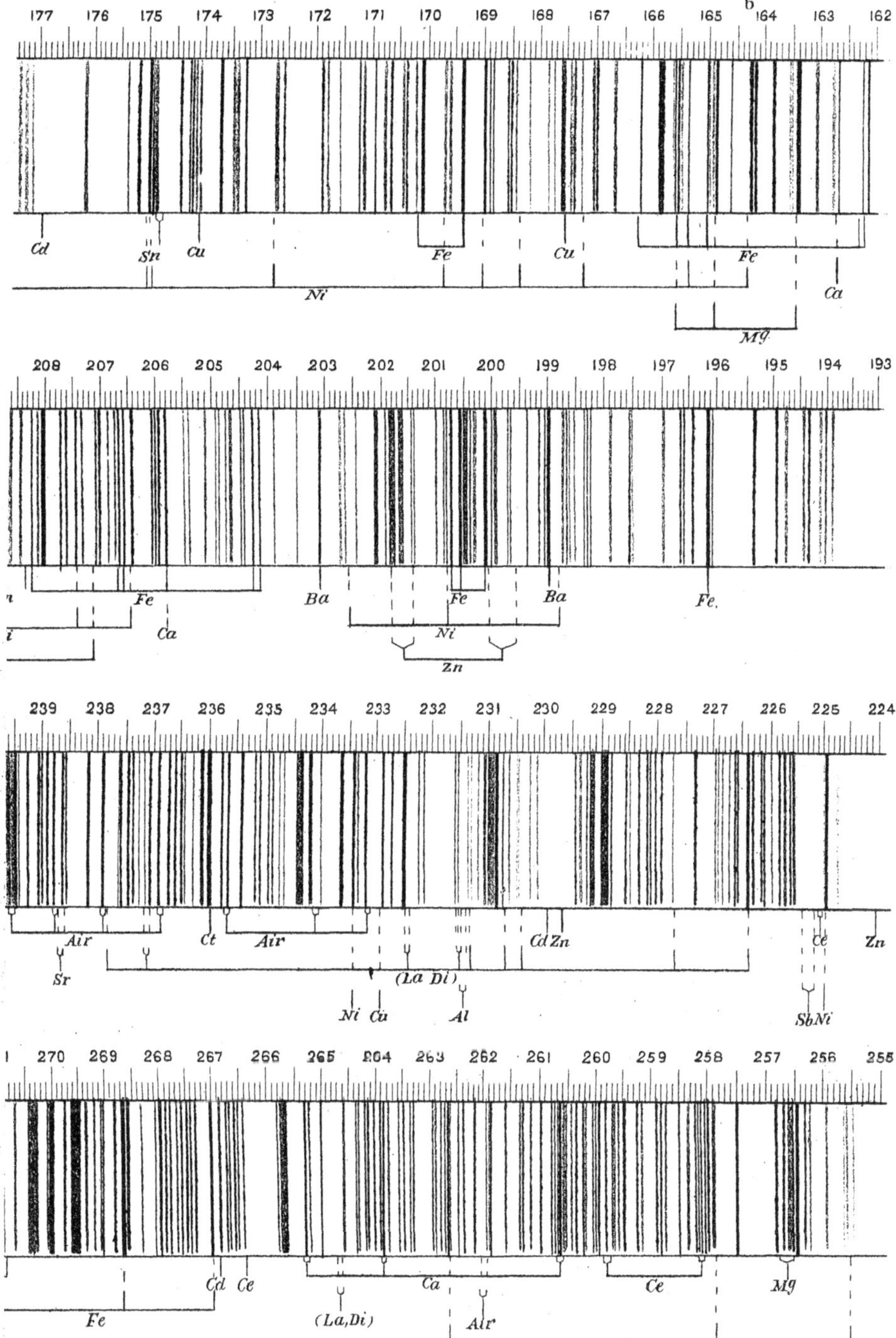

b
177 176 175 174 173 172 171 170 169 168 167 166 165 164 163 162
Cd
Sn
Cu
Fe
Cu
Fe
Ni
Ca
Mg
208 207 206 205 204 203 202 201 200 199 198 197 196 195 194 193
Fe
Ba
Fe
Ba
Fe.
Ca
Ni
Zn
239 238 237 236 235 234 233 232 231 230 229 228 227 226 225 224
Air
Ct
Air
Cd Zn
Ce
Zn
Sr
(La Di)
Ni
Cu
Al
Sb Ni
270 269 268 267 266 265 264 263 262 261 260 259 258 257 256 255
Cd
Ce
Ca
Ce
Mg
Fe
(La,Di)
Air
Pt
Pd
Be

In tabulating these measures, Kirchhoff employed as a basis a scale divided into millimetres, and selected an arbitrary starting-point: each millimetre corresponded to a division on the micrometer-screw head. The drawings published by Kirchhoff embrace a portion of the spectrum extending from the line D to a little beyond F, and occupy a length of four feet. The remaining portions, from A to D and from F to G, have been observed and measured by Hofmann, a pupil of Kirchhoff's, with the same instrument, and according to the same method as the first portion, and they occupy a similar length, so that the whole of the solar spectrum is exhibited in a very accurate drawing of about eight feet in length.

Fig. 87 is a greatly reduced copy of Kirchhoff's scale, with the principle Fraunhofer lines; Plates II. and III., for permission to publish which we are indebted to the kindness of Prof. Kirchhoff, and to which we shall again refer in § 44, give the lines measured by Kirchhoff and Hofmann according to their width and intensity; these maps are about half the size of the original drawings.*

The principal Fraunhofer lines are numbered on this scale as follows:

A	405	E	1522.7	h	3371
a	505	b_1	1633.4	H_1	3568 (?)
B	593	b_2	1648.3	H_2	is, according to Kirchhoff, uncertain.
C	694	b_3	1655.0		
D_1	1002.8	F	2080		
D_2	1006.8	G	2855		

43. Ångström's Normal Solar Spectrum

It is a grave objection to the plan of mapping the solar spectrum according to the positions and relative distances of the dark lines—their *indices of refraction* (p. 49)—that the position of these lines is considerably affected by the number and composition of the prisms employed; and therefore the appearance of the spectrum, and the drawings made from it, vary according to the construction of the instrument. Fraunhofer was the first to undertake the determination of the wave-lengths of those colors, the places of which are occupied by the principal dark lines of the solar spectrum; the subsequent labors of Ditscheiner, Van der Willigen, Mascart, and Gibbs, perfected this method, and ap-

* **Monatsberichte der Berliner Akademie der Wissenschaften, 1859.**

plied it to a greater number of lines, until at length the task was completed, with the aid of the best instruments, by Ångström, of Upsala, whose work is characterized by such accuracy and completeness as to render it worthy of the highest admiration, to be regarded as a pattern to all investigators.*

The number of dark lines measured by Ångström, with the aid and coöperation of Thalén, amount to 1,000; and the wave-lengths of the colors corresponding to these lines are accurately determined in units of a *ten-millionth of a millimetre.* In the original maps† [Plates IV., V., VI.], the whole solar spectrum from *a* to H_2 is represented in eleven parts, which when joined together form a length of about eleven feet. The upper edge of each part is provided with a scale divided into millimetres; each millimetre of the scale represents a difference of wave-length equal to the ten-millionth of a millimetre (0.0000001), and as the tenth of a millimetre may be estimated with sufficient accuracy, the scale used by Ångström will show, with approximate correctness, the wave-lengths of lines to the hundred-millionth of a millimetre.

As the red rays (*a*, B, C) have a greater wave-length than the blue (G), or the violet (H), the numbers denoting the divisions of the scale decrease in succession from red to violet, in the reverse order of Kirchhoff's uniform scale. An eighth part of the original drawing, in which the line F is included, is given in Fig. 88. This line is situated close to the division of the scale marked 4860, whence it may be concluded that the wave-length of the greenish-blue color corresponding to the F-line amounts to 0.0004860 of a millimetre. The lines to the right of F possessing a greater wave-length are toward the red, while those to

* [For the preparation of his normal solar spectrum, which is described in the text, and which is represented in an atlas of six maps, Ångström employed, in place of a prism, a *grating*—that is, a piece of plain glass ruled closely with fine lines. This grating was placed in the position in which usually a prism is placed, between the object-glass of the collimator and that of the observing telescope. Three gratings were employed by Ångström, one containing 4,501 lines within the length of nine Paris lines, a second having 2,701 lines, and a third 1,501 lines, within the same length. The spectrum from a grating by diffraction, unlike that produced by a prism, is always truly normal—that is, the relative distances of the Fraunhofer lines correspond precisely with the differences of wave-length of the light in the parts of the spectrum where they occur.]

† Recherches sur le Spectre solaire, par A. J. Angström. Spectre Normal du Soleil, Atlas de six planches. Upsal, W. Schultz. (Berlin, F. Dümmler, 1869.)

Fig. 88.

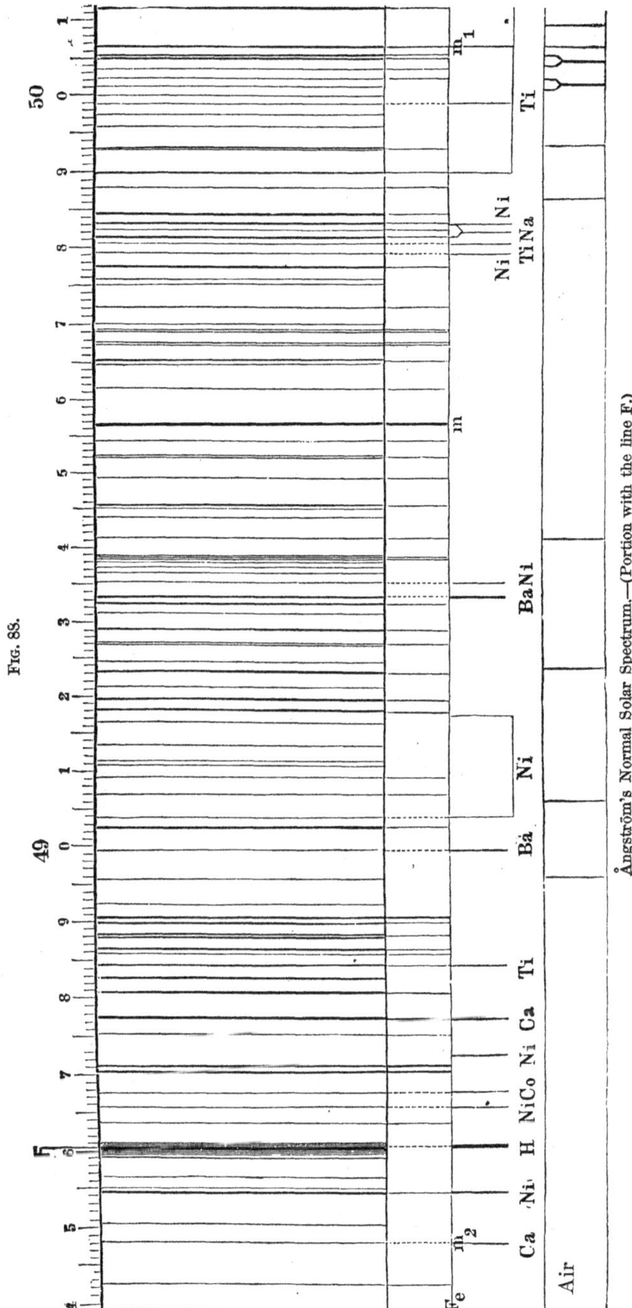

Ångström's Normal Solar Spectrum.—(Portion with the line F.)

the left are in the direction of the violet. The line marked m in the figure corresponds to a color possessing a wave-length of 0.00049565 of a millimetre, that marked m_1 to a wave-length of 0.00050064 of a millimetre, that marked m_2 to a wave-length of 0.00048481 of a millimetre, etc.

Ångström determined the wave-lengths of the principal lines in the solar spectrum to be as follows:

A	0.00076009 Mm.	b_1	0.00051830 Mm.
a	0.00071850 "	b_2	0.00051720 "
B	0.00068668 "	b_3	0.00051667 "
C	0.00065618 "	F	0.00048606 "
D_1	0.00058950 "	G	0.00043072 "
D_2	0.00058890 "	h	0.00041012 "
E	0.00052689 "	H_1	0.00039680 "
		H_2	0.00039328 "

[These maps are given in Plates IV., V., and VI.: they are about one-half the size of the original drawings, and are inserted by the translators with the kind permission of Prof. Ångström.]

44. Coincidence of the Dark Fraunhofer Lines with the Bright Spectrum Lines of Terrestrial Elements.—Kirchhoff's Maps.

From the coincidence previously observed by Fraunhofer of the two dark lines in the solar spectrum designated by him D, with the two bright lines which Kirchhoff and Bunsen discovered to be those of sodium, Kirchhoff was induced to put this coincidence to the most direct test by obtaining a tolerably bright solar spectrum, and then bringing a sodium-flame in front of the slit of the spectroscope.

"I saw," says Kirchhoff, "the dark lines D change into bright ones. The flame of a Bunsen lamp showed the sodium lines on the solar spectrum with an unexpected brilliancy. In order to find out how far the intensity of the solar spectrum might be increased without impairing the distinctness of the sodium lines, I allowed direct sunlight to fall upon the slit through the sodium-flame, and saw to my astonishment the dark lines D standing out with extraordinary clearness. I replaced the light of the sun by Drummond's light, the spectrum of which, like that of every other incandescent solid or liquid body, contains no dark lines; when this light was allowed to pass through

ANGSTROM'S AND THALÉN'S MAPS OF THE SOLAR SPECTRUM FROM α TO a.

α

70 71 72 73

0 1 2 3 4 5 6 7 8 9 0 1 2 3 4 5 6 7 8 9 0 1 2 3 4 5 6 7 8 9 0 1 2

Fe

B

67 68 69 70

8 9 0 1 2 3 4 5 6 7 8 9 0 1 2 3 4 5 6 7 8 9 0 1 2 3 4 5 6 7 8 9 0

Fe

Ca

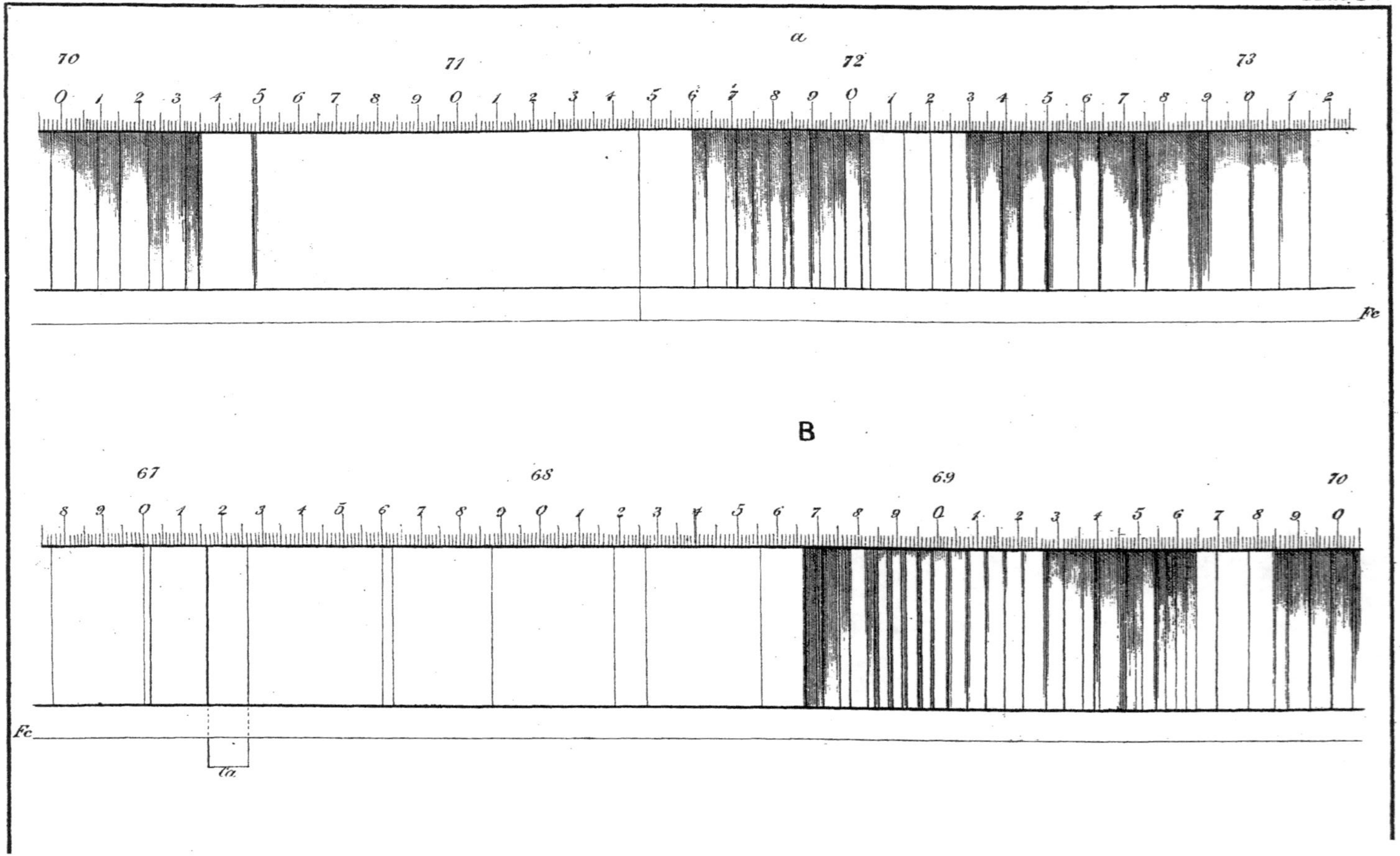

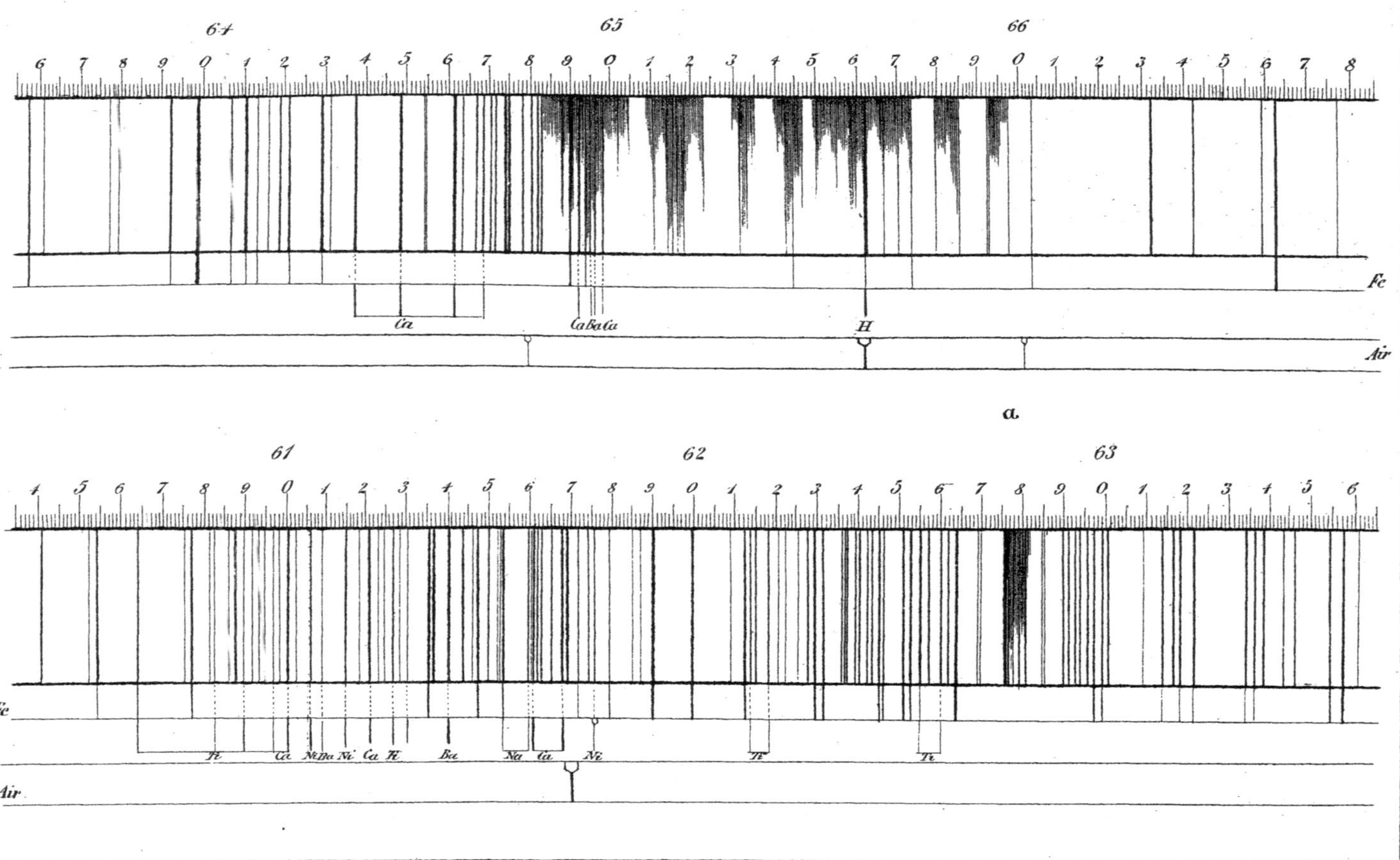

64
65
66
Ca
CaBaCa
H
Fe
Air
a.
61
62
63
Fe
Ca
Ba
Na
Ca
Ni
Air

Plate V.

ANGSTROM'S AND THALEN'S MAPS OF THE SOLAR SPECTRUM FROM D TO F.

D

58 59 60

Fe

Atmospheric Zone

Ba Ca Ba Ca Ti Na Ni Na Ti Ti Mn

Air

54 55 56 57

Fe

Ti Cr Ti Ti Ni Ti Ti Ba Mg Ba Ti Ca Ti Na Ti Ti

Air

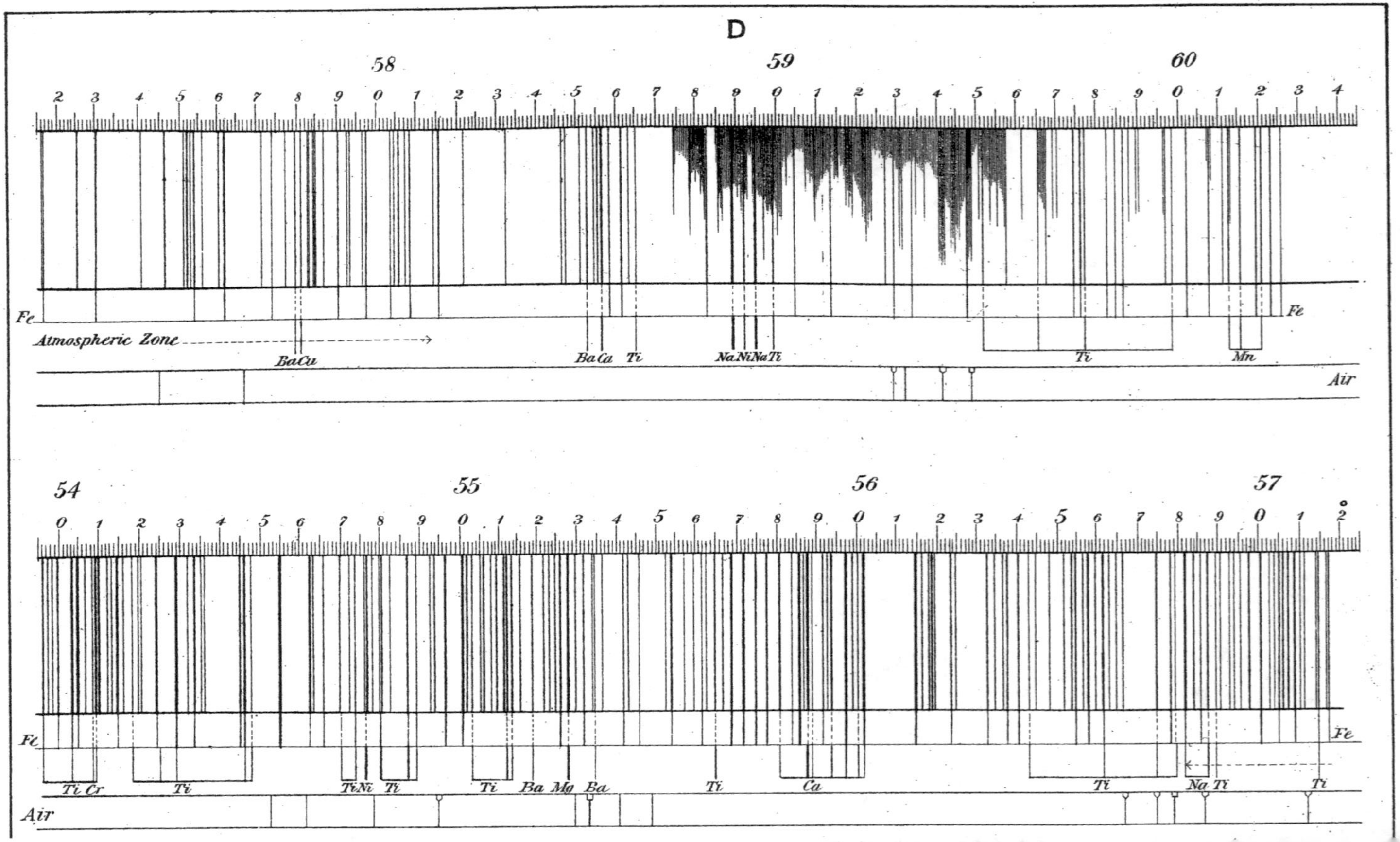

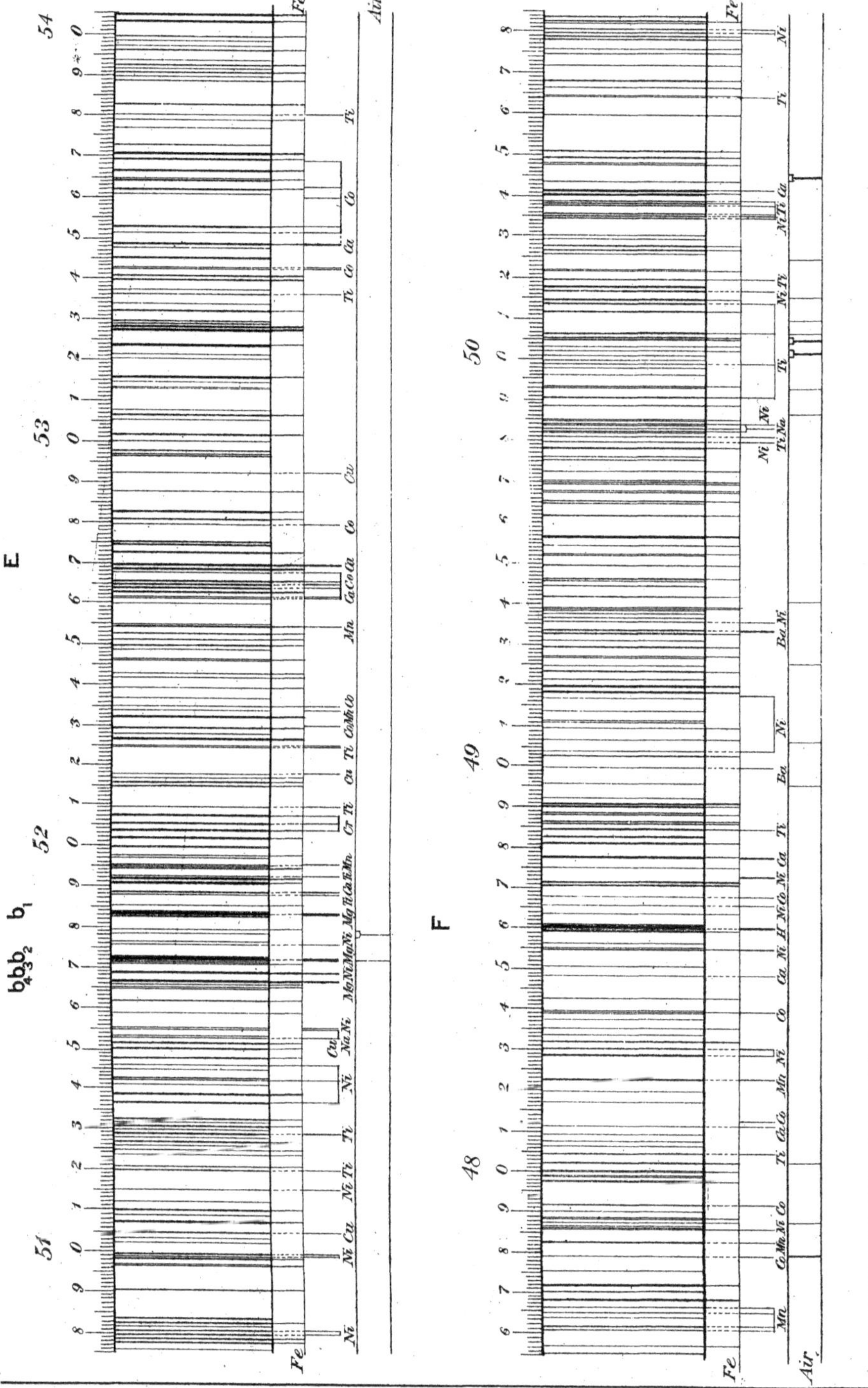

ÅNGSTRÖM'S AND THALÉN'S MAPS OF THE SOLAR SPECTRUM FROM G TO H_2

Plate VI.

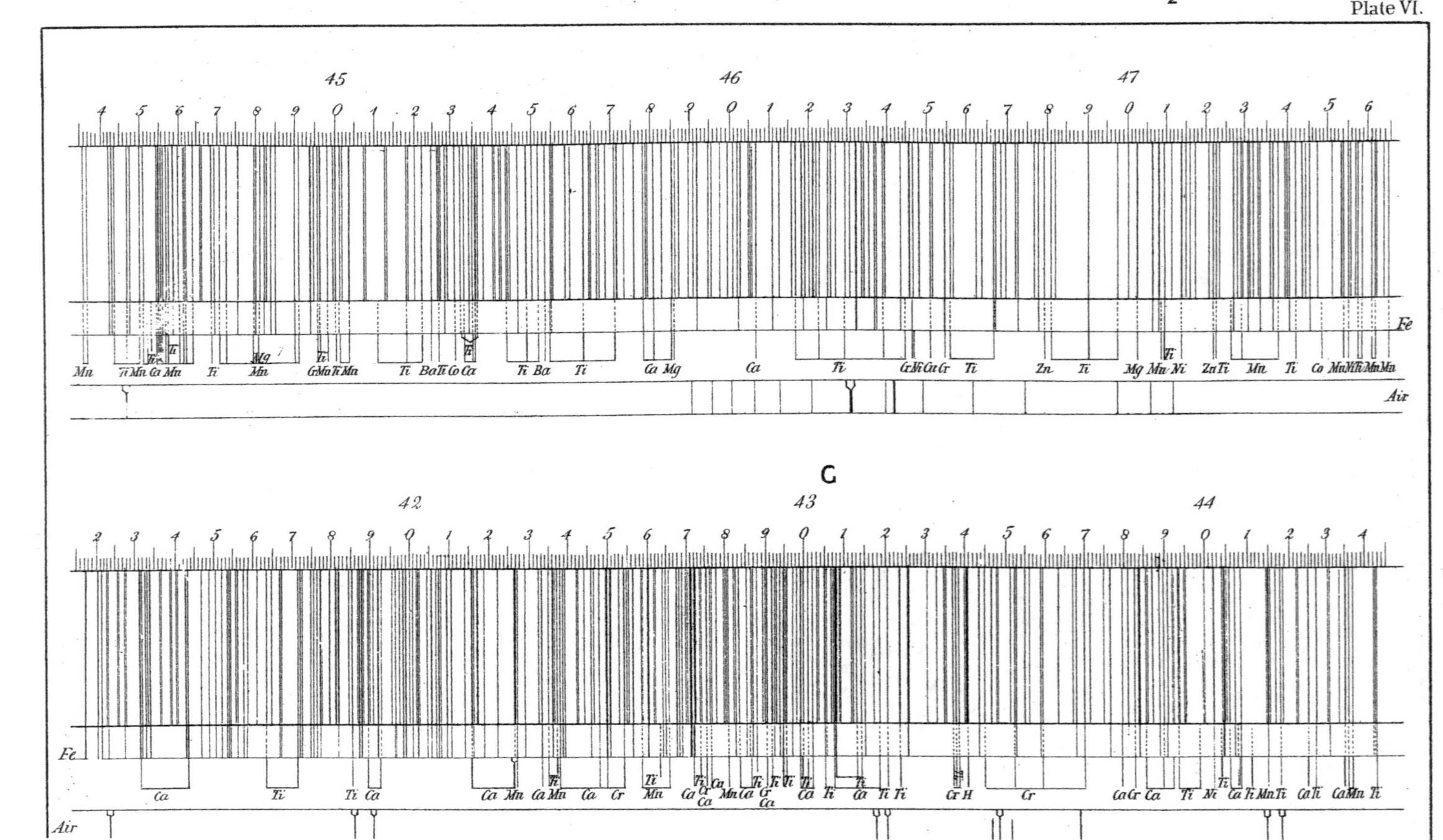

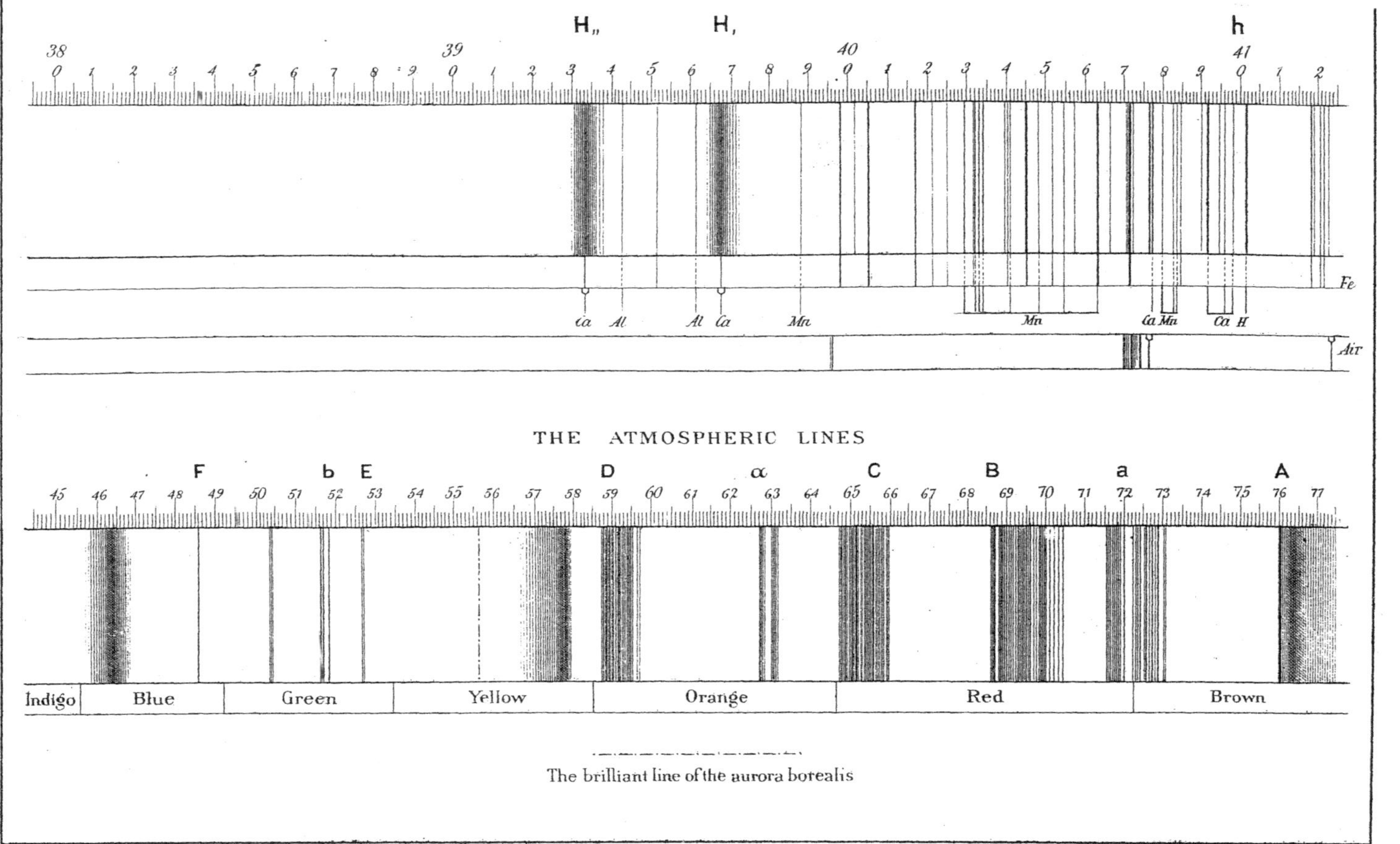

THE ATMOSPHERIC LINES

a flame in which salt was burning, dark lines appeared in the spectrum in the position of the sodium lines. The same thing occurred when, instead of a cylinder of incandescent lime, a platinum wire was used, which, after being made to glow in a flame, was brought nearly to its melting-point by the electric current."

Kirchhoff could no longer doubt, from these observations, that the existence of the dark lines D in the solar spectrum was due to the presence of vapor of sodium in the sun, and that they must be produced in the sun by *reversion* (absorption), in a manner similar to that shown in the experiments already described with terrestrial sodium.

After the existence of sodium had been thus suspected in the sun with so great an amount of probability, Kirchhoff commenced the arduous undertaking of comparing the spectra of a variety of terrestrial substances with the spectrum of the sun, to determine whether any of the spectrum lines of these substances, and if so which of them, coincided with the Fraunhofer lines; that is to say, if they appeared in the spectroscope in the same place, and were of similar breadth and intensity.

We have already made acquaintance with the method by which such a comparison may be made by means of two spectra in the same instrument (§ 28). Kirchhoff allowed the light of the sun to fall directly into the spectroscope, and on to the first large prism through the *lower* half of the slit, while the *upper* half was covered by the small prism for comparison: the rays from an artificial source of light placed at the side were so reflected by the prism into the instrument that, while the solar spectrum with the Fraunhofer lines was seen in the upper half of the field of view in the (inverting) telescope, there appeared below, and in immediate contact with it, the spectrum of the artificial light. In this way the position of the bright lines of this spectrum could be compared with great accuracy with that of the dark lines of the solar spectrum.

The artificial light employed by Kirchhoff was almost exclusively that of the induction spark from a powerful Ruhmkorff coil, with electrodes of small pieces of such metals as he wished to volatilize in order to obtain their spectra.

By the comparison of these spectra with the dark lines of the solar spectrum, Kirchhoff arrived at the surprising result, that the bright lines of several metals were entirely coincident with the same number of lines in the solar spectrum.

The coincidence of the two sodium lines D is shown in Fig. 89; the upper part represents that portion of the solar spectrum with the two dark D-lines which is situated in the yellow, between 100 and 101 millimetres of Kirchhoff's scale; the lower

FIG. 89.

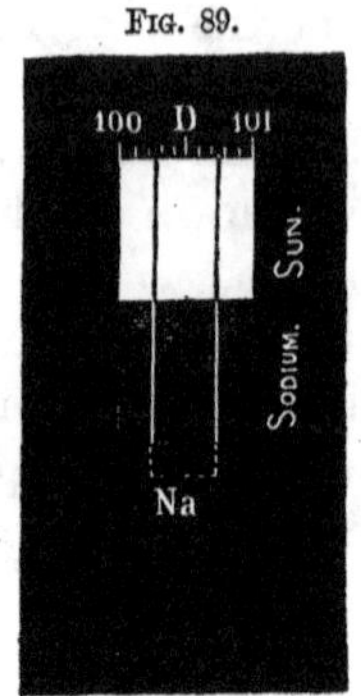

Coincidence of the Fraunhofer D-Lines with the Lines of Sodium.

part shows the bright lines given by sodium-vapor rendered luminous either by the electric spark or the flame of a lamp; and both pairs of lines occupy so precisely the same position in the spectrum that one forms the exact prolongation of the other. In a very perfect instrument, another fine line, corresponding to a bright line given by nickel, appears between the two dark lines.*

Two portions of the spectrum, the one situated in the yellow between 120 and 125 of Kirchhoff's scale, and the other in the green between 150 and 154, are represented in Fig. 90. The lower thirteen bright lines, designated Fe.=Ferrum (iron), are lines in the spectrum of iron; they fall in exact accordance with an equal number of dark lines in the solar spectrum. The remaining twelve bright lines indicated by dots belong to the spectrum of calcium, and are coincident with as many dark lines in the solar spectrum. Between these dark lines in Kirchhoff's drawing are several other lines, some of which coincide with the bright lines of terrestrial substances, while others are due to some other effects of absorption.

* [There is at least one fine line between D_1 and D_2 which belongs to sodium, and which may be seen as a bright line when a source of light containing sodium is examined.]

Plates II. and III. contain all the dark lines measured by Kirchhoff in the spectrum of the sun, and below the solar spectrum are marked in black the lines of those terrestrial elements with which he had compared them in the usual manner. These substances are designated by their chemical symbols: thus, Fe.

FIG. 90.

Coincidence of the Fraunhofer Lines with the Lines of Iron and Calcium.

= Ferrum (iron), Ca. = Calcium, Pb. = Plumbum (lead), Hg. = Hydrargyrum (mercury), Na. = Natrium (sodium), Ba. = Barium, Mg. = Magnesium, Au. = Aurum (gold), H. = Hydrogenium (hydrogen gas), etc. The horizontal lines by which the lower ends of the vertical spectrum lines are grouped together indicate that all lines thus bracketed belong to the same substance, the chemical symbol of which is placed below.

The wave-lengths of the bright spectrum lines of terrestrial substances have in the same manner been determined by Ångström and Thalén, the latter of whom has devoted himself especially to this subject; the coincidence of these lines with the dark lines of the solar spectrum has been proved by these observers, and recorded in their maps by inserting them beneath the solar spectrum (*vide* Fig. 88, Plates IV., V., VI.).

Even in the portion of the spectrum published by Kirchhoff there are some sixty bright lines of iron, all of which coincide with as many of the dark Fraunhofer lines; the continuation made by Hofmann contains thirteen additional very striking coincidences, and Ångström and Thalén, who volatilized iron in the electric arc, found a coincidence of more than 460 bright lines of iron, with an equal number of the Fraunhofer lines.

The complete coincidence of so many bright lines in one and

the same substance with the same number of dark lines of the solar spectrum, shows conclusively that it cannot be the effect of chance. A glance at Fig. 91, in which the coincidence is shown of more than sixty of Kirchhoff's observed lines of iron, with as many dark lines in various parts of the solar spectrum between C and F, justifies the conclusion that those dark lines are to be ascribed to the absorptive effect of the vapor of iron present in the atmosphere of the sun. The likelihood that such a coincidence of sixty lines is a mere chance, bears a proportion to the supposition that these lines really make known the presence of iron in the sun's atmosphere, according to the doctrine of probabilities, of 1 to 2^{60}, or in other words in the ratio of 1 to 1,152,930,000,000,000,000.

Fig. 91.

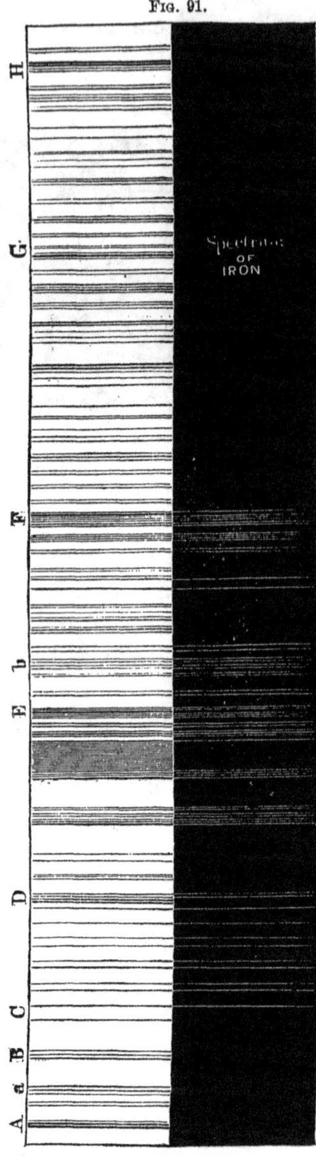

Coincidence of the Spectrum of Iron with 65 of the Fraunhofer Lines.

The most striking coincidences between the spectrum lines of terrestrial elements and the dark lines of the solar spectrum are shown in iron, sodium, potassium, calcium, magnesium, manganese, chromium, nickel, and hydrogen; the spectrum lines of these substances not only agree exactly with the dark lines in *position* and *breadth*, but proclaim their relationship to them by a similar degree of intensity. The brighter, for instance, a spectrum line appears, so much the darker will its corresponding line be in the solar spectrum.

A partial coincidence only of the bright and dark lines is shown in the spectra of the metals zinc, barium, copper, cobalt, and gold, where the brightest lines only correspond with the dark lines of the solar spectrum. Thalén has lately discovered that the greater number of the 170 bright lines given by the metal titanium correspond with as many of the Fraunhofer lines; his investigations, which extend over forty-five metals, fully confirm the observations of Kirchhoff.

The spectra of the metals silver, mercury, antimony, arsenic, tin, lead, cadmium, strontium, and lithium, show no coincidence with the Fraunhofer lines, and this is also the case with the two non-metallic substances silicon and oxygen.

45. Kirchhoff's Theory of the Physical Constitution of the Sun:

It had long been assumed that the gaps in the colors of the solar spectrum which form the Fraunhofer dark lines were due to an absorption of the corresponding colored rays in the atmosphere of the sun; but no explanation could be given of this phenomenon. The cause of this absorption was ascertained by Kirchhoff in his discovery that a vapor absorbs from white light just those rays which it emits when luminous (§ 40), and he proved the whole system of the Fraunhofer lines to be mainly produced by the overlying of the reversed spectra of such substances as are to be found in the earth. He thus arrived at a new conception of the physical constitution of the sun which is entirely opposed to the theories held by Wilson and Sir William Herschel in explanation of the solar spots.

According to Kirchhoff, the sun consists of a *solid* or *partially-liquid* nucleus in the highest state of incandescence, which emits, like all incandescent solid or liquid bodies, every possible kind of light, and therefore would of itself give a *continuous* spectrum without any dark lines. This incandescent central nucleus is surrounded by an *atmosphere* of lower temperature, containing, on account of the extreme heat of the nucleus, the vapors of many of the substances of which this body is composed. The rays of light therefore emitted by the nucleus must pass through this atmosphere before reaching the earth, and each vapor extinguishes from the white light those rays which it would itself emit in a glowing state. Now, it is found when the sun's light is analyzed by a prism that a multitude of rays are extinguished, and just those rays which would be emitted by the vapors of sodium, iron, calcium, magnesium, etc., were they made self-luminous; consequently the vapors of the following substances, sodium, iron, potassium, calcium, barium, magnesium, manganese, titanium, chromium, nickel, cobalt, hydrogen, and probably also zinc, copper, and gold, must exist in the solar atmosphere, and these metals therefore must also be present to a considerable extent in the body of the sun. According to the investigations of Ångström, the number of the bright lines of the following substances coincident with an equal number of the Fraunhofer dark lines is as follows: sodium 9, iron 450, calcium 75, barium 11, magnesium 4, manganese 57, titanium 118, chromium 18, nickel 33, cobalt 19, hydrogen 4, aluminium 2, zinc 2, copper 7.

It appears therefore indubitable that the substances composing the body of the sun are similar to those of which the earth is formed, for though there may be between F and G some conspicuous dark lines the origin of which is as yet unknown, it would be premature to say that they were occasioned by substances foreign to this earth.

Could the light from the sun's nucleus in any way be set aside, and only that of the incandescent vapors of the sun's atmosphere be received through the slit of the spectroscope, a spectrum would then be obtained composed of the actual spectra of these substances, that is to say, the same system of bright-colored lines which now appear as the dark Fraunhofer lines. The occurrence of a total solar eclipse affords an opportunity of applying such a test for Kirchhoff's theory, for, as the sun's disk is then completely covered by the moon, and all light from the body of the sun is intercepted, no light can be received except from the solar atmosphere and the glowing vapors by which the nucleus is surrounded.

The results of the observations of the solar eclipses of 1868 and 1869 did not fulfil the expectations that had been entertained; for, though the Fraunhofer lines ceased to be visible the moment when, with the disappearance of the last rays of the sun, total darkness commenced, the system of bright lines did not appear in their stead, which, as the spectra of the glowing vapors of the solar atmosphere were still in view, was to be expected.*

* [At the total eclipse of 1870, Prof. Young observed all the Fraunhofer lines reversed. His observations, which seem to enable us to fix with precision the birthplace of the Fraunhofer lines, are described by Prof. Langley as follows:

"With the slit of his spectroscope placed longitudinally at the moment of obscura-

It would, however, be premature to form a conclusion against Kirchhoff's theory from these negative results; for it may easily be presumed that the vapors of the solar atmosphere do not possess that degree of heat which would be necessary to produce a light sufficiently intense for creating gas-spectra at such an enormous distance (ninety-two million miles); indeed, the great darkness and even blackness of many of the Fraunhofer lines justifies the conclusion that the difference of temperature must be very considerable between the sun's nucleus and the atmosphere of vapor by which, according to Kirchhoff's theory, it is surrounded. And if on other grounds, to which reference will be made hereafter, it were admitted that the supposition of the sun's nucleus being an incandescent solid or liquid body were untenable, yet Kirchhoff's explanation of the Fraunhofer lines, and his proof of the presence of elements in the sun similar to those found in the earth, would still remain unaffected. Even if the nucleus of the sun were, as the French astronomer Faye supposes, neither solid nor liquid, but in a condition of vapor or gas, there is still no doubt that either the ball of gas itself in consequence of the extreme heat is incandescent, and would therefore emit rays of every shade of color—proof of which has been furnished by the experiments of Frankland, Deville, and Wüllner (p. 117), in accordance with the views of De la Rue, Stewart, and Loewy—of which rays those corresponding to the Fraunhofer lines would be absorbed by the cooler outside strata, or else the ball of gas, if non-luminous, is surrounded by a stratum of vapor partially condensed, forming a cloud in a condition of extreme heat, called the *photosphere*, whence emanates the white solar light, and in which the absorption of the vapors composing it takes place in the same way as occurs in the direct volatilization of sodium by the electric light (p. 148).

tion, and for one or two seconds later, the field of the instrument was filled with bright lines. As far as could be judged, during this brief interval, every non-atmospheric line of the solar spectrum showed bright; an interesting observation confirmed by Mr. Pye, a young gentleman whose voluntary aid proved of much service. From the concurrence of these independent observations, we seem to be justified in assuming the probable existence of an envelope surrounding the photosphere, and beneath the chromosphere, usually so called, whose thickness must be limited to two or three seconds of arc, and which gives a discontinuous spectrum consisting of all, or nearly all, the Fraunhofer lines showing them, that is, *bright* on a dark ground."]

We shall enter upon these theories more in detail hereafter, but this much may be said here: that every explanation of the physical constitution of the sun must always be based upon the discoveries of Kirchhoff; and the various details of any theory in explanation of the solar spots, the faculæ, the prominences, etc., must be in strict accordance with the phenomena established by Kirchhoff of the absorption of the colored rays and the reversal of the spectrum.

46. The Atmospheric Lines in the Solar Spectrum as observed by Brewster and Gladstone.

The Italian physicist Zantedeschi, of whom we have already spoken, was the first to remark that the dark lines in the solar spectrum are not all invariable, and that the changes occurring in number, position, intensity, and breadth, in some of them are due to the varying condition of the earth's atmosphere. This subject has since occupied the attention of Brewster and Gladstone, Piazzi Smyth, Secchi, and preëminently the French physicist Janssen, but their investigations have not as yet led to any satisfactory result.

Brewster and Gladstone (1860 *) found that new dark lines and bands made their appearance in the solar spectrum when the sun approached the horizon, and that certain dark bands were more strongly marked in the morning and evening than at noon when the sun stood high in the heavens. As the sun when near the horizon must transmit its rays through a stratum of air nearly fifteen times as thick as when at a high altitude at noon, the idea was suggested that the atmospheric air, though colorless, might exercise an absorptive influence upon the light, and obstruct the rays as vapors do (§ 38), in proportion as the stratum increases in thickness and density through which the solar rays have to pass.

The solar spectrum published by Brewster and Gladstone in 1860, nearly five feet in length, contains more than 2,000 visible dark lines or bands, easily distinguishable one from another. The violet end extends as far as in Fraunhofer's map, while in the direction of the red it is of considerably greater length.

* [Brewster in 1832 discovered that certain dark lines, seen under the conditions mentioned in the text, in the solar spectrum, were caused by atmospheric absorption.]

The Fraunhofer lines retain their original designations A, a, B, etc., while the lines and bands interspersed between them, and clearly separable one from the other, are marked by figures after the letters A, B, C, etc., in succession toward the violet, always commencing with 1. Thus between A and a there lie three bands, marked A_1, A_2, A_3; between a and B there are eight lines or bands, marked a_1, a_2, . . . a_8. There are seven lines between B and C, sixteen between C and D, twenty-nine between D and E, ten between E and b, thirty between b and F, fifty between F and G, fifty-three between G and H, four between H and k, and ten between k and I, each line marked by a number, beginning always with 1. Besides these prominent lines, there are many very fine lines interspersed among them which are not enumerated. Those lines and bands which are preëminently influenced by atmospheric conditions, and are, therefore, more or less prominent according to the altitude of the sun, are designated by the letters of the Greek alphabet.

The solar spectrum given in Fig. 92 is taken from a reduced drawing by Brewster, and represents not only the Fraunhofer lines, but also all the variable lines and bands of any importance which are easily discernible, and which are here marked by the Greek letters; the numbers are omitted. The drawing shows the spectrum as it appears when the sun is near the horizon; all the lines and bands marked by the Greek letters disappear from the spectrum, or become more or less pale as the sun attains a meridian altitude. These bands were named by Brewster and Gladstone *atmospheric* lines, to indicate that they were formed by the absorptive power of the earth's atmosphere; these observers did not succeed, however, in ascertaining to what elements in the atmospheric air this selective absorption was to be ascribed.

FIG. 92.—The Brewster-Gladstone Solar Spectrum, with the Atmospheric Lines.

In the least refrangible portion of the spectrum two intensely dark bands appear at sunrise in front of A, bordered on both sides by a fine line Y Z. A increases much in breadth, and preserves this width even when the sun has a considerable altitude. When A is observed at noon, it appears as a double line, or like two dark spaces separated by a narrow band of light; when the sun is setting, this bright stripe disappears, and the line is seen as *one* band of uniform width and intensity. The group *a* increases in intensity toward sunset, but the individual lines do not subside into one band. The strongest absorption takes place close to B. C and most of the lines between C and C_6 become darker, and C_6 (in the orange) is especially remarkable, as it deepens in intensity while the sun is yet high in the heavens. In England, this line is visible during the whole day in winter, but not in summer; at sunrise and sunset it is one of the darkest and best-defined lines in the whole spectrum. C_{15} increases toward evening to a black band, and the double line D becomes at the same time very prominent. Behind D_2, a band, marked δ, begins, which is specially characteristic of the spectrum of light that has passed through a thick stratum of air. Even in a small spectroscope, this band may be readily seen at any hour of a dull day in the diffused light, but it is particularly dark and well defined during heavy rain or a thunder-storm, and at sunset it becomes almost black. The same is noticed in the bands ϵ and ζ, as also in the line η, which is very distinct at evening, and from its proximity to E, which remains unaffected by the atmosphere, may easily be mistaken for it. On the farther side of *b* are several other remarkable atmospheric bands, particularly *i* and *x*. F loses its sharpness at sunset, and seven bands from λ to ς become visible between F and G. At G the only change is a loss of brightness toward evening, but a still greater amount of absorption takes place beyond, in the violet rays.

The western sky, immediately after sunset, affords the best opportunity for observing these dark atmospheric lines, especially the bands δ and ζ in the bright parts of the spectrum. If at that time the sky be red, the lines C, C_6, D, δ, appear generally as four very dark bands, but when the sky is yellow they are much less distinctly marked.*

* [Mr. J. H. Hennessy, to whom a spectroscope was intrusted by the Royal Society for observations of the atmospheric lines of the solar spectrum at different

47. The Telluric Lines in the Solar Spectrum and the Spectrum of Aqueous Vapor, as observed by Janssen.

The investigations of Brewster and Gladstone were resumed by the French physicist Janssen, in 1864, for the purpose of discovering what substance in the atmosphere produced the selective absorption of the solar spectrum. With an instrument of his own construction, composed of five prisms, he succeeded at once in resolving the dark bands noticed by the English observers into very fine lines, and in ascertaining that their intensity was perpetually varying. He found them to be darkest at sunrise and sunset, and less intense in the middle of the day, but they were never entirely absent from the spectrum, a periodicity of change which at once proves their atmospheric origin. To procure still more decisive evidence on this point, Janssen resolved to pursue his observations on the solar spectrum from the top of a high mountain, whence the absorptive influence of the lower and denser stratum of the atmosphere would be excluded, and the effects of absorption consequently would be manifested in a more moderate degree than on the plain.

For this purpose, in the year 1864 Janssen remained for a week at the summit of the Faulhorn, at a height of 3,000 metres (about 9,000 feet) above the sea, and convinced himself that the variable dark lines in the solar spectrum were, in reality, much fainter there than in the plain. But, in order to discover the real origin of this absorption, and to obtain proof that these lines were produced only by the earth's atmosphere, he devoted himself to the examination of artificial light, since the light of the sun in travelling to the earth has to pass for millions of miles through foreign media.

In October, 1864, he caused a large pile of pine-wood to be set on fire at Geneva, at a distance of 21,000 metres (about thirteen miles) from his place of observation, and observed the flame in the spectroscope; when viewed near, the fire gave a continuous spectrum without dark lines, but at the full distance some of the dark lines appeared which Brewster had observed in the spectrum of the setting sun.

altitudes of the sun at the favorable position of Mussoorie has sent in a first report of his observations, together with a chart of the atmospheric lines as seen by him at sunset. This map has been printed in "The Proceedings of the Royal Society," vol. xix., p. 1, and may be found of assistance to those who are studying these lines.]

It remained now for Janssen to determine with yet greater certainty whether this atmospheric absorption was to be ascribed to the air, or to the aqueous vapor contained in the air, an investigation beset with unusual difficulties, which could only at last be accomplished when, in 1866, the Gas Company of Paris placed their apparatus at his disposal.

An iron cylinder 118 feet long, after being exhausted of air by forcing steam through it under a pressure of seven atmospheres, was filled with steam, and closed at both ends by pieces of strong plate glass. The cylinder was surrounded with sawdust to prevent radiation, and additional contrivances were also adopted to preserve the steam from condensation, and so to maintain its transparency. A very bright flame (produced by sixteen united gas-burners) was placed at one end of the cylinder, and the spectroscope at the other, so that the rays from the flame had to pass through a stratum of aqueous vapor 118 feet thick before reaching the slit of the instrument. The spectrum of the light in the air was entirely free from absorption lines; but, seen through the cylinder of steam, there at once appeared groups of dark lines between the extreme red and the line D, similar to those seen in the spectrum of the setting sun. By this means, not only was the proof furnished that a large number of the variable lines in the solar spectrum are due to the presence of aqueous vapor in the earth's atmosphere, but also a method secured for detecting the presence of aqueous vapor in the heavenly bodies.

Fig. 93 represents the solar spectrum between the lines C and D as drawn by Janssen; the upper half is the spectrum of the sun in the meridian, the lower half that of the sun at the horizon (*vide* p. 177). Those lines which present the same appearance in both halves belong exclusively to the sun, while those which are darker in the lower than in the upper half are *telluric lines.*

It has been further shown by Janssen that almost all telluric lines are produced by the *aqueous vapor* of the earth's atmosphere; that an absorptive influence is also exerted by this vapor on the invisible portion of the solar spectrum beyond the red (that is to say, in the heat-spectrum), where it produces absorption lines; and, finally, that it affects the whole of the violet portion of the spectrum in a manner more nearly uniform than selective.

The absorption spectrum of aqueous vapor consists, therefore, of all the lines introduced into the continuous spectrum by the aqueous vapor of the earth's atmosphere: it is an absorption spectrum which may be easily constructed for the portion between C and D by leaving out all those lines from the lower part of Fig. 93 which agree exactly in appearance with those in the upper half. It has been proved that the groups marked C β and D arise from the aqueous vapor in the atmosphere; the *telluric* character of the central group C γ has been also established by Janssen beyond a doubt, but as yet it remains uncertain whether they are likewise to be attributed to aqueous vapor.

The investigations of Janssen were not confined merely to that portion of the solar spectrum included between C and D; he continued the spectrum in another map, where it reaches below the line B and beyond D; in this spectrum are included also the three groups marked by Brewster α, β, γ, δ (Fig. 92). Janssen has extended his observations to the light of the moon and fixed stars,* with the view of ascertaining if the stellar light, which differs from that of the sun, be subject to similar changes in its passage through the earth's atmosphere.

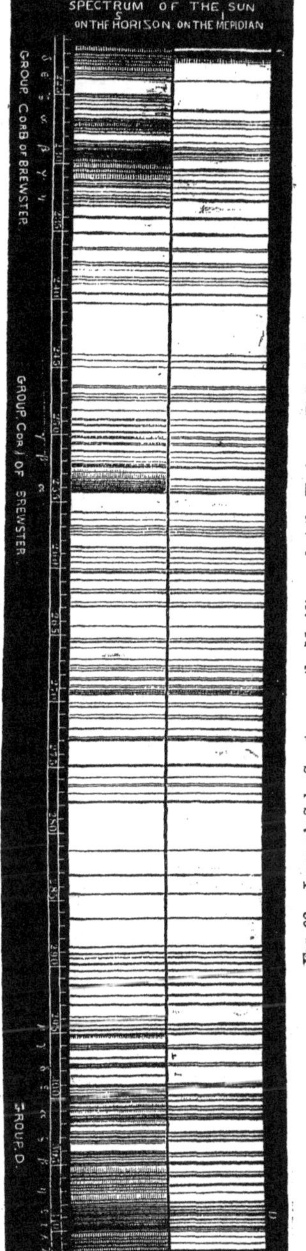

Fig. 93.—Janssen's Solar Spectrum on the Meridian and at the Horizon. (Telluric Lines.)

* Janssen, "Rapport sur une Mission en Italie." Paris, Imprimerie impériale, 1868.

With this object Janssen attached a small direct-vision spectroscope to a powerful astronomical telescope, in the manner described more in detail in the section on stellar spectroscopes, and examined the spectrum of Sirius, as the star appeared above the horizon. In its very bright spectrum were several dark bands, which when measured were found to occupy precisely the same position as the dark bands that appeared in the solar spectrum at sunrise and sunset. In proportion as Sirius gained in altitude, the intensity of these telluric bands gradually diminished, until as the star passed the meridian they entirely disappeared.

Fig. 94 gives the spectrum of the sun (I I) and the spectrum of Sirius (I) as they appeared in the small spectroscope when observed in the meridian and at the horizon. The telluric bands will be recognized at once on comparing the two spectra of the same object; the dark bands marked 1, 2, 3, are evidently telluric absorption bands common to both the sun and Sirius when near the horizon.

Secchi has also been occupied for many years in observing the telluric lines of the solar spectrum. From the first he expressed an opinion that the existence of these dark lines, which vary with the place of the sun, the position of the observer, and the amount of humidity in the air, were to be ascribed to the absorptive action of the aqueous vapor contained in the atmosphere. The influence of the weather was apparent in the fact that some of

Fig. 94.

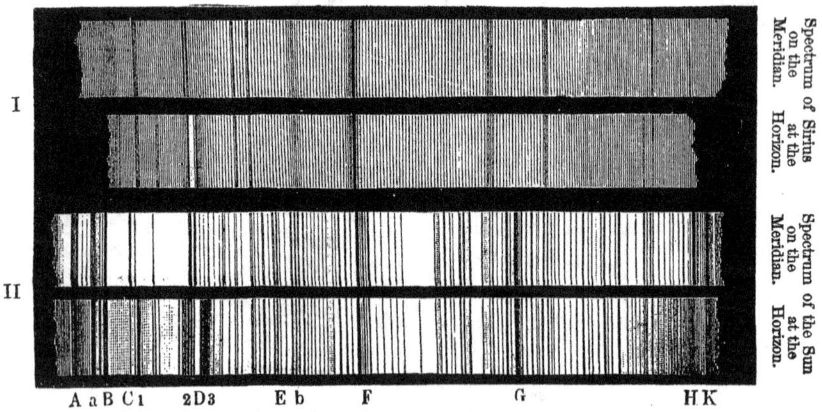

these lines were invisible in clear weather with a north wind, while they were strongly marked on dull days with the wind in the south. Secchi has also observed and measured the dark absorption lines during rainy weather in the spectrum of a flame distant 2,000 metres ($1\frac{1}{4}$=mile), as well as in that of large fires kindled on the mountains.

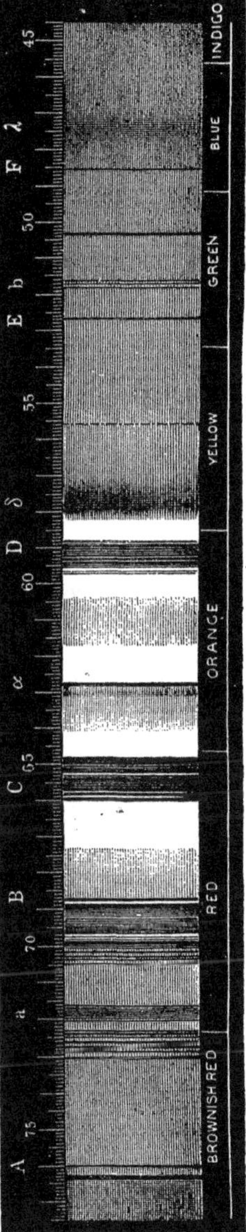

Fig. 95.—The Telluric Lines in the Solar Spectrum, after Ångström.

Ångström, of Upsala, has also instituted careful investigations of the telluric lines in the solar spectrum, and has introduced these lines into his maps (§ 43, Plate VI.), measured according to the wave-lengths of the colors they absorbed. In Fig. 95 a map of these lines is given on a reduced scale; the lines and bands there shown are all atmospheric lines with the exception of the Fraunhofer lines C, D, E, *b*, F. The order of the phenomena produced by the absorptive power of the atmosphere as the sun approaches the horizon is thus described by Ångström:

The violet portion of the spectrum disappears as far as G; the absorption then keeps advancing toward the red, and intensifies the dark bands near F and D. At the same time the lines A, B, and *a*, which are always visible in the red part of the spectrum, become much darker, and the lines of aqueous vapor both at C and D continually augment. At last the only parts remaining bright lie between B and *a*, between *a* and δ, and in the greater portion of the greenish yellow in the vicinity and to the right of δ, while the portion between B and δ is more or less shaded by dark bands. The part of the spectrum least affected by the telluric absorption lies between D and δ.

Ångström concurs with Brewster that nearly all the changes of color observed in the red glow of sunrise and sunset find a simple explanation in the phenomena of atmospheric absorption, whereby all the ingenious and elaborate explanations hitherto attempted are completely set aside.

Ångström is of opinion that the bands A, B, *a*, and *δ*, are not produced by the aqueous vapor of the atmosphere, since they are very constant, and are not affected apparently by changes of temperature; whether other gases contained in the atmospheric air, as, for instance, carbonic-acid gas, exercise an influence upon them, has yet to be investigated.

It is fully admitted that other heavenly bodies besides the earth may be surrounded by an atmosphere; Janssen's discovery of the spectrum of aqueous vapor furnishes the means of ascertaining whether this vapor, indispensable to the maintenance of all the living organisms of our planet, is also present in the other celestial bodies. Repeated observations undertaken by Janssen on the high mountains of Italy and Greece have already furnished proof that aqueous vapor is present in the atmospheres of the planets Mars and Saturn.

48. The Solar Spots—The Faculæ and their Spectra.

It would lead us too far from our subject were we to dwell upon the phenomena of the solar spots, important as they are for acquiring a knowledge of the physical constitution of the sun, or enter upon a full description of their form, their mode of formation and disappearance, their motion, their connection with the sun's rotation upon its axis, their periodic occurrence, and the various hypotheses that have been formed as to their nature; but, on the other hand, we must still less be silent on the subject, since spectrum analysis has investigated these wonderful appearances with a success which has added much to our knowledge of the constitution of the sun.

A number of excellent photographs and drawings have been made by Secchi, Nasmyth, Warren De la Rue, and others, of remarkable spots, showing very clearly the characteristic forms they assume, and the phenomena which accompany them. By means of a magnifying lantern and an intense light, these photographs may be thrown upon a screen and exhibited to a large audience. Spots similar to those shown in Fig. 96 and following figures consist principally of a dark, almost black, central portion, the *umbra*,* surrounded by a space somewhat less dark, called the *penumbra:* the umbra has generally an irregular form, while the penumbra exhibits a structure radiating toward the centre.

Fig. 96.

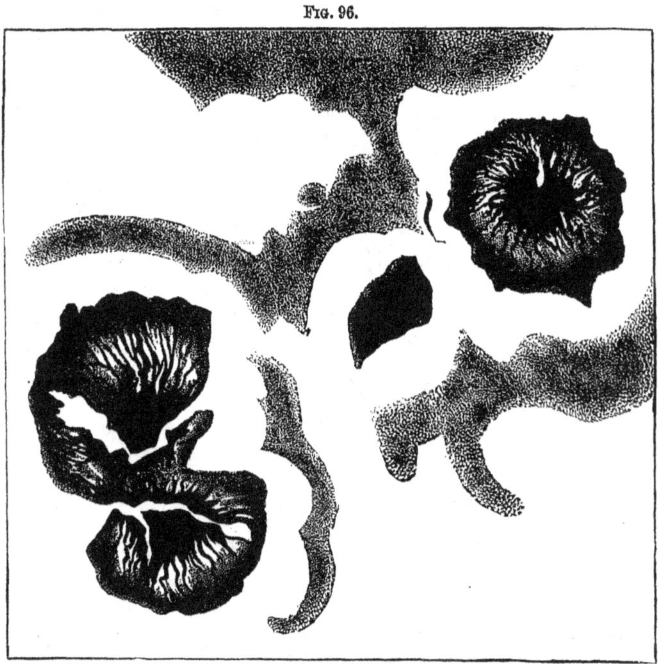

Solar Spot seen through a Large Telescope by Secchi, at Rome, April 3, 1858.

If the sun be observed with a high power, the surface presents by no means a uniform appearance; a multitude of bright and dark stripes cross each other in all directions, and the luminous surface appears like a net of bright meshes interwoven with dark threads and small dark pores. The brightest portions (Fig. 97) show a more or less elongated form (compare Fig. 101), which suggested to Nasmyth the name of "willow-leaves," while

* [The dark central part of a spot, called by the author "kern," has been distinguished throughout by the name *umbra*, in accordance with the usual custom of astronomers. Mr. Dawes showed that within this part of a spot one or more darker spots may generally be observed, to which he gave the name of *nucleus*.]

Dawes compares them to "bits of straw," and Huggins calls them merely "granules." *

Fig. 97.

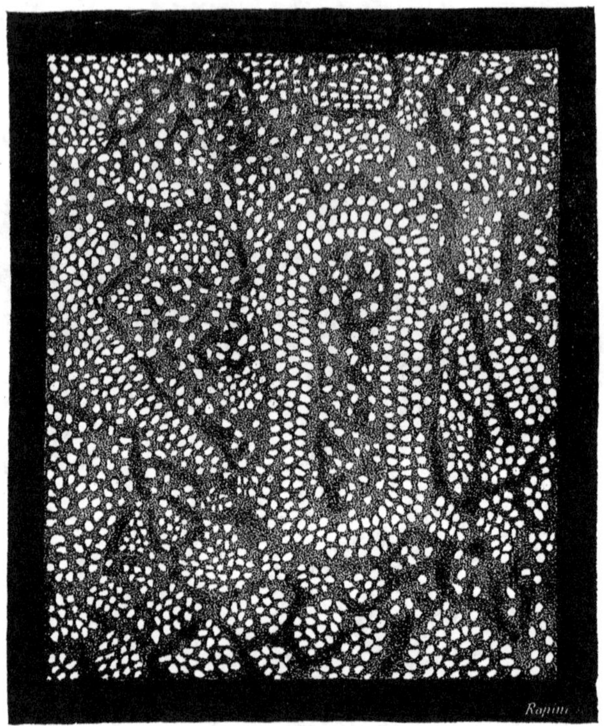

Granules and Pores of the Sun's Surface, after Huggins.

On this uneven and ever-varying bright background the spots make their appearance in the greatest variety of form and size. The penumbra not unfrequently stretches across the black

* [Dawes restricted the name *straws* to the objects of that shape in the immediate neighborhood of the spots, which appear to be formed either by the elongation of the normal granules, or by an aggregation of them under the influence of the forces which are present in the spots. The term *granules*, adopted by Huggins, was first suggested by Dawes for the solar particles in their *normal* form, that is, as they appear on the general surface of the sun, because, as he observed, "the appellation granulation or granules assumes nothing either as to their exact form or precise character." The observations of these astronomers agree in representing the granules to be generally of an oval form, but that irregularly-shaped masses of almost every form frequently present themselves. The average size of these particles may be taken to be about 1″ in diameter, and the average longer diameter of the more oval particles at about 1″.5.

central portion in various places, Fig. 98, and generally appears much darker at the outer edges, where the spot touches the bright part of the sun's surface, than in other places. Very often the penumbra is traversed by few or more bright curved bands,

FIG. 98.

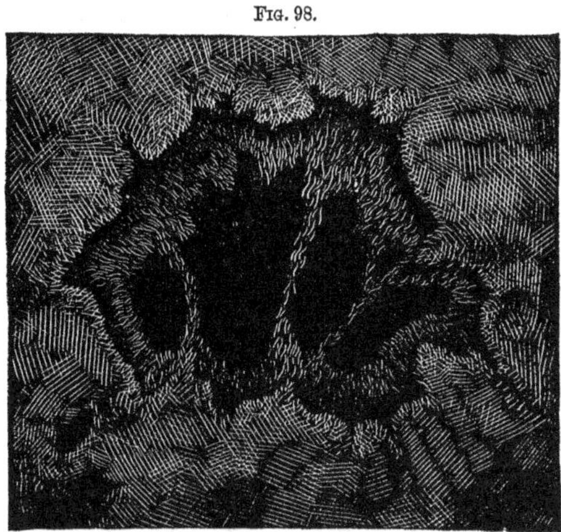

Solar Spot, after Nasmyth, with Three Bridges of Light.

stretching from the outer edge toward the nucleus, generally at right angles to the confines of the nucleus and penumbra (Fig. 99) which give the spot the appearance as if a number of streams

FIG. 99.

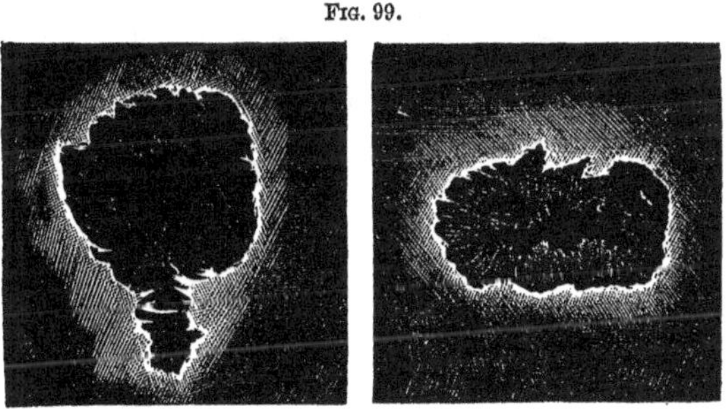

Solar Spots, after Capocci; Furrows in the Penumbra.

of some luminous matter had broken through the dam formed by the penumbra, to fall into the abyss of the umbra. Even the umbra itself is often crossed by one or more broad luminous bands, called *bridges*, by which it is divided into several portions (Figs. 96, 98, 101).

Besides the dark spots, and chiefly in their immediate neighborhood, bright places make their appearance on the sun's surface, which have been called *faculæ.* They are generally the attendants of solar spots, and are especially to be seen at the extreme edge of the penumbra when the spot has reached the sun's limb: that they are not the effect of contrast between the dark spot and the neighboring brightness is proved by the circumstance that every spot is not accompanied by faculæ, and

FIG. 100.

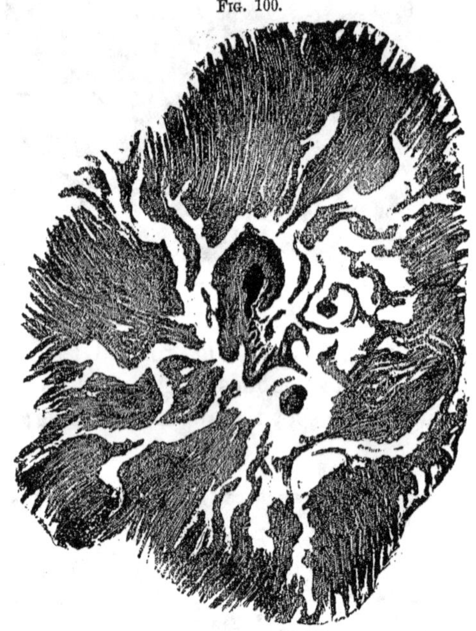

Faculæ in the Neighborhood of a Spot, after Chacornac.

that very frequently isolated faculæ are to be seen which are almost always the precursor of a coming spot.

The faculæ, like the spots, vary considerably in form; generally they are round and concentrated, but often they have the appearance of long stripes of light (Fig. 100), disposed like veins, converging from all sides toward a spot.

The wreathed faculæ are almost always followed in a few

days by the appearance of a group of spots; among the vein-like waves of light visible in many places, more especially toward the sun's limb, there is first developed a dull, scar-like place out of which the spots are formed, sometimes singly, sometimes in groups; and not unfrequently the formation of a spot may be predicted from the increased intensity of light at that place on the sun's disk.

When a spot is observed near the sun's limb in the midst of the surrounding faculæ, it is difficult to avoid the impression that the spot lies in a hollow between bright overhanging mountains; and it was observed by Secchi, on the 5th of August, 1865, that the faculæ, when they reached the western limb of the sun, appeared like small projections and irregularities upon the sharply-defined limb of the sun.

Although the real connection between the faculæ and the spots is not yet fully understood, it may be safely concluded, from these observations, that the spots lie deeper in the solar surface than do the faculæ, and that these faculæ are mountainous elevations of the luminous matter forming the photosphere, by which the spot is surrounded in a wide circuit as by a wall.

A representation of a group of solar spots observed and drawn by Nasmyth, on the 5th of June, 1864, is given in Fig. 101, in which all the details characteristic of a spot are to be recognized—the black umbra, the penumbra in a variety of forms, composed of the "leaves" directed toward the umbra, and the surrounding luminous surface of the sun presenting its usual granulated appearance. This surface is called the *photosphere*, a name given without reference to any particular theory as to its physical constitution or structure. The photosphere is entirely covered with *pores*, or small spots, less luminous than the other parts: where they congregate, and become conspicuous by forming a black umbra and shaded penumbra, they constitute the ordinary *solar spot;* where the portions of greater brilliancy than the surrounding parts of the photosphere congregate, they form the *faculæ*, and these generally accompany the spots or precede their formation.

If a solar spot be watched in the telescope from day to day, or from hour to hour, it will soon be seen to change in form; it increases or diminishes, or completely vanishes away, while new spots make their appearance. In the process of disappearing the

Fig. 101.

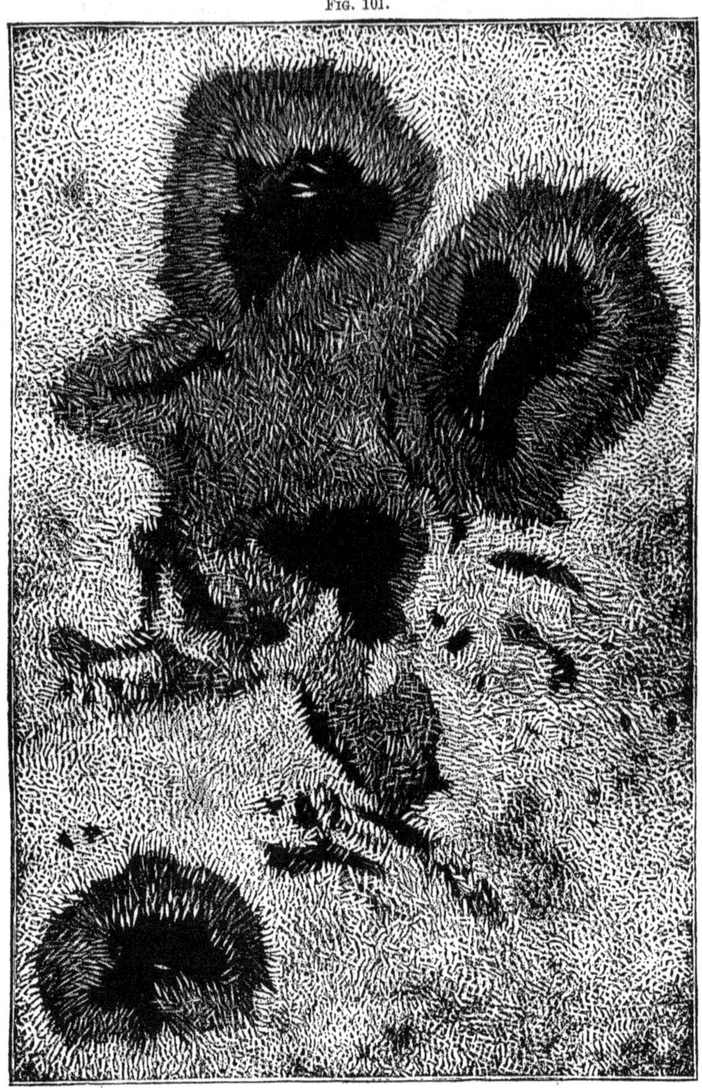

Group of Solar Spots observed and drawn by Nasmyth, June 5, 1864.

dark umbra first gradually contracts until it becomes invisible, leaving the dusky penumbra perceptible for some time longer. Not unfrequently a spot breaks up into several spots, and occasionally a group unites to form one; and sometimes, even as was observed by Weiss, on the 12th of March, 1864, and by Haag on the 13th, 15th, and 16th of April, 1869, one spot is seen to pass over another, partially covering it, and then withdrawing from it. In all these changes the spots exhibit an amount of mobility displayed in general only by liquid or vaporous masses.

Fig. 102.

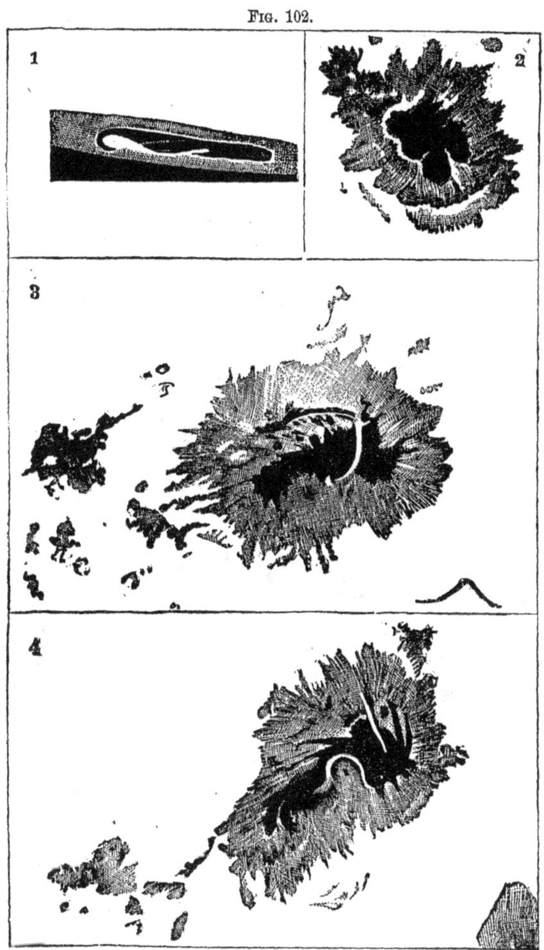

The Great Solar Spot of 1865. (From 7th October to 16th October.)

The great changes which sometimes occur in a solar spot are shown in Fig. 102, representing four drawings of the large spot, more than 46,000 square miles in area, that appeared in 1865.

The drawings are numbered in order of date. No. 1 shows the form of the spot on the 7th of October, when it was first visible on the eastern (left) limb of the sun; Nos. 2 and 3 as it appeared on the 10th and 14th of October (central view), when a bridge had been already formed across the nucleus; and No. 4 as it was seen on the 16th of October.

The formation and changes in the configuration of a spot may often be watched during the course of observation, and it not unfrequently happens that the appearance of a group of spots is so entirely changed from one day to another that it can no longer be recognized in the new form it has assumed. An

Fig. 103.

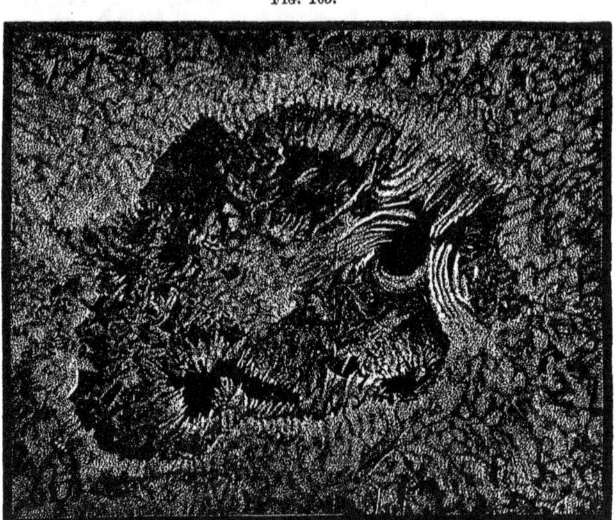

Solar Spot of July 30, 1869.

example of this is given in Figs. 103 and 104, consisting of drawings of the same group of spots observed by Secchi at noon on the 30th and 31st of July, 1869.

On the other hand, there are spots presenting scarcely any change, which preserve nearly the same form for many days together. Spots of this kind are of the highest value to the astronomer, as they afford the only means of ascertaining the time of the revolution of the sun upon its axis, the position of this axis, and its inclination to the earth's orbit.

If a spot be observed even for a short time, it will soon be remarked that it apparently advances on the sun's disk from east to west—that is to say, from the left to the right limb of the sun: in an inverting* (astronomical) telescope the motion will appear to be in the opposite direction, namely, from right to left.

FIG. 104.

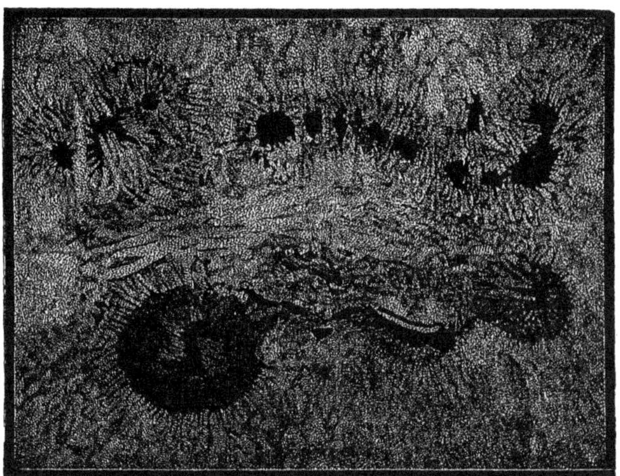

Solar Spot of July 31, 1869.

The form of a spot on its first appearance on the eastern limb of the sun is that of a small dark streak the length of which is much greater than the breadth. For the first few days it appears to move but slowly toward the middle of the sun's disk; its speed afterward increases from day to day till it has accomplished half the journey across the disk. The motion then slowly diminishes until the spot again assumes the form of a narrow streak, and disappears at the opposite (western) limb of the sun. It not unfrequently happens that the same spot which has been observed to disappear on the western limb has in the course of about fourteen days been seen to reappear on the eastern limb, and in the lapse of another fourteen days has disappeared a second time on the western limb, a phenomenon that proves beyond a doubt that the spots are connected with the surface of the sun,

* In an astronomical telescope the highest point of the sun's disk appears as the lowest, and the lowest appears to be the highest; in the same way the eastern limb appears to the right, and the western limb to the left of the observer.

and that the sun itself has a revolution upon its axis. If the time required for the earth's motion round the sun be allowed for in this revolution of the spot, the result will show according to Spörer a mean time of rotation for the sun amounting to twenty-five days, five hours, thirty-eight minutes.

Kirchhoff, whose views Prof. Spörer, one of the most industrious observers of solar spots, has in the course of his investigations adopted with increasing confidence, considers these forms to be cloud-like condensations in the sun's atmosphere, which are produced by the loss of the solar heat by radiation, in the same way as the aqueous vapors of the earth's atmosphere are formed into mist and cloud. When such clouds arise over the bright and glowing surface of the sun, they obscure the light of the sun at that spot, and it is but natural that these cloudy masses, so irregularly formed, should also become further condensed, or be dispersed with the same amount of irregularity, according as they come in contact with cooler or warmer streams of gas.

Those physicists who differ from Kirchhoff in their views of the physical constitution of the sun, and consider, with Faye, that the actual nucleus of the sun is a non-luminous ball of gas, entertain a different theory of the nature of the solar spots, regarding them as rents or openings in the bright *photosphere* surrounding the *dark* ball of gas through which this dark nucleus is seen.

The elder and younger Herschel have both recorded observations of a depression or notch in the sun's limb when a spot has been disappearing round the edge of the sun. If the idea has been once entertained that a solar spot is a cavity or funnel-like depression in the luminous photosphere, it is difficult to resist the optical illusion arising from the fact that a dark spot on a bright background always conveys the impression of a hole.

Fig. 105 shows a spot observed and drawn by Secchi at Rome, on the 5th of May, 1857, which resembles a gigantic whirlpool or a funnel, into the interior of which the substance of the photo sphere appears to be rushing with an eddying motion. Warren De la Rue has taken two photographic pictures of the same spot at an interval of two days, and, if these pictures be placed together and looked at through a stereoscope, the spot exhibits the form of a funnel with remarkable exactness. Other photographic pictures, taken of similar spots when at the extreme edge of the sun, also convey the idea of the existence of real depressions in the photosphere.

FIG. 105.

Spiral Solar Spot observed by Secchi.

The opinion that the solar spots are funnel-shaped depressions in the outer stratum of the sun's envelope, or photosphere, finds support not so much from observations of this kind as from the different appearances they present in their apparent motion across the sun's disk, without any actual change occurring in their form, size, or grouping.

Were a spot to make its appearance upon the *surface* of the sun, and become visible on the eastern limb, the preceding or western part of the penumbra would first come into view, owing to the sun's rotation from east to west; then the western portion of the umbra would appear, and the umbra itself would gradually increase from west to east; finally, the most eastern portion of the penumbra, that which was farthest from the line of sight, would be revealed. In the same way, on disappearing round the western limb of the sun, the preceding or western part of the penumbra would first become invisible, the western penumbra would then gradually decrease, after which the umbra would diminish in the direction of west to east, and finally the following or western part of the penumbra would entirely disappear from view.

In reality, however, the exact contrary is observed. On the

appearance of a spot at the eastern limb, the eastern portion of the penumbra is first visible, then follows the umbra in the form of a dark streak, which gradually widens in the direction of east to west, till at length, when the umbra is wholly visible, the western side of the penumbra begins to appear. On the disappearance of the spot at the western limb of the sun, the eastern portion of the penumbra, that which is turned toward the centre of the sun's disk, first diminishes, and the umbra again contracts into a narrow streak, while the western side of the penumbra has scarcely at all decreased. Only when the umbra is entirely lost to sight does the western penumbra begin to diminish, and finally disappear.

In Fig. 106 the drawings marked I represent the varying phases through which a spot surrounded by a penumbra usually passes from the moment of its first appearance on the eastern limb of the sun until it appears again at the western limb. They show that the theory of the spot being above the surface of the sun, as a cloud in the solar atmosphere, or being on the surface itself, is untenable; the phenomena observed, however, can be at once explained by the supposition that the spot is a conical-shaped depression in the outer surface of the sun (the photosphere), which expands from the inside, and contains in its deepest recesses the cause of the dark umbra, while its sloping sides are composed of what appears to us as penumbra. The drawings marked II represent such a conical-shaped cavity in a globe shown in perspective in the same positions as those occupied by the spot on the sun's disk in the first set of drawings. It is needless to remark that the size of the spot in reality bears no such proportion to the size of the sun as for the sake of clearness has been adopted in the drawings.

We cannot any further follow the reasons for or against these hypotheses concerning the cloud-like or funnel-formed appearance presented by the solar spots, without first becoming acquainted with the results which spectrum analysis has already furnished in connection with these mysterious phenomena.

William Huggins, whose invaluable labors in the province of stellar spectrum analysis will be discussed hereafter, made an examination of the spectrum of a solar spot on the 15th of April, 1868, and then found, in accordance with the previous observations of Secchi and Lockyer, that, notwithstanding the darkness

Fig. 106.

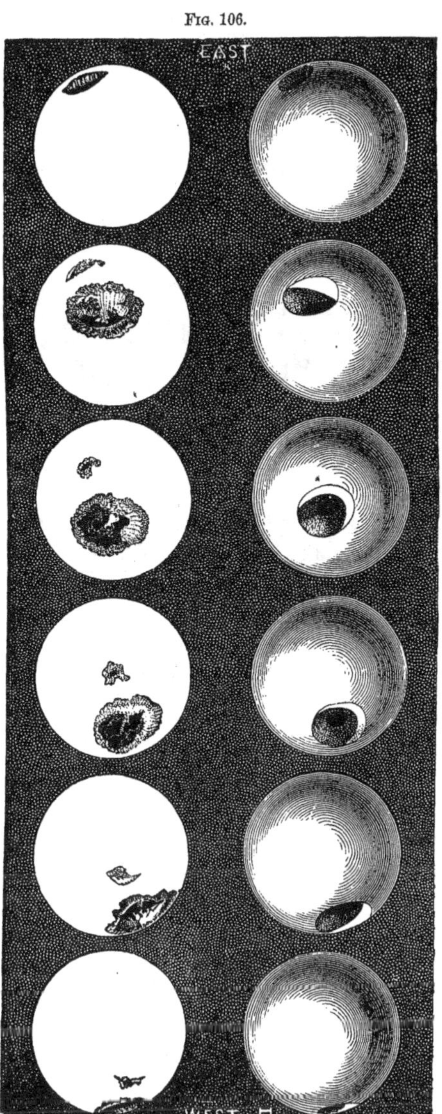

The Changes in the Appearance of a Spot caused by the Rotation of the Sun.

of the spot, the continuous solar spectrum did not disappear, but that several dark lines increased in *breadth* and *intensity*, as shown in Fig. 107 for the double D-line. New lines did not appear in the spectrum formed by the light of the umbra of a spot, but no single line was missing from the normal solar spectrum; bright lines were scarcely ever to be seen. These phenomena cannot well be reconciled with Faye's hypothesis that a spot is formed by the eruption of streams of gas from the interior of the sun, by which the bright photosphere is pushed on one side, and the *dark* ball of gas composing the nucleus of the sun exposed to

Fig. 107.

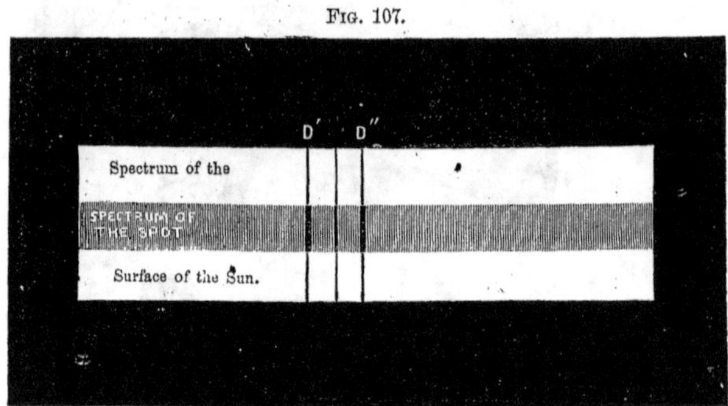

The D-lines in the Spectrum of a Solar Spot.

view; for how can the persistence of the continuous spectrum be explained if by the rending of the photosphere a *dark* body be exposed which can yield no light for the formation of a spectrum? According to Faye's theory, a solar spot must either show no spectrum, or if the inner *gaseous* portion of the sun emit any light it must yield a spectrum composed of *bright lines;* neither of which is the case. The continuous spectrum crossed by the Fraunhofer lines proves that the umbra allows a considerable portion of the sun's ordinary light to pass through it, and the widening of the dark lines shows indisputably that the spot occasions an *increased absorption of the light*, arising from the condensation of the same vaporous substance which produces the dark absorption bands in the ordinary solar spectrum.

More significant are the recent investigations of Secchi. In examining with his great spectroscope the neighborhood of a large spot, he saw groups of three, four, or six cloudy bands, equally distant from each other, appear in the red and orange of the spectrum. These bands usually disappeared when the slit of the instrument was directed away from the spot on to the clear disk of the sun; their appearance in the spectrum was always a sure sign of the proximity of a spot even when it was not itself within the field of the instrument. On the 6th of January, 1869, Secchi was surprised to observe the same bands on the clear disk of the sun, the cause of which was soon apparent by the passage of a cirrus cloud over the sun, and on a closer examination these bands were seen to show themselves in all parts of the disk; as the cloud passed away, the bands disappeared from the spectrum. It was thus proved that *aqueous vapor* had some share in producing the phenomena of the cloudy bands, and this was demonstrated still more unequivocally by another observation made in the beginning of February, when Secchi, observing the sun through a tolerably thick fog, noticed that these bands were visible on every part of the disk, but decidedly more prominent in the vicinity of the spot. Secchi concludes, therefore, that the absorptive power in the sun producing these bands is intensified by the absorptive action of the aqueous vapor contained in the earth's atmosphere; where the earth's mist and the solar spot coincide, this action is increased; the cause of the absorption in the sun in the neighborhood of the solar spots is therefore the same as that which is present in a fog—namely, aqueous vapor; consequently it seems proved that *aqueous vapor exists in the atmosphere of the sun in the vicinity of large spots.**

Secchi also carefully analyzed the fine group of solar spots which appeared in the middle of March, 1869, with a spectrum apparatus consisting of a powerful telescope and three very widely dispersive prisms, and arrived at the following results:

1. Several dark lines which were very narrow and well defined on those parts of the sun free from spots appeared swollen and widened in the spectrum of the spot; other lines were fainter, and not so sharply defined at the edges, as in the spectrum of other parts of the sun.

2. Most of the exceedingly fine dark lines scarcely visible in the solar spectrum appeared very dark and broad in the spectrum of the spot.

3. The relative intensity of the bright portions was considerably altered in the spot: while some lost much in brilliancy, others retained their full intensity.

4. The apparent loss of brilliancy in the bright portions was produced more by the increased width of the dark lines than

* [This result appears to the editor to need confirmation.]

by an actual diminution in the light. The widening of the two lines D_1 and D_2, forming the sodium line D, for example, was so great that the space between them seemed to have almost quite disappeared, while in places away from the spot these two lines were widely separated.

Similar observations were made on a spot visible from the 11th to the 13th of April. The spot had a double oval umbra, and a large penumbra, and was surrounded by a number of smaller spots. The two principal portions of the umbra were separated by a very narrow and very bright *bridge*, which, dividing the spot into two parts, extended through the whole of the penumbra from one end to the other. The interior of the umbra appeared as if filled with rose-colored veils, twisted confusedly and spread about in every possible way.

Under very favorable atmospheric circumstances, Secchi was able to confirm all the foregoing spectrum observations of a spot, both with regard to the widening of the dark lines, and the conversion of the fine lines into cloudy bands. The lines most affected were those numbered 719.5 and 864 in Kirchhoff's spectrum; they were at least three times as black and broad on the spot as in other places, though the edges were still sharply defined.

When the slit of the spectroscope was placed at right angles to the bridge of the spot, so that the light of the bridge, the umbra, and the penumbra, fell simultaneously upon the prism, Secchi saw in the field of the instrument three kinds of spectra at the same moment, each sharply separated from the other, as shown in Fig. 108, where they are represented with the Fraunhofer lines and Kirchhoff's numbers.

No. 1: the ordinary solar spectrum given by the luminous bridge, except that the hydrogen lines $H\alpha = C$, $H\beta = F$, $H\gamma$ near to G, were *bright* instead of dark.

No. 2: the spectrum of the umbra with the dark lines widened and intensified, some new striped bands and some *bright* double lines in the green; the bright hydrogen line of the adjoining spectrum of the bridge No. 1 projected for some distance into the spectrum of the umbra, a phenomenon which was observed also in the C-line by Rayet on the 12th of April, 1870.

No. 3: the spectrum of the penumbra in which the hydrogen lines were not visible; they did not appear either as dark lines or as bright lines, but were altogether wanting.

Besides the thickening of the dark lines, several absorption bands made their appearance also in the spectrum of the umbra: one in the red near C toward B; another near D, and a very dark zone half-way between C and D. A wide dark space was seen in the green, and it is specially deserving of notice that several *bright* lines made their appearance upon this dark background, two and two together, at moderate distances from each other, and so brilliant that their light had not apparently suffered any absorption; a dark band was also visible in the blue near F.

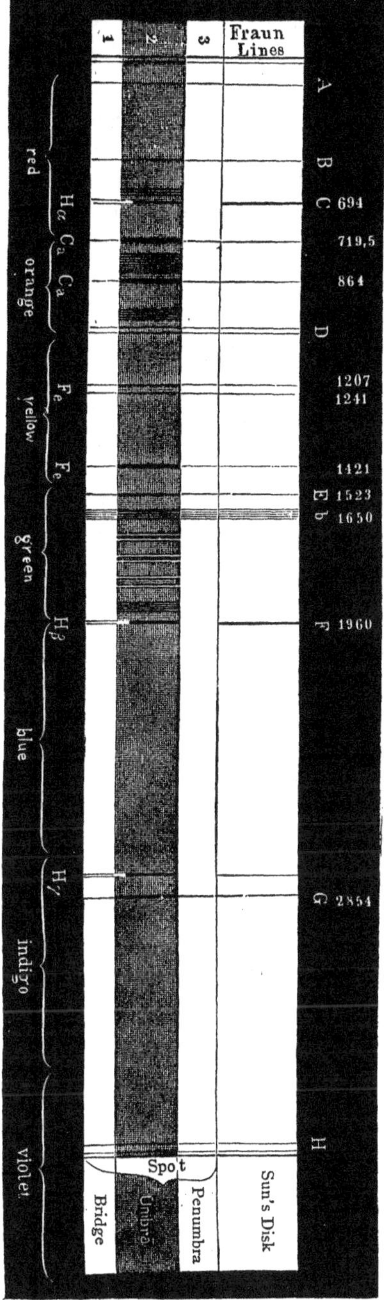

FIG. 108.—Spectrum of the Solar Spot of 11–13th April, 1869, observed by Secchi.

Other dark lines become wider and darker in the umbra of a spot besides the two already mentioned belonging to calcium 719.5 and 864 of Kirchhoff's scale: this phenomenon has been observed with remarkable distinctness in the neighboring group of iron, in the group between the lines 1207 and 1241 (Kirchhoff), as well as in that group extending on both sides of the line 1421. Secchi has identified a number of these lines with those of iron; they were all more influenced by the absorptive action of the substance of the spot than the two D-lines of sodium, which, though also considerably widened, had lost the sharpness of their edges: the magnesium lines *b* scarcely underwent any change in the spectrum of the spot.

Lockyer found in a spot which he observed on the 20th of February, 1869, that the magnesium as well as the barium lines were increased in breadth, and he agrees with Secchi in the opinion that this widening of the Fraunhofer lines which takes place in the spectrum of a spot arises from an increased absorption in those substances out of which the spot is composed, and that in general the spots are deep recesses in the surface of the solar body, filled with concentrated masses of those substances (iron, calcium, barium, magnesium, sodium, hydrogen), the lines of which undergo an increase of breadth and intensity in the spectrum, and over which floats the lighter hydrogen gas.

Prof. C. A. Young, of Dartmouth College, Hanover (America), also found, when investigating with the spectroscope, a large group of spots, on the 9th of April, 1870, that the hydrogen lines C and F were reversed in the umbra—appearing bright. C was very bright, F much fainter; the remaining hydrogen lines, H γ (2796 Kirchhoff) and H δ or *h* (3365.5 K.), were not reversed, but appeared as somewhat finer lines. He remarked also that many dark lines had become wider and darker, while others remained unchanged, among which were *a*, B, E, 1472 (K.), the lines *b*, 1691 (K.), and G. The two sodium lines D_1 and D_2, as well as 850 (iron), were evidently widened, but not to any considerable extent.

The lines most affected by the increased absorption in the substance of the spot were as follows: 864 (Ca.), 877 (Fe. ?), 885 (Ca.), 895 (Ca.), 1580 (Ti.), 1599 (Ti.), 1627 (Ca.), and 1629 (Ti.). The lines of titanium which were identified by Ångström's map were very prominent, and this was the more remarkable as they are not visible in the ordinary solar spectrum; the same observation was made with regard to the calcium lines.

The results of the spectrum observations of Secchi, Lockyer, and Young, important and valuable as they are, remain as yet too isolated and unconnected with telescopic observations of the spots and faculæ to yield material sufficient for explaining the nature of these forms. This much, however, may be regarded as certain, that the phenomena of the increase in the width and intensity of the Fraunhofer lines, as well as the appearance of new dark bands in the spectrum of the umbra, *are produced by the increased absorptive power exercised by the substances of which the spot is formed.*

When the white light of the sun's nucleus which has already suffered absorption from the absorptive stratum passes through the vaporous matter of a spot, it undergoes a yet further absorption from the additional matter which the spot contains. As, therefore, the lines of calcium and iron are considerably affected in the spectrum of a spot, the sodium lines in a smaller degree, and, to some extent, those of magnesium, it may be concluded that the substance forming the solar spots is composed preeminently of vapors of calcium, iron, titanium, sodium, barium, and magnesium, and that these substances occur in layers of varying thickness, and in very different proportions.

That hydrogen gas constitutes an important element in the formation of the spots is shown in the most unequivocal manner by the spectrum. The hydrogen lines are most affected in the parts that lie close to the umbra, in the bridge when one is formed, and in the penumbra. In the spectrum of the bridge (No. 1) the three characteristic lines H α, H β, H γ, are *very bright*, in the spectrum of the penumbra (No. 3) they are often entirely wanting, while, in the spectrum of the surface of the sun and of the umbra (No. 2), they appear as the well-known dark Fraunhofer lines C, F, and the one near to G.

An explanation * of this phenomenon is offered by the supposition that hydrogen gas breaks forth from time to time from the interior of the incandescent solar nucleus. Owing to its extreme lightness, this gas would rise in enormous pillars of flame (prominences) over the absorptive vaporous stratum of the photosphere, and, in consequence of the cooling ensuing from expansion, would enter into a variety of chemical combinations, especially with oxygen; the uncombined part would then flow to the side, while that in combination with oxygen (steam) and the other solar substances would form gaseous or vaporous masses, which, from their nature as well as from their continued cooling, would be heavier than the hydrogen gas, and would sink down, from their greater gravity. It is to be expected that the

* [The editor reminds the readers of the book that he is not responsible for the views and explanations of the author.]

stream of gas, on rising, would carry up with it a quantity of those substances that exist in the sun's nucleus and the surrounding stratum of absorptive vapor (the photosphere); if these substances, themselves incandescent, were present in sufficient quantities in the luminous hydrogen gas, their characteristic lines would be seen as bright lines in the spectrum of the pillars of flame. During the recent total eclipses, many such lines were in fact observed, together with the bright hydrogen lines, in the prominences, a description of which will be given farther on; they can now be observed daily, sometimes in great numbers, upon the sun's disk.

When the force of the gas-eruption has somewhat subsided, and the chemical combinations ensue, producing vaporous precipitations of many kinds, the formation of the spot begins. The heavier portions of these precipitations sink down, and form the *umbra* of a spot at the place of greatest condensation, while the parts which are less dense constitute the *penumbra.* The vaporous umbra, however, though apparently quite black, is yet able to transmit a considerable amount of sunlight; indeed, according to Zöllner's measurements, the black umbra of a spot emits four thousand times as much light as that derived from an equal area of the full moon. This statement is fully confirmed by the results of spectrum analysis, for even the blackest umbra yields a spectrum exhibiting all the details of full sunlight.

Where the spot is broken through by the overflowing masses of the photosphere, a bright band is formed, called a *bridge,* which extends across the whole of the penumbra. The rays of light emitted by the luminous hydrogen as it flows to the edges of the spot from the neighboring parts of the bridge, and breaks over the absorptive stratum of the bridge, are not further absorbed, and illuminate the dark Fraunhofer lines C, F, and one near G; these lines, therefore, in the spectrum of the bridge (No. 1) are reversed from dark to bright. In the umbra of the spot the free hydrogen is no longer present in sufficient quantity or at a sufficiently high temperature for its lines H α, β, γ, to overpower the dark Fraunhofer lines C, F, and the one near G, or even to weaken them perceptibly; on the other hand, the intensity of the light and the temperature of the hydrogen in the parts belonging to the penumbra are sufficient to cause its three bright lines coincident with the dark lines C, F, and the one near

G, to be of the same intensity as the neighboring parts of the spectrum, and therefore they become invisible. In the spectrum of the bridge (1) these lines are generally bright, in that of the umbra (2) they remain dark, while they are frequently entirely wanting in the spectrum of the penumbra.

The various remarkable changes which the lines of hydrogen, magnesium, sodium, calcium, and iron, suffer in the spectrum of the umbra, seem to show that, in the cloud-like and vaporous substances constituting the spot, the new combinations are disposed in layers according to their specific gravity. Thus hydrogen gas occupies the highest stratum; aqueous vapor, magnesium, and sodium follow in thinner layers below; and the heavier vapors of calcium, titanium, and iron, form the lowest and densest stratum, the base of the spot.

The formation of a spot will accordingly immediately follow an eruption of hydrogen; the spot itself is a dense, cloudy, luminous mass, probably of a semi-fluid consistency, composed of many constituents—according to Zöllner, a kind of scoria—which sinks by its gravity a certain depth into the photosphere, or outer portion of the sun, and partially intercepts the light from the lower stratum of the photosphere, therefore presenting to us the appearance of a dark mass projected upon the disk of the sun, in the same way as the exceedingly intense light of the oxyhydrogen lime-light appears black when seen against the sun.

The enormous dimensions of these dense masses of vapor, which extend sometimes in all directions, account for the length of time the spots continue visible, not unfrequently remaining during several rotations of the sun. Their disappearance is to be explained partly by the substance of the photosphere flowing into the cavity of the spot, partly by the complete subsidence of the vapors into the nucleus of the sun, where, in consequence of the enormous heat, the compound substances which may exist in them are broken up into their original elements.

These conjectures are by no means intended to afford a complete explanation of all the phenomena of a solar spot. Though it certainly is of the highest interest for us to acquire a knowledge of the physical nature of that heavenly body whence we derive light, heat, motion, and life, we must yet be cautious of receiving for truth what is only the result of speculation, especially as the theories on this subject rest on isolated observations which are too unconnected to point to any certain conclusion. The suggestions here thrown out are only intended, therefore, to cast some light upon the results hitherto obtained by the spectrum observations of Secchi, Huggins, Lockyer, and Young, and, by affording an unconstrained interpretation of them, to bring them into harmony with the phenomena observed during the total solar eclipses of 1868 and 1869.

49. Total Solar Eclipses.

The reason why our knowledge concerning the nature of the sun is still so imperfect that it is scarcely possible to decide between the diametrically opposed theories of Kirchhoff and Faye is, that the remarkable phenomena occurring on the sun's limb are so completely overpowered by the blinding light of the solar nucleus or photosphere that they remain invisible even in the most powerful telescopes. It is not sufficient to get rid of the sun's rays by the interposition of an opaque screen, because the diffused light of the sky cannot be eliminated by this means, and this light even is so intense as to conceal the faint light of the sun's appendages. It is quite otherwise, however, during a *total eclipse* of the sun; then the moon covers the whole of the sun's disk, and includes a large tract of the earth's surface in the cone of its shadow, revealing to the observer, who is no longer hindered by the light of day, a display of phenomena round the sun which can be seen in no other way, and the study of which is peculiarly fitted to throw light on the nature and physical constitution of the sun.

When at the commencement of a total solar eclipse the moon in her course from west to east passes over the disk of the sun, the observer perceives, by the use of a simple dark glass, the first contact of the moon's disk on the west—that is to say, right—side of the sun; if he employ an astronomical telescope, the image is reversed, and the eclipse appears to begin at the left side. If, however, he continue to observe it by direct vision only, the moon is seen to advance over the sun's disk from west to east, and the obscuration increases until the whole of the sun is covered, and the last rays disappear from the sun's eastern limb. Between this moment, the commencement of *total* darkness, and that when the following edge of the moon touches the sun's western limb, where at the same instant the solar rays reappear and the total darkness is at an end, are comprised the few precious moments for the sake of which costly expeditions are prepared, and the interest of learned and scientific men of every nation greatly aroused, since in these moments a unique opportunity is afforded for the investigation of the central body of our system, and the successful use of this opportunity is entirely dependent upon the weather, for a momentary veil of cloud or a fleeting whisp of vapor, may render unavailing all the trouble and expense incurred.

We will not suffer ourselves to be detained by a description of those changes that pass over the landscape as the darkness advances, nor dwell upon the deep impression which the sudden disappearance of the last rays of the sun, and the equally sudden reappearance of the light, make both upon men and animals.

The diameter of the cone of the shadow thrown by the moon toward the earth amounts, at the spot where it touches the earth's surface on the equator during the time of totality, to about 122 miles: as, however, the moon, which throws the shadow, only completes its course in the heavens round the earth from west to east in one month, and the earth, which receives the shadow, accomplishes its revolution from west to east in one day, it follows that the motion of the moon's shadow is very much slower than that of the earth's surface. It therefore happens that the earth appears to run away from under the moon's shadow, or that the moon's shadow seems to run over the earth from east to west. From an elevated position the shadow of the moon is seen to approach with enormous rapidity, and the sensation as though a material substance, such as a terrific cloud of smoke, were rushing over the earth's surface, fills the uninitiated spectator with fear and dread. A few minutes before the commencement of the totality, the brightest stars become visible, and the sharply-defined black edge of the moon appears surrounded on all sides by a very narrow but very brilliant ring of light of silver whiteness, which is called the *corona*. From the corona faint rays of light, irregular in length and breadth, stream out in all directions, surrounding the moon's disk like a glory, whence this crown of rays is usually designated the glory (*gloires, aigrettes*) or *halo*.

Fig. 109 is taken from a very carefully-prepared drawing by Dr. B. A. Gould, and represents the total eclipse of the 7th of

August, 1869, as it appeared to the unassisted eye at Des Moines, in North America.

When the total darkness has commenced, the *prominences* make their appearance, which are cloud-like masses of a rose or pale coral color, disposed either singly or in groups at various places on the moon's limb.

They pierce the corona in the most wonderful forms, sometimes as single outgrowths of enormous height, sometimes as low projections spreading far along the moon's limb. The prom-

Fig. 109.

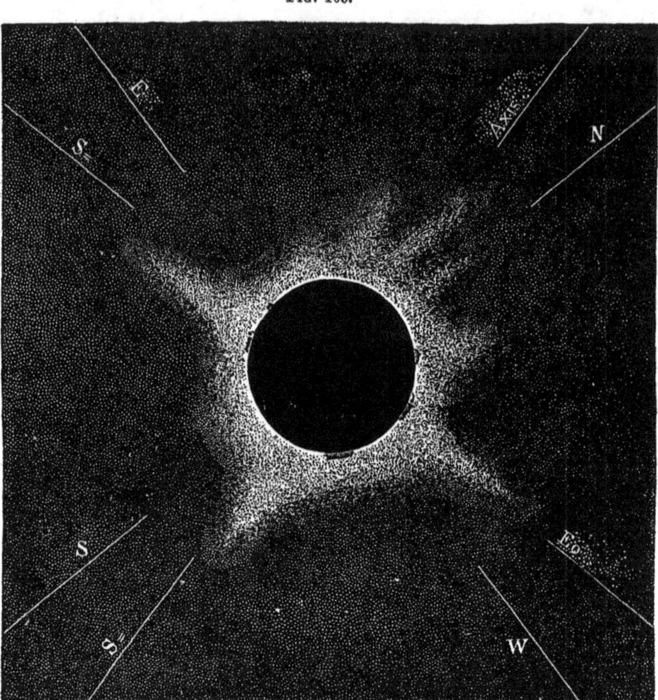

Total Solar Eclipse of August 7, 1869.

inences are generally first seen on the eastern (left) side of the sun, where at the commencement of the totality the moon only grazes the sun's edge, and the space immediately surrounding the sun is yet uncovered; in proportion as the moon advances to the east (E), the space immediately surrounding the western parts (W) of the sun becomes free, and the prominences are then seen also on that side in greater number, and developed with much greater distinctness.

There remains now no longer any doubt that these remarkable phenomena belong to the sun, and are great accumulations of the luminous gaseous material by which the solar body is wholly surrounded; it cannot therefore greatly astonish us that their forms have been seen to change even during the short duration of the totality; that which calls much more for wonder is the enormous height to which these pillars of gas extend beyond the limb of the sun, a height which in some instances exceeds 90,000 miles.

50. Photographic Pictures of Total Solar Eclipses.

Besides the important observations of the first, second, third, and fourth contacts, especially needed by astronomers for a more precise determination of the diameters of the sun and moon, and the direction of the moon's course, careful attention is also given, during a total eclipse, to the corona and halo (Corona nebst Strahlenkranz), and especially to the prominences. The telescope was formerly the exclusive means of observation: photography was first made use of at the great solar eclipse of 1860, in Spain, where it was employed, with very good results, by Secchi and De la Rue at different stations.

It will in future be extensively applied to the record of important eclipses, since photographic pictures taken of the sun through the telescope at different periods of observation give a faithful transcript of the phenomena taking place; and when the pictures are taken at rapidly-succeeding intervals, and at stations far removed from each other, they afford, when collected together, a vivid picture of the whole course of the eclipse, as well as of the phenomena which have occurred during the totality.

The apparatus needed for astronomical photography is as follows: 1. An astronomical telescope; 2. A driving clock to carry the telescope in a direction contrary to the revolution of the earth, at such a speed that a star placed on a wire, or in the axis of the instrument, should not alter its position, notwithstanding the motion of the earth on its axis, and that the telescope, without any interference on the part of the observer, should follow precisely the apparent motion of a star, or any other object in the heavens; 3. The photographic apparatus, which, in its connection with the telescope, consists only of a contrivance for holding the slide containing the prepared plate in the place where the

Fig. 110.

Browning's Photographic Telescope.

image is formed by the object-glass, and upon which the eye-piece is usually directed; this slide is so arranged that the light may be admitted on to the glass plate for either the fraction of a second, or for a much longer period, according to the will of the observer.

This contrivance must be fixed at the upper or lower end of the tube, according as the telescope is a reflector or a refractor—that is to say, whether the image be formed by a mirror or a lens.

In Fig. 110 is shown the photographic reflecting telescope made by Browning for the Indian Government, with which Colonel Tennant took photographs of the eclipse of the 18th of August, 1868, at Guntoor. The tube A A is constructed of iron, in three pieces, connected together by the two rings C C, and contains at the lower end the concave mirror B, of silvered glass (Fig. 111). By means of two projecting screws, this mirror can be easily so adjusted that the rays reflected from it to the

FIG. 111.

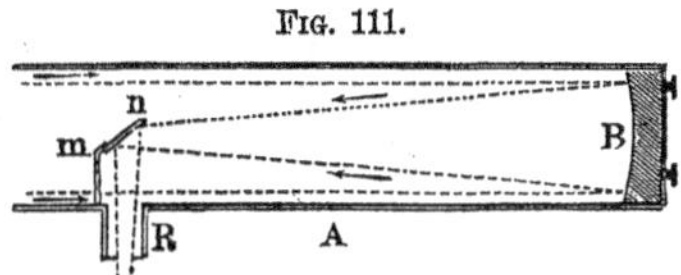

Path of the Rays through the Telescope.

plane mirror *m n*, and thence to the opening R, shall there form a small sharp image of the object to be observed, the sun, for instance.

The telescope A A is attached to the declination axis, and is counterbalanced by the weight D ; close to this counterpoise is fixed the declination circle, by which the angle the tube makes with the direction of the pole is measured.

The hour-circle E is fastened to the polar axis G G, and registers the right ascension on the fixed vernier H. On the under side of this circle are three friction-wheels, two of which are shown in the drawing, by which the friction of the polar axis, placed parallel to the axis of the earth, is so reduced, that a weight of 9 lb. hung at D on the declination axis is sufficient to set in motion the movable part of the instrument, weighing about 5 cwt. The weight of the instrument is counterbalanced by the massive weight N attached to the end of the polar axis, and the telescope, counterpoise D, and the circle E, with its driving-screw, are thus held in equilibrium. The polar axis G G carries the driving-wheel I, made of gun-metal, which is set in motion by means of an endless screw placed underneath; the axle-bed S of this screw can be moved aside to allow it to be placed either in or out of contact with the teeth of the driving-wheel I, a contrivance requisite for enabling the observer to turn the telescope by hand in any direction, and fix it on the object to be observed: when this has been accomplished, and the screw S is pushed back into

Fig. 112.

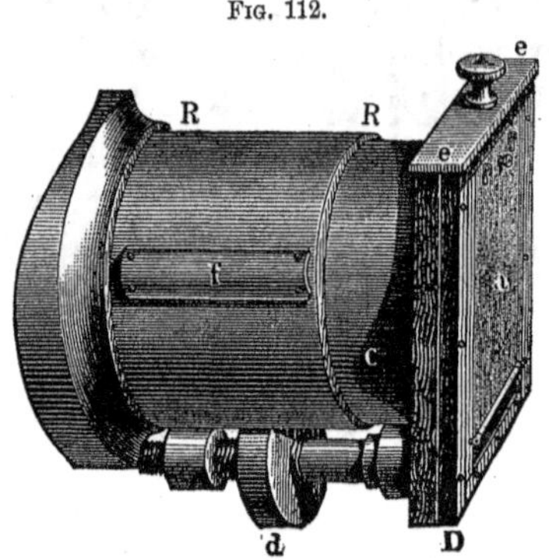

Eye-piece Tube of the Photographic Telescope.

the toothed wheel I, the telescope can only be moved as the clock drives it. The works are enclosed in the square bronze case T, and are propelled by means of the driving-weight U; the governing balls K serve to regulate the clock which sets in motion the endless screw, and turns the driving-wheel I and the polar axis G G.

The solar rays falling parallel on the mirror B, the diameter of which is 9½ inches, will, as shown in Fig. 111, be reflected so as to unite at the focus of the mirror, distant 5 ft. 9 in. Intercepting the rays close in front of the focal point is placed the diagonal mirror *m n*, by which the converging rays are reflected sideways, and thrown into the eye-tube R. The rays unite somewhat beyond the tube R to form an image which is a point when the luminous object has no sensible diameter, but, as the sun subtends an angle of about 32′, its image formed at the focus is somewhat more than three-quarters of an inch in diameter.

The eye-piece tube R serves for the reception of the photographic slide, and for this purpose contains a tube *c* (Fig. 112), which is entirely closed from both light and dust by means of two springs *f*, and which can be moved in and out by the use of the powerful screw *d*. At the end of this inner tube C is the slide *e e* (Fig. 113), which holds the sensitive plate prepared for the reception of the photographic image. The construction of this

FIG. 113.

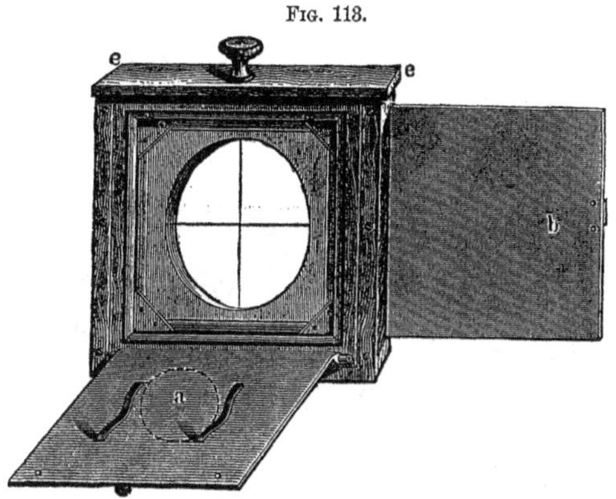

Slide of the Photographic Telescope.

dark slide will be easily understood from the drawing. When the opaque shutter *b* has been pushed in so as to cover the four fine silver wires, the prepared plate is laid upon the silver ledges fixed at the corners, and the door *a* shut: the slide is then inserted at the end of the tube *c* (Fig. 112), the shutter *b* drawn out, and the plate exposed to the action of the light; after a suitable exposure, *b* is again pushed in, and the slide taken away, and replaced in the telescope by another containing a newly-prepared plate.

In order to avoid delay during the short duration of totality, six dark slides with as many sensitive plates were prepared beforehand for photographing the phenomena. To secure the perfect definition of the cross marked by the four silver wires on each plate, the purpose of which was to show the exact position of the sun's axis upon each photographic picture, the wires were placed at a distance of only $\frac{1}{100}$ of an inch from the surface of the prepared plate, without, however, interfering with the action of the exceedingly thin shutter *b*, which moved up and down with safety between the wires and the plate, touching neither the one nor the other. The focus required for the plate—that is to say, the distance the tube *c* (Fig. 112) had to be withdrawn from R R—was ascertained by previous trials; for this purpose a round sliding shutter was constructed at the back of the door *a* (Fig. 110), which when opened allowed of a view into the interior of the dark slide on to the ground glass.

The two pictures represented in Fig. 114 are faithful copies of the photographs taken by De la Rue at Rivabellosa, in Spain, on the 18th of July, 1860: the first shows the appearance of the

FIG. 114.

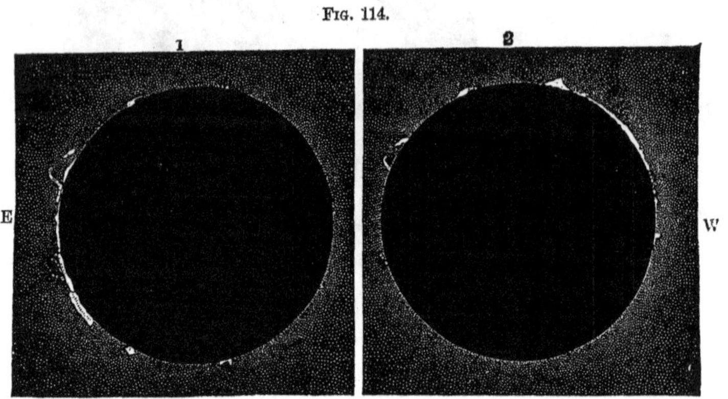

Total Eclipse of July 18, 1860.—(Photographed by De la Rue.)

eclipse at 3h. 0m. 40s.; the second at 3h. 3m. 50s., G. M. T. The corona appears as a soft gentle light round the intensely black moon; the prominences stand out conspicuously in different parts of the corona, and among them one at the upper left side assumed the form compared by De la Rue to a Turkish cimeter, and reached the enormous height of 70,000 miles. The rays of the halo emanating from the corona appeared with great beauty in the telescope and to the unassisted eye, but the light was too faint to make any impression on the photographic plates.

Since these pictures were taken, spectrum analysis has entered the service of astronomy, and has been rendered, mainly by the labors of Kirchhoff, so indispensable to all investigations of the sun that the spectroscope forms now an important part of the requisite apparatus for observing the phenomena of a total solar eclipse. When it is remembered that astronomers have now in addition the self-registering electric chronograph for recording time, as well as the newly-invented photometer (by Zöllner) for measuring the amount of light, it may be supposed that for the efficient use of so many delicate instruments, and the observation of so many phenomena, several experienced astronomers, photographers, and physicists, are required at each station, and therefore the outfitting of an expedition for observing a total solar eclipse is both a difficult and expensive undertaking.

51. The Total Solar Eclipse of August 18, 1868.

This eclipse afforded a remarkable combination of advantageous circumstances, and excited considerable interest from the fact that it could be well observed from many stations widely separated; and also that the duration of totality, being 6m. 50s., was very nearly the greatest that can ever occur in an eclipse of the sun.

A *total* solar eclipse is a phenomenon of rare occurrence at any fixed spot; the last visible in London took place in 1715, and the first in this century to be seen at Berlin will not occur till the 19th of August, 1887, while in Paris there will not be one during the whole of the nineteenth century. The eclipse of the 18th of August, 1868, offered sufficient inducement therefore to assemble the scientific men of all nations for its observation, and it might perhaps be asserted that it excited the interest of all nations in a higher degree than any other astronomical phenomenon of this century. The zone of total darkness passed over the southern part of Asia from Aden, across Hindostan, Malacca, Borneo, Celebes, etc., in a breadth of 138 miles, and expeditions furnished with efficient and costly instruments were sent out by the North-German Confederation, Austria, France, and England, under the superintendence of well-known astronomers.

The zone of totality from Aden to Torres Straits is represented in Fig. 115, in which the various stations are marked: the central dark line denotes the middle of the shadow where the duration of totality was greatest. According to a calculation previously made by Dr. Weiss, of Vienna, the sun rose eclipsed in that region of Abyssinia where the Blue Nile begins its northward course. The nucleus of the shadow grazed Gondar with its northern edge, passed over the lake of Zaka, and by the straits of Bab-el-Mandeb to Aden, the first station marked in the map;

then it crossed the Arabian Gulf to Southern India, where the districts Jamkandi, Beejapoor, Moolwar, Guntoor, Masulipatam, lay near the central line, and the duration of totality varied from 5m.

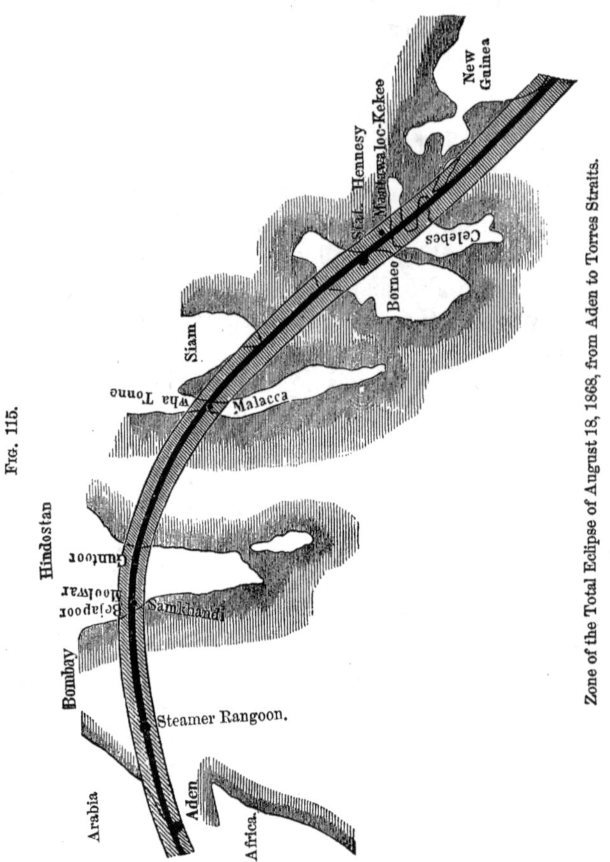

Fig. 115.

Zone of the Total Eclipse of August 18, 1868, from Aden to Torres Straits.

10s. to 5m. 45s. In the Bay of Bengal and in theMalay peninsula (Wha Tonne) the duration of total darkness increased till in the Gulf of Siam it attained its maximum of 6m. 50s. The zone of totality passed then through the southern point of the Anamba Islands, over the northern portions of Borneo and Celebes, and through the middle of the Molucca group. The cone of shadow passed farther over the southern bay of New Guinea, the northern point of Australia, and finally over the Pacific Ocean to the New Hebrides, where the sun must have set while still eclipsed.

1. The North-German Confederation sent out two expeditions, one of which, consisting of Dr. Thiele from the observatory at Bonn, and the Berlin photographers Drs. Vogel, Zenkler, and Fritsch, selected Aden as a station; while the other, with Prof. Spörer of Anclam, Dr. Tietjen of Berlin, Dr. Engelmann of Leipsic, and Koppe of Berlin, repaired to Moolwar, in the Bombay presidency, four miles south of Beejapoor.

2. The Austrian expedition, under Dr. Weiss, Dr. Oppolzer, and a naval officer, Lieutenant Rziha, remained at Aden with the first division of the North-German Confederation.

3. France also sent out two expeditions; the first was under the superintendence of Janssen, an observer greatly experienced in spectrum investigations, who selected the station of Guntoor; the second, comprising Stéphan, director of the observatory at Marseilles, and among others the physicists Rayet and Tisserand, and the engineer Hall, was sent farther east, and stationed themselves at Wha Tonne, a small place near the sea, in the peninsula of Malacca.

4. The English expeditions were also admirably prepared: the one under the conduct of Captain Herschel took up its position on the western coast of Southern India, at Jamkandi, in the neighborhood of Belgaum; another detachment, under Captains Haig and Tanner, was stationed at Beejapoor; while a third, superintended by Colonel Tennant, and equipped especially for photographic purposes, occupied a locality farther east at Guntoor, where Janssen also was stationed.

5. The Jesuits at Manilla, in the Philippines, fitted out a small expedition, consisting of Fathers Fauro, Nonell, and Ricart, stationed at Mantawaloc-Kekee, a coral island at the entrance of the Gulf of Tomini or Garontola, where in company with Captain Charles Bullock, of H. M. S. Serpent, the eclipse was observed with good results. This station was in 0° 32′ 50.1″ south latitude and 123° 27′ 27.5″ east longitude from Greenwich.

Besides these very complete expeditions, furnished with every requisite instrument for scientific investigation, there were many private individuals, some possessed of very good telescopes, who, happening to be in the line of totality, observed the eclipse with praiseworthy zeal, and obtained some good results. Among these was Captain Rennoldson, who crossed the line of shadow in mid-ocean in the steamer Rangoon, and the four sketches he took during the totality were among the first pictures published of the eclipse. The eclipse was observed also by the Governor of Labuan, Mr. J. Pope-Hennessy, on the west coast of Borneo, in company with Captain Reed and others, and the account he gave of the phenomena of the eclipse, with the readings of the barometer and thermometer during its course, is of the greatest interest. At Adoni, a town near Bellary, in 15° 37′ north latitude and 77° 20′ east longitude, Lieutenant Warren, possessing a good telescope, watched the phenomena of the eclipse with care, and has published his observations, including the variations of the thermometer. The Dutch doubtless sent an expedition to the zone of totality from their settlements in the islands of the Archipelago, but no published account of their proceedings has yet appeared.

With the purpose we have in view, we must pass over the results of the various expeditions as far as they are purely astronomical, such as the measures in position and height of the prominences, and the observations of the polarization of light in the corona, as well as those that relate to the variations of light and heat, the changes in the density of the atmosphere, etc., in order to dwell in detail on those phenomena registered by photography and spectrum analysis, since they are of such high importance that their full significance cannot as yet be fully realized.

Photographic pictures of the eclipse of the 18th of August, 1868, were taken by the following expeditions:

1. The North-German expedition at Aden, under Drs. Vogel, Zenker, Fritsch, and Thiele.

2. The English expedition at Guntoor, under Colonel Tennant.

3. The expedition of the Jesuits from Manilla, at Mantawaloc-Kekee.

The results obtained by Dr. Vogel, the first on the list, shall be narrated in his own words; he wrote as follows, from the steamer in which he and his party returned to Suez: "We rose early, by four o'clock on the morning of the 18th of August. About nine-tenths of the sky was overcast. In a spirit of resignation we commenced our preparations. . . . The task before us consisted of taking as many pictures of the phenomena as possible during the three minutes, the duration of totality at Aden.

For this purpose we had regularly drilled ourselves in the use of the photographic telescope, like so many artillerymen at a gun. Dr. Fritsch prepared the plates in the first tent; Dr. Zenker undertook the insertion of the dark slide into the tube; Dr. Thiele attended to the exposure of the plate in the telescope, which by means of the clock followed the course of the sun with such precision that its image remained immovable upon the prepared plate; and I developed the pictures in the second tent. We had proved by experiment that it was possible in this way to take six pictures in three minutes. The decisive moment came nearer and nearer; to our great joy the clouds we had been watching with so much anxiety began to break, and the sun, already partially eclipsed, appeared occasionally as a crescent. A strange light overspread the landscape, something between sunlight and moonlight. The chemical action of the light was exceedingly small. . . . The crescent kept diminishing—the breaks in the clouds seemed to increase; we began to hope. The minute before totality, which commenced at 6h. 20m., flew rapidly by. Dr. Fritsch and I hastily crept to our tents, and remained there, seeing unfortunately nothing of the totality under these circumstances. Our work began. The first plate was exposed five and ten seconds, to test the right amount of exposure. Mohammed, our black servant, brought me the first dark slide with the plate that had just been exposed. I poured the developing solution of iron over it, looking eagerly for the expected image. My lamp at this moment went out. 'Light! light!' I called—'light!' but no one heard; every one had enough to do. I caught at the outside of the tent with one hand—holding the plate in my left—and happily found the oil-lamp which I had placed there lighted in case of accident; then I saw the small image of the sun appearing on the plate (Fig. 116). The dark edge of the moon was surrounded by a range of remarkable elevations at one side, while on the other there was an extraordinary horn or protuberance. Both phenomena were perfectly analogous in the two pictures on the same plate. My delight was great, but it was no time for rejoicing. The second plate was soon brought me, and a minute later the third was also in my tent. 'The sun is coming!' called out Zenker, and the totality was over. All seemed but the work of a moment, so rapidly had the time flown. The second plate gave in developing only faint traces of an image, and showed peculiar markings; this was explained by thin passing clouds which had almost entirely interrupted the photographic action. The third plate (Fig. 117), taken during the third minute of totality, showed two suc-

Fig. 116.

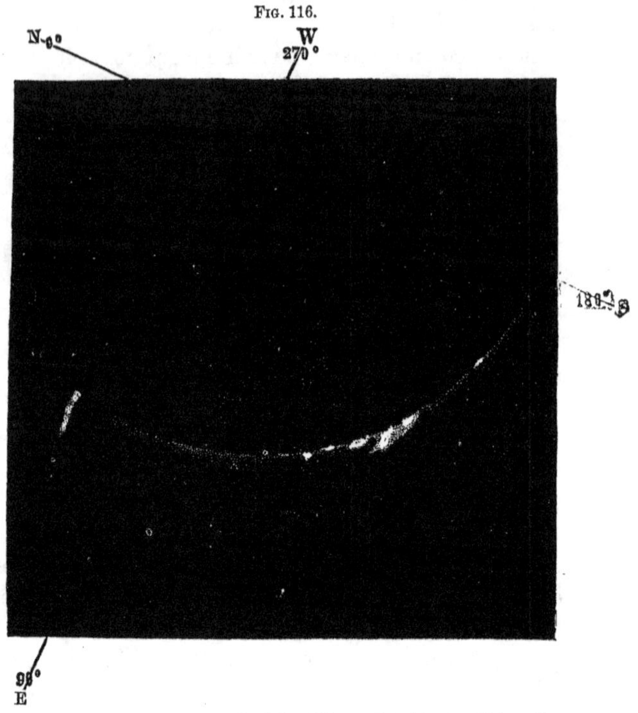

Total Solar Eclipse of August 18, 1868.—(Observed at Aden.) (Picture 1.)

cessful pictures, with prominences on the lower limb, as seen in an inverting telescope. The fourth picture (Fig. 118) was taken at the last moment of totality, and exhibited yet more plainly the prominences that had already appeared on the western limb of the sun."

By uniting in one drawing (Fig. 119) the various photographic pictures taken during the totality, a very correct conception may be formed of the way in which the prominences were arranged round the sun's limb at the time of the eclipse. The chemical action of the light of the corona was not sufficiently powerful to leave any impression on the prepared plate during the short time of exposure; but through the telescope, and even with the unassisted eye, this phenomenon was seen at every station in all its glory.

FIG. 117

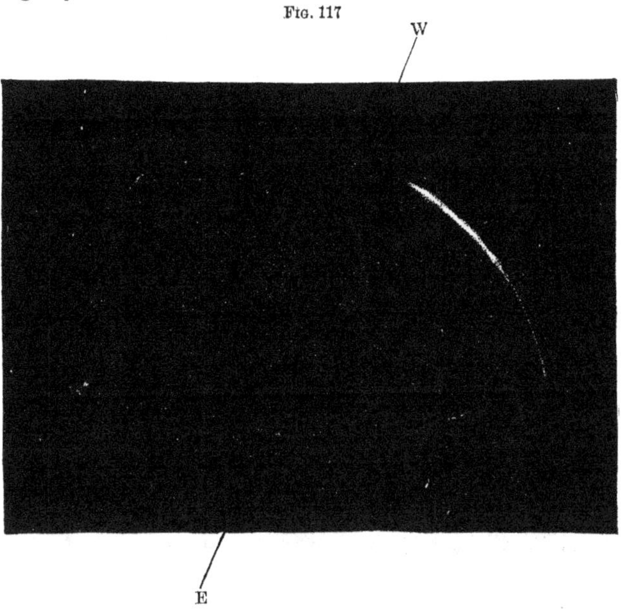

Total Solar Eclipse of August 18, 1868.—(Aden.) (Picture 2.)

The great prominence on the eastern limb of the sun had an elevation of about one-fourteenth of the sun's diameter, or about 60,000 miles.

In the various drawings of the totality, more or less carefully executed, which have been contributed by different observers, the prominences are very differently represented both as to size and position. After rejecting those unworthy productions prepared for sale which are finished merely for effect according to the fancy of the artist, the chief cause of these discrepancies will be found to arise from the fact that the sun's disk assumes a different position with respect to the horizon according as it is observed at sunrise, noon, or sunset. The same prominence, therefore, appears to occupy a different position with respect to the horizon in a picture taken early in the morning at Aden to that in which it appears in one taken at mid-day at Celebes.

Another cause of discrepancy is to be found in the difference of time (about seven hours) between the extreme ends of the central line of totality or zone of observation, one of which was at

Fig. 118.

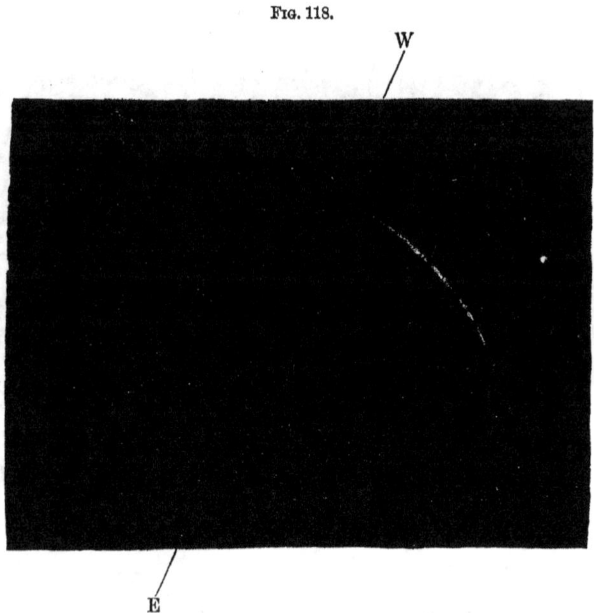

Total Solar Eclipse of August 18, 1868.—(Aden.) (Picture 3.)

Aden and the other at Celebes, and during this time great changes may have occurred in the position and size of the prominences. When it is remembered also that the image of the eclipsed sun appears inverted in an astronomical telescope, the upper part being seen below, and the right side reversed to the left, it will easily be understood that the various drawings of the eclipse present different appearances according to the place whence the phenomena were seen, and whether observed by the unassisted eye or by an inverting telescope.

When the sun at noon has reached its greatest altitude, the highest point is the true north, the lowest point the true south. Standing face to the sun, the east lies 90° from the north point to the left, and the west as many degrees to the right. A glance at Fig. 120 will show this more clearly; supposing the sun's circumference to be divided into 360°, and the north point reckoned as 0°, the point of due east lies 90° to the left of north, the south point 180°, and the west 270°.

Fig. 119.

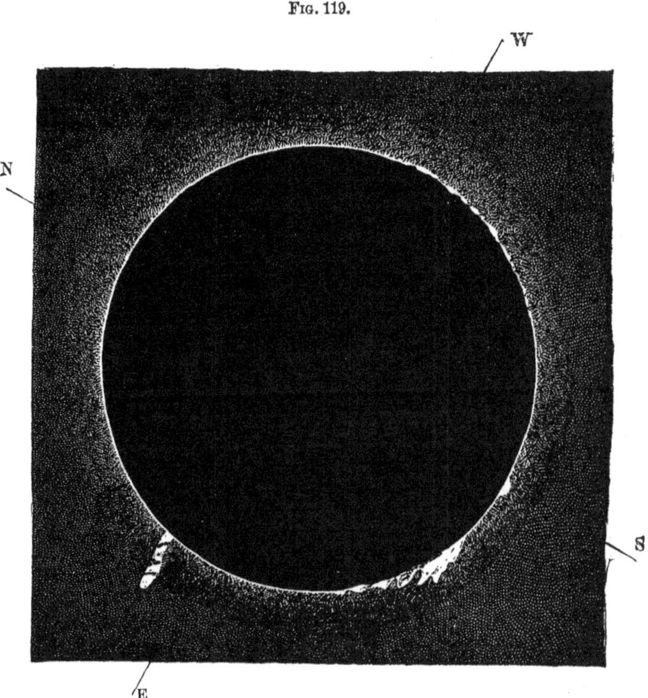

Union of the Prominences in one Drawing.

If the sun be observed at any other time of day, a vertical line represented by the cross-wires forms the apparent north and south line, the upper end of which is called the apparent north point, and the lower end the apparent south point. It is therefore easy for astronomers to calculate the true north for any time and place from the apparent north by means of the latitude and the time of observation, as well as to determine, by the use of a telescope provided with a suitable micrometer, the angle which the apparent north and south line makes with any other line drawn from the centre of the sun to its circumference. If, therefore, this angle—that is to say, the *apparent* position of any particular object on the limb or disk of the sun, a prominence or a solar spot for instance—be measured and reduced to the true north and south line, and the angle thus determined, or the *true* position be drawn out upon a diagram of the sun's disk, divided into degrees (*vide* Fig. 120), the correct place which the object occupied on the sun will then be found, whatever the position of the sun in the heavens may have been at the time of observation.

Fig. 120.

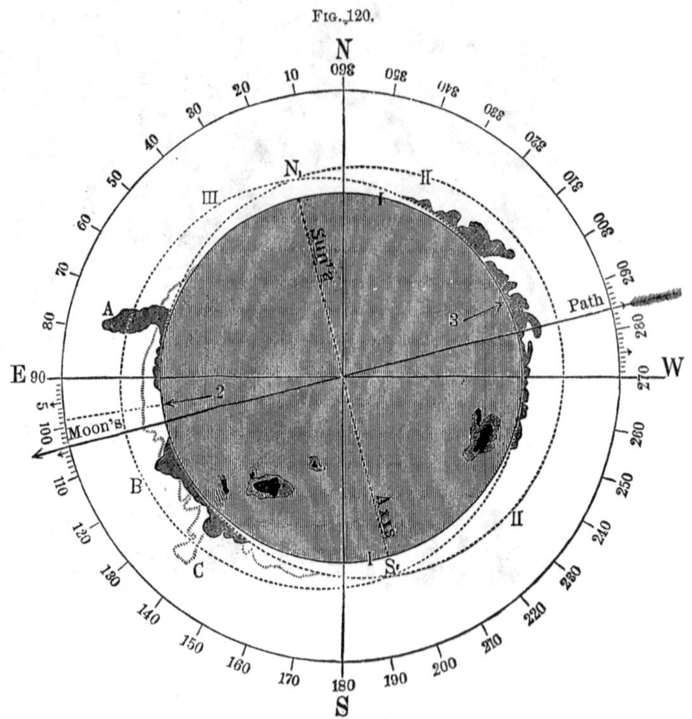

Tennant's Photographic Pictures collected into one Drawing.—(Guntoor, August 18, 1868.)

Fig. 109 gives a picture of the total eclipse of the 7th of August, 1869, taken at Des Moines at five o'clock in the afternoon, at which hour the apparent north point was considerably removed from the true north.

As the disk of the sun was never during any part of the totality concentric with that of the moon, a further correction is necessary for transferring the angles measured with the circumference of the moon to that of the sun. The angle of position for the great prominence (Figs. 116 and 120) was about 80°. To

TOTAL SOLAR ECLIPSE (India)
1868 August 18.

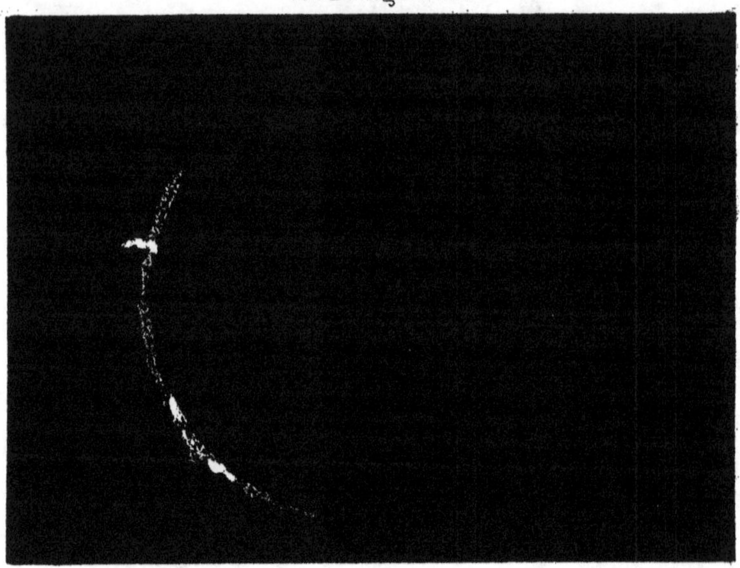

Guntoor (Col[l] Tennant) Commencement of Totality.
Time of Exposure 5 Sec.

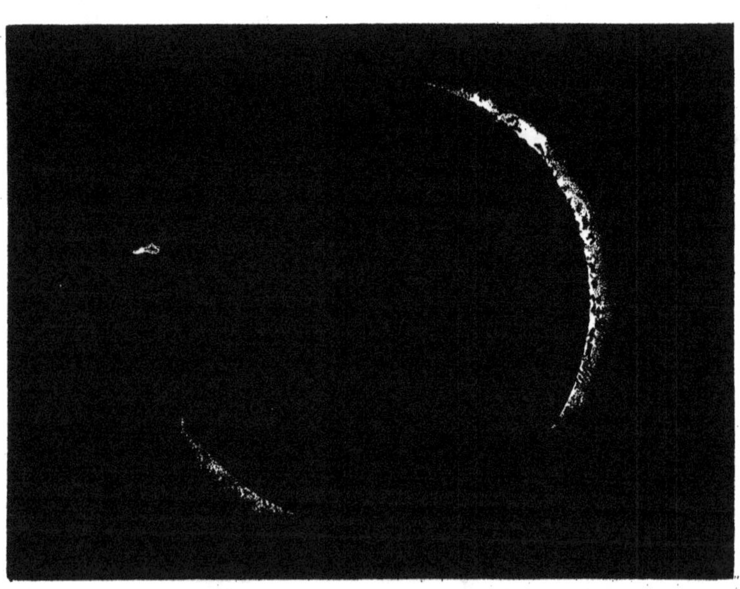

Guntoor (Col[l] Tennant) Towards the end of Totality.
Time of Exposure 1 Sec.

assist in estimating the positions, the four true points of the sun are given in Fig. 116 and following pictures of the eclipse.

The photographs obtained by Colonel Tennant at Guntoor appear at first sight to have been less successful than those taken at Aden. He exposed six plates, in all of which the prominences were sufficiently well marked to allow of the photographs being compared one with another. Plate VII. exhibits exact copies of these photographs, published with the coöperation of Warren De la Rue; the upper picture shows the eclipse at the commencement of the totality, and the lower one immediately before its cessation. In all the pictures the same large prominence appears which is to be seen in the photographs taken by the German expedition, while the configuration of the smaller prominences also seen in each plate presents a different appearance in every picture.

Warren De la Rue has superposed magnified copies (something more than two inches in diameter) of Tennant's six original photographs, and, by a careful estimation of the sun's centre and the exact coincidence of the large prominence in all the pictures, has composed a drawing (Fig. 120) which not only gives a representation of the prominences that made their appearance during the course of the eclipse, but also shows clearly by the first and second inner contacts the beginning and the end of the total darkness. In the figure the shaded disk I, I represents the sun; II, II denotes the moon's disk * at the moment of second contact 2 (first inner contact), when the totality began, and the large prominence A appeared on the sun's eastern limb; III, III is the moon's disk at the third contact 3 (second inner contact); the drawing also gives the position of the sun's axis, the direction in which the moon's centre was travelling from west to east, and indicates by the dotted lines over the prominences a peculiar faint glimmering light which appeared on the eastern side, and was invisible in the telescope on account of the brilliancy of the corona and prominences, a phenomenon the nature of which, unknown as yet, may perhaps be discovered at some future eclipse. The spots drawn on the sun's disk are those which were photographed at the Kew Observatory on the day of the eclipse. The corona and the halo are both wanting in these photographs.

The expedition of the Jesuits from Manila did not arrive at

* For the sake of clearness, the disk is drawn a little larger than it was in reality.

the plaçe of observation, owing to an accident to the machinery of the vessel, till the evening of the 17th of August, the day before the eclipse, so that no photographic experiments could be previously made on the spot selected as a station. The eight

FIG. 121.

Total Solar Eclipse of August 18, 1868, at Mantawaloc-Kekee.

instantaneous pictures of the principal phases of the eclipse were successful; but, of the four plates exposed during the totality, the second only, which was exposed twelve seconds, showed any trace of the corona. This loss was fortunately, however, repaired to some extent by immediately tracing upon the focussing-glass of the camera the image of the totality as it appeared upon the smoothly-ground glass, and permanently fixing the drawing thus made.

Fig. 121 gives a view of the totality as it was seen at Manta-waloc-Kekee during the last 2m. 25s., therefore just before the reappearance of the sun's rays. "Scarcely had the last ray of sunlight disappeared," writes Father F. Fauro in reporting the results of this expedition to Secchi, in Rome,* "when the magnificent corona or aureola burst into view, as by enchantment, round the black edge of the moon. The form that it assumed is shown in Fig. 121, but the color was beyond the power of any artist to paint. All observers agree that it resembled mother-of-pearl, or pure unpolished silver, but far more beautiful and more intensely brilliant. The corona consisted of three principal divisions: the first was a narrow circle of intense white light, forming an even band round the edge of the moon; the second extended farther out, gradually diminishing in intensity, but preserving tolerable regularity of form; the third was composed of a very large number of rays which possessed various degrees of intensity, and radiated with great irregularity, some reaching to a distance equal to more than double the diameter of the moon. The aspect of the rays changed slightly from one moment to another, and it deserves special notice that a somewhat brighter line was seen to cut obliquely through the lower (?) stratum of rays. This line represented a ray of light which made its appearance five minutes after the commencement of the totality, and remained visible as long as the darkness lasted." †

From the communications received from the various expeditions, it seems conclusive that the halo of the corona presented a different appearance at each station; but, as the drawings of this phenomenon were made from estimations taken merely by the eye, their accuracy is not sufficient to warrant any conclusions being deduced from them. We shall enter more fully upon this subject when we come to speak of the spectroscopic

* The full account is to be found in "Natur und Offenbarung," 1869, p. 145, and also in the "Wochenschrift für Astronomie und Meteorologie" (Halle, 1869), in papers communicated by Prof. Heiss, from the "Bulletino meteorologico dell 'Osservatorio del Collegio Romano" (vol. vii., No. 12).

† Similar phenomena were observed by Mazette and Dalbiez, at Perpignan, during the total eclipse of 1842; and by Stenglein, at Pobes, in the eclipse of the 18th of July, 1860.

16

observations of the corona, and the various theories that have been propounded as to its nature.

With regard to the inner portion of the corona, the observations made at all the above-mentioned stations concur in this—that all light was not extinguished during the totality, but that immediately after the disappearance of the sun (contact 2) the intensely black disk of the moon was surrounded by a very white and brilliant narrow ring of light, from which the pale-red prominences projected at various places. The Austrian observers, as well as the French observers Stéphan, Tisserand, and Janssen, speak very decidedly of the formation of an intensely bright and very narrow ring of light immediately round the edge of the

Fig. 122.

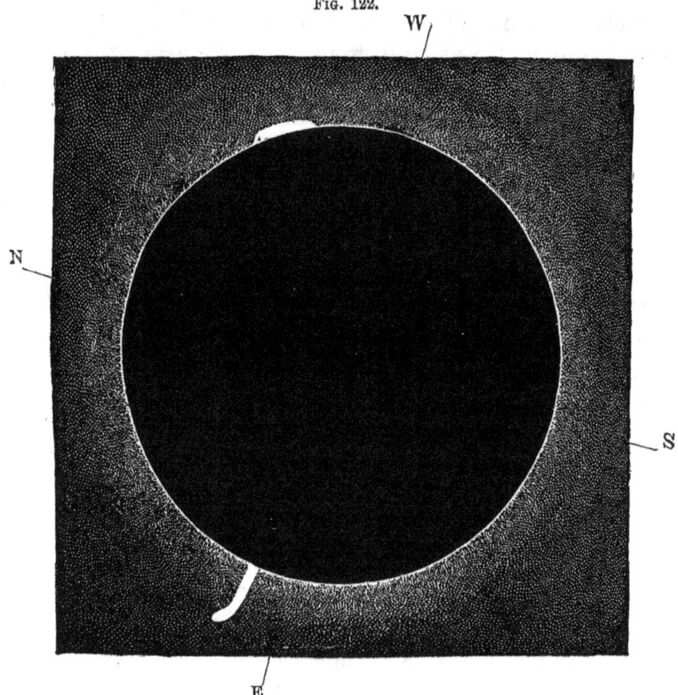

Solar Eclipse of August 18, 1868, observed from the Steamer Rangoon.

moon; there is, therefore, scarcely any doubt that the lower part of the corona belongs to the sun, and that this *close appendage of the sun is highly luminous, but that the intensity rapidly diminishes at a little distance from the edge.*

The observations of the total solar eclipse of the 18th of July, 1860, in Spain, when the prominences were photographed (Fig. 114), as well as examined telescopically by many eminent astronomers, left scarcely any doubt that these remarkable forms are of a gaseous nature, and belong, not to the moon, but to the

Fig. 123.

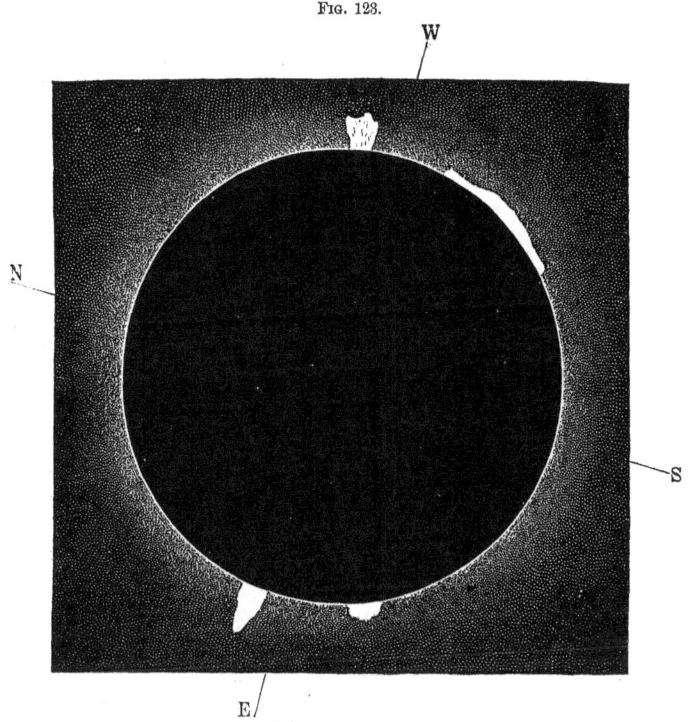

Solar Eclipse of August 18, 1868, observed at Wha-Tonne by Stéphan.

sun. The eclipse of the 18th of August, 1868, afforded an opportunity for acquiring complete certainty on this subject.

At the same instant that the corona started into view, the prominences also became visible on the eastern limb of the sun, precisely at the spot where the last rays of light disappeared at the commencement of the totality. The first of these prominences, to the left of the vertical line (Fig. 116), was of an extraordinary height, and shone with an intense rose-colored light; the other prominence at the right side of the vertical line was of a similar color, and of equal brilliancy, but was neither so high nor so beautiful in form.

Fig. 122 shows the great prominence as observed from the steamer Rangoon at the beginning of total darkness, when another prominence, much less in height, but spreading much farther along the sun's limb, made its appearance almost simultaneously upon the opposite side.

Fig. 123 represents the prominences as they were drawn by Stéphan during the course of the totality at Wha-Tonne.

Fig. 124 is in connection with the more complete picture of

FIG. 124.

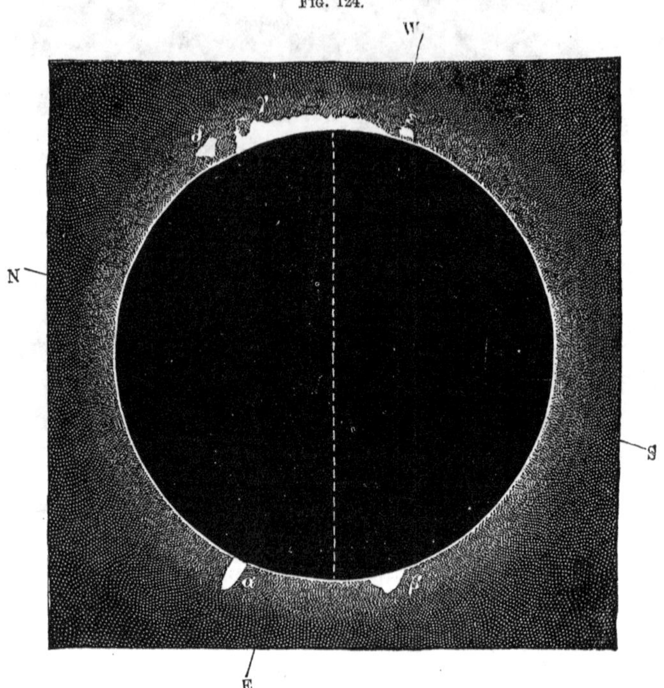

Solar Eclipse of August 18, 1868, observed at Mantawaloc-Kekee.

the totality shown in Fig. 121, and merely represents the prominences as they were observed at Mantawaloc-Kekee by the Jesuits from Manila 2m. 25s. before the reappearance of the sun. In explanation of this picture, we give an abstract of Father Fauro's communication to Secchi.

The breadth of the great prominence α was 1° 40′, that of the second one β amounted to 9° at the base. Scarcely had these prominences made their appearance when a third prominence γ broke out from the western limb of the sun, and gradually increased in size and beauty as the moon passed over the sun from west to east (*vide* Fig. 120). The phenomenon of the gradual disappearance of the prominences from the eastern side, and the simultaneous increase and extension of those on the western side, was distinctly seen by all observers. The height of the two prominences α and β, the moment they appeared in view, was respectively 3′ 10″ and 1′ 15″, and on repeating the measurements after an interval of 3′ 10″, when the totality was about half over, their height was found to be 2′ 12″ and 0′ 18″.* The prominence γ, which was seen at first with difficulty, was gradually disclosed as the moon passed on, and when fully visible presented the appearance of a long chain of mountains. It terminated very abruptly to the left, as if suddenly cut off, while toward the right it gradually diminished in height until it was lost behind the dark disk of the moon at the spot where the corona exhibited the greatest amount of irregularity.

In the same picture, Fig. 124, a fourth prominence δ is seen to the left of γ; it was completely separated from the other prominences, and presented the appearance of a cloud:† the color was neither so brilliant nor so uniform as that of the others, and it exhibited some dark streaks similar to those observed in other prominences; its breadth amounted to 5° 30′. Finally, a small prominence ϵ made its appearance half a minute before the end of the totality, to the right of the chain of rose-colored peaks; it was perfectly detached, and bore a great resemblance to δ.

The color of the prominences was described in very different terms by the various observers; it was designated by most of them as pale red, by some as scarlet, by others again as rose-red or pale coral-red, and by Tennant as white.

* One second = 450 miles.† As a rule, one second of the measured angle of an object seen upon the sun from the earth may be reckoned roundly at 100 German geographical miles, and one minute of the arc of the sun's circumference as 122 miles.

† In later observations by Zöllner, Lockyer, and Young, to which we shall have occasion again to refer, the same forms are repeatedly exhibited.

† [More accurately, 1″ is equal to 445 miles.]

52. The Total Solar Eclipse of August 7, 1869.

This eclipse was likewise invisible in Europe; the zone of totality stretched from Alaska, where the eclipse began at noon, over British America and the southwest corner of Minnesota, then crossed the Mississippi near Burlington (Iowa), and passed through Illinois, Western Virginia, and North Carolina, reaching the Atlantic Ocean in the neighborhood of Beaufort.

The event excited the most lively interest among astronomers and photographers throughout the whole of North America, and occasioned the equipment of a number of scientific expeditions, which were also supplemented by the valuable labors of many private individuals. The observers were in almost every instance favored with the finest weather, and their efforts were rewarded by a large collection of photographic pictures, and many valuable spectroscopic and other observations. That portion of the zone of totality which traversed the inhabited parts of the United States was studied everywhere with telescopes, spectroscopes, and other instruments of observation, so that the whole of this tract of country became one vast observatory. Although the duration of totality was less than in the eclipse observed in India (1868), yet the phenomenon was attended on the whole with many more favorable circumstances; the heat was less intense, the places suitable for observation were much more conveniently situated, and the sun's altitude was not so great as in the eclipse of 1868. The most important points of investigation had reference to the scrutiny of the prominences by means of photography and the spectroscope, the examination of the nature of the corona, and the search for planets between Mercury and the sun.

The most complete expeditions were those sent out from Washington, one from the Nautical Almanac Office, the astronomical department being under the charge of Prof. Coffin, while the photographic arrangements were conducted by Prof. Henry Morton, of Philadelphia: another expedition was dispatched from the United States Naval Observatory, under the superintendence of Commodore B. F. Sands.

The first expedition, under the guidance of Prof. Morton, selected stations in the State of Iowa, as follows:

1. Burlington, where the observers were Prof. Mayer, and

Messrs. Kendall, Willard, Phillips, and Mahoney, together with Dr. C. A. Young, professor of Dartmouth College (Hanover), well known as an experienced spectroscopist, and Dr. B. A. Gould, to whose charge the photographic department was committed.

2. Ottumwa, where Prof. Himes, and Messrs. Zentmeyer, Moelling, Brown, and Baker, were stationed.

3. Mount Pleasant, occupied by Prof. Morton, and Messrs. Wilson, Clifford, Cremer, Ranger, and Carbutt, as well as by some other professors, including Pickering, who were desirous of making astronomical observations on the physical phenomena of the eclipse.

Stations selected by the second expedition:

1. Des Moines (Iowa), where Prof. Newcomb undertook the observation of the corona and the search for intermercurial planets, Prof. Harkness the spectroscopic investigations, and Prof. Eastman the meteorological department. Several other gentlemen skilled in solar photography associated themselves with these observers.

2. Bristol (Tennessee), where Bardwell, who undertook the observation of the corona, and other observers, were stationed.

Besides these important expeditions, furnished with the most admirable and complete means of observation, several scientific men were engaged at various points in the zone of totality, either in observing the astronomical details of the eclipse, or in investigating the prominences, the corona, and their spectra. Among these may be mentioned Dr. Edward Curtis, who at Des Moines obtained no fewer than 119 pictures of the different phases of the eclipse; W. S. Gilman, by whom some most valuable observations were instituted at St. Paul Junction (Iowa) upon the connection between the solar spots, the faculæ, and the prominences; J. A. Whipple, who with Prof. Winlock and several assistants procured at Shelbyville (Kentucky) eighty photographic pictures, six of which were taken during the totality, one of them exhibiting a complete and magnificent corona; as well as Prof. G. W. Hough, director of the Dudley Observatory, who in company with nine fellow-observers recorded all the details of the eclipse at Mattoon (Illinois).

Out of the mass of materials afforded by the observations of this eclipse it will only come within our province to communicate those results which have reference to the physical constitution of the sun, and were obtained partly by photographic delineation, and partly by the help of the spectroscope. Here, as in § 51, the phenomena of the eclipse as exhibited in the telescope and on the photographic plates will first be described, while the details of the prominences and the corona revealed by the spec troscope will be deferred to a future page. The course of the eclipse and the photographic work carried on at Mount Pleasant, where the totality lasted two minutes, forty-eight seconds, is described by Wilson nearly as follows:

"For some days prior to the eclipse the sky was overcast and threatened rain, but the 7th of August was bright, without a cloud, such a day as had not occurred for months, and the sun shone with remarkable clearness and warmth. The moment of first contact arrived; the first plate was already placed in the tube; Prof. Watson signalled to us the moment for exposure by a motion of the hand; the instantaneous shutter was opened and closed, and the first picture was taken. We thus commenced a series of pictures taken at intervals of five or ten minutes till the commencement of totality, after which the series was continued on the reappearance of the sun till the termination of the eclipse. Darkness came on with the totality, but not the darkness of night; still it rendered reading impossible. The amount of light upon the landscape was scarcely equal to that of bright moonlight, yet it was sufficient for us to pursue our work. An instant before the commencement of totality the thin crescent of the sun was still quite dazzling; then the light went out as from an expiring candle.

"There, between heaven and earth, hung face to face the two great luminaries, sun and moon, a large black round spot encircled by a brilliant ring of deep gold-colored light, interrupted here and there by the brighter spots of the flesh-colored prominences of irregular size and form, and surrounded by the magnificent corona, which shot out rays in every direction, faintest where the prominences were most conspicuous, but enveloping the whole with a glory which was marvellously beautiful, as if the Creator were about to show His omnipotence in this wonder. The phenomenon resembled a gigantic image from a magic-lantern received upon the heavens as a screen. Four plates were exposed, when suddenly the full significance of those words was

TOTAL SOLAR ECLIPSE (North America)
1869 August. 7.

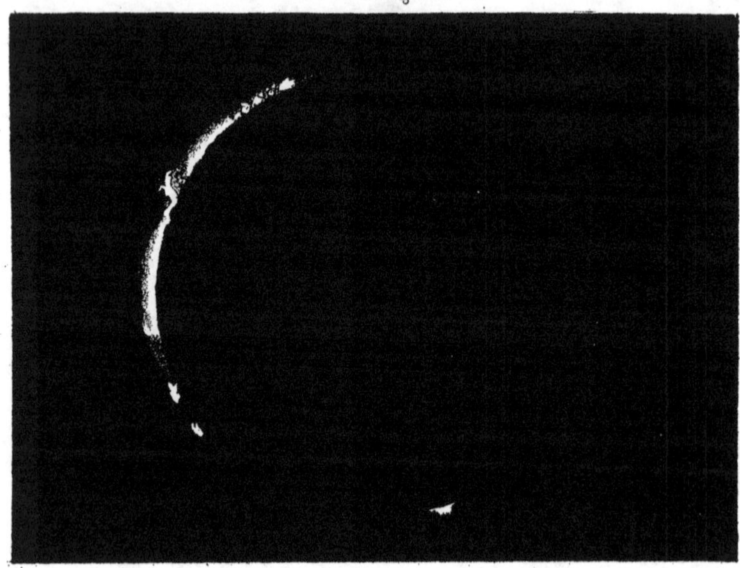

Burlington (Iowa) Commencement of Totality.
Time of Exposure 5 Sec.

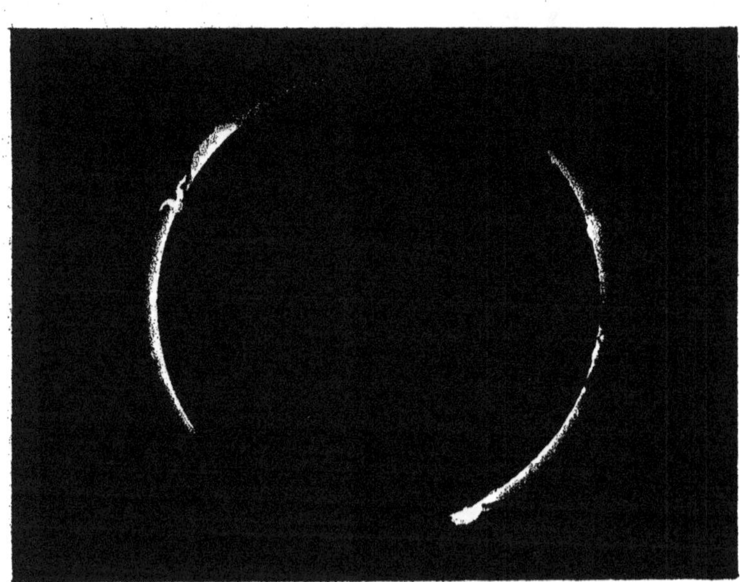

Burlington (Iowa) Towards the end of Totality.
Time of Exposure 7 Sec.

realized, 'Let there be light, and there was light,' for a mighty flood of brilliant light gushed forth like the rushing, foaming waters of Niagara. The sun came forth like a conqueror from a battle with the Titans, and was greeted with acclamations by the assembled spectators."

The three pictures of the totality taken at Mount Pleasant were not remarkably sharp, as the telescope was not furnished with a clock-movement: much better results were obtained by the observers stationed at Ottumwa and Burlington; at Ottumwa forty negatives were taken, four of which were during the totality; and, of the forty pictures obtained at Burlington, six were taken while the totality lasted; so that the expedition under Morton contributed thirteen pictures of the totality, several of which were of great excellence.

A picture of this magnificent spectacle has been already given in Fig. 109, showing the prominences and corona after drawings made by Dr. Gould; the photographic plates, which were exposed for the brief space of from five to sixteen seconds, give only faint traces of the corona, on account of its light being too weak to produce in so short a time any chemical action on the prepared plates. Plate VIII. contains correct copies of the two photographic pictures taken at Burlington at the commencement of the totality and immediately before its termination. In the upper picture the first prominences are just becoming visible on the eastern limb of the sun, while those on the western limb are still covered by the moon; by the farther advance of the moon from west to east, the eastern prominences are shown in the lower picture to be gradually disappearing, while those to the west are being revealed with increasing distinctness.

Fig. 125 unites in one picture all the prominences as they appeared on the sun's limb during the course of the totality, whether as single and isolated flames, or in less definite forms as wide-spread luminous masses, arranged according to the measures obtained and the estimations made of their angles of position (p. 223). The prominences are numbered from 1 to 12, beginning at north and passing by east and south to west; among them Nos. 4, 5, and 8 are especially remarkable from their form and height. No. 4, called "the eagle," rose to a height of 82″. No. 5, "a nebulous cloud of flame" extending from B to C, attained a height of 136″; while No. 8, compared to "the head of an albatross," measured 75″ in height, whence it may be calculated that the actual height of these prominences must have been respectively 37,000 miles, 61,000 miles, and 34,000 miles.

Fig. 125.

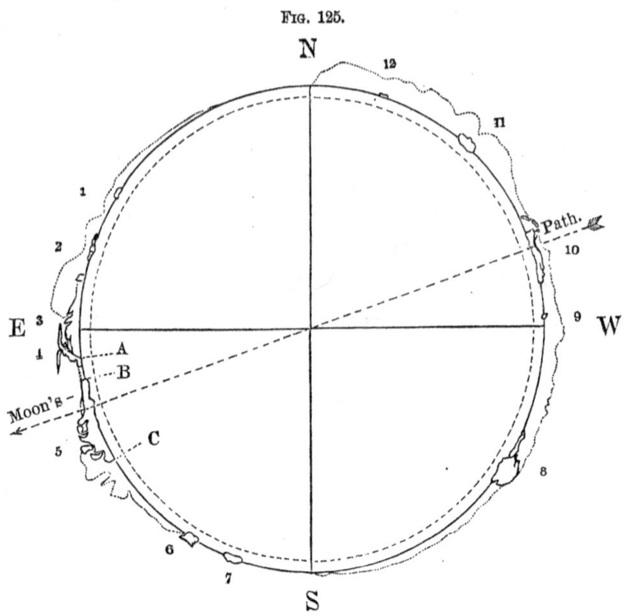

Union of the Prominences in one Drawing.—(Total Eclipse of August 7, 1869.)

In the photographic pictures there was to be seen a glow of light of indefinite form (represented in Fig. 125 by an irregular dotted line), which extended from the point N toward the east nearly as far as S, and attained a maximum elevation of 2′ 15″ about half-way between the prominences 2 and 4, and again at a few degrees south of 5. In the vicinity of the prominences 3 and 5, near the points where the luminous appendage had attained its greatest elevation, several tongues of vivid flame, separated one from another, rose high above the lower portions of the mass of light. The white nebulous cloud of light between B and C attained a height of at least 64,000 miles. A similar luminous cloud was seen in the pictures along the western side, extending from south to north; it reached a maximum height between the prominences 11 and 12, and at the point N was cut off almost perpendicularly.

The dotted surface within the moon's edge shows the proportional size of the sun, as well as its position in the middle of totality. The arrow marks the direction of the moon's course; but the fact, that the disks of the sun and moon were never perfectly concentric during the eclipse, has not been disregarded in the drawing.

In the photographic pictures the bases of the prominences, with the exception of No. 4, project within the circle formed by the moon's edge, as shown in Fig. 125. The explanation of this remarkable phenomenon was thought to be found in the circumstance that the photographic telescope, by following the motion of the prominences by clock-work, kept their image immovable on the photographic plate, while the image of the moon, owing to its angular motion being different to that of the sun, continued to advance over the plate. Dr. Curtis, however, has strikingly shown, by photographing from an artificial eclipse in which the moon was represented by black paper, notched for the prominences and corona, that this projection of the prominence-images on the disk of the moon is caused by a kind of *photographic irradiation* on the prepared plate, and is therefore an entirely mechanical action which always occurs where an intensely bright object is in immediate contact with a dark one, and the duration of the action of the light (time of exposure) has exceeded the proper limit.

The eclipse of 1868 observed in India, though furnishing so many valuable details concerning the prominences, was almost without results with respect to the corona. The various observers of the eclipse in America were all the more eager, therefore, to examine the details of this remarkable phenomenon, its form, its spectrum, and especially its connection with the prominences.

The photographs of short exposure (from one to seven seconds) show the corona only in its brightest parts close to the edge of the sun; still they give, especially those taken at Ottumwa, a tolerably distinct image of it, with nearly the same form as it presented to the unassisted eye. The curved path of the rays, and the varying intensity with which they stream out from the different points, can be distinctly traced in these pictures. The most brilliant rays agree strikingly in position with the light of those prominences which have the form of a pointed flame, while where the prominences resemble rounded masses a shadow seems cast upon the corona. It is clearly evident, from these pictures, that the corona does not move along with the moon during the totality, but that it remains concentric with the sun. It becomes more and more covered at the eastern edge in proportion as the moon advances, and in the same proportion is gradually revealed on the opposite side.

In order to obtain a complete photographic picture of the entire corona in all its parts, not only must the time of exposure considerably exceed that requisite for the intensely bright prominences, but the image of the corona must not be magnified before falling on the photographic plate. J. A. Whipple, of Boston, accordingly arranged his telescope for photographing the corona at Shelbyville (Kentucky) in such a manner that the prepared plate was placed in the main focus of the object-glass, and he employed forty seconds as the time of exposure. In this way a picture was obtained in which the prominences appeared only as bright spots, while the inner ring of light, as well as the outline of the whole corona, and the peculiar curve of its rays, are clearly shown. Fig. 126 is an exact copy of this picture, with the excep-

Fig. 126.

Photographic Picture of the Corona, August 7, 1869.

tion that in the original the light fades away more gradually, and the rays are not so sharply defined.

When the corona is observed through a large telescope, only a small portion of it can be seen at once, and the instrument must be gradually turned round the entire limb of the moon in order to obtain a general view of the whole. Prof. Eastman, who instituted observations of this kind at Des Moines, has published two pictures of the corona, one of which, represented in Fig. 127, was taken at the commencement of the totality, and the other just before its termination. The instant the totality began, the corona made its appearance as a light of silvery whiteness, with an exceedingly tender flush of a greenish-violet hue at the extreme edges, and not the slightest change was perceptible during the totality in the color, the outline, or the position of the rays—an observation confirmed by Prof. Hough at Mattoon (Illinois), by Gill, and by several others.

FIG. 127.

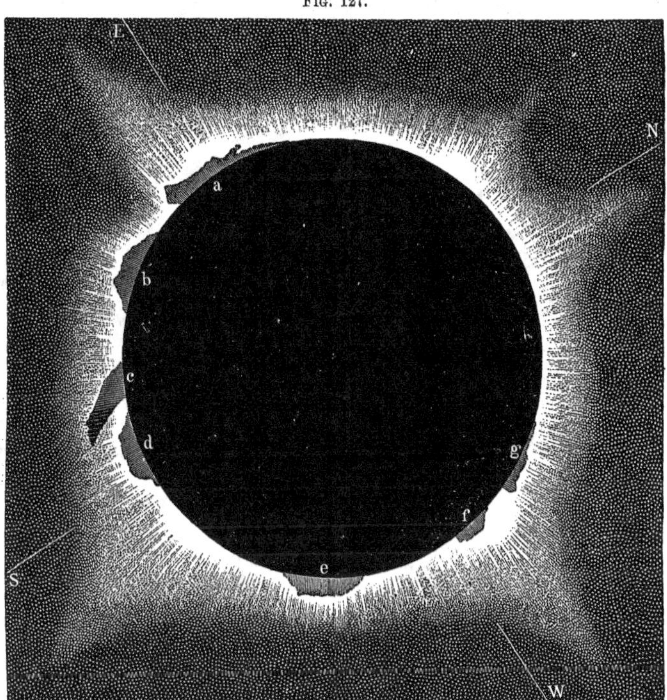

The Corona of the Eclipse of August 7, 1869, at Des Moines.

The corona appeared to consist of two principal portions: the inner one, next to the sun, was nearly annular, reaching an elevation of about 1′, and in color of a pure silvery whiteness; the outer portion consisted of rays, some of which grouped themselves into five star-like points, while the others assumed the appearance of radiations, and were the most sharply defined; the corona was scarcely visible between the prominences *a* and *b*. The star-like rays attained a height equal to half the diameter of the sun.

FIG. 128.

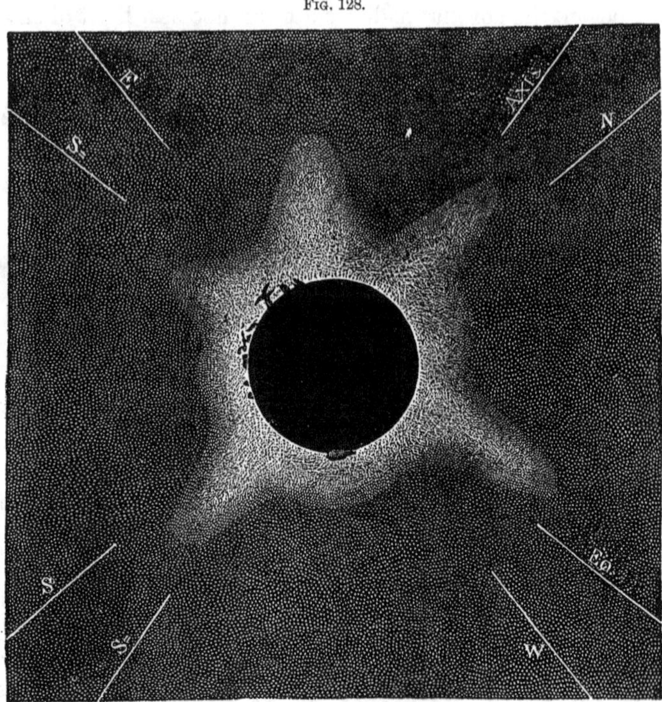

Gould's Drawing of the Corona of August 7, 1869 (4h. 58m.).

Dr. B. A. Gould observed the corona with the unassisted eye at Burlington, and made three complete drawings of it during the totality, at intervals of one minute. In Figs. 128 and 129 two of the pictures are given, one representing the corona at the commencement of the totality, at 4h. 58m., and the other at 5h., immediately before its termination. These pictures by Gould appear to be opposed to the observations cited above, that the corona preserved the same appearance throughout the totality, inasmuch as they seem to show some evidence of change. This observer therefore maintains that, owing to the long exposure of forty seconds, the sharp photographic picture (Fig. 126) does not represent the corona, but another luminous atmosphere of the sun—the chromosphere. Against this opinion of Gould's, it must first of all be remarked that it is not possible to draw a correct picture of the corona in all its details merely by the unassisted eye, without the aid of instruments of measurement, for which reason all the drawings of the various observers made

Fig. 129.

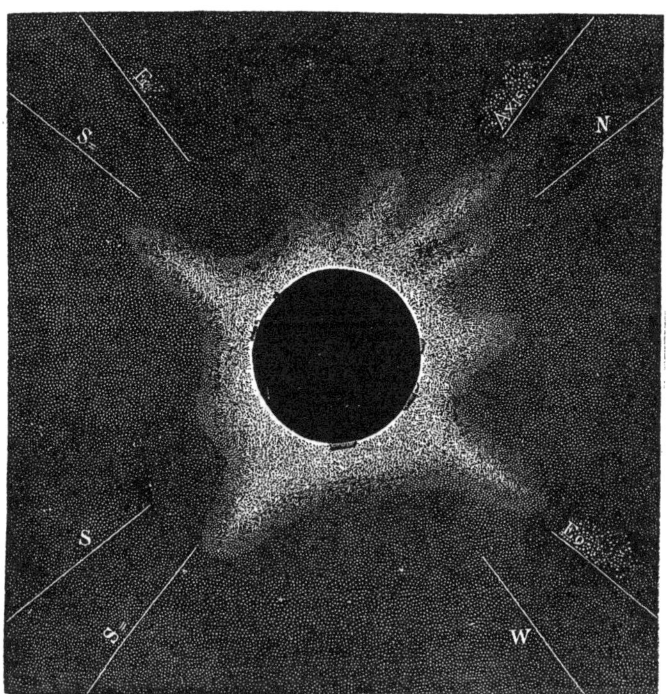

Gould's Drawing of the Corona of August 7, 1869 (5h.).

merely by the eye differ one from the other, and from the photographs;* then, again, the photographic picture taken by Whipple, that has been alluded to, cannot possibly represent the chromosphere, since this appendage of the sun, as will be seen farther on, is not higher than 10″ (4,450 miles),† while the rays of light in the photograph attain a height of 10′ (277,000 miles). Dr. Curtis has, after a very complete and searching investigation, ar-

* [The differences between the pictures of the corona made by different observers are often greater than can be accounted for by the reasons given in the text.]

† [The whole question rests upon the meaning assigned to the word *chromosphere*. See note at the beginning of § 56.]

rived at the conclusion that Gould's three drawings of the corona are not perfectly accurate, and that his views as to the variability of the corona, and his explanation of Whipple's photograph, cannot be justified; but that, on the contrary, the corona did not change its form during the whole period of total darkness, and that the photograph referred to could represent nothing else but the corona.

53. The Prominences and their Spectra.

In the total eclipse of the 18th of August, 1868, the spectrum of the prominences was observed by Herschel at Jamkandi, by Haig at Beejapoor, by Tennant and Janssen at Guntoor, by Rayet and Hall at Wha Tonne, and was found by these observers to consist of a few bright lines, from which they concluded that these forms are composed of *luminous gases* of which hydrogen gas is the chief constituent. The spectrum of this gas is characterized, as is well known, by three bright lines (Frontispiece No. 7), of which the first, *red*, is coincident with the Fraunhofer line C; the second, *greenish blue*, coincides with the line F; while the third, *dark blue*, lies in the vicinity of the line G (*vide* Fig. 69, No. 2).

Fig. 130 contains, in addition to the two comparison spectra No. 1 (the principal lines of the solar spectrum), and No. 2 (the principal lines of hydrogen gas), the spectra of the prominences Nos. 3, 4, 5, and 6, as observed by Rayet, Herschel, Tennant, and Lockyer.

Rayet, who preferred to keep his direct-vision spectroscope pointed exclusively to the great prominence, and employed the instrument in all positions, perceived nine bright lines, consisting of those corresponding to the dark lines B, D, E, *b*, F, G, of a green line between *b* and F, and a blue one near G (No. 3). These lines appeared very bright upon the dark background, so that their position could be determined with ease. The bright lines D, E, F, were seen in the inverting telescope of the spectroscope to be prolonged downward below the rest, as finer and fainter lines, and were thus turned away from the sun's limb, a phenomenon which seems to indicate that a portion of the mass of glowing gas composing the prominence stretches far upward into the sun's atmosphere in a state of extreme rarefaction.

Herschel (No. 4) made use of a spectroscope specially constructed for these observations, and for the measurement of the spectrum lines. At the first glance the spectrum of the prominence appeared as a spectrum of three very brilliant lines, of which the orange line coincided with D, while the red line was not coincident with either B or C, nor did the blue line coincide with F.

FIG. 130.

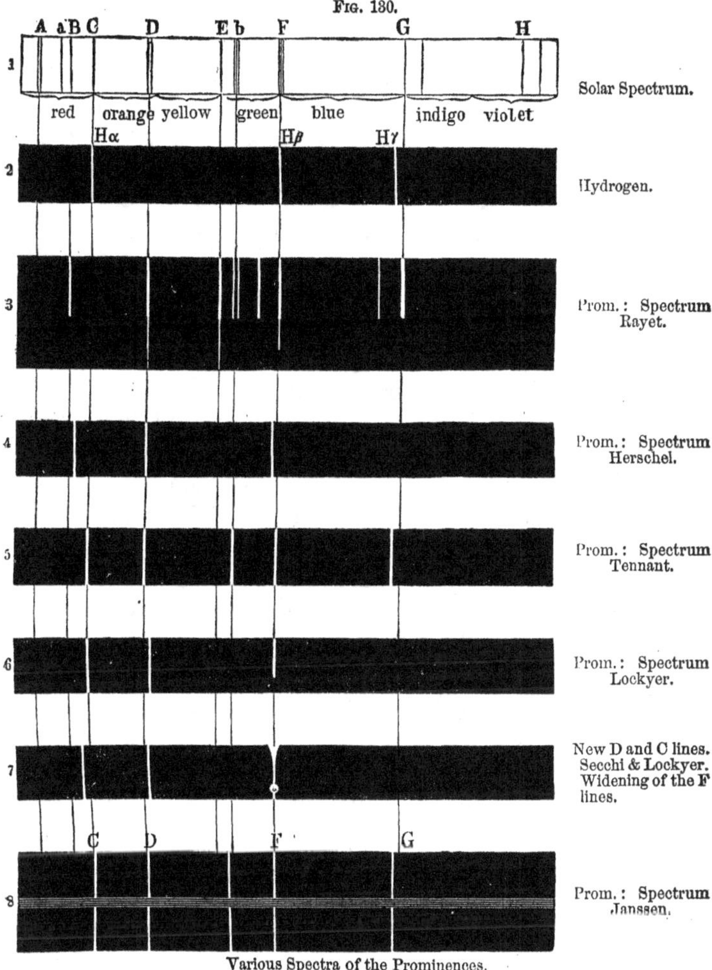

Various Spectra of the Prominences.

Tennant (No. 5) employed a spectroscope similar to that used by Huggins in his investigations on the spectra of the nebulæ and the fixed stars. The spectrum of the prominence appeared to him as a spectrum of five bright lines, three of which were in exact coincidence with C, D, and *b*, while the greenish-blue line lay very near to F, and the dark-blue line near to G. Time did not allow of a more accurate measurement of these two doubtful lines, but from the observations of Rayet it is almost certain that the first of them was actually coincident with F, and the other with the hydrogen line H γ, near to G.

Janssen sent the first telegraphic announcement to Europe that the spectrum of the prominences consisted of bright lines, and that therefore these remarkable forms are enormous columns of luminous gas, of which hydrogen constitutes the chief element. In readiness for the observation, the slit was held close to the advancing limb of the moon, at a tangent to the point where the last rays of the sun would disappear. With the extinction of the last rays, two new spectra started suddenly into view, each consisting of five or six bright lines (Fig. 130, No. 8); the lines were red, yellow, green, blue, and violet, and the two spectra, which were separated by a dark space, were exactly coincident line for line. When Janssen left the spectroscope to look for a moment through the finder, or small telescope, he saw that both spectra belonged to two magnificent prominences which shone out at the black edge of the moon to the right and left of the point where the last ray of sunlight had disappeared. One of these attained a height of 3′, and resembled the flame of a furnace as it breaks forth vehemently under the influence of a powerful blast; the other presented the appearance of an extended chain of snow mountains, which seemed to rest on the moon's limb, and glowed as if illuminated by the red light of the setting sun. As the principal lines of the spectrum coincided with the Fraunhofer lines C and F, Janssen declared at once that hydrogen gas forms an important element in the constitution of the prominences.

From the circumstance that the space between the spectra of the two prominences was dark, Janssen was brought to the conclusion that the results of his investigations were not in accordance with Kirchhoff's theory. He imagined that the space between these prominences must have been filled with what Kirchhoff had assumed to be the solar atmosphere, and therefore that this space, instead of being dark in the spectroscope, ought to have yielded a spectrum of bright lines. As this was not the case, then, Kirchhoff's theory, that the white light of the solid or incandescent solar nucleus was partially absorbed by the glowing vapors of an atmosphere, had become untenable; this absorption could not, therefore, have taken place outside the photosphere or light-giving portion of the sun, but necessarily within it, and had been produced by the glowing vapors from which the condensed solid or liquid particles of the cloud-like mass of the actual photosphere were formed.

In reply to this objection of Janssen's, it may be remarked that, though he obtained no spectrum from the immediate neighborhood of the sun, it was to be attributed to the very narrow setting of the slit he employed, for the sake of seeing the bright lines of the prominences distinctly, which was too narrow to allow of a spectrum from the other much fainter portions of the sun being received at the same time. Rziha, as well as Tennant, obtained indubitable though faint spectra from the immediate neighborhood of the sun. Janssen's observations seem, therefore, only to strengthen the conclusion arrived at by the other observers, that the light of the prominences is much more intense than that of the solar atmosphere, even when in closest proximity to the sun's limb, or than the corona.

If all the spectrum observations of the prominences made on the 18th of August, 1868, be collected together, and those of least importance be set aside, the following results are obtained:

1. The spectrum of the prominences consists of some bright lines of intense brilliancy, among which the hydrogen lines $H\alpha = C$, $H\beta = F$, and $H\gamma$, near to G, are especially noticeable.

2. The prominences are masses of luminous gas, principally luminous hydrogen gas; they envelop the entire surface of the solar body, sometimes in a low stratum extending over exceedingly large tracts of the sun's surface, sometimes in accumulated masses rising at certain localities to a height of more than 80,000 miles.

In the eclipse of the 7th of August, 1869, observed in America, the spectra of the prominences were investigated by Prof. Harkness at Des Moines, as well as by Prof. Young at Burlington, who devoted himself with especial attention to this work. Prof. Harkness employed an ordinary simple spectroscope, consisting of a single prism of 60°, to which had been added a micrometer in preparation for the eclipse. Owing to the small dispersive power of such an instrument, the measures taken of the distances between the lines of the spectrum, as compared with Kirchhoff's scale, can make no claim to great accuracy. Harkness compared the divisions of his micrometer, by means of the principal Fraunhofer lines, with the millimetre numbers of the same lines in Kirchhoff's map, and marked the bright lines seen in the prominences given in Fig. 127 by the following numbers of Kirchhoff's scale:

Prominence *a* gave approximately the lines:
693, 1007, 1497 (Kirchhoff).
Prominence *c* gave approximately the lines:
693, 1007, 1497, ——, 2069.
Prominence *e* gave approximately the lines:
693, 1007, 1497, 1611, 2069, 2770.
Prominence *f* gave approximately the lines:
693, 1007, 1497, ——, 2069, 2770.

If these readings, though only approximately correct, be compared with Kirchhoff's numbers for the most important of the Fraunhofer lines given in p. 165, it will be found that the bright lines observed in the prominences may very probably have been as follows: 694 = C (H α), 1017 = D_3 (beyond D_2), 2080 = F (H β), 2796 = H γ, as well as the line 1474 (instead of 1497) less refrangible than E. Whether an error had occurred in the measurement of the position of the green line 1611 (between E and *b*), or whether this line be identical with that observed by Winlock in the spectrum of the Aurora Borealis marked 1680 in Huggins's scale (1608, Kirchhoff), must still be left in doubt. According to these observations, therefore, it appears that the bright lines in the various prominences vary in number, but not in position, and that hydrogen gas is the principal constituent of the prominences.

The observations and measurements made by Young were much more accurate and complete: he was provided with an instrument consisting of five prisms of 45° each, the lateral surfaces of $2\frac{1}{4}$ and $3\frac{1}{4}$ inches, and the method by which this compound spectroscope P was connected with the telescope A, a comet-seeker of 4 inches aperture and 30 inches focus, is shown in Fig. 131. The collimator C was furnished with an adjustable slit one-eighth of an inch in length, through one-half of which the prism of comparison introduced into the instrument the light of any terrestrial substance rendered luminous in the electric spark, or of a Geissler's tube; by means of the conducting wires L, the platinum electrodes could be placed in connection with an induction coil. Immediately in front of the slit there was placed at S

FIG. 131.

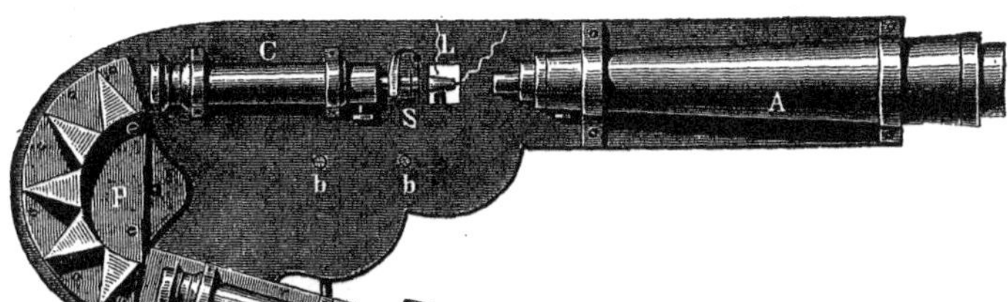

Young's Telespectroscope.

a divided disk, in the centre of which was a circular opening one-eighth of an inch wide, a contrivance by means of which the image of the sun could be kept exactly on the slit, and any portion of the solar image directed upon it at will. The dispersive power of the five prisms amounted to 80° between the lines A and H, and the total deviation for the D-line nearly to 165°. The prisms were so adjusted one with another, and the plate P carrying them secured to the telescope A in such a manner by the bolts *b*, *b*, that all lines occupying the middle of the field of view should be in the most advantageous position; the field of view included at the same time the lines D and E. By means of the micrometer-screw T, the telescope E, turning upon a pivot, could be directed upon any of the lines of the spectrum; the eye-piece was furnished with a micrometer, M.

The solar spectrum appeared about an inch and three-quarters in width, and 45 inches in length, and showed all the lines contained in Kirchhoff's map. The readings of the instrument had been compared with Kirchhoff's maps by repeated measurements at forty-two intervals between the principal lines along the whole length of the spectrum from A to G.

Before the commencement of totality, the slit *s s* (Fig. 132) was placed on the limb M N of the sun, in a perpendicular direction to the tangent, *a c*, at that point where, by the advance of the moon on to the sun's disk (in an inverting telescope at the left side) the first contact would take place. With such an arrangement the spectrum consists, as will be described more in detail hereafter, of two halves in juxtaposition, one of which is the very intense solar spectrum *a b c d*, and the other the very faint spectrum *a e f c* of the diffused atmospheric light rendered extremely pale by the powerful dispersion of the light. Both spectra are crossed equally by the Fraunhofer lines, as shown in Fig. 133, where the portion of the spectrum between B and C is more fully represented. When the one half of the slit happens to fall upon a prominence, *p*, the *bright* lines of the luminous gases in the prominence immediately appear upon the faint spectrum of the atmosphere, especially the hydrogen lines H *α* (red) upon C, H *β* (green) upon F, and H *γ* (blue) near G, as well as the bright lines of the other incandescent substances that may be present in the prominence.

FIG. 132.

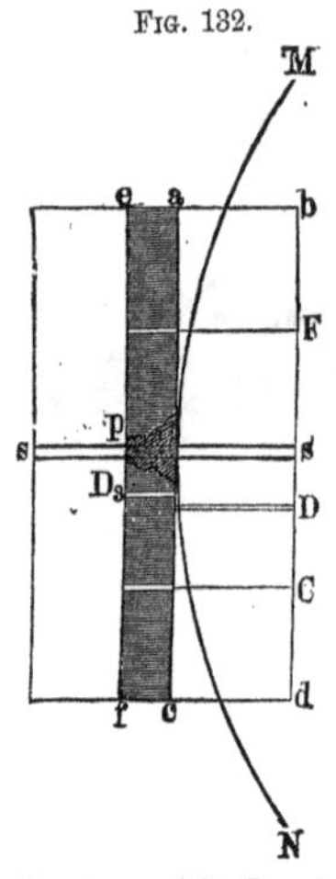

Spectrum of the Prominences.

Before the moon's entrance on the sun's disk, Young observed, as he directed the telescope upon the line C in the spec-

FIG. 133.

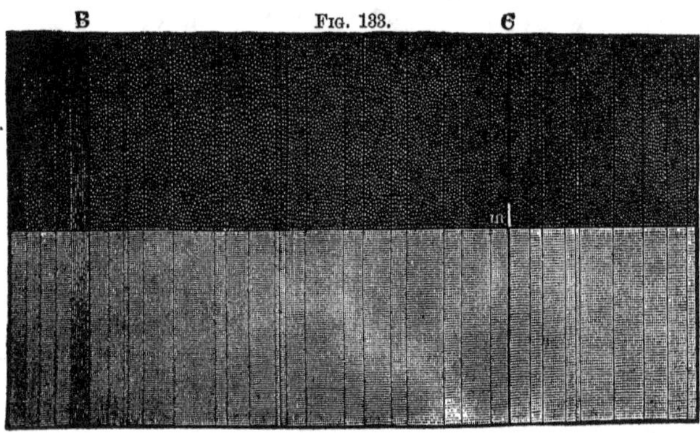

Young's Observation of the Prominence-Spectrum.

trum, a very bright red line, *m*, upon the dark spectrum of the sky, forming an exact prolongation of the dark line C of the solar spectrum, an evidence that at this spot the sun was surrounded by a stratum of luminous hydrogen, the height of which, reckoned by the length of the line *m*, must have been from 5,000 to 12,500 miles.

Now; it is evident that the moon in its approach to the sun must first pass over this stratum of hydrogen. The observer notices the entrance of the moon upon this stratum, and her progress over it by the shortening of the bright-red line *m*, and he is able to determine with great accuracy the moment of first contact of the moon and sun by noticing the time when this line disappeared completely. The same phenomenon may be observed if, instead of the line C, the F-line be brought into the field of view, but the red line H *α* is better suited for this observation than the greenish-blue line H *β*.

This plan of observation employed by Young had already been devised in theory by Faye, who had suggested this method as an accurate means of observing the first contact of the moon, Venus, or any other planet, with the sun's limb. Shortly before the commencement of totality, the slit was directed on to the prominence marked *d* in Fig. 127, and the line C brought into the field of view. When the totality began, the red line H *α* became exceedingly intense, but, owing to the slight elevation of the prominence, it did not extend across the whole width of the spectrum. No bright lines were perceptible either between C and A or between C and D. Immediately beyond the second sodium line (D_2) appeared the orange-colored line D_3 on 1017.5 of Kirchhoff's scale, which was followed immediately by two faint yellowish-green lines, estimated at 1250 $\pm$ 20 and 1350 $\pm$ 20 (Kirchhoff). The green line following at 1474 (K.) was very bright, though fainter than C and D_3; it crossed the whole breadth of the spectrum, and *remained visible without undergoing any change* when the slit was turned from the prominence to the corona, while the line D_3 disappeared. Proof was thus afforded that this line did not belong exclusively to the spectrum of the prominence, but also to that of the corona. Young is of opinion that the two preceding faint lines remained also unaffected, and therefore belonged equally to the spectrum of the corona, which was observed simultaneously with that of the prominence.* While the slit was directed upon the prominence

* [Young, in a "Note on the Solar Corona," published May, 1871, says: "I have ex

e (Fig. 127), the magnesium lines *b* were not visible, so that no bright lines were perceived by Young at this part of the prominence-spectrum. The greenish-blue line F (H β) was truly splendid, wide at the base, and terminating above in a point; it was followed by a blue line at 2602 $\pm$ 2 (K.) almost as bright as the green line 1474, by the third hydrogen line H γ, near G at 2796 (K.), and finally by the very distinct but much less bright hydrogen line *h* (H δ) at 3370.1 (K.).

The nine bright lines observed by Young in the spectrum of the prominences are given in their natural colors in Plate IX., No. 1, annexed to the solar spectrum according to Kirchhoff's scale given above, and they afford an accurate representation of the spectrum of a prominence as it appears during the totality of a solar eclipse. The upper half of the picture, that is to say, the solar spectrum, is of course invisible at such a time, and in its stead a faint continuous spectrum without a trace of any dark lines—belonging, without doubt, to the corona—appears to adjoin the spectrum of the prominence. If the bright prominence-lines as observed by Young be tabulated in their order of succession from red to blue, they will be found to correspond with the following numbers of Kirchhoff's scale:

1. 694 . . . C = H α.
2. 1017.5 . . D_3 (belonging neither to hydrogen nor sodium).
3. 1250 $\pm$ 20 } Apparently belonging to the corona.
4. 1350 $\pm$ 20 }
5. 1474 }
6. 2080 . . . F = H β.
7. 2602 $\pm$ 2 (observed also by Captain Herschel between F and G during the eclipse of the 18th of August, 1868).
8. 2796 . . . H γ.
9. 3370.1 . . *h* = H δ.

The spectroscopic observations of the prominences during the eclipse of 1868, given in p. 245, have been fully confirmed by the observations of 1869, when further results were obtained, the import of which will be more attentively considered in the following section.

perienced some annoyance during the past year at seeing these lines in several publications put upon the same footing as 1474. I was never at all confident as to their coronal character."]

54. The Corona and its Spectrum.

In the eclipse of 1868 the observers were too much occupied with the spectroscopic investigations of the prominences to pay any adequate attention to the examination of the corona. The few observations that were obtained, some of which were made by Rziha at Aden, and some by Tennant at Guntoor, are in complete agreement as to the sudden disappearance of all the dark lines from the spectrum on the commencement of the totality, and as to the fact that the light of the corona gave only a *faint continuous* spectrum. Tennant admits that this spectrum might also have contained faint lines which he was unable to perceive, because, in order to insure seeing something, he had employed a rather wide opening of the slit, and consequently some of the lines may have run one into the other.

The eclipse of 1869 has furnished many valuable details on the spectrum of the corona, throwing much light upon its nature, and fully confirming the previous observations that its spectrum is free from dark lines.

Pickering, Harkness, Young, and others, are agreed that with the extinction of the last rays of the sun all the Fraunhofer lines disappeared at once from the spectrum. The small instruments employed by Pickering and Harkness, in which the field of view was large, exhibited a spectrum obtained at once from the corona, the prominences, and the sky in the neighborhood of the sun. These instruments showed during the totality a faint continuous spectrum, free from dark lines, but crossed by *two* or *three bright* lines.

Young, whose spectroscope consisted of five prisms (Fig. 131), observed the three bright lines in the spectrum of the corona which are represented in Plate IX., No. 2, where they are drawn in the colors in which they appeared according to Kirchhoff's millimetre scale introduced above. These lines were 1250 $\pm$ 20, 1350 $\pm$ 20, and 1474. It has been already explained in p. 249 why the last and brightest of these lines is thought to belong to the spectrum of the corona, and not to that of the prominences; and it seems probable that the other two lines belong also to the light of the corona, from the fact that they are both wanting in the spectrum of the prominences when observed without an eclipse.

But what invests these three lines with a peculiar interest is the circumstance that they appear to coincide exactly with the first three of the five bright lines observed by Prof. Winlock in the spectrum of the Aurora Borealis (Plate IX., No. 3). These lines of the Aurora were determined by Winlock according to Huggins's scale; if these numbers be reduced to Kirchhoff's scale, the position of the lines will be found to be 1247, 1351, and 1473, while the lines observed by Young were registered as 1250, 1350, and 1474. Now, if it be borne in mind that Young found the positions of the two fainter lines more by estimation than by measurement, the coincidence between the bright lines of the corona and those of the Aurora Borealis will be found to be very remarkable. The brightest of these lines, 1474, is the reversal of a strongly-marked Fraunhofer line which has been ascribed both by Kirchhoff and Ångström to the vapor of iron.

What, then, is the nature of the corona, this magic circle of rays of silvery whiteness, which surrounds like a halo the black disk of the moon at the time of a total eclipse, and invests the whole phenomenon with an indescribable charm? It has been thought that while the inner bright circle of light closely surrounding the moon's limb belonged to the solar body itself, the rays streaming from the luminous ring were merely the rays of the sun reflected from the dark and uneven surface of the moon, and brought by a sort of refraction into the earth's atmosphere, whence they were reflected to the eye of the observer.

In opposition to this theory is the fact that, whereas the halo ought then to pass through great changes by the advance of the moon during the totality, no such changes were noticed by any of the observers, Gould excepted, nor were they to be traced in any of the photographs taken during the totality; in addition, it would not be difficut to prove geometrically that none of such rays as might be reflected from the moon's limb could possibly reach the small terrestrial zone of the totality.

The light of the corona cannot be that of reflected sunlight, since none of the dark Fraunhofer lines are contained in its spectrum. A comparison of several of the photographic pictures leads further to the conclusion that, in proportion as the moon advanced, the corona around the eastern limb of the sun became gradually covered, while on the west it was more and more revealed; the ring of light did not therefore move with the moon, but remained invariable during the whole of the totality. If it be also taken into consideration that, as shown by the careful investigations of Prof. Pickering, the light of the whole surrounding sky, almost up to the edge of the corona, was polarized, while that from the corona itself was not polarized, the conclusion will be arrived at that the corona is *self-luminous* and *belongs to the sun*, and therefore is not to be regarded as an optical phenomenon caused by the combined action of the sun's rays, the moon, and the earth's atmosphere.

From the bright lines in its spectrum, it is probably of a *gaseous* nature, and forms a widely-diffused atmosphere round the sun. If this were the case, even its most remote particles would be a hundred times nearer the sun than the earth is, and would therefore receive ten thousand times the amount of heat. Such a temperature would suffice to resolve every known substance of our planet either into a state of incandescence or into a gaseous form.

It has been supposed, from the coincidence of the three bright lines of the corona with those of the Aurora Borealis, that the corona is a *permanent polar light, existing in the sun*, analogous to that of our earth. Lockyer, however, justly urges against this theory the fact that, although the brightest of these three lines, which is due to the vapor of iron,* is very often present among the great number of bright lines occasionally seen in the spectrum of the prominences, it is by no means constantly visible, which ought to be the case were the corona a permanent polar light in the sun. A yet bolder theory is the ascription of such a polar light in the sun to the influence of electricity, which has been proved, as is well known, by the agitation of the magnetic needle, and the disturbance of the electric current in the telegraph-wires, to play an important part in the phenomena of the Aurora Borealis.

In the present state of our knowledge on this branch of science, the question as to the nature of the corona still remains unanswered: the solution of this problem must be reserved till, by the careful observation of future total eclipses, fresh data

* [This line is coincident with one of the faintest of the numerous lines usually seen in the spectrum of iron, but it cannot on this account be considered certainly to show the presence of the vapor of iron.]

shall be collected, which may either confirm the theories already received, or else suggest new ones in their stead.

[THE TOTAL ECLIPSE OF DECEMBER 22, 1870.

The following account of the observations of this eclipse is taken from the Report of the Council of the Royal Astronomical Society to the Fifty-first Annual Meeting of that Society:

"As this eclipse would be total at several places within easy reach of England, namely, the south of Spain, Sicily, and the north coast of Africa, it appeared to the Council an occasion on which they should take steps to assist observers, and, if necessary, organize an expedition provided with suitable instruments for attacking the important problem which still remained unsolved —the extent and nature of the Coronal Light. At the meeting of the Council held in March, the Council resolved itself into a committee to consider the preparations to be made for the observation of the Solar Eclipse of December 22. In the following month this committee united itself with a committee appointed for a similar purpose by the Royal Society. At a meeting held by this joint committee on June 16th it was resolved that the Government be solicited to grant two ships for the conveyance of observers to Spain and Sicily, and also a sum of money for the preparation and transport of instruments. To this application, which was made, in accordance with former usage, to the Admiralty, an unfavorable answer was received on August 10th. Absence from town of some members of the joint committee, and other circumstances, prevented any farther steps being taken until November 4th, when the joint committee met, and resolved that an application for means of transit for the expedition and for a pecuniary grant in aid of the funds voted by the Royal and Royal Astronomical Societies should be made to the Lords Commissioners of Her Majesty's Treasury. To this renewed application a favorable reply was returned by the Government, who placed H. M. troop-ship Urgent at the service of the expedition for the conveyance of observers and instruments to Spain and Africa, and the sum of £2,000 in aid of the travelling expenses of the overland party to Sicily, and for the preparation and transport of instruments.

"At this late moment, a few weeks only before the expedition should leave England, the greatest energy was needed to organize a party of observers, and procure the special instruments needed for the proposed observations. A small organizing committee was appointed, which met almost daily up to the departure of the expedition. The successful and very complete arrangements ultimately made were due in great measure to the unflagging zeal of the secretary, Mr. Lockyer, and of the assistant-secretary, Mr. Ranyard; and the Council wish here to state how much in their opinion is owing to the valuable suggestions and assistance afforded by Prof. Stokes. The opticians, Mr. Browning, Mr. Grubb, Mr. Ladd, and Mr. Slater, afforded very valuable assistance to the expedition by the preparation and loan of instruments, for which they deserve the grateful thanks of the Society.

"Distinct observing parties, in charge of Mr. Lockyer, Rev. S. J. Perry, Captain Parsons, and Mr. Huggins, were appointed for the four stations, Sicily, Cadiz, Gibraltar, and Oran. Prof. Tyndall accompanied the Oran party as an independent observer.

"Lord Lindsay, taking with him several skilled observers and a very complete photographic apparatus, went to Cadiz independently, at his own expense.

"Besides these English expeditions, there was an American expedition, with Prof. Peirce at its head, consisting of two parties, one in Sicily, under Prof. Peirce himself, and one in Spain, under Prof. Winlock. Independent observations were taken by Prof. Newcomb at Gibraltar, and by a party consisting of Profs. Hall, Eastman, and Harkness, in Sicily.

"At no former eclipse have preparations been made on so complete a scale, or the work to be done so skilfully divided among observers trained to carry out efficiently the parts assigned to them. All the parties were prepared to attack the corona by the several methods of the spectroscope, the polariscope, photography, and eye-drawings. With favorable weather it was not too much to expect from these expeditions a searching and almost exhaustive examination of the coronal light by these different methods of attack.

"The weather was not propitious; at all the stations the sky was more or less obscured by clouds. On the African Continent, where there had been grounds for confidently anticipating a cloudless sky, the English party and M. Janssen, who had escaped with his instruments from Paris in a balloon, at Oran, and Drs.

Weiss and Oppolzer at Tunis, saw nothing of the eclipse at the time of totality, though the earlier phases were visible at Oran.

"At Cadiz and in Sicily successful photographs of the totality were obtained by Lord Lindsay, Mr. Willard, of the American expedition, and Mr. Brothers. At these stations, and also at Estepona, some observations were obtained of the spectrum and polarization of the corona.

"Although the gain to our knowledge of solar physics is much less full and decided than doubtless it would have been if the observers had been favored with a coludless sky, the new information which comes to us from the eclipse is very valuable, and well repays the large amount of thought, time, and money, which were so freely bestowed upon the preparations.

"The present time is too early for a complete analysis of the different observations with a view to eliciting from them the new teaching which they may contain of the extent and nature of the coronal light, still it may not be undesirable to give a short account of some of the more important observations.

"In the last Annual Report, in the account of the Eclipse of August, 1869, attention was called to the two apparently distinct portions besides the prominences in the light seen round the Moon during totality. The American pictures showed similar indications of brighter portions near the sun's limb, within which the eruptions of hydrogen forming the prominences take place, to those which were visible in the photographs taken by Mr. De la Rue in 1860, and by Colonel Tennant and Dr. Vogel in 1868. A distinction between different portions of the coronal light was observed as early as 1706 by MM. Plantade and Capiés, at Montpellier. 'As soon as the sun was eclipsed there appeared around the moon a very white light forming a corona, the breadth of which was equal to about 3′. Within these limits the light was everywhere equally vivid, but beyond the exterior contour it was less intense, and was seen to fade off gradually into the surrounding darkness, forming an annulus around the moon of about 8′ in diameter.' In 1842 M. Arago considered this distinction to be sufficiently marked to sanction the subdivision of the corona into two concentric zones, the inner zone equally bright and well defined at the outer border, while the exterior zone gradually diminished in brightness until it was lost in the surrounding darkness.

"The observations of the eclipse of last December confirm these earlier descriptions as to the apparent subdivision of the coronal light, though the breadth of the inner zone varies considerably as described by different observers. In our future remarks we shall restrict the word *corona* to the inner brighter ring, and for the faint exterior portion use the term *halo*.

"It may conduce to clearness in our interpretation of those observations which appear to differ from each other, if we consider that the imperfect transparency of our atmosphere must cause a scattering of a portion of the light of the corona seen through it, and form a more or less brightly-illuminated screen between the eye and the eclipsed sun. This atmospheric light will interfere especially with the observer's appreciation of the form and extent of the faint halo. There may exist at least three distinct sources of the light seen about the sun, in addition to the prominences, the corona, a solar halo overlapping the corona or beginning at its exterior limit, and an atmospheric halo produced by the scattering of the light by our atmosphere. The corona and solar halo would probably not alter greatly in the short time between observations of the same eclipse at different stations, but the scattering of light would be peculiar to each station, and be mixed up with the effect of haze or light cloud present at the time. It is *possible* that, without the earth's atmosphere, some scattering of light may arise from the imperfect transparency of interplanetary space, not to speak of the possible existence of finely-divided matter more densely aggregated in the neighborhood of the sun. It may be that in these and some other considerations will be found the key to the interpretation of the widely-different descriptions of the solar surroundings which come to us from different observers.

"Prof. Watson observing at Carlentini describes a bright corona about 5′ high; observations at Cadiz give a breadth of about 8′; Lieutenant Brown, observing with Lord Lindsay, found the inner zone, which he saw defined in its outer margin, to vary from 2′ to 5′ in breadth; Mr. Abbatt at Gibraltar at about 5′ high. Some of the observers describe the exterior contour of the corona to be affected by the prominences bulging out over the loftiest of these. In the photographs a defined zone is also seen—in Lord Lindsay's photographs and the one taken by Mr. Willard, it extends rather more than 1′. In the photograph by Mr. Brothers the height of the brighter zone varies from 3′ to 5′.

"We will now speak of the photographs of the totality, which are very instructive.

"The photographs taken at Cadiz by Lord Lindsay were obtained by placing the sensitive surface at the focus of a silvered glass mirror 12¼ inches in diameter and 6 feet focal length, giving an image of the sun about three-quarters of an inch in diameter. The other photograph, taken near Cadiz by Mr. Willard of the American expedition, was obtained at the focus of an achromatic object-glass of 6 inches diameter, specially corrected for actinic rays.

"Mr. Brothers, at Syracuse, employed a photographic object-glass of 30 inches focal length and 4 inches diameter, lent to him by the maker, Mr. Dallmeyer.* This lens gave a brilliant image of the sun about three-tenths of an inch in diameter, which was received upon a plate 5 inches square. The camera was mounted on the Sheepshanks equatorial, belonging to the Society.

"The photograph taken at the commencement of totality by Lord Lindsay had an exposure of twenty seconds. It shows around the moon's advancing limb a bright corona extending about 1′ from the moon's limb, in which the prominences are distinctly marked, and outside this a halo of faint light diminishing rapidly in brilliancy, with indications of a radial structure which can be traced as far as 15′ from the moon's limb. On the other side of the moon, where it overlaps the sun sufficiently to conceal the prominences and the bright corona, *the halo is almost absent.* It may be suggested that such portion of the halo as appears around the advancing limb of the moon has its origin on this side of the moon. As a pure speculation, the explanation may perhaps be hazarded, that the true solar halo, as some spectroscopic observations would suggest, was less powerfully actinic than the scattered light of the prominences and corona, in which the halo on the one side of the moon only as seen on the plate may have its origin.

"The photograph taken by Mr. Willard was exposed during a minute and a half, and therefore must contain mixed up several successive appearances. The prominences are distinctly shown, and a defined corona of rather more than 1′ in height. In the halo there are indications of portions of unequal brightness, and a radial structure, but the most remarkable feature is a V-shaped

* These lenses are constructed by Mr. Dallmeyer for photographic copying.

rift or dark space in the halo on the southeast, beginning from the outer boundary of the bright corona; a second similar dark space is faintly traceable on the south. The same dark gaps are also recorded in an eye-sketch by Lieutenant Brown. Similar dark rifts * are also shown in Mr. Brothers's photograph taken at Syracuse, a representation of which is given in Plate X.† The photograph taken by Mr. Brothers is very valuable, since it shows the halo extending toward the northwest, about two diameters of the moon, and on the east and south about one diameter; the halo, therefore, is not concentric with either the sun or moon, but extends to the greatest distance in the direction from which the moon is moving. It shows in many parts traces of a radial structure. The stronger light about the moon is much broader on the west and northwest, and assumes a somewhat stellate appearance, with rays gradually softening down, as if combed out into the fainter halo. This photograph was taken in eight seconds, from the 93d to the 101st second after the commencement of totality, and therefore presents a true representation of the different phenomena at the time—that is, as regards their relative actinic power, which may possibly differ in a sensible degree from the relative brightness they present to the eye. The eye-sketches made at different stations show remarkable differences, especially in the form of the outer part of the halo; some represent it as consisting of separate rays, others give to it an almost true geometrical contour; in some of the Spanish sketches a tendency to assume a roughly quadrangular form can be detected, while in most of the Sicilian drawings there is a tendency to an annular form.

"We pass to the spectroscopic observations of the corona and halo.

"Prof. Winlock, using a spectroscope of two prisms on a five and a half inch achromatic, found a faint continuous spectrum. Of the bright lines, the most persistent was 1474 Kirchhoff. This bright line, and the continuous spectrum without dark lines, were followed from the sun to at least 20′ from his disk. Prof. Young estimates the least extension of this line to a solar radius.

* [Subsequent comparisons of Mr. Willard's photograph with that taken by Mr. Brothers leave little doubt of the absolute agreement in position of these dark rifts or gaps. Prof. Young remarks, "If this be so, it certainly bears very strongly in favor of those theories which assign a purely solar origin to the whole phenomena."]

† The thanks of the translators are due to Mr. Brothers for his kind permission to introduce this drawing, and also for the care he has taken in correcting the proofs.

18

Captain Maclear, observing with a direct-vision spectroscope attached to a four-inch telescope, saw a faint continuous spectrum and bright lines in position about C, D, E, and F, to a distance of 8′ from the moon's limb, and also the same lines, but much fainter, *on the moon's disk.* This observation would seem to show, as has been already suggested, that some of the light from the true surroundings of the sun is scattered by some medium between the eye and the moon, and therefore the distance from the moon to which these lines can be traced does not imply necessarily an equally great extension of the true halo.

"Lieutenant Brown, of Lord Lindsay's party, saw only a continuous spectrum without bright lines, from 4½′ to 25′ from the moon's limb. Mr. Carpmael, observing at Estepona, saw three bright lines in the spectrum of the corona. He considers the one in green to correspond with 1359 Kirchhoff.

"The observations with the polariscope show that a portion of the coronal light is polarized; and though the results as to the plane of polarization are interpreted differently by different observers, there seems reason to suppose with Mr. Ranyard and Mr. Peirce that the light is polarized radially, showing that the corona and halo may possibly reflect solar light as well as emit light of their own.

"There is one observation made by Prof. Young which is of so much importance that it will be well to give an account of it in Prof. Langley's words:

"'With the slit of his spectroscope placed longitudinally at the moment of obscuration, and for one or two seconds later, the field of the instrument was filled with bright lines. As far as could be judged, during this brief interval every non-atmospheric line of the solar spectrum showed bright; an interesting observation confirmed by Mr. Pye, a young gentleman whose voluntary aid proved of much service. From the concurrence of these independent observations we seem to be justified in assuming the probable existence of an envelope surrounding the photosphere, and beneath the chromosphere, usually so called, whose thickness must be limited to two or three seconds of arc, and which gives a discontinuous spectrum consisting of all, or nearly all, the Fraunhofer lines showing them—that is, *bright* on a dark ground.'

"Rapid and imperfect as this early sketch must necessarily

be of the observations of the last eclipse, it shows a distinct and important gain to our knowledge of solar physics."

Prof. Young considers it to be shown by the observations of this eclipse that "one important element of the corona consists in a solar envelope of glowing gas reaching to a considerable elevation," at least to 8′ or 10′ on the average, with occasional prolongations of double that extent, and it may turn out to have no upper limit whatever. He states: "There was an important difference between the behavior of the hydrogen line and that of 1474. At the edge of the chromosphere there was a sudden and very great falling off in the brightness of the former, while no such boundary was observed for the latter; the line grew regularly and continuously more faint as the distance from the sun increased, until it simply faded out." Prof. Young says, "I have no hesitation in affirming that the corona as it appeared to me in December was a very different phenomenon from what I saw the year before, and far more complex." He considers the spectrum of the corona to consist of at least four superposed elements:

"1. A continuous spectrum without lines either bright or dark, due to incandescent dust—that is, particles of solid or liquid meteoric matter near the sun.

"2. A true gaseous spectrum, consisting of one (1474) or more bright lines, which may arise from the vapor of the meteoric dust, but more probably from a solar atmosphere through which the meteoric particles move as foreign bodies.

"3. A true sunlight spectrum (with its dark lines), formed by photospheric light reflected from the solar atmosphere and meteoric dust. To this reflected sunlight undoubtedly is due most of the polarization.

"4. Another component spectrum is due to the light reflected from the particles of our own atmosphere. This is a mixture of the three already named, with the addition of the chromosphere-spectrum; for, while at the middle of the eclipse the air is wholly shielded from photospheric sunlight, it is of course exposed to illumination from the prominences and upper portions of the chromosphere.

"5. If there should be between us and the moon, at the moment of eclipse, any cloud of cosmical dust, the light reflected by this cloud would come in as a fifth element."

Mr. Proctor ("Monthly Notices," vol. xxxi., p. 184) considers that we have evidence of vertical disturbance, with reference to the sun's globe, in the objects which surround the sun, and that these are not of the nature of concentric atmospheric shells. The observations, he remarks, of Zöllner and Respighi show that the prominences, as respects their first formation, are phenomena of eruption. The velocity with which the gaseous matter of the prominences must pass the photosphere must be in many cases at least 200 miles per second, and its initial velocity probably not less than 300 miles per second. Dense gaseous matter flung out with the hydrogen would probably retain a velocity of, say, 240 miles per second, and reach a height exceeding that indicated by the greatest extension of the radiations observed last December. From an examination of the original negative taken by Mr. Brothers, Mr. Proctor considers that this photograph favors the view that the coronal radiations are phenomena of eruption.]

55. The Telespectroscope, and Method of observing the Spectra of the Prominences in Sunshine.

As early as October, 1866, Mr. J. Norman Lockyer communicated to the Royal Society a method for observing the spectrum of the solar prominences at any time when the sun was visible, but his labors were unproductive, owing to the insufficient dispersive power of his instrument.*

In observing the solar eclipse of 18th August, 1868, Janssen

* [Though to Mr. Lockyer is due the first publication of the idea of the possibility of applying the spectroscope to observe the red flames in sunshine, as a matter of history it should not be passed over that, about the same time, the same idea occurred quite independently to two other astronomers, Mr. Stone, of Greenwich, and Mr. Huggins. These observers were, however, unsuccessful in numerous attempts which they made to see the spectra of the prominences, for the reason probably that the spectroscopes they employed were not of sufficient dispersive power to make the bright lines of the solar flames easily visible. When the position of the lines was known, Huggins saw them instantly with the same spectroscope (two prisms of 60°) which he had previously used in vain.

It does not seem that Janssen was aware of Lockyer's suggestion in 1866, or that he had seen the following description of the experiments of Huggins, published some six months before the eclipse (February, 1868) in the "Monthly Notices of the Royal Astronomical Society" (vol. xxviii., p. 88): "During the last two years Mr. Huggins has made numerous observations for the purpose of obtaining a view of the red prominences seen during a solar eclipse. The invisibility of these objects at ordinary times is supposed to arise from the illumination of our atmosphere. If these bodies are was surprised by the remarkable brilliancy of the prominence-lines, and exclaimed, as the sun reappeared and the prominences faded away, "Je reverrai ces lignes là en dehors des éclipses!" Clouds prevented him carrying out his intention on that day, but on the 19th of August he was up by daybreak to await the rising of the sun, and scarcely had the orb of day risen in full splendor above the horizon than he succeeded in seeing the spectrum of the prominences with perfect distinctness. The phenomena of the previous day had completely changed their character: the distribution of the masses of gas round the sun's edge was entirely different, and of the great prominence scarcely a trace remained. For seventeen consecutive days Janssen continued to observe and make drawings of the prominences, by which it was proved that these gaseous masses changed their form and position with extraordinary rapidity. Janssen's paper communicating his discovery to the French Minister of Education is dated from Cocanada, the 19th of September.

Lockyer, in the mean time, had caused some improvements to be made in his instrument, and only received it again into his possession on the 16th of October, 1868, long after the news of Janssen's discovery had reached Europe. On the 20th of October the *telespectroscope** was sufficiently in order to allow of its being employed for observation, and on the same day Lockyer wrote in a communication to the Royal Society as follows:

"I have this morning perfectly succeeded in obtaining and observing part of the spectrum of a solar prominence. As a result I have established the existence of three bright lines in the following positions (Fig. 130, No. 6): 1. Absolutely coincident with C; 2. Nearly coincident with F; 3. Near D."

This third line near D, always a very fine line, is more refrangible by nine or ten degrees of Kirchhoff's scale than the most refrangible of the two D-lines (that is to say, it lies nearer to the green), and is designated D_3.

gaseous, their spectra would consist of bright lines. With a powerful spectroscope the light scattered by our atmosphere near the sun's edge would be greatly reduced in intensity by the dispersion of the prisms, while the bright lines of the prominences, if such be present, would remain but little diminished in brilliancy. This principle has been carried out by various forms of prismatic apparatus, and also by other contrivances, but hitherto without success."]

* We designate by this expression the combination of a telescope, moved by clockwork, with a spectroscope of great dispersive power.

In a subsequent communication to Mr. Warren De la Rue, Lockyer states that the prominences are merely local aggregations of a luminous gaseous medium which entirely envelops the sun, and that the characteristic spectrum of the prominences could be obtained on all sides of the sun. He estimates the thickness of this gaseous envelope to be about 5,000 miles, and remarks that the pure spectrum of a prominence consists of *short* bright lines, but that if the slit of the instrument be directed on to the limb M N of the sun as already explained in Fig. 132, and kept perpendicular to the tangent *a c* of this spot, a narrow stripe *a b c d* of the solar spectrum will be seen fringed by the faint spectrum *a e f c* of the air and the prominence *p*. As in this way the bright lines of the prominence are so closely joined to the solar spectrum as to form prolongations of the Fraunhofer lines, it is easy to ascertain with great accuracy which of the lines coincide with the Fraunhofer lines and which do not. If the spectroscope be directed according to this method to the extreme edge of the sun, and the slit carried round the sun, the spectrum of the prominences will be immediately recognized; and as the lines appear only where an accumulation of hydrogen is present, from the greater or less length of these bright lines a drawing of the form and position of the prominences round the sun may be made with almost the same accuracy as during an eclipse.

A prominence thus observed and sketched by Lockyer is shown in Fig. 134. As the length of the bright lines depends

FIG. 134.

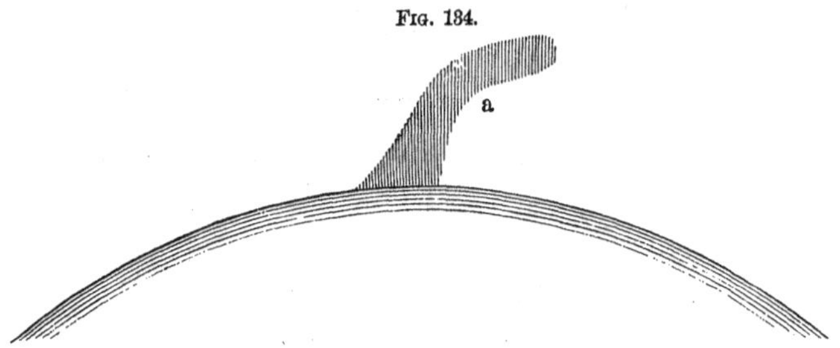

Sketch of a Prominence by means of its Spectrum Lines.

upon the height of the prominence upon which the slit of the spectroscope is directed, and these lines appear only in the field of the instrument when the light of the luminous gas falls into the slit, it is easy to see that attention need only be directed to one of these bright lines, the bluish-green F-line for instance, in order to determine the form of a prominence. If such a line be observed to be of some length, a prominence is then in view; and if the slit be turned slowly to the right and to the left, the line will lengthen or shorten according as the prominence is higher or lower; it will also appear interrupted, divided, or as at the point *a* isolated from the solar spectrum according as the prominence itself is interrupted or separated from the sun's limb.

Lockyer was undoubtedly the first to suggest the possibility of observing the spectrum of the prominences in ordinary sunlight, and to furnish a method for the purpose; Janssen was the first to accomplish the fact. Under such circumstances it is needless to discuss to whom the priority of this important discovery is due; the fame connected with it is sufficiently great to be shared by these two observers.

The possibility of observing the lines of the prominences in bright sunshine lies in the difference between the spectrum of the solar light and that of the prominences; while the former is continuous, crossed with the dark lines, the latter consists merely of a few bright lines. If both spectra be formed in the spectroscope at the same time, the intense brightness of the continuous spectrum will in an ordinary instrument completely overpower the one consisting of lines, and prevent its being visible. It has, however, been shown (p. 163) that, by increasing the number of prisms, the spectrum may be greatly extended, whereby the continuous spectrum becomes considerably diminished in intensity, and may, indeed, by the use of a sufficient number of prisms, be rendered almost invisible; the light of the prominences, on the contrary, consists of very few colors, which, though becoming farther separated one from another by the increased dispersion of the light, are yet merely displaced, and do not suffer any very perceptible loss of light, but remain still visible in the spectroscope as very bright lines. It therefore follows that by the use of a spectroscope of highly-dispersive power, the dazzling light of the sun is modified, while the lines of the prominences retaining their intensity may be observed even on the disk of the sun. The greater, therefore, the dispersive power of the instrument, the brighter will the colored lines of the prominences appear to be.

It was on these considerations that Lockyer based his plan of observing the spectra of the prominences in full sunlight by means of a telespectroscope (Fig. 135). For this purpose the slit of a highly-dispersive spectroscope, *d c e h*, firmly attached by the rods *a a b* to an equatorially mounted telescope L T P, driven by clock-work, is directed perpendicularly on to the edge of the sun's image formed in the telescope. By moving the tube *e* of the

Fig. 135.

Lockyer's Telespectroscope.

spectroscope from end to end of the spectrum, and setting the focus each time, the bright lines of the prominences may be seen as prolongations of the dark lines of the spectrum of the sun's disk on a background of the exceedingly faint spectrum of the earth's atmosphere. In the picture, S is the finder, *g* a handle for moving the telescope in declination, *d* the tube containing the slit, *h* a small telescope for reading the divisions on the micrometer-screw head, partly concealed by the rod *a a*.

The telescope, an excellent refractor of $6\frac{1}{4}$ inches aperture, and $98\frac{1}{2}$ inches focal length, is driven by clock-work. The spectroscope, constructed by Browning with his well-known ability, is represented on an enlarged scale in Fig. 136. The eye-piece is separated from the telescope, and the small image of the sun is

FIG. 136.

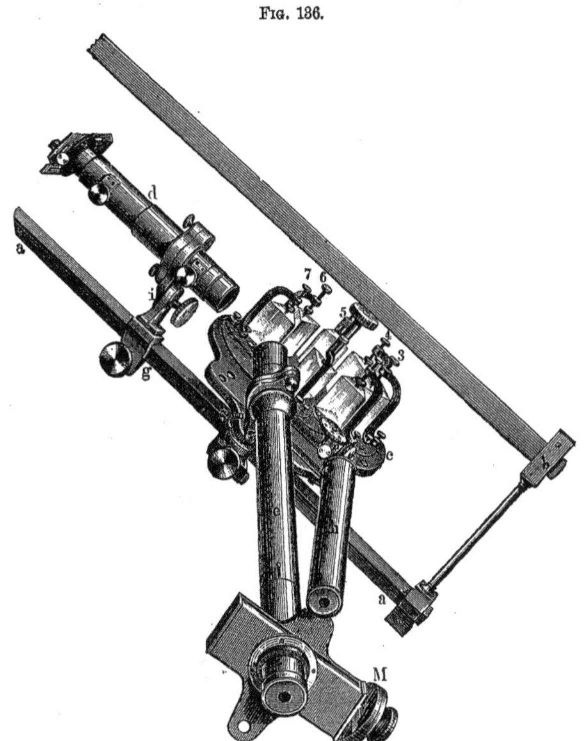

Lockyer's Telespectroscope constructed by Browning.

therefore formed beyond the tube of the telescope, and can, if necessary, be easily received upon a screen. The slit of the collimator *d* is fixed precisely on the edge of this image, and the small telescope *e* so far turned round the pivot *m* by the driving-screw *n* as to bring the dark line C or F of the solar spectrum into the middle of the field of view. The adjustment of the spectroscope to the telescope allows of the slit being brought either radially or tangentially on to any part of the sun's limb as required. The system of prisms C consists of seven prisms of dense flint glass* of 45° each, and possesses a refracting angle of more than 300°: when a still greater dispersion is needed, Lockyer employs an eighth prism of 60°, and in some special cases even makes use in addition of a system of direct-vision prisms, which is introduced into the telescope-tube *e*.

Fig. 137, in connection with Fig. 132, will explain more clearly this method of observing the prominences. S represents the solar image as formed by the object-glass of the telescope; *p p* the image of the immediate neighborhood of the sun, which is rendered invisible owing to the overpowering light of day. The slit *s s* is placed perpendicularly to the sun's limb, and is therefore in the direction of the sun's radius, so that one half

FIG. 137.

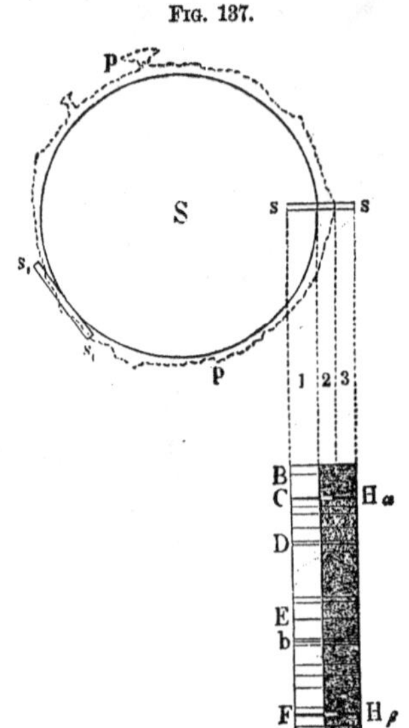

Method of observing the Prominences.

falls on the sun's disk, while the other half extends beyond it on to the surrounding envelope of glowing hydrogen (the prominences). In spectrum 1, which is still bright, though very much weakened by the great dispersion of the light, the Fraunhofer lines are very strongly marked. The other half of the field of

* The glass had a specific gravity of 3.91, a refractory index of 1.665, and a dispersive power of 0.0752.

view contains the spectrum of the air 2, 3, which is extremely faint, and which by a sufficient increase in the number of prisms may be very nearly extinguished. The spectrum 2 of the prominence stratum *p p* appears upon this spectrum in immediate contact with the spectrum 1 of the sun's disk, and it has been found by observation that spectrum 2 consists of several *bright* lines, among which the hydrogen lines are at all times particularly brilliant, of which H α (red) forms the exact prolongation of C, H β (greenish blue) the equally accurate prolongation of F, and H γ (blue) less refrangible than G (not represented in the drawing); there is also to be seen the line as yet unknown D_3, immediately following the sodium line D_2.

In Plate IX., No. 4, is represented the spectrum of the sun, and that of its immediate neighborhood, as it usually appears in a large telespectroscope with a radial slit. In the latter spectrum, besides the four bright lines of luminous hydrogen, other bright lines are generally visible, being the reversal of the Fraunhofer lines; among these, the yellow line D_3 beyond D is usually present, and frequently a green line due to iron, 1475 (Kirchhoff), besides the three magnesium lines *b*, and, according to an observation by Rayet, the two sodium lines D_1 and D_2. From the circumstance of the spectrum of the prominences, as well as that of the gaseous stratum *pp* immediately surrounding the sun, being composed of colored lines, Lockyer has given to this gaseous envelope the name of *chromosphere.*

The slit may also be placed in a position *tangential* to the sun's limb, as at s_1 s_1 (Fig. 137), and the light admitted either exclusively from the immediate neighborhood of the sun, namely, from the chromosphere, or else in conjunction with that from the extreme edge of the sun.

Instead of examining the direct image of the sun as formed by the object-glass, a magnified image may be obtained by drawing out the eye-piece of the telescope and directing the slit on to this enlarged image.

The telespectroscope employed by Prof. Young (Fig. 131) is essentially of the same construction as that just described, used by Lockyer.

Merz, the celebrated optician of Munich, constructs direct-vision spectroscopes of great dispersive power, for the spectroscopic observation of the prominences; they afford the advantage * of viewing directly the object to be observed—as, for instance, the sun's limb, a prominence or a spot—and are introduced into the telescope in place of the eye-piece. Fig. 138 shows the interior construction of such a spectroscope. The system of prisms P has a dispersive power from D to H = 8°; the collimating lens is placed at C; one-half of the slit *s s*, adjustable by the screw S, is covered by the reflecting prism *r*, which receives the light used for comparison, whether that of a flame or a Geissler's tube, from the side opposite to where the screw S is placed; L is a cylindrical lens employed for stellar observations, but withdrawn for observations on the sun. The telescope F, of which the object-glasses have a focal length of four inches, and an aperture of seven lines, is provided with the positive eye-piece O of one inch, and furnished with a micrometer of points *m m*, with the necessary delicate adjustments. By means of the screw *g*, the tube F, under pressure of the opposing spring *f*, can be so far turned toward either side as to be fixed on any part of the spectrum from the extreme red to the violet.

In this form the instrument acts as an ordinary highly-dispersive spectroscope, particularly when it is screwed into the place of the eye-piece of a telescope in order to observe the spectrum of a faint object, such as the moon, the planets, or the brightest of the fixed stars.

When the instrument is required for the observation of the solar prominences, its dispersive power must be doubled by the

Fig. 138.

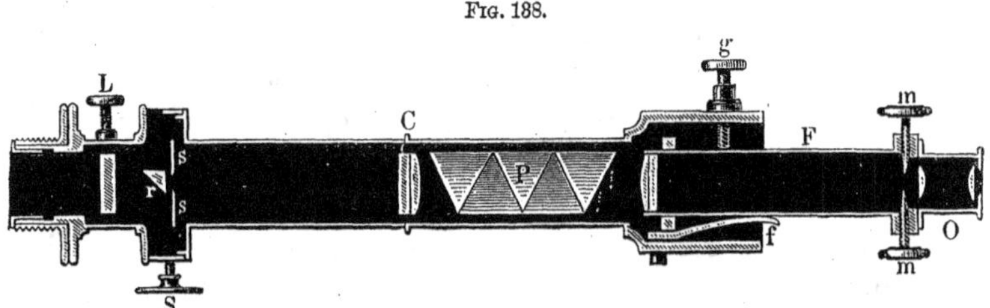

Merz's Simple and Compound Spectroscope.

introduction of a second direct-vision system of prisms similar to that marked P between the collimating lens C and the first system of prisms. In this compound form the instrument shows

* [There is no advantage in this; on the contrary, the position of the observer is less convenient, especially when the sun is high.]

very distinctly in a clear atmosphere the fine nickel line between the two sodium lines D_1 and D_2. To assist in directing the instrument on to any part of the sun's limb, a divided position-circle is attached within the tube at the part where it is screwed on to the telescope.

According to Carpmael, one of Browning's direct-vision system of seven prisms, similar to that contained in the spectroscope described in page 85, suffices, when combined with the two-inch object-glass of a good telescope, to show in sunlight the two bright prominence-lines H α and H β. When the instrument is so mounted as to be turned with convenience on to the sun, a blue glass is placed before the slit, so as to exclude all but blue light from the spectroscope. When the image of the sun formed within the telescope passes over the slit, and the slit is placed in the right position, the bright greenish-blue line H β will be seen as a prolongation of the F-line of the solar spectrum. By substituting red glass for blue, the red line H α will be seen in a similar manner as the prolongation of the line C.

Immediately upon the arrival of the news by telegraph of Janssen's discovery, Secchi, at Rome, began a series of spectrum investigations of the prominences. He employed a spectroscope of two excellent flint-glass prisms of highly-dispersive power, capable of showing the fine Fraunhofer lines situated between B and A, and placed it in combination with an excellent equatorial. Even on the first attempt, as the narrow slit was fixed on the sun's limb, the lines C and F were observed to be reversed in the spectrum of the air, and appeared therefore as bright lines.

Secchi then carried the slit completely round the disk of the sun, placing it alternately in a direction parallel and perpendicular to the sun's limb. He observed that the bright line C (red) was everywhere visible; with the slit in a position perpendicular to the sun's limb, this line was always from 10″ to 15″ in length, excepting in a zone of 45° on each side of the equator; in this region, where the solar spots and faculæ are known to abound, this line was four times its ordinary length. In many places the C-line was separated from the sun's limb; when the slit was placed at a tangent to the limb, this line always appeared as a bright line crossing the entire spectrum, and sometimes was cut up in single pieces when the slit was removed from the sun's limb, but always appeared complete and unbroken when the slit was again brought in contact with the limb of the sun.

This proves what the observations of solar eclipses * and the researches of Lockyer had already shown, that the stratum of glowing gas (the chromosphere) surrounding the sun is really continuous, though distributed very unevenly. Where a bright line attains the height of 60″ or more in the spectrum, it proclaims the existence of a prominence in that place, and where a bright line is broken into fragments, it is an indication of the presence of isolated masses of glowing gas—of solar clouds at a considerable height above the sun's surface.

56. The Chromosphere and its Spectrum.

By the term chromosphere is designated that luminous, gaseous envelope by which the sun is entirely surrounded.† As already mentioned, its spectrum consists of a number of bright lines, among which those of hydrogen are always present, and are especially noticeable from their length and brilliancy. If

* [Prof. Swan, discussing his observations of the total solar eclipse of July, 1851, wrote (April, 1852): "Obviously the simplest view that can be taken of this phenomenon is to regard the red fringe and the red protuberances as of the same nature; and all the observations will then confirm the idea that the matter composing those objects *is distributed all round the sun.*" Prof. Grant, in his "History of Physical Astronomy" (date of preface March 2, 1852), expresses a similar opinion. Leverrier in 1860 wrote: "The existence of a bed of rose-colored matter, partially transparent, covering the whole surface of the sun, is a fact established by the observations made during the totality in the eclipse of this year."]

† [This term was used originally to denote the red flames and stratum of red light connecting them. Recently it has been suggested to extend it to the whole of the light surrounding the sun, which gives a spectrum of bright lines. At the present time, however, it is more important than ever to be able to distinguish with precision the different objects which make up the sun's surroundings.

Prof. Young writes: "One important element of the corona consists in a solar envelope of glowing gas reaching to a considerable elevation. For this envelope the name of 'leucosphere' has been proposed; it seems a suitable term and well worthy of adoption. It has been objected to on the ground that 'chromosphere' covers the whole bright-line region around the sun; but, when the latter name was first proposed, there was evidently no idea that above the envelope of hydrogen there lay another from twenty to a hundred times as extensive, and it would be very convenient to restrict it to the lower hydrogen stratum, and retain the new term for the more elevated mass of gaseous matter."

Mr. Proctor suggests that "the relation between the prominences and the layer of colored matter at a lower level is such as to render the term *Sierra*, employed by those who discovered the layer, altogether more appropriate than *chromosphere*, which during the observation the slit of the spectroscope be placed *radially*, as in Fig. 137, so that, while one half extends over the sun's limb, the other half falls on the chromosphere, the double spectrum of the sun and chromosphere will then be received as shown in Plate IX., No. 4. So great a power of dispersion is

FIG. 139.

The Spectrum of the Sun's Disk (below) and that of the Chromosphere (above) near the C-line.

requisite in a spectroscope suited to this purpose, in order to subdue the spectrum of diffused daylight formed at the same time, that only a small portion of the spectrum of the chromosphere can be in the field of view at once, and therefore the telescope must be brought in various directions on to the system of prisms, in order to examine the different sections of the entire spectrum.

Figs. 139, 140, and 141, represent, after Lockyer's drawings, those portions of the spectrum which are usually observed, since they are those best suited for the examination of the prominences and the chromosphere, and for noticing the changes occurring in them. Fig. 139 shows that part of the solar spectrum which includes the C-line, together with the similar portion of the chromosphere exhibiting the hydrogen line H α, equally broad

seems to imply that the colored layer forms a spherical envelope. I see no reason why the fine word *Sierra* should not be restored to its place in our books of astronomy, and the brighter and fainter pacts of the corona should not be called *corona* and *glory;* or else the Astronomer Royal's mode of describing them might be adopted, and one called the *ring-formed corona*, the other the *radiated corona*."]

and somewhat pointed at its termination. Fig. 141 exhibits the F-line and solar spectrum in its immediate neighborhood, and above it the hydrogen line H β of the chromosphere: this line

Fig. 140.

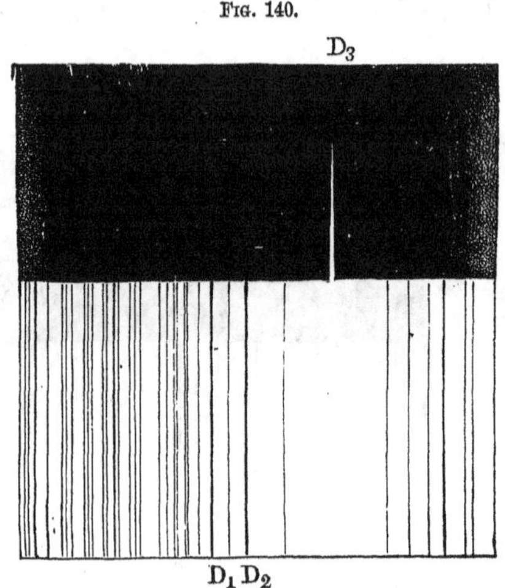

The Spectrum of the Sun's Disk (below) and that of the Chromosphere (above) near the D-line.

Fig. 141.

The Spectrum of the Sun's Disk (below) and that of the Chromosphere (above) near the F-line.

is spread out at the base, and terminates above in an arrow-shaped point, while the line H α, on the contrary, remains, as a rule, of the same width throughout as the C-line. Fig. 140 represents that portion of the spectrum beyond the double sodium line D, where about midway between two very fine dark lines of the solar spectrum the yet unknown line D_3 is situated in the spectrum of the chromosphere.

While the red line H α is always brilliant and easily seen, the greenish-blue line H β, though also very bright, is yet much fainter and frequently also much shorter than H α. The F-line, as well as its corresponding line H β, is subject to a variety of changes, such as becoming inflated, bent, widened, twisted, and broken up—a full description of which will be found in § 57.

Besides these bright lines constantly occurring in the spectra of the prominences and the chromosphere, there appear from time to time in various places of the spectrum many other bright lines, very marked and brilliant, among which is a line in the red between B and C, but nearer to C * (Fig. 130, No. 7), another in the green between E and F (Fig. 130, Nos. 3, 5, 8), the iron line 1474 (K.), the magnesium lines, etc.

In the same way the third hydrogen line H γ (blue) near G (Fig. 130, No. 2; Frontispiece No. 7), No. 2796 (K.), appears very brilliant under favorable circumstances; and when the air is transparent and free from vapor, and a high prominence is present, there is also seen the fourth hydrogen line H δ (blue, 3370.1 K.), which coincides precisely with the dark line marked *h* by Ångström, of a wave-length of 0·00041011 of a millimetre; this line was seen by Rayet with great distinctness on the 30th of April and on the 1st and 20th of May, 1869. The red line near C does not correspond with any of the dark Fraunhofer lines.

The remarkable yellow line D_3 (Fig. 140) is seen as constantly in every part of the circumference of the sun's disk as the hydrogen lines; the luminous gas to which it is due must therefore, like hydrogen, form a constituent of the chromosphere. Lockyer has been unable to find any corresponding dark line in the solar spectrum for this line, notwithstanding the most careful micrometric measurements, and the most painstaking comparisons with the maps of Kirchhoff and Gassiot.

* [Prof. C. A. Young, on December 21, 1870, saw, in the spectrum of a very bright but small prominence on the N. W. limb of the sun, the line below C, which he had seen twice before, but had often looked for in vain. It is the reversal of the dark line, 656, of Kirchhoff's map.]

The position of this line has been determined by Rayet, as well as by Lockyer and Secchi. If with Rayet the distance between the sodium lines D_1 and D_2 be taken as the unit, then the distance of the line D_3 from $D_2 = 2.49$. If the wave-lengths of the lines D_1 and D_2 be taken at 590.53 and 589.88 millionth of a millimetre, then the wave-length of the line D_3 will be 588.27 millionth of a millimetre. The position of this line in Kirchhoff's scale is according to Young 1017.5, according to Rayet 1016.8.

A series of observations upon this line has lately been instituted by Lockyer, who in conjunction with Frankland had previously ascertained, by comparisons with the spectrum given by a tube filled with hydrogen, that it could not be attributed to hydrogen gas. The results obtained were as follows:

1. With the slit tangential to the sun's limb, the line D_3 appeared bright at the lower part of the chromosphere, while at the same time the C-line was dark in the same field of view.

2. In a prominence over a spot on the sun's disk the lines C and F were bright, while the yellow line D_3 was invisible.

3. In a prominence which burst forth under high pressure from the sun, the motion indicated by change of the wave-length (§ 57) was less for the line D_3 than for either C or F.

4. In one case the C-line appeared long and continuous, while the line D_3, though of equal length, was broken and interrupted.

It follows from this that the line D_3 is certainly not occasioned by hydrogen gas, and its source is therefore at present still undiscovered.

The reversal of the sodium lines D_1 and D_2 (*vide* Plate IX., No. 4) has been observed by Lockyer, and subsequently also by Rayet, in the spectrum of the chromosphere; that is to say, they have been seen as bright lines. With a tangential slit, Rayet saw both these lines dark upon the sun's limb; at the base of a magnificent prominence 3′ high, which appeared to rest upon the sun's limb, both these lines were still dark and fading away, though already somewhat fainter; when nearly two-thirds from the base they had entirely disappeared, but, by a slight displacement of the slit, they were discovered in the form of bright-yellow lines. At the summit of the prominence they were again dark lines.

The four magnesium lines b_1, b_2, b_3, b_4,* are seen not unfrequently as bright lines in the spectrum of the chromosphere, but almost always as very short lines, which seems to show that the vapor of magnesium does not rise to any great height in the chromosphere. When these bright lines are visible, the first three, b_1, b_2, b_3, appear of about equal length, while the fourth line, b_4, is much shorter (Plate IX., No. 4). It has been found by Lockyer and Frankland that a similar phenomenon to that observed in the chromosphere is to be noticed in the spectrum of terrestrial magnesium when formed by the passage of the electric spark through the air between electrodes of this metal, and the poles too far separated to allow of the spectrum extending from one pole to the other, but each pole surrounded by a luminous vapor of magnesium. In observing at a short distance the spectrum of this luminous gaseous envelope, the most refrangible of the three magnesium lines that made their appearance was always the shortest, and shorter still were several other lines which have not been observed as yet in the spectrum of the chromosphere. Of the many iron lines occurring as dark lines in the solar spectrum, only a few appear as bright lines in the spectrum of the chromosphere; among these, the line 1474, so often referred to, which shows itself as a short green line, is that most frequently observed.

At certain times, when powerful eruptions from the interior of the sun extend into and even beyond the chromosphere, the spectrum of the latter becomes very complicated. Phenomena of this kind have been frequently observed by Lockyer with a *tangential* slit. This position offers the advantage of viewing at one time a much larger extent of the sun's limb, or chromosphere, than can be obtained by a slit placed radially, although the latter position is advantageous when the object of the observer is to watch the changes occurring in the chromosphere, or to observe especially the form and height of the prominences. When the slit is placed tangentially upon the sun's limb, so that portions of the sun and chromosphere are visible at the same time to an equal height in the slit, the spectra of the sun and chromosphere are no longer seen side by side, but are partially superposed, the one obscuring the other. An instance of this is

* [Three only of these lines belong to magnesium, b_3 consists of lines of nickel and iron.]

given in Fig. 142, as observed by Lockyer in that portion of the spectrum containing the C-line, when the slit encountered a prominence; the dark C-line was completely annihilated, and

FIG. 142.

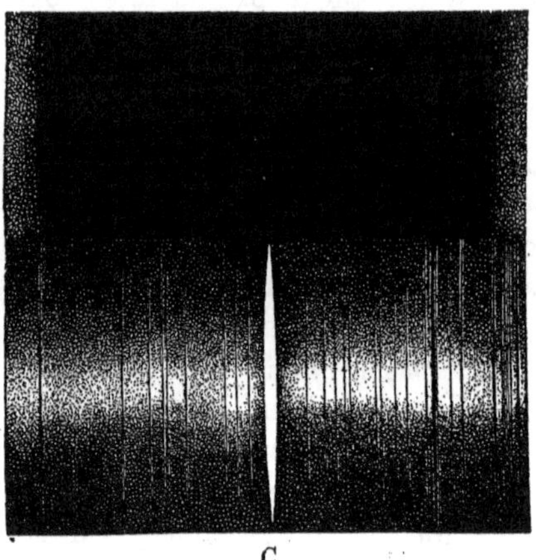

Covering of the dark C-line with H α.

replaced by a bright band. The F-line, as shown in Fig. 143, was differently affected. In the spectrum of the light emitted from the extreme edge of the sun, the bright F-line H β appears to be of greater refrangibility than the dark F-line itself, but, at a short distance from the sun's limb, the dark F-line in the spectrum of a prominence was also completely replaced by the corresponding bright line of hydrogen gas. Not only the hydrogen lines, but also many other lines, appear bright, under similar circumstances, in the spectrum of the chromosphere, and, on the 17th of April, 1870, hundreds of such bright or reversed Fraunhofer lines were observed by Lockyer at a spot in the chromosphere where a prominence was situated. The complications in the spectrum of the chromosphere were most remarkable in the regions more refrangible than C, and in those extending from the line E to beyond *b*, and as far as the neighborhood of F; the vapor of iron under extreme pressure seems to be an important agent in this phenomenon.

Among the most remarkable phenomena observable in the bright lines of hydrogen gas seen in the spectrum of the chromosphere is that of the widening at the base and pointed arrow-like termination of the greenish-blue line H β, as well as the narrowing to a point of the other bright lines H α and D_3, as represented in Figs. 139, 140, and 141. The causes affecting the width of the spectrum lines have been pointed out in § 32; these have been found to consist partly in the density dependent upon pressure, and partly in the temperature of the gas, yet, according to some experiments made by Secchi, the temperature is found to exercise the most important influence upon the width of the lines. At a given temperature, and at a certain degree of rarefaction, the spectrum of hydrogen consists of the three character-

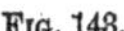

FIG. 143.

Partial Covering of the dark F-line with H β.

istic lines H α, H β, H γ. With an increase of temperature, the line H γ is the first to begin to widen on both sides, then H β becomes similarly affected, while H α remains unchanged, even when H γ has passed into a broad, ill-defined violet band. When the gas is rarefied, then H α is the first to disappear, while H β remains unaffected. On the other hand, it seems to be proved from Secchi's experiments that, with the same density of gas, a decrease of temperature is followed by a narrowing of the three lines, and that, with a given density, there is a limit to the decrease of temperature at which they will entirely disappear. The pointed termination of the bright lines in the spectrum of the chromosphere indicates therefore that the temperature of the chromosphere decreases as it recedes from the sun, and, at the same time, that the density of the hydrogen envelope is greater at the base of the chromosphere than in the higher regions.

The phenomena observed in the C- and F-lines of the hydrogen gas in the chromosphere and prominences do not, however, consist merely in the widening of the lines and their pointed termination, but also frequently in several other changes, such as their becoming swollen out in several places and assuming a twisted appearance, or being broken up into separate pieces—phenomena which must be regarded as an indication of violent eruptive or stormy action taking place in the interior of the

Fig. 144.

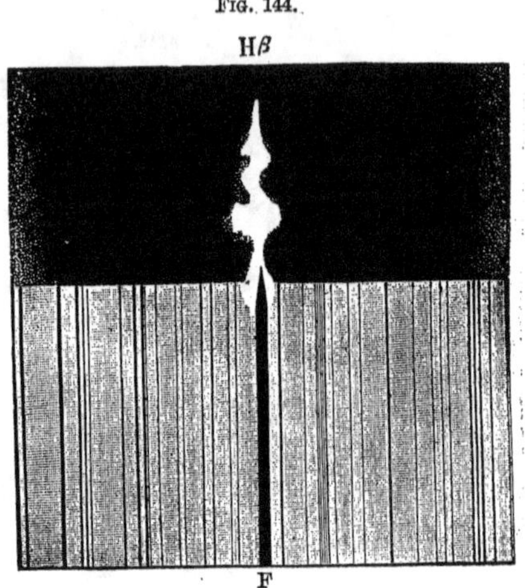

Changes in the Line H β, after Lockyer.

gaseous mass. Among other observers, Lockyer has made many observations of this kind, and he has recorded the appearance presented by these lines. An instance is given in Fig. 144, where the F-line of the solar spectrum is accompanied by the corresponding bright prominence-line H β, which, in addition to the usual arrow-pointed termination, has assumed the form of a twisted wavy line, the lower part of which spreads out over the sun's disk: the C-line of the same prominence remained, in the mean while, unaffected, being neither spread out at the base nor twisted in form.

A similar phenomenon in a very brilliant prominence was

noticed by Prof. Young on the 19th of April, 1870. The red C-line (H α) was remarkably bright, so as to admit of its form being observed with a tolerably wide opening of the slit, but in no part was the line either twisted or broken. The F-line (H β), on the contrary (Fig. 145), though equally brilliant, was everywhere broken up into pieces, and at the base was three or four times wider than usual.

FIG. 145.

Changes in the Line H β, after Young.

It will presently be shown in what manner the displacement of a spectrum-line and the phenomena, depicted in Figs. 144 and 145, are connected with the *motion* of the luminous gaseous mass to which these lines in the spectroscope owe their origin. When, however, as in these instances, only one of the spectrum lines (H β) is so affected, and the other line (H α) remains unchanged, it is scarcely credible that the cause of this phenomenon is to be found in the eddying motion of the gas whence the light is emitted. Young is of opinion that phenomena of this kind are to be attributed to some local absorption, by which a line (color) which is much spread out by the influence of pressure and temperature is particularly affected. By means of his powerful spectroscope, composed of five prisms, Young was able to watch the above phenomenon for half an hour at a time.

A series of similar but still more complicated phenomena occurring in the bright spectrum-lines of a prominence, the causes of which will be dealt with more in detail in § 57, were observed by Lockyer in April, 1870, when some sketches were taken of them by an experienced draughtsman. In this instance the phenomena were confined chiefly to the red C-line, to which Lockyer directed his attention almost exclusively.

When the air is exceedingly tranquil in the neighborhood of

a large solar spot, or over a large region in the sun's disk, absorption bands are seen to traverse the whole length of the spectrum (Fig. 107) crossing at right angles the Fraunhofer lines; they vary in width and in depth of shade, according as a pore, a depression, or a completely-formed spot, is found opposite the corresponding place in the slit. Here and there, in the brightest portions of the spectrum, there suddenly appears a lozenge-shaped light (Fig. 146, No. 2) in the middle of the absorption line. It is thought by Lockyer to be caused by luminous hydrogen which is subjected to a more than usual pressure, and this may, therefore, possibly be the cause of those extremely bright points which are to be observed in the faculæ in the neighborhood of the sun's limb.

Fig. 146, No. 1, shows the dark F-line at the base of a prominence as observed with a tangential slit. In it are to be seen two or three of those lozenge-shaped stripes of light, which are

FIG. 146.

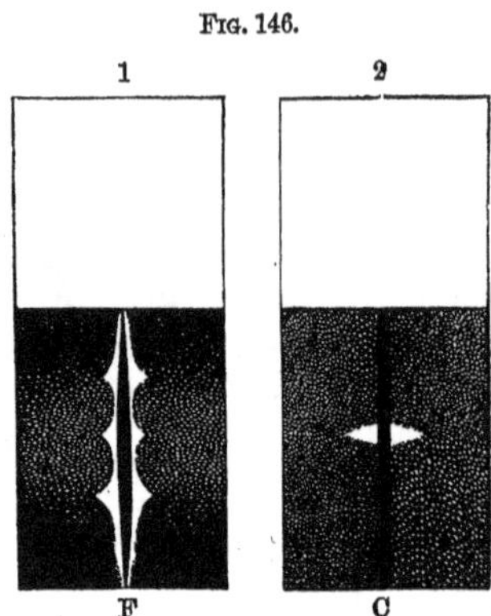

Reversal of the C- and F-lines.

due apparently to the greater pressure of the gas; they were more elongated in the direction of the dark line than was the case in the line C.

A precisely similar phenomenon was observed by Young in both the D-lines. On the 22d of September, 1870, he saw, in the spectrum of the umbra of a large spot near the sun's eastern limb, the two sodium lines D_1 and D_2 reversed, or as bright lines in the manner represented in Fig. 147. The C- and F-lines were also reversed at the same time—a phenomenon which has been frequently observed in the spectra of the solar spots (p. 202) with Young's new spectroscope, an instrument possessing a dispersive power equal to thirteen prisms of dense flint glass.

The line D_3 was not visible in the umbra of the spot, but showed itself distinctly in the penumbra as a dark shadow. On the afternoon of the 28th of September, the following lines were seen, bright or reversed, in the spectrum of the umbra of the same spot, in the following order of brightness: C, F, D_3, 2796

FIG. 147.

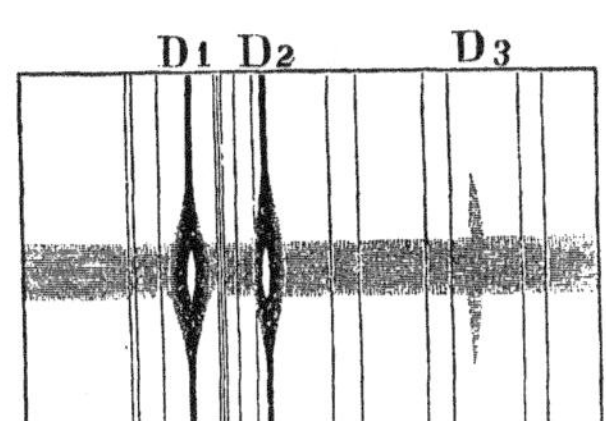

Young's Observation of the Reversal of the D-lines.

(K.), or H γ; b_3, b_1, b_2; D_1, D_2; h, b_4, and 1474 (K.). The cause of this phenomenon was soon revealed by the appearance of two gigantic prominences which were observed as brilliant objects in the spectroscope on the sun's disk; one extended into the umbra of the spot, the other only as far as the penumbra.

A simple method of illustrating the occurrence of the simultaneous observation of the spectra of the immediate appendage of the sun (the chromosphere) and the sun itself has been devised by Lockyer. He noticed that the flame of an ordinary tallow or stearine candle is surrounded by an envelope of sodium-vapor not ordinarily visible, but which can be perceived, immediately on the application of the spectroscope, by the existence of the yellow sodium lines. If the slit of the instrument be moved slowly from the slide into the flame, at the spot a little above the place where the wick bends outward, the bright line D will at once appear against a dark background: by a further movement of the slit into the flame itself, a second spectrum, the continuous spectrum of the flame, is formed, and there will be seen, side by side, in the same field of view, the two spectra—that of the flame, and that of the sodium-vapor by which it is enveloped. If the flame be agitated so as to produce a flickering, the bright D-line may be made to pass through similar changes to those observed in the hydrogen lines of the chromosphere.

It may at first sight appear strange that the lines of oxygen, nitrogen, and carbon, have never been perceived either in the spectrum of the sun or in that of the chromosphere, seeing that these substances are found in such abundance upon the earth. In his large maps of the solar spectrum (Plates IV., V., VI.), Ångström has also included the spectrum of the atmospheric air as obtained from the electric spark, whence it may at once be seen that the lines given by air, the components of which are nitrogen and oxygen, are nowhere coincident with any of the Fraunhofer lines. The non-appearance of the lines of any substance in the spectrum of a self-luminous composite body in no way justifies the conclusion that such a substance is entirely absent.

From Ångström's investigations it appears that the spectrum of the atmosphere is not visible when the electric spark is formed in the free air between the carbon-points of a Bunsen battery of fifty elements, and can in general only be produced by the employment of a Geissler's tube filled with rarefied air when the electricity is at a high tension; * that is to say, under circumstances that accompany an extremely high temperature. In the same way the spectrum of carbon cannot be obtained by the mere incandescence of carbon in the electric current; the spectrum thus produced consists partly of the continuous spectrum of the incandescent solid particles of carbon, and partly of the spectra of carburetted hydrogen and of cyanogen. The heat of the voltaic arc of flame (§ 10) is therefore insufficient to convert carbon into a gaseous form.†

* [The spectrum of the air is not seen when the electricity from the battery passes between carbon-points, because the voltaic arc present under these circumstances consists of a bridge of the vapor or fine particles of the substance of the electrodes over which the electricity passes, and which by the resistance it offers becomes vividly incandescent. When a spark, as that of an induction coil, can pass *through free air*, the spectra of the gases of the atmosphere are always visible, as is the case when an induction spark passes between metallic electrodes, the spectre of the atmospheric gases, oxygen and nitrogen (and the red line of hydrogen from the aqueous vapor always present in ordinary air) being then seen together with the spectrum of the metal employed. The invariable presence of the atmospheric spectrum when a spark passes *through free air* led Huggins to use this spectrum as a scale of reference in his maps of the spectra of the chemical elements. The small amount of carbonic-acid gas present in the atmosphere cannot be detected by the spectroscope.]

† [See note in § 68.]

By applying these phenomena to the sun, we are led, with Ångström to the conclusion that the temperature of that luminary is on the one hand too high to permit of such combinations as carburetted hydrogen, cyanogen, etc., being formed, and, on the other hand, too low to allow of carbon being converted into a gaseous state, so as to form its spectrum, or to produce the spectra of oxygen and nitrogen.

Similar results have been arrived at by Wüllner, Secchi, and Zöllner,* Wüllner by means of experiment (p. 122), Zöllner by ingenious reasonings upon the behavior of hydrogen, nitrogen, and oxygen in the sun as affected by variations in their density, specific gravity, and emissive power, founded upon the supposition that the eruptive forms of the prominences are to be regarded as the result of hydrogen gas rushing to the outer surface from the interior of the sun, and that the cause of these eruptions is to be sought for in the difference of pressure to which the gas is subject in the interior, and on the surface of the sun. Calculations made on this hypothesis, taking into account the amount of hydrogen present in the sun, would lead us by analogy to regard the amount of oxygen and nitrogen in that stratum where the hydrogen spectrum begins to be continuous as extremely small in comparison with the amount of hydrogen. Those rays, therefore, which are given out by a stratum of hydrogen yielding a continuous spectrum, pass through so small an amount of incandescent particles of oxygen and nitrogen in coming to our eye, that the absorption they suffer is extremely small, and therefore not perceptible. For this reason, even supposing the sun to possess an atmosphere of nitrogen and oxygen similar in density and temperature to its atmosphere of hydrogen, the lines of nitrogen and oxygen would still fail to be visible either as dark Fraunhofer lines in the spectrum of the sun, or as bright lines in the spectrum of the chromosphere. It must not be concluded, therefore, from the absence of the lines of nitrogen and oxygen in both these spectra, that these substances are not present in either the sun or the chromosphere.

From all these observations the following results may be deduced concerning the nature of the chromosphere:

1. The body of the sun, or its light-giving envelope the photo-

* Zöllner, Ueber die Temperatur und physische Beschaffenheit der Sonne. Bericht der Königl. Sächs. Gesellsch. der Wissenschaften vom 2 Juni 1870.

sphere, is completely surrounded by a gaseous envelope in which hydrogen constitutes the chief element, and which is called the chromosphere. Its mean thickness is between 5,000 and 7,000 miles.

2. The prominences are local accumulations of the chromosphere, and therefore preëminently of hydrogen gas, which appear to break forth from time to time from the interior of the sun in the form of monster eruptions, forcing their way through the photosphere and chromosphere. As this gas on effecting a passage rises with great rapidity, it becomes quickly rarefied in a direction away from the sun's limb.

3. As in the spectrum of the chromosphere the greenish-blue line H β, coincident with the Fraunhofer line F, takes in general the form of an arrow-head, the base of which rests on the sun's limb, and the widening of this line is caused by an increase of pressure as well as by a rise of temperature, therefore the pressure and the temperature of the gas in the lowest stratum of the chromosphere must be greater than in the upper part. From the experiments undertaken by Lockyer, Frankland, Wüllner, and Secchi, it appears that *even in the lowest stratum of this gaseous envelope the pressure is smaller than that of our atmosphere, therefore that the gas of the chromosphere is in a state of greater attenuation.*

4. The greenish-blue line H β, which under normal conditions is of the same width as the lines H α and C, sometimes in a prominence swells out in a globular form, and is twisted over the chromosphere line (Fig. 144), the cause of which is probably the sudden and violent meeting or damming up of streams of gas, and their consequent condensation.

5. The three characteristic lines of hydrogen H α, H β, H γ, as well as a fourth blue line, are all observed with complete certainty in the spectrum of the chromosphere and that of the prominences; in good instruments, and under favorable atmospheric circumstances, the first two lines sometimes extend into the spectrum of the regions underlying the chromosphere, and thus cause the corresponding Fraunhofer lines C and F to appear as bright lines upon the sun's disk. The yellow line D_3 of the chromosphere is neither due to sodium nor to hydrogen, nor is the red line less refrangible than C a hydrogen line; it has not yet been ascertained to what substances they belong.

6. Under the chromosphere lies the luminous cloud-like vaporous or nebulous *photosphere*, which contains all the substances, the spectrum lines of which appear as absorption lines in the solar spectrum. These substances—among which iron, magnesium, and sodium, are especially prominent—often burst forth in a state of incandescence, and are carried up to a certain distance into the chromosphere and into the basis of the prominences, though not in general to any considerable elevation.

Secchi has been led to believe from his observations during the total eclipse of 1860, as well as from those recently undertaken with his large instrument, that the chromosphere does not immediately rest on the sun's limb, but is separated from it by a very thin space of white light from 2″ to 3″ in thickness (40,000 miles), which gives a continuous spectrum. Secchi is of opinion that Kirchhoff's assumed *atmosphere* of luminous vapors, in which the white light of the sun suffers the selective absorption producing the dark lines, is to be found in this stratum of white light.*

This view is opposed by Lockyer, who denies the existence of this stratum of light separating the chromosphere from the sun's limb. According to him, the photosphere, a very narrow stratum of mixed luminous vapors which yield reversed spectra of the Fraunhofer lines, forms the border or upper surface of the solar nucleus upon which the chromosphere or stratum of glowing hydrogen gas immediately rests.

Kirchhoff's theory, that the solar nucleus is surrounded by a very expanded, non-luminous, and comparatively cool absorptive atmosphere, must therefore give place to that of the glowing and light-emitting photosphere being surrounded by a luminous and intensely hot stratum of gas, the chromosphere, the spectrum of which consists mainly of that of hydrogen gas. Lockyer is of opinion that, from the extremely rarefied condition of this gas, the existence of any other atmosphere extending beyond it, as might

* [Prof. Young, in describing his observations of the total solar eclipse of December 22, 1870, says: "Prof. Langley has so well stated what we saw (see note on page 174) that it is not necessary to repeat it; but I cannot refrain from putting on record that the sudden reversal into brightness and color of the countless dark lines of the spectrum at the commencement of totality, and their gradual dying out, was the most exquisitely beautiful phenomenon possible to conceive, and it seems to me to have considerable theoretical importance. Secchi's *continuous spectrum* at the sun's limb is probably the same thing modified by atmospheric glare; anywhere but in the clear sky of Italy, so much modified, indeed, as to be wholly masked."]

be inferred from the corona, is very improbable, and that the thickness of the chromosphere would be indicated by the height of its spectrum lines, the bright hydrogen lines H α, H β, H γ; these lines being broad at the limb of the sun, and running to a point at the top, lead to the conclusion that the temperature of the chromosphere, at the height indicated by the termination of the lines, is insufficient to keep hydrogen gas in a state of luminosity. It has been ascertained (p. 122) that an increase of temperature imparts to hydrogen the power of widening its spectrum lines, while, on the contrary, a decrease of temperature produces a narrowing of the lines. Now, the spectrum lines of a prominence are broad at the base in the neighborhood of the sun's limb, and terminate in a point (Figs. 140, 141); the temperature at the point must therefore be lower than at the base. The envelope of hydrogen may manifestly extend far beyond the limit of the bright lines without its existence being revealed to us by the lines of its spectrum, and for this reason these bright lines afford no sufficient measure for the thickness of the chromosphere; it is much more probable that, owing to a continuous decrease in its temperature and density, the chromosphere stretches out into space to a distance far beyond our power of recognition.*

57. Modes of observing the Prominences in Sunshine.—Form of the Prominences.

As early as 1866, Lockyer attempted to observe the prominences in full sunshine by means of a Herschel-Browning spectroscope placed in combination with a telescope. The method he employed, and which he laid before the Royal Society in a special communication,† depends, as we have previously mentioned (p. 264), on the specific difference between the light of the prominences and that of the sun itself.

The light of an incandescent solid or liquid body which passes through the slit of a spectroscope will be spread out by the prism

* [This seems the place to call attention to the valuable paper by Mr. Johnstone Stoney, published in 1867, in which he anticipated from theoretical considerations some of the results since obtained from observation.—*See* Abstract, "Proceedings Royal Society," vol. xvi., p. 25, and vol. xvii., p. 1.]

† [In Lockyer's communication to the Royal Society in October, 1866, there was no statement of a method of observation or of the principles on which the spectroscope might reveal the red flames. His suggestion consisted only of the following

into a band of greater or less length, and form a *continuous* spectrum.

The light of a gaseous or vaporous body will by the same means, on the contrary, be decomposed into a few only, sometimes even into a very few, bright *lines*.

In the first case, the greater the length of the spectrum, the less will be its intensity in comparison with that of the source of light; in the second case, especially when the spectrum consists only of a couple of lines, the intensity of each line is little less than half that of the light itself.

If, therefore, an equal amount of light from two self-luminous bodies, one of which is solid or liquid, and the other gaseous or vaporous, enter the slit of the spectroscope at the same time, the bright lines of the latter will be more brilliant than the color of the corresponding portion of the continuous spectrum.

Now, by increasing the number of prisms, the continuous spectrum may become so elongated, and consequently diminished in light, that, as we have already mentioned (p. 163), the once brilliant solar spectrum may be reduced to the verge of visibility, while the same amount of dispersion produces on a spectrum of lines from glowing gas only an increase in the *distance between the lines*, and no considerable diminution of their brilliancy.

The reason why the prominences round the sun's limb cannot be seen through a telescope at any time by screening off the intense light of the sun is owing to the extreme brilliancy with which the sun illuminates the earth's atmosphere, the particles of which scatter so large an amount of light as quite to overpower the fainter light of the prominences, and prevent them making any sensible impression on the eye.

In a total eclipse of the sun the light of this atmosphere is so considerably reduced as to allow the larger prominences beyond the limb of the sun to be observed by the unassisted eye. The possibility of reducing the glare of sunlight at any other time without extinguishing the light of the prominences rests on the circumstance already mentioned, that the light of the sun consists of rays of every color, and therefore produces in a spectroscope

question: "May not the spectroscope afford us evidence of the existence of the 'red flames' which total eclipses have revealed to us in the sun's atmosphere; although they escape all other methods of observation at other times?"—"Proceedings Royal Society," vol. xv., p. 258.]

of highly dispersive power a long and faint spectrum, while the light of the prominences, consisting in general of only three or four kinds of rays, remains even after the greatest dispersive power still concentrated into the same number of lines (H α, H β, H γ, D_3).

It was on these principles, first announced by Lockyer,* that Janssen succeeded the day after the eclipse of August 18, 1868, in observing the *spectrum* of the prominences in sunshine. That the method he employed was no other than that suggested by Lockyer is evident from his own communication to the French Academy, dated Calcutta, the 3d of October, 1868, in which he expresses himself as follows: "The principle of the new method rests upon the difference between the spectrum peculiarities of the light of the prominences and that of the photosphere. The light of the photosphere, which is derived from incandescent solid or liquid particles is incomparably stronger than that of the prominences which is derived from gases. On this account it has been impossible hitherto to see the prominences except during a total solar eclipse. By the employment, however, of spectrum analysis the circumstances of the case may be reversed. *In fact, by the process of analyzation the light of the sun is dispersed over the whole range of the spectrum, and its intensity becomes considerably lessened. The prominences, on the contrary, furnish only a few detached groups of rays which are bright enough to bear comparison with the corresponding rays of the solar spectrum.* It is for this reason that the lines of the prominences may be seen easily in the same field of the spectroscope with the solar spectrum, while the direct images of the prominences are invisible on account of the overpowering light of the sun. Another circumstance very favorable to this new method of observation lies in the fact that the bright lines of the prominences correspond with the dark lines of the solar spectrum: they can, therefore, not only be more easily recognized in the field of the spectroscope along the edges of the solar spectrum, but also detected on the solar spectrum itself, and their traces even followed on the very surface of the sun."

As soon as Janssen and Lockyer had succeeded by this method in observing the *spectrum* of the prominences independently of a total eclipse, it became a question whether it would

* [See note on page 262.]

not be possible not merely to see the lines of the prominences, but also to make their actual forms visible during sunshine.

The length of the bright lines of a prominence, the line H β for instance, corresponds with the height of that part of the prominence which lies in the direction of the slit, and it has been already shown (p. 264) how by passing the slit over the surface of the prominence, and mapping down the varying height of the line H β, Lockyer succeeded in constructing the outline of a prominence.

Janssen, on the contrary, proposed to bring the slit successively over every part of the surface of a prominence by means of the quick rotation of a direct-vision spectroscope, so that when the motion was sufficiently rapid he might be able, owing to the duration of the impression of light upon the eye, to see the complete outline at one view. The same idea occurred both to Lockyer and Zöllner: the former, without interfering with the spectroscope, merely gave the slit a rapid revolution in a direction at right angles to that of the instrument; the latter accomplished the same end by giving the slit an oscillatory motion by means of a spring. But these experiments, though giving promise of success, were soon abandoned for other methods, partly on account of the mechanical difficulties they entailed, partly because it soon appeared that the object could be far better attained by a much simpler process.

Huggins had already been working for two years in another direction. As the prominences were pale red or pink in color, it occurred to him that it might be possible to see them fully during sunshine, if he could succeed, by the intervention of colored glasses, in eliminating the intense yellow, green, and blue rays from the white light of the sun. Were this accomplished, it was to be expected that the *red* light of the prominences would alone pass unobstructed through the glasses, and be no longer overpowered by the remaining atmospheric rays, so that the forms of the prominences themselves would be seen direct by the aid of a telescope or an opera-glass.

After selecting with great care, by means of prismatic analysis, a number of colored glasses and fluids suitable for this purpose, Huggins examined the sun by their aid, both by viewing it through them directly, and also by projecting the image of the sun upon a screen in a dark room, after the white light had previously been sifted, so to speak, by means of the system of colored media.*

This plan, however, failed in accomplishing its object, and in the winter of 1868 Huggins resumed his labors by employing as a medium a ruby-colored glass which permitted only the extreme red rays of the spectrum to pass through. On February 13, 1869, he first succeeded in bright sunshine in seeing a prominence with sufficient distinctness to determine its form and draw its outline.

For this investigation he made use of a spectroscope in which a narrow slit had been introduced between the prisms and the object-glass of the small telescope, close in front of the latter.† This slit admitted into the telescope only those rays of a refrangibility exactly corresponding to that of the line C. As the *bright* C-line (H α) always occurs in the spectrum of a prominence, Huggins knew that when he saw this line visible in the instrument a prominence was in the field of the slit: when he *widened* the slit of the spectroscope so as to view the whole form of the prominence, the spectrum became so impure that the image could only be traced with difficulty, and the light from the neighborhood of the C-line became at the same time so intense as to interfere injuriously with the susceptibility of the eye. He then applied a deep ruby-colored glass to absorb the rays of a different refrangibility to that of the C-line, when the

* [In a note read before the Royal Astronomical Society in 1869, Huggins says: "Subsequently, when the Indian observations had confirmed my suspicion that the prominences would give bright lines, and also show their position in the spectrum, I tried a large number of colored media. The difficulty is, to find two media which by their combination shall absorb light of all refrangibilities except precisely that of the line C or the line F. If even a small range of refrangibility besides that of the line selected be allowed to pass, the scattered light of the atmosphere overpowers and eclipses the prominences. The most promising of the media which I tested were a solution of carmine in ammonia, which cuts off very nearly all the light more refrangible than C, and a solution of chlorophyll, which gives a strong band of absorption, taking away the brighter part of the light less refrangible than C. Unfortunately, the chlorophyll band encroaches a little upon C, and so weakens the light of the prominences. The absorption band of chlorophyll, as Prof. Stokes has shown, can be moved a little in the spectrum by acids and alkalies, and differs slightly in position in the chlorophyll of different plants; but I have not been able to degrade the band sufficiently to allow light of the refrangibility of C to pass wholly unimpeded."]

† [The slit was placed in the focus of the small telescope, and not before the object-glass. This mistake was made by Huggins in his description of his observations.]

prominence was seen in a complete form with perfect distinctness. A sketch of the prominence first observed by Huggins in this manner is given in Fig. 148.

Simultaneously with Huggins, both Zöllner and Lockyer were each working independently toward the same end. Zöllner, already known to fame by his "Photometrischen Untersuchungen," and well acquainted with the construction of every kind of optical instrument, had in a treatise entitled "Ueber ein neues Spectroskop," etc.,* given expression to his ideas on the different modes of observing the forms of the prominences in

FIG. 148.

Huggins's First Observation of a Prominence in Full Sunshine.

sunlight, with a description of the experiments he had himself undertaken in this direction. He came to the conclusion that the method of diminishing the light of the earth's atmosphere by a sufficient increase in the number of prisms deserved the most decided preference over the methods of a revolving slit or an absorptive medium, but he was unable himself to put this plan immediately into practice owing to the incomplete state of the necessary instruments. The mode of procedure which Zöllner considered as most suitable consisted of a combination of Lockyer's principle with the last method employed by Huggins, namely, of first seeking out the spectrum line of a prominence, and then opening the slit so wide as to be able to see the entire prominence, or at least a portion of it, through the aperture.

When Lockyer learned on the 27th of February, 1869, that Huggins had succeeded in seeing the prominences in sunshine by *merely widening the slit*, the same idea occurred to him which Zöllner had already published on the 6th of the same month,

* Berichte der K. Sächs. Gesellschaft der Wissenschaften zu Leipzig, vom 6. Februar, 1869.

but which he had not been able to carry out practically, that the diminution of the atmospheric light would be much more completely accomplished by an increase in the number of prisms than by the use of absorptive glasses,* and that the prominences would certainly be seen in their whole extent if one of their spectrum lines, the greenish-blue line H β, or the red line H α, for instance, was brought into the field of view of a spectroscope of great dispersive power, and the slit then opened sufficiently to allow the complete form of the prominence to be seen. The admirable telespectroscope (Fig. 136), furnished with seven prisms, which was then complete and in his possession, confirmed after a few trials the correctness of this view, and he was the first to succeed, without additional mechanical help or the use of colored glasses, in observing the prominences at any time when the sun was visible, and tracing their complete outline.†

* [The author appears here not sufficiently to distinguish between the experiments by Huggins to view the prominences by the method of absorption, and those by the prismatic method, which he was carrying on at the same time. In the method of the wide slit, Huggins relied alone upon the prismatic method, and the ruby glass was used for diminishing the glare, which was painful to the eye, and prevented the forms of the prominences from being seen with the small spectroscope employed, which was furnished with only two prisms. With a spectroscope of greater dispersive power the red glass is not necessary. The method is identical with that adopted by Zöllner, and employed by Lockyer and Respighi.]

† [The editor has on several occasions since February, 1869, when he corresponded with Prof. Maxwell on the subject, attempted to apply to the sun the method of viewing an object by monochromatic light originally employed by Prof. Maxwell in his experiments on color. This method would permit a considerable portion of the sun's limb, or even the whole sun, to be seen at once. Prof. Maxwell, in a letter dated February 19, 1869, stated the general principle thus: "You make a spectroscope consisting of a set of prisms and a lens on either side of them, and a slit at the principal focus of each of the lenses. No light can get through this combination except that which can pass from one slit to the other, so that by adjusting the slits all light except that of one bright line of the prominence may be cut off." In applying this method to the sun, a spectroscope of great dispersive power, provided with a long collimator, is attached to the astronomical telescope so that the slit is placed at some distance within the principal focus, thus causing the sun's image to fall without the collimating lens somewhere among the prisms. At the principal focus of the small telescope of the spectroscope a second slit is placed. With the aid of a positive eye-piece this telescope is moved until the bright line, say C, of a prominence is seen to fall between the jaws of this second slit. The eye-piece is then removed, and the eye placed at the slit. Under these circumstances the observer sees the sun, or part of his disk, by means of light of that particular refrangibility only. By moving the small telescope the sun may be viewed by monochromatic light of any desired refrangibility. The editor has always found the false light about the sun's limb from the diffraction images

By the same means Zöllner saw the prominences for the first time on the 1st of July, 1869. He has published the results of his observations, and accompanied them by a series of highly-interesting drawings of some of the larger prominences, in which

FIG. 149.

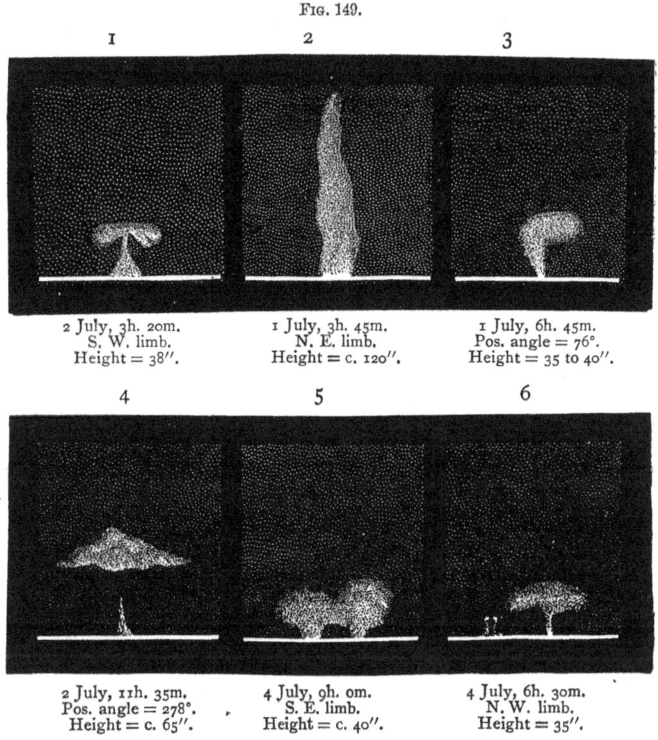

Solar Prominences observed by Zöllner.

their origin, development, and subsequent disappearance, are very clearly exhibited.

In Fig. 149 are given some of the most conspicuous forms of these masses of flame, together with the date of observation, the place of their appearance on the sun's limb, and their height in seconds (*vide* note in p. 231). With regard to these forms, Zöllner makes the following remarks:

caused by the first slit to render the prominences less distinct than when seen by the method of using a wide slit, and more than to counterbalance the advantage of viewing at once a much larger portion of the sun's limb.]

"The first prominence which I observed is represented in Fig. 149, No. 1. Over a conical mass of extreme brilliancy projecting from the sun's limb there extends a cloud-like form of less intensity. To the same type belong also the prominences No. 4 and No. 6.

"No. 4 was a very striking object from the surprisingly beautiful cloud of cumulus form which floated at some distance above the cone. The cloud was remarkably soft in texture, and traceable in its smallest details. The individual cumulus-like elements of which it was composed appeared almost like faintly luminous points.

"One of the most remarkable forms was that represented in No. 2. I could hardly trust the evidence of my eyes as I perceived in it the lambent motion of a flame. This motion was, however, slower in proportion to the size of the flame than the corresponding motion in the high flaring flames of great conflagrations. The time required for the propagation of this wave of flame from the base to the termination of the image was between two and three seconds."

It is in most cases a matter of indifference whether the red line (H α) or the greenish-blue line (H β) be selected for this method of observation; the requisite width of slit depends mainly upon the condition of the atmosphere. If the observing telescope of the spectroscope be fixed upon the C-line, and the narrow slit be so directed on to the limb of the sun that the red line H α appears in the field of view, on widening the slit, the prominence will be seen of a red color; if, on the contrary, the F-line and the line H β be observed, the same form will be visible in the color of greenish blue.

It will not perhaps be superfluous to mention that even with the smallest opening of the slit a very considerable portion of the sun's surface is included in the field of view. If this opening be not greater than $\frac{1}{250}$ of an inch, and the image of the sun, as in Lockyer's instrument, be nearly an inch in diameter, yet the rays passing through the slit would include those emitted from a space on the sun's surface of about 3,300 miles in extent.

Each of the two methods described in § 55 of observing the spectrum of the chromosphere and that of the prominences possesses peculiar advantages. If the object be merely to analyze the various lines in the spectrum of the chromosphere, then the magnified image of the sun is examined by means of the narrow slit; but, if, on the contrary, the forms of the prominences are to be observed, the small direct image of the sun formed in the principal focus of the object-glass is made use of, and a wider slit is employed.

When, as in Secchi's equatorial, the direct image of the sun is about $1\frac{1}{2}$ inch in diameter, and the slit of the spectroscope can be opened about $\frac{1}{25}$ of an inch, the whole of a prominence may be seen at once if not exceeding 40″ or 50″ (18,000 or 22,000 miles). Prominences exceeding that height must be observed piecemeal. Under such circumstances, with a wide slit radially placed, it is not easy to observe in the small image of the sun the thickness of the chromosphere, even supposing it to extend to some distance, while in the magnified image it may readily both be seen and measured.

If the widened slit be placed *tangentially*, that is to say, in a direction parallel to the sun's limb, the stratum of the chromosphere appears as a very bright red band; upon this line are seen small elevations of a form resembling such flames as are to be seen in the fields of an evening at harvest-time when the stubble is being burnt. The prominences are to be distinguished from the rest of the chromosphere by their more vivid light, and in general by their rising to a much greater elevation.

When the spectrum of the earth's atmosphere has disappeared in consequence of the powerful dispersion of the light, and the portion of the prominence then in the field of view alone is visible through the widely-opened slit, the telescope or slit is moved slowly forward, and luminous images of the most wonderful forms flit before the eye, being just as easily observed as during a total solar eclipse. In describing some of these shadow-forms Lockyer writes: "Here one is reminded, by the fleecy, infinitely delicate cloud-films, of an English hedgerow with luxuriant elms; here of a densely intertwined tropical forest, the intimately interwoven branches threading in all directions, the prominences generally expanding as they mount upward, and changing slowly, indeed almost imperceptibly. . . . As a rule, the attachment to the chromosphere is narrow, and is not often single; higher up, the stems, so to speak, intertwine, and the prominence expands and soars upward until it is lost in delicate filaments, which are carried away in floating masses."

The various forms of the prominences may be classified generally into two characteristic groups, very aptly designated by Zöllner as *vaporous* or *cloud-like* forms, and *eruptive* forms.

Through a small telescope the details of the outline and internal configuration of these forms are less clearly visible. Some

FIG. 150.

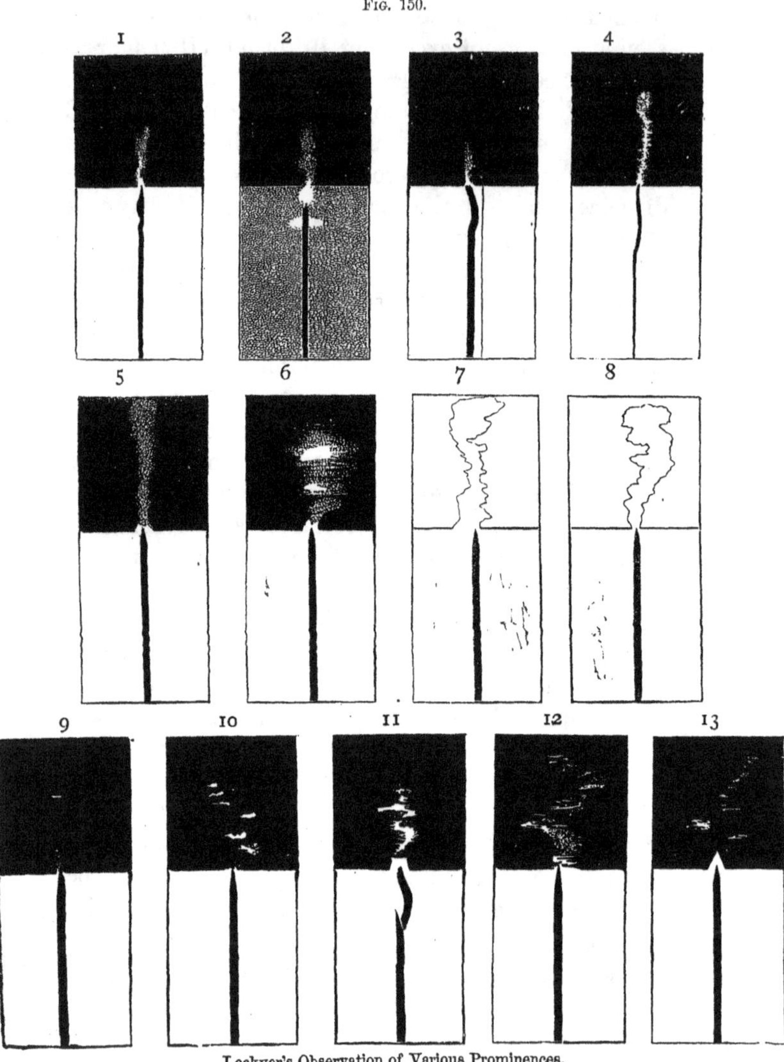

Lockyer's Observation of Various Prominences.

of these are represented in Fig. 150, Nos. 1 to 13, as they were seen by Lockyer through his telescope, when they appeared as prolongations of the C-line of the solar spectrum in the form of red flames. The upper part is the spectrum of the sky immediately surrounding the sun, reduced to the verge of visibility by the great dispersive power of the spectroscope; upon this first appeared the red line H α, which on widening the slit assumed the form of the prominence visible at that spot, represented in the drawings as white upon a black background. In some cases (No. 2) the prominence was seen to extend downward along the C-line, in others the C-line appeared waved (4), or interrupted (11), and sometimes terminated in a lozenge-shaped light of a red color; in No. 3 the dark F-line also appeared waved, and the small flame above it was of the greenish-blue color peculiar to that part of the spectrum.

Prof. C. A. Young, of Dartmouth College, Hanover, in the United States, has devoted himself especially to the observation of the forms and variability of the prominences. In Fig. 151, Nos. 1 to 8, are represented some of these characteristic forms according to the drawings prepared by Young. The observations were made early in the afternoon, on various days between the 1st of October and the 4th of November, 1869. The annexed table contains particulars of their size and position:

No.	Position Angle.	Breadth.	Height.	Remarks.
1	230°	− 68°	45″	Very brilliant.
2	267°	− 31°	60″	Bright, and in two parts.
3	270°	− 28°	30″	Faintly luminous, in form resembling a mushroom.
4	335°	+ 37°	55″	Bright, cloud-like.
5	150°	− 32°	..	An isolated cloud, 25″ above the sun's limb; 20″ in diameter.
6	350°	+ 63°	35″	Bright; a low flat arch.
7	260°	− 35°	20″	A small horn rising from a depression in the chromosphere in the neighborhood of a spot.
8	345°	+ 50°	65″	A gigantic pyramid of cloud with active internal motion.

On the 17th of September, 1869, an extended chain of prominences was seen by the same observer between + 80° and + 110° position angle, a representation of which is given in Fig. 152. These enormous masses of flaming gas extended along the sun's limb for a distance of nearly 224,000 miles, and attained a height of 50″, or 23,000 miles: the points of greatest brilliancy were at *a* and *b*.

Slight changes in the form of the prominences may be watched almost without intermission with an open slit; great changes, as a rule, take place only very slowly, or quite imperceptibly. In some cases, however, the change in the form of a prominence is

Fig. 151.

Young's Observations of Various Prominences.

so extraordinary, and occurs with such rapidity, that it can only be ascribed to extremely violent agitation in the upper portions of the solar atmosphere, compared with which the cyclonic storms, occasionally agitating the earth's atmosphere, sink into insignificance. The observation of such a solar storm has been thus described by Lockyer:

"On the 14th of March, 1869, about 9h. 45m., with a slit tangential to the sun's limb, instead of radial, which was its usual position, I observed a fine dense prominence near the sun's equator, on the eastern limb, in which intense action was evidently taking place. At 10h. 50m., when the action was slackening, I opened the slit; I saw at once that the dense appearance had all disappeared, and cloud-like filaments had taken its place. The first sketch, Fig. 153, embracing an irregular prominence with a long, perfectly straight one, was finished at 11h. 5m., the height of the prominence being 1′ 5″, or about 27,000 miles. I left the observatory for a few minutes, and on return

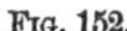

Fig. 152.

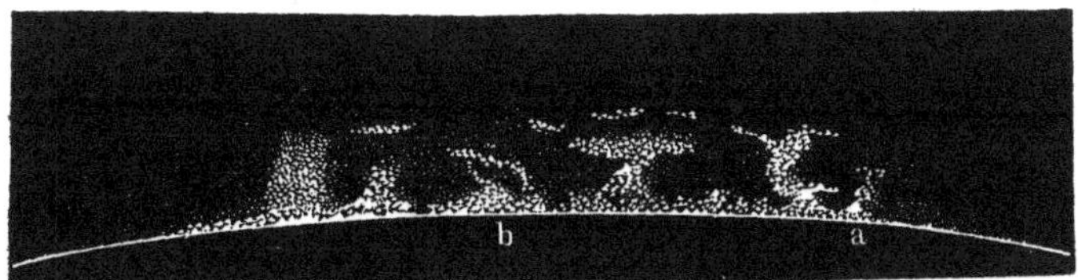

Young's Observation of a Chain of Prominences.

Fig. 153.

Solar Storm observed by Lockyer March 14, 1869.—(Picture 1.)

ing, at 11h. 15m., I was astonished to find that part of the straight prominence had entirely disappeared; not even the slightest rack appeared in its place: whether it was entirely dissipated, or whether parts of it had been wafted toward the other part, I do not know, although I think the latter explanation the more probable one, as the other part had increased, which is to be seen clearly in the second sketch that was taken, Fig. 154."

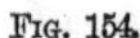

FIG. 154.

Storm observed by Lockyer March 14, 1869.—(Picture 2.)

The four drawings given in Fig. 155 were made from one and the same brilliant prominence observed by Prof. Young on October 7, 1869. Its place was estimated at 125° (position angle), its breadth was — 7°, and its height measured 75″. The changes in its form took place with extraordinary rapidity; the four drawings were made at the following epochs, 2h. 20m., 2h. 35m., 2h. 55m., and 3h. 30m. A nearly horizontal movement of the various masses of cloud was perceptible in the interior of the prominence: the form of No. 2 resembles the large prominence called "the eagle," which was observed at the total eclipse of August 7, 1869 (*vide* Plate VIII.), in the interior of which the original photographs clearly show an eddying motion in the lower part, while the upper part exhibited a centrifugal movement by which the gas was whirled off horizontally

FIG. 155.

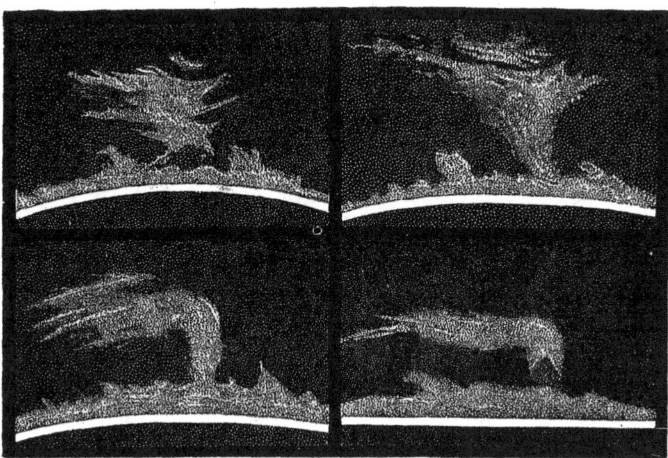
Changes in the Form of a Prominence.

In Plates XI. and XII. two prominences are represented, in their natural colors, as seen in a large telescope when the slit of the spectroscope was opened wide and directed on to the red C-line (H α). They are characteristic of the two classes, the *eruptive* and the *nebulous* class, and serve to illustrate the remarkable changes of these forms. The prominence given in Plate XI., Nos. 1 and 2, was observed and drawn by Prof. Zöllner, and is of an eruptive form, with a decided rotatory movement; the prominence represented in Plate XII., Nos. 3 and 4, is one observed by Prof. Young, and is of a cloud-like character. By means of the accompanying scale * their height can be easily ascertained.

As the meteorologist registers many times in a day the conditions of our atmosphere in the hope that a comparison of the observations may lead to a discovery of the law governing these changes, so has Respighi, director of the University Observatory at the Campidoglio at Rome, made it his daily task since October, 1869, to observe the entire limb of the sun when the weather was

* The same scale of 60,000 miles is given in both Plates XI. and XII.

favorable, including the chromosphere and prominences, and to mark upon a straight line representing the circumference of the sun the position, height, and form, of the prominences for each day. By collating these lines or circumferences of the sun one below the other, and crossing them with lines indicating the principal positions, a comprehensive picture is afforded of the distribution of the prominences round the sun's limb, which shows at a glance those regions in which the prominences abound and those in which they are least frequently to be met with.

The instrument employed by Respighi is an equatorial telescope by Merz, of 4.4 inches aperture, with a direct-vision spectroscope of great dispersive power, constructed on Hofmann's principle; at each observation the slit is placed in a direction tangential to the sun's limb, and beginning at the north point is carried round the sun, its place at the various points of observation being read off on the position-circle of the telescope. At each adjustment of the slit about 20° of the circumference could be examined, so that sixteen adjustments sufficed to survey the entire limb of the sun. The presence of a prominence was revealed in the manner previously described by the red C-line (H α) being seen to extend to a greater or less distance beyond the chromosphere when the narrow slit was removed somewhat from the sun's limb. In order to observe the form of the prominence, the slit was widened to the full height of this line. When this height exceeded 1′ the observation was made in parts from the sun's limb outward, since by a wider opening of the slit the light became too brilliant. By this method Respighi sketched in detail the whole circumference of the chromosphere point by point, and it will be seen from Fig. 156, which is an exact copy on a reduced scale of one of his original maps, how the aspects of the prominences, their distribution on the sun's limb, and their forms and heights during the space of a month, may be viewed at a glance. The prominences are represented in the drawing twice the size they really appear; in the lines (days) marked with an asterisk the observations are not trustworthy, owing to the prevalence of fog. By a comparison of the maps already constructed, Respighi has arrived at the following results:

1. In the polar regions prominences occur only exceptionally. The district from which they are absent lies between north and northeast on the one side, and south and southwest on the

other; the portion which is almost entirely without prominences has a semi-diameter of $22\frac{1}{2}°$.

FIG. 156.

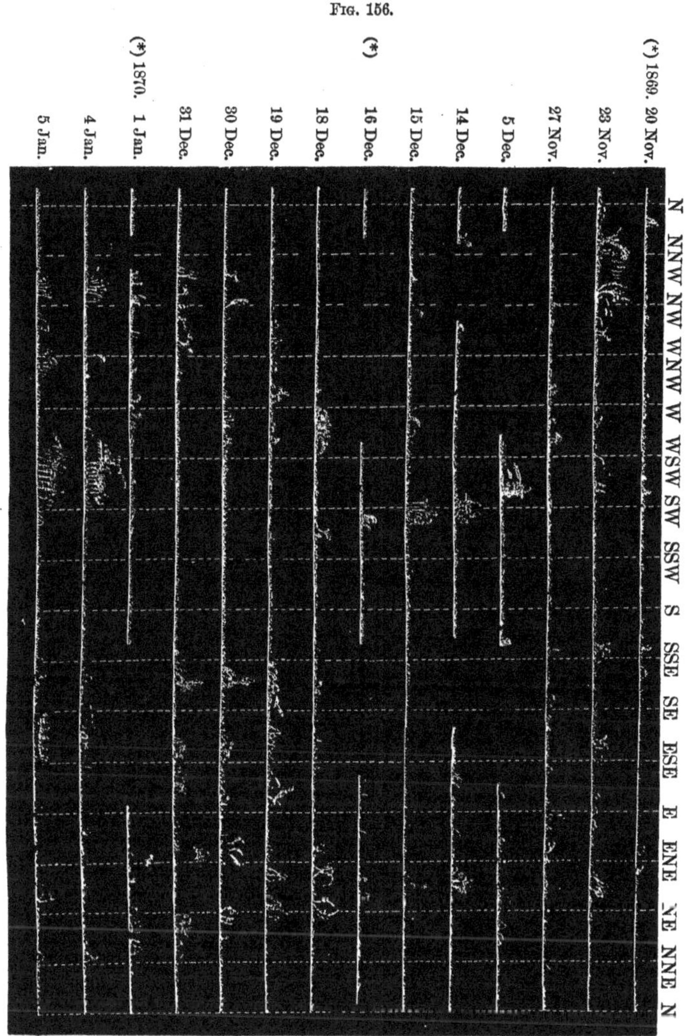

Respighi's Observations of the Prominences round the entire Limb of the Sun.

2. The district where the prominences most frequently occur lies between north and northwest, at about 45° north latitude, in a region where solar spots are rarely seen.

3. The prominences are, therefore, phenomena quite distinct from the spots; they are probably more intimately connected with the formation of *faculæ* (p. 188), an hypothesis supported by the observations of both Gilman and Lockyer.

4. The various forms of the prominences show that they are not of the nature of *clouds*, which float in an atmosphere in which they are produced by local condensations; they are much more like *eruptions* out of the chromosphere, which often spread out of the higher regions, and take the form of bouquets of flowers, some being bent over on one side and some on the other, and which fall again on to the surface of the chromosphere as rapidly as they rose from it.

5. It appears that *eruptions of hydrogen* take place from the interior of the sun; their form and the extreme rapidity of their motion necessitate the hypothesis of a *repulsive power* at work either at the surface or in the mass of the sun, which Respighi attributes to electricity, but Faye simply to the action of the intense heat of the photosphere.

On the 28th of September, 1870, Prof. Young succeeded for the first time in photographing the prominences on the sun's limb in bright sunshine. This he effected by bringing the blue hydrogen line H γ near G into the middle of the field of the spectroscope, and placing a small photographic camera in connection with the eye-piece of the telescope. As the chemicals employed were those ordinarily used in taking portraits, the requisite time of exposure was three and a half minutes, during which time the image of the prominence suffered a slight displacement on the prepared plate owing to a want of accuracy in the perfect adjustment of the polar axis. Still, however, the various forms of the prominences could be clearly discerned in the photograph, which was half an inch in diameter, so that the possibility of photographing the prominences has been proved by Young's experiment.

[The translators have inserted in Plate XIII., by the kind permission of Prof. Respighi, a reproduction in color of some of the more remarkable forms of the prominences as given in his memoir "Sulle Osservazioni spettroscopiche del bordo e delle protuberanze solari, etc. Nota III. Roma, 1871."]

58. Measurement of the Direction and Speed of the Gas-streams in the Sun.

One of the most glorious triumphs of spectrum analysis—surpassing, perhaps, in splendor all its other wonderful achievements—is the discovery that by means of accurate measurements, undertaken with the best instruments, of the position or rather of the small displacement in the position of the spectrum lines of a star or other source of light, a prominence for instance, it is possible to ascertain whether this luminous body be approaching us or receding from us, and at what speed it is travelling.

The principle on which investigations of this kind are founded was suggested by Doppler in 1842,* who sought to explain the periodic change of color in variable stars by assuming their motion to bear some comparison with that of light, and therefore that the number of ether-waves striking the eye in a second would be greater if the star were approaching us, and smaller if it were receding from us than if it were at rest. Now, as violet light produces the greatest number of vibrations in a second, and red light the fewest vibrations, it follows that, if the star be approaching, its light will be displaced in the direction of the violet, and in the direction of the red if the star be receding from us.

The pitch of a musical tone depends, as is well known, upon the number of impulses which the ear receives from the air in a given time (p. 43). Now, as a tone rises in pitch the greater the number of air-vibrations which strike the tympanum in a second, so must a sound ascend in tone if we rapidly approach it, and fall in pitch if we recede from it. The truth of this supposition may be fully proved by the whistle of a railway-engine in rapid motion. To an observer standing still, the pitch of the tone rises on the rapid approach of the locomotive, although the same note is sounded, and falls again as the engine travels away.

* [That Doppler was not correct in making this application of his theory is obvious from the consideration that even if a star could be conceived to be moving with a velocity sufficient to alter its color sensibly to the eye, still no change of color would be perceived, for the reason that beyond the visible spectrum, at both extremities, there exists a store of invisible waves, which would be at the same time exalted or degraded into visibility, to take the place of waves which had been raised or lowered in refrangibility by the star's motion. No change of color in the star could take place until the whole of those invisible waves of force had been expended, which would only be the case when the relative motion of the star and the observer was several times greater than that of light.]

As the various tones of sound depend on the rapidity of the air-vibrations, so the varieties of color are regulated by the number of ether-vibrations (p. 45). If, therefore, a luminous object, as for instance the glowing hydrogen of a prominence, be *receding* rapidly from us, fewer waves of ether will strike the optic nerve in a second than if it were stationary. If the difference in the number of ether-waves be sufficiently great to be perceived by the eye, then each color of the glowing gas must sink in the scale of the spectrum—that is to say, incline more toward the red. The individual colored rays will not then in the prismatic decomposition of the light occur in the same place of the spectrum in which they would have appeared had the light been stationary; they will all be displaced somewhat toward the *red.*

The converse takes place when the luminous body is rapidly approaching us: the number of ether-vibrations received by the eye is then increased beyond what it would be if the source of light were stationary; in the prismatic analysis of the light the colored rays will be found likewise to have changed their place in the scale of the spectrum, and taken a position in accordance with their increased refrangibility, suffering a general displacement toward the *violet.*

When it is remembered that the number of ether-waves in red light is at least 480 billion and in violet 800 billion in a second, and that moreover the wave-length of the greenish-blue light (H β), situated at the spot marked F in the solar spectrum, is only 485 millionth (more precisely 0.00048505) of a millimetre, and that instruments of sufficient delicacy to measure these minute quantities are required for this purpose, there will be little danger of under-estimating the extreme difficulty connected with observations of this displacement in the colors of the spectrum. Indeed, these observations would scarcely be possible, were it not that, in the dark lines crossing the spectra of the sun and fixed stars, the places of some of which may be accurately ascertained, we have fixed positions in the spectrum the degree of refrangibility or wave-length of which may be determined beforehand both for the sun and terrestrial substances, and also for the stars or other sources of light supposed to be at rest.

We shall presently see how Secchi and Huggins have availed

themselves of this principle to determine the rate at which a fixed star is approaching or receding from the earth.

Lockyer made use of the same plan for measuring the speed at which the glowing hydrogen gas composing the prominences streams forth from the sun's nucleus, or sinks again when the eruptive force is exhausted. The principle of this method rests on the following considerations:

The refrangibility of the greenish-blue light (H β), which with the red (H α) and the blue light (H γ) is emitted by glowing hydrogen gas (Frontispiece No. 7), is determined by the position of the line F in the solar spectrum. If any displacement be observed in the line F—that is to say, a change in the refrangibility or wave-length of the greenish-blue light—without *the neighboring dark lines suffering any displacement at the same time*, it is evident that the cause of this movement cannot be attributed either to the motion of the earth or to that of the sun, but is rather to be ascribed exclusively to the motion of the luminous hydrogen gas.

If the hydrogen gas in the sun were rapidly *approaching* us, the number of its ether-waves in a second must increase; the length of each wave will become shorter and the light be inclined toward the violet, because that color is composed of the shortest wave-lengths. *The* F-*line suffers then a displacement from its usual position in the solar spectrum toward the violet end.* If the shortening of the ether-waves of the greenish-blue hydrogen line (H β) be only $\frac{1}{10,000,000}$ of a millimetre, the consequent displacement of the F-line can be perceived, and by this means the motion of the hydrogen gas on the sun be demonstrated.

If, on the contrary, this gas be moving in the opposite direction, and be *receding* from us, the number of its ether-waves in a second will decrease, the wave-lengths will be augmented, the greenish-blue rays will approach the red, and a *displacement of the* F-*line will be produced then toward the red end of the spectrum.*

With regard to the approach or recession of the hydrogen gas in reference to an observer on the earth, there are two different circumstances to be taken into account. If the direction of the arrow a in Fig. 157 be supposed to denote a luminous stream of gas rising from the sun and *approaching* the earth, that of the arrow n, on the contrary, to represent a stream of gas sinking again into the sun and *receding* from the earth, the stream a will cause a displacement of the F-line toward the violet, and the stream n toward the red, providing the velocity be sufficiently great to alter the wave-length at least $\frac{1}{10,000,000}$ of a millimetre. Tangential or side streams, however, indicated by the arrows r and l, will have no influence in displacing the F-line; they neither approach nor recede from the eye, their direction being perpendicular to the line of sight L. If, therefore, the telespectroscope be directed to the *centre* of the sun in the direction of the line L, we shall, in the event of the displacement of the F-line, perceive only the *rising* and *falling* gas-streams a and n, the velocity of which can be measured, but neither of the lateral streams flowing at a tangent to the sun's surface.

Fig. 157.

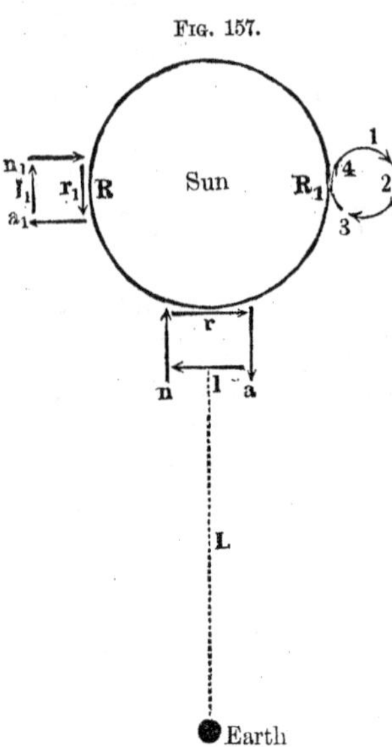

Direction and Speed of the Gas-streams in the Sun.

But, if the instrument be directed to the sun's limb at R, the case is reversed, and the rising and falling gas-streams a_1 and n_1, inasmuch as they neither approach the eye nor recede from it, and therefore produce by their motion no displacement in the F-line, cannot be perceived. If, on the contrary, the lateral or tangential streams r_1, l_1 be travelling at this spot with sufficient rapidity, the stream r_1 will approach the eye of the observer and cause a displacement of the F-line toward the violet, while the stream l_1, receding from the earth, will produce a displacement of the same line toward the red.

It is evident, therefore, that the rising and falling streams of hydrogen gas are best observed in the central part of the sun, while the lateral streams, compared by Lockyer to circular storms, whirlpools, or cyclones, the best observed on the sun's limb (R or R_1).

If it should happen that the hydrogen lines suffer a simultaneous displacement at both sides, or a uniform increase in width, it is obvious that the inference of motion in the luminous body must be received with caution: the cause of such a widening of either the bright or the dark lines must rather be sought for in an increase of density or temperature in the luminous gas (§ 32). when, however, the expansion of the lines occurs sometimes on one side only, then only on the other, and again unequally on both sides, this cannot, according to the investigations of Lockyer and Frankland, be ascribed to a change in density, since by an increase of pressure the F-line of hydrogen gas always expands equally or nearly equally on both sides.

Fig. 158, which is from a drawing by Lockyer, shows clearly what remarkable changes take place in the dark line F when the

Fig. 158.

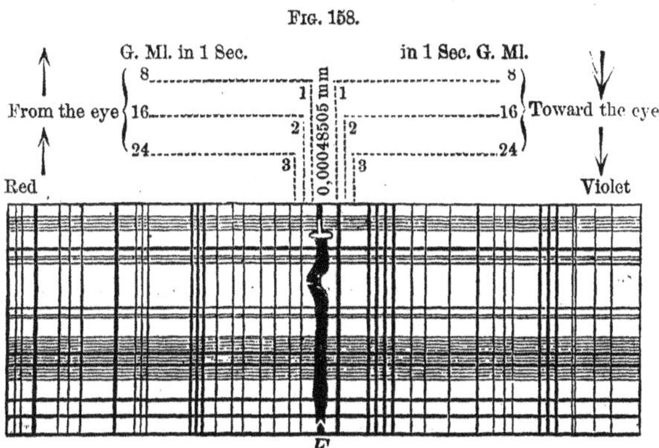

Displacement of the F-line; Velocity of the Gas-streams in the Sun.

spectroscope is directed to a solar spot in the middle of the sun. The dark band passing through the length of the spectrum is occasioned by the general absorption and weakening of the light produced by the substance of the spot. The F-line, which as a rule is sharply defined at the edges, appears in some places not merely as a bright line, but as a bright and dark line twisted together, in which parts it suffers the greatest displacement toward the red. When this occurs, there is frequently also a bright line to be seen on the violet side. In small solar spots this line sometimes breaks off suddenly, or spreads out immediately before its termination in a globular form; over the bright faculæ of a spot (the bridges) the line is often altogether wanting, or else it is reversed, and appears as a bright line (compare Fig. 108, also Fig. 143).

The same phenomena are exhibited also by the red C-line

(H α), though as the greenish-blue F-line (H β) is by an equal increase of pressure much more sensitive with regard to expansion than the red line is, and exhibits with greater distinctness the changes that have been already described, it is better adapted to observations of this kind.

All these expansions, twistings, and displacements of the F-line result, as we have already learned in § 56, from a change in the wave-length of the greenish-blue light emitted by the moving masses of incandescent hydrogen gas in the sun. The middle of this line, when it is well defined, corresponds to a wave-length of 485 millionths of a millimetre, yet it is possible by means of Ångström's maps of the solar spectrum (Plates IV., V., VI.) to measure a displacement of this line when the wave-length has only changed as much as $\frac{1}{10,000,000}$ of a millimetre, and, inversely, it is also possible to read off at once by the measured displacement of the F-line the corresponding amount which the wave-length of the greenish-blue hydrogen light has lengthened or shortened to ten millionth of a millimetre. Were the F-line to be displaced from its normal place in the solar spectrum to the spot marked 1 (Fig. 158), the wave-lengths of the greenish-blue hydrogen light would be shortened $\frac{1}{10,000,000}$ of a millimetre; the light would therefore be approaching the eye of the observer, and an eruption of gas be *ascending* at the spot (Fig. 157, *a*) observed in the middle of the sun. It is easy to calculate that such a displacement of the F-line from its normal centre to the spot marked 1 denotes a rate of motion in the glowing gas of thirty-six miles in a second.

If the F-line were to suffer an equal displacement to the left, that is to say toward the red, the wave-length of the greenish-blue hydrogen light would then be lengthened; the gas would therefore be moving away from the earth at the same rate of 36 miles in a second, and the stream of gas be sinking down to the surface of the sun, as indicated by the arrow *n* in Fig. 157.

A displacement of the F-line from its normal centre to the places marked 2 and 3 in Fig. 158, either toward the violet or the red, would justify the conclusion that the hydrogen gas was rising from the sun or sinking back to it again at a speed of 72 and 144 miles respectively in a second. From the changes actually observed in the wave-length of the greenish-blue hydrogen light, or from the measured displacements of the F-line, whether bright or dark, it appears that the speed of the gas-streams is usually about 18 miles in a second.

The observation of the *lateral* movements must be made on the bright lines of the chromosphere at the sun's limb either at R or R_1. The speed of the hydrogen gas is in this case much greater, whether it be approaching the earth as at r_1 near R, or at 2 near R_1 (Fig. 157), or whether it be receding from the earth as at n_1 near R, and at 4 near R_1. The changes in the wave-lengths of the greenish-blue hydrogen light occurring at these places are not caused by the rising and falling of the streams of gas a_1, n_1, and 1, 3, but by the lateral motion of the streams r_1, l_1, and 2, 4, and they are evident indications that the glowing hydrogen is in a state of rotatory or cyclonic movement.

It must again be remarked that even with the narrowest setting of the slit, when the opening is not wider than $\frac{1}{500}$ of an inch, a considerable portion of the sun's surface is still visible; in Lockyer's telescope the field of view, even with this exceedingly narrow slit, embraces a portion of the sun's surface about 1,800 miles in extent, and in Secchi's telescope the slit when fully open covers a space of from 20,000 to 24,000 miles.

If, therefore, a vortex of glowing hydrogen gas extending over a space of 900 or 1,000 miles be in rapid revolution in the neighborhood of the sun's limb, the whole of it may be observed with even the narrowest opening of the slit; in the telespectroscope the ether-waves which are approaching the earth may be distinguished at once from those which are receding from it, and the motion detected by a corresponding displacement of the F-line. Such a gas-cyclone (Fig. 157, 1, 2, 3, 4) has been observed by Lockyer. When the slit was directed to the middle of the storm, there was an equal expansion of the F-line both toward the red and the violet, which indicated the velocity of the stream of gas to be rather more than 36 miles in a second. When the slit was moved first to one end of the vortex and then to the other (Fig. 157, 2, 4) it was evident that the ether-waves were at one place approaching and at the other receding from the earth, for in each case the displacement of the F-line occurred only on one side. Where the displacement was toward the red, a lengthening of the ether-waves had taken place, and consequently the stream of gas (Fig. 157, 4) was receding from the earth; the displacement or expansion of the F-line toward the violet only proved, on the contrary, a shortening of the ether-waves and the approach of the stream of gas (2) toward the earth.

Fig. 159 shows such a circular storm or cyclone observed by Lockyer on the sun's limb on the 14th of March, 1869. With the first setting of the slit the image of the bright F-line (H β) in the chromosphere appeared in the spectroscope, as in No. 1; a slight alteration of the slit gave in succession the pictures 2

FIG. 159.

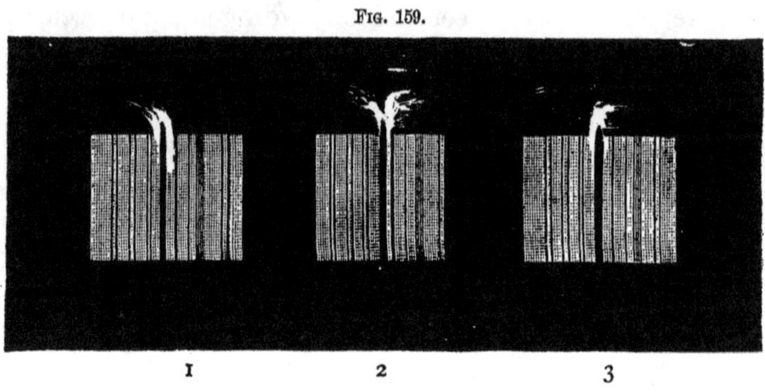

Movement of a Gas-vortex in the Sun.

and 3. There occurred also a simultaneous displacement of the bright F-line toward both the red and violet—a sign that at that place on the sun a portion of the hydrogen gas was moving toward the earth, while another portion was going in an opposite direction away from the earth toward the sun, and thus the whole action of the gas in motion resembled that of a whirlwind.

In Fig. 160 are given three different pictures of the same greenish-blue F-line of a prominence which Lockyer observed near the middle of the sun on the 12th of May, 1869, together with the dark F-line of the faint solar spectrum. In all these drawings the pointed bright line coinciding in direction with the dark F-line indicates that portion of the prominence or chromosphere which was at rest; these lines showed unequivocally that the greenish-blue light of the glowing hydrogen had undergone no change in its wave-length, and therefore that the gas was not in motion either toward or away from the earth. The bright lines diverging from these normal lines to the right or toward the violet indicate those portions of the prominences that were in motion toward the earth with very varying velocities.

The greenish-blue line of the hydrogen gas, for instance, manifestly underwent a very unequal displacement in the spectroscope; the lower portions lying close to the dark F-line showed a smaller displacement and therefore a smaller change (shortening) of the wave-length than did the upper portions—an indication that the incandescent hydrogen gas was moving from the sun toward the eye of the observer with a velocity greater in the higher and less dense regions of the solar atmosphere than in the lower strata.

FIG. 160.

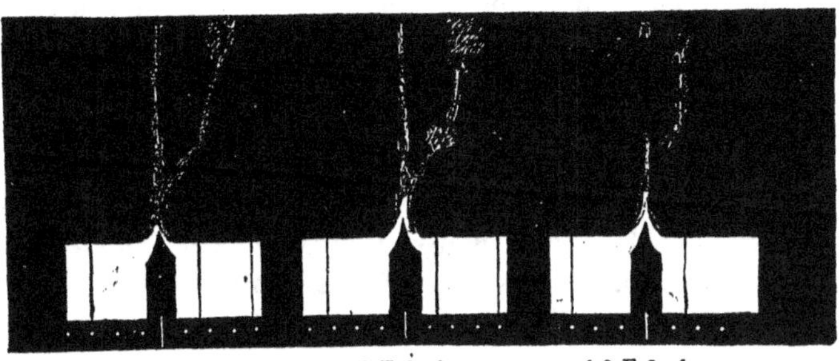

Unequal Displacement of the greenish-blue Hydrogen Line (H β).

By means of the distances from the normal dark F-line which are taken from Ångström's maps and marked by dots, it is easy to recognize the individual displacements to which the greenish-blue hydrogen line is subject in consequence of motion, and to estimate from them the velocity of the movements of the gas. Lockyer found that the farthest displacement of the bright F-line corresponded to a shortening of the wave-length that indicated a velocity in the stream of gas of at least 147 miles in a second in the direction from the sun toward the earth.

These spectroscopic observations receive an additional interest when taken in connection with those made with the telescope. On the 21st of April, 1869, Lockyer observed a spot in the neighborhood of the sun's limb. At 7h. 30m. a prominence showing great activity appeared in the field of view. The lines of hydrogen were remarkably brilliant, and, as the spectrum of the spot was visible in the same field, it could be seen that the prominence was advancing toward the spot. The violence of the eruption was so great as to carry up a quantity of metallic vapors out of the photosphere in a manner not previously observed. High up in the flame of hydrogen floated a cloud of magnesium-vapor. At 8h. 30m. the eruption was over; but an hour later another eruption began, and the new prominence displayed a motion of extreme rapidity. While this was taking place, the hydrogen lines at the side of the spot nearest to the earth were suddenly changed into bright lines, and expanded so remarkably as to give undoubted evidence of the occurrence of a cyclonic storm.

The sun was photographed at Kew on the same day at 10h. 55m.; the picture showed clearly that great disturbances had taken place in the photosphere in the neighborhood of the spot observed by Lockyer. In a second photograph, taken at 4h. 1m., the sun's limb appeared as if torn away just at the place where the spectroscope had revealed a rotatory storm.

It occurred to both Secchi and Zöllner that, from the unequal displacement of the C-line when observed at the two opposite points of the sun's equator, the speed of the sun's rotation might be ascertained. As a point on the surface of the sun turned toward the earth moves in the direction from east to west, so a point on the sun's eastern limb must be approaching an observer stationed on the earth, while a point on the western limb must be receding from him. The points upon the sun's equator would have the greatest velocity, amounting to as much as 1.92 kilometre in a second. If a spectrum line, as for instance the C-line, be observed on the eastern limb of the sun which is *approaching* the observer, it will in comparison with its position when viewed at the pole of the sun's axis, or even in the centre of the sun, appear to be displaced toward the *violet;* while, on the contrary, the same line observed on the western limb of the sun where it is receding from the earth would be seen to suffer a displacement toward the *red.* Secchi thinks he has observed similar displacements in the red H α line of the chromosphere when compared with the constant dark C-line in the spectrum of the atmosphere visible at the same time. This bright line when viewed on the *advancing* limb in the sun's equator was seen pushed toward the violet, leaving behind it a narrow strip of the dark C-line visible on the side nearest the red; when examined on the receding limb, the line was pushed toward the red, leaving behind it a narrow strip of the C-line visible on the side nearest the violet.

Although, owing to improvements introduced by Fizeau,

instruments are constructed of sufficient delicacy to measure such a displacement even when it does not exceed 0.0075 of the interval between the two D-lines, and a very ingenious contrivance (a reversion spectroscope) has been specially devised by Zöllner by which this small amount may be reduced one-half, yet observations and measurements of this kind must be received with great caution. The observations of Secchi, as far as they relate to the displacement of the line, are doubtless correct, but it is premature to ascribe this displacement to the rotation of the sun. Not merely because displacements of the bright lines are seen at all times and at all points on the sun's surface, wherever prominences exist, sometimes to one side of the spectrum and sometimes to the other, and that often on the eastern limb of the sun's equator the red C-line is seen to be displaced toward the red instead of the violet, and the reverse observed on the western limb of the sun, but also because the dark lines of the spectrum ought to suffer an equal displacement if the cause lay in the revolution of the sun upon its axis. It must therefore be concluded that, at least in the instances adduced by Secchi, the observed displacement of the red line in the spectrum of the prominence was in no way due to the rotation of the sun.

59. Spectrum Analysis of the Heavenly Bodies.—Stellar Spectroscopes.

The investigation of the spectra of the planets and fixed stars commenced by Fraunhofer has since been carried on at various times by Lamont, Donati, Brewster, Stokes, Gladstone, and others; but their labors were restricted to observing the position of the dark lines present in these spectra, as well as their relation to the Fraunhofer lines of the solar spectrum, without any suspicion of their real nature or connection with the material constitution of the heavenly bodies. It was not till Kirchhoff's discovery of the theory of the Fraunhofer lines (1859) that the sun, the planets, the fixed stars, the nebulæ, clusters, comets, and even meteors, were subjected to analysis by means of their spectra.

When it is remembered that the light of the stars, and especially that of nebulæ and comets, is very faint, and that in a northern climate there are but few nights favorable for the observation of these delicate objects, in which their light is neither overpowered by the moon nor obscured by mist or cloud; and when it is further borne in mind that, since the instruments participate in the daily revolution of the earth, a complicated driving clock is requisite for giving them a contrary motion, by which the image of a star may be kept stationary for some time in the field of view; some idea may be formed of the difficulties inseparable from the investigations of the heavenly bodies by spectrum analysis, and some proper estimate made of the services of such men as Angelo Secchi, director of the Observatory at the Collegio Romano at Rome, William Huggins, of Upper Tulse Hill, and William Allen Miller,* vice-president of the Royal Society, who have won for themselves well-merited honor by their untiring zeal and energy in overcoming so many obstacles.

It is obvious that the spectroscopes constructed in the manner most suitable for the analysis of terrestrial substances are not adapted for the investigation of stellar light. Whenever the distances of the lines in the stellar spectra have to be measured, or their position compared with the spectrum lines of any terrestrial substance, the instrument must be attached to an equatorially-mounted telescope—that is to say, a telescope made to turn at the same speed as the earth, but in a contrary direction, so as to follow any star, from its rising to its setting, upon which the instrument may be directed, and thus to keep the star stationary in the centre of the field of view. The motion of such an instrument is generally accomplished by clock-work, according to the method already described in connection with Fig. 110.

The image of a fixed star in a telescope is, as is well known, a point; now, the spectrum of a point is a line without any sensible breadth, and therefore not suitable for observation. In order to obtain a spectrum of sufficient breadth from a luminous point, the point may either first be converted into a short line of light, which is easily accomplished by the use of a cylindrical lens, and its light when projected on to the slit analyzed by a prism, or a linear spectrum may first be formed, and then a cylindrical lens employed for increasing its breadth. †

It is evident that suitable optical contrivances are requisite (a

* [On September 30, 1870, the editor sustained the great loss of his esteemed friend Dr. Miller, who died on that day after a short illness.]

† [The first method should always be employed.]

large object-glass or concentrating lens, for instance) to collect the greatest possible amount of the faint light of a star, and condense it into a short line of light, and further that on account of the faintness of the object the dispersive power of the spectroscope must under ordinary circumstances be limited, and the instrument contain only a few prisms.

A suitable contrivance is also necessary whereby in immediate connection with the spectroscope all kinds of terrestrial substances may be converted into luminous vapor, either by means of a Bunsen burner, or, which is preferable, a Ruhmkorff's induction coil, and the light thus emitted sent into the spectroscope through the prism of comparison (Fig. 57), which covers one-half of the slit, so as to enable the observer to compare the spectra thus formed with the spectrum of a star.

From these general remarks it will be easy to understand the construction of a stellar spectroscope, and become familiar with the details of its practical management.

FIG. 161

Merz's Object-glass Spectroscope.

The first stellar spectroscope was made by Fraunhofer in 1823. In order to observe the spectra of the fixed stars, and at the same time to determine the refrangibility of their light, he constructed a large instrument with a telescope $4\frac{1}{2}$ inches aperture, and placed in connection with it a flint-glass prism possessing an angle of 37° 40′, of the same diameter as the object-glass. The angle formed by the incident with the emergent ray was about 26°. Fraunhofer placed the prism in front of the object-glass of the telescope, so that the latter served only as the observing telescope to the spectrum already formed. This plan was abandoned by later observers, who, after the example of Lamont (1838), allowed the light of the star to pass unchanged through the object-glass of the telescope, and analyzed the image from the position of the eye-piece either by a prism alone or else by the use of a small telescope.

The Roman observers Respighi and Secchi have lately reverted to Fraunhofer's method, and have furnished their large refractors with an *object-glass spectroscope* constructed by the celebrated optician Merz, of Munich.

In Fig. 161 the apparatus is represented complete, ready for attachment to the object-glass of a refractor; Fig. 162 shows the

Fig. 162.

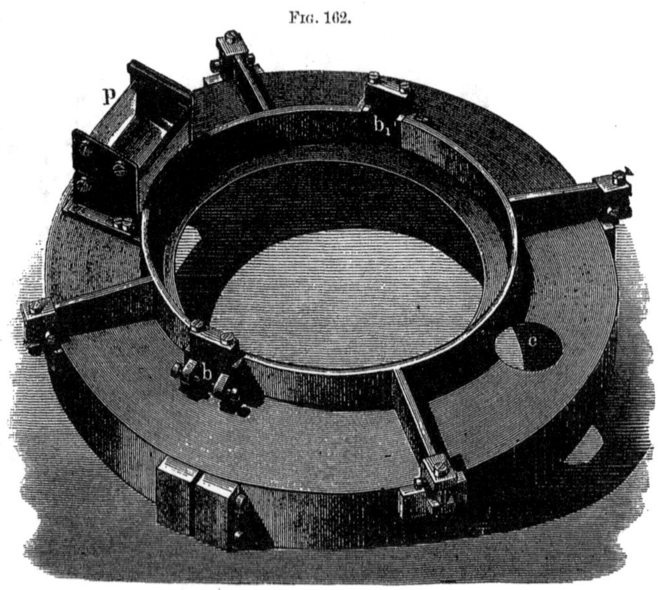

Merz's Object-glass Spectroscope.—(Mounting of the Prism.)

mounting for the prism; and Fig. 163 the prism when removed from its bed. The prism P is mounted in a ring turning on an horizontal axis, which by means of the lateral pins a, a_1, being inserted between the screws b b_1, may be fitted into a second ring. This outer ring is made to travel round the case by which the whole apparatus is placed in connection with the mounting of the object-glass, so as to allow of the prism being placed in any position or inclined in any direction with respect to the object-glass or the axis of the telescope. Since the rays falling on the object-glass are diverted by the prism, the axis of the telescope cannot be pointed direct to the star that is to be observed. In order, therefore, to facilitate the finding of a star, the case carrying the prism is constructed with an opening at c, through which the star may be viewed direct; on the side of the case opposite this aperture is attached an achromatic system of prisms p of equal refracting power with the prism P, by means of which the difficulty of finding a star is much reduced.

The prism has a refracting angle of 12°; it is composed of the purest colorless flint glass, so that the loss of light it occasions is inappreciable. Its aperture measures six Paris inches; and the mounting is provided, as shown in the drawings, with every necessary contrivance for adjustment.

Fig. 163.

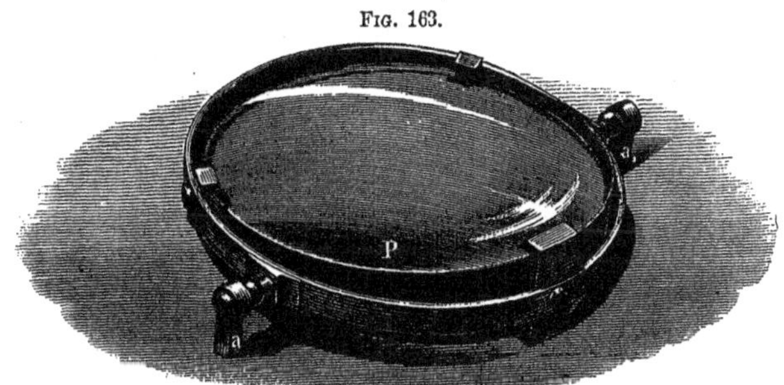

Merz's Object-glass Prism.

Although this prism reduces the effective aperture of the 9-inch refractor of the Collegio Romano to less than one-half, the amount of light obtained far exceeds that of the refractor with a direct-vision spectroscope applied in the place of the eye-piece; the dispersion is, according to Secchi, at least six times as great as the most powerful apparatus applied at the eye-piece tube.*

* [This statement needs confirmation. There may have been great loss of light in the direct-vision spectroscopes with which it was compared.]

Merz has also adapted the object-glass prism for direct-vision observation by constructing it of a combination of crown- and flint-glass prisms corrected for refraction. The slight loss of light occasioned by such a combination is unavoidable. In an instru-

Fig. 164.

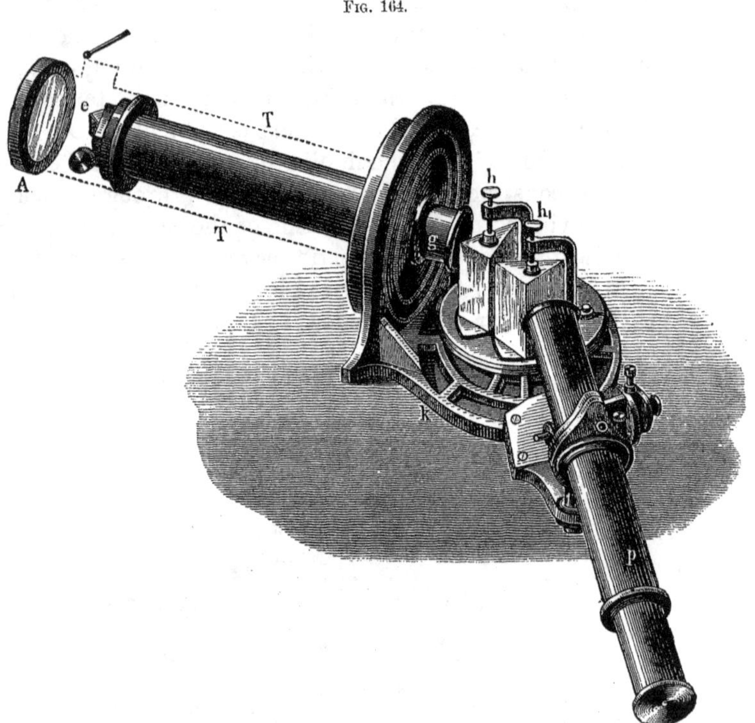

Huggins's Stellar Spectroscope.—(Perspective View.)

ment of this kind made for the observatory of Privy Counsellor L. Camphausen at Rüngsdorf, the refracting angle of the crown-glass prism is 36°, and that of the flint-glass prism 25°; the mean index of refraction for the crown glass is 1.5283, for the flint glass 1.7610.

When an eye-piece spectroscope is employed which analyzes the optical image of a heavenly body—a point of light in the case of a fixed star—by means of a system of prisms occupying the place of the eye-piece, either of the methods above described for spreading out the point of light by the use of a cylindrical lens may be adopted, and it is in most cases a matter of indifference whether this lens be placed in front or behind the slit and prisms.*

The stellar spectroscope with which Huggins made his first

FIG. 165.

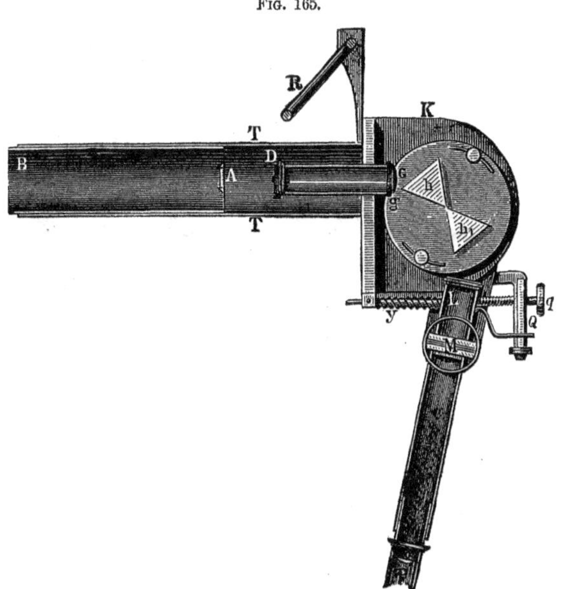

Huggins's Stellar Spectroscope.—(Horizontal Section.)

observations, and which was constructed for him by Browning,† is represented in Figs. 164, 165, and 166. The outer tube T T of the eye-piece is the only portion of the equatorial telescope given in the drawings; all the other parts are omitted. The spectroscope is attached to the eye-end T T of the telescope, a refractor of 8 inches aperture and 10 feet focal length, the whole being carried forward by clock-work.

* [This statement is not quite correct. The cylindrical lens should be placed before the slit.]

† [This telescope has now been replaced by a refractor of 15 inches aperture and 15 feet focal length, constructed by Messrs. Grubb & Son, of Dublin, for the Royal Society, by whom it has been placed in the hands of Mr. Huggins. Spectroscopes of a new form, furnished with compound prisms automatically brought to the position of minimum deviation for the part of the spectrum under observation, for use with this large telescope, are being constructed by the same opticians. One of these instruments is described in a note at p. 96, and the train of prisms represented in diagram **H.** The instrument shown at C contains one compound prism (equal in dispersive power

Within the tube T T of the equatorial there slides a second tube B, which carries a plano-convex cylindrical lens A of 1 inch aperture and 14 inches focal length; this lens is so placed in the

Fig. 166.

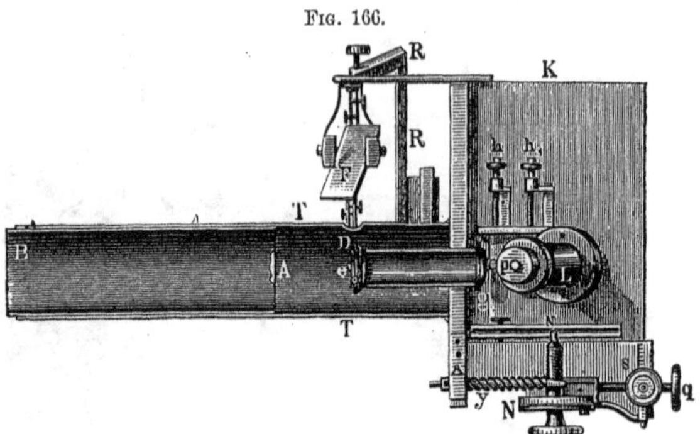

Huggins's Stellar Spectroscope.—(Partial Vertical Section.)

path of the converging rays as they emerge from the object-glass that the axis of the cylindrical surface is perpendicular to the slit D of the spectroscope, and by its means a sufficiently broad spec-

to two prisms of dense glass of 60°), and is used in the observation of nebulæ and faint stars. The spectroscope represented at D contains two compound prisms, and is filled with Grubb's automatic arrangement. The collimator, which is common to

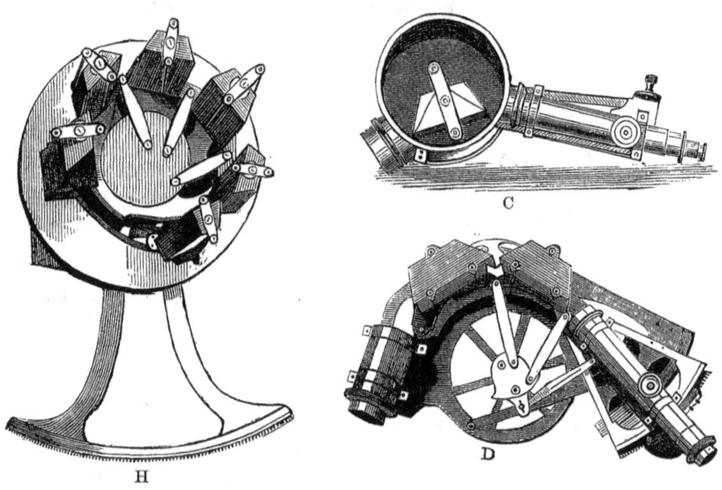

all the spectroscopes, is provided with a perforated mirror and adjustable hole for spectra of comparison, and with a cylindrical lens. It is not represented in the figures.]

trum of the line of light is formed, the slit D being placed exactly in the focus of the object-glass of the telescope. Behind the slit is placed, as usual, the collimating lens *g*, by which the rays are rendered parallel before entering the prism; the lens is achromatic, and has a focus of 4.7 inches, and an aperture of $\frac{1}{2}$ inch. By this arrangement the lens *g* receives all the light which diverges from the linear image of the star when this has been brought precisely between the two edges of the slit. The parallel rays emerging from the lens *g* pass through two dense flint-glass prisms h, h_1, possessing a refracting angle of 60°, by which they are decomposed, and a spectrum formed which is examined by means of the small achromatic telescope *p*. In order to measure the distances between the lines of the spectrum, the telescope can be turned upon a pivot by means of a fine micrometer-screw *q y*.

The object-glass of this observing telescope has an aperture of 0.8 inch, and a focal length of 6.75 inches; the eye-piece usually employed has a magnifying power of 5.7 times; the micrometer-screw is so contrived that it is possible to measure with accuracy an interval of $\frac{1}{1800}$ of the distance between the lines A and H of the solar spectrum.

The light of the terrestrial elements, the spectra of which are required for comparison with the spectrum of a star, is brought into the spectroscope in the following manner:

One-half of the slit D is covered with a small prism *e*, opposite to which is a mirror F (Fig. 166), so fastened to the spectroscope by the arm R as to be easily adjusted. This mirror receives the light emitted by the substance, which, held in the right position by metal forceps fixed into ebonite, is converted into glowing vapor by the induction spark, and reflects it through a side-opening in the tube T T into the telescope, and on to the little prism *e*. While at the same time, therefore, the light of the star passes through one half of the slit, the light from the glowing terrestrial substance passes through the other half, and in this way there are formed in the telescope *p*, at the same time, two spectra, ranged close one over the other, so that the coincidence or non-coincidence of the dark lines of the star with the bright lines of the terrestrial substance may be observed with accuracy.

In his researches on stellar spectra, Secchi employs by preference a simple direct-vision spectroscope, as a more complicated apparatus when attached to an equatorial is liable to destroy the equilibrium of the instrument, and interfere with the regularity of the clock-motion.*

The spectroscope employed by Secchi is represented apart from the equatorial in Fig. 167. M N is the principal tube, which is adapted at M to screw into the eye-piece tube G of the equatorial; to this tube is attached the arc Q B C, along the divided circle C B of which the telescope Q O is made to travel round the pivot *d* by means of a fine micrometer-screw *n*, for the purpose of measuring the lines of the spectrum.

Fig. 167.

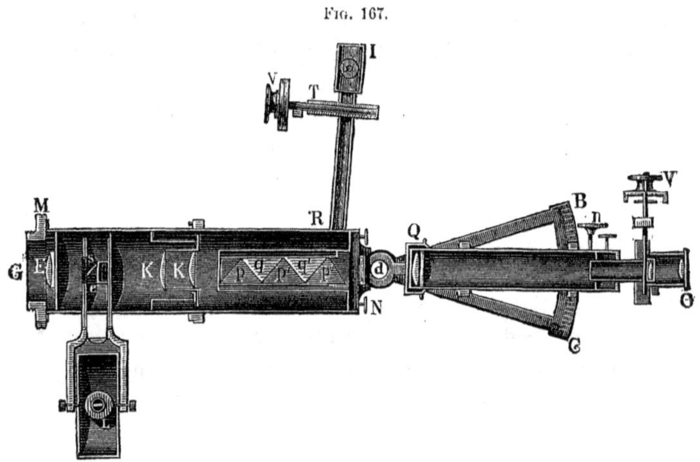

Secchi's Stellar Spectroscope.

E is an achromatic cylindrical lens, the axis of which can be placed either at right angles to the slit or parallel with it; *e* is the slit, and *s* a small glass mirror inclined to the slit at a less angle than 45°, the upper half of which being unsilvered allows the light of the star to pass through unobstructed, while the lower half, acting as a mirror, reflects from its silvered surface into the spectroscope the light of the substance made incandescent in the electric apparatus at L.

The two achromatic lenses K K, as their combined foci meet

* [When the equatorial mounting is sufficiently firm, which should be the case in all large instruments, spectroscopes of the form represented in Figs. 164, 165, are to be preferred to direct-vision instruments.]

at the slit, act as collimators, and render the rays parallel before throwing them on to the system of prisms.

The five Janssen-Hofmann direct-vision prisms $p\ q\ p^1\ q^1\ p''$ (Fig. 47) throw the prismatic rays into the observing telescope Q O in the direction G d, so that the axis of the equatorial can be directed straight upon the star.

In the lateral tube R I is the collimating lens R, in the focus of which is a small metal plate T, containing an exceedingly narrow slit, and movable backward and forward by means of a fine micrometer-screw V^1. Through this slit passes the light of an enclosed lamp at I, and forms a very narrow line of light in the inside of the tube R I, which, reflected into the telescope Q O by the front surface of the first prism p'', serves as a mark to the observer in the examination of the relative positions of the spectrum lines.

In order to see the finer dark lines of the spectra, and to compare them with the lines of terrestrial substances, instruments composed of single and compound prisms have recently been constructed both by Secchi and Huggins, suitable for application to powerful telescopes which admit of a great dispersion of the light.

A sketch of Secchi's compound spectroscope without the equatorial is given in Fig. 168: it is more particularly adapted to celestial objects of considerable diameter. By means of the screw O O^1 the instrument is attached to the eye-piece tube of the refractor; at K, as in the foregoing arrangement, is a cylindrical lens by which the image of a star appearing as a point is extended into a fine line of light, and brought precisely within the opening of the slit. F is the slit, half of which is covered with the prism for comparison, p; B the collimating lens for bringing the rays on to the first prism C in a parallel direction. Both prisms C and D are of dense flint glass, possessing a refracting angle of 60°, and are fastened on to the plate X Y Z; they throw the spectrum of the star into the axis of the direct-vision spectroscope E F H O, which contains the compound prism E F, consisting of five prisms, the observing telescope H O, and, as in the instrument previously described, the lateral tube K with a graduated scale. This scale is moved by the micrometer-screw M, and when the instrument is in use is illuminated in the usual manner by the flame of a lamp; the image of the scale is thrown by reflection from the front surface of the last prism into the telescope O, where the eye sees at the same moment the divisions of the scale and the spectrum of the star. N is a holder for receiving Geissler's tubes.

Fig. 168.

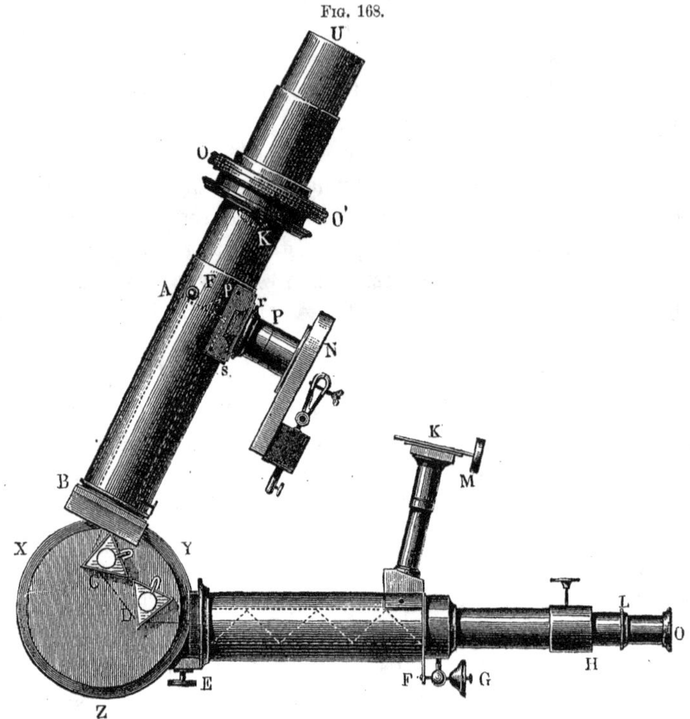

Secchi's Large Telespectroscope.

Huggins's large compound telespectroscope is shown in Fig. 169; it consists of *two* direct-vision systems of prisms, each system composed of five prisms, with a train of three excellent single prisms, two of which possess a refracting angle of 60°, and one of 45°, making thirteen prisms in all. The spectroscope is screwed in the usual manner into the eye-tube T T of an equatorial, driven by clock-work: *a* is the slit provided with a prism for comparison, and the contrivances, already described, for the simultaneous observation of the spectrum of a star, and that of a terrestrial substance produced by the induction coil; *b* is the achromatic collimating lens of 4.5 inches focus which renders parallel the rays entering the slit. The light is decomposed first by the set of prisms *d*, then further dispersed, and the individual colored rays still more separated, by the following train of three prisms *f*, *g* of 60°, and *h* of 45°, after which it again passes through a second direct-vision system of prisms *e*, to reach the object-glass of the telescope *c*. The last set of prisms *e* is placed in a tube attached to the telescope *c*; by means of a micrometer-screw the telescope can be directed to any part of the spectrum, which is a necessary contrivance in the observation of nebulæ, as these objects frequently emit light consisting only of two or three different kinds of colored rays.

Fig. 169.

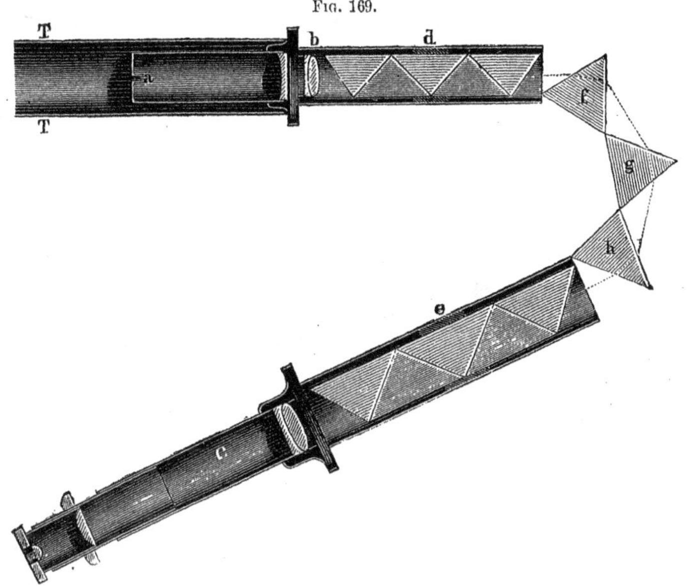

Huggins's Large Telespectroscope.

The compound prism *e* can be employed or dispensed with at pleasure, so that the dispersive power of the instrument may be made to vary within the limits of from 4½ to 6½ prisms of 60°. The advantage of being thus able to reduce the dispersive power of the instrument is found to be very great when observing faint objects, or when the atmospheric conditions are unfavorable.

The excellence of the prisms and the whole instrument is proved by the great purity and sharpness with which, even with high powers, the finest lines in the spectrum can be separated when metals are volatilized in the electric spark.

For most purposes, however, and for application to small refractors, the dispersion of the stellar light must be accomplished in much less compass than is the case with the instruments just described. The direct-vision spectroscope constructed by Merz, of Munich, for the observation of the solar prominences described at p. 270, is a very efficient instrument for this purpose, and from the simplicity of its construction is easily managed. When attached to the telescope it is screwed into the sliding-tube of the eye-piece, which has been previously removed, and the cylindrical lens L (Fig. 170), not required for the observation of the prominences, is inserted in such a manner as to project the line of light into which the image of the star has been converted exactly upon the slit *s s*. As there is no means of altering the distance between L and *s*, the exact adjustment of the line of light on to the slit is

Fig. 170.

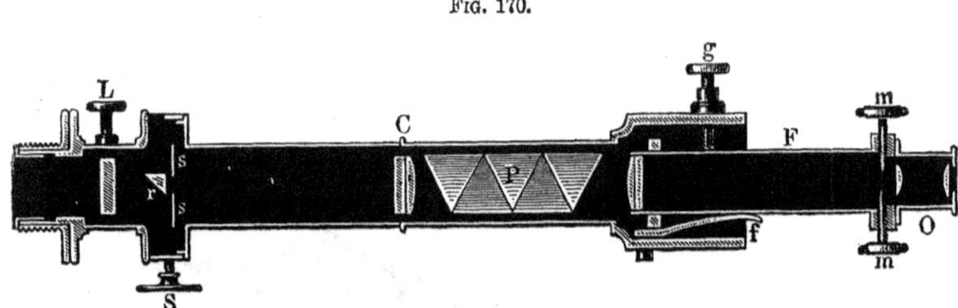

Merz's Simple and Compound Spectroscope.

accomplished by screwing the whole instrument in or out, which increases or diminishes the distance between the lens L and the image of the star. In observing the spectra of the stars, when the light is sufficient to allow of it, the dispersive power may be doubled by the introduction of a second system of prisms, without losing the advantage of a direct-vision spectroscope.

A simple stellar spectroscope is also constructed by Merz adapted specially to telescopes of small power. A drawing of this instrument is given in Fig. 171; it consists of a positive eyepiece O, an adjustable cylindrical lens L, and a direct-vision system of five prisms, the dispersive power of which amounts to 8° from D to H. It is so contrived that the prisms, when separated from the lens L and the eye-piece O, may be easily introduced between the collimator C and the system of prisms of the larger spectroscope (Fig. 170), which is furnished with a slit. The two instruments (Figs. 170 and 171) thus form a *universal eye-piece spectroscope* admirably suited to the observation of the heavenly bodies.

Fig. 171.

Merz's Simple Spectroscope.

Even Browning's miniature spectroscope, represented in Fig. 49, and described in p. 119, which, including the tube containing the prisms, measures only 3½ inches, yields a really fine spectrum when directed on to a bright star, and shows very distinctly the prominent dark lines. The construction of this little instrument is shown in Fig. 172. The outer tube carries the slit, which can be removed at pleasure, and is easily adjusted by turning round

Fig. 172.

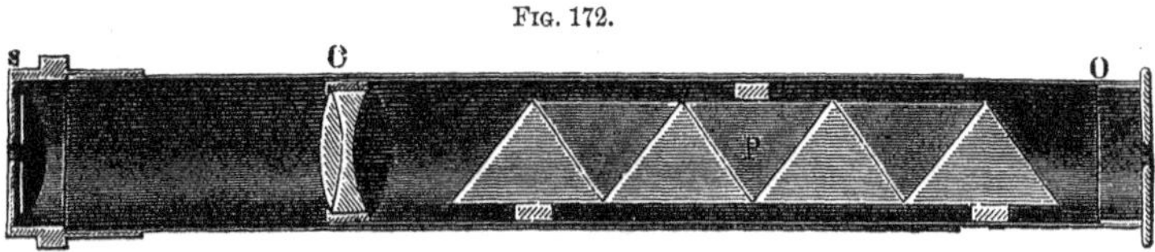

Browning's Miniature Spectroscope.

a ring; in this tube slides a second tube carrying the small achromatic collimating lens C, behind which is placed the system of seven prisms P, and an opening O for the eye-piece without any lens. To employ it in stellar observations, the tube containing the slit is removed, and the collimator tube O screwed into the place of the eye-piece of the telescope. The spectroscope is easily so adjusted that the image of the star is brought into the focus of the lens C, whence the rays are thrown in a parallel direction on to the system of prisms P, and present to the observer at O a sharply-defined linear spectrum of the star. By the introduction of a suitable cylindrical lens between the eye-hole O and the eye, a sufficient breadth is given to the spectrum for the dark lines to be visible when the instrument is properly adjusted.

We must not omit here to mention the simple spectroscopes employed both by Secchi and Huggins in those circumstances when the light is insufficient or the large instruments too cumbrous for use. Huggins has long made use of a hand spectroscope for observing the spectra of meteors and other phenomena in rapid motion in the heavens; similar instruments were also employed in the various expeditions for observing the solar eclipse of August 18, 1868, on which occasion they rendered valuable service.

These instruments as constructed by Browning consist principally, as shown in Fig. 173, of a direct-vision system of prisms *c*, and an observing telescope *a b*. The achromatic object-glass *a* has an aperture of 1.2 inch, and a focus of about 10 inches. The eye-piece *b* consists of two plano-convex lenses. As a large field of view is very important, especially when the instrument is employed as a meteor-spectroscope, the lens turned toward the object-glass *a* equals it in diameter, and is fixed in a movable tube, so that the distance between the two lenses of the eye-piece may be controlled, and thus the power of the instrument increased or diminished within certain limits. The system of

Fig. 173.

Browning's Hand Spectroscope.

prisms consists of one prism of dense flint glass and two prisms of crown glass.

The field of view of this hand spectroscope embraces a space in the heavens of about 7° in diameter: the spectrum of a bright star has an apparent length of 3°, and even the spectrum of the great nebula of Orion appears as two bright lines with a faint continuous spectrum.

For the purpose of testing the instrument as a meteor-spectroscope, Huggins observed the spectra of some fireworks at a distance of about three miles. The bright lines of the incandescent metals in the fireworks were seen with great distinctness, and showed with certainty the presence of sodium, magnesium, strontium, copper, and some other metals. The same little instrument suffices to show some of the Fraunhofer lines in the spectrum of the extreme points of the moon's cusps, as well as the dark lines in the stellar spectra. In order to give some breadth to the spectrum of a star, which in this instrument appears only as a bright line, a small cylindrical lens is placed over the eye-piece immediately in front of the eye. As the instrument is not furnished with a slit, it can only be used on bright objects of small magnitude, or on objects at such a distance that they have only a small apparent size.

60. Spectra of the Moon and Planets.

Since the planets and their satellites do not emit any light of their own, but shine only by the reflected light of the sun, their spectra are the same as the solar spectrum, and any differences that may be perceived can arise only from the changes the sunlight may undergo by reflection from the surfaces of these bodies, or by its passage through their atmospheres.

The observations of Fraunhofer (1823), Brewster and Gladstone (1860), Huggins and Miller, as well as Janssen, agree in establishing the complete accordance of the lunar spectrum with that of the sun. In all the various portions of the moon's disk brought under observation, no difference could be perceived in the dark lines of the spectrum either in respect of their number or relative intensity. From this entire absence of any special absorption lines, it must be concluded that there is no atmosphere in the moon, a conclusion previously arrived at from the circumstance that during an occultation no refraction is perceived on the moon's limb when a star disappears behind the disk. Moreover, a small telescope of only a few inches aperture suffices to show the spectrum of the moon very distinctly.

The spectra of the planets Venus, Mars, Jupiter, and Saturn, are also characterized by the Fraunhofer lines peculiar to the solar light, but contain in addition the absorption lines which are known to be telluric lines (§ 47), and are evidence of the presence of an atmosphere containing aqueous vapor.

The spectrum of Jupiter, which has been recently examined by Browning with a spectroscope attached to his 12½-inch reflector, is not of sufficient brilliancy to allow of its being observed or measured with extreme accuracy. Notwithstanding the great brilliancy with which this planet shines in the heavens, its spectrum is not so bright as that of a star of the second magnitude; this is owing to the brightness being more apparent than real, and arises from the large size of the disk compared with a star, and from the light being reflected, and not original.

As early as 1864 Huggins discovered some dark lines in the red portion of Jupiter's spectrum which were not coincident with any of the Fraunhofer lines of the solar spectrum, and among them is one that does not occur among the telluric lines.* Browning distinctly recognized these lines early in 1870, and thinks that in the green part of the spectrum, near the yellow, several fine dark lines occur which are coincident with those occasioned by the vapors of the earth's atmosphere, and which are generally visible in the corresponding portion of the solar spectrum when the sun is near the horizon. If it be supposed that Jupiter is in any way self-luminous, these lines may be occasioned by such elements in the planet as are not to be found in the sun, or, if present in the sun, have not been revealed to us by any effect of absorption.

The comparatively faint spectrum of Saturn has been examined by Huggins, who observed in it some of the lines characteristic of Jupiter's spectrum. These lines are less clearly seen in the light of the ring than in that of the ball, whence it may be concluded that the light from the ring suffers less absorption than does the light from the planet itself. The observations of Janssen, which have been supported by Secchi, have since shown that aqueous vapor is probably present both in Jupiter and Saturn. Secchi has further discovered some lines in the spectrum of Saturn which are not coincident with any of the telluric lines, nor with any of the lines of the solar spectrum produced by the aqueous vapor of the earth's atmosphere. It is not improbable, therefore, that the atmosphere of Saturn may contain gases or vapors which do not exist in that of our earth.

The spectrum of Uranus, which has been investigated by Secchi, appears to be of a very remarkable character. It consists mainly of two broad black bands, one *m* (Fig. 174) in the greenish blue, but not coincident with the F-line, and the other *n* in the green near the line E. A little beyond the band *n* the spec-

* [In 1869 Mr. Le Sueur examined the spectrum of Jupiter with the Great Melbourne Telescope, and saw the absorption lines as they are described by Huggins.]

trum disappears altogether, and shows a blank space *q p*, extending entirely over the yellow to the red, where there is again a faint reappearance of light. The spectrum is therefore such a one as would be produced were all the yellow rays extinguished from the light of the sun. The dark sodium line D occurs, as is well known, in the part of the spectrum occupied by this broad non-luminous space: is this extraordinary phenomenon, therefore, to be ascribed to the influence of this metal, or is the planet Uranus, which has a spectrum differing so greatly from that of the sun, self-luminous? Has the planet not yet attained that degree of consistency possessed by the nearer planets, which shine only by the sun's light, and, as the photometric observations of Zöllner lead us to suppose is possible, is still in that process of condensation and subsequent development through which the earth has already passed? These are questions to which at present we can furnish no reply, and the problem can only be solved by additional observations of the strange characteristics exhibited by this spectrum.*

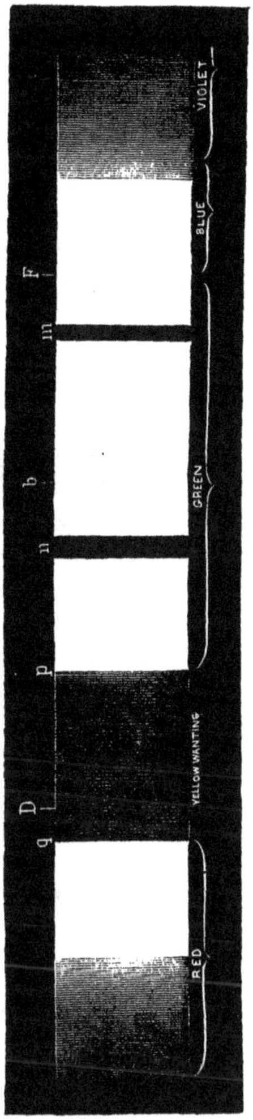

FIG. 174.—The Spectrum of Uranus.

The spectrum of Neptune, which has also been examined by Secchi, bears a great resemblance to that of Uranus. It is characterized by three principal bands. The first, which is the faintest, is situated between the green and the yellow, nearly in the centre between D and *b*; it is of considerable breadth, but very ill defined at the edges. Between this and the red there is a tolerably bright band, with which the spectrum seems suddenly to terminate, and the red is entirely wanting. Secchi

* [Huggins gives the following description of the spectrum of Uranus in a paper recently presented to the Royal Society: "The spectrum of Uranus, as it appears in my instrument, is represented in the accompanying diagram. The narrow spectrum

is of opinion that the absence of the red is not occasioned by the faintness of this planet, for other stars no brighter than Neptune show the red clearly in the spectrum. The absence of this color in the spectrum of Neptune must therefore be ascribed to absorption.

placed above that of Uranus shows the relative positions of the principal solar lines, and of two of the strongest absorption bands produced by our atmosphere, namely, the group of lines a little more refrangible than D, and the group about midway from C to D. The scale placed above gives wave-lengths in millionths of a millimetre.

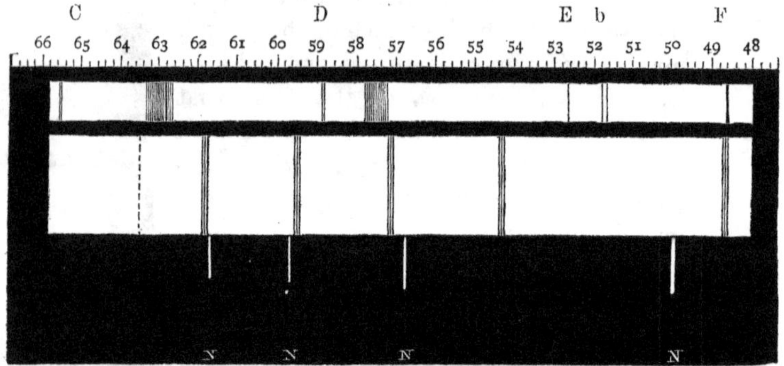

" The spectrum of Uranus is continuous, without any part being wanting as far as the feebleness of its light permits it to be traced, which is from about C to about G. On account of the small amount of light from the planet, I was not able to use a slit sufficiently narrow to bring out the Fraunhofer lines. The remarkable absorption taking place at Uranus shows itself in the six strong lines drawn in the diagram. The position of the least refrangible of these lines could only be estimated, as it occurs in a very faint part of the spectrum ; on this account it is represented by a dotted line. The measures taken of the most refrangible band showed that it was probably at the position of the solar F. By direct comparison it appeared to be coincident with the bright line of hydrogen. Three of the lines were shown by the micrometer not to differ greatly in position from some of the bright lines of air. A direct comparison was made, when the principal bright lines of the spectrum of air were found to have the positions relatively to the bands of planetary absorption which are shown in the diagram. The band, which has a wave-length of about 572-millionths of a millimetre, was found to be less refrangible than the double line of nitrogen which occurs near it. The two planetary bands less refrangible appeared nearly coincident with bright lines, but I suspected that the lines of air were in a small degree more refrangible. There was no strong line in the spectrum of Uranus at the position of the strongest of the air lines, namely, the double line of nitrogen at 500 of the scale. Measures taken with the same spectroscope of the principal bright bands of carbonic-acid gas showed the bands in the spectrum of Uranus are not produced by the absorption of this gas. There is no absorption band in the spectrum of Uranus at the place of double line of sodium. An inspection of the diagram will show that there are no bands in the spectrum of Uranus similar to those produced by the absorption of the earth's atmosphere."]

William Huggins.

Page 337.

The second absorption band occurs at the line *b;* it is tolerably well defined at the edges, but much fainter and more difficult of observation than the first band. The third band is in the blue, and is even fainter than the second.

This spectrum is in agreement with the color of the planet, which resembles the beautiful tint of the sea. A peculiar interest attaches to this spectrum from the coincidence of the dark bands with the bright bands of certain comets, and with the dark bands of stars of the fourth type. These bands may possibly be due to carbon; but accurate measurements are exceedingly difficult, and can only be attempted on the finest evenings and with the use of the most powerful instruments.

While Jupiter and his satellites, with a power of 350, give a sharply-defined image, the disk of Neptune, with the same power, ceases to be well defined, and appears with a nebulous edge.* From this it may be inferred that the planet is surrounded by a dense mist of considerable extent, the chemical nature of which has yet to be discovered, or else that, like Jupiter, Saturn, and Uranus, it has not yet attained that degree of density which must necessarily precede the formation of a solid surface.

61. Spectra of the Fixed Stars.†

The fixed stars, though immensely more remote and less conspicuous in brightness than the moon and planets, yet from the fact of their being *original sources of light* furnish us with fuller indications of their nature. In all ages, and among every people, the stars have been the object of admiring wonder, and not unfrequently of superstitious adoration. The greatest investigators, and the deepest thinkers who have devoted themselves to the study of the stars, have felt a longing to know more

* [This statement is not supported by the observations of other astronomers possessing large telescopes; Mr. Lassell has, on favorable occasions, with his 20-foot telescope, seen the disks of Uranus and Neptune as sharply defined as that of Jupiter.]

† In this section, which treats of the fixed stars and nebulæ, we have followed almost exclusively, and in some places verbally, the excellent treatise "On Spectrum Analysis applied to the Heavenly Bodies: a Discourse delivered at Nottingham, before the British Association, 1866, by William Huggins." We have also made use of the following work: "Sugli Spettri prismatici dei corpi celesti; Memoire del R. P. A. Secchi, 1868."

of these sparkling mysteries, and with the child have experienced the sentiment expressed in the well-known lines:

> "Twinkle, twinkle, little star,
> How I wonder what you are!"

The telescope has been appealed to, but in vain, for in the largest instruments the stars remain diskless, never appearing more than as brilliant points. The stars have indeed been represented as *suns*, each surrounded by a dependent group of planets, but this opinion rested only upon a possible analogy, for of the *peculiar nature* of these points of light, and of what substances they are composed, the telescope yields us no information. Spectrum analysis alone can disclose to us this much-coveted knowledge, as it gives us the means of reading, in the light emitted by these heavenly bodies, the indications of their true nature and physical constitution. In this light we possess a telegraphic communication between the stars and our earth; the spectroscope is the telegraph, the spectrum lines are individually the letters of the alphabet, their united assemblage as a spectrum forms the telegram. It is not, however, easy to comprehend this language of the stars, but through the indefatigable labors of Secchi, Huggins, and Miller, most of the bright stars, the nebulæ, and some of the comets, have been investigated by spectrum analysis, and valuable evidence obtained as to their physical constitution.

As the spectra of the stars bear in general a marked resemblance to the spectra of the sun, being continuous and crossed by dark lines, there is every reason for applying Kirchhoff's theory also to the fixed stars, and for accepting the same explanation of these similar phenomena that we have already accepted for the sun. By the supposition that the vaporous *incandescent* photosphere of a star contains or is surrounded by heated vapors which absorb the same rays of light which they would emit when self-luminous, we may discover from the dark lines in the stellar spectra the substances which are contained in the photosphere or atmosphere of each star. In order to ascertain this with certainty, the dark lines must be compared with the bright lines of terrestrial substances volatilized in the electric spark; and the complete coincidence of the characteristic bright lines of a terrestrial substance with the same number of dark lines in the stellar spectrum would justify the conclusion that this substance is present in the atmosphere of the star, a conclusion that gains all the more in certainty the greater the number of lines coincident in the two spectra.

For the purpose of exhibiting the results of his observations before a large audience, Huggins, in conjunction with Miller, prepared accurate drawings of the most remarkable stellar spectra, and had them photographed on glass of the size of about two inches. By means of these transparent photographs, colored in correspondence with the tints of the spectrum,* it is possible by the use of Duboscq's lantern and the electric or Drummond's lime-light, so to magnify these stellar spectra, and project them on to a screen, that even at a great distance the dark lines may be easily distinguished.

The brilliant spectra of two stars of the first magnitude, Aldebaran (*a* Tauri), and Betelgeux (*a* Orionis), taken from these photographs, are represented in Fig. 175. The positions of all these dark lines, about eighty in each spectrum, which cross that portion of the continuous spectrum between the Fraunhofer lines C and F, were carefully determined by Huggins and Miller through repeated and very accurate measurements. These measured lines, however, are but few compared with the innumerable fine lines which are visible in the spectra of these stars.

Beneath the spectrum of each star the bright lines of the metals with which it was compared are represented. These spectra of terrestrial elements appear in the spectroscope as bright lines upon a dark background, in the position shown in Fig. 175, that is to say, exactly in juxtaposition with the spectrum of the star, so that it can be determined with the greatest accuracy whether these bright lines are coincident or not with the dark lines of the star.

The double D-line characteristic of sodium, for example, coincides line for line with a dark line also double in both the stars; sodium-vapor is therefore contained in the atmosphere of these stars, and the metal sodium forms one of the constituent elements of these brilliant and remote heavenly bodies.

The three bright lines Mg in the green are so far as is yet known *exclusively* produced by the luminous vapor of magne-

* These are to be had from W. Ladd, 11 and 12 Beak Street, Regent Street, W.; and from J. Duboscq, 21 Rue de l'Odéon, Paris.

Fig. 175.

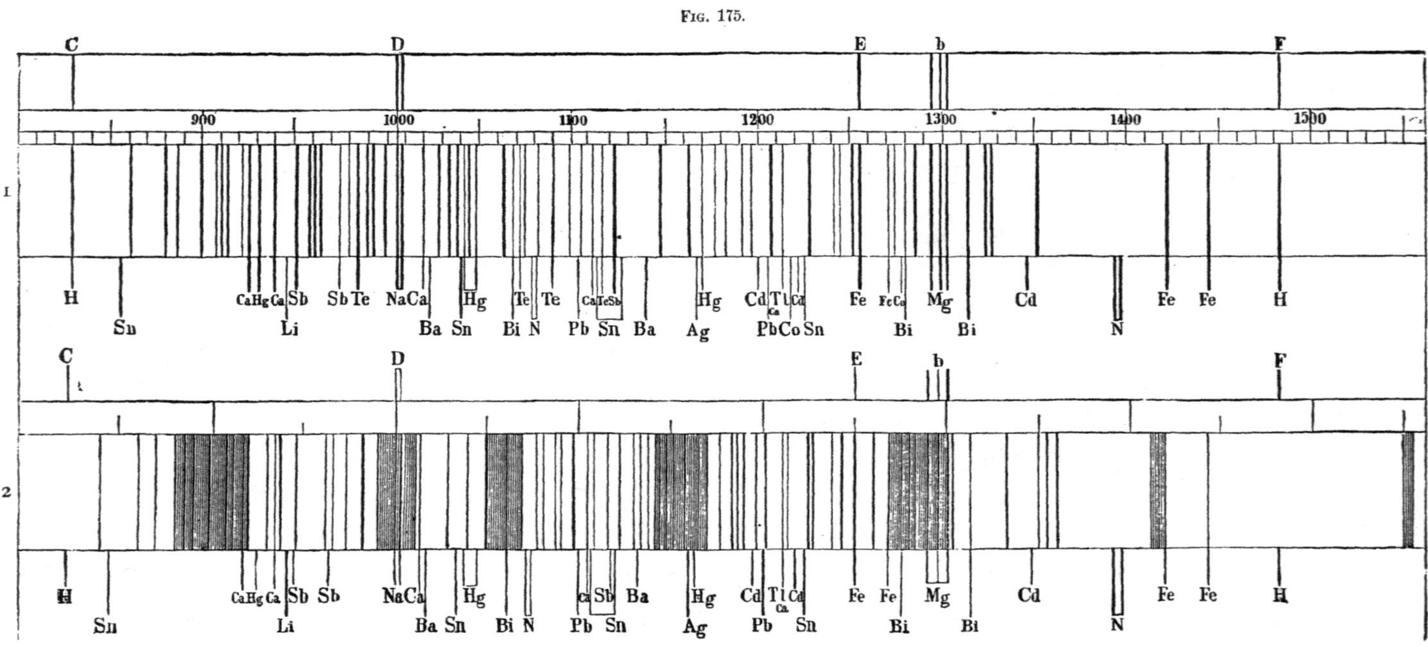

1. Spectrum of Aldebaran (α Tauri)
2. Spectrum of Betelgeux (α Orionis) } compared with solar spectrum and spectra of terrestrial elements.

sium; they agree in position exactly, line for line, with the three dark stellar lines *b*. The conclusion, therefore, would appear to be well founded that magnesium forms another of the constituents of these stars.

In the same way, the two intensely bright lines marked H, characteristic of hydrogen gas, one of which is in the red and the other in the blue limit of the green, coincide precisely with the dark lines C and F in the spectrum of Aldebaran, but not, according to Huggins, in that of Betelgeux; therefore hydrogen gas exists in the photosphere or atmosphere of Aldebaran, but is not present in that of *a* Orionis.* In a similar manner, other elements, among them bismuth, antimony, tellurium, and mercury, are known to form constituents of these stars.

It is necessary to remark here in reference to all these elements that the certainty of their presence in the stars does not rest upon the coincidence of only *one* line, which would furnish but feeble evidence, but upon the coincidence of a group of two, three, or more lines occurring in different parts of the spectrum. The coincidence of many other bright and dark lines of the same substance might doubtless be seen, as in the case of the solar spectrum, were the light of the star more intense; but the faintness of the stellar light limits the comparison to the stronger lines of each terrestrial substance.

The question might be asked, What elements are represented by the other innumerable dark lines and bands in the stars? Some of them are probably due to the vapors of such terrestrial elements as have not yet been compared with the spectra of the stars.

The fact that certain stars possess an atmosphere of aqueous vapor has been observed both by Janssen and Secchi. They belong for the most part to the class of red and yellow stars, and in their spectra, as might be supposed, the lines of luminous hydrogen are wanting. As early as 1864, Janssen had remarked the existence of an atmosphere of aqueous vapor in the star Antares; and after a more complete investigation of the spectrum of steam in 1866 (§ 47), and further observations of stellar spectra

* [No *strong* lines comparable with those seen in other stars were observed by Huggins and Miller in the spectrum of Betelgeux, and some other stars giving a similar spectrum, at the positions occupied by the lines of hydrogen, but upon this observation it is not safe to base the conclusion that that element is entirely absent.]

made after the total solar eclipse of 1868 in the remarkably dry air of the heights of Sikkim (Himalaya), he could no longer doubt that there are many stars surrounded by a similar atmosphere. Notwithstanding the dry condition of the air, the lines of aqueous vapor were more strongly marked in the spectra of these stars as seen from the heights of the Himalaya than had been observed previously, a phenomenon which cannot be ascribed to the absorption of the earth's atmosphere, and must therefore be due to that of the star.*

The results of the comparison of the two stellar spectra given above (Fig. 175), with the spectra of terrestrial elements, are given in the following table:

TERRESTRIAL ELEMENTS COMPARED WITH ALDEBARAN.

COINCIDENT.	NOT COINCIDENT.			
1. Hydrogen with the lines C and F.	Nitrogen	3	lines	compared.
2. Sodium with the double D-line.	Cobalt	2	"	"
3. Magnesium with the triple line *b*.	Tin	5	"	"
4. Calcium with four lines.	Lead	2	"	"
5. Iron with four lines and with E.	Cadmium	3	"	"
6. Bismuth with four lines.	Barium	2	"	"
7. Tellurium with four lines.	Lithium	1	line	"
8. Antimony with three lines.				
9. Mercury with four lines.				

TERRESTRIAL ELEMENTS COMPARED WITH BETELGEUX.

COINCIDENT.	NOT COINCIDENT.			
1. Sodium with the double D-line.	Hydrogen	2	lines	compared.
2. Magnesium with the triple line *b*.	Nitrogen	3	"	"
3. Calcium with four lines.	Tin	5	"	"
4. Iron with four lines and with E.	Gold?			
5. Bismuth with four lines.	Cadmium	3	"	"
6. Thallium?	Silver	2	"	"
	Mercury	2	"	"
	Barium	2	"	"
	Lithium	1	line	"

62. Secchi's Types of the Fixed Stars.

While Huggins and Miller had thus been investigating about a hundred of the brightest stars, Secchi, favored above his English fellow-laborers by the purity of an Italian sky, had already

[* These observations of the presence of lines of aqueous vapor in the spectra of some of the stars appear to the editor to require confirmation with instruments of greater dispersive power.]

P. Angelo Secchi.

Page 342.

extended his observations over more than five hundred fixed stars,* and gave the results to the world in 1867, in his work entitled "Catalogo delle Stelle di cui si è determinato lo spettro luminoso, all' osservatorio del Collegio Romano." Since then, above a hundred more stars have been added to this catalogue by this industrious astronomer, so that there exists at present a rich mass of spectrum observations of the fixed stars, which Secchi has so far provisionally arranged as to be able to group them into four principal *types*, into which all stars, with only a few very remarkable exceptions, may be classified.

The *first* type is represented by the star α Lyræ (Frontispiece No. 12), and also by the well-known brilliant star Sirius (Fig. 176, I.). Most of the stars shining with a *white* light are included in this class, such as Sirius, Vega, Altair, Regulus, Rigel, the stars of the Great Bear with the exception of α Ursæ, etc. All these stars, which are usually considered *white* stars, although they really shine with a slight tinge of blue, give a spectrum like that represented in Fig. 176, No. 1. It is composed of rays of all the seven colors, and is sometimes crossed by very numerous and mostly very fine lines, but always by four broad and very dark lines. Of these four lines, one is in the red, another in the greenish blue, and the remaining two in the violet. All the four lines are due to hydrogen, and are in exact coincidence with the four brightest lines (H α, β, γ, δ) composing the spectrum of terrestrial hydrogen as produced by means of a Geissler's tube. In Fig. 176, No. 1, the dark line C coincides with the line H α, the F-line with H β, the line V with H γ, and W with H δ. Besides these four broad lines characteristic of hydrogen, the spectra of the brightest stars of this class show also a faint dark line in the yellow, apparently coincident with the sodium line D, and also a number of still fainter lines in the green belonging to iron and magnesium.

The most remarkable peculiarity of this type is the great breadth of some of the lines, which seems to indicate that the

* [This work of Secchi and that of Huggins and Miller are not comparable. The observations of Huggins and Miller consisted of the direct comparison in the spectroscope of the lines seen in the spectrum of a star with the bright lines of terrestrial substances, an investigation which required many months' work upon a single star, and was immensely more tedious and laborious than the micrometric measures of the principal stellar lines to which Secchi's work was mainly restricted.]

Fig. 176.

Secchi's Types of the Fixed Stars.

absorptive stratum must be very thick and under considerable pressure, as well as at a very high temperature.

In the smaller stars the line C in the red is difficult of observation, on account of the faintness of the light, while the line occurring in the blue is often very broad. A slight tinge of blue pervades the color of all these stars, as before stated; consequently their spectra contain but little red and yellow, while the blue and violet predominate.*

A complete spectrum of the first type is given in Huggins's drawing of the spectrum of Sirius (Fig. 177.) Nearly half the stars in the heavens are included in this type, and their spectra may be examined even with a telescope of small power.

FIG. 177.

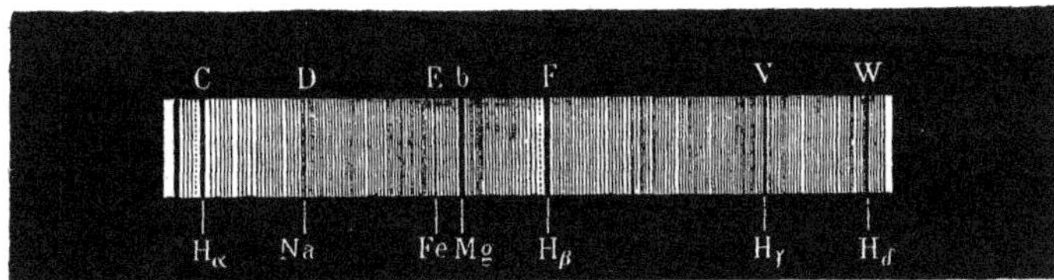

Spectrum of Sirius.

The *second* type of fixed stars, represented by the spectrum of Arcturus (*a* Bootis), is that to which our sun belongs. In this class most of the *yellow* stars are included, as, for instance, Capella, Pollux, Arcturus, Aldebaran, *a* in the Great Bear, Procyon, etc. The dark (Fraunhofer) lines are very strongly marked in the red and in the blue portions of their spectra, but are almost entirely absent in the yellow. The Fraunhofer lines in the solar spectrum (Fig. 176, No. II.) give an example of this. The space between the lines A and D is occupied, as is well known, by red and orange; yellow extends from D to E; while green and blue lie beyond. While strong absorption lines cross the spaces between A and D, and between E and G, they are almost entirely wanting in the yellow space between D and E.† It is therefore to be expected that this

* [The whole range of red and yellow rays is present, though it may be that the more refrangible parts of the spectrum are relatively brighter than in some other stars.]

† [The lines in this part of the spectrum are numerous, but are very fine, and easily escape observation.]

color should predominate in the light of these stars. The dark lines, moreover, are generally sharply defined, and only occasionally, as in the case of *a* Tauri, seem somewhat expanded.*

The stars belonging to this class are difficult to observe. The dark lines in the spectra of Capella and Pollux are extremely fine, while those in Arcturus and Aldebaran are much broader, and more easily recognized. Aldebaran may be regarded as holding an intermediate position between the second and the third type, while Procyon forms the connecting link between the stars of the first and second type.

The dark lines in the spectrum of the second type coincide so exactly with the strongest of the Fraunhofer lines, that stars of this type may be used, as suggested by Secchi, as a standard of comparison in the investigation of other spectra, and as a correction for the instrument. This close conformity to the solar spectrum undoubtedly leads to the conclusion that these stars are composed of similar elements and possess a physical constitution in other respects analogous to that of our sun. Many of them appear to yield a continuous spectrum, but this arises only from the fineness of the lines, which does not allow of their being always visible. They are, however, generally easily seen in a good instrument when the air is clear and free from tremor.

To the first type belong about one-half of all the stars hitherto observed; of the remaining half, perhaps two-thirds may be reckoned as yellow stars, to be classed accordingly under the second type.

Of the *third* type, which includes specially the stars shining with a *red* light, Secchi has given as an example the spectra of the stars *a* Orionis, and *a* Herculis (Fig. 176, and Frontispiece Nos. 13 and 14). The spectra of such stars appear like a row of columns illuminated from the side, producing a stereoscopic effect; and, when the bright bands are narrower than the dark ones, the spectrum has the appearance of a series of grooves. Red stars of even the eighth magnitude have been examined spectroscopically with Secchi's admirable instrument and show a similar constitution, while no spectrum could be obtained from white stars of the same magnitude.†

* [The lines in the spectrum of Aldebaran appear to the editor as narrow and defined as those of the solar spectrum.]

† [The meaning probably is, that in white stars of this magnitude, with Secchi's

In red stars the absorption lines are more bands than lines, and resemble the bands produced in the solar spectrum by our atmosphere. The sodium line D is not sharply defined, as in Nos. I. and II., as a single or a double line, but is very much expanded and shaded at the edges, as shown in the Frontispiece Nos. 13 and 14.* This seems to indicate that these stars are surrounded by a powerfully absorptive atmosphere, the nature of which can only be accurately ascertained when a more perfect knowledge of the influence which the temperature and density of a gas exerts upon its spectrum has been acquired.

Only about thirty bright stars belong to this type, among which are *α* Orionis, *α* Herculis, *β* Pegasi, *o* (Mira) Ceti, Antares, etc.; if stars of the second magnitude be included, their number will amount to about a hundred.

Secchi remarks as a peculiar characteristic of these stars that the darker lines of the spectrum separating the grooves occur in the same place in all the stars. The most prominent are those of magnesium (*b* in Fig. 176, No. III.), sodium (D), and iron, which, as in the solar spectrum, are often ill defined. The hydrogen lines are also present, but they do not predominate as in the foregoing types. Hydrogen gas is therefore likewise present in these stars; when its characteristic dark lines (C and F) are not visible in their spectra, an instance of which, according to Huggins, is to be found in *α* Orionis (Fig. 175, No. 2), this anomaly is to be explained by these lines being sometimes *reversed*, and appearing as bright lines, a phenomenon occasionally to be noticed in the spectrum of a solar spot. Most of the prominent lines belong to metals which are found also in the sun.

As a rule, the spectra of these stars resemble closely the spectrum of a solar spot, which has led Secchi to the conclusion that stars of the third type differ only from those of the second by the

instrument, the fine dark lines could not be recognized, whereas in red stars the close aggregations of these lines, in groups, which form the grooves of which Secchi speaks, could be seen. With superior instrumental power, the grooved appearances described in the text disappear, and the spectra of these stars are seen to be crossed by numerous dark lines, arranged in successive groups.]

* [This statement is not in accordance with the observation of the editor. In some of these stars, as *α* Herculis, the sodium line falls within a group of lines; in others, as *β* Pegasi and *α* Orionis, fine lines are present very near to D. Under unfavorable circumstances of observation, therefore, the line D may have the appearance of "being expanded and shaded at the edges."]

thickness of the envelope of vapor or atmosphere by which they are surrounded, as well as by the want of continuity in their photosphere; it seems therefore that these stars must have spots like our sun, but of proportionally much larger dimensions.

The *fourth* type, consisting of stars not exceeding the sixth magnitude, is principally characterized by a spectrum of three bright bands separated by dark spaces; the most brilliant band lies in the green, and is in general well marked and broad; the second, much fainter, and often scarcely visible, is in the blue; while the third, in the yellow, extends as far as the red, where it separates into several divisions.

All these bright bands have this peculiarity, that they are brightest on the side toward the violet, where the light terminates abruptly, while toward the red they fade gradually away into black.

The spectra of this class are therefore in direct contrast to those of the third type, in which the columnar bands are not only double in number in the same space, but the maximum of their light is turned toward the red, while the darker side is toward the violet. The spectra of the third and fourth types can therefore in no way be regarded merely as modifications of one and the same original spectrum, but must be considered as emanating from substances completely and entirely differing one from the other. The extreme faintness of these stars forbids the use of the slit, and thus the substances emitting their light cannot be ascertained with certainty; their spectra, however, bear a very close resemblance to the spectrum of carbon.

A spectrum of this fourth type is given in Fig. 176, No. IV. (No. 152 of Schjellerup's catalogue). Secchi has observed about thirty of this class, the most beautiful of which are Nos. 41, 78, 132, 152, and 273 of Schjellerup's catalogue. Great variety is noticeable in their spectra; some of them, such as the red star in the Great Bear (No. 152 Schj., in Fig. 176, No. IV.), showing intensely bright lines, two of which occur in the green and two in the greenish blue in the spectrum of this star.*

* [The description of the spectra of these stars differs from the appearance they present to the editor. He places below a diagram of the spectrum of the red star, No. 152 of Schjellerup's catalogue (Astronomische Nachrichten, No. 1591). He compared the spectrum of the star, using a narrow slit, with the brightness of sodium and carbon. The line marked D he found to be coincident with that of sodium. The less refrangible boundary of the first of the three principal bright bands in the spectrum of carbon is nearly coincident with the beginning of the first group of dark lines; the

Besides these four principal types, there are other groups of stars deserving particular notice. To these belong, for instance, the stars composing the constellation of Orion, which from the fineness of their spectrum lines ought to be classed under the second type, but which are also remarkable for the almost entire absence of the red and the yellow.* All the stars in this portion of the heavens are marked by a twofold character: they have all a very decided green color, and the lines of their spectra are so fine as to be often difficult to distinguish. The region of Cetus and Eridanus, on the contrary, is remarkable for the great number of yellow stars. It cannot be conceived that such a distribution and grouping of stars is merely the effect of chance; it is more reasonable to suppose that it depends upon the nature and condition of the substance with which the various parts of the universe are filled.

A remarkable exception to the four types above mentioned is formed by a few stars which present a *direct* spectrum of hydrogen, and may be classed, after Secchi's example, under a fifth type. The most remarkable star of this class is γ Cassiopeiæ, in the spectrum of which, according to Huggins's measurements, the bright lines H α (red), and H β (greenish blue), are visible in the places of the dark lines C and F, besides a bright line in the

second of the carbon bands is less refrangible than the second group in the star; the third band of the carbon spectrum falls on the bright space between the second and third group of dark lines in the spectrum of the star. The absorption bands are there-

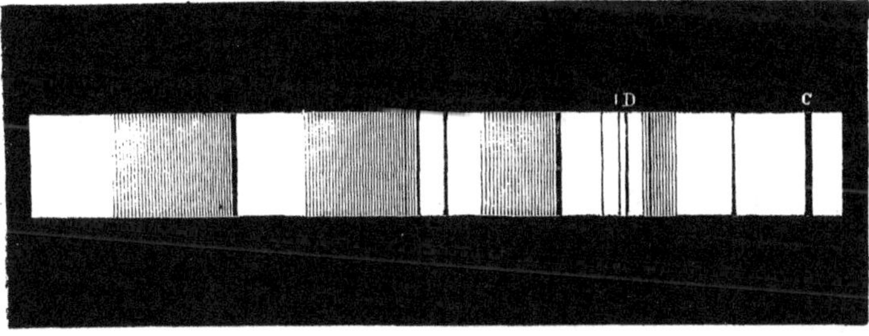

fore not due to carbon. There is a strong line about the position of C, but this part of the spectrum is too faint to permit of comparison or micrometric measurement. The comparative relative freedom of the red part of the spectrum from dark lines is in accordance with the predominance of this color in the star's light.]

* [There must be some mistake here, as the principal stars of Orion contain the red and yellow parts in their spectra.]

yellow apparently coincident with D_3* (Fig. 140). Similar spectra have been observed in the variable star β Lyræ, in η Argo, in the spectrum of which Le Sueur with the Great Melbourne Telescope saw the lines C, *b*, F, a yellow line near to D (D_3?), and the most intense of the nitrogen lines as bright lines; the same phenomena were also observed in two temporary stars, of which more will be said in § 65.

From all these observations it may be concluded that at least the brightest stars have a physical constitution similar to that of our sun. Their light radiates, like that of the sun, from matter in a state of intense incandescence, and passes in like manner through an atmosphere of absorptive vapors. Notwithstanding this general conformity of structure, there is yet a great difference in the constitution of individual stars; the grouping of the various elements is peculiar and characteristic for each star, and we must suppose that even these individual peculiarities are in necessary accordance with the special object of the star's existence, and its adaptation to the animal life of the planetary worlds by which it is surrounded.

63. Color of the Stars.—Double Stars and their Spectra.

In a transparent atmosphere, especially in a southern clime, the stars do not all appear with the white brilliancy of the diamond: here and there the eye discovers richly-colored gems, sparkling on the sombre robe of night in every shade of red, green, blue, and violet; and the astronomer, enabled by his powerful telescope to investigate the faintest objects, is lost in wonder over the variety of these colors, and their remarkable distribution in the starry heavens. This play of color is most conspicuous in the *double stars*, so called from their consisting of two or more suns kept together by the bond of mutual attraction, and revolving in orbits according to their mass, either one around the other or both round a common centre of gravity. To the naked eye their appearance is that of a single star, on account of their close proximity, but on the application of sufficient magnifying power they are found to be constituted of three, four, or more suns in intimate connection: such a system is to be found in the beautiful constellation of Orion (in the Sword), con-

* [The presence of a bright line in the yellow is not certain.]

sisting of sixteen stars, where to the unassisted eye there seems but one. In several of these double stars, the number of which already exceeds 6,000, it has been possible to calculate the time of revolution of the small star: the period of one in the Great Bear has been found to be 60 years, of another in Virgo 513 years, and of γ Leonis 1,200 years.

A peculiar interest attaches to double stars from their great diversity of color, which occasioned Sir John Herschel to remark, in describing a cluster in the Southern Cross, that it resembled a splendid ornament composed of the richest jewels. While the majority of single stars shine with a white light, but sometimes with a yellow, and even occasionally with a red hue, in double stars the companion is almost always blue, green, or red, thus contrasting with the white light of the larger or central star.

It has long been a subject of inquiry whence these colors arise. It has been supposed that they were complementary colors, and therefore that they were not inherent in the stars, but dependent on an optical illusion similar to that produced by looking upon a white wall immediately after gazing at the sun, when the wall appears covered with violet spots. But the simple expedient of covering the central star in the telescope suffices to show the incorrectness of this supposition, for the color of the small star remains unaffected by its separation from the light of the larger one. Zöllner, to whom we are indebted for a masterly work on light and the physical constitution of the heavenly bodies, was the first to express the idea that as all known substances, in their transition from a state of incandescence to that of a lower temperature, pass through the stage of red heat, so the fixed stars in their process of development from the condition of glowing gas through the period of an incandescent liquid state, and the subsequent development of floating scoriæ, or gradual formation of a cold non-luminous surface, must, together with the gradual diminution of their light, be also subject to a change of color. For many colored stars, especially for the so-called *new* stars in which the color has been known to sink in the scale from white to yellow and to red, this conjecture of Zöllner's has a high degree of probability; but that other circumstances must exercise an influence also on the color of stars is proved by a change of color having been observed to take place in the opposite direction—that is, from red to white—of which, among other stars, we have an example in Sirius, regarded by the ancients as a red star, and which is now considered as a type of the white stars, as well as in Capella, which formerly was red, and now shines with a pale-blue light. Huggins and Miller have discovered by means of the spectroscope that the color of a star not only depends upon the degree of incandescence of the intensely hot liquid or solid nucleus, but also upon the kind of absorptive power its atmosphere may exert upon the light emitted by the glowing nucleus.

As the source of stellar light, remarks Huggins, is incandescent solid or liquid matter (Kirchhoff), it appears very probable that at the time of its emission the light of all stars is alike *white*. The colors in which we see them must, therefore, be produced by certain changes which the light has undergone since its emission. It is further obvious that if the dark absorption lines are more numerous or more strongly marked in some parts of the spectrum than in others, then the peculiar colors of those places will be subdued in tone, and in any case will appear relatively weaker than in those parts of the spectrum where the absorption lines are much less numerous. While in this way certain colors would be partially extinguished from the spectrum, the remaining colors, being unaffected, would predominate, and give their own tints to the originally white light of the star.

The spectrum of Sirius, universally known as one of the most beautiful *white* stars, is given in Fig. 177. As might be expected, the spectra of these stars are remarkable for the absence of any groups of intense absorption bands. The dark lines which traverse the colored spectrum, though very numerous, and with a single exception equally distributed over all the colors, are exceedingly fine and delicate, and therefore too faint to affect the original whiteness of the light. The one exception consists of four strong single dark lines, one of which corresponds with the Fraunhofer C-line, another with the F-line, while the third lies very near to G, which, as we have already seen, indicate with certainty the presence of hydrogen.

If this spectrum be compared with that of an orange-colored star, the largest of the two stars composing the group, *α* Herculis, of which a drawing by Huggins is given in Fig. 178, the difference between this spectrum and that of Sirius will appear at a glance; for the green, blue, and even the red colors in this spectrum are subdued by groups of intensely dark bands, while the orange and yellow rays preserve nearly their original intensity, and therefore predominate in the light of this star.

After conquering many difficulties, Huggins and Miller obtained the same results from the observation of a faint telescopic double star. Fig. 179 shows the two spectra of the well-known double star β Cygni. In a large telescope the colors of these two stars contrast very beautifully; the lower spectrum is that of the orange star, the upper that of its faint but beautiful blue companion. In the orange star the dark lines are observed to be most intense, and most closely grouped in the blue and violet parts of the spectrum; the orange, therefore, which is comparatively free from these bands, gives the predominant color to the

FIG. 178.

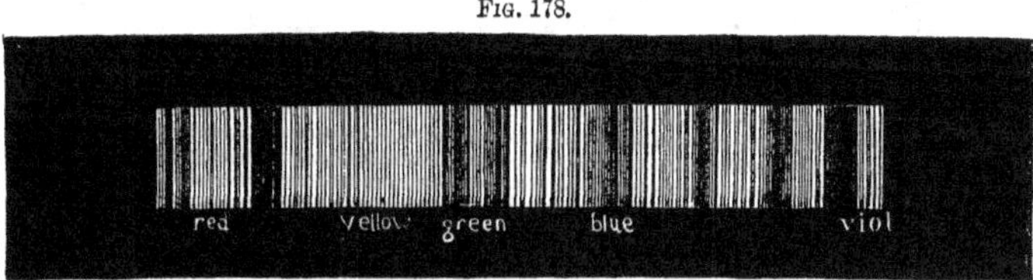

Spectrum of the Star A of α Herculis.

light. In the delicate blue companion the strongest groups of lines are to be found in the yellow, orange, and part of the red, so that it is to be expected that blue should predominate in the light of this star, and that we should see it of the hue produced by the mingling of those colors which are left after the absorption of the above-mentioned rays from the white light.

The colors of the stars are, therefore, without doubt, produced by the vapors of certain substances contained in their atmosphere; and as the chemical constitution of the atmosphere of a star depends upon the elements of which the star itself is composed, and upon its temperature, it would be possible to ascertain the chief constituents of these small telescopic worlds, if the position of the dark absorption lines could be determined with accuracy, or if these lines could be compared with the spectrum lines of terrestrial elements.

64. VARIABLE STARS.

Among the fixed stars there are several which vary from time to time in brightness as compared with neighboring stars; their light increases or diminishes, and alternates in some cases from the brilliancy even of a star of the first magnitude to complete invisibility. In some this change of brightness takes place as a constant, very slow, and regular diminution of light; in others there appears an almost sudden increase and decrease of brilliancy; while, with others, again, the change takes place within regularly-recurring periods. The *period* of variability is, therefore, the time elapsing between the two successive seasons of greatest brilliancy. The following table shows the varieties exhibited by variable stars of this latter order:

FIG. 179.

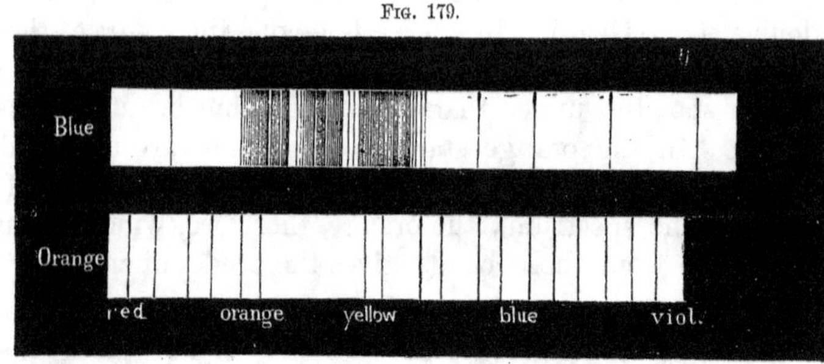

Spectra of the Component Stars of the Double Star β Cygni.

Star.	Variation of Brightness, from	to	Period of Variability.
η Argus	1 Magnitude.	4 Magnitude.	46 (?) years.
R Cephia	6 "	11 "	73 (?) "
R Cassiopeiæ	5 "	under 14	428.9 days.
O Ceti (Mira)	1 or 2 "	9.5 "	331.3363 days.
S Cancri	8 "	10.5 "	9.485 "
β Persei	2½ "	4 "	2.867 "

Of all variable stars, Mira Ceti is perhaps the most interesting, since at its maximum brightness it equals a star of the first or second magnitude. Scarcely less interesting is β Persei, which for two days thirteen hours and a half shines with the brightness of a star of the second magnitude, then suddenly decreases in light, and sinks down in three hours and a half to a star of the fourth magnitude; its light then again increases, and in a similar period of three hours and a half regains its original brilliancy. All these changes recur regularly in the space of less than three days, during which the star always remains visible to the naked eye.

Whence comes this variation in the light of a star? Zöllner, with great acuteness, and supported by numerous observations of these changes of brightness, offers a simple and unconstrained explanation in supposing the cause to lie in the configuration and distribution of dark masses of scoriæ which form on the red hot liquid body of the star in the process of cooling, and which, in consequence of the star's rotation on its axis, and the centrifugal force thus arising, would take certain definite courses on the surface of the star in a manner analogous to that which may be observed with floating icebergs on our earth. As a consequence of this peculiar relative motion, the dark masses of scoriæ would arrange themselves in a fixed order, and would produce on the surface of the star an unequal distribution of red-hot luminous matter, and accumulations of non-luminous scoriæ. Were this distribution to assume the form depicted by Zöllner in Fig. 180, and the bright liquid mass flowing in the direction of the arrows

Fig. 180.

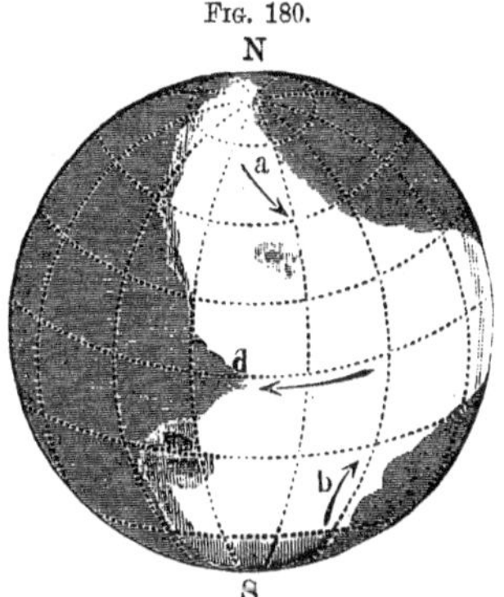

Variability of a Star according to Zöllner.

a and *b*, or against that of the star's axial rotation, after the manner of the polar streams of our earth, to become stopped in its course by the bank of scoriæ, then the change in the brilliancy of the light coming to us from this star, and the periodic recurrence with every revolution on its axis, would in most cases be easily accounted for. Others think, on the contrary, with Stewart and Klinkerfues, that the variable stars are very close double stars, and that the one in revolution, whether it be a dark body or a yet incandescent gaseous or red-hot fluid mass, would occasion, in passing before the larger star, either a partial eclipse or an atmospheric absorption of the light, such as not unfrequently happens in our own planetary system.

It is instructive to consider how these different theories have been affected by spectrum analysis. If the periodic change in the brightness of a star be occasioned by a change in its physical constitution, or by the interposition of a dark and opaque body, or should the interposing body, whether dark or luminous, be surrounded by an absorptive atmosphere, this would be made apparent by an alteration in the spectrum, consisting of an accession of absorption lines principally noticeable at the time of minimum brightness.

Secchi, and Huggins, and Miller, have given much time to investigations of this nature, and the last two observers noticed that in the spectrum of Betelgeux (*α* Orionis), Fig. 175, in February, 1866, when the star was at its maximum brightness, a group of dark bands was missing, the precise place of which had been determined with great care two years before (in Fig. 175, at No. 1069.5 of the scale, bordered by a dark line). Secchi has also noticed changes in a dark line in the spectrum of the same star during a diminution of brightness; but these observations are yet too few and isolated for any conclusion to be deduced from them as to the correctness of either of the foregoing hypotheses.

It has recently been remarked by Secchi that the spectrum of the nucleus of a solar spot (Fig. 108) bears a close resemblance to that given by several red stars, such as *α* Orionis, Antares, Aldebaran, *o* Ceti. A series of dark bands and stripes as represented in the spectrum of *α* Orionis, given in the lower part of Fig. 175, No. 2,* are present equally in the spectrum of a solar spot as in the spectra of the above-named red stars, which leads to the supposition that the red color of these stars arises from the same cause that produces the absorption bands in the spectrum of the solar spot. As nearly all these stars are variable, it is not improbable that they are also subject to spots which occur with a

* [The dark shading in Huggins's diagram referred to in the text, giving the appearance of bands, is intended to represent groups of fine lines. The spectrum of this star does not contain broad lines or bands when observed with a suitable spectroscope.]

certain degree of regularity, as the solar spots have been proved to do. The period of variability in the light would then depend upon the period of the formation of the spots, in the same way as our sun appears as a variable star, of which the period of variation in the light coincides with the regular recurrence of the spots.

65. New or Temporary Stars.

Among the variable stars must also be reckoned those which from time to time, but only at exceedingly long intervals, have suddenly flamed forth in the sky and disappeared again after a longer or shorter interval, and which always excite the greatest wonder and interest, not only from the rarity of their appearance, but also from the mighty revolutions in space which they announce. According to Humboldt, only twenty-one such stars have been recorded in the space of 2,000 years, from 134 B.C. to 1848 A.D., the most remarkable of which was that observed by Tycho Brahe (1572) in Cassiopeiæ, which surpassed both Sirius and Jupiter, and even rivalled Venus in brilliancy, but disappeared after seventeen months, without leaving a trace visible to the naked eye; * and that seen by Kepler (1604) in the right foot of Ophiuchus, which excelled Jupiter but did not quite equal Venus in brightness, and at the end of fifteen months was visible only by means of the telescope. Two similar stars which have appeared in recent times, one observed by Hind in 1848, and another seen in the Northern Crown in 1866, though they soon lost their ephemeral glory, still continue visible as stars of the tenth and ninth magnitude. A characteristic peculiarity of these temporary stars is that they nearly all flash out at once with a degree of brilliancy exceeding in some cases even stars of the first magnitude, and that they have not been observed, at least with the naked eye, to increase gradually in brightness.

Are we to suppose that these so-called *new* stars are really new creations, as Tycho Brahe believed, and that those that have disappeared are really annihilated or burnt out? Can we suppose, with Riccioli, that these heavenly bodies are luminous only on one side, which by a sudden semi-revolution the Creator at the appointed time has turned toward us? The first supposition has been set aside by later observations, which have shown by

* The telescope was not invented until thirty-seven years after this date.

the help of maps that a small star had already existed precisely in the place where the new star burst forth; the other view is too absurd to deserve in these days any further consideration. The star observed by Tycho, as well as that one seen by Kepler, is still visible; according to Argelander, the position of the first in 1865 was R.A. 4h. 19m. 57.7s.; and N.D. 63° 23′ 55″; and that of the second, according to Schönfeld, was in 1855 R.A. 17h. 21m. 57s., with a yearly variation of + 3.586s., S.D. 21° 21′ 2″, with a yearly variation of — 0.055s. If, therefore, the sudden bursting forth of a star in the heavens does not denote the creation of a new star, nor its gradual disappearance indicate its complete annihilation, we may well suppose that both phenomena are the successive effects of a violent outbreak of fire taking place in the star either in the form of an eruption of the internal red-hot liquid matter, and its suffusion over the surface, or of the ignition of gigantic streams of gas forcing their way from the interior. While such an occurrence would raise the star to a state of extreme incandescence, and cause it to emit an intense light for some time, the cooling subsequent to this combustion would ensue more or less rapidly, and the brightness consequently diminish in quick progression, until in certain conditions the star would cease to be visible.

Fortunately for science, such an occurrence has taken place since spectrum analysis has been so successfully applied to the examination of the heavenly bodies. On the night of the 12th of May, 1866, a new star, brighter than one of the second magnitude, was observed at Tuam, by Mr. John Birmingham, in the constellation Corona Borealis. On the following night it was seen by the French engineer Courbebaisse at Rochefort, and was observed a few hours earlier at Athens by the astronomer Julius Schmidt, who expressly declares that the new star could not have been visible before eleven o'clock on the night of the 12th of May, as he had been observing with his comet-seeker the star R Coronæ, and, while sweeping for some time in its neighborhood for meteors, could not have failed to notice the new star if it had been then visible. On the same night (13th of May), the light of the star sensibly decreased, and by the 16th of May it had become only of the fourth magnitude. Its brightness then waned somewhat rapidly; it decreased from 4.9 on the 17th to 5.3 on the 18th, and from 5.7 on the 19th to 6.2 on the 20th, till by the end of the month it had become a star of the ninth magnitude.

That the star was not a new one was pointed out by Schmidt, who found it marked in Argelander's "Durchmusterung des nördlichen Himmels" as No. 2,765 in + 25° declination. Argelander had observed the star on the 18th of May, 1855, and on the 31st of March, 1856, and on both occasions had classed the star as between the ninth and tenth magnitudes.*

Huggins was informed by Birmingham of his discovery on the 14th of May, and was thus enabled on the 15th inst., in conjunction with Miller, to examine the spectrum of this star when it had not fallen much below the third magnitude. The result of this investigation is as follows:

The spectrum of the star was very remarkable, and showed clearly that there were two distinct sources of light, each producing a separate spectrum. The compound spectrum (Fig. 181) is seen evidently to be composed of two independent spectra superposed; the one is a continuous spectrum crossed by dark lines similar to that given by the sun and other stars; while the other consists of *four bright* lines, which from their great brilliancy stand in bold relief upon the dark background of the first spectrum.

The principal spectrum traversed by dark lines shows the presence of a photosphere of incandescent matter probably solid or liquid, which is surrounded by an atmosphere of cooler vapors, giving rise by absorption to the dark lines. This absorption spectrum contains two strong dark bands of less refrangibility than the D-line of the solar spectrum; a group of fine lines stretches from them close up to D, while one fine line is quite coincident with D. Up to this point the constitution of this object is analogous to that of the sun and the stars; but the star has also a spectrum consisting of bright lines, which denotes the

* Mr. Barker, of London, Canada West, who announced in the *Canada Free Press* that he had observed a new star in Corona of the third magnitude on the 14th of May, now affirms, in a letter to Mr. Hind, that he had seen this star from the 4th of May, and that it had increased in brilliancy up to the 10th of May, from which time its light began to decline.†

† [Mr. Stone, now her Majesty's Astronomer at the Cape of Good Hope, stated as the result of a careful investigation of Mr. Barker's announcement: "I have not the slightest hesitation in stating that, in my opinion, Mr. Barker's observations previous to those made on May 14th are not entitled to the slightest credit."—"Monthly Notices, Royal Astronomical Society," vol. xxvii., p. 60.]

presence of a second source of light, which from the nature of the spectrum (p. 75) is undoubtedly an intensely luminous gas.

Huggins compared the spectrum of the star on the 17th of May with the spectrum of hydrogen gas produced by means of the induction spark through a Geissler's tube, and found that the strongest of the stellar lines 2 was coincident with the greenish-blue line (H β, Frontispiece No. 7) of hydrogen gas. Apparently,

Fig. 181.

Spectrum of the Temporary Star T Coronæ Borealis.—(May 15, 1866.)

also, the line 1 in the red coincided with the H α line of hydrogen, but, owing to the want of brilliancy of the line, the coincidence could not be ascertained with the same degree of certainty. The great brilliancy of these lines, compared with the parts of the continuous spectrum where they occur, proves that the luminous gas was at a higher temperature than the photosphere of the star.

These facts, taken in connection with the suddenness of the outburst of light in the star, and the immediate very rapid decline in its brightness from the second down to the eighth magnitude, have led to the hypothesis already alluded to, that in consequence of some internal convulsion enormous quantities of hydrogen and other gases were evolved, which in combining with some other elements ignited on the surface of the star, and thus enveloped the whole body suddenly in a sheet of flame. The ignited hydrogen gas in its combination with some other element produced the light characterized by the two bright bands in the red and green; the remaining bright lines, among which those of oxygen might have been expected, were not coincident with any of the lines of this gas. The burning hydrogen gas must also have greatly increased the heat of the solid matter of the photosphere, and brought it into a state of more intense incandescence and luminosity, which may explain how the formerly faint star could so suddenly assume such remarkable brilliancy. As the liberated hydrogen gas became exhausted, the flame gradually abated, and with the consequent cooling the photosphere became less vivid, and the star returned to its original condition.

Against this hypothesis it has been justly advanced that a sudden development of hydrogen in quantities sufficient to occasion the phenomenon of the outburst of a star is a very unlikely occurrence. To which it may be added that the spectrum given by the star was not that of *burning* but of *luminous* hydrogen.* Robert Meyer and H. J. Klein have, therefore, expressed the opinion that the sudden blazing out of a star might be occasioned by the violent precipitation of some great mass, perhaps of a planet, upon a fixed star, by which the momentum of the falling mass would be changed into molecular motion, or in other words into heat and light. It might even be supposed that the star in Corona, through its motion in space, may have come in contact with one of the nebulæ (§ 67), which traverse in great numbers the realms of space in every direction, and which from their gaseous condition must possess a high temperature. Such a collision would necessarily set the star on a blaze, and occasion the most vehement ignition of its hydrogen.

Rayet and Wolf, who examined the star with a large tele-spectroscope on the 20th of May, when between the fifth and sixth magnitude, confirmed Huggins's observations, and in their report to Leverrier expressed their independent opinion that the new star owed its brilliancy mainly to burning (?) gases. This brilliancy, as was to be expected, decreased faster than the light of the burning gas; when there was scarcely any trace remaining

* [The spectrum of intensely heated hydrogen would be the same whatever the nature of the source of the heat. The suggestion of combustion being *possibly* present was made in consequence of other bright lines seen in the spectrum of the star. We now know that the sun is surrounded by luminous hydrogen, and therefore bright lines similar to those seen in this star are always present in the solar spectrum. As these lines are faint as compared with the great intensity of the solar photosphere, they do but render less dark the Fraunhofer lines C and F, and are not ordinarily seen as bright lines. If we look at the dark part of a solar spot where the diminished light of the photosphere is not able to overpower that of the hydrogen, these bright lines may become visible. Hence in the star in Corona the surrounding hydrogen must have have had a great intensity relatively to the brightness of the photosphere. We now know that a similar state of things appears to be permanent, or at least of not a very temporary character, in γ Cassiopeiæ and a few other stars. It seems upon the whole probable that the so-called new stars may be but extreme instances of the periodical variation of light which we observe in a large number of stars.]

in the spectroscope of the continuous spectrum given by the photosphere, the four bright lines were still quite brilliant.*

It must not be forgotten that light, though an extremely quick messenger, yet occupies a certain time in coming to us from a star. The speed of light is 185,000 miles in a second; the distance of the nearest fixed star (*α* Centauri) is about sixteen billion miles, so that light takes about three years to travel from this star to us. The great physical convulsion which was observed in the star in Corona in the year 1866 was therefore an event which had really taken place long before that period, at a time no doubt when spectrum analysis, to which we are indebted for the information we obtained on the subject, was yet quite unknown.

Secchi has recently discovered, while examining spectroscopically the variable star R Geminorum, that its spectrum showed bright hydrogen lines just as they appeared in the spectrum of the new star T Coronæ. The star gave besides other bright bands, the most important of which coincide with the dark bands in the spectrum of *α* Orionis: one group lies in the green (*b*), and is probably due to magnesium, while another is in the yellow, and appears to be either the sodium D-line or else the new bright line D_3 of the solar prominences (p. 275). The observations were made when the star had reached its maximum brightness (somewhat above the seventh magnitude): the great interest which attaches to this phenomenon, especially to the appearance of the same bright lines that characterize the solar prominences, leads us to hope that these observations may be prosecuted during the period of variability so long as the strength of the light will permit. (*Vide* p. 350.)

66. Influence of the Proper Motion of the Stars in Space upon their Spectra.

In § 58 the principle was unfolded which, in its application to spectrum analysis, enables us, under certain circumstances, to determine, by the displacement of the spectrum lines of a star, whether it be approaching us or receding from us, and at what speed it is moving in space. It was shown that the displacement of one

* [This was not the case in the observation of the editor; he was able to see the continuous spectrum when the bright lines could be scarcely distinguished.]

of the spectrum lines toward the violet indicated that the wave-length had been shortened in its passage to the earth, and therefore that the star was approaching us; a displacement toward the red showed, on the contrary, that the ether-waves had been lengthened, and that the star was therefore receding from the earth.

Secchi, who was the first to enter on this kind of investigation, directed his telescope to Sirius, and placed the prism of the spectroscope so that the dark F-line was exactly coincident with the direct image of the star: he then turned his instrument to another fixed star of the same type in which the F-line was also visible, and observed it narrowly to ascertain whether this line were also coincident, or showed some displacement. His instrument did not, however, prove adequate to such delicate observations, and the results obtained were not decisive.

By the aid of more delicate instruments, and an apparatus better adapted for such measurements, Huggins instituted some very complete investigations on this subject.* By a series of preliminary observations he first established that a strongly-marked dark line in the spectrum of Sirius (Fig. 177) was the hydrogen line H β.† For this purpose he compared the dark line of Sirius in the usual way with the H β line of the hydrogen spectrum formed from a Geissler's tube, which is coincident with the Fraunhofer F-line of the solar spectrum, and also with the H β line of hydrogen when under atmospheric pressure. Fig. 182 shows the position of these three lines in relation to each other and to the line in Sirius. While the comparison lines coincide exactly, the *line in Sirius is displaced a little toward the red.* As this line in Sirius appears broader than the bright hydrogen line H β, which is always the case with this line when the gas is subjected to some pressure, it became of importance to determine whether the expansion of the hydrogen line H β under pressure

* [Huggins's observations, communicated to the Royal Society in April, 1868, were made quite independently, during 1867 and the spring of 1868, and nearly completed, before the statement of Secchi's work in the same direction was made public in March, 1868.]

† [That the line in Sirius belongs to hydrogen was shown by the observation that it is one of three strong lines which in a spectroscope of moderate power appear to be exactly coincident with the principal lines of hydrogen. It was only when a much more powerful spectroscope was brought to bear upon the star that the slight displacement described in the text was detected.]

takes place unsymmetrically or on both sides equally. In the first case it is obvious that the position of the Sirius line could not be regarded as a displacement due to motion, but merely as an expansion occurring on one side only; in the latter case the bright line H β ought to fall exactly in the middle of the broad

FIG. 182.

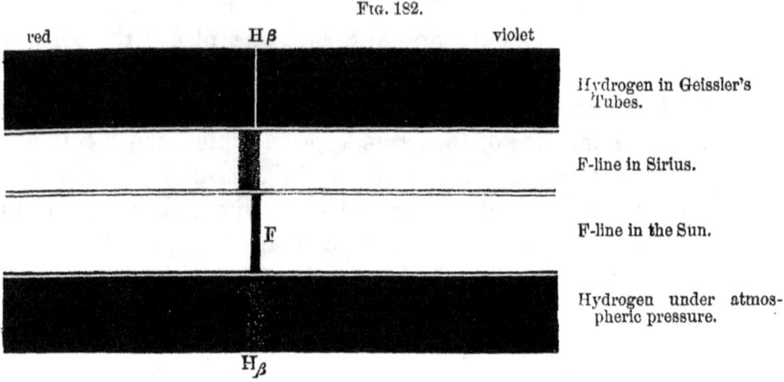

Displacement of the F-line in the Spectrum of Sirius.

Sirius line if merely the result of expansion, and a displacement had not taken place at the same time. Huggins found, however, in accordance with the researches of Lockyer and Frankland,* that, when the hydrogen line H β becomes expanded from an increase in the density of the gas, this widening always takes place on both sides equally, and the middle of the line preserves its position. It is probable that the expansion of the line in Sirius may arise from a similar cause, but at the same time there cannot be a doubt *that this whole line suffers a displacement toward the red as compared with the terrestrial hydrogen line.*

This displacement has been very carefully measured by Huggins, who found that the displacement of the F-line in the spectrum of Sirius amounted at the time of observation to about a quarter of the distance between the two D-lines. The difference between the wave-lengths of these two D-lines is 4.36 (according to some 6) millionths of a millimetre; the displacement of the F-line in the spectrum of Sirius corresponds, therefore, to an *in-*

* [Frankland and Lockyer's researches were not published until nearly a year later, in February, 1869. Huggins's experiments, in confirmation of those previously made by Plücker and Hittorf, were contained in his paper laid before the Royal Society in April, 1868.]

crease in the wave-length of 0.109 (or 0.15) millionth of a milli metre. If the velocity of light be taken to be 185,000 miles in a second, and the wave-length of the light at the line F to be 486.50 millionths of a millimetre, then the observed displacement of the line in Sirius indicates a recession of Sirius from the earth at the rate of $\frac{185000 \times 0.109}{486.50}$, or 41.4 miles in a second.

The earth has evidently some share in the rapidity of this motion. In the yearly circuit round the sun, the direction of the earth's motion changes every instant, and there are two points in the orbit separated 180° one from another, in which the direction of motion coincides with the line of sight from Sirius. In the one place the earth is approaching the star, in the other it is receding from it: while, in the two other points of the orbit 90° from the former positions, the earth's motion is at right angles to the star's line of sight, and has therefore no influence on the refrangibility of the rays.

At the time that Huggins made these observations on the line in Sirius, the earth was moving in her course away from the star at the rate of 12 miles in a second; there remains, therefore, for the proper motion of Sirius a movement of recession from the earth amounting to 29.4 miles in a second.*

Similar observations to those on Sirius were attempted by Huggins on *α* Canis Minoris, Castor, Betelgeux, Aldebaran, and some other bright stars; but, in consideration of the extreme delicacy of the investigations, and the few opportunities afforded by this climate of a sky of sufficient purity, this careful observer thinks it desirable to repeat the observations before giving them to the world.†

When it is remembered that, by employing the requisite number of prisms for producing a sufficiently long stellar spectrum, the light is so much weakened that an exact comparison of the dark lines of the stellar spectrum with the bright lines of a terrestrial element is rendered extremely difficult; and when it is further borne in mind that many dark lines in the stellar spectrum are ill defined at the edges, and often, like the F-line in the spectrum of Sirius, somewhat weak and of varying breadth, we

* [If the probable advance of the sun in space be taken into account, the motion of Sirius would be reduced to about 26 miles.]

† [The necessary spectrum apparatus is not yet completed for the continuance of these observations with the larger telescope now at his command.]

must certainly not place more than a conditional reliance upon the results of such observations, which are admitted even by Huggins to be attended with some uncertainty.

With a just appreciation of the great difficulties connected with the measurement of such exceedingly small lineal displacements as might possibly occur in the stellar spectra, Zöllner has endeavored to construct a spectroscope with such an arrangement as shall double the amount of this displacement, without diminishing at the same time the brightness of the spectrum.

The construction of this new instrument, called by Zöllner the Reversion Spectroscope,* is as follows. The line of light formed by a slit or a cylindrical lens is brought into the focus of a lens which, as in all spectroscopes, at once renders the diverging rays parallel. The rays then pass through two of Amici's direct-vision compound prisms, which are fastened near to one another in such a manner that their horizontal reflecting angles are placed at opposite sides, so that each one transmits half of the pencil of rays issuing from the collimating lens, thus decomposing the whole of the rays into two spectra, which are sent in opposite directions. The object-glass of the telescope, which unites the rays again into one image, is divided in a direction perpendicular to the horizontal position of the reflecting angles of the prisms, and each half is capable of micrometrical movement both in a parallel and perpendicular direction to the line of separation. In this way it is possible to bring the lines of the one spectrum successively into coincidence with the lines of the other, as well as to place the two spectra at will either in exact juxtaposition, so that one can be moved up and down the other in the manner of a vernier, or else brought partially one over the other. By this construction not only is the delicate and very sensitive method of a double image made use of for estimating any change of wave-length in the spectrum lines, but every such change is doubled from its influence being exerted in an opposite direction in each spectrum.

Zöllner was able to determine with the reversion spectroscope the distance between the D-lines in the solar spectrum with a probable error of only $\frac{1}{226}$ of that distance: were the distance

* Ueber ein neues Spectroskop, nebst Beiträgen zur Spectralanalyse der Gestirne, von J. C. F. Zöllner. (Berichte der Konigl. Sächs. Gesellschaft der Wissenschaften zu Leipzig, vom 6 Febr. 1869.)

between the source of light and the observer to change at the rate of sixteen miles in a second (the mean velocity of our earth), it would occasion in Zöllner's instrument a displacement of the spectrum lines amounting to one-fifth of the distance between the D-lines, a quantity nearly forty times greater than the supposed error of the instrument.

The reversion spectroscope promises not only to remove any remaining doubts as to the displacement of the dark lines being the indication of motion in the heavenly bodies,* but also, as Zöllner has pointed out, to procure for us more certain results concerning the speed of rotation of the sun, and to separate the lines of the solar spectrum produced by the absorption of the earth's atmosphere from those originating in the sun itself, since it is evident that such a displacement can occur only in the latter.

67. Spectra of Nebulæ and Clusters.

We now come to treat of the remotest realms of the universe, those regions of stellar clusters and nebulæ which can only be reached by means of the most powerful telescopes. When the starry heavens are viewed through a telescope of moderate power, a great number of stellar clusters and faint nebulous forms are revealed against the dark background of the sky which might be taken at first sight for passing clouds, but which, by their unchanging forms and persistent appearance, are proved to belong to the heavenly bodies, though possessing a character widely differing from the point-like images of ordinary stars. Sir William Herschel was able, with his gigantic forty-foot telescope, to resolve many of these nebulæ into clusters of stars, and found them to consist of vast groups of individual suns, in which thousands of fixed stars may be clearly separated and counted, but which are so far removed from us that we are unable to per-

* [As two spectra have to be formed from the light of a star, the brightness of each spectrum will be reduced to one-half. The reversion spectroscope may be found of value for the observation of bright objects, but it scarcely seems to be so well adapted for stellar work. Zöllner has succeeded with this instrument in detecting the change of refrangibility due to the sun's rotations. He has hence proposed a simpler form of the principle of reversion, which can be applied to any spectroscope. The object-glass of the telescope of the spectroscope is divided, and in front of one half a right-angled prism is placed, which reverses the spectrum seen through it by reflection.]

ceive their distance one from the other, though that may really amount to many millions of miles, and their light, with a low magnifying power, seems to come from a large faintly-luminous mass. But all nebulæ were not resolvable with this telescope, and in proportion as such nebulæ were resolved into clusters of stars, new nebulæ appeared which resisted a power of 6,000, and suggested to this astute investigator the theory that, besides the many thousand apparent nebulæ which reveal themselves to us as a complete and separate system of worlds, there are also thousands of real nebulæ in the universe composed of primeval cosmical matter out of which future worlds were to be fashioned.

Lord Rosse, by means of a telescope of fifty-two feet focus of his own construction, was able to resolve into clusters of stars many of the nebulæ not resolved by Herschel; but there were still revealed to the eye, thus carried farther into space, new nebulæ beyond the power even of this gigantic telescope to resolve.

Telescopes failed, therefore, to solve the question whether the unresolved nebulæ are portions of the primeval matter out of which the existing stars have been formed; they leave us in

Fig. 183.

The Great Nebula in Orion.

uncertainty as to whether these nebulæ are masses of luminous gas, which in the lapse of ages would pass through the various stages of incandescent liquid (the sun and fixed stars), of scoriæ or gradual formation of a cold and non-luminous surface (the earth and planets), and finally of complete gelation and torpidity (the moon), or whether they exist as a complete and separate system of worlds; telescopes have only widened the problem, and have neither simplified nor solved its difficulties.

That which was beyond the power of the most gigantic telescopes has been accomplished by that apparently insignificant, but really delicate, and almost infinitely sensitive instrument—the spectroscope; we are indebted to it for being able to say

Fig. 184.

South.

North.

Central and most brilliant Portion of the Great Nebula in the Sword-handle of Orion, as observed by Sir John Herschel in his 20-foot Reflector at Feldhausen, Cape of Good Hope (1834 to 1837).

with certainty that luminous nebulæ actually exist as isolated bodies in space, and that these bodies are luminous masses of gas.

The splendid edifice already planned by Kant in his "Allgemeinen Naturgeschichte und Theorie des Himmels" (1755), and erected by Laplace* forty-one years later, has received its

* Exposition du Système du Monde. (1799.)

topmost stone through the discoveries of the spectroscope. The spectroscope, in combination with the telescope, affords means for ascertaining even now some of the phases through which the sun and planets have passed in their process of development or transition from masses of luminous nebulæ to their present condition.

Great variety is observed in the forms of the nebulæ: while some are chaotic and irregular, and sometimes highly fantastic, others exhibit the pure and beautiful forms of a curve, a crescent,

FIG. 185.

The Large Magellanic Cloud.

a globe, or a circle. A number of the most characteristic of these forms have been photographed on glass at the suggestion of Mr. Huggins; to these have been added a few others, taken from accurate drawings by Lord Rosse;* and they may all be projected on to a screen by means of the electric or lime-light lantern, and made visible to a large audience.

* "Observations on the Nebulæ; by the Earl of Rosse. London, 1850. On the Construction of Specula of Six-feet Aperture, and a Selection from the Observations of Nebulæ made with them; by the Earl of Rosse." London, 1862. Compare Mädler in Westermann's Monatsheften, xii., 182.—The glass photographs can be procured from W. Schellen, Kevelaer (Rhenish Prussia), [and of Mr. Ladd, Beak Street, Regent Street, London].

The largest and most irregular of all the nebulæ is that in the constellation of Orion (Figs. 183, 184). It is situated rather below the three stars of second magnitude composing the central part of that magnificent constellation, and is visible to the naked eye. It is extremely difficult to execute even a tolerably correct drawing of this nebula; but it appears, from the various drawings made at different times, that a change is taking place in the form and position of the brightest portions. Fig. 184 represents

Fig. 186.

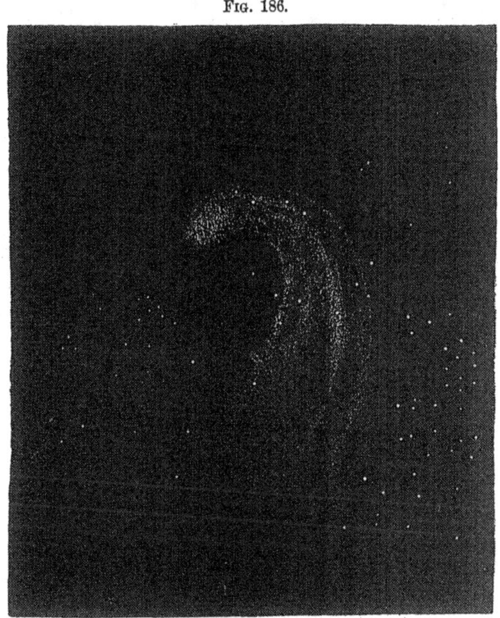

Nebula of the Form of a Sickle.—(H. 3239.)

the central and brightest part of the nebula. Four bright stars, forming a trapezium, are situated in it, one of which only is visible to the naked eye. The nebula surrounding these stars has a flaky appearance, and is of a greenish-white color; single portions form long curved streaks stretching out in a radiating manner from the middle and bright parts.

Much less irregularity is apparent in the great Magellanic or Cape clouds (Fig. 185), which are two nebulæ in the southern hemisphere, one of them exceeding by five times the apparent size of the moon. They are distinctly visible to the naked eye, and are so bright that they serve as marks for reconnoitring the heavens, and for reckoning the hour of the night.

Fig. 187.

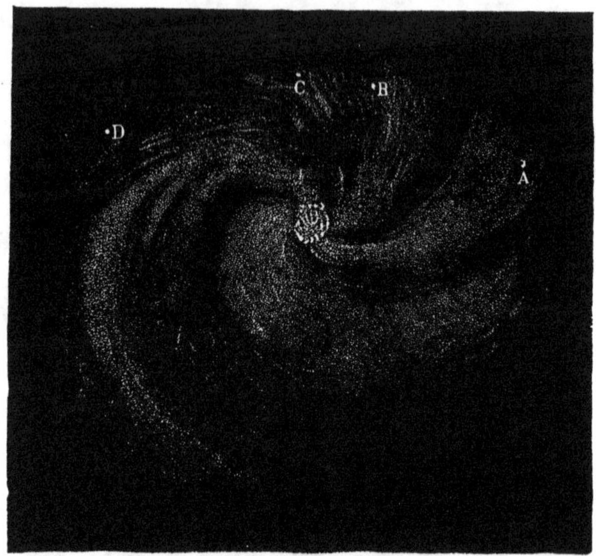

Spiral Nebula.—(H. 1173.)

Fig. 188.

Spiral Nebula in Canes Venatici.—(H. 1622.)

The interest aroused by these irregular and chaotic nebulous forms is still further increased by the phenomena of the spiral or convoluted nebulæ with which the giant telescopes of Lord Rosse and Mr. Bond have made us further acquainted. As a rule, there streams out from one or more centres of luminous

Fig. 189.

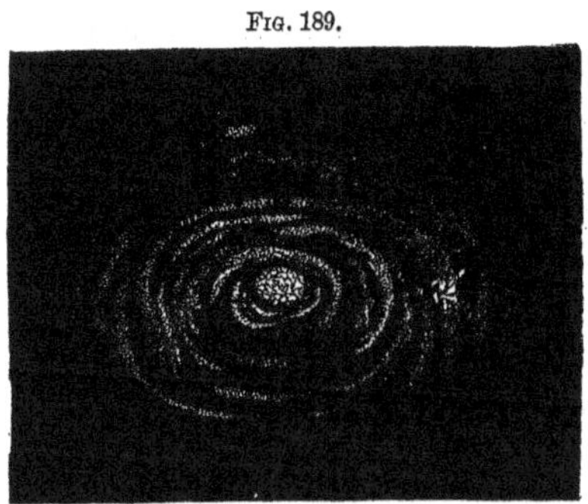

Transition from the Spiral to the Annular Form.

matter innumerable curved nebulous streaks, which recede from the centre in a spiral form, and finally lose themselves in space. Fig. 186 represents a nebula in the form of a sickle or comet-

Fig. 190.

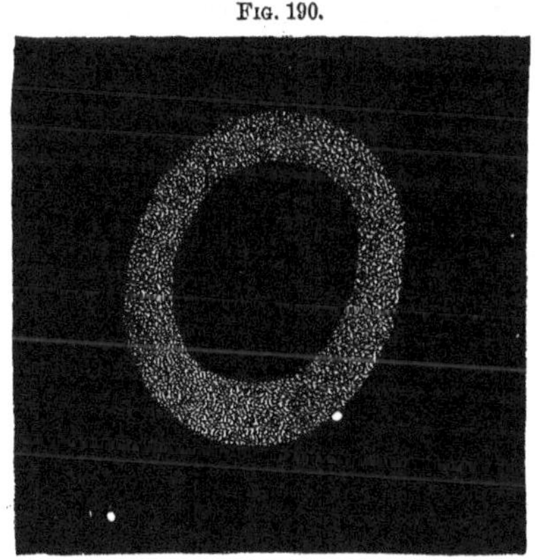

Annular Nebula in Lyra.

tail (Herschel, No. 3239), Fig. 187 a complete spiral (H. 1173), and Fig. 188 the most remarkable of all the spiral nebulæ situated in the constellation Canes Venatici (H. 1622).

It is hardly conceivable that a system of such a nebulous form could exist without internal motion. The bright nucleus, as well as the streaks curving round it in the same direction, seems to indicate an accumulation of matter toward the centre, with a gradual increase of density, and a rotatory movement. But if we combine with this motion the supposition of an opposing medium, it is difficult to harmonize such a system with the known laws of statics. Accurate measures are, therefore, of the highest interest for the purpose of showing whether actual rotation or other changes are taking place in these nebulæ; but, unfortunately, they are rendered extremely difficult and uncertain by the want of outline, and by the remarkable faintness of these nebulous objects.

The transition state from the spiral to the annular form is shown in such nebulæ as the one represented in Fig. 189 (H. 604); and they then pass into the simple or compound annular nebula of which a type is given in Fig. 190.

Fig. 191.

Nebula with several Rings.—(H. 854.)

The space within most of these elliptic rings is not perfectly dark, but is occupied either by a diffused faint nebulous light, as in Fig. 190, or, as in most cases, by a bright nucleus, round which sometimes one ring, sometimes several, are disposed in various forms. In Fig. 191 a representation is given of a compound annular nebula (H. 854), with very elliptic rings and bright nucleus.

FIG. 192.

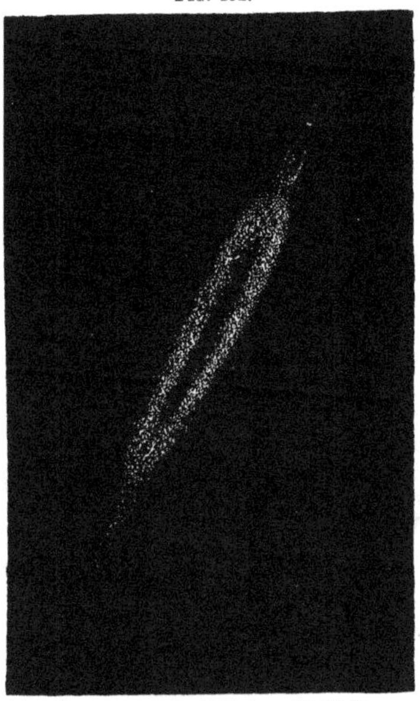

Elliptical Annular Nebula.—(H. 1909.)

According as the ring has its surface or its edge turned toward us, or according as our line of sight is perpendicular or more or less obliquely inclined to the surface of the ring, its form

FIG. 193.

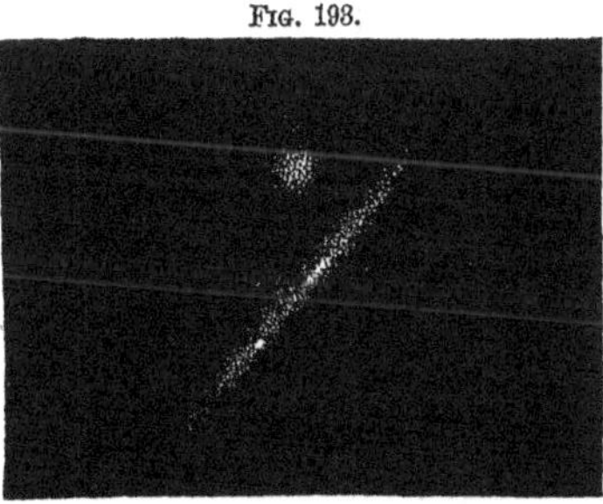

Elongated Nebula.—(H. 2621.)

approaches that of a circle, a ring, an ellipse, or even a straight line. Nebulæ of this latter kind are represented in Fig. 192 (H.

1909), and in Fig. 193 (H. 2621). When an elliptical ring is extremely elongated, and the minor axis is much smaller than the major one, the density and brightness of the ring diminish as its distance from the central nucleus increases; and this takes place to such a degree sometimes, that at the farthest points of the ring, the ends of the major axis, it ceases to be visible, and the continuity seems to be broken. The nebula has then the appearance of a double nebula, with a central spot as represented in Fig. 194 (H. 3501) and Fig. 195 (H. 2552).

Those nebulæ, which appear with tolerably sharply defined edges in the form of a circle or slight ellipse, seem to belong to

Fig. 194.

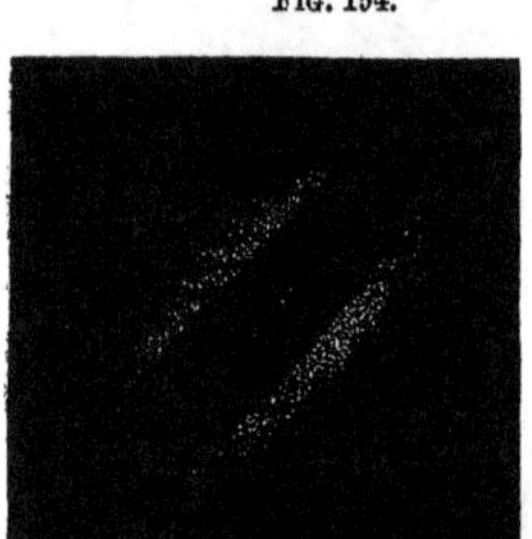

Double Nebula.—(H. 3501.)

Fig. 195.

Annular Nebula with Centre.—(H. 2552.)

a much higher stage of development. From their resemblance to those planets which shine with a pale or bluish light, they have been called *planetary* nebulæ; in form, however, they vary considerably, some of them being spiral and some annular. Some of these planetary nebulæ are represented in Figs. 196 (H. 838), 197 (H. 464), and 198 (H. 2241). The first has two central stars or nuclei, each surrounded by a dark space, beyond which the spiral streaks are disposed; the second has also two nuclei, but without clearly separable dark spaces; the third is without any nucleus, but shows a well-defined ring of light.

The highest type of nebulæ are certainly the stellar nebulæ, in which a tolerably well-defined bright star is surrounded by a completely round disk or faint atmosphere of light, which sometimes fades away gradually into space, at other times terminates abruptly with a sharp edge. Figs. 199 (H. 2098) and 200 (H. 450) exhibit the most striking of these very remarkable stellar nebulæ: the first is surrounded by a system of rings like Saturn, with the thin edge turned toward us; the second is a veritable star of the eighth magnitude, and is not nebulous, but is surrounded by a bright luminous atmosphere perfectly concentric.

Fig. 196.

Planetary Nebula with two Stars.—(H. 888.)

To the right of the star is a small dark space, such as often occurs in these nebulæ, indicating perhaps an opening in the surrounding atmosphere.

Fig. 197.

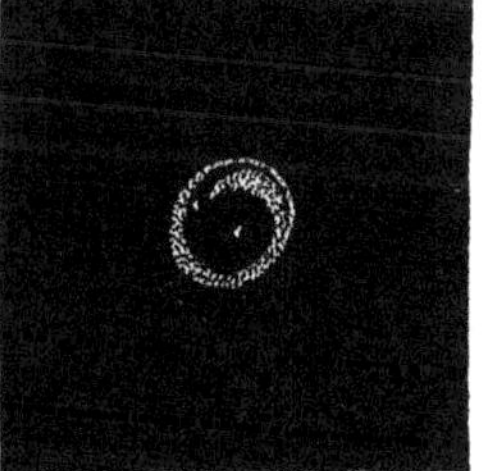

Planetary Annular Nebula with two Stars.—(H. 464.)

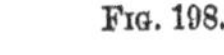

Fig. 198.

Planetary Nebula.—(H. 2241.)

We have now passed in review all that is at present known of the nebulæ, so far as their appearance and form have been revealed by the largest telescopes. The information as yet furnished by the spectroscope on this subject is certainly much less extensive, but is nevertheless of the greatest importance, since the spectroscope has power to reveal the nature and constitution of these remote heavenly bodies. It must here again be remembered that the character of the spectrum not only indicates what the substance is that emits the light, but also its physical condition. If the spectrum be a *continuous* one, consisting of rays of every color or degree of refrangibility, then the source of light is

Fig. 199.

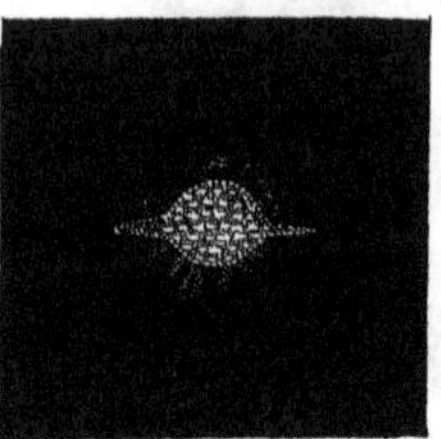

Planetary Nebula.—(H. 2098.)

Fig. 200.

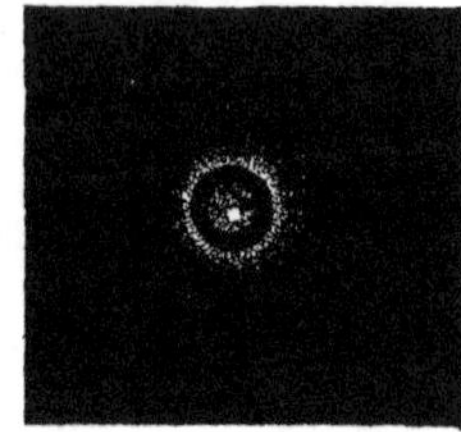

Stellar Nebula.—(H. 450.)

either a *solid* or *liquid* incandescent body; if, on the contrary, the spectrum be composed of *bright lines* only, then it is certain that the light comes from *luminous gas;* finally, if the spectrum be continuous, but crossed by *dark* lines interrupting the colors, it is an indication that the source of light is a solid or liquid incandescent body, but that the light has passed through an atmosphere of vapors at a lower temperature, which by their selective absorptive power have abstracted those colored rays which they would have emitted had they been self-luminous.

Fig. 201.

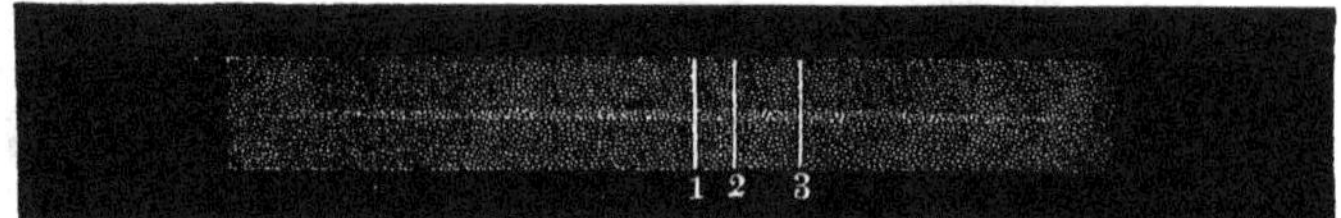

Spectrum of Nebula.—(H. 4374.)

When Huggins first directed his telespectroscope in August, 1864, to one of these objects, a small but very bright nebula (H. 4374), he found to his great surprise that the spectrum (Fig. 201), instead of being a continuous colored band such as that given by a star, consisted only of *three bright lines.*

This one observation was sufficient to solve the long-vexed question, at least for this particular nebula, and to prove that it is not a cluster of individual, separable stars, but is actually a gaseous nebula, a body of luminous gas. In fact, such a spectrum could only be produced by a substance in a state of gas; the light of this nebula, therefore, was emitted neither by solid nor liquid incandescent matter, nor by gases in a state of extreme density, as may be the case in the sun and stars, but by luminous gas in a highly-rarefied condition.

In order to discover the chemical nature of this gas, Huggins followed the usual methods of comparison, and tested the spectrum with the Fraunhofer lines of the solar spectrum, and the bright lines of terrestrial elements. A glance at Fig. 202 will show at once the result of this investigation. The brightest line

FIG. 202.

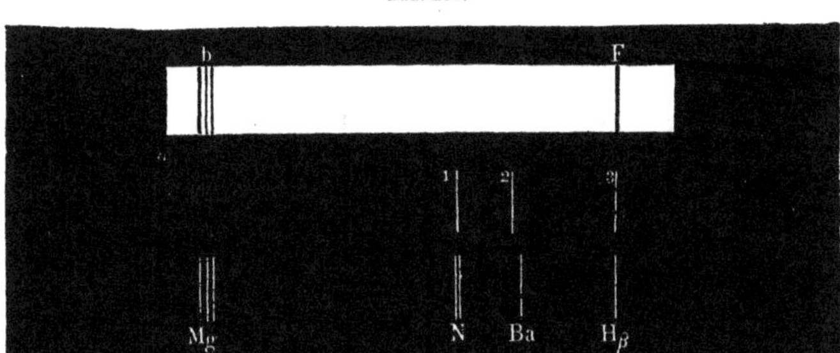

Spectrum of Nebula compared with the Sun and some Terrestrial Elements.

(1) of the nebula coincides exactly with the brightest line (N) of the spectrum of nitrogen, which is a double line. The faintest of the nebular lines (3) also coincides with the bluish-green hydrogen line H β, or, which is the same thing, with the Fraunhofer line F in the solar spectrum. The middle line (2) of the nebula was not found to coincide with any of the bright lines of the thirty terrestrial elements with which it has been compared; it lies not far from the barium line B *a*, but is not coincident with it.

The question why the characteristic bright lines of these gases are not visible in the spectrum of the nebula has long occupied the attention of Huggins; and lately Frankland and Lockyer, as well as Secchi, have devoted themselves to this subject. It has been noticed by all these observers, with the exception of Secchi, that when a Geissler's tube, in which either hydrogen or nitrogen has been made luminous by the electric spark, is held at some distance from the slit of the spectroscope, and the spectra viewed a good way off, not only does the double line of nitrogen appear as a single line, but the remaining bright lines of both gases entirely disappear, with the exception of those lines which are visible in the spectrum of the nebula.

Frankland and Lockyer have further shown that the spectrum of both hydrogen and nitrogen at a low temperature and under slight pressure consists only of one line in the green, from which it follows that *the temperature of the nebula is lower than that of our sun, and that its density is remarkably small.*

Secchi, whose work "Sulla grande nebulosa di θ Orionis" contains an accurate drawing of this nebula, has found, by comparison of the bright nitrogen line of the nebula with the spectrum of terrestrial nitrogen, that it corresponds with a dark space in the nitrogen spectrum of I. order, while it is coincident with a bright line in the spectrum of II. order.* As this spectrum of II. order is produced by an electric spark at high tension, Secchi concludes that the nebulous mass must be in the same condition as terrestrial nitrogen in an electric current of high tension. Wüllner describes this condition as that of a high temperature (§§ 31 and 32); Frankland and Lockyer maintain, on the contrary, that the spectra of II. order, composed of but few bright lines, belong to a lower temperature than the continuous spectra of I. order.†

Further investigations will be necessary before the true connection can be ascertained between the tension of the electric current and the temperature and density of the gas brought by it into a state of luminosity; or before evidence can be supplied as to the correctness of Huggins's suggestion that there may be a peculiar absorptive power in space, by which the other lines present in terrestrial hydrogen and nitrogen are extinguished in the transmission of the nebular light to our earth.‡

* [The comparison of the lines of this nebula with the lines of the spectrum of nitrogen of II. order was originally made by Huggins at the close of 1864.]

† Fresh light has been thrown on this subject by the recent investigations of Zöllner, "Ueber das Nordlichtspectrum," whose researches on the analogy between the light emitted by the nebulæ and the Aurora Borealis and that derived from Geissler's tubes warrant the conclusion that the temperature of the glowing gases in the nebulæ must be in general comparatively low, while in Geissler's tubes, on the contrary, it is high.

‡ [The early experiments of Huggins showed that in respect of the gases hydro-

Besides the spectrum containing these three bright lines, the nebula gave also a very faint continuous spectrum (Fig. 201) of scarcely perceptible width, which from its nature could proceed only from the diffused light of a faintly-glowing nucleus, either solid or liquid, or from faintly-luminous matter in the form of a cloud of solid or liquid particles.

All planetary nebulæ yield the same spectrum; the bright lines appear with considerable intensity in the spectroscope, and are of sufficient brilliancy to compare with the bright lines in the spectrum of a candle, although the nebulæ may not be brighter in the heavens than stars of the ninth magnitude.* The reason of this is, that the light of the candle is spread out into a continuous spectrum, while that of the nebula remains concentrated into a few lines; the principle is identical with that by which the spectra of the solar prominences have been since observed in sunlight simultaneously with the greatly subdued spectrum of daylight (§ 57).

During the years 1865 and 1866 more than sixty nebulæ were examined by Huggins with the spectroscope, mainly with the intention of ascertaining whether those which were clearly resolvable by the telescope into a cluster of bright points gave a continuous spectrum, or one composed of bright lines. The extreme faintness of these objects, and the circumstance that investigations of this kind can only be carried on during the absence of the moon in very clear nights, render spectroscopic observations of these heavenly bodies exceedingly difficult, and the re-

gen and nitrogen, when the intensity of their light was diminished in any way, as by the removal of the spark from the slit, or by the interposition of screens of neutral-tint glass, the line in each gas coincident with one of the lines of the nebula was the last to disappear. At present we have no certain knowledge of the state of things in the nebulæ, whether the visibility of one line only of the gases composing them (in a few nebulæ a second line of hydrogen near G is seen) is due to the diminution of their light by the imperfect transparency of interstellar space through which the light has passed, or to their original feeble luminosity. By direct comparison with the light of a candle Huggins found the intrinsic brilliancy of nebula No. 4628 to be equal to $\frac{1}{1508}$, of the annular nebula in Lyra to $\frac{1}{6032}$, and of the Dumb-bell nebula to $\frac{1}{19604}$ of the intensity of the flame of a sperm-candle burning 160 grains per hour. These results would be affected by any interstellar absorption, should such exist.]

* [Though the lines of the nebulæ are distinctly visible under favorable circumstances, the terrestrial lines to be compared with them must not be brilliant; when an induction spectra is used, the light has frequently to be diminished in intensity by a piece of neutral-tint glass.]

sults uncertain.* It is only by observations and measures many times repeated, especially when undertaken by different astronomers at various places, that the disturbing influences may in course of time be eliminated, and trustworthy results obtained.

As a result of his observations, Huggins divides the nebulæ into two groups :

1. The nebulæ giving a spectrum of one or more bright lines.
2. The nebulæ giving a spectrum apparently continuous.

About a third of the sixty nebulæ observed belong to the first group ; their spectrum consists of one, two, or three bright lines ; a few showing at the same time a very narrow, faint, continuous spectrum. They are as follows—the numbers refer to Sir John Herschel's general catalogue :

No. 4373	37 H. IV.	No. 2102	27 H. IV.
" 4390	6 Σ.	" 4214	5 Σ.
" 4514	73 H. IV.	" 4403	17 M.
" 4510	51 H. IV.	" 4572	16 H. IV.
" 4628	1 H. IV.	" 4499	38 H. VI.
" 4447	Annular nebula in Lyra	" 4827	705 H. II.
" 4964	18 H. IV.	" 4627	192 H. I.
" 4532	Dumb-bell	" 385	76 M.
" 1189	Nebula in Orion	" 386	193 H. I.
" 2102	27 H. IV.	" 2343	97 M.

Clusters and nebulæ showing a continuous spectrum without lines :

No. 4294	92 M.	No. 1949	81 M.
" 4244	50 H. IV.	" 1950	82 M.
" 116	Nebula in Andromeda	" 3572	51 M.
" 117	32 M.	" 2841	43 H. V.
" 428	55 Andromedæ	" 3474	63 M.
" 826	2 H. IV.	" 3636	3 M.
" 4670	15 M.	" 4058	215 H. I.
" 4678	18 H. V.	" 4159	1945 h.
" 105	151 H. I.	" 4230	13 M.
" 307	156 H. I.	" 4238	12 M.
" 575	156 H. I.	" 4244	50 H. IV.

* [The results contained in the following table may be accepted as trustworthy and certain so far as they go. In the case of the nebulæ, which give a spectrum apparently continuous, it is uncertain whether these excessively faint spectra contain absorption lines. The uncertainty stated in the text applies rather to the much larger number of still fainter objects observed by Huggins, but which, on account of this uncertainty, are not included in his published observations.]

No. 4256 - - -	10 M.	No. 4625 - - -	52 H. I.
" 4315 - - -	199 H. II.	" 4600 - - -	15 H. V.
" 4357 - - -	11 M.	" 4760 - - -	207 H. V.
" 4437 - - -	11 M.	" 4815 - - -	53 H. I.
" 4441 - - -	47 H. I.	" 4821 - - -	233 H. II.
" 4473 - -	Auwers 44	" 4879 - - -	251 H. II.
" 4885 - - -	56 M.	" 4883 - - -	212 H. I.
" 4526 - - -	2081 h.		

The glass photographs which Huggins has had prepared from drawings of some of the most interesting gaseous nebulæ include also their spectra of lines, so that both can be exhibited upon the screen at the same time.

Fig. 203 is the planetary annular nebulæ in Aquarius, from a drawing made by Lord Rosse (Fig. 199); the nebula, the ring of which is turned edgeways toward us, gives a spectrum of three bright lines, as in Fig. 201, one of which is due to nitrogen, and another to hydrogen.

FIG. 203.

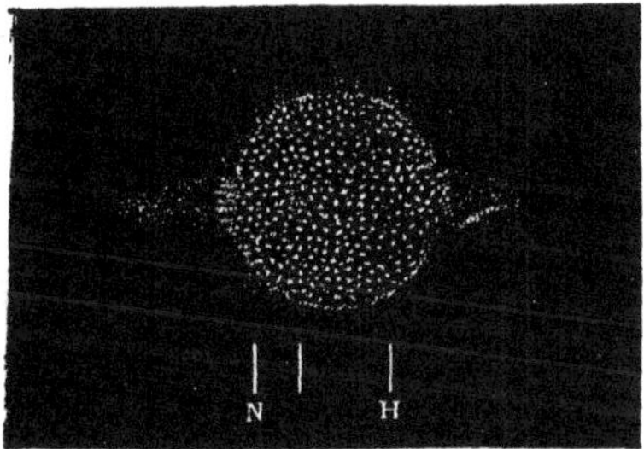

Planetary Annular Nebula in Aquarius, with Spectrum.

Fig. 204 represents on an enlarged scale the same nebula that has been already given from one of Lord Rosse's drawings in Fig. 200; its structure is essentially the same as that of the former one—a luminous gaseous mass with a central nucleus of light, and surrounded by a luminous ring, the whole surface of which, being turned toward us, causes the nebula to assume a very different form. The spectrum also consists of three bright lines.

The nebula (H. 4964) represented in Fig. 205 will be seen at a glance to be of a spiral character; it is remarkable because its spectrum contains four bright lines, two of which indicate hydrogen and one nitrogen.

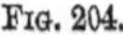
Fig. 204.

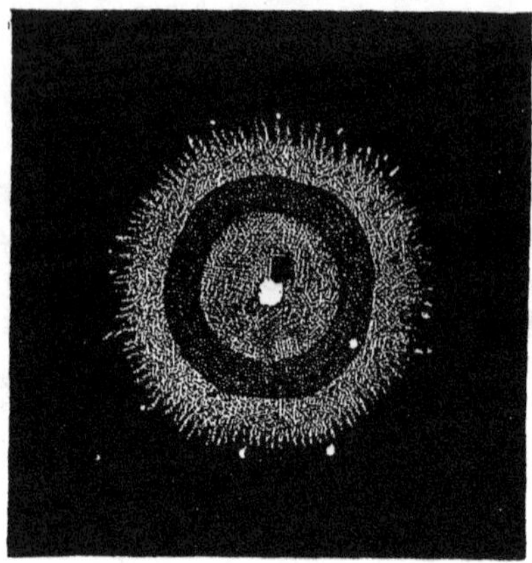

Stellar Nebula.—(H. 450.)

The spectrum of the annular nebula in Lyra (H. 4447), Fig. 206, consists, on the contrary, of only one bright line, that of nitrogen. When the spectroscope is so directed to the nebula

Fig. 205.

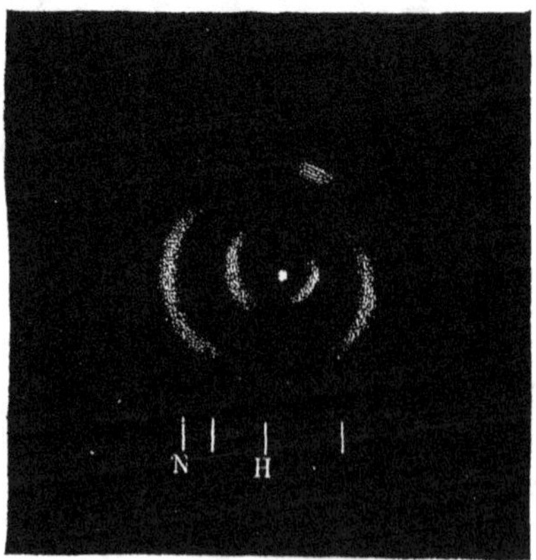

Spiral Nebula (H. 4964), with Spectrum.

that the slit cuts straight through it, the bright line appears to be composed of two brilliant lines corresponding to the upper and lower segments of the ring. These two lines are united by a small band, which shows that the faint inner portion of the nebula is of the same substance as that of the surrounding ring.

The great nebula of Orion (Figs. 183 and 184) has been the

Fig. 206.

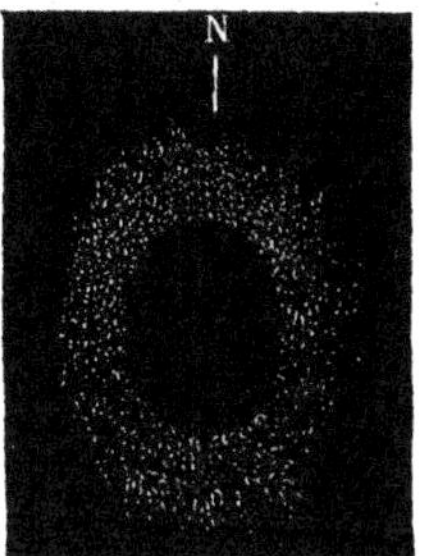

Annular Nebula in Lyra, with Spectrum.

subject of spectroscopic investigations. Its spectrum consists of three very conspicuous bright lines, one of which again indicates nitrogen and another hydrogen.

Huggins has lately repeated his former observations with instruments of much greater power, and compared especially these two lines with those of the terrestrial gases, under circumstances which gave him a spectrum four times the length of the one he obtained in his earlier investigations. The result of these observations, continued for several nights, was to show the complete coincidence, even in this greatly-extended spectrum of the nebular lines, with those of both gases, so that there can be no remaining doubt as to the identity of the lines.

Recently a fourth line has been seen in this nebula by Captain Herschel in India, by Lord Rosse, and also by Prof. Winlock, of Harvard Observatory—the same line which Huggins had before observed in the nebula H. 4964 (Fig. 205), and which belongs apparently to hydrogen. It has been suggested by the last-named observer that very probably other faint lines exist in this spectrum which can only be revealed by more powerful instruments.

All actual clusters of stars, separable by the telescope into individual bright points, give a continuous spectrum, without either gaps or bright lines. There are, however, some instances where resolvable nebulæ—the cluster in Hercules, for example—

give different and peculiar spectra, consisting of bands and dark lines.* It would therefore be interesting to inquire how far and in what manner the classification of nebulæ, as given by the spectroscope, is in accordance with the classification made by the telescope.

This information is given in the following table, drawn up by Lord Oxmantown,† by whom a revision has been undertaken of all the observations made with his father's great telescope of such of the nebulæ and clusters as had been examined by Huggins.

	Continuous Spectrum.	Spectrum of Lines.
Clusters - - - - - - - -	10	0
Resolved, or apparently resolved - - -	10	0
Resolvable, or apparently resolvable - -	5	6
Blue or green, no resolvability - - -	0	4
No resolvability apparent - - - - -	6	5
	31	15
Not observed through Lord Rosse's telescope	10	4
Total - - -	41	19

Half of the nebulæ giving a continuous spectrum have been resolved into stars, and about a third more are probably resolvable; while, of those yielding a spectrum of lines, not one has been certainly resolved by Lord Rosse. Considering the extreme difficulty attending investigations of this kind, there is scarcely any doubt that there is a complete accordance between the results of the telescope and spectroscope; and therefore those nebulæ giving a continuous spectrum are clusters of actual stars, while those giving a spectrum of bright lines must be regarded as masses of luminous gas, of which nitrogen and hydrogen form the chief constituents.

68. Comets and their Spectra.

Besides the planets, which, already cold or in process of cooling, derive their light from the incandescent sun around which

* [The spectrum of this cluster ends abruptly in the orange at about the position of D. The spectrum appears unequal in brilliancy, which suggests the presence of bright or dark lines, but no lines have been certainly detected.—*Phil. Trans.*, 1866, p. 382.]

† The present Earl of Rosse, whose successful researches on the heat of the moon give promise of the good work we may expect from his use of the noble instruments now in his hands.]

they revolve in their appointed orbits, all travelling nearly in one plane among the fixed stars in regular progress from west to east, there appear from time to time certain other wandering stars of peculiar aspect, which, from their rapid change of form and size, their fantastic contour, and their brilliant light, usually excite the greatest attention. These remarkable visitors are comets; and though their laws of motion have been well ascertained, yet their physical constitution has presented greater difficulties to astronomers than even that of the nebulæ. When they first become visible their motion is evidently round the sun, but frequently in orbits of such great elongation as hardly to be called elliptical, travelling, besides, in all possible planes and directions—sometimes, like the planets, from west to east, sometimes in the reverse way, from east to west. Several of these extraordinary objects move in closed orbits round the sun with a regular period of revolution; others come quite unexpectedly from the regions of space into our system, and retreat again to be seen no more. The periodic comets are as follows:

Comet.	Period.	Distance from the Sun.	
		Perihelion.	Aphelion.
	Years.	Miles.	
Encke's	$3\frac{1}{3}$	289 millions.	350 millions.
Winnecke's	$5\frac{1}{2}$	69 "	501 "
Brorsen's	$5\frac{3}{5}$	55 "	516 "
Biela's	$6\frac{3}{4}$	78 "	564 "
Faye's	$7\frac{1}{2}$	156 "	543 "
Halley's	$76\frac{1}{6}$	52 "	3175 "

While these comets have but a short period, there are others, such as the comets of 1858, 1811, and 1844, the calculated periods of which amount respectively to 2,100, 3,000, and 100,000 years. Differences of quite a proportionate magnitude are observable in relation to the points of nearest approach to and greatest distance from the sun. Encke's comet is twelve times nearer the sun at its perihelion than at its aphelion. Some of them, with an orbit extending beyond Jupiter, approach so close to the sun as almost to graze the surface. Newton estimated that the comet of 1680 came so near to the sun that its temperature must have exceeded by two thousand times that of melted iron.

At its nearest approach it was removed from the sun by only a sixth of his diameter. The comet of 1843, also, was so near the sun at its perihelion as to be seen in broad daylight.

FIG. 207.

Donati's Comet on July 2, 1858.

Most comets exhibit a planetary disk, more or less bright, which is called the nucleus, and this is surrounded by a fainter cloudy or nebulous envelope, the coma; the nucleus and coma form the head of the comet. In almost all comets visible to the naked eye, there streams out from the head a fan of light—the tail, consisting of one or more luminous streaks, which vary in width and length, are sometimes straight, sometimes curved, but almost always turned away from the sun, forming the prolongation of a straight line connecting the sun and the comet. While telescopic comets are usually without a tail, which causes them to assume the appearance of a more or less irregularly-shaped nebula possessing a nucleus, an example of which is given in Donati's comet (Fig. 207), as it appeared when first seen on the 2d of June, 1858, the comet of July, 1861, exhibited two tails (Fig. 208), and the comet of 1844 had even six.

FIG. 208.

July Comet on July 3, 1861.

Comets are transparent in every part, and cause no refraction in the light of the stars seen through them. Bessel saw a fixed star through Halley's comet, and Struve one through

Biela's comet, when distant only a few seconds from the centre of the nucleus, which passed over the star in both instances without either rendering it invisible or even perceptibly fainter; from accurate measures taken at the time, and the calculated motion of the comet, it was evident that the position of the star had not been changed by any refraction of the light.

Similar observations were made with respect to Donati's comet of 1858 (Fig. 209), and the comet of July, 1861 (Fig. 210).* Close to the head of the former, where the tail at its commencement was about 54,000 miles in thickness, Arcturus was seen to shine with undiminished brightness; while in both comets a number of fixed stars appeared in full brilliancy through even a much thicker portion of the tail. The comet of 1828 possessed a nucleus about 528,000 miles in diameter, and yet Struve saw a star of the eleventh magnitude through it, a fact which seems to

FIG. 209.

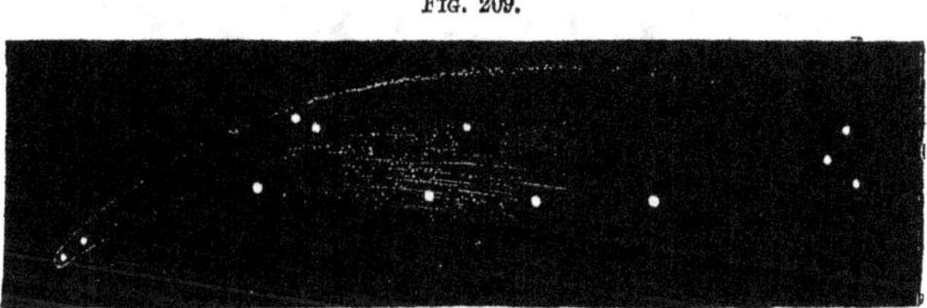

Donati's Comet on October 5, 1858.

justify the conclusion of Babinet, drawn from his own observations, that a comet has no influence upon the light of a star, and that stars of the tenth and eleventh magnitude, and some even fainter, may be seen through their greatest mass without losing in the smallest degree either their light or their color.

The nucleus of a comet is greatly affected both in size and density by its approach to the sun; but, from the want of any sharply-defined edge, it is difficult to measure its diameter with any accuracy. The comets of 1798 and 1805 each possessed a nucleus the diameter of which was twenty-two and twenty-six miles respectively; that of the great comet of 1811 attained a diameter of 380 miles, while that of 1843 reached 4,680 miles, and the comet of 1845 as much as 7,468 miles. Donati's comet

* See Westermann's Monatsheften, v., p. 277, and xi., p. 568.

measured on September 1, 1858, 13,894 miles in diameter; while on the 25th of the same month it did not exceed 1,526 miles.

The nebulous envelope, or coma, is also subject to changes in form and size, according as the comet approaches or recedes from

FIG. 210.

July Comet on July 2, 1861.

the sun. It might be expected that the coma on approaching the sun would expand and become rarefied by the extreme heat; but, as in the nucleus, exactly the reverse has often been observed. In Encke's comet, for instance, in the year 1838, the diameter of the coma on the 9th of October was 285,480 miles;

FIG. 211.

Position of the Tail of a Comet as regards the Sun.

on the 25th of the same month it was 122,616 miles; on the 23d of November it measured 39,302 miles; and on the 17th of December it was only 3,038 miles.

The tail is a prolongation of the coma, and is in most cases turned away from the sun (Fig. 211), whether the comet be approaching or receding from the sun in the course of its orbit.

A drawing by Prof. John Müller, given in Fig. 212, shows this position of the tail very clearly. In the map the position of

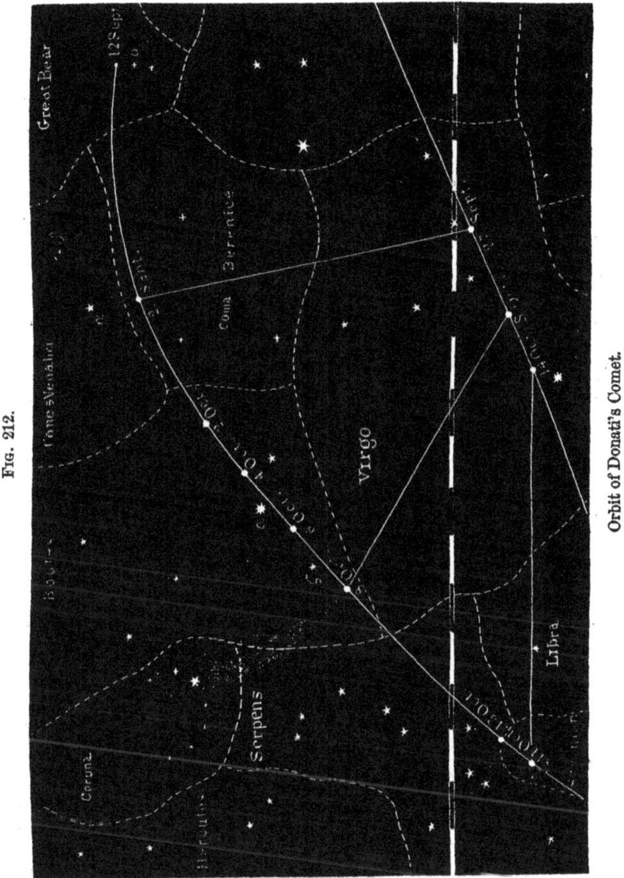

Fig. 212.

Orbit of Donati's Comet.

the sun is marked on the lower line to the right for the 27th of September, and the 8th and 14th of October, and these places are connected by straight lines with the places of the comet for those dates. The tail appears always curved, with the convex side turned toward the direction of the comet's motion. At the same time this preceding edge is much more sharply defined than the concave side, just as if some resisting medium had impeded the advance of the tail, and forced it back. But the tail does not always maintain this position; comets have been observed where the tail has been turned toward the sun, and others again possessed several tails, all turned in opposite directions.

As a comet approaches the sun, the tail regularly increases, from which it appears that the sun, whether by the action of heat or other means, contributes essentially to the formation of the tail, and produces a separation of material particles from the head of the comet. The length of the tail is rarely less than 500,000 miles, and in some cases it extends as far as 100,000,000 or 150,000,000 miles. The breadth of the tail of the great comet of 1811 at its widest part was nearly 14,000,000 miles, the length 116,000,000; and that of the second comet of the same year even 140,000,000 miles. And yet the formation of the tail takes place in a very short space of time, often in a few weeks, or even days.

The influence exercised on the formation of the tail by its approach to the sun was shown in the comet of 1680, for at its perihelion it travelled at the rate of 1,216,800 miles in an hour, and as a consequence put forth a tail in two days 54,000,000 miles in length.

It is easily conceivable that under such circumstances the mass of a comet must be exceedingly small. It is very probable that our earth actually passed on the 30th of June, 1861, through part of the tail of the magnificent comet called the July comet (Fig. 213), which suddenly appeared in the heavens as if by

Fig. 213.

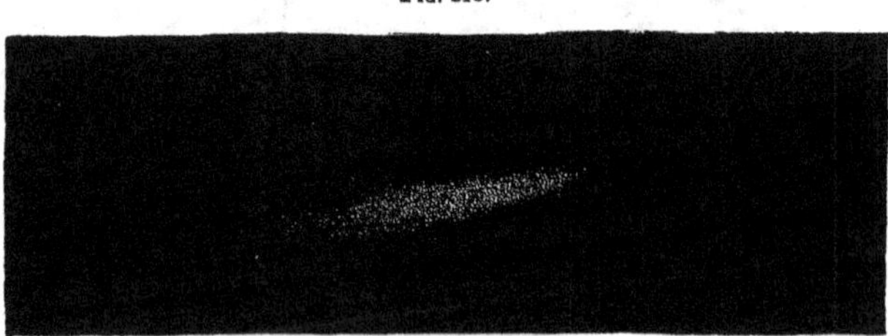

July Comet on June 30 and July 1, 1861.

magic on the 29th of June, and no indication of such a contact was evinced beyond a peculiar phosphorescence in the atmosphere which was noticed by Mr. Hind, and also at the Liverpool

Observatory. In the same way the comet of 1776 passed among the satellites of Jupiter without disturbing their position in the slightest degree. This was not the case, however, with the comet, for the influence of the planet was so great on its small mass as to send it quite out of its course into an entirely new orbit, which it now accomplishes in about twenty years.

We must now consider the remarkable phenomenon of a comet being divided into two parts, each part becoming a separate comet, and pursuing an orbit of its own. Such an occurrence happened to Biela's comet while under observation in the year 1845. When observed on the 26th of November of that year, it appeared as a faint nebulous spot, not perfectly round, with an increased density toward the middle. On the 19th of December it was rather more elongated, and ten days later it had become divided into two separate cloudy masses of equal dimensions, each furnished with a nucleus and tail, and for three months one followed the other at a distance of one-tenth, subsequently one-fifth, of the moon's diameter. The pair made their appearance again in August, 1852, after having travelled together in one common orbit round the sun for more than six years and a half; but the distance between them had much increased, and, from 154,000 miles, it had now reached 1,404,000 miles. Nor is this all: in conformity with its known period, the return of this comet was expected in the year 1859, and again in 1866, when it must have been visible from the earth as its path crossed the earth's orbit at the place where the earth was on the 30th of November. Notwithstanding the most diligent search, however, the comet could not be found, and it would seem that either, like Lexell's comet, it has been drawn out of its orbit by some member of the solar system, or else, as analogy suggests, it has ceased to be a comet, and has passed into some other form of existence.

We must enter a little further than might seem needful for our purpose into the important phenomena observed in comets, partly by the naked eye, but more especially by the telescope, in order to obtain some ground for answering queries as to the physical nature of these heavenly bodies, as well as to acquire a standard by which to compare the facts collected by telescopic observation with those gathered by spectrum analysis.

These questions are directed in the first place to the consideration of whether comets, like fixed stars and nebulæ, are self-luminous, or whether, like planets, they shine by the reflected light of the sun; in the second place, to the consideration of their material composition and physical constitution. That the nucleus of a comet cannot be in itself a dark and solid body such as the planets are, is proved by its great transparency; but this does not preclude the possibility of its consisting of innumerable solid particles separated one from another, which, when illuminated by the sun, give by the reflection of the solar light the impression of a homogeneous mass. It has therefore been concluded that comets are either composed of a substance which, like gas in a state of extreme rarefaction, is perfectly transparent, or of small solid particles individually separated by intervening spaces through which the light of a star can pass without obstruction, and which, held together by mutual attraction, as well as by gravitation toward a central denser conglomeration, moves through space like a cloud of dust. It is not impossible that comets without a nucleus are masses of gas at a white heat, of similar constitution to the nebulæ, while those possessing a nucleus are composed of disengaged solid particles. In any case, the connection lately noticed by Schiaparelli between comets and meteor-showers seems to necessitate the supposition that in many comets a similar aggregation of particles exists.

It has been thought that the polarization of light furnished a means for ascertaining whether the light of an object was inherent or reflected; and, supported by the observations made on the nuclei of comets for this purpose, the opinion has been confidently expressed that comets shine by reflected light, and not by any light of their own. But observations of this kind are in no way decisive, because in all polariscopes diffused, *irregularly* reflected light appears, just as little polarized as that given out by an independent source.

Spectrum analysis could at once answer this question, were a comet bright enough to form a complete spectrum. If the light of the comet were only reflected sunlight, the spectrum would then be like that of the moon and planets, a continuous one crossed by the Fraunhofer lines. But for the formation of such a spectrum a very narrow slit is necessary, and none of the comets which have appeared within the last few years have been bright enough to allow of their spectra being examined with a close setting of the slit. On this point, therefore, the question remains at present undecided.

Donati, at Florence, was the first to examine spectroscopically the light of comets: he compared the spectrum of the comet I., 1864, with the spectra of metals in which the dark places were wider than the luminous parts, and he found that the entire spectrum consisted of three bright lines.

Tempel's comet was observed in January, 1866, by Secchi and Huggins, who found that it yielded a continuous spectrum exceedingly faint at the two ends, in which three bright lines were seen by the former observer and only one by Huggins. The line seen by both observers was the brightest, and was situated about half-way between *b* and F of the solar spectrum. Secchi's view of this spectrum is given in Fig. 214; none of the three bright lines coincided with those of the nebula in Orion. It appears from this that the nucleus is at least partially self-luminous, and is composed of gas in a luminous condition. On the other hand, the continuous spectrum proves that some of the light is reflected sunlight, for it cannot be admitted that the coma is formed of incandescent solid or liquid particles.

The spectroscope gives no information as to the nature or condition of a substance from which we receive only reflected light: it is, however, probable that the coma and tail are of the same substance as the nucleus. These observations, therefore, yield no further result than that a gas in a state of luminosity is

FIG. 214.

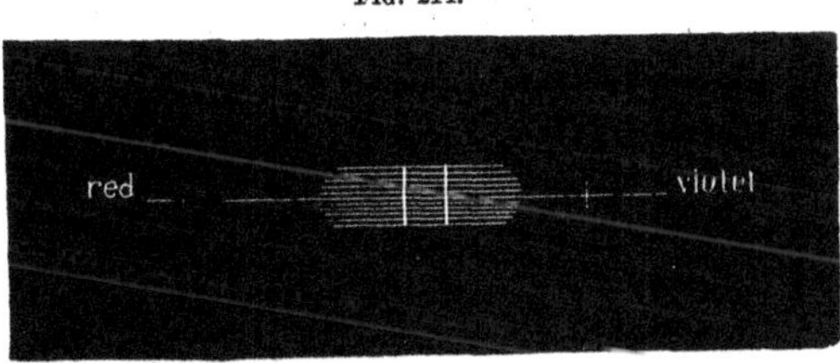

Spectrum of Tempel's Comet (1866.)

present in the comet, but that at the same time, either from this gas or from other portions of the comet which are non-luminous, sunlight is also reflected.

In the years 1866 and 1867, Huggins observed the spectra of two small comets, and found them to consist of a continuous spectrum, as well as of one of bright lines. The light of these comets was therefore, like Tempel's comet, composed partly of reflected light and partly of the comet's own light.

The year 1868 brought the return of two periodic comets of greater brilliancy, the comet of Brorsen (I.), and that of Winnecke (II.).

Fig. 215.

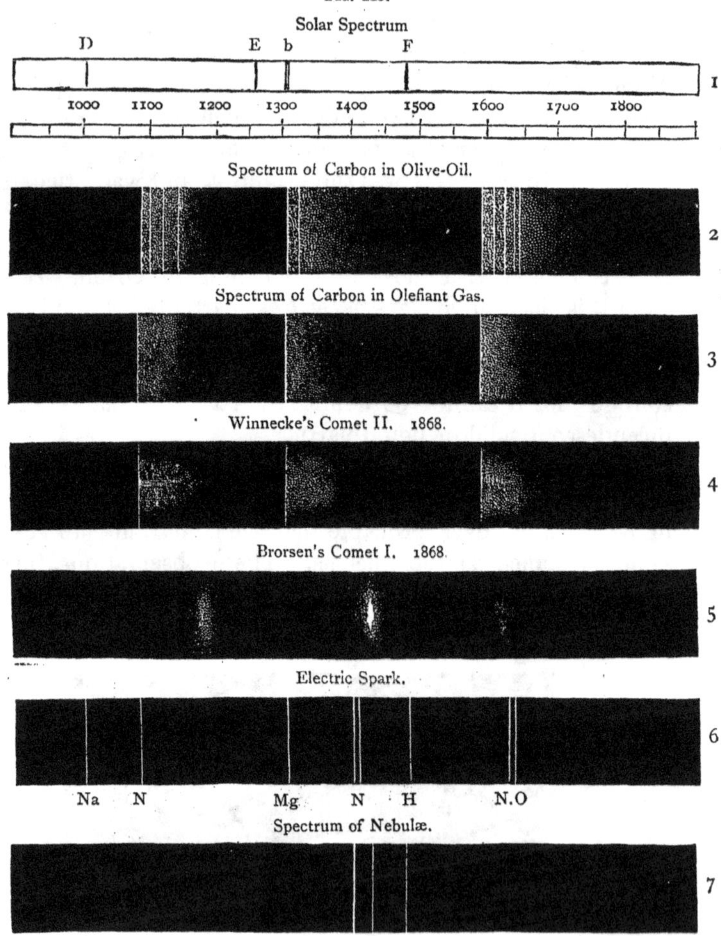

Spectra of Brorsen's and Winnecke's Comets compared with the Spectra of the Sun, Carbon, and the Nebulæ.

Brorsen's comet (I., 1868) had in the telescope the appearance of a nearly circular nebula, in which the brightness rapidly increased toward the centre, but in which the existence of a nucleus was doubtful; there was only the faint trace of a tail, or more properly merely a slight expansion of the coma on the side away from the sun.

Secchi examined this comet with a simple direct-vision spectroscope, and compared the spectrum with that of Venus, bringing the planet and the comet alternately into the same place in the instrument.

Huggins observed the same comet from the 2d to the 13th of May, and found, with Secchi, that the spectrum (Fig. 215, No. 5) was discontinuous, consisting of three bright bands; the length showed that the light of the centre of the head, as well as that of the coma, had entered the spectroscope. The brightest band of light was the middle one in the green, about half-way between the Fraunhofer lines *b* and F. When the sky was very favorable, this band was reduced to a single bright line of the apparent width of the comet's nucleus.* The second band, less intense, but still very bright, was situated in the yellow-green, nearly in the middle of the space between the Fraunhofer lines *b* and D. Occasionally another band could be traced in the red, but it was difficult to fix its place. The third band was in the blue, toward the violet, about a third of the distance between F and G.

An extremely faint light, not shown in the drawing, was apparent at the same time over the whole space of the spectrum, the indication of a very faint continuous spectrum.

By narrowing the slit, these luminous bands could not be resolved into lines, which is the case with the bright bands of the nebulæ; it only produced a weakening of the bands of light until they completely disappeared.

The spectrum of Brorsen's comet bears a great resemblance to that observed by Donati; but it differs essentially from the spectrum of a nebula, not only in its character, but also in the position of the bands of light. A comparison of these two spectra (No. 5 and No. 7) shows this at a glance.

The comet II., 1868, was first observed on the night of the 13th–14th of June, by Dr. Winnecke, in Carlsruhe, and soon attained sufficient brightness to be seen by the naked eye as a star of the seventh or eighth magnitude. The diameter of the

* [Doubtful.]

coma, including the extremely faint luminous envelope, amounted to about 6′ 20″, the length of the tail being more than 1°. The tail, as shown in Fig. 216, went straight out from the coma, and

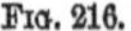

Fig. 216.

Winnecke's Comet (II., 1868).

seemed to have no connection with the bright nucleus. The following side, that turned away from the direction of motion, was sharply defined, while the other side gradually lost itself in space.

When Secchi examined the comet on the 21st of June with a simple spectroscope without a slit, the spectrum was seen to consist of three brilliant bands of light, the brightest of which was in the green, another less bright in the yellow, and the faintest was situated in the blue. When this instrument was exchanged for one of Hofmann's direct-vision spectroscopes, the three bands were well defined, and the dispersed light had disappeared. On comparing the position of these lines with those exhibited by the spectra of various metals, it was found that the middle one lay very near to the magnesium line *b*, but the spectrum, as a whole, could not be brought to agree with that of any metal. He perceived, however, a great resemblance between the spectrum of the comet and that of carburetted hydrogen, which made him conclude that the light from the self-luminous part of the comet was produced by that substance.

Huggins investigated Winnecke's comet with a spectroscope consisting of two prisms of 60°, and has given a drawing of the comet (Fig. 216), as well as of its spectrum, together with the spectra of the substances with which it was compared. In Fig. 215, No. 4 is the spectrum of the comet; No. 2 that of the electric spark, in olive-oil; No. 3 the electric spark, in olefiant gas; No. 6 gives the principal lines of some of the substances brought into comparison by means of the electric spark (N. = nitrogen, O. = oxygen, H. = hydrogen, Mg. = magnesium, Na. = sodium).

The apparatus employed by Huggins for these comparisons is shown in Fig. 217. The olefiant gas was contained in the glass bottle *a*, whence it flowed through the tube *b*, into which were soldered two platinum wires *e* and *f*. At the place where the spark was to pass, a hole was bored through the glass tube, the edges of the opening carefully ground, and the opening closed by a smooth plate of glass. The light of the glowing gas was reflected by the small mirror *c* on to the reflecting prism in the interior of the tube, by which it was thrown on to the lower half of the slit, while the light of the comet was received upon the upper half. By this means the spectrum of the olefiant gas produced by the electric spark was brought into close juxtaposition with the spectrum of the comet, so as to admit of an exact comparison.

Secchi's observations have been completely confirmed by those of Huggins; the spectrum of the comet consisted of three broad bright bands, which were sharply defined at the edge toward the red, but faded away gradually on the opposite side; Huggins, however, did not succeed in resolving the bands into sharp lines, but the middle and brightest band appeared to commence with a well-defined bright line. When the slit was placed on the edge of the coma the three bands were still distinguishable, but when the slit was directed to the fainter light of the tail the spectrum appeared to be continuous.

FIG. 217.

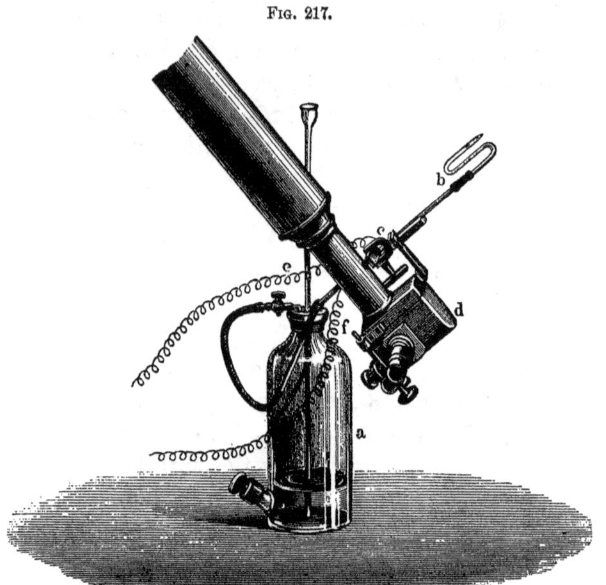

Huggins's Apparatus for observing the Spectra of Hydrocarbons.

If the spectrum of the comet be compared with that of carbon which has been disengaged from olive-oil or olefiant gas by the heat of the electric spark, there is no great resemblance to be observed between them;* the lines of hydrogen, moreover,

* [This statement is not correct. Huggins found, as may be seen in Fig. 215, the spectrum of this comet to be apparently *identical* with that of carbon as obtained by the passage of the induction spark in olefiant gas, not only in the position in the spectrum of the bands, but also in their general characters and relative brightness. The spectrum of Brorsen's comet, as shown in the diagram No. 5, does not agree with that of carbon. The spectrum of carbon as obtained when the spark passes in olive-oil, No. 2, differs from No. 3 only in that the bands are resolvable into fine lines. The bands in the spectrum of the comet were like those obtained when olefiant gas is used, irresolvable into lines. The lines of the other component of olefiant gas, hydrogen, are omitted in the diagram. The lines of hydrogen were not visible in the spectrum of the comet. It appears to be right to consider this spectrum of bright bands to be that of carbon, and not that of any stable hydrocarbon, for Huggins

belonging to the spectrum of olefiant gas are not present in the spectrum of the comet.

The same comet was spectroscopically observed by H. M. C. Wolf at Paris. It was remarked also by him that the three bright bands separated from each other by perfectly dark spaces could not be condensed into lines by narrowing the slit, and thus the spectrum offered no analogy to that of a nebula.

The spectrum of the comet I., 1870 (Winnecke), was examined by Wolf and Rayet; it consisted, like the spectra of earlier comets, of three bright bands which spread out upon a continuous spectrum.*

It would be premature to draw decisive results from these comprehensive but as yet isolated observations. The spectrum of the three bright bands is derived unquestionably from the light of the comet's nucleus, and not from that of the coma, which is far too faint and ill-defined to produce such a spectrum; it may therefore be assumed that the nucleus is self-luminous, and that it is very possibly composed of glowing gas containing carbon. This theory has already been opposed by Prazmowski, who instituted some experiments on light reflected from faintly-illuminated strips of colored paper, and found that the spectrum of a body faintly illuminated by the sun presented exactly the same appearance which was observed by Secchi and Huggins in the comet of 1868; the spectrum of bands, therefore, given by this comet is not a proof of its being self-luminous, and even the light

found the same bands, together with the lines of nitrogen, when the spark was taken in cyanogen, and a spectrum essentially the same, but less complete, when compounds of carbon with oxygen were employed.]

* [Huggins gives the following description of the spectrum of comet I., 1871 (Proceedings R. S., 1871):

"On April 7th, a faint comet was discovered by Dr. Winnecke. I observed the comet on April 13th and May 2d. On both days the comet was exceedingly faint, and on May 2d it was rendered more difficult to observe by the light of the moon and a faint haze in the atmosphere. It presented the appearance of a small faint coma, with an extension in the direction from the sun. When observed in the spectroscope, I could detect the light of the coma to consist almost entirely of three bright bands. A fair measure was obtained of the centre of the middle band, which was the brightest; it gives for this band a wave-length of about 510 millionths of a millimetre. I was not able to do more than estimate roughly the position of the less refrangible band. The result gives 545 millionths. The third band was situated at about the same distance from the middle band on the more refrangible side. It would appear that this comet is similar in constitution to the comets which I examined in 1868."]

emitted by the nucleus may also be a reflected light.* Secchi maintains, on the contrary, that the dark and bright absorption bands which are seen in the spectrum of light reflected from colored substances never have those sharp edges which are observed in the spectra of comets; in his fine polariscope, polarization was observed principally in the coma, and scarcely at all in the nucleus, which, had it reflected the sun's light, would have shown the greater amount of polarization.

By collating these various phenomena, the conviction can scarcely be resisted that the nuclei of comets not only emit their own light, which is that of a glowing gas, but also, together with the coma and the tail, reflect the light of the sun. There seems, therefore, nothing to contradict the theory that the mass of a comet may be composed of minute solid bodies kept apart one from another in the same way as the infinitesimal particles forming a cloud of dust or smoke are held loosely together, and that, as the comet approaches the sun, the most easily fusible constituents of these small bodies become wholly or partially vaporized, and in a condition of white heat overtake the remaining solid particles, and surround the nucleus in a *self-luminous* cloud of glowing vapor. Spectrum analysis will not be able to afford any more certain evidence regarding the physical nature of comets until the appearance of a really brilliant comet which can be examined in the various phases it may present.

It would lead us too far from our purpose were we to describe more minutely the extremely interesting phenomena which the telescope has revealed of the separation of cometic matter, and the gradual formation of the coma and tail;† nor can we enter more fully here into the causes of the changes produced in the form of a comet by its approach to the sun, or to one of the larger planets;‡ but we cannot pass over the extremely ingenious hypothesis brought forward by Prof. Tyndall before the Philo-

* [Prazmowski's objection is untenable. Huggins has remarked that a spectrum of bright bands might be given by a gas in a fluorescent state, but the circumstance of the coincidence of the cometary spectrum with that of carbon would remain unexplained.]

† Mädler, "Die Ausströmungen der Kometen," in Westermann's Monatshefton, vol. vii., p. 392.

‡ Linder, Théorie des Comètes fondée sur la seule loi de l'attraction universelle, Les Mondes, xxi., p. 562.

sophical Society of Cambridge, on the 8th of March, 1869.* This admirable investigator had already proved, by a series of interesting experiments, that concentrated solar light, or the electric light, decomposes the volatile vapors of many liquids, producing almost instantly a precipitate of cloudy matter, in which some very peculiar phenomena of light are displayed. The quantity of vapor may be so small as to escape detection, but the concentrated light falling upon it soon forms a blue cloud from the moving atoms of vapor which now become visible, and appear, according to the nature of the vapor, in a variety of forms as precipitations of matter on the beams of light.

It is very striking in this experiment to see the astonishing amount of light that an infinitesimal amount of decomposable vapor is able to reflect. When the electric light is admitted into the tube, nothing is to be seen for the first moment; but soon a blue cloud shows itself, which is formed of almost infinitely small particles, either of vapor, or, what is more probable, of the molecules set free by its decomposition, and after some minutes the whole tube is filled with this blue color. The vaporous particles gradually augment in magnitude, and after some time (from ten to fifteen minutes) a dense white cloud fills the tube, which discharges so great a body of light that it is scarcely conceivable how so small a quantity of matter can possibly reflect so much light.

"Nothing," says Tyndall, "could more perfectly illustrate that 'spiritual texture' which Sir John Herschel ascribes to a comet than these actinic clouds. Indeed, the experiments prove that matter of almost infinite tenuity is competent to shed forth light far more intense than that of the tails of comets." Upon these facts Tyndall has constructed a theory which offers an unforced explanation of many of the phenomena that have been observed, as, for instance, the formation and motion of the tail, etc., but which also stands in complete contradiction to many of the facts discovered by Schiaparelli.

69. Falling Stars, Meteor-Showers, Balls of Fire and their Spectra.

Whoever has observed the heavens on a clear night with some amount of attention and patience, cannot fail to have noticed the

* Philosophical Transactions, 1870, p. 323; Philosophical Magazine, 1869, No. 249; Naturforscher, ii., No. 33.

phenomenon of a falling star, one of those well-known fiery meteors which suddenly blaze forth in any quarter of the heavens, descend toward the earth, generally with great rapidity, in either a vertical or slanting direction, and disappear after a few seconds at a higher or lower altitude. As a rule, falling stars can only be seen of an evening, or at night, owing to the great brightness of daylight; but many instances have occurred in which their brilliancy has been so great as to render them visible in the daytime, as well when the sky was overcast as when it was perfectly cloudless. It has been calculated that the average number of these meteors passing through the earth's atmosphere, and sufficiently bright to be seen at night with the naked eye, is not less than seven million and a half during the space of twenty-four hours, and this number must be increased to four hundred million if those be included which a telescope would reveal. In many nights, however, the number of these meteors is so great that they pass over the heavens like flakes of snow, and for several hours are too numerous to be counted. Early in the morning of the 12th of November, 1799, Humboldt and Bonpland saw before sunrise, when on the coast of Mexico, thousands of meteors during the space of four hours, most of which left a track behind them of from 5° to 10° in length; they mostly disappeared without any display of sparks, but some seemed to burst, and others, again, had a nucleus as bright as Jupiter, which emitted sparks. On the 12th of November, 1833, there fell another shower of meteors, in which, according to Arago's estimation, two hundred and forty thousand passed over the heavens, as seen from the place of observation, in three hours.

Only in very rare instances do these fiery substances fall upon the surface of the earth; when they do, they are called balls of fire; and occasionally they reach the earth before they are completely burnt out or evaporated; they are then termed meteoric stones, aërolites, or meteoric iron. They are also divided into accidental meteors and meteoric showers, according as to whether they traverse the heavens in every direction at random, or appear in great numbers following a common path, thus indicating that they are parts of a great whole.

It is now generally received, and placed almost beyond doubt by the recent observations of Schiaparelli, Le Verrier, Weiss, and others, that these meteors, for the most part small, but weighing occasionally many tons, are fragmentary masses, revolving, like the planets, round the sun, which in their course approach the earth, and, drawn by its attraction into our atmosphere, are set on fire by the heat generated through the resistance offered by the compressed air.

The chemical analysis of those meteors which have fallen to the earth in a half-burnt condition in the form of meteoric stones proves that they are composed only of terrestrial elements, which present a form and combination commonly met with in our planet. Their chief constituent is metallic iron, mixed with various silicious compounds; in combination with iron, nickel is always found, and sometimes also cobalt, copper, tin, and chromium; among the silicates, olivine is especially worthy of remark as a mineral very abundant in volcanic rocks, as also augite. There have also been found, in the meteoric stones hitherto examined, oxygen, hydrogen, sulphur, phosphorus, carbon, aluminium, magnesium, calcium, sodium, potassium, manganese, titanium, lead, lithium, and strontium.

The height at which meteors appear is very various, and ranges chiefly between the limits of 46 and 92 miles; the mean may be taken at 66 miles. The speed at which they travel is also various, generally about half as fast again as that of the earth's motion round the sun, or about 26 miles in a second: the maximum and minimum differ greatly from this amount, the velocity of some meteors being estimated at 14 miles, and that of others at 107 miles in a second.

When a dark meteorite of this kind, having a velocity of 1,660 miles per minute, encounters the earth, flying through space at a mean rate of 1,140 miles per minute, and when through the earth's attraction its velocity is further increased 230 miles per minute, this body meets with such a degree of resistance, even in the highest and most rarefied state of our atmosphere, that it is impeded in its course, and loses in a very short time a considerable part of its momentum. By this encounter there follows a result common to all bodies which while in motion suddenly experience a check. When a wheel revolves very rapidly, the axletree or the drag which is placed under the wheel is made red-hot by the friction. When a cannon-ball strikes suddenly with great velocity against a plate of iron, which constantly happens at target-practice, a spark is seen to flash from the ball even in daylight; under similar circumstances a lead bullet becomes partially melted. The heat of a body consists in the vibratory motion of its smallest particles; an increase of this molecular motion is synonymous with a higher temperature; a lessening of this vibration is termed decreasing heat, or the process of cooling. Now, if a body in motion, as for instance a cannonball, strike against an iron plate, or a meteorite against the earth's atmosphere, in proportion as the motion of the body diminishes and the external action of the moving mass becomes annihilated by the pressure of the opposing medium upon the foremost molecules, the vibration of these particles increases; this motion is immediately communicated to the rest of the mass, and by the acceleration of this vibration through all the particles the temperature of the body is raised. This phenomenon, which always takes place when the motion of a body is interrupted, is designated by the expression *the conversion of the motion of the mass into molecular action or heat;* it is a law without exception that where the *external* motion of the mass is diminished, an inner action among its particles or heat is set up in its place as an equivalent, and it may be easily supposed that even in the highest and most rarefied strata of the earth's atmosphere, the velocity of the meteorite would be rapidly diminished by its opposing action, so that shortly after entering our atmosphere the vibration of the inner particles would become accelerated to such a degree as to raise them to a white heat, when they would either become partially fused, or if the meteorite were sufficiently small, it would be dissipated into vapor, and leave a luminous track behind it of glowing vapors.

Haidinger, in a theory embracing all the phenomena of meteorites, explains the formation of a ball of fire round the meteor by supposing that the meteorite, in consequence of its rapid motion through the atmosphere, presses the air before it till it becomes luminous. The compressed air in which the solid particles of the surface of the meteorite glow then rushes on all sides, but especially over the surface of the meteor behind it, where it encloses a pear-shaped vacuum which has been left by the meteorite, and so appears to the observer as a ball of fire. If several bodies enter the earth's atmosphere in this way at the same time, the largest among them precedes the others, because the air offers the least resistance to its proportionately smallest surface; the rest follow in the track of the first meteor which is the only one surrounded by a ball of fire. When by the resistance of the air the motion of the meteor is arrested, it remains for a moment perfectly still; the ball of fire is extinguished, the surrounding air rushes suddenly into the vacuum behind the meteor, which, left solely to the action of gravitation, falls vertically to the earth. The loud detonating noise usually accompanying this phenomenon finds an easy explanation in the violent concussion of the air behind the meteor, while the generally received theory, that the detonating noise is the result of an explosion or bursting of the meteorite, does not meet with any confirmation.

The circumstance that most meteors are extinguished before reaching the earth seems to show that their mass is but small. If the distance of a meteor from the earth be ascertained, as well as its apparent brightness as compared with that of a planet, it is possible, by comparing its luminosity with that of a known quantity of ignited gas, to estimate the degree of heat evolved in the meteor's combustion. As this heat originates from the motion of the meteor being impeded or interrupted by the resistance of the air, and as this motion or momentum is exclusively dependent on the speed of the meteor as well as upon its mass, it is possible when the rate of motion has been ascertained by direct observation to determine the mass. Prof. Alexander Herschel has calculated by this means that those meteors of the 9th and 10th of August, 1863, which equalled the brilliancy of Venus and Jupiter, must have possessed a mass of from five to eight pounds, while those which were only as bright as stars of the second or third magnitude would not be more than about ninety grains in weight. As the greater number of meteors are less bright than stars of the second magnitude, the faint meteors must weigh only a few grains, for, according to Prof. Herschel's computation, the five meteors observed on the 12th of November, 1865, some of which surpassed in brilliancy stars of the first magnitude, had not an average weight of more than five grains; and Schiaparelli estimated the weight of a meteor from other phenomena to be about fifteen grains. The mass, however, of the meteoric stones which fall to the earth is considerably greater, whether they consist of one single piece, such as the celebrated iron-stone discovered by Pallas in Siberia, which weighed about 2,000 lb., or of a cloud composed of many small bodies which penetrate the earth's atmosphere in parallel paths, as shown in Fig. 218, and which, from a simultaneous ignition and descent upon the earth, present the appearance of a large meteor bursting into several smaller pieces. Such a shower of stones, accompanied by a bright light and loud explosion, occurred at L'Aigle, in Normandy, on the 26th of April, 1803, when the number of stones found in a space of 14 square miles exceeded 2,000. In the meteoric shower that fell at Kúyahinga, in Hungary, on the 9th of June, 1866, the principal stone weighed about 800 lb., and was accompanied by about a thousand smaller stones, which were strewed over an area of 9 miles in length by 3¼ broad.

Fig. 218.

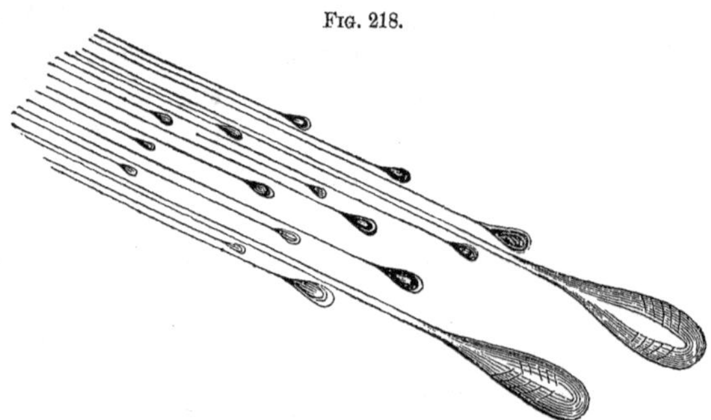

Balls of Fire seen through the Telescope.

It must not be supposed, however, that the density of such a cosmical cloud is as great when out of the reach of the attraction of the sun and the earth as when its constituents fall upon the earth's surface. Schiaparelli calculates, from the number of meteors observed yearly in the month of August, that the distance between any two must amount, on the average, to 460 miles. As the cosmical clouds which produce the meteors approach the sun in their wanderings from the far-off regions of space, they increase in density some million times, therefore the distance between any two meteors, only a few grains in weight, before the cloud begins to be condensed, may be upward of 40,000 miles.

The most striking example of such a cosmical cloud composed of small bodies loosely hung together, and existing with hardly any connection one with another, is exhibited in the meteoric showers occurring periodically in August and November. It is an ascertained fact that on certain nights in the year the number of meteors is extraordinarily great, and that at these times they shoot out from certain fixed points in the heavens. The shower of meteors which happens every year on the night of the 10th of August, proceeding from the constellation of Perseus, is mentioned in many old writings. The shower of the 12th and 13th of November occurs periodically every thirty-three years, for three years in succession, with diminishing numbers; it was this shower that Alexander von Humboldt and Bonpland observed on the 12th of November, 1799, as a real rain of fire. It recurred on the 12th of November, 1833, in such force that Arago compared it to a fall of snow, and was lately observed again in its customary splendor in North America, on the 14th of November, 1867. Besides these two principal showers, there are almost a hundred others recurring at regular intervals; each of these is a cosmical cloud composed of small dark bodies very loosely held together, like the particles of a sand-cloud, which circulate round the sun in one common orbit. The orbits of these meteor streams are very diverse; they do not lie approximately in one plane like those of the planets, but cross the plane of the earth's orbit at widely different angles. The motion of the individual meteors ensues in the same direction in one and the same orbit; but this direction is in some orbits in conformity with that of the earth and planets, while in others it is in the reverse order.

The earth in its revolution round the sun occupies every day a different place in the universe; if, therefore, a meteoric shower pass through our atmosphere at regular intervals, there must be at the place where the earth is at that time an accumulation of those small cosmical bodies, which, attracted by the earth, penetrate its atmosphere, are ignited by the resistance of the air, and become visible as falling stars. A cosmical cloud, however, cannot remain at a fixed spot in our solar system, but must circulate round the sun as planets and comets do; whence it follows that the path of a periodic shower intersects the earth's orbit, and the earth must either be passing through the cloud, or else very near to it, when the meteors are visible to us.

The meteor-shower of the 10th of August, the radiant point of which is situated in the constellation of Perseus, takes place nearly every year, with varying splendor; we may therefore conclude that the small meteors composing this group form a ring round the sun, and the earth every 10th of August is at the spot where this ring intersects our orbit; also that the ring of meteors is not equally dense in all parts: here and there these small bodies must be very thinly scattered, and in some places even altogether wanting.

FIG. 219.

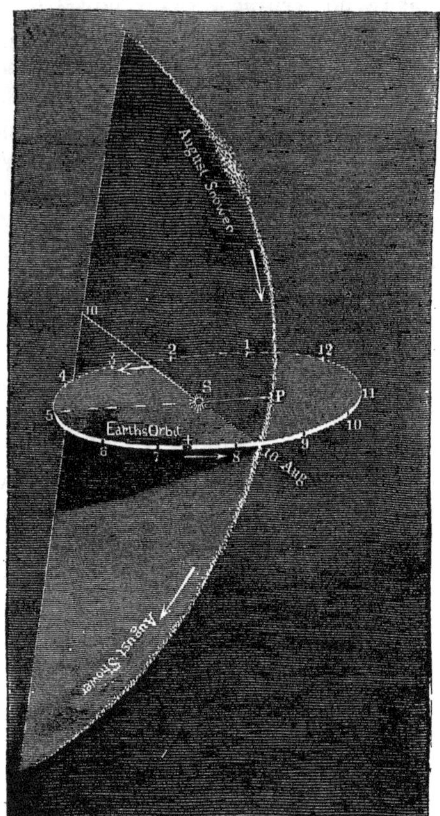

Orbit of the Meteor-Shower of the 10th of August.

Fig. 219 shows a very small part of the elliptic orbit which this meteoric mass describes round the sun S. The earth encounters this orbit on the 10th of August, and goes straight through the ring of meteors. The dots along the ring indicate the small dark meteors which ignite in our atmosphere, and are visible as shooting-stars. The line *m* is the line of intersection of the earth's orbit and that of the meteors; the line P S shows the direction of the major axis of their orbit. This axis is fifty times greater than the mean diameter of the earth's orbit; the orbit of the meteors is inclined to that of the earth at an angle of 64° 3′, and their motion is retrograde, or contrary to that of the earth.

The November shower is not observed to take place every year on the 12th or 13th of that month, but it is found that every thirty-three years an extraordinary shower occurs on those days, proceeding from a point in the constellation of Leo. The meteors composing this shower, unlike the August one, are not distributed along the whole course of their orbit, so as to form a ring entirely filled with meteoric particles, but constitute a dense cloud, of an elongated form, which completes its revolution round the sun in thirty-three years, and crosses the earth's path at that point where the earth is every 13th of November.

When the November shower reappears after the lapse of thirty-three years, the phenomenon is repeated during the two following years on the 13th of that month, but with diminished splendor; the meteors, therefore, extend so far along the orbit as to require three years before they have all crossed the earth's path at the place of intersection; they are, besides, unequally distributed, the preceding part being much the most dense.

A very small part of the elliptic orbit, and the distribution of the meteors during the November shower, is represented in Fig. 220. As shown in the drawing, this orbit intersects that of the earth at the place where the earth is about the 14th of November, and the motion of the meteors, which occupy only a small part of their orbit, and are very unequally distributed, is retrograde, or contrary to that of the earth. The inclination of this orbit to that of the earth is only 17° 44′; its major axis is about ten and one-third times greater than the diameter of the earth's orbit, and the period of revolution for the densest part of the meteorites round the sun S is thirty-three years three months.

From all we have now learned concerning the nature and constitution of comets, nebulæ, cosmical clouds, and meteoric swarms, an unmistakable resemblance will be remarked among these different forms in space. The affinity between comets and meteors had been already recognized by Chladni, but Schiaparelli, of Milan, was the first to take account of all the phenomena ex hibited by these mysterious heavenly bodies, and with wonderful acuteness to treat successfully the mass of observations and calculations which had been contributed during the course of the last few years by Oppolzer, Peters, Bruhns, Heis, Le Verrier, and other observers. He not only shows that the orbits of meteors are quite coincident with those of comets, and that the same

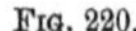

Fig. 220.

Orbit of the November Meteor-Shower.

object may appear to us at one time as a comet and at another as a shower of meteors, but he proves also by a highly-elegant mathematical calculation that the scattered cosmical masses known to us by the name of nebulæ would, if in their journey through the universe they were to come within the powerful attraction of our sun, be formed into comets, and these again into meteoric showers.

We should be carried away too far from our subject were we to enter fully into the consideration of this bold and ingenious theory of the Milan astronomer, supported though it be by a series of facts; but while we refer the reader to vol. xx. of "Naturwissenschaftlichen Volksbücher" by A. Bernstein, in which this subject, "die Räthsel der Sternschnuppen und der Kometen," is fully treated of in a very clear and attractive manner, we shall confine ourselves to the following short statement of Schiaparelli's theory:

Nebulæ are composed of cosmical matter in which as yet there is no central point of concentration, and which has not become sufficiently dense to form a celestial body in the ordinary sense of the term. The diffuse substance of these cosmical clouds is very loosely hung together; its particles are widely separated, thus constituting masses of enormous extent, some of which have taken a regular form, and some not. As these nebulous clouds may be supposed to have, like our sun, a motion in space, it will sometimes happen that such a cloud comes within reach of the power of attraction of our sun. The attraction acts more powerfully on the preceding part of the nebula than on the farther and following portion; and the nebula while still at a great distance begins to lose its original spherical form, and becomes considerably elongated. Other portions of the nebulous mass follow continuously the preceding part, until the sphere is converted into a long cylinder, the foremost part of which, that toward the sun, is denser and more pointed than the following part, which retains a portion of its original breadth. As it nears the sun, this transformation of the nebulous cloud becomes more complete: illuminated by the sun, the preceding part appears to us as a dense nucleus, and the following part, turned away from the sun, as a long tail, curved in consequence of the lateral motion preserved by the nebula during its progress. Out of the original spherical nebula, quite unconnected with our solar system, a comet has been formed, which in its altered condition will either pass through our system to wander again in space, or else remain as a permanent member of our planetary system. The form of the orbit in which it moves depends on the original speed of the cloud, its distance from the sun, and the direction of its motion, and thus its path may be elliptical, hyperbolical, or parabolical; in the last two cases, the comet appears only once in our system, and then returns to wander in the realms of space; in the former case, it abides with us, and accomplishes its course round the sun, like the planets, in a certain fixed period of years. From this it is evident that the orbits of comets may occur at every possible angle to that of the earth, and that their motion will be sometimes progressive and sometimes retrograde.

The history of the cosmical cloud does not, however, end with its transformation into a comet. Schiaparelli shows in a striking manner that, as a comet is not a solid mass, but consists of particles each possessing an independent motion, the head or nucleus nearer the sun must necessarily complete its orbit in less time than the more distant portions of the tail. The tail will therefore lag behind the nucleus in the course of the comet's revolution, and the comet, becoming more and more elongated, will at last be either partially or entirely resolved into a ring of meteors. In this way the whole path of the comet becomes strewed with portions of its mass, with those small dark meteoric bodies which, when penetrating the earth's atmosphere, become luminous, and appear as falling stars. Instead of the comet, there now revolves round the sun a broad ring of meteoric stones, which occasion the phenomena we every year observe as the August meteors. Whether this ring be continuous, and the meteoric masses strewed along the whole course of the path of the original comet, or whether the individual meteors, as in the November shower, have not filled up entirely the whole orbit, but are still partially in the form of a comet, is in the transformation of a cosmical cloud through the influence of the sun only a question of time; in course of years the matter composing a comet which describes an orbit round the sun must be dispersed over its whole path; *if the original orbit be elliptical, an elliptic ring of meteors will gradually be formed from the substance of the comet of the same size and form as the original orbit.*

Schiaparelli has in fact discovered so close a resemblance between the path of the August meteors and that of the comet of 1862, No. III., that there cannot be any doubt as to their complete identity. The meteors to which we owe the annual display of falling stars on the 10th of August are not distributed equally along the whole course of their orbit; it is still possible to distinguish the agglomeration of meteoric particles which originally formed the cometary nucleus from the other less dense parts of the comet; thus in the year 1862 the denser portion of this ring of meteors through which the earth passes annually on the 10th of August, and which causes the display of falling stars, was seen in the form of a comet, with head and tail as the densest parts, approached the sun and earth in the course of that month. Oppolzer, of Vienna, calculated with great accuracy the orbit of this comet, which was visible to the naked eye. Schiaparelli had previously calculated the orbit of the meteoric ring to which the shooting-stars of the 10th of August belong before they are drawn into the earth's atmosphere. The almost perfect identity of the two orbits justifies Schiaparelli in the bold assertion that *the comet of* 1862, No. III., *is no other than the remains of the comet out of which the meteoric ring of the* 10*th of August has been formed in the course of time.* The difference between the comet's nucleus and its tail that has now been formed into a ring, consists in that, while the denser meteoric mass forming the head approaches so near the earth once in every hundred and twenty years as to be visible in the reflected light of the sun, the more widely-scattered portion of the tail composing the ring remains invisible, even though the earth passes through it annually on the 10th of August. Only fragments of this ring, composed of dark meteoric particles, become visible as shooting-stars when they penetrate our atmosphere by the attraction of the earth, and ignite by the compression of the air.

A cloud of meteors of such a character can naturally only be observed as a meteor-shower when in the nodes of its orbit—that is to say, in those points where it crosses the earth's orbit—and then only when the earth is also there at the same time, so that the meteors pass through our atmosphere. The nebula coming within the sphere of attraction of our solar system would, at its nearest approach to the sun (perihelion), and in the neighboring portions of its orbit, appear as a *comet*, and when it grazed the earth's atmosphere would be seen as a *shower of meteors.*

Calculation shows that this ring of meteors is about 10,948 millions of miles in its greatest diameter. As the meteoric shower of the 10th of August lasts about six hours, and the earth travels at the rate of eighteen miles in a second, it follows that the breadth of this ring at the place where the earth crosses it is 4,043,520 miles. In Fig. 221, A B represents a portion of the orbit of the comet of 1862, No. III., which is identical with that (Fig. 219) of the August shower.

The calculations of Schiaparelli, Oppolzer, Peters, and Le Verrier, have also discovered the comet producing the meteors of the November shower, and have found it in the small comet of 1866, No. I., first observed by Tempel, of Marseilles. Its transformation into a ring of meteors has not proceeded nearly so far as that of the comet of 1862, No. III. Its existence is of

Fig. 221.

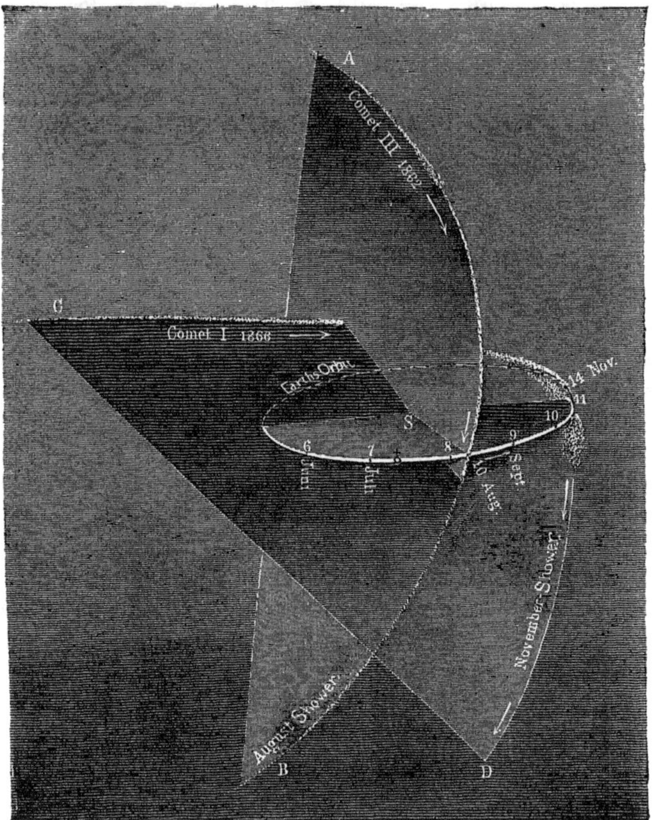

Orbits of the August and November Meteor-Showers.
(Orbits of Comets III., 1862, and I., 1866.)

a much more recent date; and, therefore, the dispersion of the meteoric particles along the orbit, and the consequent formation of the ring, is but slightly developed.

According to Le Verrier, a cosmical nebulous cloud entered our system in January, 126, and passed so near the planet Uranus as to be brought by its attraction into an elliptic orbit round the sun. This orbit is the same as that of the comet discovered by Tempel, and calculated by Oppolzer, and is identical with that in which the November group of meteors make their revolution.

Since that time, this cosmical cloud, in the form of a comet, has completed fifty-two revolutions round the sun, without its existence being otherwise made known than by the loss of an immense number of its components, in the form of shooting-stars, as it crossed the earth's path in each revolution, or in the month of November in every thirty-three years. It was only in its last revolution, in the year 1866, that this meteoric cloud, now forming part of our solar system, was first seen as a comet.

The orbit of this comet is much smaller than that of the August meteors, extending at the aphelion as far as the orbit of Uranus, while the perihelion is nearly as far from the sun as our earth. The comet completes its revolution in about thirty-three years and three months, and encounters the earth's orbit as it is approaching the sun toward the end of September. It is followed by a large group of small meteoric bodies, which form a very broad and long tail, through which the earth passes on the 13th of November. Those particles which come in contact with the earth, or approach so near as to be attracted into its atmosphere, become ignited, and appear as falling stars. As the earth encounters the comet's tail, or meteoric shower, for three successive years at the same place, we must conclude the comet's track to have the enormous length of 1,772 millions of miles. In Fig. 221, C D represents a portion of the orbit of this comet which is identical with the orbit (Fig. 220) of the November meteors.

By the side of these important conclusions, which the observation and acuteness of modern astronomers have been able to make concerning the nature and mutual connection of nebulæ, comets, meteors, and balls of fire, the results of spectrum analysis as applied to meteors will seem to be exceedingly scant. This is easy to understand when we reflect how rapidly these fiery meteors rush through our atmosphere, and how difficult it is to lay hold of them with the spectroscope during their instantaneous apparition. Before the instrument can be directed to a meteor or ball of fire, and the focus adjusted, the object has disappeared from view. The application, therefore, of spectrum analysis to these fleeting visitors is left almost entirely to chance, and is mainly confined to those nights in which yearly, or at certain known periods, an extraordinary shower of falling stars is expected to occur.

In the year 1865, Alexander Herschel drew attention to the expected fall of meteors in the ensuing year, and suggested that they should be observed with the spectroscope, on the ground that some few spectroscopic observations previously made had shown the spectrum of a meteor to be a continuous one, without any dark lines. Browning, a master in the art of constructing spectrum apparatus, undertook the investigation, and observed in the nights of the 9th and 10th of August, as well as during the early morning hours of the 14th of November, at his observatory at Upper Holloway, near London, as many as seventy spectra of meteors and their trains.

The hand-spectroscope of Huggins, described at p. 332, and represented in Fig. 173, as constructed by Browning for the direct observation of the solar appendages during an eclipse, is well adapted for these investigations; but a still better instrument is that drawn in Fig. 222, especially constructed by Brown-

Fig. 222.

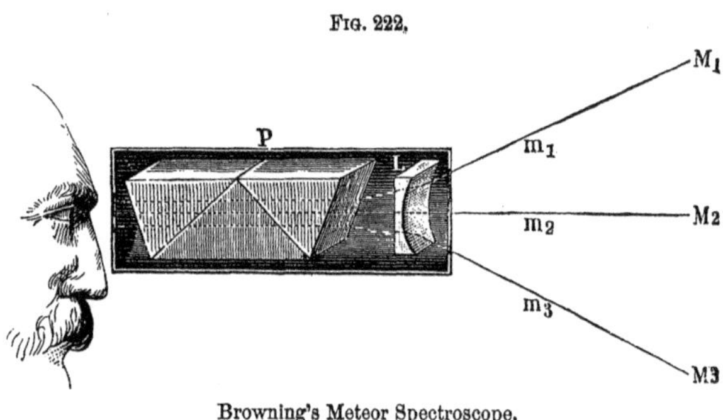

Browning's Meteor Spectroscope.

ing for his own use in the observation of meteors, in which the apparent angle caused by the velocity of the meteor is diminished, and which, on account of the large field of view, greatly facilitates the observation of a falling star.

This instrument consists of a direct-vision compound prism P, and a plano-concave cylindrical lens L. M_1, M_2, M_3 denote three successive places in the flight of a meteor, and m_1, m_2, m_3 show the path of the rays from the meteor to the lens L, while the dotted lines indicate the course taken by the rays in their passage through the refracting media. The ray m_1 reaches the eye viewing it through the prism at the same moment as the ray m_3; the eye, therefore, commands the large space in the heavens included between M_1 and M_3, and can observe accordingly a meteor shooting over that space without the instrument being moved. In such a spectroscope the meteor appears to be stationary, and its spectrum can be observed without difficulty. Browning was able with this instrument to observe the spectra of some fireballs thrown into the air only a few feet from him. Although the angular velocity of such balls was very great, yet the characteristic lines of their component metals, barium, strontium, etc., were very clearly seen. If a bi-concave lens of longer focus than the cylindrical lens be placed immediately in front of L, and turned toward the heavens, rays of a still greater convergence, reaching beyond M_1 and M_3, will be brought within the range of the eye, and the field of view of the instrument considerably increased by this means.

Instead of observing the spectrum with the unassisted eye, a small telescope may be employed, the position and direction of which with regard to the prisms is represented in Fig. 173.

In conducting these investigations, Browning directed the instrument to that point in the heavens whence the meteors proceeded, and thus succeeded in retaining a few of the great number that fell in the field of the spectroscope, and observing the character of their spectra.

The spectra of the heads of the meteors were mostly continuous, in which all the prismatic colors of the solar spectrum were visible excepting violet. In certain instances, however, the yellow preponderated in the spectrum; in others the spectrum consisted almost entirely of one homogeneous yellow hue, though nearly every other color, from red to green, was very faintly visible. In two instances the spectrum presented a homogeneous green tint. No remarkable difference in the light of the nuclei of the August and November meteors was perceptible.

In most of the August meteors only one yellow line of intense brilliancy remained in the spectrum of the tail or track of light left behind, when it began to dissipate—the unmistakable sign of the presence of luminous gas, a line which could only be compared to the line of glowing sodium.

In the November meteors, on the contrary, the spectrum of the train was characterized by continuity and breadth, but by a deficiency of color. The light, which was mostly blue, green, or steel-gray, appeared in general to be homogeneous; but this appearance might arise from the light being too weak to yield a visible spectrum, as in the case of stars below the second and third magnitude, where the red and blue rays are wanting in the spectrum, though doubtless present in the light of the star. The yellow line given by the train of the August meteors was altogether absent in that of the November meteors.

The principal result of these investigations is confined, therefore, to the establishment of the fact that meteors consist of incandescent solid bodies, and that a difference is discernible in the chemical composition of the August and November meteoric showers.

The November shower of 1868 was observed by Secchi. Among the numerous meteors that left a train of light behind them was one the track of which lasted fifteen minutes, and was at first sufficiently bright to allow of examination by a prism. Secchi found the spectrum to be discontinuous, and the principal bright bands and lines were red, yellow, green, and blue. Besides this observation, Secchi was so fortunate as to see two meteors in the spectroscope: the magnesium line appeared with great distinctness, besides which some lines were also seen in the red.

On account of the great difficulty of observing meteors with a narrow setting of the slit, ordinary spectroscopes are not suited to this purpose. The hand-spectroscope described at p. 332, however, cannot show any sharp lines, even when the meteor contains elements which in an ordinary spectroscope would yield bright lines.* The only resource, therefore, is to substitute a cylindrical lens for the slit, and there can be no doubt that an apparatus of this kind will be employed in future with great success in the investigation of meteors by means of spectrum analysis.

* [In the case of meteors which have a small apparent diameter, the bright images appear sufficiently narrow for identification, as is found to be the case when the instrument is directed to distant fireworks.]

70. Spectrum of Lightning.

From the close connection between lightning and the electric spark, it was to be anticipated that a flash of lightning would yield a spectrum closely allied to that of the ordinary electric discharge when passed through the air, and that it would therefore consist of the bright lines belonging to the atmospheric air, and therefore preëminently those of nitrogen. This was, in fact, proved to be the case by Captain Herschel during a storm when the flashes of lightning were very numerous, on which occasion he found, by the use of a hand-spectroscope (Fig. 172), that, among the numberless bright lines visible, the blue nitrogen line was the brightest, while the red line of hydrogen, H α, was also present. Besides this spectrum of lines, there was visible at the same time a bright continuous spectrum exhibiting the principal colors.

The ordinary spectrum of lightning produces the impression of green and blue, or rather of greenish-blue; but, as in bright flashes all the prismatic colors are visible, it must be supposed that the part between the lines E and F is so much brighter than the rest as to cause the impression of those colors to predominate in the spectrum. The variation of relative brightness of the continuous spectrum and of the spectrum of lines is very surprising: at times the lines are scarcely visible; and at other times, with the exception of the lines, there is scarcely any spectrum to be seen.

The difficulty of distinguishing the many fainter lines is considerably increased by the instantaneous character of the phenomenon. Before a certain line has been selected, the faint impression upon the retina has disappeared, and the remembrance of the line half determined upon has passed away before another flash succeeds, so that there remains no standard of comparison.

The most complete observations that have yet been made on the spectra of lightning are those by Prof. Kundt, of Zürich, by whom upward of fifty flashes of lightning have at different times been observed with a pocket-spectroscope. In addition to the spectra consisting of bright lines, there always appeared other spectra formed of a great number of fainter bands, somewhat broader than the lines, and disposed regularly at equal intervals one from another.

The spectra of lines consisted of one and sometimes of two

lines in the extreme red, a few very bright lines in the green, and some less bright in the blue, besides a still greater number much fainter, most of which, however, were sharply defined. The spectra of different flashes were so fàr different, that while certain lines were very brilliant in one flash, they were entirely wanting in another, where they were replaced by a set of lines which were invisible in many other flashes.

The spectra of bands were quite as dissimilar, the colored bands in some flashes appearing in the blue and violet; in others in the green as well, and occasionally only in the red.

In most cases each flash had only one of these spectra. The spectra of lines were usually given by the forked flashes, while sheet-lightning yielded the spectra of bands. In only two cases did the same flash first give a bright spectrum of lines very sharply defined, and then suddenly show a spectrum of bands evenly distributed throughout.

The two kinds of spectra correspond with the different colors in which both descriptions of lightning appear to the unassisted eye: the light of forked lightning is usually white, while that of sheet-lightning is mostly red, but sometimes violet and bluish. This is in conformity with the different colors exhibited by the discharges of electrical machines, according to the form in which they appear, whether as a spark or a brush of light. While the light of a spark discharged into the air is more or less white according to the nature of the bodies between which it passes, the color of the electric brush is red or violet, and that of the electric glow is violet or bluish. The light of the electric spark always gives a spectrum of lines, while that of the brush or glow discharge exhibits a spectrum of bands.

The investigations of Kundt lead to the conclusion that the difference in the spectra of lightning depends upon the mode in which the electricity of the atmosphere is discharged, whether through the earth or between the clouds. When an electric cloud discharges itself into the earth, the discharge occurs at a state of high tension, and, accompanied by a great development of heat, darts to the ground in the form of a forked flash, passing on its way through the atmospheric air, that is to say, through a gaseous mixture of oxygen, nitrogen, watery vapor, and carbonic acid. According as one or other or several together of these gases are raised by the flash to a glowing state, the spectrum of the lightning assumes a different form. When, on the contrary, the discharge takes place from one cloud into another, it occurs usually in the form of a brush, because in consequence of the previous electrical attraction both clouds have received pointed and indented forms, and in such circumstances a high degree of tension is rarely attained, and the current frequently passes as a rapid succession of discharges which take the form of a brush of light. The various kinds of electrical discharges are accompanied by a corresponding variety in the report; if in the form of a spark, it is well known that a single sharp crack is heard; the brush discharge is never accompanied by a single clap, but always by a hissing or rushing noise, with a series of faint cracks in rapid succession: the glow-discharge is perfectly noiseless.

All these phenomena lead to a simple explanation of the various kinds of lightning, whether in the form of forked flashes, sheet-lightning, or summer-lightning, as well as of the sounds by which they are accompanied, of the simple clap and the peal of thunder; but the few observations yet made upon the spectra of lightning suggest a number of questions which can only be answered by a series of additional observations.

71. Spectrum of the Aurora Borealis.

The splendid phenomena exhibited by a brilliant display of the Aurora Borealis are always accompanied by a greater or less disturbance of the magnetic needle, so that the Aurora has long been supposed to be occasioned by the noiseless passage of electricity through the rarefied portions of the upper regions of the atmosphere—a kind of glow-discharge or electric display, such as is exhibited by discharging a quantity of electricity through a Geissler's tube filled with highly-rarefied air.

Ångström's spectrum observations of this object do not seem to confirm this conjecture, for the luminous arch skirting the dark segment, and never absent in a faint show of Aurora, gives a spectrum of one bright line situated to the left of the well-known calcium group of the solar spectrum. Besides this comparatively very intense line, Ångström observed, with a wider slit, traces of three very faint bands reaching nearly to the Fraunhofer F-line, but only once did faint lines appear in this region during the undulations of a very flickering arch. The light of the Aurora Borealis is therefore almost homogeneous (monochromatic). A special interest attaches to these observations, made in the winter of 1867–'68, from the circumstance that the zodiacal light gave the same line as observed by Ångström for a week together, in March, 1867, at Upsala, where it was seen with remarkable intensity for that latitude, and in one brilliant starlight night, when the whole heavens appeared to be phosphorescent, traces of this homogeneous light were visible in the spectroscope, from the faint light proceeding from all parts of the sky.

The bright line mentioned above, the place of which has been determined by Struve to be No. 1259 of Kirchhoff's scale (between D and E), with a probable error of ten or fifteen units, corresponds, according to Ångström, to a wave-length of 0.0005567 of a millimetre, and is not coincident with any known line of a terrestrial element. This line is introduced into Ångström's spectrum of the telluric lines, Fig. 95, as a dotted line between δ and E at 556. (*Vide* Plate VI.)

The display of the Aurora Borealis on the 15th of April, 1869, visible in Western Europe, Russia, and America, and which at New York exhibited an appearance of extraordinary beauty, was observed there by Prof. Winlock with the spectroscope. In opposition to the observations made in Europe, he found the spectrum to consist of five bright lines, the positions of which he has determined, according to Huggins's scale, to be 1280, 1400, 1550, 1680, and 2640. The divisions of Kirchhoff's scale 1247, 1351, and 1473, correspond to the first three numbers, consequently Winlock's spectrum of the Aurora approaches very closely the representation given in Plate IX., No. 3, where it stands in connection with the spectrum of the corona No. 2, and that of the prominences No. 1, as observed by Young in the total eclipse of the 7th of August, 1869. Of these lines the third (1474 K.) is the brighest. The spectrum of the Aurora has been repeatedly observed in America by D. K. Winder. A bright line in the yellow was nearly always seen by him close to D, but less refrangible, and was coincident with one of the dark lines in the telluric group which appears in the solar spectrum when the sun is near the horizon; beside this line, there was a fainter one in the green, and on one occasion a line appeared also in the red.

The Aurora Borealis was observed by Rayet and Sorel on the 15th and 16th of April, 1869, when the spectrum showed very clearly the characteristic auroral line (wave-length, 5567 ten millionth of a millimetre—Ångström), as well as the atmospheric lines.

The Aurora of the 6th of October, 1869, was examined by Flögel with the spectroscope. On this occasion also the light appeared to be homogeneous, though with a moderate opening of the slit the spectrum showed only the yellow characteristic line, the position of which was estimated at about 1230 (K.). When the slit was opened as much as 1.3 millimetre, a faint green light made its appearance, which was roughly estimated to extend as far as the F-line. This light could not be concentrated into a line of light by any contraction of the slit. No such faint light was perceptible in the direction of the red, a fact which precludes the possibility of this light being occasioned by some stellar light finding its way into the spectroscope through the slit.*

On the 5th of April, 1870, a display of the Aurora was examined by A. Schmidt, at Lennep (Rhenish Provinces). The spectrum here, again, consisted of one remarkably bright and broad line, somewhat to the right of D toward E, which varied in intensity, at times appearing very faint, and immediately afterward shining out with great brilliancy. From the neighborhood of this line to F, there stretched a continuous band, which became resolved frequently into three lines, bright, though fainter than the first line.

A magnificent exhibition of the Aurora Borealis was visible on the 24th and 25th of October, 1870, over the greater part of Europe, which for beauty and extent has hardly ever been exceeded in this portion of the globe. On the 24th of October it extended over the northern and western portions of the sky, and

* [The spectrum of the Aurora was observed by Mr. Ellery, of Melbourne, on April 5, 1870. "The red streamers," he writes, "were gorgeous, and emitted light enough to read a newspaper by. The most remarkable and brightest of the lines in the spectrum was a red line more refrangible than C; a greenish band or two in the position of the green calcium lines, and a cloudy band, more refrangible, appeared as if irresolvable into lines. The dark segment rested on the sea-horizon. Above this was an arch of greenish auroral light, and from a well-defined boundary of this the rose-colored streamers started zenithward. The red line disappeared immediately the spectroscope was directed to any point below this boundary, and only the green lines remained. The loss and reappearance of the red line was as sharp as possible as the slit passed from the red to the green region."]

covered more than a fourth of the whole horizon. Upon the luminous red background there appeared three deep-red streamers very sharply defined, to which the cloudless heavens and the brilliancy of the stars upon the red sky gave an additional splendor.

On the 25th of October the phenomenon offered the rare spectacle of an *auroral crown.* A number of flaming streamers of the Aurora, which shot out on all sides, were united at a point in the heavens a little to the south of the zenith. On that evening all the large streamers, most of which were of a crimson hue, crossed by white rays, converged toward that central point which preserved unchanged its position with regard to the horizon.*

Prof. Förster, of Berlin, found that the spectrum of the Aurora of the 25th of October consisted only of the same narrow greenish-yellow band of light the position of which has been already determined, and which is not coincident with any of the lines of known elements. In those portions, however, of the sky which to the eye seemed unilluminated, the spectroscope revealed very clearly the characteristic line of the Aurora. Dr. Tietjen states that some weeks previously, in the same observatory, upon evenings when no trace of Aurora was visible, the spectroscope showed the same line in several places in the sky.

On the same evening, Capron at Guilford observed in the spectrum of the Aurora a very bright line in the green, which was distinctly visible in all parts of the sky, but which appeared with remarkable brilliancy in the silver-white rays of the Aurora. Besides this line, there was also a much fainter line in the red, which is the lithium line.

An observer at St. Mary Church, Torquay, describes the spectrum as consisting of four lines in the red and one line in the green ; of these a strongly-marked red line was near C, a strongly-marked pale-yellow line near D, a paler one near F, and a still fainter one beyond; there was also a faint continuous spectrum that extended from D to beyond F. The line near C was the brightest of all the lines; in position and color it lay between the red lines of lithium and calcium. The observer is of opinion that two spectra were here superposed, one produced by the red rays, consisting of the four lines and the faint continuous spec-

* This point, as observed at Maidenhead, was situated to the south of υ Cygni, by one-third of the distance between that star and α Cygni.—(Translators' Note.

trum, the other given by the remaining light, showing the greenish line near D.

Gibbs, observing in London on the same evening, saw only a line in the red very similar to the C line (H *a*), and another line in the pale-green part of the spectrum.

Elger, in Bedford, also observed a red band near C, a very bright white band near D, apparently the characteristic line of the Aurora mentioned before as being visible on the 25th of October in every portion of the sky, a faint and ill-defined line near F, as well as an exceedingly faint line about midway between these last two lines. The red band was absent from the spectrum of the white rays of the Aurora, whereas the remaining three lines were always visible. These observations establish the supposition that the different rays of the Aurora Borealis produce different spectra.

On the same evening the Aurora was observed by Zöllner at Leipsic with one of Browning's miniature spectroscopes (Figs. 49 and 172), when he obtained the spectrum represented in Fig. 223. In order to collect sufficient light, the slit was opened tolerably wide; and, for the purpose of securing an approximate estimate

Fig. 223.

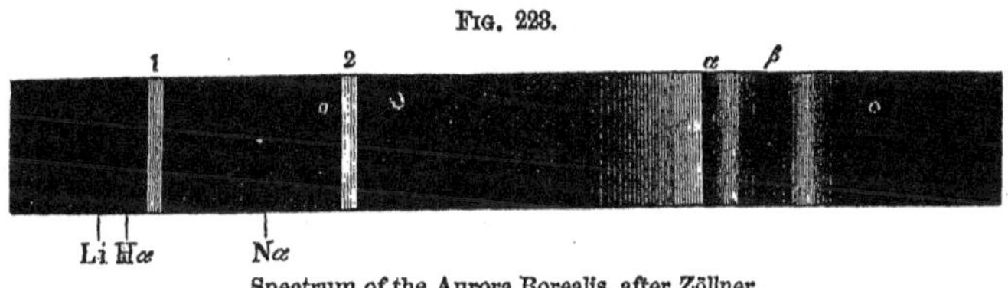

Spectrum of the Aurora Borealis, after Zöllner.

of the position of the lines of the Aurora, those of lithium and sodium were produced simultaneously by means of a spirit lamp. The line (2) in the green part of the spectrum is in all probability the characteristic auroral line (1474 K.); the red line (1) in this case also was only well seen when the instrument was directed to those parts of the sky which appeared to be deep red, while the green line (2) was brilliant in every part of the Aurora. In the blue parts of the spectrum the faint bands *a*, *β* were only occasionally seen, of which the most striking was the broad dark band *β* as it appeared against a bright background.

The English observers speak of some remarkably faint, ill-defined *bright* bands near F and a little beyond it, as well as of a continuous spectrum between D and F; Zöllner, on the contrary, regards these ill-defined bands in the blue as the remains of the continuous spectrum which has been broken up by the *dark* absorption bands α, β.

It was not till after the disappearance of the Aurora that Zöllner was able to observe in *the same* spectroscope the spectra of hydrogen, nitrogen, oxygen, and carbonic acid in Geissler's tubes; nevertheless this observer was convinced, in consequence of the simultaneous observation of the spectrum of sodium and that of lithium, that the red line of the Aurora (1) was not coincident with the brightest parts in the spectra of any of these four gases. It is more refrangible than the red hydrogen line H α, which is acknowledged also by the English observers, and may possibly, according to Zöllner, lie near the position of the group of dark telluric lines α (Ångström, Fig. 95, Plate VI.), situated between C and D in the solar spectrum, the mean wave-length of which is 0.0006279 of a millimetre.

Since the chief lines in the spectrum of the Aurora Borealis are not found to be coincident with those of any of the spectra hitherto observed of terrestrial elements, Zöllner concludes that, if the light developed by the Aurora be chiefly of an *electric* character analogous to the gases made luminous in a vacuum-tube, it must belong to a temperature lower than that at which it is possible to observe the spectra of gases rendered luminous in a Geissler's tube. *The spectrum of the Aurora Borealis is not therefore coincident with any of the known spectra of gases of our atmosphere, because it is a spectrum of an order that has not yet been artificially produced.*

For a further explanation of the mysterious phenomenon of the Aurora Borealis, more complete measurements of the position of the various lines of its spectrum are necessary, made at various distances from the North Pole, especially within the polar circle; while, on the other hand, physicists will feel impelled to test by suitable experiments the ingenious and well-grounded theory of Zöllner, and compare the results of their investigations with the spectroscopic observations of the Aurora Borealis.

APPENDIX A.

ON THE CAUSE OF THE INTERRUPTED SPECTRA OF GASES.

BY G. JOHNSTONE STONEY, M. A., F. R. S.*

In the *Philosophical Magazine* for August, 1868, there is a paper "On the Internal Motions of Gases," † by the author of the following communication, in which a comparison is instituted between these motions and the phenomena of light, from which the conclusion is drawn that the lines in the spectra of gases are to be referred to periodic motions within the individual molecules, and not to the irregular journeys of the molecules among one another.

Mr. Stoney thinks it possible now to advance another step in this inquiry, and has given to the Royal Irish Academy an account of which the following is an abstract, of the grounds upon which he founds this hope:

A *pendulous* vibration, according to the meaning which has been given to that phrase by Helmholtz, is such a vibration as is executed by the simple cycloidal pendulum. It is, accordingly, one in which the relation between the displacement of each particle and the time is represented by the simple curve of sines, of which the equation is—

$$y = C_0 + C_1 \sin (x + a),$$

where $y - C_0$ is the displacement of the particle from its central position; C_1 is the amplitude of the vibration; x stands for $2\pi \frac{t}{\tau}$, where t is the time from a fixed epoch, and τ the period of a complete double vibration; and a

* From the Proceedings of the Royal Irish Academy, read January 9, 1871.

† In reading that paper, the reader is requested to correct 16^2 into $\sqrt{16}$ at the end of paragraph 2.

is a constant depending on the phase of the vibration at the instant which is taken as the epoch from which t is measured.

Now, we may not assume that the waves impressed on the ether by one of the periodic motions within a molecule of a gas are of this simple character. We must expect them to be usually much more involved. And, whatever may happen to be the intricacy of their form near to their origin, they will retain substantially the same complex character so long as they advance through the open undispersing ether, in which waves of all lengths travel at the same rate. But it would seem that a very different state of things must arise when the undulation enters a dispersing medium, such as glass.

Let us suppose that the undulation * before it enters the glass consists of plane-waves. Then, whatever the form of these waves, the relation between the displacement of an element of the ether and the time may be represented by some curve repeated over and over again. This curve may be either one continuous curve, or parts of several different curves joined on to one another. In the latter case (which includes the other) one of the sections of the curve may be represented by the equations—

$$\left.\begin{array}{l} y = \phi_0(x) \text{ from } x = 0 \text{ to } x = x_1, \\ y = \phi_1(x) \text{ from } x = x_1 \text{ to } x = x_2, \\ \text{and so on to} \\ y = \phi_1(x) \text{ from } x = x \text{ to } x = 2\pi, \end{array}\right\} \quad . \quad . \quad . \quad . \quad . \quad . \quad (1)$$

y being the displacement, and x being an abbreviation for $2\pi\frac{t}{\tau}$, where τ is the complete periodic time of one wave.

The undulation *in vacuo* will then be represented, according to Fourier's well-known theorem, by the following series:

$$\left.\begin{array}{l} y = A_0 + A_1 \cos x + A_2 \cos 2x + \dots \\ \qquad + B_1 \sin x + B_2 \sin 2x + \dots \end{array}\right\} \quad . \quad . \quad . \quad . \quad (2)$$

where the coefficients are obtained from equations (1) by the definite integrals

$$\left.\begin{array}{l} \int_0^{2\pi} y \cos nx, \, dx = \pi A_n, \\ \int_0^{2\pi} y \sin nx, \, dx = \pi B_n. \end{array}\right\} \quad . \quad . \quad . \quad . \quad (3)$$

Equation (2), the equation of the undulation before it enters the glass, may be put into the more convenient form—

$$y - A_0 = C_1 \sin(x + \alpha_1) + C_2 \sin(2x + \alpha_2) + \quad . \quad . \quad . \quad (4)$$

where $y - A_0$ is the displacement from the position of rest, and the new constants are related to those of equation (2) as follows:

$$C_n = \sqrt{A_n + B_n}, \qquad \alpha_n = \tan^{-1} \frac{A_n}{B_n} \quad . \quad . \quad . \quad . \quad . \quad . \quad (5)$$

---

* By the term *undulation* is to be understood a series of waves.

The first term of expansion (4) represents a pendulous vibration of the full period τ; the remaining terms represent harmonics of this vibration; i. e., their periodic times are $\frac{1}{2}\tau$, $\frac{1}{3}\tau$, etc. All of these also are pendulous; so that equation (4) is equivalent to the statement that, whatever be the form of the plane undulation before entering the glass, it may be regarded as formed by the superposition of a number of simple pendulous vibrations, one of which has the full periodic time τ, while the others are harmonics of this vibration.

Moreover, these vibrations will coexist in a state of mechanical independence of one another, if the disturbance be not too violent for the legitimate employment of the principle of the superposition of small motions. So long as the light traverses undispersing space, these constituent vibrations will strictly accompany one another, since in open space waves of all periods travel at the same velocity. The general resulting undulation will therefore here retain whatever complicated form it may have had at first. But when the undulation enters such a medium as glass, in which waves of different periods travel at different rates, the constituent vibrations are no longer able to keep together, each being forced to advance through the glass at a speed depending on its periodic time. Thus there arises a physical resolution within the glass of series (4) into its constituent terms.* And if the glass be in the form of a prism, the pendulous undulations corresponding to the successive terms of series (4) will emerge in different directions, so that each will give rise to a separate line in the spectrum of the gas.

We thus find that one periodic motion in the molecules of the incandescent gas may be the source of a whole series of lines in the spectrum of the gas. The nth of these lines is represented by the term

$$C_n \sin (nx + \alpha_n),$$

in which C_n is the amplitude of the vibration; and consequently C_n represents the brightness of the line. If some of the coefficients of series (4) vanish, the corresponding lines are absent from the spectrum. This is analogous to the familiar case of the suppression of some of the harmonics in music, and

---

* Other expansions similar to Fourier's series can be conceived, in which the terms, instead of representing pendulous vibrations, would represent vibrations of any other prescribed form; and hence a doubt may arise whether the physical resolution effected by the prism is into the terms of the simpler series. That it is so may, perhaps, not be susceptible of demonstration; but the following considerations seem to show it to be probable in so high a degree that it is the hypothesis which we ought provisionally to accept. For, first, the form of the emerging vibrations is independent of the material of the prism, since the lines correspond to the same wave-lengths as seen in all prisms; and, secondly, it is independent of the amplitude of the vibration within very wide limits, since the positions of the lines remain fixed through great ranges of temperature, and in many cases, when the temperature falls so low that the lines fade out through excessive faintness. The first consideration shows the series to be the same under varying circumstances; and the second consideration suggests, as in the theory of the superposition of small motions, that this series is a series of *pendulous* vibrations.

appears to be what usually occurs in those spectra which are called by Plücker spectra of the Second Order.

In spectra of this kind the lines which fall within the limits of the visible spectrum appear at first sight to be scattered at irregular intervals. This may arise, and probably does in most cases arise in part, from the circumstance that there may be several distinct motions in each molecule of the gas, each of which produces its own series of harmonics in the spectrum, which by their being presented together to the eye give the appearance of a confused maze of lines. But it appears also to arise in part from the absence of most of the harmonics, so that it is not easy to trace the relationship between the few that remain. To do so without the assistance of spectra of the First Order, requires that we should have at our disposal determinations of the wave-lengths of the lines made with extraordinary accuracy; and perhaps in a few cases, as, for example, in the case of hydrogen, the marvellous determinations which have been made by Ångström may have the requisite precision.

The ordinary spectrum of hydrogen consists of four lines, corresponding to C in the solar spectrum, F, a line near G, and h. To these it is possible that we ought to add a conspicuous line in the solar prominences which lies near D, but which has not yet been found in the artificial spectrum of hydrogen. Of these lines, three, viz., C, F, and h, are to be referred to the same motion in the molecules of the gas.

In fact, the wave-lengths of these lines, as determined by Ångström,* are:

$$h = 4101.2 \text{ tenth-metres.}$$
$$F = 4860.74 \quad ''$$
$$C = 6562.10 \quad ''$$

These are their wave-lengths in air of standard pressure and 14° temperature, determined with extraordinary precision. We must correct these for the dispersion of the air, so as to arrive at the wave-lengths *in vacuo* which are proportionate to the periodic times. Now, by interpolating between Ketteler's observations † on the dispersion of air, we find—

$$\mu_h = 1.000\ 29952,$$
$$\mu_F = 1.000\ 29685,$$
$$\mu_C = 1.000\ 29383,$$

for the refractive indices of air of standard pressure and temperature for the rays h, F, and C. From these we deduce that if the air be at 14° of temperature, the refractive indices will become

$$\mu_h = 1.000\ 2845,$$
$$\mu_F = 1.000\ 2820,$$
$$\mu_C = 1.000\ 2791.$$

---

* Ångström's "*Recherches sur le Spectre Solaire,*" p. 31. A tenth-metre means a metre divided by 10^{10}; similarly a fourteenth-second is a second of time divided by 10^{14}.

† Phil. Mag., 1866, vol. xxxii., p. 345.

Multiplying the foregoing wave-lengths by these values, we find for the wave-lengths *in vacuo*—

$$h = 4102.37 \text{ tenth-metres,}$$
$$F = 4862.11 \quad ``$$
$$C = 6563.93 \quad ``$$

which are the 33d, 27th, and 20th harmonics of a fundamental vibration whose wave-length *in vacuo* is

0.13127714 of a millimetre,

as appears from the following Table:

Observed wave-lengths reduced to wave-lengths *in vacuo*.	Calculated values.	Differences.
Tenth-metres.	Tenth-metres.	Tenth-metres.
$h = 4102.37$	$\frac{1}{32} \times 131277.14 = 4102.41$	$+0.04$
$F = 4862.11$	$\frac{1}{27} \times 131277.14 = 4862.12$	$+0.01$
$C = 6563.93$	$\frac{1}{20} \times 131277.14 = 6563.86$	-0.07

Thus the outstanding differences are all fractions of an eleventh-metre, an eleventh-metre being the limit within which Ångström thinks that his measures may be depended on.

The wave-length 0.13127714 of a millimetre corresponds to the periodic time 4.4 fourteenth-seconds, if we assume the velocity of light to be 298,000,000 metres per second.

Hence we may conclude, with a good deal of confidence, that 4.4 fourteenth-seconds is very nearly the periodic time of one of the motions within the molecules of hydrogen.

The other harmonics of this fundamental motion in the molecules of hydrogen—viz., the 19th, 21st, 22d, etc., harmonics—are not found in this spectrum of hydrogen. But two other spectra of hydrogen are known to exist in which there are a great number of lines; and possibly the missing harmonics will be found among them when their positions shall have been sufficiently accurately mapped down. A far more moderate degree of accuracy will suffice in this case than was required by the foregoing investigation.

But it is from the examination of spectra of the First Order that the most copious results may be expected. These spectra consist of lines ruled close to one another, and presenting in the aggregate the appearance of patterns which often resemble the flutings on a pillar. When these spectra are more carefully examined, it is probable that the whole series of lines occasioning one of the fluted patterns will be found to be the successive harmonics of a single motion in the molecules of the gas. It may readily be shown that such patterns as are met with in nature may in this way arise. For this purpose it is only necessary to make some suitable hypothesis as to the original undulation impressed by the gas upon the ether. Thus, if the law of this undulation were the same as that of the motion of a point near the end of a violin-string, and of a periodic time sufficiently long (as, for example, two million-millionths of a second), this undulation, when analyzed by the prism, would give a spectrum covered with lines ruled at intervals about the same as that between the two D-lines, and of intensities varying so as to become gradually brighter and then gradually fainter several times in succession in passing from line to line along the spectrum. These alternations would give a fluted appearance to the spectrum; and, from appropriate hypotheses as to the original vibration, all the patterns met with in nature would result. Possibly it may prove to be practicable to trace back from the appearances presented within the limits of the visible spectrum to the character of the original motion to which they are all to be referred. But, however this may be, it will be easy in a spectrum of this kind, in which we have a long series of consecutive harmonics, to determine at least the *period* of this motion; and it is in the examination of these spectra that the most easily-obtained results may be expected. But the necessary observations are at present almost altogether wanting. The only case in which the author had been able to arrive at any result was that of the nitrogen spectrum of the First Order, observed by Plücker. It would appear from his observations* that the more refrangible of the two fluted patterns observed by him is due to a motion in the gas having a wave-length of about 0.89376 of a millimetre, which corresponds to a periodic time of three twelfth-seconds, one of the flutings consisting of the thirty-five harmonics from about the 1960th to the 1995th.

This result, however, does not command the confidence which the preceding determination of one of the periodic times in hydrogen does; but it will suffice to show the character of the much easier investigation which has to be made in the case of gases which produce spectra of the First Order.

NOTE.—Since the foregoing communication was made to the Royal Irish Academy, Mr. Stoney and Mr. J. Emerson Reynolds, of Dublin, have published an account of a detailed examination of the absorption spectrum of the vapor of chlorochromic anhydride at atmospheric temperatures. (*See Phil. Mag.* for July, 1871.) This vapor, which is of a brown color, absorbs very little of the red, while it entirely obliterates the other end of the spectrum, shutting out the blue, indigo, and violet; and in the interval between these two regions, extending over the orange, yellow, and green, there are about 120 or 130 lines. The positions of 31 of these, distributed irregularly over nearly the whole of this range, were measured. In doing this, those lines were selected of which the positions could be determined accurately with the most ease, and in every one of these cases the position of the line was found to be that which Mr. Stoney's theory assigns to it.

According to the theory, the whole series of lines is due to a single motion in the molecules of the vapor. And the periodic time of this motion as given by the observations is $\frac{\tau}{2.70}$, where τ is the time which light takes to advance one millimetre. The authors are of opinion that this determination cannot be in error by more than one five-hundredth part of its amount, and it indicates, if the theory can be depended on, that the fundamental motion is executed rather more than eight hundred thousand millions of times in each molecule of the vapor every second of time.

In order to complete this picture, we should bear in mind that, according to the

* Philosophical Transactions for 1865, p. 7, § 16.

most recent estimates of physicists, the number of molecules in each cubic millimetre of the vapor is about a million times a million of millions.

Messrs. Stoney and Reynolds have also attempted to extract some information about the *character* of the motion, from the succession of intensities of the lines in the spectrum; and they arrive at the conclusion that it bears a curious relation to the motion of a certain point upon a violin-string while the bow is being drawn, viz., a point that lies at a distance of nearly but not quite two-fifths of the length of the string from one end.

APPENDIX B.

PRELIMINARY CATALOGUE OF THE BRIGHT LINES IN THE SPECTRUM OF THE CHROMOSPHERE.

BY C. A. YOUNG, PH. D., PROFESSOR OF ASTRONOMY IN DARTMOUTH COLLEGE.

(*Added by the Translators from the Philosophical Magazine for November*, 1871.)

THE following list contains the bright lines which have been observed by the writer in the spectrum of the chromosphere within the past four weeks. It includes, however, only those which have been seen twice at least; a number observed on one occasion (September 7th) still await verification.

The spectroscope employed is the same described in the *Journal of the Franklin Institute* for November, 1870; but certain important modifications have since been effected in the instrument. The telescope and collimator have each a focal length of nearly 10 inches, and an aperture of $\frac{7}{8}$ of an inch. The prism-train consists of five prisms (with refracting angles of 55°) and two half-prisms. The light is sent twice through the whole series by means of a prism of total reflection at the end of the train, so that the dispersive power is that of twelve prisms. The instrument distinctly divides the strong iron line at 1961 of Kirchhoff's scale, and separates B (not *b*) into its three components. Of course it easily shows every thing that appears on the spectrum-maps of Kirchhoff and Ångström. The adjustment for "the position of minimum deviation" is automatic; i.e., the different portions of the spectrum are brought to the centre of the field of view by a movement which at the same time also adjusts the prisms.

The telescope to which the spectroscope is attached is the new equatorial recently mounted in the observatory of the college by Alvan Clark & Sons. It is a very perfect specimen of the admirable optical workmanship of this celebrated firm, and has an aperture of $9\frac{4}{10}$ inches, with a focal length of 12 feet.

In the table, the first column contains simply the reference number. An asterisk denotes that the line affected by it has no well-marked corresponding dark line in the ordinary solar spectrum.

The second column gives the position of the line upon the scale of Kirchhoff's map, determined by direct comparison with the map at the time of observation. In some cases an interrogation-mark is appended, which signifies not that the *existence* of the line is doubtful, but only that its precise place could not be determined, either because it fell in a shading of fine lines, or because it could not be decided, in the case of some close double lines, which of the two components was the bright one, or, finally, because there were no well-marked dark lines near enough to furnish the basis of reference for a perfectly accurate determination.

The third column gives the position of the line upon Ångström's normal atlas of the solar spectrum. In this column an occasional interrogation-mark denotes that there is some doubt as to the precise point of Ångström's scale corresponding to Kirchhoff's. There is considerable difference between the two maps, owing to the omission of many faint lines by Ångström, and the want of the fine gradations of shading observed by Kirchhoff, which renders the coördination of the two scales sometimes difficult, and makes the atlas of Kirchhoff far superior to the other for use in the observatory.

The numbers in the fourth column are intended to denote the percentage of frequency with which the corresponding lines are visible in my instrument. They are to be regarded as only roughly approximative; it would, of course, require a much longer period of observation to furnish results of this kind worthy of much confidence.

In the fifth column the numbers denote the relative brilliance of the lines on a scale where 100 is the brightest and 1 the faintest. These numbers also, like those in the preceding column, are entitled to very little weight.

The sixth column contains the symbols of the chemical substances to which, according to the maps above referred to, the lines owe their origin.

There are no disagreements between the two authorities; in the majority of cases, however, Ångström alone indicates the element; and there are several instances where the lines of more than one substance coincide with each other and with a line of the solar spectrum so closely as to make it impossible to decide between them.

In the seventh and last column the letters J., L., and R., denote that, to my knowledge, the line indicated has been observed, and its place published by Janssen, Lockyer, or Rayet. It is altogether probable that a large portion of the other lines contained in the catalogue have before this been seen and located by one or the other of these keen and active observers; but, if so, I have as yet seen no account of such determinations.

I would call especial attention to the lines numbered 1 and 82 in the catalogue; they are very persistently present, though faint, and can be distinctly seen in the spectroscope to belong to the chromosphere as such, not being due, like most of the other lines, to the exceptional elevation of matter to heights where it does not properly belong. It would seem very probable that both these lines are due to the same substance which causes the D^3 line.

I do not know that the presence of titanium-vapor in the prominences and chromosphere has before been ascertained. It comes out very clearly from the catalogue, as no less than 20 of the whole 103 lines are due to this metal.

HANOVER, N. H., *September* 13, 1871.

PRELIMINARY CATALOGUE OF CHROMOSPHERIC LINES.

Reference Number.	Kirchhoff.	Ångström.	Relative Frequency.	Relative Brightness.	Chemical Elements.	Previous Observer.
1	534.5	7060.0 ?	60	3		
2	654.5	6677.0 ?	8	4	....	L.
3	C	6561.8	100	100	H	L. J.
4	719.0	6495.7	2	2	Ba	
5	734.0	6454.5	2	3		
6	743.?	6431.0	2	2		
7	768.?	6370.0	2	2		
8	816.8	6260.3	1	1	Ti	
9	820.0	6253.2	1	2	Fe	
10	874.2	6140.5	6	8	Ba	L.
11	D_1	5894.8	10	10	Na	L.
12	D_2	5889.0	10	10	Na	L.
*13	1017.0	5871.0	100	75	....	L. J.
14	1274.3	5534.0	6	8	Ba	R. L.
15	1281.5	5526.0	1	1	Fe	
16	1343.5	5454.5	1	2	Fe	
17	1351.3	5445.9	1	2	Fe, Ti.	
18	1363.1	5433.0	1	1	Fe	
*19	1366.0	5430.0	2	3		
20	1372.0	5424.5	3	4	Ba	L.
21	1378.5 ?	5418.0 ?	1	2	Ti ?	
*22	1382.5	5412.0	1	1		
23	1391.2	5403.0	2	2	Fe, Ti	
24	1397.8	5396.2	1	2	Fe	
25	1421.5	5370.4	1	2	Fe	R.
26	1431.3	5360.6	2	2	....	R.
27	1454.7	5332.0	2	2	Ti	
28 }	1462.9	5327.7	1	3	Fe	
29 }	1463.4	5327.2	1	3	Fe	
30	1465.0 ?	5321.0	2	2		
31	{ Corona line 1474.1 }	5315.9	75	15	Fe ?	L.
32	1505.5	5283.0	5	4		
33	1515.5	5275.0	7	5	....	L. R.
34	{ E_1	5269.5	1	3	Fe, Ca	
35	} E_2	5268.5	1	2	Fe	
36	1528.0	5265.5	3	2	Fe, Co	L.
37	1561.0	5239.0	1	1	Fe	
38	1564.1	5236.2	1	1	....	
39	1567.7	5233.5	2	2	Mn	R.
40	1569.7	5232.0	1	2	Fe	
41	1577.3	5226.0	1	2	Fe	
42	1580.5 ?	5224.5	1	1	Ti ?	
43	1601.5	5207.3	3	3	Cr, Fe ?	
44	1604.4	5205.3	3	3	Cr	
45	1606.5	5203.7	3	3	Cr, Fe ?	
46	1609.3	5201.6	1	2	Fe	
47	1611.5	5199.5	1	1		
48	1615.6	5197.0	3	2	....	L. R.
49	{ *b*	5183.0	15	15	Mg	L.
50	{ *b*	5172.0	15	15	Mg	L.
51	{ *b*	5168.5	12	10	Ni	L.
52	{ *b*	5166.5	10	10	Mg	L.

PRELIMINARY CATALOGUE OF CHROMOSPHERIC LINES—*Continued.*

Reference Number.	Kirchhoff.	Angström.	Relative Frequency.	Relative Brightness.	Chemical Elements.	Previous Observer.
53	1673.9	5153.2	1	1	Na	
54	1678.0	5150.1	1	2	Fe	
55	1778.5	5077.8	1	1	Fe	
56	1866.8	5017.5	2	3	....	R.
57	1870.3	5015.0 ?	2	2	....	R.
58	1989.5	4933.4	8	5	Ba	L.
59	2001.5	4923.2	5	3	Fe	R. L.
60	2003.2	4921.3	1	1		
61	2007.1	4918.1	3	3	....	L.
62	2031.0	4899.3	6	4	Ba	L.
63	2051.5	4882.5	2	2	....	L.
64	F.	4860.6	100	75	H	J. L.
65	2358.5	4629.0	1	1	Ti	
66	2419.3	4583.5	1	1		
67	2435.5	4571.4	1	1	Li	
68	2444.0	4564.6	1	1		
69	2446.6	4563.1	1	2	Ti	
70	2457.8	4555.0	1	1	Ti	
71	2461.2	4553.3	3	3	Ba	
72	2467.7	4548.7	1	3	Ti	
73	2486.8	4535.2	1	1	Ti, Ca ?	
74	2489.5	4533.2	1	1	Fe	
75	2490.6	4531.7	1	1	Ti	
76	2502.5	4524.2	2	2	Ba	
77	2505.8	4522.1	1	2	Ti	
78	2537.3	4500.4	1	3	Ti	
79	2553.0 ?	4491.0 ?	1	1	Mn ?	
80	2555.0 ?	4489.5 ?	1	1	Mn ?	
81	2566.5	4480.4	1	2	Mg	L.
82	2581.5 ?	4471.4	75	8	A band rather than a line.	
83	2585.5	4468.6	1	1	Ti	
84	2625.0	4443.0	1	1	Ti	
85	2670.0	4414.6	1	1	Fe, Mn	
86	2686.7	4404.3	1	2	Fe	
87	2705.0	4393.5	3	2	Ti	
88	2719.0 ?	4384.8	1	1	Ca ?	
89	2721.2	4382.7	1	2	Fe	
90	2734.0 ?	4372.0	1	1		
91	2737.0 ?	4369.3 ?	1	1	Cr ?	
92	2775.8	4352.0	1	1	Fe, Cr	
93	2796.0	4340.0	100	50	H	L. J.
94	G.	4307.0	1	2	Fe, Ti, Ca	
95	2770.0	4300.0	1	1	Ti	
96		4297.5	1	1	Ti, Ca	
97		4289.0	1	2	Cr	
98		4274.5	1	2	Cr	
99		4260.0	1	1	Fe	
100		4245.2	1	1	Fe	
101		4226.5	1	1	Ca	
102		4215.5	1	2	Fe, Ca	
103	*h*	4101.2	100	20	H	R. L.

LIST OF WORKS ON SPECTRUM ANALYSIS.

I.

LECTURES OR MEMOIRS RELATING TO THE SUBJECT OF SPECTRUM ANALYSIS GENERALLY.

BREWSTER, SIR D.: Data toward a History of Spectrum Analysis. Compt. Rend., lxii., 17.

DELAUNAY, M. CH.: Notice sur la Constitution de l'Univers. Première Partie: Analyse Spectrale. Annuaire (1869) publié par le Bureau des Longitudes. Paris, Gauthier-Villars.

DIBBITS, H. C.: De Spectraal-Analyse. Academisch Proefschrift. Rotterdam, Tasselmeyer, 1863.

GRANDEAU, L.: Instruction pratique sur l'Analyse Spectrale. Paris, Mallet-Bachelier, 1863.

HERSCHEL, ALEX. S.: On the Methods and Recent Progress of Spectrum Analysis. Chem. News, xix., 157.

HOPPE-SEYLER: Die Spectralanalyse. Ein Vortrag. Berlin, 1869, Lüderitz'scher Verlag.

HUGGINS, W.: Spectrum Analysis, applied to the Heavenly Bodies. A Discourse delivered at Nottingham before the British Association. 1866.

JAMIN: Leçons sur l'Analyse Spectrale. Journal Pharm., Third Series, xlii., 9. 1862.

LIELEGG, A.: Die Spectralanalyse. Weimar, Friedr. Voigt. 1867.

LORSCHEID, J.: Die Spectralanalyse, Münster, Aschendorff, 1870.

MILLER, W. A.: Lectures on Spectrum Analysis, 1862. Pharm. Journ., Second Series, iii., 339. Chem. News, v., 201–214.—A Course of Four Lectures on Spectrum Analysis, with its Applications to Astronomy. Delivered at the Royal Institution of Great Britain, May–June, 1867. Chem. News, xv., 259, 276; xvi., 8, 20, 47, 71.—Exeter Lecture, 1869. Popular Science Review, Oct., 1869.

MOIGNO, FR.: Sur l'Analyse Spectrale. Cosmos, xxii., 23, 52, 75.

MORTON, H.: Spectrum Analysis. Journ. of the Franklin Institute, 1869 (3), lviii., 56, 136.

MOUSSON, A.: Résumé de nos Connaissances Actuelles sur le Spectre. Arch. des Sciences Nat. de Genève. T. x., 221.

ROSCOE, H. E.: Lectures on Spectrum Analysis, delivered at the Royal Institution of Great Britain, 1861. Chem. News, iv., 118.—Ditto, 1862. Chem. News, v., 218, 261, 287.—Spectrum Analysis. Six Lectures, delivered in 1868, before the Society of Apothecaries of London. London, Macmillan, 1869.—Deutsche Ausgabe, bearbeitet von C. Schorlemmer, Braunschweig, Vieweg und Sohn, 1870.

SCHELLEN, H.: Die Spectralanalyse in ihrer Anwendung auf die Stoffe der Erde und die Natur der Himmelskörper. 2. Auflage. Braunschweig, G. Westermann, 1871.

SECCHI, A.: Résumé des resultats de l'Analyse Spectrale. N. Arch. Ph. Nat., xxiii., 145.

SIMMLER, R. TH.: Beiträge zur chemischen Analyse durch Spectralbeobachtungen. Chur, 1861.

THALÉN, R.: Spektralanalys exposé och Historik, med en Spektralkarta. Upsala, 1866.

VALENTIN, G.: Der Gebrauch des Spectroskops zu physiologischen und ärztlichen Zwecken. Leipzig und Heidelberg, Winter'sche Buchhandlung, 1863.

II.

MEMOIRS RELATING TO THE APPLICATION OF SPECTRUM ANALYSIS TO TERRESTRIAL SUBSTANCES.

1. *Relating to Spectra generally, and the Direct Spectra of the Elements.*

ALLEN, O. D.: Observations on Cæsium and Rubidium. Sill. Journ., Nov., 1862.

ÅNGSTRÖM, A. J.: Optische Untersuchungen. Pogg. Ann., xciv., 141. (The electric spark is shown to give a double spectrum, that of the atmospheric air or gas through which the sparks pass, and that of the incandescent metallic particles of the electrodes.)

ATTFIELD: On the Carbon Spectrum. Phil. Trans., 1862, p. 221.

BECQUEREL, EDM.: La lumière, t. i. et ii. Paris, Firmin Didot Frères, 1867 et 1868. (Valuable on account of the investigation of the spectra of phosphorescent substances.)

BRASSACK: Ueber die elektrischen Spectra der Metalle. Zeitschrift f. d. ges. Naturw., ix., 185.

BREWSTER, SIR D.: On the Action of Various Colored Bodies on the Spectrum. Phil. Mag. (4), xxiv., 441.

BUNSEN, R.: Entdeckung der neuen Alkalimetalle. Berliner Monats-Ber. 10 Mai, 1860, p. 221. (The discovery of Cæsium.)—Ueber das Atomgewicht des Cæsiums. Pogg. Ann., cxix., 1.—Ueber ein fünftes der Alkaligruppe angehörendes Element. Berl. Mon.-Ber., 1861, p. 273. (Rubidium.)—Ueber Darstellung der Rubidiumverbindungen. Ann. Chem. Pharm., cxxii., 347.—Ueber das Vorkommen von Lithium in Meteoriten. Ann. Chem. Pharm., cxxxi., 253.

BUNSEN UND BAHR: Ueber das Erbiumspectrum. Ann. Chem. Pharm., cxxxvii., 1.

CAPPEL, E.: Einfluss der Temperatur auf die Empfindlichkeit der Spectralreaction. Pogg. Ann., cxxxix., 628.

CHANTARD: Phénomènes observés dans les Spectres produits par la Lumière des Courants d'Induction traversant les gaz rarefiés. Compt. rend., lix., 383.

CHRISTOFLE AND BEILSTEIN: Sur le Spectre du Phosphore. Ann. Chim. Phys. (4), iii., 280.

COOKE, J. P.: On the Projection of the Spectra of the Metals. Sill. Jour. (2), xl., 243.

CROOKES, W.: On a Means of increasing the Intensity of Metallic Spectra. Chem. News, v., 234.—On the Existence of a new Element, probably of the Sulphur

Group. Chem. News, iii. 193.—The Discovery of the Metal Thallium. Chem. News, 1863, p. 13.—On Thallium and its Compounds. Chem. Soc. Journ., xvii., 112.

Debray, H. H.: Sur la Projection des Raies brillantes des Flammes Colorées par les Métaux. Ann. Chem. Phys. (3), lxv., 331; Sill. Jour. (2), xxxiv., 407.

Diacon, M. E.: Recherches sur l'Influence des Eléments électro-négatifs sur le Spectre des Métaux. Ann. Chim. Phys. (4), vi., 1. (With drawings of the Spectra of Copper Chloride and Bromide).

Diacon and Wolf: Sur les Spectres des Métaux Alcalins. Mém. de l'Acad. de Montpellier, 1863.

Dibbits: Ueber die Spectra der Flammen einiger Gase. Pogg. Ann., cxxii., 497.

Ditscheiner, L.: Ueber die Krümmung von Spectrallinien. Wien. Ber., li. 2, p. 368. Les Mondes, viii., 471.

Fizeau: Note sur la Lumière émise par le Sodium brûlant dans l'Air. Compt. rend., liv., 493.

Frankland, E.: On the Combustion of Hydrogen and Carbonic Oxide in Oxygen under Great Pressure. Proc. Roy. Soc., xvi., 419.—On the Blue Band of the Lithium Spectrum. Ph. Mag. (4), xxii., 472.

Frazer, W.: On the Spectrum of Osmium. Chem. News, July 18, 1863.

Gladstone, J. H.: On an Optical Test for Didymium. Chem. Soc. Journ., 1858, 219. —On the Use of the Prism in Qualitative Analysis. Chem. Soc. Journ., x. 79. Zeitschr. f. Naturw., x., 52.—On the Violet Flame of many Chlorides. Phil. Mag. (4), xxiv., 417.

Gottschalk, F.: Ueber die Möglichkeit, Uebereinstimmung unter den Spectral, apparaten zu erzielen. Pogg. Ann., cxxi., 64.

Grandeau, L.: Recherches sur le Présence de Rubidium et Cæsium dans les Eaux Naturelles, les Minéraux et les Végétaux. Ann. Chim. Phys. (3), lxvii.

Hinrichs, G.: On the Distribution of Lines in Spectra. Sill. Journ., July, 1864.

Huggins, W.: On the Spectra of some of the Chemical Elements. Phil. Trans., 1864, p. 139. Pogg. Ann., cxxiv., 275, 621. (Valuable treatise, giving exact measurement of the spectrum lines of twenty-four metals, with maps.)

Ketteler: Wellenmessungen der Metalllinien, Monatsber. der Berl. Akad. d. Wissensch., 1864, p. 632.

Kirchhoff and Bunsen: Chemische Analyse durch Spectralbeobachtungen. I. Theil. Pogg. Ann., cx., 161. II. Theil. Pogg. Ann., cxiii., 337.

Kindt: Phosphorescenzlicht. Pogg. Ann., cxxxi., 160.

Lamy, A.: De l'Existence d'un Nouveau Métal, le Thallium. Ann. Chim. Phys. (3), lxvii., 385.

Leeds, A. R.: On the Spectra of Certain Metallic Compounds. Journ. of the Franklin Inst., lx., 194.

Lielegg, A.: Beiträge zur Kenntniss der Flammenspectren kohlenstoffhaltiger Gase. K. Akad. d. Wiss. Wien, April, 1868.

Mascart: Bestimmung der Wellenlängen der Metalllinien vermittelst des Gitterspectrums. Ann. scient. de l'École Normale supérieure. Paris, iv., 1868.

Melville, Th.: On the Examination of Colored Flames by the Prism. Edinburgh, Phys. and Lit. Essays, ii., 12 (1752). (One of the first investigations by Spectrum Analysis.)

Merz, S.: Ueber des Farbenspectrum. Pogg. Ann., cxii., 654. (The D-line is resolved into seven lines.)

Miller, W. A.: Note on the Spectrum of Thallium. Proc. Roy. Soc., xii., 407.

Mitscherlich, Al.: Beiträge zur Spectralanalyse. Pogg. Ann., cvi., 499; cxvi., 499.—Ueber die Spectren der Verbindungen und der einfachen Körper. Pogg. Ann., cxxi., 459.

Morren, M. A.: De la Flamme de quelques Gaz Carbures et en particulier de celle de l'Acetylène et du Cyanogène. Ann. Chim. Phys. (4), iv., 305. (With drawing of the Carbon Spectrum.)

Mulder, E.: Ueber die Spectren von Phosphor, Schwefel und Sellen. Journ. f. pract. Chem., xci., 111.

Müller, J.: Bestimmung der Wellenlänge einiger hellen Spectrallinien. Pogg. Ann., cxviii., 641.—Wellenlängen von Metalllinien. Fortschr. d. Physik., 1863, p. 191; 1865, p. 229.—Wellenlänge der blauen Indiumlinie. Pogg. Ann., cxxiv., 637.

Plücker, F.: Analyse Spectrale. Cosmos, xxi., 283, 312.—Messungen der Wellenlängen von Metalllinien. Wiedemann, Galv., ii., 875.—Ueber die Constitution der elektrischen Spectra der verschiedenen Gase und Dämpfe. Pogg. Ann., ciii., 88; civ., 113, 622; cv., 67; cvii., 77, 415.—On Spectral Analysis. Rep. Brit. Assoc., 1862, 2, p. 15.

Plücker and Hittorf: On the Spectra of Ignited Gases and Vapors, with regard to the Different Spectra of the same Elementary Gaseous Substance. Phil. Trans., 1865, 1. Jahresbericht, 1864, 110. (With drawings of the Spectra of the various orders.)

Roscoe and Clifton: On the Effect of Increased Temperature upon the Nature of the Light emitted by the Vapor of certain Metals or Metallic Compounds. Chem. News, v., 233.

F. Reich and Th. Richter: Vorläufige Notiz über ein neues Metall (Indium). Erdmann's Journ., lxxxix., 441.—Ueber das Indium. Erdmann's Journ., xc., 172. Phil. Mag. (4), xxvi., p. 488.

Secchi, A.: Spectrum des Gasgemische. Naturforscher iii., 93; Les Mondes, xxii., 144, 187.

Seguin, J. M.: Note sur les Spectres du Phosphore et du Soufre. Compt. rend., liii., 1272.

Simmler, R. T.: Beiträge zur chemischen Analyse durch Spectralbeobachtungen. Pogg. Ann., cxv., 242.

Sorby, H. C.: On Jargonium, a New Element, accompanying Zirconium. Chem. News, xix., 121. Proc. Roy. Soc., xvii., 511.—On some Remarkable Spectra of Compounds of Zirconia and the Oxides of Uranium. Proc. Roy. Soc., xviii., 197.

Steinheil: Wie vollständige Uebereinstimmung in den Angaben der Spectralapparate leicht zu erreichen sei. Pogg. Ann., cxxii., 167.

Stokes, G. G.: On the Discrimination of Organic Bodies by their Optical Properties. Roy. Instit., March 4, 1864. Phil. Mag. (4), xxvii., 388.

Swan: On the Blue Lines of the Spectrum of the Non-luminous Gas-flame. Edinburgh Phil. Trans., iii., 376; xxi., 353 (1857). (Giving accurate measurements of the lines.)—On the Prismatic Spectra of the Flames of Compounds of Carbon and Hydrogen. Proc. Edinb. Soc., iii., 376. Pogg. Ann., c., 306.

Talbot, H. Fox: Some Experiments on Colored Flames. Brewster's Journ. of Science, v., 1826.—On a Method of obtaining Homogeneous Light of Great Intensity. Phil. Mag. (3), iii., 35.—On the Flame of Lithia. Phil. Mag. (3), iv., 11.—On Prismatic Spectra. Phil. Mag. (3), ix., 3.

Thalén, R.: Mémoire sur la Détermination des Longueurs d'Onde des Raies Métalliques. Nova Acta Reg. Soc. Sc. Upsal. (3), vi. Published in a separate form by

W. Schultz, Upsala, 1868. (An admirable memoir on the wave-lengths of the metallic lines.)

TYNDALL AND FRANKLAND: On the Blue Band of the Lithium Spectrum. Phil. Mag. (4), xxii., 151, 472.

WARTMANN, E.: Sur les Lignes Longitudinales du Spectre. Arch. d. sc. ph. et nat., vii., 33; x., 302. Ph. Mag., xxxii., 499.

WATTS, W. M.: On the Spectra of Carbon. Phil. Mag. (4), xxxviii., 249.

WEINHOLD, A.: Ueber eine vergleichbare Spectralskala. Carl's Rep. d. Exp. Phys., vi., 84.

WOLF AND DIACON: Note sur les Spectres des Métaux Alcalins. Edin. Journ., lxxxviii., 67.

WÜLLNER, A.: Ueber die Spectra einiger Gase in Geissler'schen Röhren. Pogg. Ann., cxxxv., 174; cxxxvii., 362. (Describing the spectra of various orders, and the influence of density and temperature.)—Die Spectra des Wasserstoffs und des Aluminiums. With drawings by Bettendorff. Festschrift der Neiderrhein. Ges. f. Nat.- u. Heilkunde. Bonn, Markus, 1868.

ZANTEDESCHI, F.: Sur les Causes des Lignes Longitudinales du Spectre, etc. Arch. d. sc. ph. et nat., xii., 43; Corresp. scient. di Roma, Nr. ix., p. 69.

ZÖLLNER, F.: Ueber den Einfluss der Dichtigkeit und Temperatur auf die Spectra glühender Gase. Ber. Sächs. Ges. d. Wiss. (Math. Phys. Kl.) October 31, 1870.

2. *Relating to Absorptive Phenomena, the Emissive and Absorptive Powers of Various Substances, and the Reversal of their Spectra.**

ÅNGSTRÖM, A. J.: On the Discovery that a Glowing Gas emits Rays of the same Refrangibility as those it has power to absorb. Memoir of the year, 1853.

BAHR AND BUNSEN: Ueber Erbinerde und Yttererde. Ann. D. Chim. (4), ix., 484. Comp. Leib. Ann., cxxxv., 376.

BUNSEN, R.: Ueber die Umkehrung des Absorptionsspectrums des Didyms. Ann. Chem. Pharm., cxxxi., 255.—Ueber die Absorptionsspectra der Didymsalze. Pogg. Ann., cxxviii., 100.

BREWSTER, D.: Observations on the Lines of the Solar Spectrum, and on those produced by the Earth's Atmosphere, and by the Action of Nitrous Gas. Edin. Trans. Roy. Soc., xii. (1834), 522. Pogg. Ann., xxxiv., 233; xxxviii., 50.—On the Action of various Colored Bodies in the Spectrum. Phil. Mag. (4), xxiv., 441

CROOKES, W.: On the Opacity of the Yellow Soda Flame in Light of its own Color. Phil. Mag. (4), xxi., 55. Pogg. Ann., cxii., 344.

DELAFONTAINE: Ueber die Absorptionsspectra des Didyms, des Erbiums und des Terbiums. Ann. Chem. Pharm., cxxxv., 194.

FEUSSNER: Ueber Absorption des Lichtes bei verschiedenen Temperaturen. Mon. Ber. Berl. Akad. d. Wiss. Berlin, 1865, March.

FIZEAU: Note sur la Lumière émise par le Sodium brûlant dans l'Air. Pogg. Ann., cxiv., 492; Cosmos xx., 307. (Reversal of the D-line.)

FOUCAULT: The Reversal of the double Sodium-line in the Spectrum of the Electric Arc. Instit., 1849, 45.

GAMGEE, A.: On the Action of Nitrides on the Blood. Phil. Trans., 1868, 589.

GLADSTONE, J. H.: On an Optical Test for Didymium. Chem. Soc. Journ., 1858, 219.—On the Emission and Absorption of Rays of Light by certain Gases. Rep. Brit. Assoc., 1861, 2, p. 79.

* For the absorptive phenomena of aqueous vapor and the telluric lines of the solar spectrum, *vide* III., 1, A; of Blood, etc., *vide* IV., 6.

HAERLIN, J.: Ueber das Verhalten einiger Farbstoffe in Sonnenspectrum. Pogg. Ann., cxviii. (1863), 70.

HOPPE-SEYLER, F.: Ueber die Absorptionslinien im Blutspectrum. Schmid's Jahrb. ges. Med., cxiv., 3 (1862).

KIRCHHOFF, G.: Ueber das Verhältniss zwischen dem Emissionsvermögen und dem Absorptionsvermögen der Körper für Wärme und Licht. Pogg. Ann. cix., 275.—Ueber den Zusammenhang zwischen Emission und Absorption von Licht und Wärme. Mon.-Ber. d. Berl. Akad. 27 Oct., 1859. (The discovery of the cause of the Fraunhofer lines.)

MADAN, N. G.: On the Reversal of the Spectra of Metallic Vapors. Phil. Mag. (4), xxix., 338. (Compare Phil. Mag. (4), xxx., 390.)

MELDE, F.: Ueber die Absorption des Lichtes durch gefärbte Flüssigkeiten. Pogg. Ann., cxxiv., 91; cxxvi., 264.

MILLER, W. HALLOWS: On the Absorption Bands of Nitrous-Acid Gas, etc. Phil. Mag. (3), ii., 381.

MILLER, WILL. ALLEN: Experiments and Observations of some Cases of Lines in the Prismatic Spectrum produced by the Passage of Light through colored Vapors and Gases, and from certain Colored Flames. Phil. Mag. (3), xxvii., 81; Pogg. Ann., lxix., 1846.

MORREN: Ueber die im Sonnenlichte beim Durchgange durch Chlor erzeugten Absorptionslinien. Pogg. Ann., cxxxvii., 165.

ROOD, O. N.: On the Didymium Absorption Spectrum. Sill. Journ. (2), xxxiv., 129.

SIMMLER, R. TH.: Beiträge zur chemischen Analyse durch Spectralbeobachtungen. Chur, 1861. Absorption des Chlorophyls. Pogg. Ann., cxv., 1862, 611.

SORBY, H. C.: *Vide* Microspectroscopic Investigations, iv., 3.

STEWART, BALFOUR: Report on the Theory of Exchanges. Brit. Assoc. Rep. 1861.—On the Theory of Exchanges, etc. Trans. Roy. Soc. Edinburgh, 1858; Rep. of Brit. Assoc., 1861, 2, p. 97.

STOKES, G. G.: On the Reduction and Oxidation of the Coloring Matter of the Blood. Proc. Roy. Soc., xiii., 355.

THALÉN, R.: Das Absorptionsspectrum des Joddampfes. Kongl. Svenska vetensk. Acad. Handl. f. 1869. (With Drawings.) Pogg. Ann., cxxxix., 503.

VIERORDT, C.: Die Messung der Lichtabsorption durchsichtiger Medien mittelst des Spectralapparates. Pogg. Ann., cxl., 172.

WEISS, A.: Ueber die Aenderungen, welche die Lage der Linien in Spectrum der Untersalpetersäure erfahren, wenn man die Dichte derselben ändert. Pogg. Ann., cxii., 153.

WÜLLNER, A.: Zur Absorption des Lichtes. Pogg. Ann., cxx., 158. Phil. Mag. (4), xxvii., 44.

III.

MEMOIRS RELATING TO THE APPLICATION OF SPECTRUM ANALYSIS TO THE HEAVENLY BODIES.

1. *Relating to the Spectrum Analysis of the Sun, the Spots, Eclipses, the Chromosphere, the Prominences, etc.*

A. *The Solar Spectrum.*

AIRY, G. B.: Wave-lengths of Lines in Kirchhoff's Maps. Phil. Trans., 1868, p. 29.

ÅNGSTRÖM, A. J.: Mémoire sur les Raies Fraunhoferiennes du Spectre Solaire. Oefvers, af K. Vet. Akad. Förh., 1861, p. 365; 1863, 41. Pogg. Ann., cxvii., 290.—Sur les Raies Telluriques et les Raies Lumineuses que présente le Spectre Electrique de l'Air. Compt. rend., lxiii., 1866, p. 647.—Recherches sur le Spectre normal du Soleil, avec Atlas de 6 pl. Upsal, W. Schulz, 1868.

BERNARD, F.: Mémoire sur la Détermination des Longueurs d'Onde des Raies du Spectre Solaire, etc. Compt. rend., lviii., 1153; lix., 32.

BREWSTER, SIR D.: Observations of the Lines of the Solar Spectrum, and on those produced by the Earth's Atmosphere, and by the Action of Nitrous-Acid Gas. Phil. Mag. (3), viii., 384.

BREWSTER AND GLADSTONE: On the Lines of the Solar Spectrum. Map of the Solar Spectrum giving the Absorption Lines of the Earth's Atmosphere. Phil. Trans., 1860, cl., p. 149.

COOKE, J. P.: On the Aqueous Lines of the Solar Spectrum. Phil. Mag. (4), xxxi., 327.

CROOKES, W.: Photographic Researches on the Solar Spectrum, etc. Pogg. Ann., xcvii., 616. Cosmos viii., 90.

DITSCHEINER, L.: Wellenlängemessungen der Fraunhofer'schen Linien. Sitz.-Ber. der Wiener Akad., l., 2, p. 296 (1864).—Eine absolute Bestimmung der Wellenlängen der Fraunhofer'schen D-Linien. Wien. Ber., lii., 2, p. 289.

DRAPER, W.: On the Variation in Intensity of the Fixed Lines of the Solar Spectrum. Phil. Mag. (4), xxv., 342.

FRAUNHOFER, J.: Bestimmung des Brechungs- und des Farbenzerstreuungs-Vermögens verschiedener Glasarten. Denkschriften der Münchener Akademie, v., 1814, 1815. München, 1817, 4, pp. 103–226. (An abstract, with map, of the Solar Spectrum in Gilbert's Ann. der Phys., 1817, xxvi., 264.)

GIBBS, WOLCOTT: On the Normal Solar Spectrum. Sill. Journ., January, 1867.—On Wave-lengths. Sill. Journ., March, 1869; July, 1870.

GLADSTONE, J. H.: Notes on the Atmospheric Lines of the Solar Spectrum, and on certain Spectra of Gases. Proc. Roy. Soc., xi., 305.—On the Fixed Lines of the Solar Spectrum. Rep. of Brit. Assoc., 1858, p. 17.

GLAISHIER, J.: Scientific Balloon Ascent. The Lines in the Spectrum. Month. Not., xxiii., 191.

JANSSEN, M. J.: Mémoire sur les Raies Telluriques du Spectre Solaire. Compt. rend., liv., 1280; lvi., 213.—Sur le Spectre de la Vapeur d'Eau. Compt. rend., 1866, lxiii., 289. (With map.)—Sur quelques Spectres Stellaires remarquables par les Caractères optiques de la Vapeur d'Eau. Compt. rend., lxviii., 1545.—Rapport sur une Mission en Italie, etc. Paris, imprimerie Impériale, 1868. (With Plates. Contains a collection of Janssen's observations on the telluric lines of the solar spectrum with those on the spectrum of aqueous vapor.)

KIRCHHOFF, G.: Ueber die Fraunhofer'schen Linien. Abh. der Berl. Akad., 1861, p. 63; 1862, p. 227. Published in a separate form by Dümmler, Berlin, 1866.—Untersuchungen über das Sonnenspectrum und die spectren der chemischen Elemente. (With four plates of the solar spectrum, with Hofmann's continuation.)—Zur Geschichte der Spectralanalyse und der Analyse der Sonnenatmosphäre. Pogg. Ann., cxviii., p. 94.

LOCKYER, J. N.: Spectroscopic Observations of the Sun. Proc. Roy. Soc., xv., 256; xvii., 91, 128, 350, 415; xviii., 74.—Spectroscopic Observations of the Sun. Phil. Trans., 1869, 425. (With drawing of his Telespectroscope.)

MASCART: Sur les Raies du Spectre Solaire ultra-violet. Compt. rend., lvii., 789; lviii., 1111.—Détermination de la Longueur d'Onde de la Raie A. Pogg. Ann., cxviii., 367.

MERZ, S.: Ueber das Farbenspectrum. Pogg. Ann., cxviii., 654.

MÜLLER, J.: Ueber die Photographie des Spectrums. Pogg. Ann., xcii., 135; cix., 151.

RAYET: Sur le Spectre de l'Atmosphère Solaire. Compt. rend., lxviii., 1321.

ROSCOE, H. E.: On the Opalescence of the Atmosphere for Chemically Active Rays. Chem. News, xix., 158.

SECCHI, A.: Sur l'Origine des Raies Atmosphériques du Spectre Solaire. Arch. Sc. Phys., xxviii., 49.—Sur l'Influence de l'Atmosphère sur les Raies du Spectre et sur la Constitution du Soleil. Compt. rend., lx., 379.—Raies Spectrales Atmosphériques. Les Mondes, vii., 142.—Observations sur le Spectre Solaire. Les Mondes, viii., 645.—Spectrum Observations on the Rotation of the Sun. Naturforscher, iii., 205, 237; Monthly Not. Roy. Ast. Soc., xxx., p. 197 (1870).

VAN DER WILLIGEN; Bestimmung der Wellenlängen. Arch. du Musée Teyler. Vol. i., p. 1.

WEISS, A.: Kurze Notiz über eine Beobachtung über das Sonnenspectrum. Pogg. Ann., cxii., 153.

WOLLASTON, W. H.: On a Method of Examining Refractive and Dispersive Powers by Prismatic Reflection. Phil. Trans., 1802, p. 365. (Containing the first discovery of the dark solar lines.)

ZANTEDESCHI, FR.: De mutationibus quae contigunt in spectro solari fixo elucabratio. München Abh., viii., 99.

B. *The Spectra of Solar Spots and Faculæ.*

LOCKYER, J. N.: In almost all his "Spectroscopic Observations of the Sun," *vide* III., A; as well as in his paper entitled "On Recent Discoveries," etc., *vide* III., E.

RAYET: The Reversal of the C-line. Compt. rend., April 18, 1870.

SECCHI, A.: Le Soleil, etc., *vide* III., E. (This memoir contains detailed observations of the spots and faculæ, with plates.) Also Compt. rend., lxviii., 764, 959, and especially 1082.

YOUNG, C. A.: Spectroscopic Notes. Franklin Journ., lviii., 287; lix., 132; lx., 64, 232 (*a–b*).—Papers in the Periodical Der Naturforscher, Berlin, ii., 109, 181, 199, 297; iii., 212.

C. *Total Solar Eclipses of August* 18, 1868.

FAURA, F.: Account of the Expedition of the Jesuits from Manila, contained in Bulletino meteor. dell. Osservatorio del Collegio Romano, vol. vii., No. 12; in Heis' Wochenschrift für Astron. und Meteorol., Halle, 1869; also in Natur und Offenb., Münster, Aschendorf, 1869, 145.

HERSCHEL, ALEX.: On the Total Eclipse of the Sun of August 18, 1868. Proc. Roy. Instit., 1868–'69.

HERSCHEL, CAPTAIN JOHN: On the Solar Eclipse of 1868, seen at Jamkandi. Roy. Ast. Soc. Mem., vii.

JANSSEN, M. J.: Eclipse du 18 Août, 1868. (Cocanada, Sept. 19, 1868.) Compt. rend., 26 Oct., 1868.—Account of the Solar Eclipse of 1868, observed at Guntoor, in the Annuaire du Bureau des Longitudes, 1868, p. 584.—See also III., 1, A and D.

TENNANT, COLONEL: Report on the Indian Eclipse, 1868. Roy. Ast. Soc. Mem., vii.—Report on the Total Eclipse of the Sun, August 17–18, 1868. As observed at Guntoor. Mem. Roy. Ast. Soc., xxxvii., Part 1. (With several plates.)—Papers in the Periodical Der Naturforscher, Berlin, i., 311, 319, 327, 351, 369, 393, ii., 59.—Papers in the Periodical Les Mondes, Paris, xviii., 130, 168, 272, 296, 362, 413.

Of August 7, 1869.

Hough, G. W.: The Total Eclipse of August 7, 1869; Albany, J. Munsell, 82 State Street, 1870.

Journal of the Franklin Institute, ed. by Prof. Henry Morton; (3) lviii., 149, 150, 200, 224 (Abstr. of Prof. Young's Rep.), 226 (Phot. of the Corona), 249 (Rep. of Prof. Meyer), 276 (Rep. of Prof. Himes), 281 (Rep. of Prof. Pickering), 354 (Rep. of Mr. Brown), 356 (Rep. of Mr. Willard); lix., 58 (Rep. of Prof. Hough), 417 (with drawing of the "Anvil" prominence).

Lockyer, J. N.: Remarks on the Recent Eclipse of the Sun as observed in the United States. Proc. Roy. Soc., xviii., 179.

U. S. Naval Observatory, Washington: Reports on Observations of the Total Eclipse of the Sun, August 7, 1869, conducted under the direction of Commodore B. F. Sands. Appendix ii., Washington, 1869, Government Printing-Office. (This valuable work contains, with several drawings, the official communications of Commodore Sands, Prof. S. Newcomb, W. Harkness, J. R. Eastman, E. Curtis, J. H. Lane, W. S. Gilman, F. W. Bardwell, A. J. Meyer, A. Hall, and Rogers.)

Young, C. A.: On a New Method of Observing Contacts at the Sun's Limb and other Spectroscopic Observations during the Recent Eclipse. Amer. Journ. of Science and Art (2), xlviii., 370.—Papers in the Periodical Der Naturforscher, Berlin, ii., 253, 379, 533,; iii., 16, 53, 142, 163, 175.—Papers in the Periodical Les Mondes, Paris, xxi., 238, 600.—Papers in the Periodical Nature, London, i., 14, 170, 203, 336, 532.

D. *Prominences, Corona, Chromosphere.*

Herschel, Captain J.: Spectroscopic Observations of the Solar Prominences. Proc. Roy. Soc., xviii., 62.

Huggins, W.: On a Possible Method of viewing the Red Flames without an Eclipse. Monthly Not. Roy. Ast. Soc., xxix., 4.—Note on a Method of viewing the Solar Prominences without an Eclipse. Proc. Roy. Soc., xvii., 302.

Janssen, M. J.: Sur les protubérances solaires et la constitution du Soleil, etc. Compt. rend., lxviii., 93, 112, 181, 245, 312, 367, 731.

Lockyer, J. N.: Spectroscopic Observations of the Sun (*vide* III., 1, a).—Notice of an Observation of the Spectrum of a Solar Prominence. Proc. Roy. Soc., xvii., 91, 104, 128.

Norton, W. A.: On the Corona seen in Total Eclipses of the Sun. Sill. Journ. (2), l., 250.

Rayet: Sur le Spectra des Protubérances Solaires. Compt. rend., lxviii., 62.—Sur la Réfrangibilité de la Raie jaune brilliante de l'Atmosphère Solaire. Compt. rend., lxviii., 320.—Sur le Spectre de l'Atmosphère Solaire. Compt. rend., lxviii., 1321. —Renversement des Raies D dans une Protubérance. Les Mondes, xxiii., 399; Naturf., iii., 262, 278.

Respighi, L.: Observations of the Prominences round the Entire Limb of the Sun. Compt. rend., lxix., 1178; Nature, i., 292; Naturforscher, iii., 39, 189.

Secchi, A.: Existence d'une Couche donnant un Spectre Continu entre la Couche rose et le Bord Solaire. Compt. rend., lxviii., 580.—Nove Ricerche sulle Protuberanze

Solari. Bulletino Meteorol. dell' Osserv. del Coll. Romano x., Nr. 9. (September 30, 1870.)

YOUNG, C. A.: Spectroscopic Notes. Journ. of the Franklin Inst., lviii., 141, 287, 416 (drawing of prominence); lx., 64, 232 (*a–b*); (lx., No. 5, with drawings of a new Telespectroscope and Prominence.)

ZÖLLNER, F.: Beobachtungen von Protuberanzen der Sonne. Ber. d. Sächs. Ges. d. W., 1 Juli, 1869. Pogg. Ann., cxxxvii., 624. With drawings.—Papers in the Periodical Der Naturforscher, Berlin, i., 417; ii., 9, 33, 51, 74, 91, 116, 133, 213, 245, 338; iii., 39, 175, 189, 205, 262, 263, 278.—Papers in the Periodical Les Mondes, Paris, xviii., 362, 413; xix., 213, 215, 232, 498.—Papers in the Periodical Nature, London, i., 172, 195, 607; ii., 131.—On the Corona specially: Naturforscher, Berlin, ii., 167, 253, 379, 395; iii., 91, 392. Les Mondes, Paris, xxi., 345, 602; xxii., 142. Nature, London, i., 15, 139, 146, 533, 543; ii., 114, 164, 277; iii., 163, 175, 262, 263, 278. Phil. Mag., xxxviii., 281; xxxix., 17. Monthly Not. of the Roy. Ast. Soc., xxx., 193.

E. *Physical Constitution, Temperature of the Sun.*

BERNAERTS: Ueber die Beschaffenheit der Sonne. Sitz. der Belg. Akad., March 3, 1870.

CHACORNAC: Sur la Constitution Physique du Soleil. Compt. rend., lx., 170.

FAYE: Sur la Constitution Physique du Soleil. Compt. rend., lx., 80, 138, 468.

FRANKLAND AND LOCKYER: Preliminary Notes of Researches on Gaseous Spectra in Relation to the Physical Constitution of the Sun. Proc. Roy. Soc., xvii., 288.—Researches on Gaseous Spectra in Relation to the Physical Constitution of the Sun, Stars, and Nebulæ. Proc. Roy. Soc., xvii., 453; xviii., 79.

GOULD, B. A.: The Physical Constitution of the Sun. Journ. of the Franklin Inst., lix., 228.—On Faye's Theory of the Physical Constitution of the Sun. Compt. rend., lxix., 1176.—The Sun. A Course of Five Lectures before the Peabody Inst. of Baltimore. Franklin Journal, lx. (August, 1870, and following Nos.).

GUILLEMIN, A.: Le Soleil. Paris, 1869, Hachette et Cie.

KIRCHHOFF, G.: Untersuchungen über das Sonnenspectrum. Berlin, Dümmler, 1866. (Contains Kirchhoff's views on the physical constitution of the sun.)

LALLEMAND, M.: Constitution Physique du Soleil. Conférence. Montpellier, J. Martel aîné, 1867. (Pamphlet.)

LOCKYER, J. N.: On Recent Discoveries in Solar Physics made by means of the Spectroscope. Roy. Inst. of Great Britain, May 28, 1869.—Reply to some Remarks of Father Secchi on the Recent Solar Discoveries. Phil. Mag., January, 1870.

MAIBAUER, R. O.: Ueber die physische Beschaffenheit der Sonne. Berlin, 1866. Lüderitz' Buchh. (Pamphlet.)

RAYET: La Constitution Physique du Soleil. Déherain, Annuaire scientifique. Paris, Masson, 1870 (ix.).

REIS, P.: Die Sonne. Zwei physikalische Vorträge. Leipzig, Quandt und Händel, 1869.

SECCHI, A.: Le Soleil; Exposé des principales Découvertes modernes sur la Structure de cet Astre, etc. Paris, 1870. Gauthiers-Villars.—Sulle ultime Scoperte Spettroscopiche Fatte nel Sole. Lettura all' Academia Tibernia. Roma, Typ. delle Belle Arti, 1869.

STONEY: On the Physical Constitution of the Sun and Stars. Proc. Roy. Soc., xvi., 25; xvii., 1.—On the Bearing of Recent Observations upon Solar Physics. Phil. Mag. (4), xxxvi., 447.

TYNDALL, J. : On the Physical Basis of Solar Chemistry. Proc. Roy. Inst., June 7, 1861. Phil. Mag. (4), xxii., 147.

WARREN DE LA RUE, STEWART, AND LOEWY: Researches on Solar Physics. Phil. Trans., London, 1869, clix., 1; 1870, clx., 389.

ZÖLLNER, F. : Ueber die Temperatur und die physische Beschaffenheit der Sonne. Ber. K. Sächs. Ges. d. Wiss. Leipzig. (Math. Phys. Klasse, 2 Juni, 1870.) Naturf., iii., 311.—Papers in the Periodical Der Naturforscher, Berlin, iii., 93, 189, 233, 311.

2. *Relating to the Spectrum Analysis of the Moon and Planets.*

FRAUNHOFER, J. : Resultate von Versuchen mit dem Farbenspectrum des Mondes, etc. Gilb. Ann., 1823, xiv., 374.

HUGGINS, W. : On the Spectrum of Mars. Month. Not. Roy. Ast. Soc., xxvii., 178.

JANSSEN, J. : Application de l'Analyse Spectrale à la Question concernant l'Atmosphère Lunaire. Compt. rend., lvi., 962.

LE SUEUR: On the Spectrum of Jupiter. Proc. Roy. Soc., xviii., 245. Nature, i., 517.

SECCHI, A. : Sur les Raies Atmosphériques des Planètes. Compt. rend., lix., 182.—Sur les Raies du Spectre de la Planète Saturn. Compt. rend., lx., 543.—Observation du Spectre de Jupiter. Compt. rend., lix., 309.—Resultats fournis par l'Analyse Spectrale de la Lumière d'Uranus. Compt. rend., lxviii., 761.—Sur le Spectre du Neptune. Compt. rend., Novbr., 1869, lxix., 1051.—Le Soleil (*vide* III., I, E), p. 342.—Papers in the Periodical Der Naturforscher, Berlin, ii., 125, 197; iii., 26, 149.

3. *Relating to the Spectrum Analysis of the Fixed Stars.*

AIRY, G. B.: Measurements of Stellar Lines. Monthly Not. Roy. Ast. Soc., xiii., 190, and further in xxiii., 188.

DONATI: Intorno alle Strie degli spettri Stellari. Il Nuovo Cimento, xv., 292. (With a lens 41 centimetres in diameter.)—Memorie Astronomiche. Month. Not., xxiii., 100. (Researches on the Spectra of Fifteen Stars.)

FRAUNHOFER, J. : Resultate von Versuchen mit den Farbenspectris vom Sternenlichte. Gilb. Ann., 1823, xiv., 374.

HUGGINS, W. : On the Disappearance of the Spectrum of ε Piscium at its Occultation on January 4, 1865. Month. Not. Roy. Ast. Soc., xxv., 60.—Further Observations on the Spectra of some of the Stars and Nebulæ, with an Attempt to determine therefrom whether these Bodies are moving toward or from the Earth. Phil. Trans., 1868, 529.—Spectrum Analysis, *vide* I.—On some Further Results of Spectrum Analysis as applied to the Heavenly Bodies. Chem. News, xix., 187.

HUGGINS AND MILLER: On the Lines of the Spectra of some of the Fixed Stars. Proc. Roy. Soc., xii., 444.—On the Spectra of some of the Fixed Stars. Phil. Trans., 1864, 413; Phil. Mag., June, 1866.—On the Spectrum of the Variable Star α Orionis. Month. Not. R. Ast. Soc., xxvi., 215.—On the Spectrum of a New Star in Corona Borealis. Proc. Roy. Soc., xv., 146.

JANSSEN, M. J. : Sur quelques Spectres Stellaires remarquables par les Caractères optiques de la Vapeur d'Eau. Compt. rend., lxviii., 1845.

LAMONT: Untersuchungen über das Spectrum der Fixsterne. Jahrbuch der Sternwarte bei München, 1838, p. 190.

LE SUEUR: On the Spectrum of η Argo with Bright Lines. Nature, i., 517.

RUTHERFURD, L. M.: Measurements of the Stellar Spectra. Sill. Journ. (2), xxxv., 71, 407; xxxvi., 154.

SECCHI, A.: Notes sur les Spectres Prismatiques des Corps Célestes. Compt. rend., lvii., 71.—Sur les Spectres Stellaires. Compt. rend., lxiii., 364, 621; lxiv., 774; lxv., 662; lxvi., 124, 398; lxii., 373.—Catalogo delle Stelle, etc. Parigi, 1867, Gauthier-Villars.—Sugli Spettri prismatici delle Stelle fisse. Memoria, i. e ii. Atti della Soc. Ital., 1868, Rome.—La Soleil, Paris, Gauthier-Villars, 1870, p. 385.

WOLF AND RAYET: Sur la Spectroscopie Stellaire. Compt. rend., lxv., 292.—Papers in the Periodical Der Naturforscher, Berlin, i., 59, 127, 215, 279, 357; ii., 199, 215, 353; iii., 343.

4. *Relating to the Spectrum Analysis of the Nebulæ and Clusters.*

HERSCHEL, CAPTAIN J.: On the Spectra of Southern Nebulæ, etc. Proc. Roy. Soc., xvi., 416, 451; xvii., 303.

HUGGINS, W.: On the Spectra of the Nebulæ. Phil. Trans., 1864, p. 437.—On the Nebula in the Sword-Handle of Orion. Proc. Roy. Soc., xiv., 39.—Further Observations on the Spectra of some of the Nebulæ, with a Mode of determining the Brightness of these Bodies. Phil. Trans., 1866, p. 381; 1868, 529. Phil. Mag. (4), xxxvi., 57.—Q'uest ce qu'une Nébuleuse. Les Mondes, ix., 18.

LE SUEUR: On the Nebulæ of Argo and Orion. Proc. Roy. Soc., xviii., 245.

SECCHI, A.: Sur la Lumière Spectrale de la Nébuleuse d'Orion. Compt. rend., lx., 543.—Sulla grande Nebulosa di Θ'Orione. Firenze, Stamperia Reale, 1868, p. 29. —Le Soleil (*vide* III., I, E), p. 400.—Spettro di alcune Nebulose. Sugli spettri prism. dei Corpi celesti. Mem. I. Roma, 1868, p. 33.—Papers in the Periodical Der Naturforscher, Berlin, i., 279; ii., 279, 356.

5. *Relating to the Spectrum Analysis of Comets.*

DONATI: Ueber das Spectrum des Kometen II., 1864. Astr. Nach., lxii., 375.

HUGGINS, W.: On the Spectrum of the Comet I., 1866. Proc. Roy. Soc., xv., 5.—Spectre de la Comète de Tempel. Les Mondes (2), i., 251.—On the Spectrum of the Comet II., 1867. Monthly Not. Roy. Ast. Soc., xxvii., 288.—On the Spectrum of Brorsen's Comet, 1868. Proc. Roy. Soc., xvi., 386. Phil. Mag. (4), xxxvi., 60.—Spectrum of the Comet II., 1868. Phil. Trans., 1868, 529.

HUGGINS, W., AND TYNDALL, J.: On Cometary Theory. Phil. Mag. (4), xxxvii., 241.

SECCHI, A.: Le Soleil (*vide* III., I, E), p. 360.—Spectre de la Comète de Tempel. Compt. rend., lxii., 210.—On the Spectrum of Brorsen's Comet. Ph. Mag. (4), xxxvi., 75.

WOLF AND RAYET: Spectre de la Comète de Winnecke (I., 1870). Compt. rend., 4 Juillet, 1870.—Papers in the Periodical Der Naturforscher, Berlin, i., 263, 295; iii., 302.—Papers in the Periodical Les Mondes, Paris, xvii., 95, 270; xxiii., 498.

6. *Relating to the Spectrum Analysis of Meteors and Falling Stars.*

BROWNING, J.: On the Spectra of the Meteors of November 13–14, 1866. Phil. Mag. (4), xxxiii., 234.

BROWNING-HERSCHEL: The Coming Meteor Shower; the Spectra of Meteors. Intell. Observ. Rev., London, x., 38.

HERSCHEL, A. S.: Prismatic Spectra of the August Meteors, 1866. Int. Obs. Rev., x., 161.—Spectre d'une Étoile filante. Les Mondes, vii., 139.—Papers in the Periodical Der Naturforscher, Berlin, ii., 2, 99, 404.

IV.

MEMOIRS RELATING TO VARIOUS OTHER SPECTRUM OBSERVATIONS, AND THE APPLICATION OF SPECTRUM ANALYSIS TO TECHNOLOGY, INDUSTRY, PHYSIOLOGY, ETC.

1. *Relating to Spectrum Apparatus and the Various Appliances connected therewith.*

ABBE, E.: Ueber einen Spectralapparat am Mikroskop. Jena'sche Zeitschr. v. Hft., 4, 459. (Manufactured by C. Zeiss in Jena.)

BROWNING, J.: On a Spectroscope in which the Prisms are automatically adjusted to the Minimum Angle of Deviation for the Particular Ray under Examination. Monthly Not. of the Roy. Ast. Soc., xxx., 198 (1870).

COOKE, J. P.: On the Construction of Spectroscopes. Sill. Journ., xl., 305; Phil. Mag. (4), xxxi., 110.—An Improved Spectroscope. Chem. News, 1863, 4 July. Sill. Journ. (2), xxxvi., p. 266.

CROOKES, W.: On Spectroscopes. Mech. Mag., June, 1861, p. 308.—Binocular-Spectrum-Microscope. Phil. Mag. (4), xxxviii., 383.

GASSIOT, J. P.: Description of a large Spectroscope. Proc. Roy. Soc., 1863, xii., 536. (Compare Proc. Roy. Soc., xiv., 320.)—Spectroscope with Eleven Prisms. Proc. Roy. Soc., xiii., 183. Phil. Mag. (4), xxviii., 69.—On an Automatic Spectroscope. Les Mondes, xxiii., 95.

GIBBS, WOLCOTT: Description of a Large Spectroscope. Sill. Journ. (2), xxxv., 110.

HOFMANN, J. H.: Spectroscope à Vision Directe. Cosmos, xxii., p. 984.

HUGGINS, W.: Description of a Hand Spectrum Telescope. Proc. Roy. Soc., xvi., 241.—A New Telespectroscope. Nature, i., 145.

JANSSEN, M. J.: Note sur de Nouveaux Spectroscopes; Spectroscope à Vision Directe, à Reflexion. Compt. rend., 1862, October 6. (The first construction of a direct-vision spectroscope.)

LITTROW, O.: Eine neue Einrichtung des Spectralapparates. Wien. Ber. xlvii. (2), 26.

LOCKYER, J. N.: Spectroscopic Observations of the Sun. Phil. Trans., 1869, 425. (Contains description and drawing of a large telespectroscope.)

MATHIESSEN, A.: Du Lentiprisme. Cosmos ii. (A complete spectroscope, 1844.)

MERZ, S.: Objectiva Spectralapparat. Carl's Rep. f. Exp. Phys., vi., 164. Compt. rend., lxix., 1053.—Kleines Universal-Stern-Spectroskop. Carl's Rep. f. Exp. Phys., vi., 273.—Spectralapparat für Mikroskope. Carl's Rep. f. Exp. Phys., v., 390.

MEYERSTEIN, M.: Das Spectrometer. Göttingen, 1870, Deuerlich.

PICKERING: Comparative Efficiency of Different Forms of Spectroscopes. Sill. Journ., May, 1868.

PROCTOR, R. A.: The Use of the Spectroscope in Astronomical Observation. Pop. Sc. Review, 1869, April, p. 141. (With drawings.)

ROOD, O. N.: On the Use of Prisms of Flint Glass and Bisulphide of Carbon for Spectrum Analysis. Sill. Journ. (2), xxxv., p. 356.

RUTHERFURD, L. M.: On the Construction of the Spectroscope. Amer. Journ. of Sc. and Art, xxxix., 129. Sill. Journ. (2), xxxv., 407.

SECCHI, A.: Sugli Spettri Prismatici dei Corpi celesti. Roma, 1868. (Contains a discussion on stellar spectroscopes, with a drawing.)

SIMMLER, R. Th.: Ein Hand und Reisespectroskop. Pogg. Ann., cxx., 623.

STEINHEIL: Ueber Verbesserungen in der Construction der Spectralapparate, München Ber., 1863, 1, 47.

VOIT: Ueber Spectralapparate. Carl Rep. d. Phys. Techn., i., 65.

WINLOCK: A Reliable Finder for a Spectrotelescope. Journ. of the Franklin Instit. (3), lx., 295.

YOUNG, C. A.: A New Form of Spectroscope. Journ. of the Franklin Instit., lx. (3), 538. (With a drawing of a new spectroscope equal to thirteen prisms.)

ZANTEDESCHI, FR.: Ricerche fisico-chimiche-fisiologiche sulla luce. Venezia, 1846, Antonelli.—Descrizione di uno Spettrometro, e degli esperimenti esequiti con esso, etc. Atti del Inst. Veneto, xv., 793 (1855–'56). Published in a separate form by A. Sicca, Padova, Sept., 1856. (With drawing of one of the earliest spectroscopes.)

ZÖLLNER, J. C. F.: Ein neues Spectroskop (Reversionsspectroskop) nebst Beiträgen zur Spectralanalyse der Gestirne. Ber. Kgl. Sächs. Ges. d. Wiss. Leipzig, 1869. (Math. phys. Klasse vom 6 Februar.)

2. *Relating to the Spectrum of the Electric Light and Discharge.*

ÅNGSTRÖM, A. J.: Optische Untersuchungen. Pogg. Ann., cxiv., 141.—Das Prismatische Spectrum des elektrischen Funkens. Zeitschr. f. Math., 1856, 1, p. 57.—Berl. Ber., 1853, p. 251.

BRASSAC, F.: Das Luftspectrum, eine prismatische Untersuchung des zwischen Platinaelectroden überschlagenden Funkens. Zeitschr. f. Nat., xxviii., 1.

DANIEL: Analyse Spectrale de l'Étincelle Électrique produite dans les Liquides et les Gaz. Compt. rend., lvii., 98.

FOUCAULT, L.: Note sur la Lumière de l'Arc Voltaique. Ann. d. Chim. (3), lviii., 476.

MASSON: De la Nature de l'Étincelle Électrique.

PLÜCKER, F.: Spectrum des elektrischen Funkens. Pogg. Ann., civ., 117. Wiedemann, Galv. ii., 874. (With drawings.)

ROBINSON, F. R.: On Electric Spectra. Phil. Trans., 1862.—On Spectra of Electric Light as modified by the Nature of the Electrodes and the Media of Discharge. Proc. Roy. Soc., xii., 202.

SCHIMKOW, A.: Ueber das Spectrum des electrischen Büschel- und Glimmlichtes in der Luft. Pogg. Ann., cxxix., 508.

SÉGUIN, J. M.: Note sur le Spectre de l'Étincelle Électrique dans les Gaz composés. Compt. rend., lix., 933.—Sur les Spectres de l'Étincelle Électrique dans les Dissolutions des Sels. Rev. des Soc. sav. (Sc. Math. Phys., nat. iv., p. 305, 13 Nov., 1863).—Sur l'Analogie de l'Étincelle d'Induction avec les autres Décharges électriques. Ann. Chim. Phys. (3), t. lxix.—Sur la Lumière Stratifiée et sur l'Étincelle d'Induction. Grenoble, Maisonville et Fils, 1867.—Experiences sur l'Étincelle Électrique. Compt. rend., 16 Nov., 1868.

STOKES, G. G.: On the Long Spectrum of the Electric Light. Phil. Trans., 1862, 599

VAN DER WILLIGEN: Ueber das elektrische Spectrum. Pogg. Ann., cvi., 610.

WALTENHOFEN, A. VON: Spectren des elektrischen Funkens in verdünnten Gasen. Dingl. Polyt. Journ., clxxvii., 38.

WHEATSTONE, C.: On the Prismatic Decomposition of the Electric, Voltaic, and Electromagnetic Sparks. Brit. Assoc., Dublin, August 12, 1835. Chem. News, iii., 198.—Papers in the Periodical Der Naturforscher, Berlin, iii., 50.

3. *Relating to the Spectrum Analysis of Lightning.*

HERSCHEL, CAPT. J.: On the Spectrum of Lightning. Proc. Roy. Soc., xvii., 58.

KUNDT: Ueber das Spectrum des Blitzes. Pogg. Ann., cxxii., 497.

LABORDE: Spectre de la Lumière des Éclairs. Les Mondes viii., 299.—Papers in the Periodical Der Naturforscher, Berlin, i., 384; ii., 17, 289.

4. *Relating to the Spectrum Analysis of the Aurora Borealis.*

ÅNGSTRÖM, A. J.: Spectre de l'Aurore Boréale. Recherches sur le Spectre Solaire. Berlin, Dümmler, 1869, 41. Pogg. Ann., cxxxviii., 161.

DAVIS, A. S.: On the Possible Cause of the Bright Line observed by M. Ångström in the Spectrum of the Aurora Borealis. Phil. Mag. (4), xl. 33.

STRUVE, O. v.: Beobachtungen eines Nordlichtspectrums. Bull. Acad. Imp. Science. Petersbourg, xiii., 49.

ZÖLLNER, FR.: Ueber das Spectrum des Nordlichtes. Ber. d. Sächs. Ges. d. Wiss. (Math. Phys. Kl.), 31 October, 1870, p. 254.—Papers in the Periodical Der Naturforscher, Berlin, i., 392; ii., 261, 369; iii., 390.—Papers in the Periodical Les Mondes, Paris, xxi., 293.—Papers in the Periodical Nature, London, iii., 6, 28.

5. *Relating to the Microspectroscope and Microspectroscopic Investigations.*

CHURCH: Microspectroscopic Investigations. (Letter.) Intell. Obs. Rev., ix., 291.

HERAPATH, W. BIRD: On the Use of the Microspectroscope in the Discovery of Blood-stains. Chem. News, xvii., 113, 123.

HUGGINS, W.: On the Prismatic Examination of Microscopic Objects. Quart. Journ. Micros. Soc., July, 1865.

MERZ, S.: Spectralapparat für Mikroskope. Carl's Rep. f. Exp. Phys., v., 390.

SORBY, H. C.: On the Application of Spectrum Analysis to Microscopical Investigations, etc. Chem. News, xi., 186, 194, 232, 256.—On a Definite Method of Qualitative Analysis of Animal and Vegetable Coloring Matters by means of the Spectrum-Microscope. Proc. Roy. Soc., xv., 433.—On a New Microspectroscope, and on a New Method of printing a Description of the Spectra seen with the Spectrum-Microscope. Chem. News, xv., 220.

6. *Relating to the Application of Spectrum Analysis to Physiology, Histology, and Pathology.*

ASKENAY, E.: Beiträge zur Kenntniss des Chlorophylls und einiger dasselbe begleitender Farbestoffe. Bot. Zeit., 1867. Nos. 29 and 30. (Plate with eleven spectra.)

BENOIT, R.: Études Spectroscopiques sur le Sang. Montpellier.

COHN, F.: Ueber den Farbstoff der Phycochromaceen. Archiv für mikr. Anat. v. M. Schultze, iii., 6 (1867).

HOPPE-SEYLER, F.: Ueber das Verhalten des Blutfarbestoffs im Spectrum des Sonnenlichtes. Virch. Arch., xxiii., 446; xxix., 233 (Z. f. Chem., 1865, 214).—Handbuch der physiologisch- und pathologisch-chemischen Analyse. 3 Aufl. Berlin, 1870.—Erkennung der Vergiftung mit Kohlenoxyd. Z. f. anal. Chem., iii., 439. Phil. Mag. (4), xxx., 456.—Weiteres über die optischen und chemischen Eigenschaften des Blutfarbstoffes. Centr.-Bl. f. d. med. Wiss., 1864. Nos. 52 and 53.

MAXWELL: Investigations on Color Blindness by means of the Spectrum. Phil. Mag. xxi., 1861, p. 145. Compare Helmholtz, Phys. Optik., p. 294.

SACHS, J.: Durchleuchtung der Pflanzentheile. Hdb. d. Exp. Phys. d. Pflanzen. Leipzig, 1865, p. 4.

VALENTIN, G.: Histiologische und physiologische Studien. Abth. ix., Zeitschrift für

Biologie, vi. (The first eight treatises appeared in Henle and Pfeuffer's Zeitschrift für rationelle Medizin.)—Einige neue Beobachtungen über das Erkennen des Blutes durch das Spectroskop. Virch. Arch., xxvi., 580.—Gebrauch des Spectroskops zu physiologischen und ärztlichen Zwecken. Leipzig, 1863.

7. *Relating to the Application of Spectrum Analysis to Technology and Industry.*

LIELEGG, A.: Ueber das Spectrum der Bessemer-Flamme. K. Akad. Wiss. Wien, Jan., 1867.

ROSCOE, H. E.: On the Spectrum produced by the Flame evolved in the Manufacture of Steel by the Bessemer Process. Phil. Mag. (4), xxv., 318.

SILLIMAN, J. M.: On the Examination of the Bessemer Flame with Colored Glasses and with the Spectroscope. Sill. Journ. (2), l., 217.

SORBY, H. C.: Application of the Spectroscope to Technological Researches, and the Discovery of Adulterations in Food, etc. Deutsche Vierteljahrschrift für öffentl. Gesundhtspfl. ii., 1. Heft. Dingler's Journ., 1870. November part.—Investigations on the Adulteration of Liquids. Quart. Journ. of Micros. Soc., October, 1869.

WATTS, W. M.: On the Spectrum of the Bessemer Flame. Phil. Mag. (4), xxxiv., 437. —Ueber das Spectrum der Bessemer-Flamme. Naturforscher, i., 71; ii., 106; Les Mondes, xv., 696, 705.

THE END.

www.ingramcontent.com/pod-product-compliance
Lightning Source LLC
LaVergne TN
LVHW021318110826
845150LV00003B/613

* 9 7 8 1 4 2 5 5 5 7 1 7 1 *